TEACHING THE BIBLE
THROUGH POPULAR CULTURE AND THE ARTS

Society of Biblical Literature

Resources for Biblical Study

Susan Ackerman,
Hebrew Bible/Old Testament Editor

J. Ross Wagner,
New Testament Editor

Number 53

TEACHING THE BIBLE
THROUGH POPULAR CULTURE AND THE ARTS

TEACHING THE BIBLE
THROUGH POPULAR CULTURE AND THE ARTS

Edited by

Mark Roncace and Patrick Gray

Society of Biblical Literature
Atlanta

TEACHING THE BIBLE
THROUGH POPULAR CULTURE AND THE ARTS

Library of Congress Cataloging-in-Publication Data

Teaching the Bible through popular culture and the arts / edited by Mark Roncace, Patrick Gray.
      p. cm. — (Society of Biblical Literature resources for biblical study ; no. 53)
    Includes bibliographical references and index.
    ISBN: 978-1-58983-244-2 (paper binding : alk. paper)
    1. Bible—Study and teaching. 2. Popular culture—Religious aspects—Study and teaching. 3. Arts and religion—Study and teaching. I. Roncace, Mark. II. Gray, Patrick, 1970–.
    BS600.3.T43 2007
    220.071—dc22   2007036077

15 14 13 12 11 10 09 08 07   5 4 3 2 1
Printed in the United States of America on acid-free, recycled paper conforming to ANSI/NISO Z39.48-1992 (R1997) and ISO 9706:1994 standards for paper permanence.

CONTENTS

CONTRIBUTORS

Bryan Bibb
Furman University
Greenville, South Carolina

Dan W. Clanton Jr.
University of Denver
Denver, Colorado

Jaime Clark-Soles
Perkins School of Theology
Southern Methodist University
Dallas, Texas

Nicola Denzey
Harvard University
Cambridge, Massachusetts

Ira Brent Driggers
Pfeiffer University
Misenheimer, North Carolina

Patrick Gray
Rhodes College
Memphis, Tennessee

Lynn R. Huber
Elon University
Elon, North Carolina

Mark Roncace
Wingate University
Wingate, North Carolina

Brent A. Strawn
Emory University
Atlanta, Georgia

Jane S. Webster
Barton College
Wilson, North Carolina

Introduction

Mark Roncace and Patrick Gray

Relatively few resources offer specific, innovative ideas for teaching particular texts and topics in courses devoted to the Bible. In our own effort to provide such a resource (*Teaching the Bible: Practical Strategies for Classroom Instruction* [SBLRBS 49; Atlanta: Society of Biblical Literature, 2005]), we drew on the expertise and experience of nearly one hundred college, university, and seminary professors. One trend that came to our attention in the process of editing that collection is the increasing use of various nonbiblical media—music, film, art, and literature—in biblical studies classrooms. The present volume, which focuses on the incorporation of popular culture and the arts, is thus a supplement to our first volume. Both works assume an academic approach to the Bible but represent a wide range of methodological, theological, and ideological perspectives. The primary objective of each is to present an eclectic compendium of engaging classroom strategies for teaching the Bible in undergraduate, seminary, church, and synagogue settings. Whereas the first volume is organized according to the standard divisions of the Jewish and Christian canons, this volume features chapters devoted to the various media that serve as intertexts for study alongside the biblical writings.

Each section includes an introduction surveying the ways in which the Bible intersects with works in a given medium and highlighting common pedagogical objectives well-suited to that medium. Concluding the introductory essays are bibliographies listing general studies, anthologies, and secondary literature cited in the discussions of particular works in the subsequent chapters.

Part 1 ("Music"): one chapter discusses classroom strategies for use with several dozen examples of popular music; a second chapter considers a selection of classical compositions.
Part 2 ("Film"): one chapter examines renderings of biblical narrative into film (so-called "sword and sandal" movies); a second chapter considers Hollywood releases bearing less explicit connections to the Bible

and the ways in which particular scenes may be employed in the class-room.

Part 3 ("Art"): one chapter discusses works of art that depict scenes and characters from the Bible; a second chapter examines works that generate conversation about a variety of concepts arising in biblical studies courses, despite the fact that the artists make no attempt at representing subjects typically considered "biblical."

Part 4 ("Literature"): one chapter explores the heuristic uses of poetry with direct or indirect links to biblical themes; a second chapter discusses the pedagogical potential of a smaller sampling of prose excerpts (fiction and nonfiction).

Part 5 ("Other Media"): a final chapter briefly introduces material such as comic strips, the Internet, and television programs, resources for biblical studies courses that have until recently remained largely untapped.

Each chapter consists of a catalogue of entries focusing on one or more literary, cinematic, artistic, or musical works. Entries concisely lay out specific strategies for deploying these works in classroom settings or related assignments. While the introductions outline generic sets of questions that could be applied, say, to any artistic image or musical composition, individual entries briefly describe and include discussion questions or exercises tailored to the particular works under consideration. Although the chapters do not function as primers in the technical skills of literary or film criticism, there is sufficient background for enhancing one's teaching repertoire through the integration of the diverse materials surveyed in the following pages.

The contributors to this volume have not attempted to catalogue all creative works that allude to, interpret, depict, or spur reflection on some aspect of the Bible; nor do all biblical texts receive equal attention. To accomplish either task would have entailed a project of encyclopedic proportions. The items discussed here represent a relatively small selection of the possibilities. (Since the volume is organized according to genre, the Scripture index is the most efficient way to find the broadest range of entries dealing with specific biblical texts.) In addition to the entries devoted to individual works, some chapters also include lists that help instructors locate other works inspired by the Bible that might be used in the classroom. Along with ease of integration into biblical studies courses, one of the main criteria for selecting items to be included is accessibility. The vast majority of the works discussed are readily available in any library, movie rental store, or on the Internet—normally for free or at a minimal cost.

In addition to providing analogies for various approaches to the study of the Bible, using comparative texts from popular culture and the arts, broadly defined, helps students to become critical and creative readers and thinkers. Drawing on such material does not represent a "dumbing down" of education. Rather, by failing to incorporate it, many instructors miss valuable opportunities to capitalize on their students' natural interests and to nurture their capacity to engage and analyze classic texts like the Bible and the traditions informed by it. By challenging students to compare the Bible and the worldviews it embraces with those expressed in more familiar cultural forms, these intersections encourage them to attend to the gaps—both real and apparent. How broad, exactly, is Lessing's "ugly, broad ditch" (*der garstige breite Graben*)? What is required to bring about Gadamer's "fusion of horizons"? Our hope is that this collection provides instructors with a resource for grappling with these and other, less theoretical questions that regularly arise in a biblical studies curriculum.

Finally, we want to express our gratitude to series editors Susan Ackerman of Dartmouth College and J. Ross Wagner of Princeton Theological Seminary for their helpful suggestions in the early stages of this project; to Bob Buller and Leigh Andersen of the Society of Biblical Literature for their guidance in preparing the manuscript; to student assistants Rebekah Kuhn and Eric Hagemeyer of Rhodes College, whose work in compiling the index and bibliographies has been indispensable; and to Jessica Haynes of Wingate University, who offered much help with the popular music chapter.

All abbreviations conform to the guidelines found in *The SBL Handbook of Style* (ed. Patrick H. Alexander et al.; Peabody, Mass.: Hendrickson, 1999).

PART 1:
MUSIC

Introduction: Teaching the Bible with Music

Mark Roncace and Dan W. Clanton Jr.

Although the study of the intersection between the Bible and music has until recently received relatively little attention from scholars, popular and classical music both offer a wealth of pedagogical possibilities.[1] Both categories require some definition. Popular music, as we are treating it here, includes a variety of genres—rock, country, folk, hip-hop, heavy metal, and others. The designation "classical music" is similarly expansive. Even though "classical music," strictly speaking, denotes only a certain period within the Western tradition of music (ca. 1750–1825), it is now commonly used to designate a much broader range of music (rather than simply to distinguish "classical" from Baroque or Romantic). Deciding what belongs to this larger family of musical genres does not fall within the purview of this introduction, where "classical music" will refer to the types of music most nonspecialists have in mind when they use the term. Rather, the goal here is to focus on effective use of music in the classroom. "At its most profound and best," writes Jan Swafford, "music is the ideal stimulus for humanity's eternal meditation on the

---

1. Studies of the Bible and popular music include, among others, Michael J. Gilmour, *Tangled Up in the Bible: Bob Dylan and Scripture* (New York: Continuum, 2004); Darrell W. Cluck, Catherine S. George, and J. Clinton McCann Jr., *Facing the Music: Faith and Meaning in Popular Songs* (St. Louis: Chalice, 1999); David Fillingim, *Redneck Liberation: Country Music as Theology* (Macon: Mercer University Press, 2003); Michael Gilmour, ed., *Call Me the Seeker: Listening to Religion in Popular Music* (New York: Continuum, 2005); and Raewynne J. Whiteley and Beth Maynard, eds., *Get Up Off Your Knees: Preaching the U2 Catalogue* (Cambridge, Mass.: Cowley, 2003). For classical music, see Helen Leneman "Portrayals of Power in the Stories of Delilah and Bathsheba: Seduction in Song," in *Sacred Text, Secular Times: The Hebrew Bible in the Modern World* (ed. L. Greenspoon and B. F. LeBeau; Omaha: Creighton University Press, 2000), 227–43; Bluma Goldstein, "Schoenberg's *Moses und Aron*: A Vanishing Biblical Nation," in *Political and Religious Ideas in the Works of Arnold Schoenberg* (ed. C. M. Cross and R. A. Berman; New York: Garland, 2000), 159–92; Dan W. Clanton Jr., "*Samson et Dalila*: What French Opera Reveals about the Biblical Duo," *BRev* 20/3 (June 2004): 12–19, 44–46.

mystery of its own being."[2] Indeed, because it appeals to such a wide range of students, music can provide a catalyst for engaging the multitude of questions raised in the academic study of the Bible.

Music has several practical advantages over other forms of media when it comes to teaching. No "smart classroom" or special technology is required. It is also time efficient, as it typically takes fewer than ten minutes to introduce and play a given piece. Classical music pieces sometimes run longer, but most recordings now are helpfully divided by CD track, so one can easily skip to the most illuminative portion of a particular piece. Furthermore, musical selections—especially popular songs—are remarkably accessible. For 99 cents apiece, one can purchase millions of individual songs at websites such as iTunes.com or Limewire.com.[3] The sheer amount of available music makes it possible to locate items that relate to a variety of biblical texts and themes. Song lyrics, too, are easily accessible on the Internet with a simple search for the title of the song, followed by the word "lyrics." Websites such as songlyrics.com or getlyrics.com catalogue millions of lyrics from artists in every genre. One can also use a search engine to locate background material on particular artists and songs. Especially for classical music, it is often helpful for the teacher to provide historical information about the piece as well as some biographical background on the composer in order to contextualize the work.[4]

Music offers theoretical as well as practical benefits in the classroom. Studies show that music activates different sensory receptors that prime students for learning by stimulating emotional involvement and physical movement. While songs may not generate emotional and kinesthetic responses in ways directly related to the material to be studied, music's ability to activate different senses nevertheless facilitates retention of material.[5]

---

2. Jan Swafford, *The Vintage Guide to Classical Music* (New York: Random House, 1992), 520.

3. Some of the songs discussed here have been recorded by multiple artists. If one version is difficult to locate online, finding the same title by another artist is relatively simple with any search engine.

4. Resources for gathering such information are plentiful. For example, Swafford (*The Vintage Guide to Classical Music*) presents a chronological biography of many key composers, as well as a glossary and suggestions for building a classical library. Similarly, both the *Penguin Guide to Compact Discs* and the *Gramophone Good CD Guide*, updated yearly, offer reviews of thousands of classical CDs. Finally, there are many excellent websites providing access to reviews, discographies, and information (e.g., www.classicstoday.com; www.arkivmusic.com; www.classical.net; and www.gramophone.co.uk).

5. On the physiological aspects of music and learning, see Eric Jensen, *Brain-Based Learning: The New Science of Teaching and Training* (rev. ed.; San Diego: The Brain Store,

Whatever its impact on individual learners, music also has a positive effect on learning communities. One strategy that highlights the communal benefits is to play background music as students arrive for class. For example, on days when Luke is the target text, Krzysztof Penderecki's *Passio et mors domini nostri Jesu Christi secundum Lucam* (*St. Luke's Passion*) provides a calming introduction to the session's topic. Or more upbeat popular music can be played in order to stimulate chatter among the students as they prepare for class. Lively background music cultivates an environment for active, engaged learning, in part by creating a sense of community.[6] Another approach is to play background music during small group work. This helps to encourage conversation, as students are more willing to talk when there is already some "noise" in the classroom. The music in this case functions, according to educational theorists, as a "pad" to ease students into dialogue.

The most obvious manner in which biblical studies instructors might use music, of course, is as a vehicle for discussing specific course content. The possibilities are limited only by the imagination of the instructor.[7] For example, the technique of "sampling," where one artist uses part (a sample) of an earlier song in the composition of a new song, can offer helpful ways to discuss hermeneutical issues.[8] Similarly, instances in which one artist sings an entire piece that was originally performed by someone else (called "covering") can lead to productive discussions about characteristics of biblical literature

M
U
S
I
C

2000); and idem, *Music with the Brain in Mind* (San Diego: The Brain Store, 2000).

6. Richard Howell Allen, *Impact Teaching* (Boston: Allyn & Bacon, 2001), presents empirical and anecdotal evidence for this effect; see also "Songs for Teaching," n.p. [cited 3 May 2007]. Online: www.songsforteaching.com/richallen/strategies.htm.

7. In addition to items catalogued in the following chapters, Roncace and Gray, *Teaching the Bible*, contains entries for a number of others using popular music: Donald C. Polaski, "Tom Lehrer and Historical Criticism," 26–27; idem, "Holiness as an Unknown Culture," 129; and "Hosea Meets Hank Williams," 181–82; Mark McEntire, "Isaiah and Bob Dylan on the Watchtower," 173–74; Brent A. Strawn, "Lament and Praise, Top Forty and Psychology," 201–203; idem, "Imprecatory Psalms: Ancient and Modern," 203–204; Mark Roncace, "Psalm 23 and Modern Worldviews," 205–206; idem, "The Structure of Ecclesiastes and the Views of the Teacher," 232–33; Frank M. Yamada, "The Characterization of Qoheleth in Ecclesiastes," 230–31; Emily R. Cheney, "The Gospels as Aural and Socio-Political Documents," 271–72; and Gregory Stevenson, "The Letters and Historical Context," 341–43. Entries outlining strategies using classical music include Sara Koenig, "Canonicity, Musical Polyphony, and the Book of Psalms," 206–207; Amy C. Cottrill, "Lamentations through Musical Interpretation," 224–26; and Patrick Gray, "Gospel Music," 266–67.

8. See, in Roncace and Gray, *Teaching the Bible*, Guy D. Nave Jr., "The Documentary Hypothesis and Sampling," 134–35; and Brent A. Strawn, "Ancient Near Eastern Parallels and Hip Hop Sampling," 246–47.

such as intertextuality and allusiveness.[9] Playing a song with social, political, or historical referents which students will not understand can underscore the importance of social, cultural, and historical criticism. But the most common way that music can be used in class is as a comparative "text" to be "read" alongside the Bible in order to explore a particular biblical theme or text or to open up fresh avenues of inquiry. Songwriters who quote or paraphrase biblical texts are, in effect, interpreters of the Bible, and as such they provide interesting material for studying the history of its reception. When Bob Dylan, for example, alludes to the Akedah in "Highway 61 Revisited" or Bruce Springsteen sings that "Jesus Was an Only Son," instructors have ample opportunity to place such musical instances of biblical interpretation within the broader contexts of popular and scholarly discourse.

Two caveats, one for popular music and one for classical. First, some teachers who do not feel sufficiently knowledgeable about poplar music might be hesitant to use it in their classrooms. A middle-aged white woman presenting a song by 50 Cent (a contemporary rap artist), for example, might think, "I could not play that song. Students would see right through me and laugh." This is an understandable sentiment, and not all instructors will be able to escape it. There is nothing wrong, however, with students knowing that the instructor's knowledge of popular music is the result of academic study rather than a long-standing personal subscription to *Rolling Stone*. Most students will appreciate the teacher's attempt to keep up with pop culture. (And keeping up is not terribly difficult. One hour a month with the library's copy of *Rolling Stone* goes a long way.)

Second, in many cases involving classical music, students will need access to the lyrics or the libretto of a given piece, if it contains a vocal part. This text will allow the students to not only *see* the words the composer is setting to music, but, when coupled with the music, should allow them to *hear* the text as well. Because students respond to music so differently than they do to a traditional lecture or class discussion, it is very important that teachers do not separate the words from the music. Classical music, especially opera, ideally makes a holistic demand on the listener, and to dissect it by focusing solely on the text would be a disservice not only to the composer, but it also lessens the pedagogic impact. Reading the lyrics to Handel's oratorio *Messiah*, for example, is a radically different experience without the music; it reduces the piece to nothing more than a string of loosely connected Bible verses. Many operas based on biblical texts (e.g., Schoenberg's *Moses und Aron*; Verdi's *Nabucco*)

---

9. See Brent A. Strawn, "On Covering (the Song of) Songs and the Importance of (Canonical) Context," in Roncace and Gray, *Teaching the Bible*, 216–18.

are available on DVD with closed-captioning. This makes it possible for students to be more thoroughly engaged by adding the visual component to the aural.

A single song or composition could be employed in a variety of ways, so teachers are encouraged to explore how each piece might best fit into their classrooms. The aim of the chapters on popular and classical music is to make instructors aware of the variety of possibilities and then offer a few suggestions for classroom use. Teachers and students, too, will likely think of additional avenues of inquiry in connection with any given piece. A simple but effective technique is simply to say to students: "How does this song connect to today's text?" or "Compare these lyrics to the biblical text." It is not unusual for students to make their own insightful observations. The category "popular music" covers a vast terrain, and so it can be instructive for the teacher—as well as fun for students—to assign them the task of locating and commenting on material that relates to some element of the course. Allowing students to present their findings gives them a sense of ownership of the course.

The songs discussed in the chapter devoted to popular music are drawn from a variety of genres, artists, and time periods. Some deal exclusively with a biblical text or image, others have a passing biblical reference, and still others have nothing explicitly to do with the Bible. Most of the pieces discussed in the chapter devoted to classical music are explicitly inspired by or based on biblical texts.[10] This diversity is designed to prompt consideration of additional songs that could be used successfully. The examples discussed here represent only a fraction of the possibilities open to a thoughtful pedagogue.

M
U
S
I
C

BIBLIOGRAPHY

Allen, Richard Howell. *Impact Teaching*. Boston: Allyn & Bacon, 2001.
Billig, Michael. *Rock 'n' Roll Jews*. Syracuse: Syracuse University Press, 2001.
Bullard, J. M. "Music, The Bible and." Pages 172–87 in vol. 2 of *Dictionary of Biblical Interpretation*. Edited by John H. Hayes. 2 vols. Nashville: Abingdon, 1999.
Callahan, Allen Dwight. *The Talking Book: African Americans and the Bible*. New Haven: Yale University Press, 2006.
Clanton, Dan W., Jr. "*Samson et Dalila*: What French Opera Reveals about the Biblical Duo." *Bible Review* 20/3 (2004): 12–19, 44–46.

---

10. Classical music not explicitly inspired by the Bible can also be an effective teaching device; for example, the opening of Mahler's *Symphony No. 1* or Richard Strauss's "Fanfare" sequence from *Also Sprach Zarathustra* can accompany a reading of the Prologue of the Fourth Gospel (John 1:1–18).

Cluck, Darrell W., Catherine S. George, and J. Clinton McCann Jr. *Facing the Music: Faith and Meaning in Popular Songs*. St. Louis: Chalice, 1999.

Cone, James. *The Spirituals and the Blues: An Interpretation*. New York: Seabury, 1972.

Dyson, Michael Eric. *Mercy Mercy Me: The Art, Loves, and Demons of Marvin Gaye*. New York: Basic Civitas, 2004.

Edelman, Marsha Bryan. *Discovering Jewish Music*. Philadelphia: Jewish Publication Society of America, 2007.

Fillingim, David. *Redneck Liberation: Country Music as Theology*. Macon, Ga.: Mercer University Press, 2003.

Friskics-Warren, Bill. *I'll Take You There: Pop Music and the Urge for Transcendence*. New York: Continuum, 2005.

Gilmour, Michael J. *Tangled Up in the Bible: Bob Dylan and Scripture*. New York: Continuum, 2004.

—— , ed. *Call Me the Seeker: Listening to Religion in Popular Music*. New York: Continuum, 2005.

Goldstein, Bluma. "Schoenberg's *Moses und Aron*: A Vanishing Biblical Nation." Pages 159–92 in *Political and Religious Ideas in the Works of Arnold Schoenberg*. Edited by Charlotte M. Cross and Russell A. Berman. New York: Garland, 2000.

Graves, Michael P., and David Fillingim, eds. *More Than "Precious Memories": The Rhetoric of Southern Gospel Music*. Macon, Ga.: Mercer University Press, 2004.

Ingersoll, Julie J. "The Thin Line between Saturday Night and Sunday Morning: Meaning and Community among Jimmy Buffett's Parrotheads." Pages 253–66 in *God in the Details: American Religion in Popular Culture*. Edited by Eric Michael Mazur and Kate McCarthy. New York: Routledge, 2001.

Irwin, Joyce, ed. *Sacred Sound: Music in Religious Thought and Practice*. Chico, Calif.: Scholars Press, 1983.

Jensen, Eric. *Brain-Based Learning: The New Science of Teaching and Training*. Revised edition. San Diego: The Brain Store, 2000.

—— . *Music with the Brain in Mind*. San Diego: The Brain Store, 2000.

Leneman, Helen. "Portrayals of Power in the Stories of Delilah and Bathsheba: Seduction in Song." Pages 227–43 in *Sacred Text, Secular Times: The Hebrew Bible in the Modern World*. Edited by Leonard Greenspoon and Bryan F. LeBeau. Omaha: Creighton University Press, 2000.

McCarthy, Kate. "Deliver Me From Nowhere: Bruce Springsteen and the Myth of the American Promised Land." Pages 17–45 in *God in the Details: American Religion in Popular Culture*. Edited by Eric Michael Mazur and Kate McCarthy. New York: Routledge, 2001.

McEntire, Mark. *Raising Cain, Fleeing Egypt, and Fighting Philistines: The Old Testament in Popular Music.* Macon, Ga.: Smyth & Helwys, 2006.

Sample, Tex. *White Soul: Country Music, the Church, and Working Americans.* Nashville: Abingdon, 1996.

Scharen, Christian. *One Step Closer: Why U2 Matters to Those Seeking God.* Grand Rapids: Brazos, 2006.

Seay, David. *Stairway to Heaven: The Spiritual Roots of Rock 'n' Roll—From the King and Little Richard to Prince and Amy Grant.* New York: Ballantine, 1986.

Swafford, Jan. *The Vintage Guide to Classical Music.* New York: Random House, 1992.

Sylvan, Robin. *Traces of the Spirit: The Religious Dimensions of Popular Music.* New York: New York University Press, 2002.

Terrien, Samuel. *The Magnificat: Musicians as Biblical Interpreters.* New York: Paulist, 1995.

Turner, Steve. *Hungry for Heaven: Rock 'n' Roll and the Search for Redemption.* Downers Grove, Ill.: InterVarsity Press, 1995.

Urbanski, Dave. *The Man Comes Around: The Spiritual Journey of Johnny Cash.* Lake Mary, Fla.: Relevant Books, 2005.

Weber, Eugen. *Apocalypses: Prophecies, Cults, and Millennial Beliefs through the Ages.* Cambridge, Mass.: Harvard University Press, 2000.

Whiteley, Raewynne J., and Beth Maynard, eds. *Get Up Off Your Knees: Preaching the U2 Catalogue.* Cambridge, Mass.: Cowley, 2003.

MUSIC

Popular Music

Mark Roncace and Dan W. Clanton Jr.

The songs discussed in this chapter are arranged according to the order in which their subject matter appears in the canon. The indices may be consulted to find entries with classroom strategies related to particular texts. All secondary literature cited here is included in the preceding bibliography (pp. 11–13).

Hebrew Bible

Torah

Bob Marley, "We and Dem" (Reggae, 1980)

Marley cites the biblical text which says that God gave humans "dominion" over the earth (Gen 1:26). He then decries the fact that humans are destroying the earth and will one day pay for their irresponsible actions. The song invites one to consider the meaning of the word "dominion," the fact that God gives humans (not just "man") dominion only over the animals (not "all things" as Marley sings), and that God gives plants to humans and animals for their food (Gen 1:29–30), which suggests that "dominion" over the animals does not include killing them. In general, Marley's song sets the context for a discussion of how, if at all, one appropriates the biblical text in light of a variety of contemporary environmental and ethical issues.

Esther, "Eve's Lament" (Folk, 2001)

The song expresses Eve's perspective, which invites students to consider the story from multiple points of view. Eve wonders how she was supposed to know the consequences for eating the fruit; this is an understandable question since in the biblical narrative the Lord's instructions about the Tree are given only to the man (Gen 2:16–17). Further, the deity vows death "on the day" that the fruit is eaten, which of course is not the literal, immediate consequence for the man and woman. Eve's observation that they would not have been banished if they had not eaten the fruit can lead to consideration of the main reason for banishment in the biblical version: to prevent access to the Tree of Life (which significantly complicates the logic of the story). Eve's assertion "I thought I would try something new" can open up discussion about the desire for knowledge, the reasons the deity would try to withhold it from humans, and what it means to be human. Similarly, Eve wonders why, if God had wanted her to remain innocent, would there be a serpent and the Tree in the Garden. Is the deity somehow at least partially responsible for the situation? The song also invites one to consider whether the biblical story ends on a note of "lament," per the song title, or if it offers a more hopeful conclusion.

Bob Marley, "Adam and Eve" (Reggae, 1975)

This song makes a number of extrabiblical observations, which can lead to a discussion of the importance of not following Marley's exegetical lead, even if he is in some cases supported by subsequent Christian tradition. The song refers to the devil, original sin, and asserts that "woman is the root of all evil." On a less egregious note, the first verse of the song claims that God named Adam and Eve and gave them a happy life in the Garden. The former idea is incorrect, since the man names Eve in the biblical story (Gen 3:20); and students might consider the ways in which the Garden could (or could not) be a truly happy place prior to eating the fruit. Interestingly, however, the song does hold both the man and woman responsible, saying "they" disobeyed—a notion supported by the text. A simple question such as, "Where does Marley follow the biblical story and where does he deviate?" can get the discussion moving.

Bob Dylan, "Man Gave Names to All the Animals" (Folk, 1979)

This light-hearted song details how the man named the animals. It helps one to pause over the fact that God's goal in creating the animals and bringing them to the man was to identify a suitable companion. Dylan does not mention the naming of the woman, a note which can prompt discussion about the significance of naming (does it indicate power over someone or something?) and the fact that the man names the woman with a poetic utterance (Gen 2:23). Instead, the song concludes by mentioning the man's encounter with the serpent. This raises questions: Had the man encountered the serpent prior to the incident at the Tree? Why would the deity create the serpent? If the serpent was not "good," how does that affect our understanding of the Garden? Obviously there are not clear answers to these questions, which helps students appreciate not only the gaps in the story, but how filling them can significantly alter one's understanding of the story.

Garth Brooks, "Against the Grain" (Country, 1991)

The song points to Noah as an example of a man who "bucked the system" and went "out on a limb." The song includes the popular and extrabiblical idea that Noah was ridiculed for building the ark, but continued anyway. Like the biblical text—but unlike other ancient flood stories—Brooks's version has a moral or pedagogical point. The points, however, are different and reflect the values from which they emanate. The biblical Noah escapes the flood because he is righteous; in the song, it is because he is brave enough to be different. Brooks presents a maverick (comparing him to Columbus and John Wayne); he is an American Noah who is praised for recognizing that "nothin' ventured, nothin' gained." Brooks transforms the biblical story of a man who follows God's instructions to build the ark into a figure who prides himself in the American ideals of individualism and independence.

Ice Cube, "When I Get to Heaven" (Rap, 1993)

This song, which rails against the hypocrisy of the church, features a couple of interesting lines regarding the flood story which can help students reflect on the image of the deity. Ice Cube notes that if he himself must use violence, "God won't mind" because God too "is a killer from the start. Why you think Noah had to build his ark?" These lyrics shift the focus away from the ark as a vehicle of salvation to what the salvation is from: massive death and destruction (cf. Doré's painting, *The Deluge*). Students are not accustomed to thinking about the implications of God's actions: God regrets making people and so simply wipes them all out, save eight. Ice Cube's assertion that God will approve of his use of violence raises questions about how one appropriates the biblical text. Clearly, we are uncomfortable with his reasoning, but why? Is the deity not a moral exemplar? How does one responsibly draw moral meaning from the text?

Boogie Down Productions, "Why Is That?" (Rap, 1989)

The song is a diatribe against the manner in which black youth are educated. In the process, the song cites Gen 11:10 as evidence that Shem was black and since Abraham was a decedent of Shem, he too must have been black (citing Gen 14:13). Teachers could invite closer study of these two verses and other genealogical material in a discussion about the identity/ethnicity of the patriarchs. The song then observes that since Moses passed as Pharaoh's grandson, he must have been black—which means black Egyptians were enslaving black Israelites. This observation would fit nicely with a discussion of Moses' identity, for example, how Moses seems to have difficulty identifying with the Israelites (Exod 3–4), or how liberators of oppressed people often come from positions of power or have access to it. In general, the song

M
U
S
I
C

can be employed to facilitate discussion of the origin of Israel as it relates to surrounding people groups. In a different vein, the song challenges what people are taught and why ("why is that"), which can be used to underscore the importance of considering the ideological agenda behind "facts" and who benefits from a given presentation of them. What is at stake by depicting the Israelites as light or dark skinned?

Momus, "The Lesson of Sodom (According to Lot)" (Alternative, 1986)

This is an odd and intriguing song about Lot and his daughters after the destruction of Sodom (Gen 19:30–38). Lot's wife is appropriately named "Salt," but the daughters, as in the Bible, are not named, which could lead to conversation about the anonymity of biblical women. In the song, Lot struggles to identify the lesson of Sodom—what was the point? After considering several clichéd options (spare the rod spoil the child, you can lead a horse to water…), Lot concludes that he has forgotten the lesson. The song prompts one to ask what exactly did provoke the deity's wrath: Homosexuality? Inhospitality? Or something else? If students are asked to identify the sin of Sodom, according to the text, very few will suggest homosexuality, which can lead to a discussion of how texts are (mis)appropriated in contemporary debates. Further, the song underscores the irony of Lot being saved from Sodom since he is not righteous—as the song observes, he is "exempt" from the destruction (cf. Abraham's debate with God in Gen 18:22–33). Not only did Lot offer his daughters to the angry mob (Gen 19:7–8), but in the song, he actively participates in and enjoys the incest with his daughters. Indeed, what is the lesson of Sodom? (For an exercise related to Lot's wife's perspective, see F. V. Greifenhagen, "Lot's Wife: Bringing Minor Biblical Characters Out of the Shadows," in Roncace and Gray, *Teaching the Bible*, 91–92.)

Bob Dylan, "Highway 61 Revisited" (Folk, 1965)

As with many Dylan songs, the overall meaning or purpose of these lyrics is not entirely clear. The first stanza presents an alternate version of the story of Abraham's near sacrifice of Isaac (Gen 22). Here Abraham thinks that God's instructions to kill his son must be a joke. Abraham resists God's commands, which stands in striking contrast to the reticent biblical Abraham (but compare the Abraham of Gen 18:22–33). In response, God observes that Abraham can do what he wants, but "the next time you see me coming, you better run." As with the biblical text, the song raises questions about the nature of the deity and human freedom. Highway 61 is where God commands the sacrifice to occur; elsewhere in the song, Highway 61 is representative of human trials and tragedies. The carnival beat to the song stands in odd juxtaposition to its disturbing lyrics; in some ways this parallels the biblical text. On the one hand, it

MUSIC

is a deeply troubling story; but on the other hand, the reader knows it is a test (22:1) and so does not expect that God will permit Abraham to kill Isaac.

Leonard Cohen, "Story of Isaac" (Folk, 1969)

The first part of this song is a detailed retelling of Gen 22 from the perspective of Isaac. The song fills in many elements not present in the text—the color of Abraham's eyes, the tone of his voice, what occurred on the trip up the mountain. Students can be invited to fill the gaps in their own ways and consider the different understandings of the story that emerge. Similarly, students can expand the development of Isaac's perspective begun by the biblical text (Gen 22:7) and Cohen or write a similar song or poem from the perspective of another character (e.g., Sarah). Students can compare their image of Isaac to the one presented by Cohen (a small nine-year-old boy who would submit to his father) and consider the implications of the different depictions. What would have been Isaac's relationship with Abraham (or Sarah) after this event? The final two stanzas of the song are social commentary against sacrificing sons by sending them to war. Students might be asked what they think of using Gen 22 in this way or if there are any responsible ways in which the biblical story might have meaning for a contemporary audience.

Joan Baez, "Isaac and Abraham" (Folk, 1992)

In this retelling of Gen 22 it is not clear that God commands the sacrifice—it is a voice in the troubled mind of Abraham. While this is different from the biblical narrative, it still raises the question about people who do strange and violent things, claiming that God enjoined them. The song also says that the angels did not comprehend why the righteous Isaac must die; and at the end, Abraham "most mysteriously" stops before killing Isaac and declares that he wishes he were the one to have spared the boy's life. This connects with the fact that in the biblical text it is an angel of the Lord who stops Abraham. Is this angelic figure acting independently from the deity, or is it simply the agent of the Lord? The conclusion to the song celebrates Isaac, which stands in stark contrast to the taciturn denouement of the biblical account where there is no verbal or emotional reaction from the characters. The song thus invites students to speculate about the nature of the relationship between Abraham and Isaac after this incident, as well as that of Abraham and God, who never speak again in the biblical narrative.

Grateful Dead, "My Brother Esau" (Rock, 1987)

This song employs the Jacob and Esau narrative as a commentary, seemingly, on the Vietnam War. It mentions an inheritance, birthright, paternal favoritism, Jacob's dreams, Esau's hairiness, a blessing, and fraternal com-

M
U
S
I
C

petition in which Esau is a warrior and Jacob, the voice singing, is a quiet man. Toward the end of the song, Jacob takes responsibility for "Esau's curse," seems to sympathize with his suffering, and sees himself in his brother when he says: "The more my brother looks like me, the less I understand." This can lead to a discussion about the reconciliation, or lack thereof, between Jacob and Esau in the biblical story. Has Jacob matured after his stint with Laban? Or does he remain a conniving trickster who continues to deceive his brother (Gen 33:12–17)?

Ricky Skaggs & Kentucky Thunder, "Jacob's Vision" (Bluegrass Gospel, 1999).

Skaggs's album *Soldier of the Cross* is filled with biblically based songs, complete with scriptural citations of verses referenced or alluded to in any given song. Because the album is unabashedly Christian, the Hebrew Bible texts used are all viewed as proof texts for Jesus' divinity and actions on behalf of humanity. In the case of this song, Skaggs retells the story of Jacob's vision in Gen 28, but musically connects it with Jesus' execution in the chorus: "Hallelujah to Jesus who died on the tree, to raise up this ladder of mercy for me." Skaggs even writes in the liner notes, "I believe the ladder represents the cross and the stone represents Jesus, the stone the builders rejected." Because of the Christological interpretation present here, this song can be useful not only for its retelling of Gen 28, but also for a discussion of the ways in which New Testament writers reinterpret Hebrew Bible narratives, shifting the focus to Jesus. Like Skaggs, the Gospel writers and Paul used the Torah to understand their own experiences.

Dolly Parton, "Coat of Many Colors" (Country, 1971)

This song sets up discussion of how Joseph's coat, which is referenced in the song, functions in the narrative. In both the song and the biblical story, the coat is a special gift from parent to child, a symbol of parental love. In the song, however, it is a present from a poor mother to her daughter; in the biblical text, of course, it is from a father to a son and is a symbol not only of love but also of favoritism over other children. In both stories, people resent or make fun of the coat—Joseph's brothers and the girl's schoolmates. For Joseph, however, the coat does not bring "good luck and happiness," as the parent in the song hopes; rather his brothers bring the blood-stained garment to Jacob as evidence of their brother's death. The song interweaves the story of Joseph with Parton's own humble upbringing. Students might be asked to link the biblical tale with their personal experiences, for example in terms of their relationship with siblings or parents. How would they use the text as inspiration for a song about their life?

Joan Baez, "Little Moses" (Folk, 1979)

This song gives a broad overview of Moses' life, including his rescue by Pharaoh's daughter, his subsequent return to his mother, the crossing of the Red Sea, and his standing on a mountain looking into the Promised Land. One might note the unsurprising omission of Moses as a law-giver, his most significant role both in the text and in Jewish tradition. The song's juxtaposition of the rescue by Pharaoh's daughter with the drowning of "Pharaoh's host" calls attention to the story's ambiguous attitude toward Egyptians: They save Moses and adopt him as their son, yet they are the enemy killed by the powers of God. The final stanza also fails to mention that God prohibits Moses from entering the land because of one mistake (cf. Deut 32:48–52). It says as well that Moses went to heaven upon death, which provides an occasion to explain the Hebrew concept of the afterlife. Students might be asked to fill in other crucial elements of Moses' life not mentioned by the song—for example, his reluctance to return to Egypt and free the Israelites, his near death at the hands of God (Exod 4:24–26), or his struggle to lead the recalcitrant people in the wilderness. The biblical Moses indeed is a complex character, an element which popular portrayals, such as this song, fail to capture.

Steven Curtis Chapman, "Dive" (Contemporary Christian, 2000)

Although this song has nothing explicitly to do with Moses' experience at the burning bush (Exod 3:1–6), it can serve as a comparative text illustrating the typical human response to a theophany according to Rudolph Otto's idea of *Mysterium Tremendum et Fascinans*. Both Moses and Chapman encounter a theophany—the "river" in the song—and both express fascination (Exod 3:3) and fear (Exod 3:6). Both are simultaneously attracted to and repulsed by their respective theophanies. Chapman is drawn to the river and wants to jump in, but he also describes the river as "wild and rushing," "deep," "wide," and "alive." He feels compelled to jump into the river, even though he is aware that he might get swept away and die. Fire and water are appropriate mediums for each theophany, as both can give life (thus the attraction to them), but yet both can be lethal (thus the fear). Later God attempts to kill Moses (Exod 4:24–26); indeed, the appearance of the deity can lead to death, just as Chapman knows he might die in the river—paradoxically in the river of "life."

Metallica, "Creeping Death" (Heavy Metal, 1984)

This song depicts the utter horror of the final plague, the killing of all first born of Egypt. The song makes reference to other elements of the Exodus story, but the repeated phrase "I am creeping death" gives the listener an image of the death angel that wreaks havoc on the Egyptians. The heavy metal genre is fitting. The song can serve to help students wrestle with the complexity of the biblical narrative. Must the Egyptians die in order for Israel to be saved? Can salvation be wrought without violence? Is there any irony or significance to blood on the doorpost being the sign for the death angel to pass?

Cradle of Filth, "Doberman Pharaoh" (Heavy Metal, 2003)

The song presents Pharaoh's perspective on his struggles with Moses and Yahweh. The Pharaoh is stubborn in part because of his reliance on his own deities, which can provide an opportunity to point out that the specific nature of some of the plagues (e.g., of the Nile and the sun) may have been to demonstrate the power of Yahweh over Egyptian gods. The lyrics are obscure in places, but one can follow the description of the various plagues imposed by Moses. As in Metallica's "Creeping Death," the final plague receives the most attention and the listener is forced to focus on its horror—the "carrion" and the "bleeding in the dark." Students might reflect on why it is that heavy metal bands have gravitated toward the plague narratives.

Snoop Dog, "Mac Bible Chapter 211 Verse 20–21" (Rap, 2001)

Teachers might utilize this song to illustrate that one learns a great deal about an author or community by studying their laws. Snoop Dog's list of "the gangsta's ten commandments" reflects his (gangsta) culture and values, namely, loyalty, misogyny, and respect for guns and cash, among others. The same is true of the biblical Ten Commandments. For example, one sees the obvious focus on religious matters in the first four commands and its male perspective in the final one. If one studies the laws in other Hebrew Bible texts, such as Exod 21–23, one learns about the Israelite view of slaves, women, children, violence, property, and individual rights. The song also illustrates the difficulty of understanding certain laws if one stands outside the culture. What does Snoop mean by "Thou shall flex his G's" or, in the Bible, what is the significance of the festival of unleavened bread (or what is unleavened bread) or what is the rationale for the command not to boil a goat in its mothers milk? The song can also set up a discussion in which students are asked to produce their own list of Ten Commandments for contemporary society. These too will reflect current cultural problems and values.

PROPHETS

Michael W. Smith, "Be Strong and Courageous" (Contemporary Christian, 1987)

God promises to bless and protect Joshua as he leads the people into the land that God has given them (cf. the song title and Deut 31:23). The song is a typically uncritical reading of the Joshua narrative. Smith reinscribes the

Holy War ethic of the book of Joshua. He focuses on the advice to "be strong and courageous," but does not consider the implications of what God has instructed Joshua to do: wipe out the inhabitants of the land in order to possess it. The final two lines of the song recapitulate Deuteronomistic theology: If Joshua keeps God's law in his heart, he will be invincible.

Ricky Skaggs & Kentucky Thunder, "The Joshua Generation" (Bluegrass Gospel, 1999)

This song, also found on Skaggs's album *Soldier of the Cross*, represents an anthemic interpretation of the conquest narratives found in Joshua for modern evangelical Christians. Skaggs notes here that these Christians in America have achieved societal and political prominence, and as such their behavior should parallel the holy forces of Joshua. The chorus reinforces the paradigmatic example of Joshua for modern Christians: "Let's rise up and take a stand, claiming the keys to every kingdom. We can go in and take the land....The power of God is in our hands." Because of the near militancy of Skaggs's lyrics, this song can be used to illustrate the ideological danger of the conquest narratives, both in the text itself and in later interpretations.

Bob Dylan, "With God on Our Side" (Folk, 1964)

Dylan rehearses a long list of wars in U.S. and world history, including the killing of the Native Americans, the Spanish American War, the Civil War, and both World Wars. In each case, he notes, people killed in the name of God, believing that the deity sided with them and opposed their enemies. According to the lyrics, people fight bravely, ask no questions, and do not bother to count the dead when God is on their side. The song, of course, stands in opposition to the Holy War ideology of Joshua, thus helping students to contemplate the rhetoric of the biblical book. Dylan's song also makes the important connection between the Bible and contemporary violence in the name of religion. The song ends by expressing hope that God will stop the next war, which may lead to discussion about what would, in fact, eliminate, or at least curb, religious violence; and what, if any, is the deity's role is these affairs.

Grateful Dead, "Samson and Delilah" (Rock, 1977)

The song begins with the Samson and Delilah scene (Judg 16:4–22) and then backtracks through the biblical text to discuss other events in Samson's life. The song describes Delilah's physical beauty—unlike the characteristically laconic biblical text—but it omits Samson's repeated lies to Delilah about the secret source of his strength. It also omits the biblical element that Delilah was under pressure from the Philistine lords. One can reflect on how

M
U
S
I
C

the song's simplified version alters the biblical one. The song then includes the incident in which Samson kills a thousand men—ten thousand in the song—with a jawbone of a donkey (Judg 15:14–17) and Samson's killing a lion (Judg 14: 5–9). The chorus to the song references Samson pushing down the Philistine building. One could ask which significant elements of the biblical text are omitted by the song, namely, the debacle with Samson's Timnite bride (14:10–20) and his consorting with a prostitute (16:1–4). What are the effects of such omissions?

Neil Sedaka, "Run Samson Run" (Pop, 1970)

This version of Samson and Delilah articulates the traditional misogynist reading of Delilah. She is a "cheatin' gal," a "demon," and "a devil in disguise" who brings about the strong man's demise. The dangers of female sexuality are seen as Samson is seduced by Delilah's wily ways, which leads to him "getting clipped," a perfect Freudian double entendre. The song goes one step further by outlining a moral: Every girl is a little bit like Delilah. Students can consider how the song rewrites the biblical account, noting mainly its omissions and simplifications. It also invites discussion about what motivates such retellings, and what is the moral "lesson" of the biblical tale—if there is one.

Pixies, "Dead" (Alternative, 1989)

This short song about David and Bathsheba is sung from David's perspective. Its lyrics are arcane and so asking students to connect them to the biblical tale can lead to creative insights. One could ask in what sense Bathsheba is "suffocating"? How does the word "dead" function in the song? Who is "torn down" and how?

Leonard Cohen, "Hallelujah" (Folk, 1984)

This song can prompt thought about the image of David in the biblical text. It begins with an allusion to David playing music to soothe Saul and then rehearses the episode with Bathsheba. Students might be asked about the significance of the line which says that Bathsheba "broke your throne and cut your hair." In what sense, if any, did Bathsheba "break" David's throne? Or did she help to continue it by birthing Solomon and then seeing to it that he was appointed king (1 Kgs 1–2)? The reference to "cutting hair" is presumably an allusion to the Samson and Delilah story, which invites a comparison between those two male-female relationships: Who has the power? Who acts as an autonomous agent? Is love involved? What is the outcome for each character? At the end of the song, David says that he did his best and although "it all went wrong," he will stand before the Lord and sing Hallelujah. Questions

MUSIC

for further discussion include: What is the relationship between God and David in the stories in 1–2 Samuel? In Chronicles? What are the implications of the all-too-human David being associated with the book of Psalms? Does the word "hallelujah" on David's lips ring true?

Momus, "King Solomon's Song and Mine" (Alternative, 1986)

Momus describes a man who is conscripted to work for King Solomon in the construction of the temple and palace (1 Kgs 3–9). Solomon prospers mightily at the expense of his laborers, though the singer, at least, finds the work tolerable. The song highlights the disparity between the wealthy king and his servants—compare Samuel's warning about the nature of a monarch (1 Sam 8)—witnessed, for example, when the Queen of Sheba visits Solomon. The song could open a discussion about daily life for the average Israelite during the monarchy, which, in turn, can prompt conversation about disparities between the perspective of the biblical narrator and "actual" historical conditions. On an ideological level, the song illustrates how people in power manipulate their human resources to maintain and increase power.

Sade, "Jezebel" (R&B, 1985)

As is well known, Jezebel's image has not fared well in cultural representations. This song offers a Jezebel who is confident, determined, hard working, and ambitious. Although the biblical narrator does not approve of Jezebel, in a number of ways she possesses characteristics that a contemporary audience would admire: She is tolerant of the beliefs of others (Elijah is the religious fanatic), loyal to her husband, willing to do what was necessary to acquire what she wanted, and successful in her career. The Jezebel of the song, reminiscent of the biblical figure, is a woman who "won't deny where she came from" (i.e., maintains her own religious traditions) and who declares: "I want to get what's mine" (e.g., Naboth's vineyard). The song sets the context for a discussion of the one-sided depiction of Jezebel or any number of other biblical characters.

Bob Marley, "Exodus" (Reggae, 1976)

Marley's song proclaims that it is time to leave Babylon and return to the "fatherland." Like Second Isaiah (Isa 43:16–21), Marley employs images of the Egyptian Exodus (referring to Moses and the Red Sea) to encourage a new, second Exodus. Similarly, both Marley and Second Isaiah employ the language of creation to bring about hope. Marley sings about walking on the "road of creation," which is reminiscent of texts such as Isa 40:28; 44:24; 45:7, 18. The biblical text, naturally, focuses on God's power in bringing about a new Exodus, whereas Marley's focus is on "looking within."

Derek Webb, "Wedding Dress" (Contemporary Christian, 2003)

Employing language and imagery reminiscent of Ezek 16 and Hos 2, Webb accuses the contemporary church of prostituting itself to cultural values in exchange for material wealth. The white wedding dress hides the filth underneath. The song is different from the biblical texts in one crucial way. It is sung from the perspective of the unfaithful woman, rather than the husband. Accordingly, it does not include any of the rhetoric found in the biblical text in which God violently punishes and humiliates his estranged wife. The song's metaphor thus functions differently. Students can be asked to compare their reaction to the biblical text with their response to the song. How and why does the metaphor "work" for the biblical prophets? Does it "work" today? It may also be interesting to consider the implications of a male singer taking the perspective of a "whoring" female. This can open up discussion on the gendered nature of the biblical text and how male Israelites may have heard the metaphor and identified (or not) with the woman. Are similar issues in play for men today who see themselves, as the song suggests, as the bride of Christ? Further, Webb has explained that he wrote the song in response to Bruce Wilkinson's wildly popular *Prayer of Jabez*, which he sees as an example of the church prostituting itself. Webb is the prophetic voice indicting the establishment, but if students know the book and approve of it, they will identify with the establishment and resist the song's rhetoric. Other students will agree with Webb's indictment. This can lead to a discussion of how difficult it can be to distinguish "true" prophetic voices; it can also help students understand why the message of biblical prophets was not always welcomed in ancient Israel. Does prophetic rhetoric need to shock in order to be effective? Could one identify with the content of the message (be faithful to God alone), but not endorse its form (adulterous wife metaphor)?

Mark Chesnutt, "Broken Promise Land" (Country, 1992)

Chesnutt sings about a cheating husband whose wife grows tired of waiting for him to return home and so she too is unfaithful. In the biblical metaphor (Hos 2; Ezek 16; Jer 3) the wife, Israel, is unfaithful to the husband, God. The song helps to underscore the fact that students, based on common cultural expectations, are more likely to anticipate a husband cheating (per the song and contra the biblical metaphor), which can open up discussions about the social functions of marriage in ancient Israel—that is, the ramifications of female versus male infidelity. Unlike the biblical texts, the husband in the song acknowledges his own failures and says that he will hate himself for giving her the opportunity and excuse to cheat. The song, then, can be used to raise questions about the reasons for Israel's infidelity to God. Is the male partly responsible for the female's infidelity? The biblical metaphor does not allow room for this possibility; asking why it does not can lead to consideration of the text's rhetorical function. The biblical allusion in the song's title works nicely: the covenant between Israel and God has been broken and now Israel will be exiled from the land. In short, Chesnutt invites discussion about the theological and psychological complexity of the embattled Yahweh-Israel relationship.

The Byrds, "She Has a Way" (Folk Rock, 1965)

The song describes a woman who "has a way" of running around. It works well in comparison with Ezek 16 and 23, where Israel is said to have been unfaithful from its youth (e.g., Ezek 23:3), in contrast to Jer 2, where the nation was loyal initially, in the wilderness (Jer 2:2). Students can review the wilderness narratives (Exod 16:1–4; 17:1–4; 32:1–14, 30–35; Num 11:1–6; 14:1–35; 16:41–50; 21:4–6; 25:1–9) to see how those traditions depict the early relationship. Students might consider the implications of the male/God entering into a relationship with a partner who was unfaithful "from the start," as the song says. The singer and the deity lament that they have treated the women well, only to be scorned. The singer, however, is patiently waiting, hoping for her return, while God is much more assertive and forceful. Which depiction of the male presents authentic love? Or are there problems with both?

Dom Crincoli, "Jonah" (Contemporary Christian, 2005)

The opening stanza helpfully explains that Jonah ran away because he was reluctant to help the hated Assyrians—a fact that the original audience would certainly have understood, though modern readers may miss. The song also rightly explains that the big fish is a vehicle of salvation, not of punishment, as many novice readers wrongly assume. Most of the song, however, is quite different from the biblical version, thus highlighting for students some of the key features of the canonical account. In the song, God personally calls Jonah to get his attention ("and he called me Jonah"), whereas in the Bible, "the Lord hurled a great wind" and "mighty storm" on the sea, nearly killing everyone on the boat. In the song, Jonah regrets deeply his actions and prays fervently for God "to change my course" and for release from the fish. Jonah's prayer is much more ambiguous in the biblical text (Jonah 2). The song omits any element of Jonah's continued defiance (cf. Jonah 4); instead, the prophet concludes that "the sea was a serendipitous highway leading me back to you."

M
U
S
I
C

WRITINGS

Boney M, "Rivers of Babylon" (Pop, 1978)

The song presents an alternate version of Ps 137. It follows verses 1–4 fairly closely, but instead of concluding with expressions of bitter anger and resentment toward the conquering enemy (137:7–9), the song substitutes another biblical phrase, "let the words of our mouth and the meditations of our heart be acceptable in thy sight." This censored version illustrates the reluctance in modern religious contexts to voice feelings of rage and hate. The biblical psalm represents raw, candid, human sentiments which, though harsh, are seemingly a normal and healthy part of the grieving process.

Linkin Park, "Hit the Floor" (Rock, 2002)

This song can be compared to imprecatory psalms, such as Ps 59. The singer, like the biblical writer, is angry at the injustices that surround him. Both psalmist and singer also claim that they did nothing to warrant the persecution they are experiencing at the hands of their enemies. Both also describe their adversaries with similar language—underscoring their pride, their eagerness to torment, and their persistence. The song and psalm also call for revenge to be taken against their foes, and both use explicit language in describing the desired destruction. The singer, however, intends to exact retribution himself. He will wait until the time is right and will then strike with vengeance. The psalmist, by contrast, relies on the power of God to destroy the enemies. The song, then, provides an opportunity to reflect on human expressions of anger and violence and how they might function for individuals or a community.

Evanescence, "Tourniquet" (Alternative Rock, 2003)

This song closely parallels a lament psalm in form and content. It contains an invocation (a call for God to remember), a complaint (a description of the suffering—a sense of betrayal, the bleeding, and screaming), and a petition (a plea for God to be the singer's tourniquet). It does not, however, conclude on a note of assurance or hope as most biblical laments do. In fact, the last word of the song is "suicide." Thus, the song works well as a comparison specifically to Ps 39 or 88.

U2, "40" (Rock, 1983)

This version of Ps 40 combines elements of thanksgiving—the Lord has saved me from the pit (cf. 40:1)—with the cry of lament, "How long?" The song could be used to consider the nature of Israelite faith as expressed in the psalms generally or to illustrate specifically how one individual psalm, such

M
U
S
I
C

as Ps 40, can express paradoxical sentiments. One might extend this discussion to connect with the vicissitudes of Israelite history or to consider the psychology of the psalms.

Hank Williams, "Funeral" (Country, 1952)

In recounting the funeral of a child, the song claims that God has the right to take away the child because it was only a loan from God in the first place. It counsels the child's parents not to criticize God because the deity knows best—and besides, the child is in a much better, happier place. The song thus represents a poor model for dealing with human suffering and anguish. It acknowledges none of the natural sentiments of anger, grief, bitterness, frustration, and doubt that are found in the lament psalms. The song tries to circumvent the pain, rather than confronting it and working through it; it offers the antithesis of a "biblically based" model for counseling.

Hank Williams, "Thank God" (Country, 1948)

This song's structure and content can be compared to psalms of praise. It features a call to praise ("Get on your knees and pray"), a reason for praise, specifically, as with many biblical songs, for the deity's creative power (for every flower, tree, mountain, and sea, etc.), and closes with a repeated call to worship ("Wherever you may be, thank God"). As with a number of psalms, the structure is not paradigmatic and may include other genres within it, in this case, elements of wisdom.

Johnny Cash, "Spiritual" (Country, 1996)

On Cash's last few albums (*American Recordings*), this master storyteller recorded a number of gospel and spiritual songs, including a solo gospel album titled *My Mother's Hymn Book* (2004). This song, from *Unchained*, is a five-minute, wrenching plea from a penitent to Jesus not to forget him on his deathbed. The lyrics are plain ("I don't wanna die alone," "Don't leave me here," "I know I have sinned but Lord I'm suffering"), but therein lies the usefulness of the song in the classroom. Cash's delivery is both strong and pleading, and the weariness and age in his voice reveals more about the emotional content of psalms than any academic treatise can. In conjunction with this song, students may be asked to compose their own psalm, based on either their understanding of what a psalm is, or their own religious and personal backgrounds. One could even assign them a specific psalm to work from (e.g., Ps 6). Following this, the Cash song could be played as an example of one person's religious plea for mercy from God, and as such illuminate the emotional depths of these works, so that students might feel better about sharing their psalms with the class or anonymously online. (A good resource for information about Cash is Dave Urbanski, *The Man Comes Around: The Spiritual Journey of Johnny Cash*, which includes a chapter on this album.)

John Coltrane, "Psalm" (Jazz, 1964)

The fourth movement of Coltrane's signature album *A Love Supreme* (beginning at 10:45 into the third track) is a musical recitation of Coltrane's poem "A Love Supreme." Not until recently was it widely known that Coltrane composed this movement as a wordless narration, but it is a logical way to end an album that charts a pilgrim's progress toward God, with titles such as "Acknowledgment," "Resolution," and "Pursuance." The psalm, reprinted in the liner notes, is a very personal praise of God, with a special emphasis on music: "One thought can produce millions of vibrations and they all go back to God.... everything does." Admittedly, Coltrane is no poet. However, the personal imagery in the poem, as well as the deeply felt emotion of the music, can serve as an example for students who might feel the psalms are dated, or who might like to write their own psalm. In this regard, one could ask students to pick a certain psalm and compose a simple tune for it (again, Ps 6 works well for this exercise). If students are uncomfortable composing, one could ask them to consider the ways in which music can express religious sentiment apart from the spoken word. Along this line, one could play this portion of the album and provide the text for students, asking afterward their impressions of how Coltrane's psalm compares to the canonical psalms and noting any specific similarities. One could also use this piece in conjunction with Johnny Cash's song, "Spiritual," to illustrate different genres of psalms, as Coltrane's poem is a psalm of praise, whereas Cash's is one of petition.

Tori Amos, "God" (Alternative Rock, 1994)

Amos has made it clear that this song is a direct response to patriarchy and the repression of women in religious traditions. In the song she accuses God of being unreliable and needing the help of a woman, which may lend itself to a discussion of the possibility that in ancient Israelite religion Yahweh had a female consort. The song also asks God if he will tell the woman about his creative powers regarding the "sky," which could be linked to Prov 8:22–31 which places Woman Wisdom with God at creation. Specifically she claims: "I was there . . . when he made firm the skies above" (8:27–28). The song makes an explicit link to the book of Proverbs when it quotes, in a speaking voice, Prov 31:3: "Give not thy strength unto women; nor thy ways to that which destroyeth kings." The Hebrew word rendered "strength" is the same word translated as "capable" and "excellently" in Prov 31:10, 29; thus a number of commentators note the tension between the universally negative portrayal of women in 31:3 and the poem that follows in verses 10–31. Amos's song, as does the biblical text, presents different views on women. Students might consider how the citation of Prov 31:3 functions rhetorically in the song.

Hank Williams, "Lost Highway" (Country, 1949)

Williams relates that when he was a young man he was led astray by gambling, alcohol, and a woman's lies. The woman's deception was the primary culprit for his current condition, which he describes as "alone and lost." The singer's perspective is reminiscent of the father/teacher in Proverbs who warns his son to avoid the loose woman whose paths lead to death ("boys, don't start your ramblin' around")—that is, to the "lost highway." However, unlike the biblical father, Williams admits to having "paid the cost" for his sins; he speaks not from a position of power and authority, but as a male who has succumbed to the loose woman and other worldly pleasures. He hopes his listeners will not repeat his mistakes. This notion can lead to a discussion of the nature of wisdom literature and who is in the best position to dispense counsel.

DC Talk, "That Kinda Girl" (Christian Rock, 1992)

This song is about avoiding a sexually promiscuous girl and pursuing a virtuous one. This, of course, parallels Proverbs' "loose woman" and Woman Wisdom and the "capable" woman of Prov 31. The promiscuous woman, as in Proverbs, is portrayed as the temptress who seduces the male with her appearance and her speech. As in the biblical text, her words are spoken by the male voice—that is, she is a male construct. Interestingly, the encounter with her occurs in a "garden" and she says, "I'm an apple. Would you care to take a bite?" Associating the loose girl with Eve could open up discussion about Eve's portrayal in Genesis, particularly how she plays a role more akin to Woman Wisdom in her desire for knowledge. Obviously, however, the song participates in a long tradition of denigrating Eve. The song is both like and unlike Prov 31, which it directly references. In the biblical text the "capable woman's" religiousness is mentioned only once at the end (31:30), but in the song it is her main attribute (she "loves the Lord"). Although the singer promises to treat the girl properly, ultimately, perhaps like Prov 31, the virtuous girl is "for me," the male singer, who asks that divine intervention bring her "to me."

Lost in Rotation, "Proverbs" (Alternative Rock, 2004)

The song simply sings the words of Prov 2:2, 4, and 3:3, 7. It illustrates the imperative form of a proverb, which can be contrasted with other forms found in the biblical book. It also combines elements from four different verses, that is, it is a mini-collection of sayings; this can lead to discussion of how sayings are collected in Proverbs as well as in cultural traditions more broadly. The song can also be used to consider how various parts of the body function in wisdom discourse—ear, heart, neck, and eyes appear in the song.

Elvis Presley, "Sound Advice" (Rock, 1962)

Presley warns that one should not always heed the "sound advice" that one is given, even if those giving it assure the listener that it is, in fact, sage guidance. It presents a countervoice to the wisdom-dispensing father of Prov 1–9. The song urges one to think twice about following advice from those who think they are smart and enjoy being in positions of power. This connects to the power and social dynamics at work in Proverbs: The patriarchal societal structure depends on the implied reader (the son) heeding his father's advice. Those in power do not wish for the status quo to be challenged. How is the son to identify "sound advice" and what is at stake in the decision?

Smashing Pumpkins, "Bullet with Butterfly Wings" (Hard Rock, 1995)

This Grammy-winning song mentions explicitly and draws on themes in Job. The meaning of the lyrics is abstruse (and a variety of interpretations have been proposed), but connecting them to the story of Job is not difficult. Students might be asked how the first stanza connects to the prologue (Job 1–2). It mentions "secret destroyers" (Job is unaware of the causes of his suffering), "betrayed desires" (does God "betray" Job by handing him over to the *satan*), and "the game" (the divine wager between God and the *satan*). The singer asserts that he will demonstrate his "cool" and "cold" like Job. Job indeed appears to be cool in his response to the disasters and personal suffering in chapters 1–2, but then turns "cold" in his dialogues with his friends. In the song's repeated refrain (and most audibly clear line) the singer expresses his "rage," but still feels as though he is nothing more than a confined rat. Does the rhetoric of the divine reply in Job 38–41 ("Gird up your loins and answer me"; "Surely you know…") invite Job to feel like a meaningless rodent? Or is the speech more conciliatory and consoling than that? In the end, the singer declares that he cannot be saved. The conclusion to the book of Job, of course, is more optimistic, but is there a sense in which Job too, or perhaps the reader, cannot be saved from the trauma?

Seatrain, "Song of Job" (Rock, 1970)

This song retells the biblical story of Job, but with some key omissions. It focuses exclusively on Job's remaining faithful and does not include Job's venomous accusations against the deity (e.g., Job 16) or the fact that Job holds God accountable for his sufferings and demands a response to his plight (Job 31). The song also significantly revises the theologically complex divine speech in Job 38–41 by summarizing the speech thus: "Job has proved his faith and shall live joyous days." The song helps to highlight the challenging aspects of the biblical book precisely because it glosses over them. The song also presents a one-sided, negative portrayal of the friends, which can lead to discussion of their role in the biblical tale.

Joni Mitchell, "The Sire of Sorrow (Job's Sad Song)" (Folk, 1994)

Drawing on specific language and imagery in Job's speeches to his friends, the first verse of this song focuses on Job's pain and anguish, as well as his protests directed toward the deity. The second verse parallels Job 29, in which he remembers his prosperous former days. The song continues with Job expressing his despair and frustration. The friends appear in the song, much as in the Bible, as characters who assume that Job must be guilty. The song is particularly striking in that it features no divine speech from the whirlwind or any restoration of Job. Instead, after Job describes his "festering flesh," his "terrifying visions," and his desire to die (cf. Job 3), the song ends on a note of sorrowful questioning. The song provides an excellent contrast to Seatrain's version of the story (see above).

"He's Got the Whole World in His Hands" (Traditional)

This is a children's song that can be employed as a comparative text for the divine speeches in Job. Like God's answer to Job, the song declares that God has the wind and rain, land and sea, sun and moon, night and day, and fall and spring in his hands (in the fullest version of the song). But, in contrast to the biblical text, the song claims that "he's got the little tiny baby" and "everybody here" in his hands. The children's song highlights the striking absence of any mention of humanity in God's speech to Job, much less any mention of Job's specific suffering. The song prompts reflection on the purpose and point of the deity's "answer" to Job.

Hank Williams, "Everything's Okay" (Country, 1951)

This is a story about Uncle Bill who loses everything but continues to assert that it is going to be all right. Uncle Bill's experiences have obvious connections with story of Job; however, Bill's sufferings do not arise as the result of a debate between God and the *satan*. This is a crucial difference which underscores a fact that students sometimes forget: Job is not simply suffering a string of bad luck, as Uncle Bill is. Rather, Job's misfortune comes directly from the deity's hand, as God admits (Job 2:3) and Job himself recognizes (1:21; 2:10). The song can also prompt discussion about whose response to their sufferings is more appropriate, both theologically and psychologically: Job's rancorous outbursts or Bill's passive optimism?

50 Cent, "Candy Shop" (Rap, 2005)

The song can serve as a comparison to the nature of the poetic language in Song of Songs. Both songs have a male and female voice; both have indirect descriptions of sexual acts ("I'll let you lick the lollipop"; cf. 2:3; 5:4–5; 7:8–9); both appeal to multiple senses (taste, touch, sight), including the use of "wine" imagery ("champagne campaign"; cf. 1:2; 7:9); both refer to sexual activity in multiple locations, especially outdoor "garden" areas ("on the beach or in the park"; cf. 7:11–12; 8:1, 5); both describe various aspects of the female body; and both feature reference to the girl's female friends. The two songs are also different. For instance, the biblical song features prominently the female voice—or, at least, there is balanced representation with the male perspective—while in the contemporary song the male voice dominates and the female voice is relegated to only a few lines. "Candy Shop" focuses only on the male "stick," while the biblical text offers extended gazes at the whole male body (5:11–16). Further, the biblical text seemingly presents a more meaningful, intimate encounter than the song's focus on sexual exploits. Juxtaposing the two songs can lead to discussion of similarities and differences between how human sexuality is understood in modern songs and the biblical one. In short, playing a sexually explicit song—and there are many from which to choose, including ones that are much more (porno)graphic—and comparing it to the biblical song in terms of tone and content can be a productive exercise.

Kate Bush, "The Song of Solomon" (Alternative Rock, 1993)

This song quotes lines from the biblical book by the same title in order to express the singer's (female) desire for sexual intimacy. Bush declares that she "just wants your sexuality" and "I'll come in a hurricane for you," sentiments in many ways is akin to the (sexually) aggressive woman in the biblical text (cf. 3:1–5). The song can be juxtaposed with many others that express male sexual desire, such as 50 Cent's "Candy Shop" (above), in order to weigh the perceptions of male versus female expressions of sexual desire. Male expressions traditionally receive a more sympathetic read than female ones, thus highlighting the biblical book's positive portrayal of the woman's desires.

Dave Matthews Band, "Tripping Billies" (Rock, 1996)

The song's chorus, "Eat, drink, and be merry, for tomorrow we die," echoes Ecclesiastes both in its advice to enjoy the pleasures of life and in the rationale for doing so, namely, that death is the end (cf. 3:19–22). The Teacher, however, asserts that his advice to eat and drink is sanctioned by God (cf. 3:13), whereas Matthews makes no mention of the divine. This can invite discussion about the "religious" nature of Ecclesiastes, whether or

M
U
S
I
C

not the Teacher is correct in associating pleasure with the deity, or whether there is any substantive difference between the views of Matthews and the Teacher.

Sixpence None the Richer, "Meaningless" (Pop, 1994)

Drawing on language and images from Ecclesiastes, this song expresses a sense of the futility of life. In light of this sentiment, the singer, much like the Teacher, concludes that the best course of action is to enjoy the pleasures of this life before death comes. The song, however, contains the line, "Fear your God, this is all I know." Thus, like the book of Ecclesiastes, the song contains conservative exhortations (cf. 3:17; 5:1–6; 7:18; 11:9) alongside more pessimistic observations. The biblical book, of course, concludes with the command to fear God (12:13–14) while the song ends on a note of hopelessness. The song, then, can help students consider the contradictory nature of the book of Ecclesiastes as a whole, as well as the paradoxical words of the Teacher. What are the singer and the Teacher attempting to do by juxtaposing conflicting observations? What is the editor of the biblical book trying to accomplish with the epilogue?

Kansas, "Dust in the Wind" (Rock, 1977)

Both "dust" and "wind" are important theme words in Ecclesiastes, showing the ephemeral nature of life and its absurdity (1:6, 12; 2:11, 26; 3:20, etc.). The song observes: "Same old song, just a drop of water in an endless sea," and "Nothing lasts forever but the earth and sky"; this is reminiscent of the Teacher: "A generation goes and a generation comes, but the earth remains forever" (1:4; cf. 1:2–11). Similarly, both the song and biblical text lament the fact that human accomplishments are ultimately worthless ("all we do crumbles to the ground," cf. 2:1–11). Both also note the futility of dreams (cf. 5:3, 7). Although the song and biblical text are ideologically similar in many ways, the Teacher seems to find more hope and optimism than the song, namely, with the notion that one should enjoy life precisely because "all we are is dust in the wind" (cf. 5:18; 9:9).

The Stanley Brothers, "Old Daniel Prayed" (Gospel Bluegrass, 1959)

This bluegrass gospel standard by one of the most important groups in traditional American music retells the story of Daniel in the lion's den (Dan 6). Much like the hero lists one finds in Acts 7, Heb 11, Sir 44–50, and other apocryphal texts such as 1 Macc 2, Wis 10, and 4 Macc 16 and 18, this song exhorts the listener to emulate Daniel's example of piety in the face of religious persecution. As such, the song can be used to illustrate not only Dan 6, but also the phenomenon of hero lists and typological interpretation. One might ask students to reflect on what makes Daniel a heroic figure during the Second Temple period. Or, one could have students look at the hero lists mentioned above and ruminate on the commonalities found among those included. Another exercise is for students to draw on other chronologically appropriate writings to construct their own hero list.

NEW TESTAMENT

GOSPELS

Bruce Cockburn, "Cry of a Tiny Babe" (Folk, 1990)

Cockburn's song retells Matthew's birth story, with little deviation from the basic biblical outline, although Mary becomes more of a character when she asks Joseph, "What if I were with another man?" and says that she felt the baby kick. The song's refrain interprets the significance of the birth ("redemption"), as does the final verse ("forgiveness"). One could ask students where, if at all, these theological elements may be detected or foreshadowed in Matthew's birth narrative. Or, what kind of "theology" is Matthew interested in developing with his birth story (e.g., with the fulfillment quotations)? The third verse fits better with Luke's story, as it asserts that the baby came not to kings, but to "shepherds and street people, hookers and bums." Interestingly, the song never mentions Jesus by name. Can that fact at all be linked to the nature of the biblical accounts?

Dave Matthews Band, "Christmas Song" (Rock, 1993)

The song focuses on Jesus' birth and death, so students might be invited to discuss themes that appear in both the Christmas and crucifixion story. The lyrics mix the birth narratives from Matthew and Luke, as the wise men visit Jesus in the manger; there is no mention of the virgin birth, only that a "surprise" is on the way for Mary and Joseph. When Jesus is on the cross, he calls out to "Daddy" and expresses fear that his mission has failed, which naturally can be compared to the anguish that Jesus voices on the cross in Matthew and Mark. Students can be asked about the significance of the repeating refrains "Love is all around" and "The blood of our children is all around" and how they may connect to the Gospel narratives. How are love and violence linked in the Gospels and in Christian tradition?

Pearl Jam, "Meaningless" (Rock, 1992)

In the first verse this song declares that "We're all meaningless," but then ultimately resists this conclusion, saying "We're not meaningless." The song reflects the human struggle to find meaning in life, much like the book of

Ecclesiastes. Notably, however, and quite unlike the Teacher, the song concludes that meaning can be found in love: "If you love someone, tell them,"
and "Show them how you feel." This is reminiscent of Matt 5:43–45. Here
Jesus exhorts his followers to "love your enemies," and he then provides a
reason: "for [God] makes his sun rise on the evil and on the good, and sends
rain on the righteous and the unrighteous." Jesus, like the Teacher in Ecclesiastes, recognizes the inequities of life, but rather than concluding that all is
meaningless and recommending the pursuit of pleasure, he teaches that the
absurdity of it all is actually part of the divine plan and thus we, like God,
should pursue love of everyone. If nothing else, Pearl Jam serves to underscore the different ethical principles that might emerge from the notion that
life is meaningless; the song and Jesus advocate a different, presumably higher,
ethic than the Teacher. If life is meaningless, if it has no point or purpose,
how then should one live?

Hank Williams, "A House of Gold" (Country, 1950)

This tune can be compared to the antiwealth theme in Luke. Williams
proclaims that people steal, cheat, and lie to obtain wealth, even though it will
be of no value on judgment day. Similarly, he asserts that he would rather be
saved than live in a house of gold. There is one crucial difference, however,
between Williams's song and Jesus' teaching in texts such as Luke 12:13–21;
14:15–24; 16:19–31; and especially 18:18–30. In these passages, the wealthy
people are not moral or religious failures; rather, they are condemned simply
because they are wealthy. The rich man is building bigger barns to store his
wealth; the people who do not accept the dinner invitation are tending to the
duties of life; the rich man, as he is tormented in Hades, is told simply that
he was wealthy and Lazarus was not and so now the tables are turned (cf.
esp. 16:25); and the rich ruler has kept all the commands (i.e., he is morally
and religiously upright) but is not willing to sell all that he owns. Williams's
song, by contrast, offers typical religious rhetoric: Wealth is not bad in and of
itself; rather it is bad because it will likely cause you to do bad things, such as
lie, cheat, and deny God. While students are more inclined to identify with
Williams's ideas, the song helps them appreciate Jesus' much harsher teachings about wealth.

Crash Test Dummies, "God Shuffled His Feet" (Alternative Rock, 1993)

The song tells a story about God preparing a picnic of "wine and bread"
(an obvious reference to the Eucharist) for people to eat. As the people enjoy
the food, they ask God questions about the nature of life in heaven, such as
if one needs to eat, or get a haircut, and what happens if one's body were
maimed in this life. These queries could lead to discussion of texts that deal

with bodily resurrection (1 Cor 15) and associated issues, such as body-soul dualism. In response to their queries, God tells the people a story about a boy who woke up with blue hair. The people do not understand the meaning of the story and ask if it was a parable or a subtle joke. God does not respond. The enigmatic story about the blue-haired boy can serve as basis for discussion of parabolic discourse. Jesus, too, tells stories that his listeners may have had difficulty comprehending or, at the very least, were stories that they were not expecting. The song fits nicely with Mark 4:10–12, in which Jesus explains that he speaks in parables precisely so that people will not understand.

U2, "The First Time" (Rock, 1993)

This song, according to lead singer Bono, is a version of the parable of the Prodigal Son (Luke 15:11–32). Unlike the parable, however, in the song when the wayward son returns home, he throws away the key. He rejects his father's welcome. But the song then ends by saying that for the first time, he felt love. The song not only helps one to think about the nature of the biblical parable, but also is itself a parable. It twists the expected ending both with the son's rejection and with the final line expressing love. Given the antimaterialist themes in a number of U2's songs, one wonders if the son refuses the keys because the father is a rich man who dresses the part and is eager to bestow his wealth on his son. One might employ this song in conjunction with an exercise in which students are asked to play the different roles of the characters in the biblical parable. How would they respond if they were the wayward son, the father, or the faithful son?

Johnny Cash, "Matthew 24 (Is Knocking at the Door)" (Country, 1982)

In this brief song, Cash claims that the end times are near, based on the predictions of Jesus as recorded in Matt 24 (cf. Mark 13). In cryptic and easily applicable language, Cash notes that "the rumors of war," "people getting ready for battle," and "an earthquake" are "signs of the times we're in today." Cash joins a long tradition of applying apocalyptic images to modern events, and as such this song can be used to illustrate this tradition, as well as to initiate discussions on the malleable nature of apocalyptic literature and symbols in general.

Collin Raye, "What If Jesus Comes Back Like That" (Country, 1995)

Raye's song explores the implications of Jesus returning as a hobo or a homeless person. It asks the listeners if they would embrace these people or turn their back on them. The song concludes by suggesting that Jesus will accept or reject people based on their treatment of others (i.e., the hobo and homeless). In this sense it closely parallels the parable of the Sheep and Goats, where Jesus says, "As you have done to the least of these, you have done unto me" (Matt 25:31–46), and where admittance into the kingdom is granted only to those who cared for the disenfranchised. In addition to connecting with social ethics, the song lends itself to reflection on the significance of the incarnation more generally. One might also note that if the song is taken more eschatologically, the image of the returning Jesus in Revelation is hardly that of a hobo.

Sam Cooke and the Soul Stirrers, "Jesus Gave Me Water" (Gospel, 1951)
Before Sam Cooke, arguably the most important soul singer in music history, scored pop success with hits like "Cupid," and "Wonderful World," he recorded exclusively gospel music with a group called The Soul Stirrers. This song retells the story of the Samaritan woman in John 4. In it, Jesus gave the woman "livin', lovin', lastin' water." In the Johannine account, the woman's experience seems to be downplayed in 4:39–42, but in this version, the woman's perspective retains its power, as we are told in the last verse that she "left him shoutin'" and there was "no room for doubtin'" that she would "of his wonders tell." As such, this song can be used to illustrate a feminist reading of John 4, as well as Jesus' attitude toward women during his ministry.

Sam Cooke, "Touch the Hem of His Garment" (Gospel, 1956)
This recording conflates the Gospel stories of the woman suffering from hemorrhages in Mark 5:25–34, Matt 9:20–22, and Luke 8:42b–48. The song focuses on the distress of the woman, even supplementing the Gospel accounts with new details of her unsuccessful treatment by doctors. Also, the song increases the healing of the woman, so that she is not simply healed, she is made whole. Because of the emphasis on the woman's situation and Jesus' role in her restoration, this song can be used to discuss Jesus' attitudes toward cultural and social "others," especially women, during his ministry, as well as the importance of faith in the Gospels.

Iris DeMent, "He Reached Down" (Folk Gospel, 2004)
A highly regarded singer-songwriter of Americana and traditional music, DeMent's 2004 album Lifeline contains twelve classic Christian hymns, almost all from the nineteenth century. This song is her own contribution, and it retells two well-known Gospel narratives: the Good Samaritan (Luke 10:29–37) and the Woman Caught in Adultery (John 7:53–8:11). DeMent highlights the compassionate aspects of these stories through the refrain, "He reached down and touched the pain." In the final verse, the perspective shifts to encourage hearers to emulate this altruism and emphasizes the eternal rewards for doing so. As such, the song can be used to supplement discussion

of the portrayal of Jesus, his view towards the "other" during the first century
C.E., and the practice of conflation in interpretation.

Eric Taylor, "Bread and Wine" (Folk, 2001)

This slow and intense song from Taylor's album *Scuffletown* retells Jesus'
speech to his disciples at the Last Supper in a distinctly modern parlance, for
example, "You people find yourselves a chair. We're going to go through this
just one more time. And then I've got to be somewhere." Taylor's Jesus seems
tired and disturbed by his fate, and as such can be used to cast a new light
on the Gospel accounts of this event. One way to accomplish this is to display several different Jesuses who demonstrate different attitudes toward their
respective missions, for instance, John's Jesus and the Jesus from *Jesus Christ
Superstar* as compared with Martin Scorcese's *Last Temptation of Christ*,
Mark's Jesus, and Eric Taylor's Jesus. This exercise should hammer home the
point that over time there have been a number of different Jesuses, each of
whom show varying levels of enthusiasm for their missions.

Bob Dylan, "In the Garden" (Folk, 1980)

Dylan sings primarily about Jesus' reception by the people. The song features a series of rhetorical questions asking if they saw the miracles, heard his
teaching, believed the resurrection, and so forth. The basic gist is this: How
could people have misunderstood or rejected Jesus. This is in fact an interesting question, and teachers could explore it from a historical or social angle;
for example, it could lead to a discussion of first-century Judaism as a way
to explain Jesus' mixed reception, or it could help students understand how
Jesus was only subsequently proclaimed "Lord" as Dylan seems not to recognize. From a literary perspective, one could point out to Dylan that in Mark,
Jesus goes to great lengths to keep his identity and his teaching a mystery—
that is, the Messianic Secret is a way to explain why there was not universal
understanding and belief. Indeed, the song relies on a much higher Christology than the one found in Mark.

Bruce Springsteen, "Jesus Was an Only Son" (Rock, 2005)

Springsteen imagines Jesus' last moments before his execution and
emphasizes his mother Mary's presence: "His mother Mary walking beside
him, in the path where his blood spilled." Because of the popularity of the
artist, this song can serve as a useful way to encourage students to imagine
the Passion narratives from different perspectives, as well as to initiate discussions about the role of Mary in the Gospels. The title, of course, can be
brought to bear on discussions of Jesus' brothers in various biblical texts (e.g.,
Mark 6:1–6) and later Christian tradition.

Brand New, "Jesus Christ" (Alternative Rock, 2006)

The overall meaning of the song is ambiguous, but it makes several clear biblical references. It asks what Jesus did during his three days in the tomb, which could relate to a discussion of noncanonical texts that wrestle with this question. The singer is afraid to die because of the uncertainty of what comes next; students might consider where, if at all, this issue appears in the canonical Gospel tradition. He says that Jesus will come like a thief in the night, which, of course, echoes only one of several New Testament traditions. Here the song stands in some tension with Jesus' own speech in Mark 13, which says that the coming of the Son of Man will be preceded by numerous signs, although verses 32–33 also says that no one will know the time. In addition to being lonely and worried about the afterlife, the singer also asserts that "we all got wood and nails," reminiscent of Jesus' command to "take up your cross and follow me."

Tupac and Outlawz, "Black Jesuz" (Rap, 1999)

This posthumously released song works nicely in a discussion of different images of Jesus. It illustrates how portraits of Jesus often reflect the identity of those constructing the image—whether it be an artist or an historical Jesus scholar. Tupac is searching for a "black Jesus" who will understand his pain of life in the ghetto, a Jesus who is not "too perfect," a Jesus, even, who will smoke and drink like he does—in short, a Jesus who will "understand where we comin' from." Tupac appears to be aware that his image of Jesus is a reflection of himself. The song could lead to discussion of the way various understandings of Jesus function for individuals and communities.

Johnny Cash, "If Jesus Ever Loved a Woman" (Country, 1973)

Cash takes up a current topic in this song, namely, Jesus' relationship with Mary Magdalene, as well as a perennial question, namely, how human was Jesus? The former is answered specifically: "If Jesus ever loved a woman, I think Mary Magdalene was the woman that he loved." The latter issue is addressed more obliquely, that is, Cash feels Jesus' life was perfect, sinless, without temptation, but he adds, "only did his Father know about his human needs." Cash also addresses Jesus' attitudes towards the sexes, noting, "He never did condemn a man or woman, just for being man or woman." As such, there is ample material here to further discussion of Jesus' relationships with women, biblical views on Jesus' humanity, and the role of Mary Magdalene in the early Jesus movements.

M
U
S
I
C

LETTERS

Johnny Cash, "The Man in Black"/"The Man in White" (Country, 1971/2000)

Cash here condenses his only novel, also titled *The Man in White*, into a five-and-a-half minute summary of Paul's life from the death of Jesus to his blinding on the road to Damascus (Acts 9). Several things are interesting about Cash's treatment of Paul. First, he highlights Paul's Jewish background in the first verse so that he is able to emphasize the "conversion" of Paul in similar terms to those used in Acts. Second, Cash is more interested in Paul's mission than his death, as evidenced by the last verse, in which Cash recounts (as Paul): "I go to all the world, and I let the whole world know that the Man in White appeared to me." Finally, anyone who knows anything about Cash knows that he considered himself "The Man in Black." He even recorded a song by that title in which he described himself as a symbol for the disenfranchised and downtrodden, which explains why he always wore black. The last verse of the song establishes the near-scapegoat effect Cash's choice has on his world, in which Cash states he would love to be happier than he is, "But I'll try to carry off a little darkness on my back." The dichotomy between Cash's self-understanding here and his portrayal of Jesus as The Man in White is curious, to say the least. However, "The Man in White" is perhaps more useful in the classroom, not only to orient students to Paul, but also to illustrate how helpful narrative rewriting of biblical stories can be for content-recognition purposes.

Momus, "Lucky Like St. Sebastian" (Alternative, 1986)

The first half of this song discusses the life of Paul and could serve as a comparative text for some of the narratives in Acts or Gal 1–2. The song notes Paul's persecution of Christians but, against the biblical text, asserts that Paul converted, and changed his name, because he concluded that his acts of violence were actually facilitating the growth of Christianity. The blood on Paul's hands, however, stains his letters, and Paul, unable to overcome his past, decides it is best if he dies. So he asks the authorities in Rome if they can arrange his death as a martyr. The song may give students a chance to pause and reflect on the dramatic nature of Paul's conversion—the man who is responsible for writing much of the New Testament was once one of Christianity's most adamant foes, according to the biblical image of Paul. Of course, the song does not present the biblical Paul, which is what makes it thought-provoking in the same way that alternate versions of the life of Jesus prompt debate.

Red Hot Chili Peppers, "Shallow Be Thy Game" (Alternative Rock, 1995)

The meaning of the lyrics is somewhat obscure, although they are clearly objecting to certain tenets of Christianity. One of those is original sin, which is seen as a way to make people guilty and thus more easily controlled. Rather than being born into sin, the singer asserts that that he was "not created in the likeness of a fraud." For both Paul and the song, the Genesis creation stories have something to say about human nature. Paul, however, draws from the Garden of Eden story ("By one man sin entered into the world," Rom 5), whereas the song alludes to the creation of humans in the image of God (Gen 1:26–27). Students may reflect on these different interpretive moves, the issues that are at stake, and how "original sin" functions in Paul's theology (or at least in Augustine's understanding of Pauline theology). Are the Red Hot Chili Peppers right in their rejection of original sin?

Believer, "Dust to Dust" (Christian Heavy Metal, 1990)

Using language reminiscent of Ecclesiastes, the song expresses the futility of life and the inevitability of death. But then there is a shift to Pauline concepts, asserting that Christ died to absolve human guilt, was raised, and through belief in Christ one can gain life. Students might reflect on how belief in Christ's death and resurrection may, or may not, help a person confront the meaningless struggles of this life that the song so aptly describes at the outset. Like Paul, the song focuses exclusively on the significance of the resurrection of Jesus rather than, say, Jesus' teachings. If God "molded man's flesh and soul," then one might ask of both Paul and the song why humans are guilty and in need of the redemptive violence of the cross. How or why, in other words, does one move from the fairly obvious "you are dust and will one day return to dust" to "you are guilty and need to believe in Jesus to overcome death"? Students might compare the thoughts of the Teacher in Ecclesiastes regarding death and the (lack of) afterlife.

Horace Andy, "Love Is the Light" (Reggae, 1977)

The song begins by quoting Rom 6:23—the wages of sin is death but the gift of God (Jah) is eternal life. This, of course, represents basic Pauline soteriology. But the song then shifts focus as it exhorts people to "do right" and "be good" and ends by saying only the "fittest of the fittest" will stand. It also points out that the wise man built his house on the rock (cf. Matt 7:24–27), which, again, is more reminiscent of traditional wisdom thought (cf. Proverbs) and the book of James. Perhaps in this sense the song mirrors the shape of the New Testament itself as it contains different ideas regarding salvation— is it a gift or must it be merited?

REVELATION

Lowell Blanchard with the Valley Trio, "Jesus Hits Like the Atom Bomb"
(Bluegrass Gospel, ca. 1950)

Long considered to be a novelty song, this upbeat, catchy tune connects the anxiety over nuclear weapons in the 1950s and the imminent return of Jesus. While this premise may sound kitschy, Blanchard, a popular DJ of the period, takes this opportunity to warn his listeners in the song's refrain to be less concerned about atom bombs than about the Parousia, which will be akin to an atom bomb. The second verse goes even further, noting a similarity between the bomb, the fire of Elijah, and the rainbow following the Flood. Because of these interesting connections, Blanchard's song can illustrate the continuing impact and evolution of apocalyptic thought. More specifically, it can also be used in conjunction with secondary texts such as Eugen Weber's *Apocalypses: Prophecies, Cults, and Millennial Beliefs through the Ages*, as well as various documentaries such as A&E's "Mysteries of the Bible" episode on Revelation, to exemplify how persons in a specific time period interpret Revelation's dark imagery.

Manowar, "Death Angel (Revelation)" (Heavy Metal, 1983)

The song is replete with language from Revelation as it describes the apocalyptic defeat of Satan. One could ask students to locate all the passages in Revelation to which the song refers (e.g., keys of death, hair white as wool, the four horsemen, seven plagues) and perhaps identify the very few nonbiblical elements in the lyrics. The heavy metal genre captures the violent nature of the biblical book. The song helps students understand that Revelation is less about predicting future events and more about crushing the forces of evil—ideal fodder for a band that thrives on images of carnage.

Hank Williams, "The Angel of Death" (Country, 1948)

Williams claims that the book of Revelation warns its readers that when they die, they will meet the Angel of Death (cf. Rev 14:14–20). Williams asks his listeners if they are ready for this encounter. The rhetoric here is similar to Dylan's "Are You Ready?" (see below) and in the same way, it can prompt discussion of how the song employs or reconfigures biblical imagery and rhetoric (i.e., it shifts the focus to the individual's fate). The song's Death Angel is an apocalyptic judge who decides the fate of individuals upon their death. Manowar's Death Angel (see above) destroys the powers of evil. Students might consider which depiction is more akin to the biblical image. How do the strikingly different musical genres (country versus heavy metal) relate to the images of the Angel?

MUSIC

Bob Dylan, "Are You Ready" (Folk Rock, 1980)

Dylan asks if one is prepared for "judgment," "the terrible swift sword," "Armageddon," and the "day of the Lord." The song could be used in a discussion of these terms and how they are employed and connected in biblical apocalyptic literature. One might ask students to locate New Testament passages that pose the question "Are you ready?" or "Are you prepared to meet Jesus?" or texts that clearly associate "judgment day" and whether "you want to be in heaven or in hell." Students might be surprised to have trouble identifying such passages, which can illustrate the difficulty of outlining biblical eschatology.

REM, "It's the End of the World as We Know It" (Rock, 1987)

While the title of the song indicates its connection to Revelation, its lyrics are cryptic. Teachers might employ the song as an illustration of the mysterious nature of apocalyptic discourse. Both song and book have something to do with the "the end," but after that, it is difficult to say much with any certainty. If students cannot interpret contemporary apocalyptic texts (the song), how much more difficult will it be to understand ancient ones? The singer claims that even though it is the end of the world, he feels fine. This may lead to a discussion of the social location of apocalyptic literature. Was the author or audience of Revelation "feeling fine" or a persecuted minority? Is it possible that the audience was "feeling fine" but that the author wanted to alert them to reasons to be more concerned? Why would people who are doing well in the world as we know it—those with some material wealth or power, for example—wish for the end?

Jimmy Buffett, "Apocalypso" (Country, 1994)

This song from the album *Fruitcakes* takes a uniquely light-hearted view of the Apocalypse, as one might expect from Jimmy Buffett. Unlike many other songs dealing with this topic that encourage either repentance or the more somber aspects of the end of the world, Buffett notes wryly, "When this earthly light is burning low, this dance will take you to the next plateau … We'll be dancing when we go." Because of the almost celebratory tone, this song can illustrate the joy with which many throughout time have viewed the Apocalypse.

Merle Haggard, "Rainbow Stew" (Country, 1981)

There are many songs whose reliance on Revelation is thematic rather than literary. That is, they portray an ideal, utopian future that will take place only after certain conditions have been met. This general idea is matched by apocalyptic literature in general, but found more specifically in texts such as

1–2 Thessalonians and especially Revelation. In the first two verses of "Rainbow Stew," Haggard notes a litany of ecological and financial woes and then postulates that when these woes are addressed, "We'll all be drinkin' that free bubble-ubb and eatin' that Rainbow Stew." This ecological awareness is all too rare in country music, but it parallels the transformation of the heaven and earth in Rev 21–22, as well as many postmillennial eschatological movements. As such, Haggard's song can demonstrate not only the imagery of a new creation, but also the interpretations of Revelation.

VARIOUS

B. B. King, "Ain't That Just Like a Woman" (Blues, 1976)

King blames Eve, Lot's wife, and Delilah for the "problems" they cause the men in their lives. The song is a misogynistic reading of these three female characters, but it nicely invites students to compare and contrast them. For example, Eve and Delilah are depicted as much more cerebral than their male partners. Lot's wife is the only anonymous figure and the only one who ends up dead. All three, in one way or another, defy the passive role assigned to them. The final verse of the song claims that no matter how much a man takes care of a woman, "they ain't never satisfied." Of course, Adam, Lot, and Samson are not models of male concern and compassion, but, more importantly, King's notion can help underscore the male perspective in texts such as Hos 2 and Ezek 16, where God as the husband expresses anger at Israel his wife because she does not appropriately acknowledge the care that he has provided for her—she is "never satisfied." Perhaps God and B. B. King have not figured out "what women want," and both lash out in vitriolic frustration.

Elvis Presley, "Hard Headed Woman" (Rock, 1958)

The song references the stories of Adam and Eve, Samson and Delilah, and Ahab and Jezebel in order to illustrate how a "hard headed woman (has) been a thorn in the side of man." In each instance, Presley reads the text poorly. He claims that Adam told Eve to stay away from the (apple) tree, that Samson enjoined Delilah to keep her fingers out of his hair, and that Ahab was "doin' swell" until he met Jezebel. Connecting these three women can open up discussion about their portrayal in the biblical text, in contrast to Presley's (traditional) male reading. All three women, for instance, appear more intellectually engaged and diligent than their male counterparts (cf. 1 Kgs 21 for Jezebel). Interestingly, Presley concludes by observing that he has a hard-headed woman, but he nonetheless hopes desperately that she will not leave him. One might argue, from a psychoanalytic perspective, that Presley, like the biblical text, is fascinated with and drawn to "dangerous" women, even as he wants to blame them for all his failures.

Sting, "It Ain't Necessarily So" (Rock, 1997)

This 1935 George Gershwin song covered by Sting summarizes the stories of David and Goliath, Jonah, and the birth of Moses, but expresses incredulity regarding their historical veracity (per the song title). The song also claims that "it ain't necessarily" the case that the devil is a villain and that it takes clean living to get into heaven, and it expresses doubt about Methuselah living 900 years. By drawing on stories from the primeval history (Methuselah), a fictional short story (Jonah), legendary tales from the history of Israel (Moses' miraculous birth, and David and Goliath), and disparate material from the New Testament, the song helps students to consider the different genres of biblical material, the function of those genres, and the different kinds of truth that biblical stories might present, or claim to present.

KRS-One, "The Truth" (Rap, 1995)

The song has two distinct parts. The first stanza challenges traditional understandings of the crucifixion. It explains that a cross was simply the Roman form of capital punishment. If Jesus were shot with a gun, people would wear little gold guns around their neck, or if he were electrocuted, people would kneel in front of electric chairs. The song is thus calling its listeners to contemplate the nature of the cross as a religious symbol. It is also objecting to the violence that is associated with crucifixion, as the last line of the stanza notes the paradox of calling for an end to violence while continuing to venerate a remarkably violent symbol. The song could be connected to several of Paul's discussions of the cross (e.g., 1 Cor 1; Phil 2). The second stanza addresses the issue of how the world could be populated if there were only four human beings originally—Adam, Eve, Cain, and Abel. Reading the text literally, of course, causes certain logical problems, as it would for any number of other Hebrew Bible texts. The song can lead to a discussion of other ways of reading the story, including how the Israelites themselves may have understood it.

Don McLean, "American Pie" (Rock/Folk, 1971)

While this sing-along favorite makes little or no reference to the Bible, it serves as a familiar example to use when discussing the issues raised when interpretation must take place without the benefit of the author's own commentary. Buddy Holly's death in a 1959 plane crash is the explicit inspiration of the song. Many of the allusions contained in the lyrics are obvious, but many others are not and McLean has stubbornly refused to explain the meaning of his work. (One is reminded of T. S. Eliot's response when asked what he meant in the first lines of "The Lovesong of J. Alfred Prufrock," when he described the evening as being "like a patient etherized upon a table": "It means, 'like a patient etherized upon a table.'") Into this vacuum, countless interpreters—whose efforts are easy to find on the Internet—have entered to explicate the letter and spirit of the song (www.faqs.org/faqs/music/american-pie). Many of the interpretations differ significantly, and since they cannot all be correct, one suspects that perhaps none of them are. In this respect the song is similar to biblical writings such as Daniel or Revelation. Why does McLean not step in and clear up all the confusion? Should he? (When an interviewer asked Bob Dylan about his "A Hard Rain's A-Gonna Fall," which is usually interpreted as a warning about the dangers of nuclear war, Dylan protested that it was not fallout rain but that "it's just a hard rain.") Are we obliged to pay attention to an author's intended meaning? How would our understanding of, say, Isaiah or Ezekiel change if the prophets were to preface their works with introductions like the ones found in most study Bibles? To what extent would such preface be a part of the work itself? What are we to do in the absence of an "authoritative" interpretation coming directly from the author?

Flame, "Context" (Rap, 2005)

Not many hip hop/rap songs mention hermeneutics, exegesis, eisegesis, and other standard terms and tools in biblical interpretation (like "concordance," "Bible dictionary," "commentary"), but this one does and is able to make them rhyme! Although the terms are used in the song, they are often under-introduced, so that the teacher can explain their meaning and significance. The song is also useful insofar as it illustrates a number of hermeneutical principles with which teachers or their students may not agree. For instance, the song argues the point that exegesis is (primarily) about authors and their original intended meaning; this would serve as a good entry into recent debates on the locus of textual meaning. The song also advocates using Scripture to interpret Scripture, a classic exegetical strategy of the Reformation period. This, too, would serve as an excellent entry into larger interpretive matters such as the history of interpretation or exegetical strategies in different time periods and from different theological perspectives. Finally, one should note that in addition to points where teachers or students might disagree with the song, there are also a few points of factual error ("exegesis" and "eisegesis," for example, are not, as Flame would have it, Latin words). But perhaps even this is instructive: How foolproof can interpretation be? How foolproof can instruction in interpretation be?

Joan Osborne, "One of Us" (Folk/Rock, 1995)

By far Osborne's best-known song, this tune deals with various aspects of God and how one might relate to the deity. It could be used pedagogically in a variety of ways. It asks about God's name, which could prompt discussion of Yahweh and Elohim as well as the various names for the deity in both the Hebrew Bible and New Testament. It addresses the nature of God (a "slob," lonely in heaven) and the physical appearance of God, which may lead to a discussion of the anthropomorphic deity in the Hebrew Bible or of the incarnation in the New Testament. The song queries, "What if God was one of us?" which may set up a conversation about the *imago Dei* or the incarnation. It also asks if one would want to see God if seeing entailed that one had to believe in heaven, Jesus, the saints, and the prophets. Further, the refrain of the song asserts that "God is great, God is good," though it is not entirely clear how that line functions in the song (As ironic? As a counterbalance to God being a slob?). The song, like the Bible, appears to contain a variety of theologies, or better yet, hold a variety of them in tension.

Dishwalla, "Counting Blue Cars" (Alternative Rock, 1996)

The song depicts God as feminine with the oft-repeated line: "Tell me all your thoughts on God. Cause I'd really like to meet her." Holding the pronoun "her" until the end of the sentence surprises the listener. The song thus can illustrate the significant shifts that occur when thinking of the deity as female. It can set the context for discussion about the power of metaphor—particularly the metaphorical nature of language about God—or about feminine imagery of the deity in Hebrew Bible texts (e.g., Isa 49:15).

Randy Newman, "God's Song (That's Why I Love Mankind)" (Pop, 1972)

Newman takes on the voice of God and declares that humans are worthless to God, and even though God destroys them all, humans continue to look to God for hope and salvation. In a sense, the song poses the theodicy question and may thus be connected to texts such as 2 Kgs 17 or a variety of lament psalms. God declares that humans are less significant than flowers and trees, and that human squalor and filth causes God to recoil. Such notions can be contrasted with a number of biblical texts that place a much higher value on humankind, such as Psalm 8:4 ("What are humans that you are mindful of them?") or the idea that humans are created in God's image (Gen 1:26–27). The song is reminiscent of Job's sentiments, as the people implore God, "If you won't take care of us … please let us be." God then responds that even though he has burned down cities and taken children, people still foolishly have faith in God and even consider themselves blessed, which again, connects to issues raised by the book of Job (cf. Job 1:21). In fact, the rhetoric of the song as a whole stands in opposition to Job: Newman mocks belief in God in the face of human suffering, whereas Job, ultimately, persists in his faith.

Marvin Gaye, *What's Going On* (R&B/Soul, 1971)

This entire album represents a prophetic critique of war, ecological abuse, economic injustice, and a lack of religious motivation. Specific songs like "God Is Love" and "Wholy Holy" draw on religious language (e.g., in the latter, Gaye speaks of believing in Jesus as well as makes the claim that Jesus "left us a book to believe in"). However, other, more recognizable songs, such as the title track, "Mercy Mercy Me (The Ecology)," and "Inner City Blues (Make Me Wanna Holler)," mount a more broadly based condemnation of specific practices. Because of the album's popularity and the bases for its censure, it can be used profitably to illustrate the social and religious bases of prophetic literature. Prophetic texts such as Isa 1:17 and 2:4, both of which advocate social justice and a hope for an end to military solutions to problems, might be read in tandem with the title track as students reflect on their intersection with contemporary debates about militarism. Similarly, after a discussion of Amos's cry against the privileged "Cows of Bashan" (Amos 4:1–13), an instructor could shift the focus to how the underprivileged in modern society express themselves by listening to "What's Happening Brother" or "Inner City Blues." (A good resource for this album is Michael Eric Dyson, *Mercy Mercy Me: The Art, Loves, and Demons of Marvin Gaye*.)

Judy Newton and Diane Stanton-Rich, *Songs of Bible Women: Old Testament* (Christian/Inspirational, 2004)

This album contains seventeen short songs that retell specific Hebrew Bible narratives featuring women. As such, each song offers an interesting comparative text. Students might consider questions such as: How does the song's portrayal of the woman compare to that in the biblical text? Which parts of the story are omitted or highlighted? What effect do the omissions or additions have on the depiction of the woman? How are the actions and speech of the characters rendered by the song? What function or role does the woman play in the Bible and the song? What motivates the retelling? The songs feature the stories of Eve, Hagar, Sarah, Tamar, Miriam, the daughters of Zelophehad, Rahab, Ruth, Abigail, Bathsheba, the widow of Zarephath, the woman of Shunem, Esther, and Gomer.

To give just one example from the album: In the retelling of the David and Abigail story in 1 Sam 25, the title of the song voices the perspective of David, "Abigail, I Praise the Lord for Sending You." In the biblical text, Abigail makes a long speech to David (25:24–31) to which David offers a relatively brief response (25:32–35). The speech roles are reversed in the song: Abigail speaks one line and David six lines. Similarly, in the song Abigail loses some of her autonomy and agency, as there is no mention of her acting independently of her husband (25:19). One could ask if the song's interpretation of Abigail as "joyfully" becoming David's wife is a good reading of verses 41–42. One might also consider how the song's omission of God killing Nabal (25:38) influences interpretation of the characters.

Judy Newton and Diane Stanton-Rich, *Songs of Bible Women: New Testament* (Christian/Inspirational, 2004)

This album features seventeen short songs about New Testament women, including Elizabeth, Mary Magdalene, Salome, Mary and Martha, the woman at the well, the woman caught in adultery, the persistent widow, Pilate's wife, Tabitha/Dorcas, and Rhoda. (See the previous entry for suggested general discussion questions.) To give just one example from the album: "Too Near the Cross" imagines the thoughts and feelings of the women at the crucifixion (cf. Matt 27:55–56; Mark 15:40–41; Luke 23:49; and John 19:25–27). They are sad and confused and wonder why Jesus is dying and whether he will come back. Nonetheless, they make the theological observation that Jesus forgives them all and that Jesus must surely be God (cf. the centurion in Matt 27:54). They also point out that Jesus' male disciples are too ashamed to approach the cross. Following the song's lead, students might be asked to develop creatively the perspective of the women at the cross. Is the song's depiction of women in keeping with their portrayal elsewhere in the Gospels? How does their portrayal here compare to their depiction after the resurrection (Luke 24:1–12; John 20:1–18)?

M
U
S
I
C

CLASSICAL MUSIC

Dan W. Clanton Jr. and Bryan Bibb

Works by classical composers inspired by the Bible—concertos, cantatas, oratorios, symphonies, motets, tone poems, operas, even ballets—number well into the hundreds. In the space available here, it will be possible to discuss only a small, selective sample of this gargantuan body of work. (Discussion of pedagogical strategies in connection with specific works begins on p. 56.) The list of works below is provided as a resource for instructors desiring to broach specific biblical texts through the medium of classical music.

TORAH

C. Saint-Saëns, *The Deluge* [Gen 6–9]
A. Rubinstein, *Tower of Babel* [Gen 11]
I. Stravinsky, *Babel* [Gen 11]
A. Schoenberg, *Jacob's Ladder* [Gen 28]
G. F. Handel, *Joseph and His Brethren* [Gen 37–50]
G. F. Handel, *Israel in Egypt* [Exod 1–15]
A. Rubinstein, *Moses*
G. Rossini, *Moses in Egypt*
C. P. E. Bach, *Israelites in the Wilderness*
E. Bairstow, "Sing Ye to the Lord" [Exod 15]
J. Rutter, "The Lord Bless You and Keep You" [Num 6]
J. Brahms, "Wo ist ein so herrlich Volk" ("Where is such a nation?") [Deut 4]

PROPHETS

G. F. Handel, *Joshua*
I. Pizzetti, *Debora e Jaele* [Judg 5]
G. F. Handel, *Jephtha* [Judg 10–11]
M. Seter, *The Daughter of Jephthah* [Judg 10–11]
G. F. Handel, *Saul* [1 Sam 9–31]
C. Nielsen, *Saul and David* [1 Sam 16–2 Sam 1]

T. Tomkins, "When David Heard" [2 Sam 18]

A. Honegger, *King David*

F. Bartoni, *David Poenitans* [2 Sam 24; 1 Chr 21]

G. F. Handel, "Zadok the Priest" [1 Kgs 1]

G. F. Handel, *Solomon*

E. Bloch, *Schelomo*

R. Starer, *Ariel, Visions of Isaiah*

L. Bernstein, *Jeremiah*

H. Purcell, *Let Mine Eyes Run Down with Tears* [Jer 14]

Verdi, *Nabucco* [Jer 21; 30; 50; the exile]

S. Peter, "Ich will euch wie en Thau seyn" ("I will be unto you as a dew") [Hos 14]

H. Purcell, "Blow Up the Trumpet in Sion" [Joel 2]

J. Tavener, *The Whale* [Jonah]

G. F. Handel, "Thus Saith the Lord" (from *Messiah*) [Hag 2; Mal 3]

G. F. Handel, "Rejoice Greatly, O Daughter of Zion" (from *Messiah*) [Zech 9]

G. F. Handel, "But Who May Abide the Day of His Coming?" and "And He Shall Purify" (from *Messiah*) [Mal 3]

WRITINGS

A. Pärt, *Psalms of David*

G. F. Handel, *Messiah* [Pss 2; 16; 22; 24; 68; 69]

L. Bernstein, *Chichester Psalms* [Pss 2; 23; 102; 108; 122; 131]

J. Brahms, "Herr, Lehre Doch Mich" (from *A German Requiem*, movt. 3) [Ps 39]

I. Stravinsky, *Symphony of Psalms* [Pss 39; 40; 150]

A. Pärt, *Psalm 51*

T. Avni, *De Profundis* [Ps 130]

G. Verdi, "Va Pensiero" (from *Nabucco*) [Ps 137]

C. Parry, *Job*

L. Dallapiccola, *Job*

H. Purcell, *My Beloved Spake* [Song of Solomon 2]

A. N. Boskovich, *Ruth and Boaz*

G. F. Handel, "Behold, and See If There be Any Sorrow" (from *Messiah*) [Lam 1]

I. Stravinsky, *Threni* [Lam 1; 3; 5]

G. F. Handel, *Esther*

G. F. Handel, *Belshazzar* [Dan 5]

W. Walton, *Belshazzar's Feast* [Dan 5]

F. McBeth, *Daniel in the Lion's Den* [Dan 6]

APOCRYPHA

J. Haydn, *Return of Tobit*
T. Arne, *Judith*
C. Parry, *Judith*
E. Reznicek, *Holofernes* [Judith]
G. F. Handel, *Susanna*
C. Floyd, *Susanna*
G. F. Handel, *Judas Maccabeus*

GOSPELS AND ACTS

J. S. Bach, *Christmas Oratorio* [Matt 1–2; Luke 1–2]
O. Messiaen, *La Nativité du Seigneur* [Matt 1–2; Luke 1–2]
H. Berlioz, *The Childhood of Christ* [Matt 1–2; Luke 1–2]
J. Rheinberger, *The Star of Bethlehem* [Matt 1–2]
G. F. Handel, "And Lo, the Angel of the Lord Came Upon Them" (from *Messiah*) [Luke 2]
A. Stradella, *San Giovanni Battista* [Luke 1–3]
C. Franck, *Beatitudes* [Matt 5]
R. Strauss, *Salome* [Matt 14]
B. Britten, *Church Parables* [Luke 15]
H. Alfven, *The Prodigal Son* [Luke 15]
C. Debussy, *L'Enfant Prodigue* [Luke 15]
J. S. Bach, *St. Matthew Passion*
C. Wood, *St. Mark Passion*
A. Pärt, *St. Luke Passion*
A. Pärt, *St. John Passion*
J. S. Bach, *St. John Passion*
F. Martin, *Pilate*
J. Haydn, *The Seven Last Words of Christ*
L. v. Beethoven, *Christ on the Mount of Olives*
J. Taverner, "Dum Transisset Sabbatum" [Mark 16]
J. S. Bach, *Easter Oratorio*
J. S. Bach, *Ascension Oratorio* [Luke 24; Acts 1]
E. Elgar, *The Apostles*

LETTERS

F. Mendelssohn, *St. Paul*
G. F. Handel, "If God Be for Us" (from *Messiah*) [Rom 8]

M
U
S
I
C

G. F. Handel, "O Death, Where Is Thy Sting? But Thanks Be to God" (from
   Messiah) [1 Cor 15]
H. Schutz, *Es ist erschienen die heilsame Gnade Gottes* [Tit 2]
G. F. Handel, "Unto Which of the Angels Said He at Any Time" (from *Messiah*) [Heb 1]
J. Brahms, "Denn Wir Haben Hie Keine Bleibende Statt" (from *A German
   Requiem*, movt. 6) [Heb 11; 13]
J. Brahms, "Denn alles Fleisch, es ist wie Gras" (from *A German Requiem*,
   movt. 2) [1 Pet 1]

REVELATION

J. Tavener, *The Apocalypse*
J. Langlais, *Cinq Méditations sur l'Apocalypse* [Rev 1; 2; 9; 22]
G. F. Handel, "Hallelujah" (from *Messiah*) [Rev 11; 19]

The works discussed in this chapter are organized according to the order
in which their primary subject matter appears in the canon. (A number of
works deal with multiple texts; discussion of these pieces appear toward the
end of the chapter.) The indices may be consulted to find entries with classroom strategies related to particular texts. All secondary literature cited here
is included in the preceding bibliography (pp. 11–13).

HEBREW BIBLE

Joseph Haydn, *The Creation* (*Die Schöpfung*), Hob.XXI:2 (1798)
   This oratorio, one of only two Haydn composed, is generally regarded
as one of his greatest accomplishments. In three parts, it retells the first story
of creation, narrated in Gen 1:1–2:4a. Haydn's piece begins with the wonderfully expressive instrumental "Representation of Chaos," and then proceeds
to narrate the Genesis material through the voices of Gabriel, Raphael, and
Uriel. Each biblical section is complemented by an elaborative aria or recitative that expounds on the mostly familiar biblical passages. For example, after
Gabriel recites Gen 1:20, he sings, "On mighty pinions rising, / the proud eagle
/ cleaves the air / and soars in swiftest flight / towards the sun." In much this
same way, Haydn narrates the creation of humans in part 2; yet he conflates
the creation of humans in Gen 1:26–27 with the account of Adam and Eve in
Gen 2–3. However, perhaps owing to the laudatory tone of his subject, Haydn
stops short of scoring the disobedient act in the Garden. Instead, the listener
is presented with an exultant Adam and Eve, reveling in the sensual delights of
their new existence, urging all of creation to worship God. Unlike the Eve of

M
U
S
I
C

Genesis, however, this is a fully submissive Eve who is quite comfortable being at the beck and call of Adam: "O thou, for whom I was created! / My shelter, my shield, my all! / Thy will is my law, / for so hath God disposed, / and in obedience to thee I find joy, / good fortune and honour." The story of these first humans concludes on a foreboding note, uttered by Uriel, when he sings, "O happy pair, happy for evermore if vain delusion lead you not astray to want more than you have and know more than you should!" Here students might ponder whether or not "vain delusion" is the best way to render Eve's actions in the biblical narrative. This foreshadowing does not sour the jubilance of the piece, as it finishes with a gorgeous praising of God by the chorus.

Due to its length, it is unlikely that teachers will have time to play the entire piece for a class, but the individual Parts are broken down into discrete units, so that one could focus on a specific biblical text and its elaborative companion. One could also use this piece to discuss the theological category of creation itself, since Genesis is not exactly filled with praises for creation, as is the book of Psalms. One could easily match a section in Haydn's piece with a specific psalm in order to examine an aspect of creation. Finally, and most obviously, one could utilize this piece to discuss the relationship(s) between Adam and Eve. Given that Haydn's interpretation of their relationship is vastly different from modern, feminist readings, there is ample material here to illustrate musically an alternative viewpoint, as well as a conflated reading of Gen 1–3.

Aaron Copland, "In the Beginning" (1947)

Aaron Copland was born in Brooklyn, of Lithuanian Jewish ancestry and received musical training in Paris. His compositional voice is distinctly American, as he drew upon jazz and country-western musical themes as well as American history and folklore. His public reputation survived accusations that he was a member of the Communist Party, and his masterpieces, *Fanfare for the Common Man* and *Rodeo*, can be heard throughout American popular culture. Copland wrote the short choral work, "In the Beginning," at the request of the Harvard Symposium on Music Criticism held in 1947. The original request had been for a musical setting of a Hebrew text, but Copland chose instead to create an extended *a cappella* choral rendering of the first chapter of Genesis (with a few verses from Gen 2). It alternates between a mezzo-soprano who voices God's speech and a chorus who fills in the narrative text. This structure leads to a complex interaction between a single pure voice and a larger plurality that is sometimes harmonious and sometimes filled with dramatic tension. As the days of creation progress, there are changes in the tempo and mood, reaching a vibrant climax in the creation of humanity: "And man became a living soul" (beginning around the ten-minute mark). Aside from being beautifully evocative of the mood of the creation story, this work is effective as part of a classroom discussion of the genre of Gen 1. By paying attention to the repetition, cadence, and rhetorical structure of the passage, readers may recognize in the chapter an element of orality, perhaps taking the form of a sermon or other liturgical recitation. This performative quality of Gen 1 leads naturally into the kind of dramatic presentation in Copland's "In the Beginning."

Copland's piece reinforces the ordering of creation and the dramatic, sweeping nature of Gen 1. Students can ponder how Copland has divided the material and emphasized particular phrases or ideas. They may also consider how Copland, as well as Gen 1 itself, places humanity at the pinnacle of creation. Then students can answer the same questions regarding the Yahwist creation story that begins in Genesis 2:4b: How is creation ordered and structured? What is the place of humanity in the creation? What is the style and tone of the story as compared with Gen 1? In short, Copland's majestic rendering of Gen 1 helps bring the differences between the Priestly and Yahwistic creation stories into sharper relief. Finally, the nature of Copland's piece also invites students to contemplate the power of divine speech in biblical narrative, from Genesis to John.

MUSIC

Gabriel Fauré, *La Chanson d'Eve*, Op. 95 (1907–10)

This cycle of ten songs based on the poems by Charles van Lerberghe is scored for piano and voice and stems from the final period of Fauré's compositional output. Like Beethoven, Fauré was plagued by hearing loss late in life, but his own hearing loss was accompanied by terrific distortion of tones, so that what little he could hear was not accurate. Given this, it is all the more remarkable to listen to these delicately impressionistic songs that, according to one of Fauré's biographers named Émile Vuillermoz, "should be among the highest products of universal thought." The songs certainly depict a very different Eve from the one we find in Genesis. Here, the listener sees the new creation through the eyes of Eve, who has been commissioned by God to "bestow a word from your lips / on all things that I have created, / a sound for them to be known by" (from the first song, "Paradise"). In other words, Eve's discovery of and marvel at the newly created earth are at the service of providing it an identity through sound. This service to God is in contrast to the naming of the animals performed by the man in 2:19–20, and it allows teachers to offer a different perspective on these primeval events by highlighting Eve's God-given duty. One might consider the deity's lack of direct interaction with Eve in the biblical text, the significance or power associated with naming, and whether or not the woman is more "qualified" to carry out this function given her curiosity about knowledge and the man's lack of it.

The remainder of the song-cycle is a first-person recounting by Eve of the marvels of God's creation, as she witnesses them for the first time. As Eve encounters roses, sunlight, twilight, and even death (all subjects of individual songs), the hearer can ponder how this earliest creation may have appeared, in contrast to the rather sparse description in the biblical text. This literary effervescence can also allow students to consider the newly created earth from Eve's perspective and to ask questions about Eve's innate knowledge and how this knowledge is enlarged by natural phenomena, especially the idea of death. This emphasis on death is particularly important, given the prescription of God in 2:16–17, as well as the importance of this theme in other renderings of the Garden, most notably George Bernard Shaw's play *Back to Methuselah*. More generally, this piece could instigate discussion of the traditionally negative views of Eve found in Jewish, Christian, and Muslim traditions.

Stephen Hartke, *Sons of Noah* (1996)

Hartke's piece has been described as a miniature opera, similar in style to other twentieth-century composers like Igor Stravinsky and Judith Weir. The music is transparent in tone—scored as it is for quartets of guitars, bassoons, and flutes—and at first listen sounds a little odd; after all, one soprano is singing multiple parts in English. Upon adjusting to the style of the piece, however, one discovers the intent behind the words. Hartke found a nineteenth-century short story by the Brazilian author Machado de Assis and gave it to the poet Philip Littell, whose resulting libretto is the basis for this piece. The story reputes to be three lost chapters that tell the story of what happens on the Ark after Noah and his family set sail. The majority of the piece is concerned with the arguments and brutal fighting that erupts once the brothers begin discussing who will get what land, and how much will be allotted to whom after the flood. At one point, Japhet and Shem argue over ten measly acres, and one says to the other, "I would rather shed your blood / than even cheat myself like that!" Even the animals, who heretofore had been living peacefully on the ark, now recall that they are supposed to mistrust each other. Tellingly, the piece ends with a prayer from Noah after he breaks up a bloody fight between the sons and their wives. Noah says, "My God they're fighting over land they haven't got yet, / land they don't even own!" In order to connect this primordial contest over land in the name of religion with similar modern conflicts, Noah then says, "Oh Lord / can you imagine what will happen in / _____ and _____ and _____ and _____ and...?" Hartke inserts a note in the libretto here that reads "fill in the blanks with whatever current territorial aggressions come to mind." In this way, this piece can be used profitably not only to illustrate the narrative ellipses in the flood story in Gen 6–9 but would also be a wonderful resource when discussing the impact of biblical narratives on modern geopolitical and ideological issues. For example, this piece could supplement discussions of texts such as Stephen R. Haynes's *Noah's Curse: The Biblical Justification of American Slavery* or Regina Schwartz's *The Curse of Cain: The Violent Legacy of Monotheism*, both of which discuss how the Bible's stories about the flood and land have been used to justify violence and hatred.

Benjamin Britten, *War Requiem* (1962)

Benjamin Britten was commissioned to write the *War Requiem* to celebrate the rebuilding of Coventry Cathedral, which had been destroyed in World War II. It was performed inside the new cathedral on May 30, 1962, and featured solos by a British tenor, a German baritone, and a Russian soprano. Britten's purpose was to express his antiwar convictions, and using nationals from the three major European participants in World War II indicated that his concern was for the world generally, not just peace for Britain. He also expressed this pacifist ideology through a creative editing of the traditional text of the Latin mass, into which he inserted nine poems written by an infantry soldier killed during the last week of World War I, Wilfred Owen. Musically, Britten calls for an orchestra and chorus to sing the parts of the mass, soloists to sing the Owen poetry, and a boys choir to float at a distance above the chaos. The music alternates between slow, brooding sections and loud, chaotic representations of warfare and violence. Emotions range among fear, anger, bitterness, and panic, with moments of serenity and acceptance. It is musically challenging and yet quite affecting. It creates a stark and instructive contrast with some of the other famous Requiems.

The text of the *War Requiem*, however, provides the most interesting possibilities for conversation, especially the topic of why Britten includes particular poems where he does within the liturgy. After the initial *Requiem aeternam*, we hear Owen's poem, "Anthem for Doomed Youth." In this selection, Owen laments the young soldiers who "die as cattle" with only rifle shots and whistling shells as musical accompaniment. The *requiem* asks for "perpetual light" to shine upon the dead, but these war casualties experience only the "drawing-down of blinds" into darkness. The *Dies irae* contains four different poems, "Voices," "The Next War," "Sonnet On Seeing a Piece of Our Artillery Brought Into Action," and "Futility." In this long sequence, the poems bring the various parts of the liturgy together into an overall theme: what we hope for in heaven is very far from what we experience in the messy violence of this world. On the Day of Judgment, God will come with trumpets blaring, but in the war the bugles are "saddening" and "sorrowful." In this final scene of judgment, God brings the world to completion as "everything hidden becomes apparent," and "nothing remains unavenged." In war, however, death is an animating force that spurs the men onward toward more killing and dying. The *recordare* section presents the image of gentle Jesus "sinking down" to die on the cross to save the faithful supplicant. Owen's poem, however, describes the powerful gun "towering toward heaven" and "lifted up" to crush "arrogance." The poem ends by calling on God to curse the gun and remove it from the soul of humanity. Finally, the *Lacrimosa* describes the "day full of tears" when the guilty man arises from the ashes to be judged by God. Owen's poem "Futility," however, expresses the despair of moving the body of a dead comrade into the sun, with the bitter thought that he might awake from the sun's touch like a seed. The reality of the dead body causes the poet to wonder why the sun brings things to life to begin with, if they must end with such futility. There is no hope of resurrection. This basic pattern of alternation continues throughout, with clear keyword and theme associations connecting the sections.

The most interesting section to discuss might be the poem that is paired with the *Offertorium*, in which the boys announce their sacrifices and prayers to God for those who have died, asking God to "pass them from death to life" as he had promised Abraham and his seed. In the middle of this section, however, Britten includes the poem, "The Parable of the Old Man and the Young," which is a bitter retelling of the story in Gen 22, the binding of Isaac. At the end of the poem when the angel calls for Abraham to spare the boy and sacrifice the ram instead, "the old man would not do so, but slew his son, And half the seed of Europe, one by one." This is a kind of "reversal" that is seen commonly in prophetic literature, in which the prophet draws the audience in with a familiar theme and then turns the tables at the last moment. In a section that specifically connects the sparing of Isaac and the sacrifice of Jesus, it is quite unsettling to hear a version in which Abraham kills Isaac, thus extinguishing the promise and derailing God's whole plan for humanity. In this juxtaposition, Britten's antiwar sentiment could not be more apparent.

One way to begin class is to print a version of Gen 22 that subtly changes the ending so that Abraham ends by killing Isaac and have a student read the text aloud. Gauge the group's reaction when the ending is suddenly different, and ask them how the new ending changes their view of Abraham. Then, after playing the Britten *Offertorium* including Owen's poem, students can reflect on how the surprising narrative change affects the way we hear the theme of sacrifice in the *Offertorium*. Is Britten's description of the modern world accurate when he suggests that there is no compassion among humanity and no hope for divine reconciliation or salvation? This would work as a way to begin a discussion of biblical views of war and peace. Like Abraham-gone-wrong, to what extent are modern people willing to sacrifice what is most precious to achieve their political, military, or religious goals?

Arnold Schoenberg, *Moses und Aron* (ca. 1932)

This piece is the sole opera by one of the most influential composers of the twentieth century. Schoenberg tells the story of the relationship between Moses and Aaron and their bitter feud over (1) who should lead the people, and (2) whose conception of God is the most appropriate for the people. Moses insists on a very philosophical, abstract notion of God, as he says in act 1: an "infinite, omnipresent, unperceived, and inconceivable God." Aaron, on the other hand, is motivated more by his love for the people rather than devotion to the idea of God, and as such, he longs to show them a comforting God that can be grasped and beheld through God's actions. Their conflict comes to a head at the wildly frantic Golden Calf scene, where Aaron argues: "You also would have loved this people, had you only seen how they lived when they dared to see and feel and hope. No folk is faithful, unless it feels." Moses remains unmoved by Aaron's plea for the people and insists that "they must comprehend the idea! They live for that end!" Aaron retorts that "no folk can grasp more than just a partial image, the perceivable part of the whole idea." Moses then asks the central question behind the whole exchange: "Am I to debase the idea?" Aaron offers to present the idea in a way that the people will understand, but Moses will not listen. Moses even smashes the tablets of law when Aaron comments that "they're images also, just part of the whole idea." In fact, act 2 ends with a reversal of the biblical narrative: Aaron leading the people away from Moses, to the Promised Land. However, in the unscored act 3, we see Moses addressing a chained Aaron, saying to him, "You have betrayed God to the gods, the idea to images, this chosen folk to others, the extraordinary to the commonplace." Aaron then dies, and the people return to the wasteland to commune with their revitalized idea of God.

Even though this piece is both innovative and powerful, it is very difficult to listen to. The chords are dissonant, and all of Moses' dialogue is given in *sprechgesang*, or speech-song. Given these limitations, one can still make marvelous use of this piece in several ways. First, given that the opera is basically a philosophical musing on the nature of God, teachers can use Moses' and Aaron's speeches in act 2 to compare and contrast various ideas of God in the Exodus narrative. Second, this opera can be employed to evaluate the relationship between Moses and Aaron in Exodus. Since most source-critical scholarship finds evidence of this relationship in at least two different sources, the relationship is unstable and uncertain. By allowing students to hear a very different rendering of both Moses and Aaron, teachers can generate reflection on these key characters and how they both work to better their people. Finally, by exposing students to such a philosophical exegesis of Exodus, teachers can (one hopes) stimulate more advanced reflection on the new conception of God set forth in the narrative, as well as the new relationship between God and the people.

Camille Saint-Saëns, *Samson et Dalila* (1867–76)

This opera by one of France's most important musical figures focuses exclusively on the story of Samson and Delilah. Saint-Saëns takes tremendous liberties with the biblical text in his attempt to shift the story from its focus on the downfall of Samson due to his failings with women to a broader story of conflicting religious loyalties and doomed love. For example, in the Samson stories in Judges, Samson usually comes off as an oaf who is more interested in women and fighting than any religious identity. In the opera, however, Samson is portrayed as not only a prophetic figure, but also a highly religious one (act 1, scenes 1–2). Similarly, Delilah is shown in Judg 16 to be rather calculating in her dealings with Samson. She is in it for the money; she never expresses love for Samson and could simply be acting out of patriotic pride. Saint-Saëns alters the nature of their relationship so that Samson and Delilah had once been lovers—for example, in act 1, scene 6, Delilah takes pains to flirt with and seduce Samson—but now their respective religious beliefs have come between them. Delilah in the opera is emotionally unstable and vindictive, and she is looking for a way to harm Samson (act 2, scene 1). In fact, after being offered money to secure the secret of Samson's strength, Delilah laughs and says, "What matters your gold to Delilah? And what could a whole treasure if I was not dreaming of vengeance. . . for, as much as you, I loathe him!" Samson even admits that he still loves Delilah, and in a moment of weakness, succumbs to her charms. Of course, she betrays him, and when we see him at the beginning of act 3, his hair is shorn, and his eyes have been put out. The opera ends with Samson praying to God to forgive him as he pushes down the pillars of the temple, killing everyone inside, including himself.

Teachers could ask students to note the differences between the Bible and Saint-Saëns's version and to consider the rhetorical emphasis of each account. Since the opera is relatively long at close to two hours, one would need to focus on certain scenes. More generally, the opera could also be employed to illustrate larger trends in biblical interpretation, namely, the afterlives of either Samson or Delilah, so that students can learn an important lesson: One's knowledge of biblical stories and characters is often heavily influenced by cultural retellings.

Felix Mendelssohn, *Elijah*, Op. 70 (1846–47)

One of the great examples of musical conservatism during a period of growing romantic excesses, Mendelssohn not only did much to renew the classical tradition of Bach and Handel, but he also promoted their works in performance and, more indirectly, through his own compositions. Born in 1809 to a family with an illustrious Jewish background—his grandfather was the great thinker and activist Moses Mendelssohn, founder of the Jewish Enlightenment (*Haskalah*) movement—his parents nevertheless chose to have him and his sister baptized as Christians. As such, it might be surprising that of his two major religious works, *Elijah* was not only more successful, but has also survived better historically than his other oratorio, *Paulus* (see below).

Mendelssohn saw much to admire in this rather bizarre prophet whose story is told in 1 Kgs 18–21. We know Mendelssohn was basically a conservative humanist, terribly concerned about not only the state of music in the nineteenth century but also the morality of his times. In his notes to the recent Decca recording of this piece, Nicholas Temperley offers a plausible explanation for Mendelssohn's preoccupation with Elijah: He not only thought that his culture could use someone like Elijah to address the decline in morality, but he may also have viewed himself as an Elijah-like figure when it came to guarding against musical excesses and preserving the time-honored traditions of composers like Bach and Handel. Mendelssohn had a more specifically religious emphasis, as he ends the oratorio not with Elijah, but rather with several beautifully christocentric choruses that shift the focus of the piece from a celebratory ode to Elijah to a devotional experience directed at Christ. As such, one could use these last pieces to discuss not only the ways in which the Gospels present Jesus as a new Elijah, but also the phenomenon of messianic exegesis more generally, or triumphalist readings of the Hebrew Bible. One may also use the oratorio to supplement the biblical text by playing an excerpt, say, the healing of the widow's son, as a way of offering an audio illustration of the text. More fruitful, perhaps, would be to focus on various attempts to render 1 Kgs 19:12, which the NRSV translates as "a sound of sheer silence." Mendelssohn's libretto uses the KJV's "still small voice," but the real usefulness of the piece is in the way it represents Elijah's theophanic experience on Mount Horeb. The music exhibits a wide range of emotions, as the chorus is both violent and tender. This allows students to engage and experience the text in a new way, in a sense beyond translations, so that they can develop a deeper understanding not just of Elijah, but perhaps of theophanies in general.

Ralph Vaughan Williams, *Job: A Masque for Dancing* (1927–30)

Vaughan Williams was one of England's most important composers in the early to mid-twentieth century. Early on in his compositional career, he rejected the fashionable trend of writing in the Germanic style and decided instead to focus his efforts on (re)discovering an indigenous English music. After the turn of the century, he began an intensive field study of English folk music which would eventually lead him to reshape his own music into a more emphatically nationalistic mold. He enlisted in the Royal Army Medical Corps in World War I and after the war composed one of his most beautiful and characteristic pieces, the Symphony No. 3, dubbed "A Pastoral Symphony." This elegiac and serene piece paved the way for his next large-scale work, *Job: A Masque for Dancing*. In this roughly forty-five-minute work, divided into nine scenes, Vaughan Williams musically translates the 1820–26 watercolor series on Job created by William Blake into staged dances, incorporating folksong elements as well as the tonal tension that was to highlight his next major work, the rather apocalyptic-sounding Symphony No. 4 (1935). The nine scenes of *Job* relate the biblical account in sequence, beginning with "Scene I: Introduction—Pastoral Dance—Satan's Appeal to God—Saraband of the Sons of God," and ending with an Epilogue in Scene IX in which Job is reunited with his family and blesses them.

Because Vaughan Williams composed no libretto for this piece, the textual references are, admittedly, abstract. However, given the emphasis in the present volume on appealing to students who are visual and auditory learners, innovative teachers can still use this piece profitably. One way to do so would be to discuss a portion of Job that Vaughan Williams scores. Then, play the corresponding Scene from *Job* and exhibit the Blake watercolor. This way students can experience the text as word, sound, and image. Teachers can also experiment with more kinesthetic learning as well, given the suggestive instructions included in the score of *Job*. Namely, one could ask the students to act out Vaughan Williams's dance instructions, so that the text of Job could be experienced bodily as well. A wonderful resource in all this would be the score of *Job* published in 1934 by Oxford University Press in London, which contains not only a synopsis of each movement, but also the Blake illustrations that correspond to each movement.

Felix Mendelssohn, *Three Psalms*, Op. 78 (1843–44)

This work comprises three psalms in German: "Warum toben die Heiden," (Ps 2, "Why do the heathen rage"), "Mein Gott, warum hast du?" (Ps 22, "My God, why have you forsaken me?"), and "Richte mich, Gott" (Ps 43, "Judge me, O God"). They were very popular pieces during the composer's lifetime and showcase a lively interaction between a solo voice and a full choir, totally *a cappella*. The tone of these compositions is generally pastoral and soothing, with the choir gently responding to the heartfelt request of the supplicant. Psalm 22 would be especially useful in a classroom setting

M
U
S
I
C

because the Romantic style of composition does not express the sharpness or anguish that we often associate with the lament psalm in general or with Jesus' cry on the cross in particular. In fact, this contrast raises the question of how interpreters have reconstructed Jesus' emotional state on the cross from the words that he speaks. The various "last words" of Jesus in the Gospels may express confusion and doubt ("My God, why have you forsaken me?"), resignation ("It is finished"), or compassion ("Father, forgive them"). When Jesus quotes Ps 22, does he do so for theological reasons—simply because there is something in Ps 22 that he wants to bring into the mind of readers? Or, is he actually experiencing a moment of doubt and confusion? In the Gospels, how much does Jesus really know about his identity, his future, and what will happen when he dies? The answer to this may depend on the particular Gospel one reads, and on the interpreter's relative emphasis on Jesus' humanity versus his divinity.

Gregorio Allegri, *Miserere mei Deus* (1638)

Gregorio Allegri was born in Rome and spent his life from age nine singing in chapel choirs, beginning and ending his career at the Papal Chapel in the Vatican. In addition to his vocal performance, Allegri composed a large number of choral pieces, the most famous of which is his rendering of Ps 51, the *Miserere mei Deus*. It is a haunting work that became famous in the eighteenth and nineteenth centuries as European pilgrims visited Rome on their Grand Tour. The history of *Miserere mei Deus* is analogous, generally speaking, to that of many biblical writings

Many legends grew around the piece, including the story that the Papal Choir performed secret embellishments to the official score that were only known to the performers and passed down confidentially through generations of singers. King Leopold I of Portugal wrote in 1770 that Mozart had secretly copied down the score after listening to the piece and given it to him, but that he would not share with anyone else "one of the secrets of Rome." Other traditions indicate that Mozart passed the score to a British historian, Charles Burney, who in fact published the composition in 1771. Burney's edition did not reflect the embellishments used by the Papal Choir, although those were eventually published as well in the mid-nineteenth century. Even so, certain musical elements in the piece are still of disputed authenticity. One question is about the so-called "top C," a transposition of part of the verse up a fourth, which evidently is the result of a transcription error in a late-nineteenth-century dictionary of music.

The complex textual history of this piece might be a good way to discuss the question of what one ought to consider the "real" *Miserere mei*: the one Allegri composed, the one sung with embellishments by the Papal Choir, the

M
U
S
I
C

plain original publication, or the one commonly performed now with more modern changes. The final version of a complex textual or artistic creation always bears the imprint of editing, revision, copying, and transmission from one context to another. These changes, far from being interlopers that must be rooted out of the "original" text, often bring new richness or interest to the work.

The text of Allegri's *Miserere mei Deus* is taken from Ps 51, which begins, "Have mercy on me, O God, according to your great mercy." This prayer for forgiveness is identified in the psalm's apocryphal title as the one offered by David after his affair with Bathsheba. As with many classical pieces, the first question students might consider is whether the musical interpretation of biblical themes "matches" the tone or spirit of the original text. In one sense, the music is serene and otherworldly, befitting a performance in the Papal Chapel and matching the beauty and majesty of that liturgical setting. In the solo voice, however, one can hear an overtone of melancholy and resignation that may correspond to David's attitude in 2 Sam 12. David seems rather callous when he abruptly concludes his fasting and prayer after the death of his son. However, one might read his reaction as rooted in a strong sense of God's righteousness and sovereignty. In any case, the serenity and quiet of this prayer for forgiveness raises the issue of whether the supplicant's emotional state might affect the outcome of a penitential psalm.

One way to address the issue of David's "tone" in class is to begin with a dramatization of the story. One might allow a particular group of students to stage the scene of David's penitence and comments after the baby's death in 2 Sam 12 as well as a portion of Ps 51. A quicker option would be to have a dramatic reading of the passages by two different students who are instructed to perform the dialogue "with feeling." After the dramatization, students can express what tone they heard in David's voice and what that tone implies about the state of his emotions during the episode. Then, they may consider the question: How did Allegri interpret the words of contrition in Ps 51, and is his interpretation on target?

Arnold Schoenberg, "De Profundis" (1954)

Like much modern classical music, this is a complex and difficult piece, but its spare strangeness and haunting choral parts create a very effective musical setting for Ps 130, "Out of the depths, I cry to you, O Lord." An adaptation of the Hebrew text of the psalm, the soaring, overlapping choral parts create the effect of echo and reverberation that describes a cavernous sonic space, the tangible "depths" from which the music emanates. Schoenberg alternates between lilting soprano voices and ponderous choral exclamations that sound almost like accusations or incantations. It is a short piece, and one that is usually followed in class by silence as students ponder what they just heard. After playing the piece, but before telling students where it is from, they can guess which kind of psalm is being sung. Some will accurately perceive the music as a lament psalm; more specifically, Ps 130 is a "penitential psalm," which is a type of lament that begins with the confession of sin. The "depths" is a metaphor for the chaos into which sin has flung the psalmist, and only God can bring the supplicant back from such a dreadful location. Schoenberg's setting of the psalm certainly captures the sense of chaos and despair, and as such is a nice way to illustrate the emotional content of the psalm.

William Walton, *Belshazzar's Feast* (1931)

Unlike his countryman and fellow composer Edward Elgar, Walton had little use for religion or religious music. It is a little surprising, then, that his first large-scale choral work focuses on a rather obscure portion of Daniel. However, if one parses the libretto (compiled from the KJV by Sir Osbert Sitwell), one quickly realizes that Dan 5 is merely the catalyst for a more specific focus on the great symbol of civilized decadence and idolatry in the Bible: Babylon. In both the text and the bombastic orchestral writing, Walton emphasizes the fall of Babylon through an array of biblical citations and rousing music. For example, he begins with two citations from Isaiah (39:7 and 13:6), both of which speak to the suffering and trials of the Babylonian exile in the sixth century B.C.E. Next, he includes an extended selection from Ps 137 before jumping ahead to Rev 18:12–13. Only after these selections from two of the most anti-Babylon sections in the Bible do we finally come to the retelling of Dan 5 from which the piece takes its name. After recounting the story of Belshazzar and the bizarre handwriting at his banquet, but curiously omitting any mention of Daniel, Walton returns again to more generic Babylon-bashing, with texts from Ps 81:1–3 and Rev 18. Due to the prominence of Babylon in many biblical texts as a symbol of evil, rampant sexuality, and everything impure, Walton's piece can be used in the classroom as an illustration of this theme. Furthermore, *Belshazzar's Feast* is an excellent example of homiletic writing, in that he and Sitwell have constructed an amalgamation of biblical texts around a basic theme. It may thus be used as an example of that type of biblical interpretation.

NEW TESTAMENT

Johann Sebastian Bach, *The Magnificat* (1723)

Bach wrote this piece to be performed on Christmas Day in 1723 in Leipzig. It follows the Latin text of the *Magnificat*, the hymn that Mary sings

M
U
S
I
C

in Luke 1:46–55 after Elizabeth, perceiving through the Holy Spirit that Mary is carrying the Messiah, proclaims her to be "blessed among women." The title is taken from the first word of Mary's response ("My soul magnifies the Lord"). Bach's setting of the *Magnificat* is truly monumental and embodies the grandiose sentiment of the Baroque period. He alternates arias and choruses in a way that is familiar to audiences from Handel's *Messiah*, revolving around the central affirmation, "Fecit potentiam" (he has showed strength). Throughout, the music embodies the spirit of Mary's hymn in emphasizing the majesty, grandeur, and power of God. There is nothing personal or intimate about the musical setting to Mary's speech, and students might be led to consider how Bach interprets the tone and emotion in Luke and whether it matches their own reading.

In this context, one possible way of promoting discussion of Mary's emotional and intellectual state is by comparing Bach's *Magnificat* with contemporary Christian songs about Mary, most notably Amy Grant's "Breath of Heaven (Mary's Song)" and Mark Lowry and Buddy Greene's oft-covered "Mary, Did You Know?" Grant's song is told from Mary's point of view and emphasizes her fear and weariness, while Lowry and Greene juxtapose the image of Mary tenderly gazing on her infant son with the image of Jesus performing great works of power later in life. A good way to begin a class on the birth narratives, or about the literary portrayal of Mary in particular, would be to contrast these with Bach's *Magnificat* and have students write their own short hymn, prayer, or "diary entry" from Mary's point of view.

G. F. Handel, *The Messiah* (1741)

George Handel was born in Germany but lived most of his life in England after he followed his patron, George, the Elector of Hanover, to London when the latter became George I, King of England. *The Messiah* is Handel's most famous work, and is perhaps one of the most performed sacred pieces in all of classical music. Although it was written originally for performance during the Easter liturgical season, it is now performed almost exclusively during Advent. Handel follows a libretto by Charles Jennens that brings together thematically related texts from the KJV. A large percentage of the passages come from the book of Isaiah, but there are also excerpts from the Gospels, Job, and Revelation.

There are two ways that Handel's *Messiah* might be used in a classroom setting. First, it makes excellent "entrance music" for classes in which the topic is either Isaiah or the Gospels, or in any case during the Advent season. While the music plays, students who enter the room will already begin the process of thinking and focusing so that they will be primed to consider the instructor's first question or comment, especially if it is rooted in the musical

M
U
S
I
C

selection that has been playing. *The Messiah* is especially good for this because it is recognizable and the English text is easily understood by listeners without the libretto in front of them. Second, almost any passage could be adapted for a classroom discussion of Christian interpretation of prophecy. Three particular sections merit attention here, "Behold, A Virgin Shall Conceive," "And with His Stripes We Are Healed," and "I Know That My Redeemer Liveth," although the same kind of analysis would apply to any section of the work.

(1) Section No. 8 in the first part of *The Messiah* follows the text, "Behold, a virgin shall conceive, and bear a son, and shall call his name Emmanuel, God with us," quoting Isa 7:14 and Matt 1:23. The Isaiah prophecy about Immanuel/Emmanuel was one of the most controversial translation issues in twentieth-century scholarship, and the instructor could begin this discussion by looking at various modern translations to see how they handle the text. In brief, as is well known, the Hebrew word used in Isa 7:14 means "young woman," but the Septuagint translators used a Greek word that also carries the connotation of "virgin." Matthew uses the Septuagint translation to support his claim that Jesus was born of a virgin in fulfillment of the prophecy originally given to Isaiah. After reading from various modern translations that use "virgin," "young woman," or "maiden" in Isa 7:14, one can play this passage from the Messiah and ask students to imagine that the young woman described in Isaiah is not a virgin when she gives birth (i.e., that she conceived in the natural way). Would such an interpretation of Isa 7:14 undermine Matthew's claim about Jesus, echoed by Handel? After this, the conversation can be expanded to include the whole prophecy of Immanuel in Isa 7:10–17. Students should note that this child is the second of three children mentioned in Isa 7–8. Both Immanuel and the third child, Maher-Shalal-hash-baz, serve as "time stamps" in the prophecy, indicating that Isaiah's prediction of the end of the Syro-Ephraimite threat would come to pass within a couple of years.

A historically oriented reading of Isa 7, therefore, does not support the conclusion that Isaiah was predicting a child to come hundreds of years in the future. Given the broader meaning of the Hebrew term used for the woman, it is not at all required for her to conceive miraculously and give birth as a virgin for the "time stamp" function of Immanuel to be fulfilled. Therefore, this text reveals a fundamental rift between a "reading forward," in which Isaiah is read in its historical context without reference to Jesus, and a "reading backward," in which Matthew (and Handel) read Christian beliefs about Jesus back into earlier texts. There is also a contrast between the "proof-texting" approach used by Matthew and a more contextual, literal reading of Isa 7–8. By lifting this particular verse and using it in an unexpected way, Matthew has in essence created a whole new text, and it is this text that is used in Handel's *Messiah* and is familiar to modern Christians. This classroom exercise brings together discussion of Matthew's use of the Hebrew Bible and the historical context of Isaiah with the powerful musical tradition of Handel. In this way, the instructor will be able to make the point that a christological reading of Isaiah follows interpretive rules that are different from other reading strategies. However, such a reading cannot simply be dismissed because it is centrally important to Christian theology and liturgy.

(2) Sections 23–26 in part 2 follow the text of Isa 53:4–6, including the phrases "He was wounded for our transgressions" and "With his stripes we are healed." Like Isa 7, the history of interpretation of the Suffering Servant songs in Second Isaiah shows that Christians read this passage in startling new ways in light of their experience with and developing beliefs about Jesus. Commonly, Christian readers have difficulty seeing the reference in Isa 53 to be anything but Jesus, so one must spend time looking at the small details in each of the Servant songs to show that other interpretations are possible, including the common Jewish reading of interpreting the Servant as Israel itself.

One can use the beginning of the second part of Handel's *Messiah* to make the point that Christians interpreted Hebrew Bible texts very differently in light of Jesus, often by reading clearly nonmessianic texts in a messianic light. The unit begins with John 1:29, "Behold the Lamb of God, that taketh away the sin of the world," and then launches directly into Isa 53 as an illustration of Jesus' redemptive suffering. The libretto continues with quotations from Pss 16, 22, 24, 69, and others, none of which were originally intended as prophecy. After playing a selection of these prophetic passages about Jesus' sacrificial death, ask the group to discuss why, if the prophecy was so clear, did Paul suggest that "Christ crucified" was hard for Jews to comprehend (1 Cor 1:23)? The answer is ultimately that Christians were reading these passages in dramatically new ways, linking the royal messianic passages with the Suffering Servant image and the lament psalms to suggest a new way of defining "the Messiah." The contribution of Handel's *Messiah* in this discussion is its powerful expression, of course, but it also provides a direct example of Christian exegesis of the Hebrew Bible.

(3) The third part of *The Messiah* begins with Job 19:25–26 ("I know that my Redeemer liveth, and that He shall stand at the latter day upon the earth") and moves immediately to descriptions of Jesus' resurrection in 1 Cor 15. The Hebrew in Job 19:25–26 is difficult to translate and it is even more difficult to interpret Job's meaning. Even the NRSV capitalizes "Redeemer" in verse 25, which may subtly promote a christological reading of the verse, as that term is one of the most important titles for Jesus in Christian proclamation. Thus, it is easy to see how a christological reading of this passage works, but it does so at the expense of the larger conceptual worldview in the book of Job, and in the Hebrew Bible in general.

Handel draws a direct line from Job 19 to 1 Cor 15 on the subject of Jesus' resurrection, the model and guarantee of the resurrection of all believers at the second coming. Other than this passage, there is nothing on the subject of resurrection or most any other aspect of the afterlife in Job. In the context of Job's legal complaint against God, the "redeemer" in Job 19:25 could be the same (nonexistent?) mediator as the "umpire" in Job 9:33 and the "witness" in Job 16:19. In other words, Job desperately wants there to be a third party that can judge between him and God, but no objective observer exists, so Job is left only to appeal to God in his wretchedness. One can certainly understand why Christians would identify Jesus as just the one to judge between a powerful God and helpless humanity, but that is a later reading that imports Christian doctrine back into Job. Further, the idea of resurrection itself is found in the Hebrew Bible clearly only in Dan 12, and the Christian view of resurrection depends heavily on developments within Judaism during the intertestamental period.

Therefore, the link that Handel's *Messiah* draws between Job and 1 Corinthians depends on a long history of christological interpretation that lies underneath the surface. After playing the relevant sections in *The Messiah* and reading the passages from Job and 1 Corinthians, students may be asked whether they see the strong link themselves. How might modern interpreters respect the importance and power of the interpretive tradition embodied in *The Messiah* without losing touch with the historical reality of the Hebrew Bible itself?

Robert Kyr, *The Passion according to Four Evangelists* (1998)

Robert Kyr is an American-trained composer, currently teaching at the University of Oregon's School of Music and Dance. In the mid-1990s, he accepted a commission from the Boston-based Back Bay Chorale for a large-scale choral work and decided to compose a very different type of Passion. In the Western classical music tradition, there are many works that retell the story of Jesus' passion and crucifixion, and the vast majority of them are told from the viewpoint of one of the Gospel writers, for example, Bach's *St. John Passion*. The form is usually simple; a recitative (i.e., a recited section of biblical text) is followed by a more inventive vocal piece, sung by one of the characters in order to invite the audience to delve more fully into the emotions of the narrative. The overall intent is celebratory in that even though Jesus' torment and suffering is emphasized, the listener is well aware that the piece is but a prelude to Jesus' resurrection. Kyr revises these long-standing practices, and instead of telling the story from only one viewpoint, he weaves all four Gospel stories together in what looks like a musical version of the Gospel Parallels of which all New Testament teachers are so fond. And if it looks different on paper, it sounds different as well, for Kyr wants to emphasize the role of women in this story. To do so, he has scored the voices of Matthew and Mark for soprano and alto respectively (Luke is a tenor and John is a baritone), but he has also included several sections in which women's voices and characters are highlighted.

Kyr has arranged the Passion into three sections (The Judgment, The Way of the Cross, and The Crucifixion). Not only are the two main Evangelists women, but in parts two and three, women are featured prominently. In the former, Kyr accentuates female characters by way of a scene titled "Daughters of Jerusalem." It is in part 3, though, that women really come to the fore. The final scene in part 3 is an eleven-minute piece titled "Witness," in which the female voices of Matthew and Mark join together to sing Ps 88, while a women's chorus sings an intertwining lyric from the traditional *Stabat Mater*. As Kyr has written, "this scene focuses on the women at the cross who mourn the death of Jesus; these final moments of the work are a musical pieta expressing the lamentation of Jesus' mother and friends." After Ps 88 is sung, the entire chorus joins in to close the piece with Ps 130 and an epilogue. Kyr labels the former a "Psalm of Desolation," and in it the psalmist begs God for help but is left with no answer, only waiting. Similarly, Ps 130 petitions God to "hear my voice," and notes, "My soul longs for you / More than those who watch for daybreak." Following these texts, the piece concludes with the full chorus, scored elegantly but not bombastically, singing a few sparse words describing God: "O one! O eternal! O One eternal living God ever and always within! Alleluia."

Given the unique textual arrangement and the emphasis on women found in the piece, Kyr has provided teachers of the Bible a wonderful tool for classroom use that is musically accessible. Obviously, this piece can be used to address the roles and functions of women in the story of Jesus, but perhaps the most useful aspect of this piece is its innovative textual arrangement. One of the axioms of modern New Testament scholarship is that there exists a mimetic relationship among the Gospels. Teachers routinely assign students papers and worksheets on this relationship, and usually students use one or more Gospel Parallels to accomplish these tasks. Like the writers of the canonical Gospels, Kyr has taken elements of preexisting (Gospel) stories to fashion his own narrative. Teachers may thus use Kyr's piece to illustrate the process of Gospel formation as well as provide more auditory learners with an example of a Gospel parallel that might be more engaging than an ordinary worksheet.

Finally, since Kyr ends his Passion not with a resurrection, but rather with two maudlin psalms and a titular epilogue, teachers can ask students to ponder how these choices might affect hearers who are expecting more "traditional" endings, namely, with the resurrection of Jesus and perhaps even subsequent appearances. This consideration, in turn, could help students understand the varying responses within early Christian writings to Jesus' death and resurrection, for example, Mark's empty tomb as opposed to Luke's bodily resurrection and ascension.

Giovanni Pierluigi da Palestrina, *Stabat Mater* (1590)

Giovanni Pierluigi was born in Palestrina, near Rome, and became known as the greatest Italian composer of his century. He composed the *Stabat Mater* for Pope Gregory XIV near the end of his life, and for centuries it has been performed during Holy Week and on September 15, the feast day of Our Lady of Sorrows. The hymn "Stabat Mater Dolorosa" ("The Grieving Mother Stood") originated in the thirteenth century and contains twenty couplets that describe the mother of Jesus standing before the cross in mourning. The stanzas focus on her grief and anguish as Christ hangs in pain on the cross. The characteristics attributed to Mary throughout the prayer include noble resignation, enduring patience, sorrowful meditation, and loving devotion. Mary's grief emerges from her love of her son, and this love in turn fills her with a spirit of patience and hope.

The purpose of the hymn can be seen in the latter half, in which the supplicant asks Mary to create in one's heart a mirror of Mary's own devotion and love for Christ, and thus the emotional identification with Christ's suffering: "Grant that I may sincerely weep with you, mourn the crucified as long as I live." Identification with Mary leads the faithful person to have more love for Christ, and thus more sorrow at his death, and finally a greater share of Mary's own compassion on the Day of Judgment. The supplicant asks for Mary to be near upon the person's death and to intercede with her son so that one may be received "with the fruits of victory" into "glorious paradise." By recognizing the true compassion that Mary exhibits toward Christ, and participating spiritually with it, the believer unites with Mary and Christ in their familial bond. Literal and dynamic translations of the Latin text are available in liturgical books and on the Internet.

Together the music and text provide a way for students to describe how they imagine the crucifixion scene, perhaps in comparison with popular cinematic depictions. Due to his balanced and beautiful Renaissance style, Palestrina's *Stabat Mater* does not induce the intense grief and shock of the scene found in some music and movies. How does this serene and lilting musical score connect emotionally or theologically with its subject matter? Also, the hymn raises the question of what Jesus' death means in the Gospels, both for him and for believers. What is the nature of Christ's "sacrificial" suffering and death, and how are disciples called to participate in it?

One might begin a class on the subject of the crucifixion with the question of whether the students find purpose or meaning in human suffering. As they answer the question, certain particulars can be pressed: What meaning is there in the death of an innocent child, in the carnage of a natural disaster, or in the deaths of those people who die fighting in a war? One could assemble various quotations from Christian and perhaps Muslim martyr texts that encourage believers to be ready to suffer for the true faith. As the *Stabat Mater* plays, students may reflect on what suffering they would be willing to live through to support their faith, political beliefs, or family. Why would a Christian want to identify so closely with the suffering of Jesus and of his mother? Are such believers motivated mostly by the desire to make it to their "glorious paradise"? Would they feel the same urgency if they knew it would have no direct "payoff"?

Felix Mendelssohn, *Paulus*, Op. 36 (1836)

Perhaps Mendelssohn's familial background, not to mention growing anti-Semitism in German society, led Mendelssohn to compose the earlier of his two great oratorios on the subject of Paul (see above for discussion of *Elijah*). Since Mendelssohn focuses almost exclusively on the account of Paul in Acts, the theme of conversion and newfound moral and religious knowledge must have appealed to him. *Paulus* was extremely well-received when it premiered in 1836 and was performed frequently in the following year.

In part 1, the oratorio focuses on the story of Stephen from Acts 6, including a moving Recitative and Chorus detailing his death. Saul is then introduced, as in Acts 7:58, and his experience on the road to Damascus is scored with great emotion, as the Chorus and a Bass vocalize the exchange between Jesus and Paul in Acts 9. As part 1 ends, Saul has been healed by Ananias and is preaching in the Damascus synagogues (Acts 9:19–20). In part 2, we meet Paul as he embarks on his missionary activities. In keeping with the laudatory tone of part 2, Mendelssohn ends the piece prior to Paul's arrest and subsequent trial(s) in Acts 21:27ff. Instead, we see Paul leaving for Jerusalem willingly, even though he acknowledges he is heading toward affliction and death.

There are several scenes one may use effectively in the classroom, such as Stephen's *apologia* in part 1 and his subsequent stoning. One can play Mendelssohn's version of Paul's conversion as a way of illustrating the differences between the account(s) in Acts and Paul's own account in Gal 2. Also, one could use this piece to initiate a discussion on how biblical interpretation is conditioned by the background(s) of the interpreter. For example, as Ralf Wehner has noted, Mendelssohn uses different compositional styles when scoring Jews and Gentiles, especially when he is retelling stories like

M
U
S
I
C

Acts 14. Wehner claims the Gentile voices are scored quite simply, with minimal ornamentation, but "in the choruses of the Jews Mendelssohn unfurls an astonishing range of compositional details." If one adds this musicological observation to what we know of Mendelssohn's background, one can easily initiate a discussion on the nature of biblical interpretation. Bold instructors could introduce students to Richard Wagner's infamous tract *Judaism in Music*, published pseudonymously in 1850, in which he attacks Mendelssohn's religious music. Finally, Mendelssohn's biography can be compared to Paul's, or at least the Paul that is presented in Acts. There has been, for some time now, a difference of opinion about Paul's identity, namely, did Paul remain Jewish while preaching Christ or did he "convert" to a new religious identity, leaving his Judaism behind? By introducing students to a brief biographical sketch of Mendelssohn, and then his music about Paul, one can invite students to consider the nature of Paul's religious identity, even as they are absorbing some of the greatest choral and vocal writing of the nineteenth century.

Olivier Messiaen, *Quatuor pour la Fin du Temps* (*Quartet for the End of Time*) (1940)

It is difficult to place Messiaen, a French Catholic composer, into any of the modern trends in music. Equally fascinated by Catholic mysticism and the songs of birds, his music can sometimes be difficult to listen to, but at the same time, there are moments of profound depth and beauty as well. This piece has an especially interesting history. As a captured member of the French forces during World War II, Messiaen found himself imprisoned in a German POW camp in Görlitz. A pianist, Messiaen began to compose works for the instruments which other inmates knew how to play. This compositional limitation accounts for the somewhat odd scoring of this piece for violin, cello, clarinet, and piano.

Messiaen reports that his inspiration for the piece came from Rev 10:1–7, an interlude between the sixth and seventh trumpets. Here, the seer describes an angel descending from heaven, who announces that "in the days when the seventh angel is to blow his trumpet, the mystery of God will be fulfilled" (10:7). Given Messiaen's situation as a POW, as well as his interest in Catholic mysticism, we can well imagine that he thought the end of time could be coming soon. However, the *Quartet* is not filled with doom and gloom. The piece is divided into eight movements, each with an evocative title; for example, the second movement is a "Vocalise for the Angel Who Announces the End of Time." Messiaen also takes this opportunity not to dwell on the coming end, but to ponder the divinity of Jesus through music. In movements 5 and 8 he provides a "Praise to the Eternity of Jesus," and a "Praise to the Immortality of Jesus." Per the former, Messiaen noted in the score,

"Jesus is considered here as the Word. A broad phrase, infinitely slow, on the violoncello, magnifies with love and reverence the eternity of the Word, powerful and gentle." The eighth movement is described as follows: "Expansive solo violin, counterpart to the violoncello solo of the fifth movement. Why this second encomium? It addresses more specifically the second aspect of Jesus, Jesus the Man, the Word made flesh.... Its slow ascent toward the most extreme point of tension is the ascension of man toward his God, of the child of God toward his Father, of the being made divine toward Paradise." In the third movement, Messiaen includes music to praise his beloved birds, and the sixth movement portrays the sounds of the Apocalypse itself. Messiaen described it as follows: "The four instruments in unison take on the aspect of gongs and trumpets (the first six trumpets of the Apocalypse were followed by various catastrophes, the trumpet of the seventh angel announced the consummation of the mystery of God). Use of added [rhythmic] values, rhythms augmented or diminished ... Music of stone, of formidable, sonorous granite..." Aside from the title and textual inspiration of the piece, it is this sixth movement that ties most directly into Revelation.

Teachers can use this piece in several different ways to teach not only Revelation, but also other New Testament texts. Given that most scholars think the earliest New Testament texts are pre-Pauline hymns quoted in places such as Phil 2:6–11, one could accompany a discussion of these hymnic fragments (which could have been vocalized via music) with a hearing of either the fifth or eighth movements, both of which contemplate the character of Jesus through music. Also, a teacher could use the sixth movement to accompany a discussion of Revelation. Because the piece is by nature abstract, one could ask students a number of "listening questions," such as what they imagine they are hearing, how they feel the piece relates to the text(s) at hand, or how they "hear" the Apocalypse, that is, what sorts of sounds or music come to mind when reading Revelation? Such questions not only draw students into the text in a different way, but they also ask them to reconstruct creatively the text for themselves, using their own musical identities to do so. Such engagement might allow them to connect with the text in a more personal and immediate fashion.

Franz Schmidt, *Book of the Seven Seals* (1937)

Schmidt is not (yet) a well-known composer, but his pedigree certainly speaks for itself. A student of Bruckner and one of Mahler's favorite cellists, his compositions represent some of the last vestiges of the great European tradition of Romanticism. In this piece, his last great work, he attempts what no other composer in history had ever accomplished: to create what he called a "comprehensive setting" of the book of Revelation. And in fact, this lengthy piece (over one hundred minutes) surely does so, albeit with a few cuts; for example, the seven letters in Rev 2–3 are edited into an initial address by John. Schmidt was adamant that these cuts did not reflect any disrespect for Revelation. In conjunction with the première of the piece in 1938, he prepared some explanatory comments, among which one finds the following claims: "My approach to the work had always been that of a deeply religious man and of an artist.… If my musical setting of this unparalleled work, which is as relevant today as it was at its creation eighteen and a half centuries ago, should succeed in bringing the hearer spiritually closer to it, then that will be my greatest reward." Unfortunately, Schmidt did not live long enough to see the success of his work; he died in 1939.

Because of the length and complexity of the piece, a summary here would be unwieldy. However, there are several ways in which Schmidt's work can prove useful in the classroom. The opening of the first Four Seals, with their accompanying riders on horseback, include various observations and conversations by individuals (along with wonderfully expressive music) so that students can experience the terror and emotions of these events in a more significant way than simply reading them. One of the more dramatic sections in Revelation is the seven angels blowing seven trumpets (8:6–9:21; 11:14–19); Schmidt scores these sections into a lush, nine-minute portion of part 2 which features solos, quartets, and a chorus, all expressing the simultaneous dread and hope of God's Day of Wrath. This section is a prime example of the more general tone of apocalyptic literature, with its mix of emotions and wonderfully strange imagery, and can be appreciated by students who do not normally like classical music due to its almost simplistic vocal writing and its luxuriant orchestral scoring.

VARIOUS

Johannes Brahms, *Ein deutsches Requiem,* Op. 45 (1865–68)

The great German composer wrote only one Requiem, and it differs significantly from the official text of the Catholic Requiem Mass that had been established in the mid- to late-1400s. In that official text (which can be heard in many versions, such as Mozart's magnificent K. 626 or even Fauré's sublime Op. 48) the emphasis is on the dead who pray and supplicate Jesus to be pardoned "in die illa tremenda" ("on that awful day"). As such, the traditional setting borrows from biblical images and texts, specifically those dealing with Jesus' divinity and the coming Judgment. However, in the mid- to late-1860s, Brahms finalized his very personal, idiosyncratic Requiem and discarded the traditional Latin text in favor of an amalgam of texts from Luther's Bible and the Apocrypha.

Perhaps not coincidentally, the Requiem took shape in the aftermath of the deaths of two extremely important people in Brahms's life: his mentor Robert Schumann and his mother Christine Brahms. Owing to their deaths, and especially to his humanistic agnosticism, his Requiem reflects not only a pride in the German language to express ultimate grief, but it also focuses almost exclusively on "they that have sorrow" (from movement 1). Brahms thus excludes any overt emphasis on the dead in favor of offering comfort to those who mourn for them. In doing so, he musters an impressive array of biblical texts, and it is this interplay that can prove useful for Bible teachers. For example, in part 2 of the Requiem, Brahms weaves together three different New Testament texts (1 Pet 1:24; Jas 5:7; and 1 Pet 1:25). Together they offer the one who grieves an image of hope in the "Coming of the Lord," but the texts are intertextually linked by the agricultural image of the farmer and the harvest. Additionally, in part 5 Brahms links disparate texts (e.g., John 16:22; Sir 51:27; Isa 66:13) in order to offer comfort to the mourner, but the texts are connected through images of suffering, labor, and motherhood. In this way, teachers can employ the Requiem to illustrate not only the influence of the Luther translation on even an agnostic, nationalistic composer, but also the way in which texts can be intertextually interpreted. Much in the same way that early Jewish followers of Jesus read and adapted the Torah in order to address a perceived existential crisis in their community, Brahms turns to the Luther Bible to offer a message of comfort to those who, like him, are grieving for lost friends and relations.

Dave Brubeck, *The Gates of Justice* (1969)

Dave Brubeck's 1959 album *Time Out*, with its instantly recognizable title track, cemented his place as one of the great American jazz composer-musicians of the twentieth century. In the late 1960s, the Union of American Hebrew Congregations and the College Conservatory of Music at the University of Cincinnati jointly commissioned Brubeck to write an extended cantata. Brubeck was troubled by the unrest brought about by the Civil Rights struggle as well as the deteriorating relationship between American Jews and African Americans. As such, he set about composing a generically hybrid piece containing texts from the Bible, the *Union Prayer Book*, the great Jewish sage Hillel, his wife Iola, and speeches of Martin Luther King Jr. As Brubeck wrote in his original program notes, "The essential message of *The Gates of Justice* is the brotherhood of man. Concentrating on the historic and spiritual parallels of Jews and American blacks, I hoped through the juxtaposition and amalgamation of a variety of musical styles to construct a bridge upon which the universal theme of brotherhood could be communicated." This bridge is constructed by focusing on the ethical issues that concerned Brubeck during the 1960s, but which also find expression in the Hebrew Bible. To connect the two, Brubeck has scored vocal parts for a Hebrew cantor—whose melodies stem from the Jewish liturgical tradition and who symbolizes the ethical-prophetic tradition—and a black baritone—whose melodies stem from the musical tradition of the spirituals and blues and who symbolizes the ethical concerns of modern humans. The interplay of these musical styles and emphases serves to present the listener with a fusion of music that is both intriguing and accessible.

For the Bible teacher, Brubeck's piece offers a variety of options. For instance, one could focus specifically on the texts Brubeck uses and ask students to reflect on the relationship and themes found within certain movements; for instance in "Open the Gates," Brubeck utilizes Ps 118:19–23 and Isa 62:10; 57:14. It would be fairly easy to play this four and a half minute piece and pose questions about shared themes or images. Teachers may also employ this piece to discuss the relationship between Jewish and African American interpretation of the Bible. A prime movement for that emphasis would be the longest piece in *The Gates of Justice*, specifically, "Shout unto the Lord." This movement combines biblical texts (Pss 95–98; Isa 2:4; 50:8; 57:19) with the words of Hillel and Martin Luther King Jr. By examining not only the texts used, but also the musical styles, a fruitful discussion could be initiated on how different communities have interpreted and responded to key passages in biblical literature in an attempt to illustrate the continuing influence of the Bible on communal identities. For instance, Brubeck's work could set the stage for conversation about how the Bible has been used in the Jewish communities of which Brubeck is a part in comparison to the ways in which biblical images and literature have been central to the formation of certain African American identities. One could develop that discussion with a corresponding emphasis on the role of music in those identities, focusing specifically on liturgical Jewish music and "secular" black music, such as jazz and blues. (Useful resources for these discussions include Marsha Bryan Edelman's *Discovering Jewish Music*; James Cone's classic *The Spiritual and the Blues*; and Allen Dwight Callahan's *The Talking Book: African Americans and the Bible*.)

John Rutter, *Requiem Aeternam* (1985)

John Rutter is a master of short choral pieces and carols, but his full length *Requiem* is also highly regarded among contemporary performers and audiences. Like Brahms and others before him, Rutter departs from the traditional liturgy of the "mass for the dead," by integrating other texts into the *Requiem*, in this case the Book of Common Prayer and certain biblical passages. Rutter opens the *Requiem Aeternam* with a dramatic and somewhat dark passage, with a steady drum beat underneath the voices. This quickly resolves in an angelic chorus which brightly continues the phrase: *requiem aeternam dona eis, Domine*, "Grant them eternal rest, Lord." This continues into the *Kyrie eleison* in which the chorus proclaims confidently, "Lord, have mercy." This opening indicates well the mood and theme of the whole work, which is hopeful and compassionate. In contrast to the dark and bleak mood of Mozart's *Requiem* or the sadness of Britten's *War Requiem*, Rutter expresses the hope that those who have died are peaceful and safe in God's protection. Rather than an ominous or threatening call for God's mercy, this *requiem* states the faith of believers plainly and with reverence. The second movement is a setting of Ps 130 in English: "Out of the deep have I called unto thee, O Lord." The textual and musical climactic moment is the phrase, "I look for the Lord.... In his word is my trust." After the *Pie Jesu, Sanctus, Benedictus*, Rutter moves to a thoughtfully sad rendition of the *Agnus Dei*, a reflection on Jesus' sacrificial death. He intersperses the traditional Latin text (translated, "Lamb of God, who takes away the sins of the world") with quotations from the 1662 Book of Common Prayer that begin, "Man that is born of a woman hath but a short time to live and is full of misery," and "I am the resurrection and the life, saith the Lord" (cf. Job 14:1; John 11:25). As in the Anglican liturgy for burial, death is considered a release from the limited and painful nature of human life when seen in the light of eternal life in the presence of Christ. After a soothing setting of Ps 23, Rutter emphasizes again the blessing that the dead receive through Christ in the closing section, the *Lux aeterna*, "Let eternal light shine on them." He incorporates into the Latin liturgy the English text from the Book of Common Prayer that begins, "Blessed are the dead who die in the Lord" (after Rev 14:13).

Like other Masses that depart from the traditional Latin text, Rutter's *Requiem* provides an opportunity to talk about the importance of redaction and editing to the "final form" of a composite text. How does Rutter change our interpretation of the original Latin prayers by including these particular biblical passages? Also, what is the effect (to an English speaking audience in particular) of a concert that alternates between Latin and English? How does the listening experience differ when one does or does not know the meaning of the text being sung?

One promising way to use this *Requiem*, as well as any other Mass text, is to play the same textual unit in two very different musical settings. The *Kyrie eleison* in this piece, for example, presents a stark contrast with the same passage in *requiem* settings of Mozart, Verdi, and Britten. Since the text is in Latin, and not understandable to many students, one might begin by asking students to listen to two different sounding pieces and to write down what they think the piece is trying to communicate to listeners. After this, students can share their interpretations of the piece and group similar thoughts in a mind map on the board. How many students recognized the text as being the same? Did they mention key ideas in the *requiem* mass such as death, hope, forgiveness, or judgment? One may use this exercise as a way to introduce the range of biblical ideas about death and dying, such as the sanguine view of Qoheleth in Eccl 3:19–21, the graphic descriptions of death as judgment in Nahum, and the hopeful resurrection of the persecuted dead in Rev 20:4–6.

Wolfgang Amadeus Mozart, *Requiem* (1791)

This piece may be familiar to American audiences because of the 1984 movie *Amadeus*, a fictionalized account inspired by the circumstances surrounding the composition of the *Requiem*. A wealthy Count Walsegg commissioned the work anonymously through a servant, hoping to pass the work off as his own at a memorial service for his deceased wife. Mozart only fully completed the initial *Requiem* and *Kyrie* sections before his death, but his wife Constanze wanted to profit from the work and so she enlisted the help of other composers to finish the work without acknowledging their role in the final product. Constanze maintained that Mozart had left explicit instructions for the work's completion, but the truth of this is unclear, and some sections were certainly written largely by Franz Xaver Süssmayr. Whatever the circumstances of its composition, Mozart's *Requiem* is one of the most recognizable choral pieces within sacred music. The opening two movements are the most famous and have made their way into many films and television shows. Many students will be familiar with the music even though they might not know what it is.

There are at least two possibilities for using this piece in discussing the Bible. First, it raises questions about death, the relationship between God and humanity, and possibilities for the afterlife. Unlike Rutter's *Requiem*, which focuses almost exclusively on pastoral expressions of hope and comfort, Mozart's *Requiem* follows the liturgical text more fully and includes the scenes of final judgment in the sequence of the *Dies irae, Tuba mirum, Rex tremendae, Recordare, Confutatis, and Lacrimosa.* These sections clearly outline the fateful decision that God will make on the day of final judgment, a "day of wrath." Drawing on prophetic language about the Day of the Lord, the liturgy describes the arrival of God as righteous judge who examines all people in light of the information written in the secret book. The middle parts of this sequence contain the faithful person's prayer for mercy and salvation, appealing first to God, the "tremendously majestic king" who has the power to save, and Jesus, who is bidden to "remember" (*recordare*) that his death on the cross has already secured redemption for the penitent sinner. The supplicant prays to be among the blessed when the guilty are tossed into the flames of punishment. It might help to make the Latin text and English translation available as students listen to sections of Mozart's *Requiem* so that they can discuss how the music emphasizes aspects of the theology of the prayer. Especially when compared directly with other requiems by Rutter and Brahms, one can discern the relative emphasis on God's merciful nature versus God's righteous judgment.

Second, Mozart's work is especially suited for conversation about the nature of revelation. Listening to a good recording of the *Requiem* is an awe-inspiring event. Some of the beauty of this composition comes from the liturgical text that he is setting to music, but the *Requiem* would be just as powerful without any words at all. Where does such genius originate? Like the best artists and writers, Mozart began with what had been done before and moved it to a new level that no one had envisioned before him. Such arguments have been made about so-called "religious geniuses" like Moses, Isaiah, Jesus, Augustine, and Martin Luther. After Mozart's death, the *Requiem* was finished by other composers, and in recent decades musicologists have attempted to uncover and remove "inferior" accretions. How does this compare with the modern impulse to find the original layer of authentic tradition in the Gospels, the "historical Jesus," or the "authentic" oracles of Isaiah of Jerusalem? Similarly, what should be identified as the "real" *Requiem*?

M
U
S
I
C

PART 2:
FILM

Introduction: Teaching the Bible with Film

Patrick Gray

College and seminary courses on "The Bible and Film" have become quite popular in recent years, and while curricular limitations often preclude entire courses devoted to the subject, an increasing number of instructors are incorporating movies into existing biblical studies courses on an ad hoc basis. The catalogues that comprise the following chapters are intended to serve as resources for use in these settings. One chapter suggests teaching strategies for use with more or less conventional "Bible epics." A second chapter offers pedagogical suggestions for use with films bearing relatively little, if any, explicit connection to the Bible. These catalogues are by no means exhaustive. Many other movies lend themselves to use in a biblical studies course.[1] The films discussed here are intended to stimulate further reflection on the intersection of the Bible and film in the classroom.[2]

A few basic questions arise when considering this intersection: (1) What objectives are best suited to the use of film in teaching the Bible? (2) What are some common pitfalls? (3) What are the underlying assumptions in various pedagogical approaches to the Bible via the medium of film?

---

1. In addition to those catalogued here, Roncace and Gray, *Teaching the Bible*, contains entries for a number of other films: *Blade Runner* (Tod Linafelt, "The Human Condition in Genesis 2–3 and in *Blade Runner*," 73–75); *Breaking the Waves* (Carleen Mandolfo, "Film as a Resource for Theological Reflection on Biblical Texts," 321–24); *Ferris Bueller's Day Off* (Philip A. Quanbeck II, "The Letter to the Romans and Pauline Theological Concepts," 360–62); *The Godfather* (Ronald A. Simkins, "Patronage in 1 Kings 17 and 2 Kings 8," 158–60); *It's A Wonderful Life* (William Sanger Campbell, "Mark and the Movies," 324–26); *The Lord of the Rings* (Brad E. Kelle, "Remembering Deuteronomy," 130–31); *Pale Rider* (Rolf Jacobson, "Imagery and the Psalms," 197–98); *Wall Street* (Michael Barram, "Jesus, Wealth, and Wall Street," 293–95); *The Shawshank Redemption* (Brent A. Strawn, "Second Isaiah and the Exilic Imagination," 175–76); and *Star Wars* (John B. Weaver, "Teaching the Unity of 'Luke-Acts,'" 330–31).

2. In most cases, the discussions will include not only a general overview but also attention to specific scenes that are suitable for use in classroom contexts.

As one surveys the range of strategies commonly employed in the class-room, a handful of broad objectives seem particularly well served by the incorporation of film:

Using movies helps to cultivate close reading skills. The simplest way to pursue this objective involves one or more of the dozens of "sword and sandal epics" that have been produced over the past century. It is very easy to show a clip from, say, *The Ten Commandments* or *The Greatest Story Ever Told* and have students write or comment on its fidelity (or lack thereof) to the biblical text. Biblical narrative tends to be quite sparse—as Eric Auerbach puts it, "fraught with background"[3]—and discussing various attempts at translating it into another medium helps students to appreciate this quality. In the case of the Gospels, of course, it quickly becomes clear that in most films the director is presenting a composite version. It is one thing to tell students that there are four different versions of the gospel in the New Testament and to alert them to a few of the problems with the harmonizing impulse, but it is quite another thing for them to discover it on their own and to witness what difference it can make for the tone, plot, and overall message. Even the most conscientious efforts to present "the text, the whole text, and nothing but the text" (for example, Pasolini's *Il Vangelo secondo Matteo* or Saville's *The Gospel of John*) inevitably entail interpretive decisions. Movies make this palpably clear.

With appropriate adjustments, the following questions might be used with almost any film belonging to this "biblical narrative" genre: Is there anything from the biblical text that this film omits? Is there anything it adds? Is there anything about the text—particular scenes, characters, or speeches—that this film helps you see that you did not see previously? What is it about the text that obscures this aspect? What is your reaction to the film's portrayal of _____ (Jesus, Moses, Abraham, Peter, Judas, etc.)? Is there something about the gospel that the medium of film will always miss, no matter how conscientious the director tries to be in representing the text? Is there something about a story as a written text that imposes certain limitations when trying to stage it on the screen? Are there motifs that are repeated that you had not noticed when reading the text over an extended period? Is there anything implicit in the text that the film makes explicit? What about the language? Does the translation used by the screenwriters lend a more "realistic" feel to the action and dialogue? Does it feel stilted? Are there particular lines that seem to work very well or very poorly? How do you assess the artistic license exercised in the invention of minor characters? How does the director handle large blocks

---

3. E. Auerbach, *Mimesis: The Representation of Reality in Western Literature* (trans. W. R. Trask; Princeton: Princeton University Press, 1953), 12.

of material that is lacking in dramatic action? In what way, if any, does the film anachronistically inject later Christian or Jewish theological notions into the story? How does this film reflect the context in which it was made? Could you have guessed correctly had you not known its release date in advance? How do you assess the use of background music in the film?

The cultivation of close reading skills is not the only objective served by film. Watching movies also helps to make the strange familiar and the familiar strange. A hurdle to be cleared by most teachers is the students' familiarity (both real and imagined) with the biblical text. It can be difficult even to get students to read texts that, in their minds, they already know. Movies can help in this regard. The notion that Jesus' suffering provides some vicarious benefit for others does not seem as shocking as it perhaps should until one sees, in Lars von Trier's *Breaking the Waves*, a depiction of unimaginable sacrifice as a means of salvation (in the form of a woman's willing sexual degradation at the request of her paralyzed husband). Those consumed by the question of the historicity of the Eden narrative in Gen 1–3 might overlook the profound existential questions it raises about the nature of human knowledge and mortality found also in a number of science-fiction movies such as *I, Robot*.

At the same time, much of the Bible and the world that produced it seems so utterly alien to most students that they write it off as being irrelevant or unintelligible. To counter this sentiment, some teachers have found that showing the opening scene of *The Godfather* helps to explain the ancient patron-client system or that *Twelve Monkeys* can help to acquaint students with the standard elements of the apocalyptic genre.

In addition, movies often provide excellent analogies for specific concepts, methods, or patterns one encounters in the field of biblical studies. When we interpret the Bible, for example, should we concern ourselves with the final product or should we delve into the compositional history of the text?[4] Do the biblical authors retain some kind of veto power over what the text means? May other factors such as the tradition in which the text has been canonized or the social location of the individual reader come into play when determining the meaning? Or, translated into cinematic terms, is the movie shown at theaters the real thing, or should we wait until the director's cut is released on DVD, complete with commentary and deleted scenes? Should we take into account prerelease screenings that aim at gauging initial audience reaction before the final version is produced? While some students may be

---

4. See, for example, Brad Kelle's use of the *Star Wars* episodes to illuminate how Isaiah should be read as three separate works as well as to emphasize the ways in which the entire book functions together as a whole ("Introducing the Book of Isaiah," in Roncace and Gray, *Teaching the Bible*, 172–73).

suspicious of theories about Priestly redactors or Matthew's use of Mark, it is easy to illustrate the process and the goals of redaction criticism by viewing movies based on biblical narrative.[5] How has the director edited the narrative and what overall effect do the changes have? Does it change the tenor of, say, the story of the woman caught in adultery (John 7:53–8:11) when, in *The Last Temptation of Christ*, Martin Scorsese leaves out the final line ("Go forth and sin no more")? Is the shift in emphasis intended or accidental? Does it fit into a pattern of other tendencies?

The incorporation of movies can also provide a painless way for teachers to include group work in their courses. Group work is anathema to many professors and also to many students. Requiring students to watch movies is one way to make a pedagogical virtue out of a logistical necessity: In most cases, only one or two copies of a movie will be available, and so the formation of viewing groups is essential if the students are to be prepared for subsequent in-class discussion. Small groups are moreover conducive for generating and articulating detailed insights about the film in response to any questions posed by the instructor. For whatever reason, students are frequently more ready, willing, and able to participate substantively in discussions about movies. An additional advantage is that integrating movies—which, for practical reasons, must be viewed outside of class—allows a teacher to make greater demands on the time of students without causing undue resentment. Recent surveys reveal the woefully small amount of time most college students spend on coursework. Together with philosophical commitments to a learner-centered model of teaching, this has caused many instructors to seek out ways to shift more responsibility for learning to the student outside the classroom. Time spent viewing movies is perhaps not "quality time," but then again, it may be that the five total hours spent by the average college student on all courses combined is not all "quality time," either.[6]

Notwithstanding the objectives for which movies have proven conducive, there are at least two practical pitfalls. First, many teachers have found that follow-up discussion can flounder if they have not primed the pump by

---

5. For the use of Jesus movies to introduce students to redaction criticism, see these entries in Roncace and Gray, *Teaching the Bible*: Marianne Meye Thompson, "Comparing Synoptic Texts Using 'Jesus Film' Clips," 261–62; and Jeffrey L. Staley, "How to Read a Gospel by Viewing a Miracle Story in Film: An Exercise in Redaction/Narrative/Feminist Criticism," 273–74.

6. According to a recent survey, sixty-five percent of students reported spending fewer than six hours per week on homework and studying. See "The American Freshman: National Norms for Fall 2001," n.p. [cited 3 April 2007]. Online: www.gseis.ucla.edu/heri/norms_pr_01.html.

distributing a list of specific questions and viewing suggestions before the students go off to watch the movie. Second, while movies may provide a way to create distance, to make the familiar text of the Bible appear in all its foreignness, and to help students overcome preconceived ideas about what the Bible is and how one interprets it in a critical manner, it is sometimes possible to invoke analogies or parallels of such utter strangeness that the average student throws up a wall of resistance and is unable to consider matters in a dispassionate manner.[7]

Finally, it may be helpful to articulate a few of the underlying (and perhaps unacknowledged) assumptions that appear to be at work in various strategies for using film in the biblical studies classroom:

First, it is assumed that incorporating movies has pedagogical value in that it humanizes the professor. We are not only teaching a subject; we are at the same time teaching students. Students like watching movies. Therefore, if we show movies, students will enjoy the course. Since most students perform better when they enjoy the task or are favorably disposed toward the taskmaster, movies can help to accomplish course objectives.

Second, there is a widely held assumption that students are more eager to broach weighty theological questions when they appear in the guise of a movie. What is the proper relation of creature to creator? Play *Blade Runner*. What would it look like to serve mammon rather than God? Watch Michael Douglas's performance in *Wall Street*. Do we interpret the text or does the biblical text stand over and interpret us? Consider Samuel Jackson's recitation of Ezek 25:17 at the close of *Pulp Fiction*.

Third, it is generally assumed that the process of "reading" a film is a good analogy for reading a text. On this score, it would seem that many professors are simply putting into practice one of the foundational principles of critical exegesis (famously articulated in 1860 by Benjamin Jowett in *Essays and Reviews*) to read the Bible "like any other text." Or, conversely, it may be the case that the impressive level of pedagogical energy and innovation seen in cinematic approaches to the study of the Bible actually demonstrates the implicit assumption that the Bible is not, in fact, just like any other book. After all, how often does one see movies in classes devoted to Aristotle or Dostoevsky?

It may be too early to tell whether we are seeing a kind of paradigm shift in the increased popularity of movies in biblical studies courses. It is the

---

7. For example, more than one colleague has reported mixed results (at best) from attempts to explore certain discursive practices in biblical literature with reference to the proclivity of Canadian directors for stories involving pedophilia, incest, and necrophilia.

nature of things that paradigm shifts become fully visible only in hindsight. Our hope is that the discussions in the following pages not only aid other teacher-scholars in planning their classes, but also provide some empirical basis for deliberations about what is (or ought to be) happening on the ground when we teach the Bible.

BIBLIOGRAPHY

1. BIBLICAL NARRATIVE IN FILM

Babington, Bruce, and Peter Williams Evans. *Biblical Epics: Sacred Narrative in Hollywood Cinema*. New York: St. Martin's, 1993.

Bach, Alice. "Calling the Shots: Directing Salome's Dance of Death." *Semeia* 74 (1996):103–26.

———. "'Through Them to the Lions, Sire': Transforming Biblical Narratives into Hollywood Spectaculars." *Semeia* 74 (1996): 1–13.

Baugh, Lloyd. *Imaging the Divine: Jesus and Christ-Figures in Film*. Kansas City: Sheed & Ward, 1997.

Beal, Timothy K., and Tod Linafelt, eds. *Mel Gibson's Bible: Religion, Popular Culture, and "The Passion of the Christ."* Chicago: University of Chicago Press, 2005.

Campbell, Richard H., and Michael R. Pitts. *The Bible on Film: A Checklist, 1897–1980*. Lanham, Md.: Scarecrow, 1981.

Christianson, Eric S., P. Francis, and W. R. Telford, eds. *Cinéma Divinité: Religion, Theology and the Bible in Film*. London: SCM-Canterbury, 2005.

Corley, Kathleen, and Robert Webb, eds. *Jesus and Mel Gibson's* The Passion of the Christ: *The Film, the Gospels and the Claims of History*. New York: Continuum, 2004.

Davies, P. R. "Life of Brian Research." Pages 400–414 in *Biblical Studies/Cultural Studies: The Third Sheffield Colloquium*. Edited by J. C. Exum and S. D. Moore. Sheffield: Sheffield Academic Press, 1998.

Exum, J. C. *Plotted, Shot, and Painted: Cultural Representations of Biblical Women*. Sheffield: Sheffield Academic Press, 1996.

Forshey, Gerald E. *American Religious and Biblical Spectaculars*. Westport, Conn.: Praeger, 1992.

Fraser, Peter. *Images of the Passion: The Sacramental Mode in Film*. Westport, Conn.: Praeger, 1998.

Goodacre, Mark. "The Synoptic Jesus and the Celluloid Christ: Solving the Synoptic Problem through Film." *Journal for the Study of the New Testament* 80 (2000): 31–43.

FILM

Gunn, David M. "Bathsheba Goes Bathing in Hollywood: Words, Images, and Social Locations." *Semeia* 74 (1996): 75–101.

Humphries-Brooks, Stephenson. *Cinematic Savior: Hollywood's Making of the American Christ*. Westport, Conn.: Praeger, 2006.

Kinnard, Roy, and Tim Davis. *Divine Images: A History of Jesus on the Screen*. New York: Citadel, 1992.

Koosed, Jennifer L., and Tod Linafelt. "How the West was Not One: Delilah Deconstructs the Western." *Semeia* 74 (1996): 167–81.

Kozlovic, A. K. "'What Good Can Come from Nazareth?': The Via Negativa Pedagogic Advantages of Using Popular Biblical Films in Religious Education." *Journal of Religious Education* 49.2 (2001): 41–48.

Malone, Peter. *Movie Christs and Antichrists*. New York: Crossroad, 1990.

Pardes, Ilana. "Moses Goes Down to Hollywood: Miracles and Special Effects." *Semeia* 74 (1996): 15–31.

Reinhartz, Adele. *Jesus of Hollywood*. Oxford: Oxford University Press, 2007.

Rumble, Patrick, and Bart Testa, eds. *Pier Paolo Pasolini: Contemporary Perspectives*. Toronto: University of Toronto Press, 1994.

Schaberg, Jane. "Fast Forwarding to the Magdalene." *Semeia* 74 (1996): 33–45.

Singer, Michael. "Cinema Savior." *Film Comment* 24 (September–October 1988): 44–47.

Staley, Jeffrey L., and Richard Walsh. *Jesus, the Gospels, and Cinematic Imagination*. Louisville: Westminster John Knox, 2007.

Stern, Richard, Clayton Jefford, and Guerric DeBona. *Savior on the Silver Screen*. Mahwah, N.J.: Paulist, 1999.

Tatum, W. Barnes. *Jesus at the Movies: A Guide to the First Hundred Years*. Santa Rosa: Polebridge, 1997.

———, and Henry Black Ingram. "Whence and Whither the Cinematic Jesus?" *Religion in Life* 44 (1975): 470–78.

Telford, William R. "The New Testament in Fiction and Film: A Biblical Scholar's Perspective." Pages 360–94 in *Words Remembered, Texts Renewed*. Edited by W. G. E. Watson, J. Davies, and G. Harvey. Sheffield: Sheffield Academic Press, 1995.

Walsh, Richard. *Reading the Gospels in the Dark: Portrayals of Jesus in Film*. Harrisburg, Pa.: Trinity Press International, 2003.

2. NONBIBLICAL NARRATIVE IN FILM

Aichele, George, and Richard Walsh, eds. *Screening Scripture: Intertextual Connections Between Scripture and Film*. Harrisburg, Pa.: Trinity Press International, 2002.

Anker, Roy M. *Catching Light: Looking for God in the Movies*. Grand Rapids: Eerdmans, 2004.

Barsotti, Catherine M., and Robert K. Johnston. *Finding God in the Movies: 33 Films of Reel Faith*. Grand Rapids: Baker, 2004.

Bergesen, Albert J., and Andrew M. Greeley. *God at the Movies*. New Brunswick, N.J.: Transaction, 2000.

Bowman, Donna. "The Gnostic Illusion: Problematic Realized Eschatology in *The Matrix Reloaded*." *Journal of Religion and Popular Culture* 4 (Summer 2003). Cited 2 October 2006. Online: www.usask.ca/relst/jrpc/art4–matrixreloaded.html.

Boyer, Mark G. *Using Film to Teach New Testament*. Lanham, Md.: University Press of America, 2002.

Brown, Dan. *The Da Vinci Code*. New York: Doubleday, 2003.

Collins, J. J., ed. *Apocalypse: The Morphology of a Genre*. Semeia 14. Missoula, Mont.: Scholars Press, 1979.

Commins, Gary. "Woody Allen's Theological Imagination." *Theology Today* 44 (1987): 235–49.

Cukrowski, Kenneth L. "What Does New Haven Have to Do with Lubbock? Texts, Techniques, and Sociology." *Teaching Theology and Religion* 3.2 (2000): 96–102.

Deacy, Christopher. *Screening Christologies: Redemption and the Medium of Film*. Cardiff: University of Wales Press, 2001.

Desser, David. "The New Eve: The Influence of *Paradise Lost* and *Frankenstein* on *Blade Runner*." Pages 53–65 in *Retrofitting* Blade Runner: *Issues in Ridley Scott's* Blade Runner *and Philip K. Dick's* Do Androids Dream of Electric Sheep? Edited by Judith B. Kerman. Bowling Green, Ohio: Bowling Green State University Popular Press, 1991.

Dirks, Tim. "Greatest Film Misquotes." Cited 12 April 2007. Online: www.filmsite.org/moments0.html.

Ehrman, Bart D. *Truth and Fiction in the Da Vinci Code*. Oxford: Oxford University Press, 2004.

Faller, Stephen. *Beyond the Matrix: Revolutions and Revelations*. St. Louis: Chalice, 2004.

Gravett, Sharon. "The Sacred and the Profane: Examining the Religious Subtext of Ridley Scott's *Blade Runner*." *Literature-Film Quarterly* 26 (January 1998): 38–43.

Greeley, Andrew M. "Images of God in the Movies." *Journal of Religion and Film* 1.1 (April 1997): 1–6.

Horton, Robert. "Snoochie Boochies: The Gospel According to Kevin Smith." *Film Comment* 35.6 (November 1999): 60–65.

Hurley, Neil P. "Cinematic Transfigurations of Jesus." Pages 61–78 in *Religion in Film*. Edited by J. R. May and M. Bird. Knoxville: University of Tennessee Press, 1982.

Jewett, Robert. *Saint Paul at the Movies: The Apostle's Dialogue with American Culture*. Louisville: Westminster John Knox, 1993.

———. *Saint Paul Returns to the Movies: Triumph Over Shame*. Grand Rapids: Eerdmans, 1999.

Johnston, Robert K. *Reel Spirituality: Theology and Film in Dialogue*. Grand Rapids: Baker, 2000.

———. *Useless Beauty: Ecclesiastes through the Lens of Contemporary Film*. Grand Rapids: Baker, 2004.

Keefer, Kyle. "Knowledge and Mortality in *Blade Runner* and Genesis 2–3." *Journal of Religion and Film* 9.2 (October 2005). Cited 13 April 2007. Online: www.unomaha.edu/jrf/Vol9No2/KeeferKnowMortal.htm.

Kozlovic, A. K. "The Bible is Alive and Well and Living in Popular Films: A Survey of Some Western Cinematic Transfigurations of Holy Writ." *Australian Religion Studies Review* 13.1 (2000): 56–71.

———. "Popular Films and Religious Education: Prospects and Prejudices." *Journal of Religious Education* 48.3 (2000): 31–38.

———. "The Structural Characteristics of the Cinematic Christ-Figure." *Journal of Religion and Popular Culture* 8 (Fall 2004). Cited 2 October 2006. Online: www.usask.ca/relst/jrpc/art8–cinematicchrist.html.

———. "The Transmogrified Bible: A Survey of Some Popular Western Cinematic Transfigurations of Biblical Characters." *Religious Education Journal of Australia* 17.1 (2001): 7–13.

Kreitzer, Larry J. *Gospel Images in Fiction and Film: On Reversing the Hermeneutical Flow*. London: Sheffield Academic, 2002.

———. *The Old Testament in Fiction and Film: On Reversing the Hermeneutical Flow*. Sheffield: Sheffield Academic Press, 1994.

Leblanc, Douglas. "Dogmatically Anti-Dogma." *Christianity Today* 44.1 (January 10, 2000): 80.

Lyden, J. C. *Film as Religion: Myths, Morals, and Rituals*. New York: New York University Press, 2003.

Marsh, Clive. *Cinema and Sentiment: Film's Challenge to Theology*. Milton Keynes, U.K.: Paternoster, 2004.

———, and Gaye Ortiz, eds. *Explorations in Theology and Film: Movies and Meaning*. Oxford: Blackwell, 1997.

Martin, J. W., and C. E. Ostwalt Jr., eds. *Screening the Sacred: Religion, Myth, and Ideology in Popular American Film*. Boulder: Westview, 1995.

May, John R. *Image and Likeness: Religious Visions in American Film Classics*. New York: Paulist, 1992.

F
I
L
M

———, ed. *New Image of Religious Film*. Kansas City: Sheed & Ward, 1997.

———, and Michael Bird, eds. *Religion in Film*. Knoxville: University of Tennessee Press, 1982.

McNulty, Edward. *Films and Faith*. Topeka: Viaticum, 1999.

Miles, Margaret. *Seeing and Believing: Religion and Values in the Movies*. Boston: Beacon, 1996.

Mraz, Barbara. *Finding Faith at the Movies*. Harrisburg, Pa.: Morehouse, 2004.

Reinhartz, Adele. *Scripture on the Silver Screen*. Louisville: Westminster John Knox, 2003.

Roche, Mark W. "Justice and the Withdrawal of God in Woody Allen's *Crimes and Misdemeanors*." *The Journal of Value Inquiry* 29 (1995): 547–63.

Rosenberg, Joel. "What the Bible and Old Movies Have in Common." *Biblical Interpretation* 6 (1998): 266–91.

Runions, Erin. *How Hysterical: Identification and Resistance in the Bible and Film*. New York: Palgrave MacMillan, 2003.

Scott, Bernard Brandon. *Hollywood Dreams and Biblical Stories*. Minneapolis: Augsburg Fortress, 1994.

Stone, Bryan P. *Faith and Film: Theological Themes at the Cinema*. St. Louis: Chalice, 2000.

Vaux, Sara Anson. *Finding Meaning at the Movies*. Nashville: Abingdon, 1999.

Walsh, Richard. *Finding St. Paul in Film*. New York: T&T Clark, 2005.

F
I
L
M

THE BIBLE IN FILM

Nicola Denzey and Patrick Gray

The films discussed in this chapter are organized according to the order in which their subject matter appears in the canon. One of the main criteria guiding our selection of films in this chapter is availability; generally, if a film is not readily available through one of the major rental companies such as Blockbuster or Netflix, it has not been included (since logistical constraints mean that most instructors will not be able to show it). An unintended and unfortunate result is that the compilation in this chapter is very light on films covering Hebrew Bible narratives. Prior to 1960, Hollywood produced a number of movies inspired by stories from the Hebrew Bible, but very few of these can now be obtained through the usual channels. Most films in recent decades have been "Jesus films" of one sort or another.

The indices may be consulted to find film entries with classroom strategies related to particular biblical texts. All secondary literature cited here is included in the preceding bibliography (pp. 92–96).

The Bible: In the Beginning (1966)

John Huston directs, narrates, and stars in (as Noah) this adaptation of Gen 1–22. Students will be familiar with most of the stories included, discussion of which may pursue the following questions:

(1) If only for practical purposes, the movie has to end *somewhere*. How appropriate is Gen 22 as a stopping point? The meaning of a text is conditioned in part by what comes before and after it. How does the story as a whole (or the last episode) change by virtue of its placement at the end?

(2) Adding details not present in the written text is, of course, unavoidable, but Huston is relatively reserved when it comes to "filling in the gaps." Assess the film's depiction of the miraculous. How might he have handled this material differently? By not trying to explain or make these elements more plausible in naturalistic terms, the film in some ways preserves what Bultmann and others would describe as the text's mythic character. Too quickly "translating" the text's specific images and categories overlooks the fact that its message comes through those very images and categories.

(3) The voice of the serpent who tempts Eve (DVD ch. 3) belongs to the same actor (Huston) who speaks God's lines. While it is unlikely that the director intends to do so, this provides an opening for discussing the theological question of responsibility. Is God to blame for "the fall" by placing the tree in the Garden? Does God intend for the couple to eat of the tree from the beginning? Is this biblical narrator a reliable narrator?

(4) Gen 1–11 is usually referred to as the Primeval History. This section has a timeless quality and addresses questions of origins of relevance to all of humanity before turning to the specific dealings of God with Israel. Does the presentation of this section have a primeval "feel"? Is there a noticeable change when the Abraham cycle begins?

(5) Gen 14 is significant in later biblical traditions because it features the figure of Melchizedek. In the film, however, he does not appear. Instead, the battle and Abraham's rescue of Lot is greatly expanded (DVD ch. 14). Considerations of genre likely influence this decision. Is it more difficult to imagine a director doing the opposite, that is, omitting a detailed battle scene and expanding the role of a shadowy character with no other apparent impact on the narrative?

(6) The binding of Isaac is one of the most gripping sections of the movie (DVD chs. 19–20). This narrative from Gen 22 is notoriously sparse in detail. How does this depiction compare with others (e.g., Kierkegaard's)? A few of the interpretive decisions made here include: Isaac is a young adolescent. Abraham questions the voice that tells him to sacrifice his son. He is distraught, even angry through most of the episode. Abraham mentions the custom of child sacrifice practiced by neighboring tribes. Sarah does not know what is about to happen.

For further discussion, see Forshey, *American Religious and Biblical Spectulars*, 145–61.

The Ten Commandments (1956)

If there is a single film that qualifies as the quintessential "biblical epic," this Cecil B. DeMille production is the one. At nearly four hours in length, there is ample material for comparison with the text of Exodus (as well as parallel accounts given in Philo and Josephus). Fodder for discussion may include the following:

(1) DeMille appears on screen to introduce the film, which he says is "the story of the birth of freedom." To what extent is this an apt summary of Exodus? He also states that his intent is not to create a new story by filling in the missing periods in the life of Moses but rather "to be worthy of the divinely inspired story." What assumptions about the nature of inspiration does this statement suggest?

(2) Only a few of the plagues are shown on screen. Most are simply reported in very brief terms (DVD ch. 34). Inasmuch as the text itself cannot literally depict the plagues in visual terms, is this device in any way preferable to trying to re-create them via special effects? (Cf. Pardes, "Moses Goes Down to Hollywood: Miracles and Special Effects," 15–31.)

(3) The physical and spiritual change in Moses after the burning bush theophany (DVD ch. 29) is stark. To what degree does this transformation match the testimony of Exodus?

(4) While the institution of the Passover ritual receives less space than it should relative to the attention it receives in Exod 12–14, it takes place as the screams of Egyptians, whose firstborn have just died, can be heard in the background (DVD ch. 37). This depiction nicely captures the awfulness of God in Exodus (in the older sense connoting awesomeness as well as dread).

(5) Pharaoh returns after the debacle at the Red Sea and dramatically declares, in reference to the victory of the God of Moses, "His God *is God*" (end of DVD ch. 42). The scene provides an opportunity to distinguish between henotheism and strict monotheism and to examine biblical texts portraying the Israelites at various points along a trajectory toward the latter (e.g., Exod 20:2–6; Deut 6:4–9; 2 Kgs 17:7–18; 21:1–16; Isa 45:14–25; Mic 4:5).

(6) Some of the Israelites are unimpressed when Moses descends from Sinai with the tablets of the law (DVD ch. 46). They want freedom, one says, not the law. Moses replies, "There is no freedom without the Law." In what sense(s) can this sentiment be squared with the perspective of Exodus? In light of his reflections in Romans and Galatians, what might Paul say if he were to view this scene?

(7) Given the title of the film, the Decalogue occupies very little narrative space. Is the film misnamed? Similarly, to what degree may it be said that the Torah (as a synonym for the Pentateuch) is centrally concerned with Torah (in the broader sense of "the law")?

For further discussion, see Forshey, *American Religious and Biblical Spectaculars*, 123–44.

The Prince of Egypt (1998)

This animated film contains a three-minute scene (DVD ch. 7) that helps facilitate consideration of identity in the Exodus story. Students naturally think of Moses as an Israelite, and for good reason. The text identifies Moses' parents as Levites (Exod 2:1), he leads the Israelites out of Egyptian bondage, and receives the laws from God. It is also clear from the text, however, that Moses is raised in the house of Pharaoh, given an Egyptian name (2:10), and is reluctant to help emancipate the Israelites (Exod 3–4). Indeed, Moses does not even know the name of the Israelite deity (3:13), and that deity subsequently tries to kill him (4:24). In this clip, Moses encounters Miriam and Aaron. Miriam is thrilled to see her brother, who she thinks has returned to help them. Moses, however, does not recognize his sister and becomes angry when she informs him, for the first time, that he is an Israelite. As Moses is departing, Miriam begins to sing a lullaby that Moses recognizes; this is the beginning of his (ethnic) identity crisis. In the next scene (DVD ch. 8) Moses returns to the palace and—through a voice-over song—expresses his affinity for his Egyptian home and family. This clip effectively depicts what is written between the lines of the biblical narrative: Moses is part Israelite and part Egyptian, and that presents a struggle.

On an "academic" level this scene launches a discussion about the Exodus and the many ways in which it is a story of Israel's forging their own identity, apart from Egypt. The narrative, for example, recounts how God distinguished between the Israelites and the Egyptians (8:22–23; 9:4; 11:7). The Israelites, however, clearly struggled with this distinction, as they were remarkably eager to return to Egypt (16:3; 17:3). On a "personal" level, students might write about their own conflicting identities—cultural, ethnic, or otherwise. This is a particularly instructive exercise for many bi- or multicultural students—not only as they engage in self-reflection, but as they share with others their experiences as well. For students not in this category in any obvious or conventional sense, one might ask them to reflect on the tensions requisite in being, for example, a student-athlete or a nontraditional student; or what struggles were inherent in having one parent Catholic, the other Protestant or Jewish or Muslim; or one religious and one not. Whenever possible, they should draw comparisons or contrasts to Moses' situation.

For a related exercise, see F. V. Greifenhagen, "Israelite And/Or Egyptian? Ethnic Identity in Exodus," in Roncace and Gray, *Teaching the Bible*, 111–12.

King David (1985)

This retelling of 1–2 Samuel starring Richard Gere is the most readily available screen portrayal of "the man after God's own heart." Items for discussion may include:

(1) The opening scene, in which Saul "negotiates" with the captured King Agag (cf. 1 Sam 15:1–31), concisely captures a number of the key themes of 1 Samuel and of the larger Deuteronomistic History. Samuel confronts Saul over his failure to carry out the gruesome command to utterly destroy the Amalekites, refers to his initial doubts about the Israelite call for a king "like other nations," and then informs Saul that God has rejected him. Saul looks like the lame duck that he is almost from his first appearance in the text.

(2) Have students comment on the characterization of Bathsheba (DVD chs. 13–14). She is frequently portrayed as a temptress. Is this reputation justified on the basis of the text (cf. 2 Sam 11:2–5)? Does the film perpetuate this image or undercut it? The director seems confused as to the function of this story line. For example, it mitigates David's guilt considerably to have Bathsheba describe Uriah as an abusive husband.

(3) The final scene, which shows David on his deathbed giving advice to his heir Solomon, is bizarre. "Be guided by the instincts of your own heart" and not by the prophets, he says, for "it is through the heart that God speaks to man." Have students comment on the fidelity of this conclusion to 1 Kgs 2:1–9 and to the rest of the David story.

The Gospel Road (1973)

Johnny Cash personally financed the production of this musical retelling of the Jesus story. It is not of the highest quality, but its distinctive character opens several avenues of discussion:

(1) This film is markedly different from other Jesus films. Is it in any apparent way reacting against or responding to others? (Perhaps compare Luke's reference to "other accounts" in the prologue to his Gospel—likely a reference to Mark.) Despite the differences, does it in any way show the influence of other films in the genre?

(2) None of the filming took place after dark, despite the fact that the Gospels clearly locate certain scenes at night (e.g., the meeting with Nicodemus, the Last Supper, Gethsemane). Does this departure have a substantial effect on the meaning or impact of these scenes?

(3) Prior to the sequence in the passion narrative, Cash shuffles the order of Jesus' sayings from the Gospels pretty freely. In what way, if any, is this analogous to the ways in which Luke and Matthew appropriate Q material for their narratives?

(4) The film's low budget made it impossible to employ large numbers of extras for the crowd scenes. In a number of scenes requiring crowds, the director goes in the other direction, frequently depicting Jesus alone with only the sound of crowds in the background. How does the lack of a visible crowd affect the audience's reaction? When one reads the Gospel accounts, in what ways do the narrators make the crowds' presence felt?

(5) Whereas the narrators of the canonical Gospels remain anonymous, viewers of the film are acquainted with Johnny Cash. Does the identity of the narrator affect either the substance of the message or the audience's reception of it? Would it make a difference to the reader to know for certain that Matthew or Mark, for example, were or were not the authors of their Gospels?

(6) With only two or three brief exceptions, there is no spoken dialogue in the film. The story is told entirely through songs and through Cash's narration. Comment on the overall effect of this presentation.

(7) In terms of narrative style and substance, which Gospel does the film most closely resemble? Mark, on account of its quick, paratactic tempo? Matthew or John, on account of the more active role of the narrator in shaping the story? Luke, on account of the use of songs by characters? One of the extracanonoical Gospels?

Jesus Christ Superstar (1973)

This rock opera focuses on the last week of Jesus' life, with special attention to his relationship with Judas and Mary Magdalene. As the music plays, a number of issues for discussion emerge:

(1) Few other films engage in the same degree of reflection on Jesus' self-consciousness. Note the famous refrain: "Jesus Christ, Superstar, do you think you're what they say you are?" The Gethsemane scene (DVD ch. 13) contains much material for comparison with the canonical Gospels as well as with the description of Jesus in Heb 5:7–9. In this text, is Jesus afraid? Would there be something culpable about fear in this situation? Does he willingly go to his death (cf. Heb 10:5–10)? Is his acquiescence to the divine will seen as a prerequisite for its efficacy as a sacrifice?

(2) The opening number sung by Judas (DVD ch. 1) concisely broaches several topics typically covered in a course on the Gospels: Did Jesus think of himself as divine or simply a man? Did his followers, both during and after his lifetime, accurately understand his teachings? Did the later church intentionally distort his teachings? Did Jesus intend to provoke the Jewish and Roman authorities in such a way that his death would result, or did he let things "get out of hand"? What was the essence of Jesus' teaching? Was it a message about God or about himself? Or both? To borrow Bultmann's terms, when did the proclaimer become the proclaimed?

(3) Mary Magdalene's signature number (DVD chs. 10, 19: "I don't know how to love him") makes for an easy transition to a discussion of the role of women in Jesus' ministry or the many imaginative theories about her relationship with Jesus. Such theories have received great attention with the popularity of Dan Brown's novel *The Da Vinci Code*. Students may benefit from examining the two chief texts upon which this speculation rests, the *Gospel of Philip* and the *Gospel of Mary*.

(4) What did Jesus teach about care for the poor? Readers frequently overlook Jesus' somewhat unexpected words on the topic (Matt 26:6–13). The film includes a scene (DVD ch. 4) in which Jesus and Judas debate the matter.

F
I
L
M

(5) Jewish characters—both the leaders and the people—are almost relentlessly opposed to Jesus. Is it fair to level the charge of anti-Semitism?

(6) The prominent role of Judas may prompt discussion of the recently published *Gospel of Judas*.

For further discussion, see Forshey, *American Religious and Biblical Spectaculars*, 104–18; Stern, Jefford, and DeBona, *Savior on the Silver Screen*, 161–93; Baugh, *Imaging the Divine*, 35–41; and Tatum, *Jesus at the Movies*, 117–30.

Jesus of Nazareth (1977)

After repeated broadcasts on television, Franco Zeffirelli's six-hour mini-series ranks as one of the most widely viewed Jesus films of all time. Because of its length, it contains more material for textual comparison than most other films.

(1) Anthony Burgess wrote a novel based on his early draft of the screenplay for the movie but containing much additional material (*Man of Nazareth*). Somewhat oddly, William Barclay also produced a novelization (*Jesus of Nazareth*) of the movie, which was in turn based on a screenplay, which was based on the Gospels! An extended student project might involve a source-critical or redaction analysis of these interdependent versions. Shorter assignments could be given for specific scenes.

(2) Peter is portrayed as something of a hothead (e.g., DVD chs. 35–38 of disc 1). What is the textual basis for this common depiction?

(3) Zeffirelli has said that one of his main reasons for making the film was to clear the Jews of the charge that they were responsible for killing Jesus (cf. Baugh, *Imaging the Divine*, 73). How has he attempted to do this, and how successful has he been? (Scenes to discuss on this score are plentiful, including DVD chs. 9–12, 16–20, and 26–31 of disc 2.)

(4) This film was made for television, which features frequent commercial breaks. Is the manner of storytelling and scene construction noticeably affected by this medium? Is this an apt analogy for the way scholars connect *Sitz im Leben* with the particular forms in which Gospel pericopes are transmitted?

(5) The Annunciation affords the opportunity to consider the phenomenology of religious experience (DVD ch. 5 of disc 1). No angel is seen or heard by the viewer or by Mary's mother, who "witnesses" it in process. How does Luke present this encounter?

(6) Does the child Jesus evince a strong messianic self-consciousness (cf. DVD chs. 23–26 of disc 1)? Is it possible to imagine this Jesus performing the deeds seen in, for example, the *Infancy Gospel of Thomas*?

(7) Much to the chagrin of Peter and others, Jesus dines with the sinners and tax collectors at Matthew's house (DVD chs. 38–39 of disc 1). The

setting becomes the occasion for a moving recitation of the parable of the Prodigal, where two very different groups listen simultaneously to his teaching on divine mercy. This visual rendition raises important questions about the audiences for Jesus' parables. Who were the original intended audiences? Were they all aimed at a generic audience? How might different hearers draw different lessons from them?

For discussion of *Jesus of Nazareth*, see Stern, Jefford, and DeBona, *Savior on the Silver Screen*, 197–229; Tatum, *Jesus at the Movies*, 135–45; and Forshey, *American Religious and Biblical Spectaculars*, 164–71.

Intolerance (1916)

Widely hailed as one of the masterpieces of the silent era, this D. W. Griffith epic mostly confounded audiences as it shifted back and forth between four parallel story lines—one set in the modern age, focusing on social reformers; one in Jerusalem at the time of Jesus; one in ancient Babylon; and one in 1572 Paris, during the persecution of the Huguenots. Each story, according to the opening credits, "shows how hatred and intolerance … have battled against love and charity." Its length may make it difficult to incorporate into some courses, but the biblical story is by far the shortest of the four and may foster discussion along the following lines:

(1) Viewers here experience the story of Jesus juxtaposed alongside three other narratives. Many modern and ancient readers of, for example, Mark's Gospel likewise experience the story of Jesus alongside three other narratives, as well as the rest of the Bible's table of contents. In what ways does this juxtaposition resemble the canonical context for much reading of the Bible?

(2) Jesus is introduced as "the greatest enemy of intolerance" before the wedding at Cana (DVD ch. 11; the scene also features the Pharisees as "meddlers" who fault Jesus for eating with sinners). Ask students to write on this topic: Would "The central idea of _____'s Gospel is Jesus' role as an enemy of intolerance" make a good thesis statement for a short essay? If so, how would you go about supporting it? If not, how would you undermine it?

(3) The Bible consists of words and no actual images. A silent film consists almost entirely of images, with very few words. To provoke creative reflection about the nature of canon, ask students to speculate about the differences that one would see if Christianity and Judaism had adopted visual (as opposed to written) canons.

(4) Film was a new genre when *Intolerance* appeared. Similarities to other genres notwithstanding, the Gospels likewise constituted a new genre. The movie seems largely unremarkable to viewers now, but this is in part because it was so successful in introducing new techniques and devices that we now

take them for granted. Which elements of the Gospels have become type-scenes that influence subsequent literature in a similar manner?

For background and discussion of the film, see Tatum, *Jesus at the Movies*, 33–43.

Il Vangelo Secondo Matteo (The Gospel according to St. Matthew) (1966)

A Marxist and atheist, director Pier Paolo Pasolini was murdered in 1975 but not before leaving behind this masterpiece. His intent was to remythologize the Gospel, to bring to it a new beauty: "I, a nonbeliever, was telling the story through the eyes of a believer." Still, it is dated and quite slow-moving for modern audiences used to color and fast edits, who may have little patience for the film's black and white and English-language dubbing.

Since this movie is a cinematic rendition of a single Gospel, it makes a nice foil for movies such as *The Greatest Story Ever Told* that rely on harmonizing techniques to tell a story. No dialogue is added. No scene is invented. One way to present this to students is to emphasize that by focusing on a single Gospel, Pasolini is doing something similar to what contemporary biblical scholars are doing when they practice redaction criticism. But one can also practice redaction criticism on the movie's "text." Pasolini does omit some scenes, and he does reorder the sequence of events in the Gospel. Thus it is useful to ask students to analyze as systematically and thoughtfully as possible how Pasolini "redacts" the Gospel. Since this requires time, attention, and multiple viewings, this sort of work is best done as a written assignment, with the movie made available on reserve. To reduce the scope of the task, one might take only one portion of this film—the infancy narrative or the Sermon on the Mount—and look at how Pasolini has worked with the biblical text to reinterpret it. A few sets of questions might sharpen classroom discussion:

(1) Why the de-emphasis on the crucifixion, compared to what we see in other films? Why do you think Pasolini chose anachronistic elements to retell the Gospel, such as medieval hats, ancient ruins, and a soundtrack that features African drumming or African American spirituals? Why does he exclude so much sayings material? Apart from questions of intent, what is the resultant effect of these decisions?

(2) A study of Pasolini's Christology would also be interesting here since it focuses only on one Gospel. Matthew itself presents, many have argued, a thoroughly Jewish Jesus, who comes as a fulfillment, not a replacement, of the law. Do students see evidence for Jesus' Jewishness here? And what sort of Jesus is this, in terms of his personality or nature?

(3) Pasolini deliberately refrained from consulting religious experts or scholars when making his film, partly because he wished to "remytholo-

gize" the story rather than to historicize it. He also meant to draw parallels between Jesus and the Jewish authorities and the political and religious conflicts in twentieth-century Italy. And yet one consequence of this is that the film includes anti-Semitic and anti-Jewish material from the Gospel often left aside in contemporary passion plays. For instance, the woes against the Pharisees in Matt 23 are here presented in their entirety. Do students find the inclusion of these elements anti-Semitic?

(4) Pasolini was a Marxist who stated explicitly in interviews that his version of the Jesus story was a Marxist film. Where, if at all, is this apparent? Does he draw this out of the biblical material? Does he inject it where it is not present? Is it hard to tell because of the text's silences or ambiguities?

For further discussion, see Fraser, *Images of the Passion*, 67–78; Stern, Jefford, and DeBona, *Savior on the Silver Screen*, 95–125; Baugh, *Imaging the Divine*, 94–106; Walsh, *Reading the Gospels in the Dark*, 95–120; and Tatum, *Jesus at the Movies*, 103–15.

Godspell (1973)

This screen version of the successful off-Broadway production bills itself as "a musical based on the Gospel according to St. Matthew." Here Jesus comes to life as a hippie clown who wanders New York City with a merry band of disciples reenacting parables from the Gospels. Points for discussion include the following:

(1) Evaluate the film as a retelling of Matthew's Gospel. Does it really "get" Matthew, despite leaving out a number of major Matthean texts (e.g., birth and infancy narratives, the giving of the "keys of the kingdom" to Peter, the Great Commission)? What of significance does it miss? Answers to this question help to clarify what is central to Matthew's version of the story and what is peripheral.

(2) Comment on the characterization of John the Baptist. (He is decidedly more jovial than the biblical Baptist.) Without any signal of a change of character, the same actor performs the deeds of Judas. What is the effect of this merging of the two roles? Is there a point in the film where the transition from John to Judas can be detected? When Jesus tells Judas, "Do what you must do" (DVD ch. 14), he appears to do so approvingly—a striking interpretive move in light of the recently published *Gospel of Judas*.

(3) The company's reenactments of various parables take up much of the script: the hard master (Matt 25:14–30) at DVD ch. 4; the sheep and the goats (25:31–46) at DVD ch. 5; and the sower (13:3–9) at DVD ch. 8. Parables from Luke's Gospel also appear: the Good Samaritan (10:30–37) and Lazarus and the rich man (16:19–31) at DVD ch. 6; and the Prodigal (15:11–32) at DVD ch. 9. Why are Lukan parables included in a musical based on Mat-

thew? What is the effect of seeing the parables acted out instead of hearing or reading them? Does it alter their meaning when someone other than Jesus is narrating them?

(4) One critic has observed that *Jesus Christ Superstar* stresses the humanity of Jesus while *Godspell* stresses his divinity. Is this an accurate assessment?

(5) To what extent, if any, does the film's presentation of Jesus as a clown communicate Paul's message about the "foolishness" of the gospel in 1 Cor 1:18–25?

(6) Several camera shots focus on the World Trade Center. For many viewing the film after September 11, 2001, these shots evoke strong memories. Is this in any way an apt parallel to the experience of those reading the Gospels after the Roman destruction of the temple in Jerusalem? Many references to the temple in the Gospels are incidental, while other episodes more explicitly remind the reader of its demise.

(7) Ask students to summarize the plot. When they are limited to summarizing purely on the basis of what is said or shown in the film, they realize that it essentially has no plot of which to speak. Jesus comes; Jesus teaches; Jesus dies—that, in a nutshell, is the whole story. Viewers must import the necessary background and transitions to produce a coherent narrative. To some degree, the viewer is like the audiences of the Gospels who already know the story before they hear it. There are no miracles and no resurrection. Instead of a retelling of Matthew, then, perhaps the film is better compared to Q or the *Gospel of Thomas*. Jesus is a teacher and little else. What might a community look like if *Godspell* were its only "Gospel"? (Note the partial parallel to Q and *Thomas*: Is it conceivable that any real community would have read one of these documents and nothing else? Would these documents or the film represent the sum total—no more, no less—of any group's theological convictions?)

For discussion of *Godspell*, see Walsh, *Reading the Gospels in the Dark*, 69–93; Baugh, *Imaging the Divine*, 42–47; and Tatum, *Jesus at the Movies*, 117–30.

The Greatest Story Ever Told (1965)

Max von Sydow stars as Jesus in this star-studded film shot in the American southwest. As the story proceeds at a snail's pace, a number of issues for discussion emerge:

(1) The film begins with a shot of the interior of a church that fades into a shot of the countryside, and it ends inside a church as well. Ask students to comment on this as a way of framing the story. While no part of the story takes place within a church, there is something fitting about it in light of the church's role in remembering, transmitting, and shaping the Gospel accounts

as we now have them. Were it not for the church, how likely is it that we would know of Jesus today? (One clue: A few sentences in Josephus are the only other clear references to Jesus to survive from the first century.) In connection with this ecclesiastical setting, compare also the Last Supper (DVD ch. 25), which has almost the feel of a mass, and the chanting of Ps 23 (DVD ch. 23).

(2) The Sermon on the Mount is divided and dispersed to various parts of the story (the largest portions are in DVD chs. 8 and 17). How does it condition the audience's reception when it does not take place on a mountain? Similarly, when the rejection at Nazareth of Luke 4 does not occur in a synagogue, does it significantly affect the function of the scene (DVD ch. 18)?

(3) Very few miracles are depicted here. The best-known miracles are reported by a minor character in one fell swoop (DVD ch. 17). Perhaps this is due to the director's worries about the difficulties of presenting them in a plausible manner. What difference would it have made if the Evangelists had simply had a character report the miracles (cf. John 20:30–31)? Are they ever described in minute detail?

(4) The raising of Lazarus (DVD ch. 21) occurs to great fanfare. (An arrangement of Handel's Hallelujah chorus plays in the background.) Although the scene is more than a little melodramatic, this staging is not entirely inappropriate as a way of capturing the climactic tone of John 11, at the end of the Johannine "Book of Signs."

(5) In stark contrast to many other Jesus movies, the scenes dealing with the trial and crucifixion (DVD chs. 28–30) are almost entirely devoid of blood and violence. And after three hours of screen narrative, furthermore, the actual crucifixion is brief—less than four minutes elapse from the raising of Jesus on the cross to the point at which he gives up the spirit. Compared to other films, are these aspects more or less faithful to the way the passion is depicted in the Gospels? What is the effect of a less protracted, less violent death?

(6) On the third day, Mary Magdalene literally wakes up and remembers Jesus' prediction of his resurrection—before she finds the tomb empty (DVD ch. 32)! The scene works well as an example of how the texts do *not* describe the first Easter as well as how the earliest christological reflection did *not* take place.

For further background and analysis, see Babington and Evans, *Biblical Epics*, 139–48; Baugh, *Imaging the Divine*, 24–32; Stern, Jefford, and DeBona, *Savior on the Silver Screen*, 129–60; Tatum, *Jesus at the Movies*, 87–100; Walsh, *Reading the Gospels in the Dark*, 147–71; and Forshey, *American Religious and Biblical Spectaculars*, 94–104.

Jesus (1979)

This film is widely believed to be the most-watched movie of all time. Quite apart from any artistic quality, for this reason alone it is of special cultural significance. Now used as part of Campus Crusade for Christ's "Jesus Film Project," this movie has been translated into nearly one thousand languages, and a conservative estimate is that it has been viewed over four billion times. One advantage for use with students is that it can be viewed for free online (www.jesusfilm.org). Almost every word in the script is taken from Luke's Gospel, which affords pedagogical opportunities not available with other movies.

(1) The official website states that the non-Lukan material added to the film amounts to three verses—John 3:16; Rev 3:20; Matt 28:19. Although evangelism is a primary aim of the film rather than fidelity to Luke per se, is there anything about these additions that is particularly consonant with or contrary to the spirit of Luke's Gospel? Likewise, does the short shrift received by the birth and infancy narratives of Luke 1–2 detract from the story in a significant way? (The film acknowledges up front that it deals with "the public life of Jesus.")

(2) This film includes a number of scenes normally absent from other Jesus films (e.g., the stilling of the storm, the transfiguration, the Gadarene swine, the meeting with Zacchaeus, Jesus constantly at prayer). Do such scenes have common traits that make them ill suited to the film genre? Do these scenes display peculiarly Lukan concerns?

(3) Due to its use as an evangelistic tool in remote, non-Western areas, a large portion of the audiences for this film consist of those who are barely, if at all, familiar with the basic story. How might this affect their response to the film? Is this similar to or different from the audiences for the written Gospels in antiquity? (Close reading of Luke 1:1–4 might accompany discussion of these questions.)

(4) Because the crucifixion scene is considered too graphic for younger viewers, a children's version has been produced, which may also be viewed online. It is half the length of the original. An exercise in redaction criticism might have students assess the overall effect of the changes made in this shorter version.

For further discussion, see Tatum, *Jesus at the Movies*, 147–57.

The Gospel of John (2003)

Every word in the script for this film is taken verbatim from the Good News translation of the Fourth Gospel, which affords pedagogical opportunities not available with other movies:

(1) If students do not notice that John's Jesus is markedly more talkative than in the other Gospels, a showing of the quite lengthy Farewell Discourse of John 14–17 (DVD chs. 23–27) should help them see the difference. The director's commentary recounts the efforts to exploit even the tiniest opening in the text to shift the physical setting as Jesus talks without interruption. The flashbacks during this discourse effectively highlight the themes that recur in the narrative.

(2) After showing the scene with the woman caught in adultery (7:53–8:11; DVD ch. 11), have students write a memo to the director. Should it be included? This exercise allows for discussion of the text-critical, literary, and theological questions that arise in connection with this disputed pericope.

(3) A number of female students have commented that Jesus' encounter with the Samaritan woman has a flirtatious feel (DVD ch. 5). Does this mirror the way in which this text may have been read by the intended audience? This scene provides a starting point for discussing female characters in the Gospels, Jesus' views on women, social customs in first-century Palestine, or the theological assumptions behind various responses to a "sexual" Jesus in this text and elsewhere.

(4) Is the purpose of the Fourth Gospel the same as the purpose of this film? In John 20:30–31, the author states that he is writing "so that you may come to believe that Jesus is the Messiah" (NRSV). Some textual variants give a slightly different meaning on the basis of the verb tense: "These are written so that you may continue to believe." So which is it? Does the author intend to persuade the unbeliever? Or is the purpose to strengthen the faith of those already in the fold? Does the Gospel give any indication of which construal is the more likely? How would the responses of believing and unbelieving viewers of the film differ?

The Last Temptation of Christ (1988)

Martin Scorsese's controversial movie begins with scrolling text from Nikos Kazantzakis's novel of the same name on the "incessant, merciless battle between spirit and flesh." And then follows a disclaimer: "This film is not based upon the Gospels but upon this fictional exploration of this eternal spiritual conflict." The Last Temptation of Christ (LTC) is in some ways the most thoughtful, moving, troubling, and annoying movie about Christ ever made. At its release, LTC was boycotted by several Christian groups. If only to provide the current generation of university students with a comparison to the controversy engendered by Gibson's Passion of the Christ or the recently published Gospel of Judas, a showing of this film can be useful. LTC's depiction of a sympathetic Judas (Harvey Keitel) who has "the hardest job" (i.e., betraying his friend) and a protracted and gory crucifixion are likely to go over somewhat differently than they might have twenty years ago when the film first came out.

There is no doubt that the film was meant, in part, to shock. We see Jesus (Willem Dafoe), weak, whiny, and tormented by inner voices, in love with Magdalene the prostitute. He is shiftless and neurotic, angry at God, and comes to understand his destiny only at the film's final moment. It might be interesting to discuss with students what precisely Jesus' "last temptation" was, according to this film. Its post-Nicene theology of Christ as fully human and fully divine is not something that always comes across in the New Testament Gospels, and thus students who are more biblically oriented may have more trouble cultivating sympathy with the theological meditation here. At the same time, Jesus being fully human means that he experienced the full range of what it means to be human (cf. Heb 2:14; 4:15), and *LTC* is virtually the only film to take this low Christology seriously in a way that never stoops to satire.

Despite not being based on the Gospels, the film does in fact take a variety of scenes from the Gospels:

(1) Jesus rescues a woman taken in adultery (here, identified as Mary Magdalene) (DVD ch. 8)
(2) The Sermon on the Mount (DVD ch. 8)
(3) Jesus' baptism by John the Baptist (DVD ch. 10)
(4) Jesus is tested in the wilderness (note that the serpent has a woman's voice—in fact, it is the Magdalene) (DVD ch. 11–12)
(5) Jesus conducts various exorcisms and miracles (DVD ch. 13)
(6) The wedding at Cana (DVD ch. 13)
(7) Jesus is rejected by his hometown (DVD ch. 14)
(8) The raising of Lazarus (DVD ch. 15)
(9) The cleansing of the temple (DVD ch. 16)

Much of what we see here is a sort of Gospel harmony (e.g., all of Jesus' last words from all four canonical Gospels are used at the end), with additional creative interpretation (such as Paul killing Lazarus postresurrection). But it would be worthwhile to have students compare any or all of these scenes with what they read in the New Testament.

The scene of Jesus' Sermon on the Mount in which Jesus discovers something of his true calling might be good to compare with Matthew's text—not in terms of accuracy, but how successfully it casts Jesus as a sort of antirhetor. The scene of Jesus and Paul meeting—wholly fictional, of course—is also a fine way to broach a persistent issue: Who is the true founder of Christianity? Paul (Harry Dean Stanton), amusingly, gets the last word (DVD ch. 27).

For further discussion, see Stern, Jefford, and DeBona, *Savior on the Silver Screen*, 265–95; Babington and Evans, *Biblical Epics*, 149–68; Baugh, *Imaging the Divine*, 51–71; and Tatum, *Jesus at the Movies*, 161–74.

The King of Kings (1927)

In 1927, it was a relatively new discovery that motion pictures could be pressed into the service of Christ. Cecil B. DeMille took this on as his personal mission, choosing to open the film with a clear message to the audience: "This is the story of Jesus of Nazareth. He Himself commanded that His message be carried to the ends of the earth. May this portrayal play a reverent part of that great command." As a missionary tool, *King of Kings* had remarkable success. DeMille bragged that his movie had brought more people to Christ than had any other effort apart from the Bible itself. Indeed, the visual image of a long-haired, bearded, blue-eyed Jesus so deeply entrenched in the minds of so many people owes much to *The King of Kings*.

DeMille worked with one of the biggest budgets in history at the time and with the fanciest technology of the day. The movie is in black and white, but the final scenes of the resurrection are in Technicolor. Although the narrative does not closely follow the Gospels or the life of Christ, most "dialogue" is really quotations of chapter and verse. The cinematographer researched, and supposedly replicated, over three hundred paintings of Jesus as tableaux. The original musical score draws on a number of well-known hymns, some of which fit with the narrative context in not-so-obvious ways.

For those who enjoy working in class with Gospel harmonies, showing the crucifixion scenes alongside the canonical passion narratives makes for fruitful work. This one is shot from afar, without tight close-ups. Students might exegete the scenes, and pick out which scenes correspond to which Gospels. They might speculate why, for instance, DeMille's Jesus does not say "My God, why have you forsaken me?" They might note that certain scenes are titled with chapter and verse, other scenes are untitled and yet correspond to one or the other of the Gospels, and sometimes an event takes place in all four Gospels and yet its title corresponds to only one of the Gospels. And they are sure to be amused by the apocalyptic atmosphere of the crucifixion.

The Passion of the Christ (2004)

Is it historical? Is it faithful to the Gospels? Is it anti-Semitic? These three questions dominated public and private discussions of Mel Gibson's film at its release. Although many students might be inclined to disagree with the assessment, it is clear that the film is historically inaccurate and lacks fidelity to the Gospel accounts in several areas. One simple exercise in the classroom is to air the film, but to stop it at various points and ask for comments or for students to "match" it with biblical text. This exercise has, however, limited pedagogical value after a while. That Gibson had taken artistic liberties with Gospel materials is not a point that needs to be hammered home eight or ten or twelve times. But *where* Gibson got his wild riffs on Gospel narrative is a more interesting question. In classes with substantial time to devote to study of the Gospels, it would be good to assign Anne Catherine Emmerich's *The Dolorous Life of Our Lord Jesus Christ* alongside their Gospel reading and their viewing of this movie. The Emmerich work answers many questions about some of the more striking elements of the film—particularly its violent imagery and its emphasis on corporeal suffering and torture.

Students are frequently most fascinated by Gibson himself—what sort of a Christian he is, what sort of Roman Catholicism he espouses. Understanding Gibson's particular brand of Catholicism helps them to understand—and to be open to—the film's distinctive emphases. It is not just the influence of Emmerich on this film. It is the role Gibson assigns to the Jews in Jesus' death, the redemptive value of suffering, and the prominent visibility of women, particularly Jesus' mother Mary.

To exclude any mention of this film's impact on contemporary Christians in favor of a strict exercise comparing biblical text to movie keeps the reader from working through one of the most interesting issues surrounding the movie: its reception, particularly in the United States. It did not really provoke a *Kulturkampf* between Catholics and Protestants, although much of the media coverage skewed it that way. Divisions and differences of opinion existed within each denomination. Catholics debated the film's historical accuracy (especially the Pope's alleged endorsement of it, quickly retracted or denied by the Vatican), but also the ethics of constructing contemporary passion plays given their potential for incendiary anti-Semitism. Protestants had their own set of disputes. Some fundamentalist denominations decried the film's "idolatry" by permitting a human actor to play Jesus, or opposed its Mariolatry as offensive.

Instructors wanting to devote a portion of a syllabus to this film are blessed with several excellent resources (e.g., the online essays from the February 2004 issue of the *Journal of Religion and Film* [www.unomaha. edu/jrf/2004Symposium/Symposium.htm] and Kathleen Corley and Robert Webb's collection of essays by prominent scholars, *Jesus and Mel Gibson's The Passion of the Christ: The Film, the Gospels and the Claims of History*).

Jesus of Montreal (1989)

Depressed by the flagging popularity of a passion play that his diocese has enacted each year, a priest in Montreal sets out to update it for a modern audience. He brings in a cast of out-of-work actors headed by one Daniel Coulombe, who slowly begin to inhabit—and be profoundly changed by—the roles that they play. Their audiences, too, are transformed by their experience of viewing the narrative—to the extent that the Catholic diocese begins to find their priests inadvertently playing modern-day Pharisees and Sadducees to the actors' Jesus/Coulombe and his disciples.

Jesus of Montreal was, at its release, a controversial film. Denys Arcand's vision of Jesus (Lothaire Bluteau) as a revolutionary, a countercultural hero of the people, and a challenger of the hypocrisy he sees around him is, one could argue, biblically defensible. This construction of Jesus the revolutionary would be well supported in the classroom by secondary studies (e.g., Crossan, Freyne, Horsley) and passages from the canonical Gospels that appear to have Jesus challenging authorities. The "temple tantrum" pericopes have a nice parallel in the film as Coulombe accompanies a female friend who is auditioning for a beer commercial but is treated objectionably by the producers. Disgusted, Coulombe overturns the set and chases the businessmen from the studio (DVD chs. 18). As Daniel comes to inhabit his role more and more deeply, so too are his actor-friends caught up, transformed, and brought together into a tightly knit group of disciples who see signs of hypocrisy (particularly religious hypocrisy) everywhere.

An interesting element of *Jesus of Montreal* is that it effectively combines stagings of the passion play (the "play within a play" conceit), modern transformations of the actors in contemporary Montreal, and a running commentary during the passion play by the characters that reflects academic perspectives on Jesus' life. Coulombe does his research, even meeting up in a parking garage with members of a theology faculty who secretly pass him subversive academic articles. His new script that results from this research reads more like an academic work than a passion play (DVD ch. 10). The narrator begins "the story of the Jewish prophet Yeshu Ben Panthera" with an explanation that ancient historians like Tacitus, Suetonius, Pliny, and Josephus mention him only in passing and that "what we know was pieced together by his disciples a century later. Disciples lie; they embellish." While some of the details may be off, even here one may find fodder for discussion: Which disciples lied? How do we know? In what sense do they lie? Is there a difference between lying and embellishing?

And yet, for all this, *Jesus of Montreal* comes across as deeply religious in a way. It is a moving film to watch, and would work well in New Testament classes, viewed in its entirety. Particularly intriguing scenes are the parallels to the temptations of Jesus and the apocalyptic discourse in Mark 13 (DVD chs. 23, 27).

For further discussion, see Fraser, *Images of the Passion*, 98–106; Stern, Jefford, and DeBona, *Savior on the Silver Screen*, 299–333; Baugh, *Imaging the Divine*, 113–29; and Tatum, *Jesus at the Movies*, 177–88.

Monty Python's Life of Brian (1979)

A send-up of biblical "Life of Jesus" epics, this film was released in 1979 amidst a furor in the U.S. and the U.K. It is difficult to imagine that contemporary American students who had somehow never seen it would be too terribly offended by it, although they might find a number of scenes—particularly the chorus line "Always Look on the Bright Side of Life" at the movie's conclusion—in poor taste.

Students love *Life of Brian* and would benefit from a screening of the entire film. However, a variety of scenes work well shown in class in isolation. The brief but hilarious nativity (DVD ch. 1) can be shown along with other filmic examples of harmonized scenes. Another scene that works well in class is a brief one in which members of the People's Front of Judea gather clandestinely to discuss their grievances against Rome (DVD ch. 10: "What have the Romans ever done for us?"). This scene works nicely when laying out the political situation of first-century Judea and the effect of the Pax Romana on the Jewish population of Jerusalem. Students see how it is that the Romans can bring a civilizing force for the "good" which nevertheless breeds substantial disaffection among the indigenous population. *Life of Brian* has a number of other minor details in background scenes that get things Roman just right, from its spoof of gladiatorial games, Roman food, a background scene of the desecration of the temple with the Emperor's statue being carried in, one shot of Jerusalem's main street where various prophets on soapboxes spin out various addled but surprisingly accurate prophecies, and other arcane references to delight the *cognoscenti*. The Monty Python crew know their Roman history, which is what makes the satire so brilliant.

Another scene that works well in the classroom is a brief one in which Jesus does appear, preaching the Sermon on the Mount (DVD ch. 3). Since he is relatively far away, the gathered crowd cannot fully hear him, and the ensuing dialogue is full of absurd misunderstandings and misinterpretations ("Blessed are the *cheese*makers?" "Aha, what's so special about the cheesemakers?" "Well, obviously it's not meant to be taken literally; it refers to any manufacturers of dairy products")—a nice example of how oral traditions might have shifted Jesus' original sayings over time (and even *at* the time, as different disciples might have heard differently). Finally, the phenomenon of people blindly following a religious authority, as people seek to follow Brian and beg for signs, can resonate with many students as an example of the inherent danger in many religions.

Above all, *Life of Brian* is clever and learned—deceptively so. One example of such learned humor is a scene in which Brian asserts his Jewishness to his mother (DVD ch. 6). His mother then reveals that his father was actually a Roman soldier. "Did he rape you?" asks Brian, horrified. "At first, yes..." replies his mother. Everyone laughs at this, because the answer is so transgressive. Rape is not at all funny, of course, but here we can laugh at it anyway, because the answer is so unexpected. And since Brian is clearly meant to "be" Jesus, the laughter reflects, in part, some people's discomfort at the story of Jesus' birth from a virgin. But what is funnier, from an academic perspective, is Brian's mother's confession that echoes ancient Jewish slanders of Jesus as the illegitimate son of one Pandera or Panthera (see, e.g., the *Toledoth Yeshu*). Some controversies have been around for a long time.

For further discussion, see Stern, Jefford, and DeBona, *Savior on the Silver Screen*, 233–63.

The Robe (1953)

Like the other parabiblical epics from the 1950s (*Barabbas, Ben-Hur*), *The Robe* attempts to capture the decadent glory that was Rome during the time of Tiberius and Caligula. When the tribune Marcellus Gallio (Richard Burton) is dispatched to Jerusalem, he participates with other Roman soldiers in casting lots for Jesus' robe at the crucifixion. After Marcellus wins the robe, his guilt over his complicity in killing the Son of God drives him insane. Marcellus's slave Demetrius (Victor Mature), by contrast, is deeply inspired by his brief encounters with Jesus. Thus *The Robe* is a classic conversion narrative: really, a double conversion narrative—Marcellus's and Demetrius's. Although some students may still enjoy *The Robe*, at just over two hours it is perhaps too long and slow for the current generation. *The Robe* is based on the 1942 historical novel of the same name by the Lutheran minister Lloyd C. Douglas, who specialized in Christian inspirational literature. It was so popular upon its release that it threatened to unseat *Gone With the Wind* as box-office favorite. And yet, predictably, the movie comes across as a cultural relic of a bygone era that makes it difficult to use in the contemporary classroom.

Jesus appears only peripherally in *The Robe*, and yet his influence is undisputed and his status as the Messiah taken for granted—not only by the vast crowds around him, but quite obviously by the assumed audience of the movie. There is no sense that Jesus and those around him were Jewish—despite all the talk of him being the Messiah, it is taken for granted that an audience understands this through an exclusively Christian hermeneutic. One scene to show in the classroom is Jesus' triumphant entry into Jerusalem; it looks like a late nineteenth-century American Romantic landscape painting—lots of palms and people at a distance—but with a soundtrack of soaring choirs. One might read along with this Zech 9:9–10 and accounts of Jesus' entry into the city (Mark 11:1–11; Matt 21:1–11; Luke 19:28–44; John 12:12–19). Why does this director choose to include the elements he does? And what sort of a sense of Rome, of Judaism, and of the relations between the two of them do we get from this movie?

The Robe's crucifixion scene is a good one to play in conjunction with other more gruesome cinematic depictions (e.g., *The Passion of the Christ*). Students might be asked how this scene relates to the Gospel depictions. More interesting, however, is to note the lack of gore and what the director refuses to show us; it is a crucifixion scene that lacks a Jesus, although while the camera is behind and below him he does speak from the cross. Fifty years makes a huge difference in how filmmakers choose to depict this scene. Why the renewed emphasis on Jesus' suffering in twenty-first-century American Christianity? Put differently, why are modern cinematic accounts of the passion so much gorier? And why are the "follow up" scenes so much less dramatic than in the 1950s?

Ben-Hur (1959)

In the 1950s, a number of movies developed parabiblical stories set in the Roman Empire (e.g., *Quo Vadis*). *Ben-Hur* is one such film that takes the term "epic" seriously—which means it is *very* long. It is also dated enough that students may find it more of a relic of the past than something honestly gripping. If you inflict all 214 minutes on them, they will hate you. Nevertheless, *Ben-Hur* has its uses in the classroom.

Despite its subtitle ("A Tale of the Christ"), *Ben-Hur* is really more about Jewish resistance to Rome than about the story of Christianity and may thus help to introduce the turbulent political context of the first century. When Messala arrives in Jerusalem as the new Roman tribune, he and his childhood friend Prince Judah Ben-Hur (Charlton Heston) begin a bitter enmity over political allegiances. Ben-Hur must lead his people; Messala demands their submission to Rome. *Ben-Hur's* plot, therefore, is not unlike Ridley Scott's *Gladiator*: A hero highly placed in Rome breaks with his friends on matters of principle, suffers by being transformed into a slave and fighter, and ends up in a position of greater power against his powerful opponent.

Students might be invited to think about the Jewishness of Judah Ben-Hur. What does it accomplish for the plot? Apart from pawing at a mezuzah on the door of his old palace when he returns after many years, it is difficult to see any markers of the hero's Jewishness at all. He never mentions the temple or Torah, and apparently never keeps the Sabbath nor keeps kosher as he fraternizes with his Roman friends. The only time that he does pray, imploring God to help him, Jesus himself steps in to save him (DVD ch.

18 of disc 1). On the other hand, there is no question that we have in *Ben-Hur* a more positive vision of first-century Judaism than that which we find in many Christian movies about Jesus. How much this had to do with Hollywood ethics at the time and how much was an attempt at historical verisimilitude (*Ben-Hur* gets Judaism as a *political* entity more or less correct) is a question that merits consideration. Finally, Judah is very much of a Joseph figure, like Maximus of *Gladiator*, and so raising those parallels in class can make for a fruitful discussion. (On this and other gladiator movies, see Babington and Evans, *Biblical Epics*, 177–205.)

Barabbas (1962)

Based on a novel by Nobel laureate Pär Lagerkvist, *Barabbas* tells the story of the criminal set free while Jesus was crucified. It is a classic conversion narrative—Barabbas (Anthony Quinn) suffers a crisis of conscience when he discerns the significance of Jesus having, quite literally, died in his stead. Relentlessly downbeat, *Barabbas*'s view of Rome is cynical enough that it occasionally resembles a not-very-scary biblical horror film.

Barabbas's conversion comes as one dramatic moment framed by a series of vignettes in the post-Jesus aftermath of Jerusalem. Obsessed with whether Jesus will really rise from the dead, Barabbas accuses the disciples of having stolen the body (cf. Matt 28:11–15). To find out more about what happened to Jesus, he meets with a very creepy Lazarus. (These scenes may function as entry points for discussion of the ways in which the claims of the early Christians would have been understood by outsiders.) The woman whom Barabbas loves is a Christian who is stoned to death for her faith. Barabbas is next sentenced to hard labor in the sulphur mines, where he endures a hellish existence until he meets another Christian who leads him to convert. The movie ends on an ironic note: Barabbas, freed by Nero after his successes as a gladiator, is one of the Christians later crucified under Nero in ostensible punishment for the Great Fire of 64 C.E.

Barabbas yields a 1960s-style collection of moral tales of human ignorance and error, not likely to be appreciated by contemporary students. In terms of utility for the classroom, the gladiatorial scenes can nonetheless supplement a lecture on martyrdom and the social context of early Christian Rome. More remarkable is the adaptation of the passion narratives. Cinematographer Dino Di Laurentiis filmed the crucifixion scenes during a solar eclipse, yielding a remarkable film sequence that captures an unparalleled sense of eerie foreboding. This is mandatory viewing for a "Celluloid Jesus" course or for anyone who might ask New Testament students to exegete a filmic crucifixion.

Nonbiblical Narrative in Film

Nicola Denzey and Patrick Gray

The films discussed in this chapter, most of which deal with multiple texts and topics, are organized alphabetically rather than canonically. The indices may be consulted to find film entries with classroom strategies related to particular texts. All secondary literature cited here is included in the preceding bibliography (pp. 92–96).

Alexander (2004)

Proving that even bad art can have pedagogical value, a scene from this Oliver Stone film about Alexander the Great facilitates discussion of critical sociocultural developments that profoundly affected Judaism and Christianity in antiquity. The two-minute scene (DVD ch. 19) depicts the party after Alexander's wedding to the Bactrian princess Roxanne. Alexander (Colin Farrell) delivers a speech in which he mentions the main elements of the Hellenistic ideal whereby all in his empire would be "citizens of the world." Among these are (1) his promotion of intermarriage between his Macedonian soldiers and the women of the local peoples they have met along the way, and (2) the propagation of Greek education (*paideia*) for the offspring of such unions. Why would these practices prove to be significant? Who will they benefit? What will be some of the tangible results? Whether or not the details of the costuming are accurate, the scene visually displays the cultural mixing that is a hallmark of the age. Alexander's distinctive appearance, moreover, is a reminder that the process of Hellenization was not simply a matter of a Greco-Macedonian steamroller imposing its will on every culture it encountered between the Mediterranean and the Indian subcontinent. Greece, too, was influenced by these sustained encounters.

Discussion or in-class writing may focus on the various responses to Hellenization. How might the Greeks and Macedonians view this rapprochement with the "barbarians"? (The scene shows palpable resentment among the Macedonians.) How might the Persians see matters? In conjunction with a general survey of Second Temple Judaism or 1 Maccabees in particular, the question may be posed in this way: Imagine that you are a Jew present for Alexander's speech. Describe your reaction. Would it resemble that of the jubilant Persians in the movie? Why or why not? How would Ezra, the Deuteronomistic Historian, or the author of Ruth respond? Student responses will likely include the range of options seen in 1 Macc 1–4—enthusiastic embrace, staunch resistance, refusal to engage—thus the exercise helps students to appreciate the fact of Jewish ideological diversity in this formative period.

Apocalypse Now (1979)

Hollywood at the end of the twentieth century produced a spate of cinematic variations on apocalyptic themes, but only this film actually shares part of its title with the book of Revelation. Francis Ford Coppola's critically acclaimed film, based on Joseph Conrad's *Heart of Darkness*, follows Army Intelligence agent Benjamin Willard (Martin Sheen) upriver through Vietnam to the jungles of Cambodia, where he is to "terminate" Walter Kurtz (Marlin Brando), a renegade officer with a private army who worship him as a god. Because the film is still familiar to students, it can be used to generate discussion of apocalyptic literature as well as manifestations of apocalyptic sensibilities in contemporary culture.

Why was this title chosen for the film? While some have suggested that it is a turn on the Vietnam-era slogan "Peace Now," explanations from the film's producers are hard to find. Did Coppola expect his audience to connect the events of the film to its biblical namesake? Here it may be helpful to provide students with the well-known "*Semeia* 14" definition of apocalypse as "a genre of revelatory literature with a narrative framework, in which a revelation is mediated by an otherworldly being to a human recipient, disclosing a transcendent reality which is both temporal, insofar as it envisages eschatological salvation, and spatial, insofar as it involves another, supernatural world" (Collins, *Apocalypse: The Morphology of a Genre*, 9). Is anything particularly "apocalyptic" about the story or its screen presentation? Did the Vietnam War witness a cosmic conflict between good and evil? Is the bombing of Kurtz's camp at the end of the film (DVD ch. 19) analogous to the final battle in Rev 16? Is there a sense of violent judgment such as one finds in Rev 14, where the avenging Christ is seen "trampling out the vintage where the grapes of wrath are stored"? Does the film reveal anything to the viewer about the past (i.e., the period during the war, prior to the film's release)? about the "present" (i.e., the period just after the war's end in which the film was produced)? about the "future"? (Note how these three periods are easy to confuse.) Does the film equate apocalyptic with eschatology (cf. the Jim Morrison lyric, "This is the end," on the soundtrack as Willard kills Kurtz)? What is the apparent purpose of the film?

On the prevalence of apocalypticism in recent cinema, see the April 2000 edition of the *Journal of Religion and Film* (Online: www.unomaha.edu/jrf/vol4n1.htm).

The Apostle (1997)

Robert Duvall wrote and stars in this film that follows Sonny Dewey, a Pentecostal preacher with a magnetic, if flawed, personality. After he loses his Texas church, in a fit of rage he assaults the youth minister with whom his wife is having an affair and then leaves town to avoid arrest. He arrives in a small Louisiana town, rapidly revives an old church, and enjoys a devoted following as "the Apostle E. F." before the police catch up with him. In addition to providing an authentic sense of the atmosphere in which millions of believers encounter the biblical text, this film affords a number of points on which to engage students:

(1) The Apostle E. F.'s zeal, volatility, and indefatigable sense of mission have drawn comparisons to the Apostle Paul. What qualities and experiences do these two figures share? (Both have sometimes rocky relationships with their followers and colleagues; both have had trouble with the law; both identify themselves as apostles; et al.) This task facilitates a close reading of the letters and Acts, a text with clear sympathies for the protagonist that, like the movie, nonetheless displays some of his less-than-admirable traits.

(2) What is an apostle? On the basis of lexical and textual evidence, is it possible to construct a basic job description? Does the Apostle E. F. qualify? This can function as an exercise in using a concordance and other reference tools.

(3) What is baptism? How was it practiced in the first century and what was its purpose? Again, this can function as an exercise in using reference tools. The memorable scene in which Sonny baptizes himself in the river after faking his death (DVD ch. 14) serves as a compelling introduction to the question.

(4) Why does Sonny change his name? Is his name change similar to or different from other name changes in the Bible or in more recent times? Frequently (e.g., Abraham, Israel, Muhammed Ali) the new name is fraught with religious significance. In some cases (e.g., Paul) the reasons are obscure.

(5) As his world begins to fall apart, Sonny "yells at the Lord" in an all-night prayer session (DVD ch. 8). Why is this happening, he asks. In tone or substance, is this conversation similar to Job's debates with his friends or with God? Is it similar to Jesus' prayer in Gethsemane?

(6) Have students view the film in conjunction with a study of 2 Sam 11–12, the story of David and Bathsheba. According to tradition, Ps 51 was composed by David after Nathan confronts him with his guilt in the affair.

F
I
L
M

Like Sonny, David is a fornicator and murderer. What psycho-spiritual qualities do Sonny and David share? Would the penitential psalm seem out of place on Sonny's lips?

As Good as It Gets (1997)

What is a parable? All-encompassing definitions that capture all of the characteristics of parabolic discourse are hard to formulate. Insofar as parables represent Jesus' preferred mode of teaching, it is important to understand how the genre functions. An analytic paper treating a well-known parable alongside a kind of cinematic retelling of that parable serves as a helpful heuristic device for addressing the hermeneutical questions pertaining to genre, purpose, and meaning.

This film translates the Parable of the Good Samaritan (Luke 10:25–37) into a different idiom. Melvin (Jack Nicholson) is, as one character puts it, "an absolute horror of a human being"—a misanthropic, bigoted, obsessive-compulsive writer who despises his gay neighbor Simon (Greg Kinnear) and is cruel to animals. When Simon is hospitalized after being brutally beaten (DVD ch. 4), Melvin reluctantly agrees to take care of his dog. Later, he also helps the destitute Simon by letting him move into his apartment (DVD ch. 11). Simon in turn helps Melvin in his romantic pursuit of Carol (Helen Hunt), the only waitress at Melvin's favorite restaurant who will put up with him. Carol has to leave her job to care for her chronically sick son and eventually accepts Melvin's offer to pay for the mounting medical bills. As the movie ends, Melvin, through the influence of Carol, is making great progress in conquering the various neuroses that make him such a difficult person to be around (DVD chs. 27–28).

Students should view the film outside of class and then write an essay in which they argue that the film should, or should not, be regarded as the cinematic equivalent of the parable. Each character gives as well as receives help from a person with whom he or she is loath to have any dealings. Is this the point of the film? Is it the point of the parable? Does such a summary leave out anything essential? Do particular characters in the film stand for characters in Luke 10? Is the traditional title of the parable an apt one, that is, should the Samaritan be seen as the main character? Does the hearer have to agree with certain religious tenets—not at all present in the film—to appreciate its message? Is the point, rather, to highlight the absurdity of certain prejudices? To urge universal, unconditional compassion? To make the point that our "neighbors" are not of our own choosing? The exercise forces students to articulate their assumptions about the formal characteristics of the genre (narrative in form? univocal or multivalent? allegorical? any superfluous details permitted?), the intended purpose or effect (to clarify or to confound?), the audience (insiders or outsiders?), and so forth—that is, assumptions regarding what a parable is and is not.

According to available time and instructor inclination, the ensuing discussion may be integrated with a broader study of the history of the interpretation of parables, touching on the different approaches of, for example, Jülicher, Jeremias, Dodd, and Crossan. For other exercises on the parables, see Roncace and Gray, *Teaching the Bible*, 297–304, 326–28.

Blade Runner (1982)

Ridley Scott's masterpiece, *Blade Runner*, delves into the relationship between memory and the self. A "blade runner," or assassin, trained to track down bioengineered beings called replicants, Rick Deckard (Harrison Ford) pursues, and comes to know, his enemy—to the extent that he begins to question what it means to be human (and to be humane). The film's original release has been largely replaced by a later Director's Cut (1994) that removes Deckard's voiceover narration and the "happy ending" demanded by the studio in its first release.

Blade Runner would work well in courses that examine Genesis in depth. Direct allusions to the Bible are brief and relatively straightforward; for instance, the dancer and sex-worker replicant Zhora works with a serpent in her burlesque show, announced by an off-stage voice as the same serpent "who had once corrupted man." Some more penetrative themes germane to Genesis include a creator's responsibility to his creations, the relationship between creator and created, and the nature of good and evil.

As in Genesis, the film's protagonists contend with the limits of mortality. The replicants, dangerous because of their superior knowledge and power, are hobbled by an abbreviated lifespan. What they want, as the chief replicant Roy Batty (Rutger Hauer) makes clear, is a longer life. Here, there are perhaps echoes of God's promise to Adam and Eve in Gen 2:17. Mortality, therefore, is a consequence of the "fallen" state of the replicants—proud, intellectually superior beings who have rebelled against their own creator. Yet Batty's struggle against mortality ends with his acceptance of his own humanity, reflected in his last words: "Time to die."

Several of *Blade Runner*'s characters bear similarities with Genesis's characters. Rachel (Sean Young), like Eve, is in fact a new creation, the first of her kind; the end of the film hints that she and Deckard (as Adam) will continue together as a new "race" who possess self-knowledge, free will, and self-awareness. Tyrell is a sort of Yahweh, although in a way more reminiscent of "gnostic" interpretations of Genesis than Genesis itself. Some of the characters are polyvalent and polysemic. Batty is at once Tyrell's "prodigal son" (cf. DVD ch. 26), Lucifer, and the Christ-figure who drives a nail into his hand, saves Deckard's life, and whose soul, at death, ascends to heaven in the form of a dove.

Blade Runner also evinces a series of themes that recall the story of the fall of the angels—a well-known motif never clearly articulated in the Bible (see Jude 6 and Gen 6:1 on the Nephilim; Rev 12 on "Lucifer"; and Ezek 28). The replicants that are created "off-world" (i.e., in the "heavens") are, themselves, fallen angels; since they are neither fully human nor fully gods, humans interpret the replicants' superior knowledge and strength as malevolent. Batty even intentionally misquotes William Blake ("fiery the angels fell" rather than "fiery the angels rose," from Blake's *America, A Prophecy*). His dying speech mirrors that of a defiant yet wistful angel describing the mysteries of the cosmos: "I've seen things you people wouldn't believe. Attack ships on fire off the shoulder of Orion. I watched C-beams glitter in the dark near the Tannhauser gate. All those moments will be lost in time, like tears in rain" (DVD ch. 34). The speech underscores what Batty has seen as a sort of timeless, cosmic being, to the point that we forget he is merely four years old.

Blade Runner is now much older than most university students, and many will never have seen it. For it to "work" in the classroom, therefore, students may need more guidance and background, and perhaps a bit of prompting as to how to draw biblical themes from the movie once they have viewed it in its entirety. For further analysis, see Gravett, "The Sacred and the Profane: Examining the Religious Subtext of Ridley Scott's *Blade Runner*," 38–43; Desser, "The New Eve: The Influence of *Paradise Lost* and *Frankenstein* on *Blade Runner*," 53–65; and Keefer, "Knowledge and Mortality in *Blade Runner* and Genesis 2–3."

Bless the Child (2000)

Just after Christmas, with a portentous star shining above New York City, a young nurse named Maggie (Kim Basinger) gets a visit from her younger sister Jenna, a drug addict and new mother. Jenna runs out, abandoning her infant—a baby girl named Cody—to be raised by Maggie. Cut to a few years later. Cody exhibits symptoms of autism, and is referred to a Catholic school for special needs students. There, she begins exhibiting other remarkable talents, starting with bringing a dead dove back to life (DVD ch. 3).

The trope of the miracle-working divine child is not often expressed in secular film, particularly when it is done as positively as here—that is, very differently from *The Omen* series of the satanic child. Since Cody is so clearly a Christ-figure, it might be interesting to have students read, along with viewing this scene, selections from the noncanonical infancy Gospels (e.g., *Infancy Gospel of Thomas*) or even passages about Jesus as a child from the Qur'an (in Sura Âl 'Imran 3:46–49, Isa [Jesus] models a dove out of clay and animates it; see also Sura Al-Ma'idah 5:110; Sura Maryam 19:30; and Sura Al-Ma'idah 5:111 for other accounts of Isa's childhood).

Viewed alongside the canonical infancy narratives in Matthew and Luke, students should have fun catching and listing all the biblical parallels: the star, the "virgin birth," the slaughter of the innocents, and so on. They also might list the nonbiblical elements (for instance, the tattoos that all the antichrist's followers wear, the swarm of rats that besiege Cody's room) and discuss in class why these might have been added. This is perhaps the only movie that blends themes from the infancy narratives with popular biblical apocalyptic drawn ever so loosely from the Revelation, although the apocalyptic contribution appears to be confined to the notion of the antichrist.

Maggie's dormant but amiable Catholicism allows for much explanatory dialogue. When she asks at one point what the "slaughter of the innocents" is all about (DVD ch. 6), the detective John Travis (Jimmy Smits) responds by loosely paraphrasing Luke 2:16 (students may liken Travis to Michael the Archangel or the warrior angel of Rev 12). Maggie is the perfect foil to the evil Eric, who calmly plays Satan to Cody's Christ, including a variation on the synoptic passages (Matt 4; Luke 4) where Satan tempts Jesus from the top of the temple (actually, Cody's retort is more clever). All in all, this film makes a nice addition to any instructor's repertory of movies based directly on contemporary Christ-figures or the struggle between good and evil.

The Blues Brothers (1980)

"We're on a mission from God," the protagonists declare as they evade the police, their creditors, and sundry other characters on their way to save a Chicago orphanage. This musical comedy is not a religious movie in any conventional sense. The five-minute scene (DVD chs. 3–4) in which Jake and Elwood "see the light" during a charismatic church service (presided over by James Brown) nevertheless supplies a point of entry for considering various call narratives in the Hebrew Bible and the New Testament as well as the phenomenology of religious experience. Although the brothers are skeptical when they have been advised to "get wise" by going to the church, a bright light appears as the choir sings and Jake (John Belushi) begins to tremble involuntarily. Elwood (Dan Ackroyd) is at first oblivious; he replies, "What light?" when the preacher calls out, "Have you seen the light?" Soon, however, the spirit fills him and he is dancing in the aisles alongside his brother. The audience is not privy to any message communicated in the experience, but the significance for Jake and Elwood is clear: They can save the orphanage by reuniting their old band for a charity concert.

The scene may be used to introduce the concept of theophany when studying Exodus, for example, by suggesting ways in which to construe the descriptions of the divine presence at Horeb in the burning bush (Exod 3–4) and at Sinai (Exod 19). Is the articulation of the divine will in Exodus similar to that seen in the movie? Or does it more closely resemble the "still, small voice" heard by Elijah after the wind, earthquake, and fire (1 Kgs 19:11–18)? If a camera had recorded their encounters, what could it have captured? Would it detract from the truth of the narrative if, say, a tape recorder had not registered any audible message? Do the biblical writers present these experiences, or that of Isaiah in the temple (Isa 6), as ones which could be shared by others? And to what degree does the recipient of revelation acquiesce to or cooperate in mediating the experience? Jeremiah (20:7–9) reports that he has tried to resist the call to prophesy but is struck with burning pain when he does so.

Luke's reports of Paul's experience on the road to Damascus exhibit some of the same qualities as that of Jake and Elwood. In Acts 9, the men with Paul hear the voice but do not see anyone. When Paul retells the story in Acts 22:9, however, they see the light but hear no voice. Is this a slip on the part of the narrator, or a reflection of the fugitive character of such numinous encounters? What is the reader to make of Paul's expansion of the content of the message he received from Christ in his vision? Does Luke mean to suggest that the processing of divine revelation is something that necessarily takes time and reflection? Finally, fruitful discussion may emerge from consideration of the proper term to apply to these scenes. Is it accurate to think of Moses, Isaiah, Paul, and the Blues Brothers as having undergone conversion experiences? Or are these, rather, instances where an individual has received a specific task to fulfill within a preexisting religious framework that has not changed appreciably as a result of the encounter? Is the distinction an important one to make when reading these texts?

The Body (2001)

The Vatican dispatches a Jesuit from El Salvador named Guttierez (Antonio Banderas) to investigate (read: disprove) the claim that a recently discovered body of a first-century crucified man in Jerusalem is that of Jesus of Nazareth. The grave (and body) was discovered by an Israeli archaeologist who plans to make a career out of her remarkable find. The Vatican has other plans, as do the Israeli government and the Palestinian Liberation Organization. Everyone, it seems, wants a piece of the action—or, conversely, to silence the story.

The movie is concerned with the central question: What might the discovery of Jesus' body do to Christian faith (here, specifically the Vatican—once again presented as an outdated body of hypocritical and power-hungry evil men)? The recent "discovery" of the Talpiot tomb and the ossuaries purported to be those of Jesus and his immediate family members offers a very nice counterpoint to *The Body*. Students have been very curious about whether or not the ossuary might have belonged to Jesus, or whether the tomb held his body. A discussion of the find and how it was marketed to the public—contrasted with how professional biblical archaeologists responded to it—would make for a fun biblical archaeology "case study" in class. What is really amazing is, in fact, with a real-life scenario unfolding in 2007 that was quite like the discovery of Jesus' body in this movie, how *little* of an impact it made on the broader political and religious issues in Israel or in the world. But that was already recognized in the movie itself. As one character, the Israeli attaché Moshe Cohen wearily notes (in a scene just after the middle of the movie), Christianity will survive just fine in the event that Jesus' body is discovered. Those with faith will not believe that it is really Jesus' body despite whatever "proof" is offered; those who don't believe won't care, and in the end, perhaps nothing will change. (On the related theological issues raised by Bultmann, see the discussion of *Schindler's List*, pp. 161–63.)

Braveheart (1995)

Loosely based on historical events involving Scottish national hero William Wallace, this film contains one of the most memorable and most quoted speeches in recent cinema. Just before a pivotal battle against the English, Wallace (Mel Gibson) concludes the speech with a rousing call to arms (DVD ch. 10): "Fight and you may die. Run and you'll live. At least awhile. And dying in your beds, many years from now, would you be willing to trade all of the days from this day to that, for … just one chance to come back here and tell our enemies that they may take our lives, but they'll never take our freedom!" The speech lends itself to two exercises:

(1) To introduce students to textual criticism and the peculiar problems its practitioners have to solve, the speech may be used to "dramatize" the process of transmission, in combination with the child's game of "telephone" in which one person whispers a message to the person in the next seat, who whispers it to the next person, and so on until the message has been whispered to the last person in the queue. The original message changes, sometimes significantly, by the time it reaches the end of the line. When it reaches the end, each student writes down what they think was the original message. Discussion may then draw comparisons between "telephone" and the scribal process of copying manuscripts. What are the reasons for any distortions of the message or, depending on how much it has been altered, the reasons it did not change more than it did? (For a fuller description of a similar exercise, see Patrick Gray, "Introducing Textual Criticism," in Roncace and Gray, *Teaching the Bible*, 31–33.) The last line of the speech works well as the

"message" in this illustration. It is long, but not unreasonably so. It is also familiar, but not so familiar that every link in the human chain will be able to reproduce it verbatim whether or not they hear it clearly. Its familiarity moreover helps to simulate the influence of oral tradition on the process of textual transmission.

For use in this exercise, there is no shortage of famous movie lines that are frequently quoted or—perhaps even more pertinent—misquoted. Examples include: Marlin Brando in *On the Waterfront* ("I coulda been a contender"); Butterfly McQueen in *Gone With the Wind* ("I don't know nothin' 'bout birthin' babies"); Dustin Hoffman's neighbor in *The Graduate* ("I just want to say one word to you, just one word—'plastics' "); Humphrey Bogart in *Casablanca* ("Of all the gin joints in all the towns in all the world, she walks into mine"); Jimmy Stewart in *It's a Wonderful Life* ("I suppose it'd been better if I'd never been born at all"); Gary Cooper in *The Pride of the Yankees* ("Today I consider myself the luckiest man on the face of the Earth"). For discussion of common misquotations, see Tim Dirks, "Greatest Film Misquotes."

(2) The scene also provides an analogy of sorts to the scenario encountered in 1 Maccabees. Discussion after viewing the clip can bring out the similarities and differences between the two contexts. Wallace's speech is usually remembered as a *tour de force*, but the editing reminds the viewer that not all Scots shared the same nationalist vision. One character interrupts to endorse the "run and live" option, and the nobles, whose interests were likely to be adversely affected by any upheaval, are noticeably unenthused as Wallace whips the makeshift army into a frenzy. Jewish tradition likewise celebrates the Maccabean revolt as a nationalist triumph, notwithstanding the marked lack of solidarity among Jews in 1 Macc 1–3. Many Jews, who stand to gain by their relationship with members of the ruling class, want to join with the Hellenists and abandon the distinctive signs of Jewish identity. Many Hasideans oppose the hellenizers out of religious scruples rather than for political reasons and are massacred when they refuse to fight on the Sabbath. Mattathias and his sons also oppose these "lawless men" but are willing to do so by taking up arms against Antiochus. In each case, one sees competing notions of freedom and the good life at play among the various parties on the same side of the battle. Finally, one also sees a similar use of set speeches in both works (cf. 1 Macc 2:27–28; 3:16–22). The speeches, while inspirational and dramatic, are perhaps best seen as epitomes or idealized recitations rather than transcripts of speeches as actually delivered. (It seems unlikely that a thirty-second address would have won over all the doubters so decisively in either scenario.) What rhetorical resemblances does one see in the speeches in the two works?

A Clockwork Orange (1971)

Anthony Burgess, whose dystopian novel provides the basis for Stanley Kubrick's screen adaptation, has said that humans have the gift of free will and that it is within their power to choose evil rather than to choose good. In an interview, he has stated that one message of the novel is that "it is better for a man to do evil of his own free will than for the state to turn him into a machine which can only do good" (bu.univ-angers.fr/EXTRANET/Anthony-BURGESS/liana/ABClockwork.html). Selected scenes from the film prompt reflection on moral responsibility, freedom, and the nature of good and evil as they appear in the Bible.

Alex (Malcolm McDowell) is a vicious gang leader who lands in prison after he is arrested for murder. To shorten his sentence, he volunteers to undergo an experimental treatment. This treatment is a form of aversion therapy in which the patient is conditioned to experience extreme nausea at the thought of committing violent deeds. As part of the treatment, the patient is forced to view footage of horrible acts of the type he once committed with impunity (DVD chs. 20–22; warning: this clip contains quite graphic images). The treatment is successful in Alex's case, as is demonstrated by his inability to respond when provoked (DVD ch. 23). When an official presents the experiment as a success—Alex is now a "true Christian" who is able to "turn the other cheek"—the prison chaplain objects that the treatment is a travesty because "he ceases to be a creature capable of moral choice" (DVD chs. 24–25).

Is Alex now a good person? He wants to perform evil deeds but is physically unable to do so. This scenario relates to the theological issues at stake in four biblical texts:

(1) Were Adam and Eve truly free before they ate of the Tree in Gen 3:1–7? Were they truly free after eating of the Tree? Does the author of Genesis regard their sin as a "fortunate fall" (felix culpa) whereby the way is opened for God's plans for history to be realized? Is it necessary to be able to "sin" by making choices not in harmony with the divine will? Were they "good" before the fall if they were not capable of making free moral choices? Does the text provide any help with the difficult task of imagining the nature of prelapsarian human life? Is Alex better off when his rehabilitation is complete?

(2) Is it fair for God to punish Pharaoh for his behavior in Exodus if God has constricted his freedom to choose to act differently? What, exactly, does it mean for one's heart to be "hardened"? (The text does not spell this out, but one's evaluation would surely depend on the details.) In Exod 7–11, sometimes God hardens Pharaoh's heart, sometimes Pharaoh hardens his own heart, and sometimes the passive verb is used (7:13–14, 22; 8:15, 19, 32; 9:7, 12, 34–35; 10:1, 20, 27; 11:10; 14:8). The same issue arises in connection with

the reference to Pharaoh in Rom 9:16–18, though Paul's larger argument has less to do with moral culpability.

(3) After Job's wife urges him to "curse God and die," the narrator states that Job "did not sin with his lips" (Job 2:10). It has been suggested that the wording of this verse, after the simpler "Job did not sin" in 1:22, implies that Job did in fact sin in his thoughts, if not in his words. Does the text support this view? Would it qualify as a sin if Job were to resent God's dealings inwardly but refrain from voicing these thoughts? Alex still desires to respond to violence with violence but is physically unable to do so. Is he "cured" or is he still evil at heart?

(4) Paul's argument in Rom 7:7–26 has bedeviled scholars for centuries. What does Paul mean when he says, "I do not understand my own actions, for I do not do the deeds I want to do, but I do the very thing I hate" (v. 15)? After describing the "war" that is going on within himself, he ends the chapter by saying that he is a "slave to the law of God" with his mind but "a slave to the law of sin" in his flesh. In what sense is Alex a slave? Is it accurate to describe him as not being able to do the evil he desires but, rather, the good that he does not desire? Does his experience suggest any possibilities for understanding Paul?

Close Encounters of the Third Kind (1977)

Because they are enshrined in the canon, it may be difficult for students to appreciate the impression made by many of the prophets on their original audiences. Few prophets were as bizarre as Ezekiel. The main character of this Steven Spielberg classic manifests in a contemporary context many of the same qualities and evokes similar reactions from his friends and family. Roy Neary (Richard Dreyfuss) develops an obsession with UFOs after a "close encounter" one night in rural Indiana. His obsession takes the form of building models—out of clay, garbage, shaving cream, even mashed potatoes—of a particular mountain. (The image is that of Devil's Tower, Wyoming, but Roy only discovers this later in the story.)

A ten-minute clip at the halfway point of the film contains several elements seen also in the case of Ezekiel (DVD chs. 12–13; the clip has much the same impact if shortened to five minutes). Roy cannot understand the forces compelling him to engage in the odd behavior that causes his family to abandon him, and he finally cries out at the night sky, "I don't know what's happening to me!" Ezekiel, too, encounters skeptics and undergoes great distress (3:8–9, 12–15) when he shares his message about a great light he has seen (1:1–28). He speaks of family problems related to the strange events (16:15–34; 24:15–18). He has trouble making himself understood (3:22–27). And he shuts himself in a house and builds a model of a structure he has not actually witnessed

(3:24–4:3). (For a related approach to Ezekiel's behavior, see Johanna Stiebert, "Diagnosing Ezekiel," in Roncace and Gray, *Teaching the Bible*, 178–79).

It may surprise students that there are hundreds of books and Internet websites propounding the theory that the "vision" of Ezek 1 is in fact the record of an encounter with an alien spaceship. This bizarre subculture constitutes a ready-made body of material for a study of apocalypticism and its contemporary expressions.

Crimes and Misdemeanors (1989)

This film contains a three-minute scene that illustrates the differences between the perspectives of Proverbs and the Teacher in Ecclesiastes (DVD ch. 11). In the scene, Judah (Martin Landau) visits his childhood house, stirring memories of a family discussion that takes place at a Passover meal. (The scene is a flashback.) In the conversation, Sol, Judah's father, articulates the perspective of Proverbs: The world is orderly, meaningful, and fair; good deeds will be rewarded and bad deeds punished. His sister, May, represents the views of the Teacher in Ecclesiastes: the world is chaotic, lacks a "moral structure" (or at least one discernible by humans), and is unjust; righteous people suffer and wicked prosper (cf. Eccl 7:15). Other characters chime in, agreeing with one view or the other. Both May and the Teacher refuse to close their eyes to "reality." Sol, by contrast, claims that he will "always prefer God over the truth" (i.e., "reality").

The clip works effectively after a study of Proverbs as a means to introduce the contrasting perspectives found in Ecclesiastes. Students are asked to add their own voices to the conversation, as if they were at the dinner table. What would they say to each of the characters? With whom would they agree? Is the book of Proverbs naïve and unsophisticated (as May suggests about Sol's ideas)? Or is the Teacher cynical and nihilistic? Who would be a better parent—Sol or May? Can both be correct? Here one can point to the "traditional" wisdom that is scattered throughout the words of the Teacher (cf. Eccl 7:1–14; 10:1–11:6). One might also ask how Job, Job's friends, and the God of the whirlwind speeches would contribute to this dinner-table debate.

Finally, it may be helpful to close the conversation by noting that one of the characters argues that Sol is "relying too heavily on the Bible." This provides an opportunity to underscore the diversity within the canon: Ecclesiastes, too, is a part of Scripture. For further analysis, see Roche, "Justice and the Withdrawal of God in Woody Allen's *Crimes and Misdemeanors*," 547–63.

Dark City (1998)

John Murdoch (Rufus Sewell) awakens in a panic to find himself naked in a bathtub, unable to remember who he is or what chain of events led him there. Horrified to find a dead, mutilated prostitute in his apartment, the phone rings. A voice warns him that he is in great danger and must immediately leave. Murdoch rushes out, just before the evil "Strangers" arrive. Murdoch soon finds himself the chief subject of a serial murder investigation led by the ineffectual but generally sympathetic Inspector Bumstead (William Hurt). But he retains little memory of who he is. Murdoch soon encounters Dr. Daniel Schreber (Kiefer Sutherland), who proves to be a key to understanding Murdoch's true identity.

That the character John Murdoch presents many christological motifs and resonances has been well documented. Apart from these parallels, a few items are worthy of note:

(1) Watch for the fish symbolism. In the opening scene Murdoch stops to rescue a goldfish before fleeing from the police and the Strangers. Fish are prominent on postcards from Murdoch's childhood. To gain clues about his identity, he visits his uncle who was a champion sport fisherman. His apartment is decorated with fish fossils. Is there a connection between Murdoch and the Christ symbol of the *ichthys*? Perhaps it is also significant that the Strangers have an aversion to water. Murdoch is obsessed with the ocean and Shell Beach; his first act of creation after his awakening at the end of the film parallels God's in Genesis (he "separates the firmament" and creates an ocean apart from the land, creates the first day, and causes the sun to shine over the waters for the first time).

(2) Like Morpheus in *The Matrix*, Daniel Schreber is a John the Baptist figure. He calls the hero to awaken. He moves easily between the constructed world of illusion and the real world He is convinced that he has found "the One" to save the world. And Schreber, like John the Baptist, is not destined to awaken humankind to its enslavement, although they alone initially recognize that enslavement. They themselves need to be rescued, just as they recognize a coming Armageddon or showdown between the forces of Good and Evil.

(3) *Dark City* shares a dystopian vision of the world with films such as *Blade Runner, Metropolis,* and the *Matrix*. In a rowboat on Dark City's muddy canals, Schreber reveals the truth: that they are all trapped in that place by the Strangers, an alien race that uses human dead as their vessels. Humans are caught in their hapless enslavement, convinced that the lives they live and relive in different combinations are realities, never awakening to the horror of their condition. Schreber, terrified that the Strangers will kill them, shrieks helplessly as Murdoch and Bumstead break through the walls of the city, only to discover that nothing lies behind the walls but an open, swirling cosmos. As in the Gospel of Mark, only those specially possessed or specially gifted recognize the true situation of the world and of Murdoch's status as savior. But the cosmic dimensions of the human story of salvation are noteworthy

and might be compared to New Testament texts such as the Johannine Prologue and Eph 6:12: "We do not wrestle against flesh and blood, but against … spiritual forces of wickedness in heavenly places."

(4) The film's "demonology" is quite interesting because the Strangers resemble the fallen Watcher angels of apocryphal texts such as *1 Enoch* and the archons from Nag Hammadi documents such as the *Hypostasis of the Archons*. The Strangers, like the archons, desire to be human, and they fear Murdoch's divinity: "This man Murdoch is much more powerful than we can imagine.… he is becoming like us … so we must become like him." In this way, Murdoch is not only a Christ-figure, he is also like Adam in the classic "gnostic" myth. In the second-century *Apocryphon of John*, the evil Archons are celestial beings who possess malformed, demonic bodies but no souls. In *Dark City*, too, the Strangers are obsessed with acquiring human souls. They become jealous of humans, recognizing in them the spiritual possibilities for wholeness that they themselves lack. Yet the Strangers can only seek that salvation through manipulation and experimentation, not through their own paths to knowledge.

At the end of the encounter, Murdoch, affixed crucifix-like to the time clock, steps away from his bonds newly empowered and engages in a final, apocalyptic, telekinetic showdown with the chief Stranger. Their kingdom shattered, Murdoch works to create a new reality for the remaining humans, one filled with oceans and light and "true" new memories. Comparison with the scenarios described in Revelation would make for a nice end-of-term project in a New Testament course.

The Da Vinci Code (2006)

In Paris to give a lecture, Harvard professor Robert Langdon (Tom Hanks) is called to an unusual crime scene: a prominent curator at the Louvre has been murdered. As he lay dying, he left a secret message for his adoptive daughter, cryptologist Sophie Neveu (Audrey Tatou), to seek out Langdon. The two begin a modern-day quest for the Holy Grail, which here turns out to be not a chalice but a woman: Jesus' last living descendant.

As a novel, Dan Brown's bestseller raised eyebrows for its alternative version of Christian history. That Jesus is presented here as having married Mary Magdalene angered those who maintained that Jesus was celibate. That he might have survived the crucifixion obliterates the theology of the cross and the significance of the resurrection. Finally vexing is the movie's depiction of Constantine and the Council of Nicaea as the turning point in which the human Jesus came to be considered, overnight, the divine Christ—depicted as a self-serving and deceitful position that served the nefarious aims of the first Christian emperor.

The Da Vinci Code's producers hired academic advisors, with the result that in the film's most explicitly theological scene (in which Nicaea's Christology is "explained"), the dialogue is recast differently from the novel. By providing students with the text of the novel (for this scene, pp. 230–36) and then discussing its differences from the movie (DVD chs. 11–12), one may prepare for a discussion of the precise claims that are made and the evidence on which they are based. In the movie, Langdon plays the academic skeptic against Teabing's conspiracy theories. Teabing quotes no canonical writings but, rather, two second-century texts, the *Gospel of Philip* and the *Gospel of Mary*. Thanks to the film's advisors, he cites both accurately. Students might be asked to consider which biblical texts these second-century authors may have amplified to arrive at the portrait of Jesus and of his followers they present.

Director Ron Howard confronts the theological controversy engendered by this film head on in the closing scenes, where Langdon muses in a voiceover such thoughts as "Why couldn't Jesus have been a father and still have been capable of all those miracles?" and "Why does it have to be human or divine? Maybe human is divine." The scene is a good a conversation starter or a good entry into discussions of high versus low Christology in the Gospels and in the Epistles (e.g., John 1:1–5; Phil 2:5–11; Col 1:15–20; Heb 1:1–14; 5:5–10).

For background, it may be helpful to consult one of the many books published in the wake of the novel's success (e.g., Ehrman, *Truth and Fiction in the Da Vinci Code*).

Dead Man Walking (1995)

This film contains a one-minute scene that helps students think about hermeneutical questions, specifically, the complexity of citing the Bible in contemporary debates on moral and ethical issues. The clip (DVD ch. 3) could be employed in discussions of Hebrew Bible laws, New Testament ethics, or more general discussions of hermeneutics and the relevance of the Bible for modern faith communities. The scene depicts a conversation between Sister Helen Prejean (Susan Sarandon) and one of the prison officials where convicted rapist and murderer Matthew Poncelet (Sean Penn) awaits execution. The official is in favor of the death penalty and points out that the Bible says "an eye for an eye," to which Sister Helen responds with a list of other offences for which the Hebrew Bible law calls for the death penalty, such as adultery, profaning the Sabbath, and dishonoring parents. The nun decisively makes her point: it is problematic to cite one biblical text and ignore many others. The same issue is applicable to the New Testament, which contains a variety of injunctions which many Christians make no attempt to follow today—such as Jesus' teachings on divorce and remarriage (Mark 10:11), the command for women to be silent in church (1 Cor 14:34), or the recommendation not to marry (1 Cor 7:25–27, 37–38).

Since the film clip deals specifically with Hebrew Bible law, one could extend the conversation regarding the tension between the Bible's utter foreignness and its potential relevance by distributing photocopies of Exod 21–23 to small groups and giving the following instructions:

> Imagine that your group has been called in as legal consultants for the Israelites. They ask you to review the law code found in Exod 21:1–23:9 and to suggest which laws should be eliminated, revised, or retained as they are currently written. You are asked to respect their cultural, religious, and social systems as much as possible, but do not set aside your modern sensibilities. Perhaps think of it this way: a small group of people in the jungles of South America today adheres to the law codes in Exod 21:1–23:9 and they ask you to say what you think about their laws. On the attached photocopy, put a line through the laws that the Israelites should completely eliminate; circle the laws that need some revision (you do not need to make the revision, but circle only the part of the law that needs to be revised); and leave unmarked the laws that you deem acceptable.

Alternatively, one could make a list of biblical injunctions and ask which ones are permanent (valid across all times and cultures) and which ones are cultural (applicable only in a certain time and place). For a list of New Testament texts for consideration, see Cukrowski, "What Does New Haven Have to Do with Lubbock? Texts, Techniques, and Sociology," 96–102.

Questions to pose concerning the film clip include: Is Sister Helen suggesting we ignore the Bible all together? Presumably not, since she belongs to the Catholic Church and talks about the love of Jesus in other parts of the film. What underlying assumptions appear to influence her way of reading and applying the Bible? How would she determine what to follow and what to reject as irrelevant? Is she essentially making the same hermeneutical move as the prison official? That is, she opposes the death penalty and so makes one point about the biblical text to bolster her view; he is for the death penalty and thus handles the Bible in a way that supports his position.

Dogma (1999)

From their place of exile in Wisconsin, two fallen angels (Matt Damon and Ben Affleck), discover a (fictive) loophole in Catholic dogma: if they cross the threshold of a church in New Jersey, all their sins will be forgiven and they will be able to return to heaven. The catch, however, is that this loophole also proves the fallibility of God, and so (according to *Dogma*) the world would come to an end.

Dogma sports a wide range of familiar and not-so-familiar characters. The casting is an exercise in postmodernist transgression: Linda Fiorentino as the messiah-figure, Alanis Morrisette as God, Chris Rock as the thirteenth apostle Rufus, and George Carlin as Cardinal Glick, who wants to replace Jesus with an upbeat "Buddy Christ" who flashes a thumbs-up sign instead hanging on a crucifix. (Carlin's character might be used to discuss the ways in which many people refashion Jesus in their own image or the different responses to Paul's characterization of the cross as foolish and weak in, e.g., 1 Cor 1:18–25.)

Part of *Dogma*'s "shock value" lies in director Kevin Smith's choice of the most hilariously inappropriate pop culture heroes to fill traditional biblical roles. But can Christianity be funny, without being made fun of? Smith insists it can. In answer to his critics, Smith insisted that he was, at the time of the film's release, a regular church-goer, "so pro-faith I feel like I'm doing the Catholic League's job." While Robert Horton describes it as "an unabashedly pro-God movie" ("Snoochie Boochies: The Gospel according to Kevin Smith," 60), others argue that the replacement dogma that the film suggests is fundamentally misleading. As Douglas Leblanc comments, "God does not shrug and settle for people believing whatever they like, so long as they are sincere about it" ("Dogmatically Anti-Dogma," 80). Many students will sympathize with one or the other of these views or will fall somewhere in between, and thus the film offers a chance to introduce reader-response theory and certain critiques of author-centered approaches. How can two viewers have such radically different reactions to the same movie (cf. the responses to *The Passion of the Christ*)? Is Smith's characterization of his intentions sincere? If so, is it possible for the author to fail in accomplishing his stated objectives? Perhaps by writing essays in which they try to articulate the reasons a viewer might or might not find the film offensive, students can come to appreciate the importance of "the world in front of the text" as well as its relationship to the worlds "behind" and "of" the text, to use Paul Ricoeur's terms.

Donnie Darko (2001)

Even though this film flopped commercially, probably because the movie's advertising campaign made this neat little film about time travel, a teenage hero, and the angst of growing up in the suburbs look like a strange slasher flick, *Donnie Darko* has achieved virtually cult status among American college-aged students. (References here are to the widely available Theatrical Cut.) The story begins with the eponymous protagonist (played by Jake Gyllenhaal) waking up early in the morning on an open stretch of road near his house. We learn that he has had a number of such blackouts that have led to his diagnosis (and medication) as schizophrenic. Not so much angry and psychotic as confused and sickened by the hypocrisy and mediocrity that he sees around him at his parochial school in an affluent Virginia suburb, Donnie suffers from terrifying visions in which a giant blue grotesque rabbit named Frank speaks to him and compels him, so it seems, to commit acts of vandalism. Frank also gives him a chillingly delivered countdown as to how many days are left until the end of the world (28 days, 6 hours, 42 minutes, and 12 seconds).

In keeping with the ambivalent status of any visionary within an ignorant and insensitive society, we do not know if Donnie is truly privy to secret knowledge or whether he is simply insane (the Director's Cut clarifies that Donnie has been prescribed placebos—thus suggesting that his visions were no mere hallucinations—but the Theatrical Cut lets the ambiguity remain). Donnie offers up ill-appreciated cultural jeremiads as any prophet of doom might do, and it might be an interesting exercise to show *Donnie Darko* for any component of a course that deals with the prophetic writings and social critique (e.g., Amos) or to show an excerpt simply to draw an analogy illustrating how strange most of the biblical prophets must have appeared to their contemporaries.

The jeremiads of *Donnie Darko* extend into full-blown apocalyptic, although the explicitly Christian elements of this apocalyptic are muted in the theatrical release and come out more clearly in the film's deleted scenes and additional features (included in the DVD). In the audio commentary, the director claims that Frank's warnings signal a divine intervention; Frank is the "messenger." In one deleted scene, Donnie reads from an apocalyptic poem he has written: "A storm is coming … and I'll deliver them from the Kingdom of Pain." In another, we witness a dialogue between Frank and Donnie in which Frank calls Donnie to follow him "because the world is coming to an end" very soon.

Donnie also comes to realize that he is a savior-figure whose sole purpose in the tangential universe that had erroneously formed is to set the world back on its intended course. (When, one might ask students, does Jesus become aware that he is also a savior or messiah? When do the Evangelists present this realization taking place? The question seems to underlie texts such as the *Infancy Gospel of Thomas* that feature Jesus' messianic self-consciousness as a subtext.) In a moving montage near the conclusion of the film, Donnie's inversion of the realized (or avoided) eschaton is displayed in terms of its human consequences: The persecuted are comforted, and the evil and mediocre are brought before their own frailties.

Christians are fascinated with *Donnie Darko* because it can be read as a triumphant discourse on the nature of God's omniscience and control over fate and the future. When, at the end, Donnie meets his end laughing, many

F
I
L
M

Christians interpret his laughter as a sort of vindication: he sees that God really does create and control all things. (How does this compare with the laughing savior in the gnostic *Apocalypse of Peter*?) Non-Christians, however, may see the film's ending—and Donnie's sacrificial role—in a rather different light.

The Exorcist (1973)

This film is an almanac of what frightens us—even what makes us feel guilty. Within days of the onset of her daughter Regan's (Linda Blair) strange behavior, Chris MacNeil (Ellen Burstyn) takes her to the hospital for a thorough battery of testing; the doctor prescribes Ritalin, but Regan's bizarre bouts of acting out only intensify. The new cinematic release ratchets up the tension as we see the slow onset of Regan's possession and wait for Satan's inevitable manifestation.

There is no question that *The Exorcist* is a creepy film and that its chief aim is to shock. Satan says some pretty rude things, especially through the mouth of an adolescent girl. The scenes of exorcism are clearly movie exorcisms; they teach us little about contemporary Roman Catholicism. The young priest even rejects the very notion of an exorcism as outdated. When Regan's mother asks when the Church ceased doing exorcisms, he replies, "Well, since we learned about paranoid schizophrenia … all that stuff I learned at Harvard" (cf. DVD ch. 14). The exorcisms themselves are also remarkably Bible-free; that is to say, the demonology or Satan's manifestations are never really articulated through the framing lens of the New Testament (as one sees in *The Omen*, where they clearly are).

Since this film may be too intense for many viewers, the best way to use it in a course may be to list it as one choice among many and then to have students write on one or more questions: (1) What does this film say or assume about Satan? How does it compare with what one finds in the Bible? This question provides an opportunity to teach about using a concordance or Bible dictionary. In this case, the result is to highlight the ultimate separation of some conceptions of Satan from anything one actually finds in the Bible. (2) What does this film say or assume about demonic possession and exorcism? How does it compare with what one finds in the Bible? (3) How might one of the authors of the Gospels respond if confronted with the medical "explanation" of demon possession?

Fallen (1998)

This curious thriller pits a detective, John Hobbes (Denzel Washington), against a demon, Azazel. Though its harsh language may make some students uncomfortable, it has utility in the classroom for its demonology and its relatively unusual theodicy in which people are evil because they are possessed, not because they are inherently sinful. We first meet Azazel as he possesses various lowlife criminals, including one on death row. At the moment of his execution, Azazel jumps bodies; the implication, of course, is that evil can never be extirpated and, by extension, the death penalty is misguided since it kills an effectively innocent man while evil merely transfers to another host. This concept neatly subverts the *lex talionis* of Exod 21:23–27. The idea that demons may jump from one body to the next is also reflected in the parables of the Gerasene demoniac of Mark 5:1–20 and parallels.

Students of the Hebrew Bible and the Jewish pseudepigrapha may recognize Azazel from Lev 16:8, where the high priest Aaron mentions two goats, one consecrated to the Lord and the other to Azazel. Azazel's goat, given the sins of humankind, is sent into the wilderness (cf. Talmud *Yoma* 67B, where Azazel is the name of the cliff from where the goat is cast in a Yom Kippur ritual). Azazel (possibly meaning "arrogant against God") also appears in *1 Enoch*'s "Book of the Watchers" where he is one of the chief Watchers, a class of fallen angels who take human women as their wives (cf. Gen 6:1). He teaches women to make cosmetics, and men how to make weapons and wage war (*1 Enoch* 2:8). Humankind is corrupted by such knowledge. Eventually, Azazel is punished for his iniquity by being cast down. An essay assignment might require students to argue for or against the thesis that the screenwriter is consciously working with these sources and themes in specific ways rather than simply borrowing a demon's name from an ancient text.

In *Fallen*, Azazel is a formless demon, able to hop from body to body. Hobbes, then, faces the impossible task of trying to defeat a supernatural enemy who takes manifold forms. Hobbes is aided by a seminary professor Gretta Milano (Embeth Davidtz), an expert in demonology and, as it turns out, a member of an ancient secret society formed to keep watch on Azazel's activity. Much of Milano's explanatory demonology bears little resemblance to academic views on such matters, and student might enjoy a discussion of what they ostensibly learn about Azazel from this film compared to the primary sources in which he is mentioned.

Fiddler on the Roof (1971)

The screen version of the musical depicts a "slice of life" among peasant Jews in prerevolutionary Russia. Two scenes prompt reflection on issues arising in biblical studies courses:

(1) The opening number, "Tradition" (DVD chs. 1–2), helps to contextualize the New Testament "household codes" (Col 3:18–4:1; Eph 5:21–33; 1 Tim 2:8–15; 1 Pet 2:18–3:8). These texts represent attempts to delineate the expected roles, behaviors, and goals for members of a household, namely, for

spouses, children, and slaves. Because they promote values that at some points diverge in marked ways from widely held values in contemporary Western society, such texts are greeted with suspicion by many readers. The song in the film is essentially a household code set to music, describing in succession the duties of fathers, mothers, sons, and daughters. Introducing the clip in this way helps students to see that the assumptions built into these texts are not entirely unique to early Christianity. Surviving documents from ancient Greece and Rome likewise mirror the codes in broad terms. Placing the various texts side by side enables students to notice the common assumptions as well as ways in which first-century Christians distinguished themselves from their neighbors. What have these authors added to the general template? What have they deleted or subtly transformed?

This opening scene also helps students appreciate the challenge faced by Christian writers such as Paul (especially in Galatians) and the author of Hebrews as their respective audiences felt a newfound sense of community or the nostalgic tug of Jewish symbols and customs. "Because of our traditions," Tevye says, "every one of us knows who he is and what God expects him to do."

(2) Near the end of the movie, Tevye's third daughter, Chava, announces her intention to marry a Gentile. Tevye sorts out his emotions at this looming break from tradition and plans his response in an interior monologue (DVD ch. 30): "Can I deny everything I believe in? On the other hand can I deny my own child? On the other hand, how can I turn my back on my faith, my people? If I try to bend that far, I will break!" This moving scene hints at the tensions associated with intermarriage and assimilation in the Jewish tradition. To what extent are Tevye's concerns those of Deut 7:1–5 or Ezra 9–10? What would the author of Ruth or Jonah say if asked for advice? How do different social-historical settings affect the stance one sees on the matter of intermarriage?

Fight Club (1999)

What compelled the earliest Christians to refer to Jesus as the Christ? Some students are unaware that "Christ" is a transliteration of the Greek word for "messiah" instead of Jesus' family name. The factors that led the early church to proclaim Jesus as the Messiah are varied and complex, and most of their contemporaries appear not to have agreed with the identification. Among believers, too, not all of the qualities displayed by Jesus were considered necessary or sufficient for achieving messianic status. Modern observers sometimes regard as essential certain traits that ancient observers saw as incidental to Jesus' identity as the Messiah, and the New Testament writers themselves frequently focus on different aspects of his person and work as more or less central.

Reflection on one of the many cinematic Christ-figures brings this question to the fore. Many students mistakenly assume that there was a single, standardized job description for the Messiah (found in the Hebrew Scriptures) and that the birth of Christianity was simply a matter of consulting this checklist when candidates for the position presented their credentials. In discussing characters who have been hailed as Christ-figures, students come to realize that even today there is no unanimity when it comes to defining the central and peripheral traits of Jesus, among neither Christian theologians nor secular audiences. (For a list of twenty-five common traits of the Christ-figure identified and explicated, see Kozlovic, "The Structural Characteristics of the Cinematic Christ-Figure.")

This film is one of many on which students may write in preparation for class discussion. The question may be put this way: In what sense, if any, is it appropriate to consider the protagonist a Christ-figure? What specific traits, deeds, quotations, or plot devices support such a label? The whole class could view the same film, or the instructor may give a limited number of choices. Options familiar to most of the class will enable even those students who have not written on a particular film to argue for or against the positions taken in the discussion. Material for discussion is rarely lacking, but the instructor should be prepared with evidence. Here, Tyler Durden (Brad Pitt) is a violent, foul-mouthed anarchist—not exactly what comes to mind when one thinks of the Prince of Peace. But he also exhibits many qualities that parallel those of Jesus: He attracts scores of disciples. He speaks in aphorisms that are in turn quoted by his followers. He sends out his disciples on various missions. His movement spreads to other cities. His radical antimaterialistic message discourages his followers from "storing up treasures on earth." He is willing to become a eunuch (though not for the kingdom of heaven; cf. Matt 19:12). He instructs members of the club to keep it a secret (DVD ch. 15). He preaches a kind of salvation (from emasculating, consumerist culture). He is decidedly against the spiritual status quo. He speaks of bringing down—quite literally—key cultural institutions (cf. "Project Mayhem" in DVD ch. 23, 35). Legends about his exploits arise during his lifetime or shortly thereafter. Rumors about the bizarre activities of his followers abound. He is willing to endure great physical abuse on behalf of others.

How should we evaluate this character? Are the similarities significant? Are they sufficiently detailed to warrant comparison with Jesus? What differences militate against a serious comparison, despite any similarities?

A similar exercise could be performed with the following films, among others: *The Matrix*; *Sling Blade*; *The Green Mile*; *E.T.*; *Superman: The Movie*; *Superman Returns*; *The Shawshank Redemption*; *Cool Hand Luke*; *Shane*; *The Seventh Sign*; *Twelve Monkeys*; *The Lion, the Witch, and the Wardrobe*; *Edward*

Scissorhands; *The Terminator*; *The Lord of the Rings*; *Touch*; and *One Flew Over the Cuckoo's Nest*.

Frailty (2002)

In this modern film noir told in flashbacks, a tortured man, Fenton Meiks (Matt McConaughey), confesses to a skeptical FBI agent (Powers Boothe) that he knows the identity of a serial killer known as the God's Hand Killer: his own father (Bill Paxton) and, later, his younger brother (Jeremy Sumpter).

Paxton plays a widowed father of two sons who believes that an angel has commissioned him to murder sinners because they have been possessed by demons. When the father touches a sinner, he claims to be able to feel the power of the demon; he becomes "God's Hand." The problem is that only the father can see and experience this sinfulness. One son trusts that Dad is right, while the other son is wracked by doubts. The children are trapped in a nightmarish world of blood, gore, and the deliverance of "God's wrath" from which they cannot escape (no adult believes them over their father). Gradually, the father forces them to follow in his own ways.

Frailty plays throughout with the most sinister implication of Christian fundamentalism—when an individual feels deeply right about what God is telling him to do, regardless of the moral nature of those commands. There is no way out of Dad Meiks's righteousness; he even tells his son that if he tells anyone what is going on, according to the angel, someone else will die. The father is unwavering in his insistence that he is doing God's work—a viewpoint with which he consistently indoctrinates his boys. And, frighteningly, his faith can never be proven incorrect. Students are sure to have much to say about the nature of authority here. Does the fact that the angel of God wants Dad Meiks to murder "prove" that Meiks is merely insane? Or can God ask anything of his servants, even if it defies human morality? Is there such a thing as a righteous killing? What if Meiks is right—that the supposed innocents whom he murders are actually very bad demons? Who has the right to administer justice, according to the New Testament (cf. Rom 13:1–7)?

Frailty is worthy of screening in its entirety, but be forewarned that the movie is quite bleak and will probably disturb more sensitive viewers. Virtually all the dialogue centers around the tension between the sons and the father on the nature of God's instructions. But the film contains many ambiguities and raises moral and theological questions to be explored in class discussion or in a paper: (1) How were various biblical figures who have spoken for God been received (e.g., Noah, Moses, Elijah, Jeremiah, Jesus, Paul), whether in terms of the narratives in which they appear or in "real life"? It is not as simple as saying that everyone in the ancient world believed everything they were told about God and everyone learned to be suspicious after the Enlightenment. (2) How have ancient and modern readers dealt with God's test of Abraham requiring him to sacrifice his son? (3) Is the father really similar to other divine messengers or prophets? Notice the paradox inherent in attempts to verify "true" prophecy involving predictions in the Bible on account of its form and function (usually laying out some dire consequence if the people do not follow a certain course of action). God, through the prophets, desires for the people to turn from sin, but if the people respond to the prophet's call for repentance, then the prophecy of doom is not fulfilled, which makes the prophet look like a false prophet.

Gladiator (2000)

Biblical studies mavens recognize the Joseph story from Genesis in this account of a general who is the Roman emperor's favored son. Maximus (Russell Crowe) promises the dying emperor Marcus Aurelius (Richard Harris) that he will help usher back the Roman Republic; that is to say (very implausibly) that he plans to put an end to the "slavery" and restore freedom for all its people. But his "brother" Commodus, Marcus Aurelius's son and successor, is no fan of such democratic free-thinking, and is, in the understated words of the movie, "not a moral man." But Maximus's vengeance requires a long process of overcoming considerable adversity. It is the "journey motif" again, the same motif as in the biblical story of Joseph.

The Joseph parallels are well established early on: the theme of the favored son granted a boon by his father, that is, leadership of the people against the normal "rules" of succession. Like Joseph at the hands of his brothers, Maximus suffers a crushing loss of status at Commodus's hands when the young emperor orders his murder. Maximus escapes, only to return home to find his family murdered and his home razed to the ground. He ends up enslaved and forced into gladiatorial combat.

Plunged into the merciless "kill or be killed" environment that is the Roman amphitheater, Maximus remains, steadfastly, a good man. A foil to Commodus's bloodlust, Maximus refuses to kill his rivals in the amphitheater. Pitched against Rome's most notorious *secutor*, Maximus triumphs and, at the last minute, defies Commodus's "thumbs-down" signal that he must slice the gladiator's throat. For this, he becomes to the crowds "Maximus the Merciful," and his display of mercy underscores his nature as, like Joseph, the moral hero of the piece. Indeed, the character's decency can serve as a salutary reminder that a distinctive moral sensitivity was not the primary aspect of Judaism and Christianity that set them apart from the other religions and philosophies of antiquity. And insofar as it was a key period in the emergence and evolution of Judaism and Christianity, this film (despite any historical inaccuracies) can help students gain some sense of the political and cultural milieu of second-century Rome.

Jacob's Ladder (1990)

Jacob Singer (Tim Robbins) is a Vietnam veteran suffering from post-traumatic stress syndrome who finds himself plagued by terrifying visions of demons. In dreams that manifest with startling clarity, he suffers flashbacks to his pre-Vietnam existence as a philosophy professor, husband, and father living in the suburbs. The realism of his dream life throws him severely off kilter, and Jacob fears he is going insane until a fellow veteran reveals to him that Jacob was a victim of Army experiments in which soldiers were given drugs to enhance their aggression. Singer realizes his dreams and visions are the consequence of those experiments—but not in the way that he, and the audience, at first believes.

On a simple level, many students may notice that most of the characters in the film have biblical names. In terms of imagery, the film's demonology breaks free from typical movie genre restraints. At the same time, neither is it informed by the Bible. Points of contact with Jacob's ladder in Gen 28 do exist, but only if stretched substantially; here, the title is both literal (the codename of Jacob's experimental drug therapy is "the Ladder") and a metaphor for the development of an individual's consciousness. Only when Jacob reaches the top of the metaphorical ladder of the soul's ascent can he perceive the entire picture and the drama of his salvation. There, he realizes the need to give up fear, hatred, aggression, attachment, and the passions of the flesh. As a vision of Purgatory in which demons are really angels fighting for Jacob's release into heaven in order to reunite him with his son, *Jacob's Ladder* is powerful. Paired with noncanonical documents, including the *Apocalypse of Peter* in which the eponymous hero travels through hell and witnesses the torments of the wicked, students have a fine opportunity to ponder individual eschatology, soteriology, visions of the afterlife, and the nature of redemption.

The Chronicles of Narnia: The Lion, the Witch and the Wardrobe (2005)

Before this movie's release, a biblical studies instructor could assign C. S. Lewis's extraordinary children's book, *The Lion, the Witch and the Wardrobe*, and only then reveal that the novel was intended as Lewis's symbolic presentation of the Christian story told in the Gospels. But now the secret is out.

Students might be interested to learn more of Lewis's career as a Christian apologist and Oxford literature professor who finally realized that the finest way to preach the resurrected Christ was to cloak the Truth in a world of magical wardrobes, talking animals, and children who become kings and queens. Still, Lewis argued that *Narnia* was not meant to be a Christian allegory; it was meant to be "suppositional," a sort of alternate fantasy world that still resonates with God's gift of his Son. The chief deity of this world is a magnificent talking lion named Aslan, who epitomizes the majesty of God; he is at once loving and fierce, immanent and transcendent, incarnated and abstract. He is also a prophet, who declared long ago that two "sons of Adam" and two "daughters of Eve" would someday come to end the one-hundred-year period of darkness and winter imposed by the evil White Witch.

But it is only the appearance of the children in Narnia that initiates the chain of events that wrest the land from the White Witch's grasp. What is really needed is a protracted ritual of "Deep Magic" in which Aslan allows the witch and her minions to shame, torture, and slaughter Aslan one night. Aslan's torture and death is perhaps less wrenchingly rendered in the movie than in the children's book, but the point of the parallel with Christ is made. Sacrificed on the Stone Table, Aslan breaks the old covenant with his resurrection. If any scene might be shown in class, this would be it (DVD ch. 16–17). Students might discuss the theme of Jesus' death as a replacement of the Old Mosaic law and its demands of blood sacrifice with a new law of resurrection and atonement, as well as related issues raised by this theology (e.g., would the author of Leviticus or the Epistle to the Hebrews, especially chapters 8–10, agree with this Narnian "logic"? Would Paul? What does it imply about Judaism?) And is Lewis successful in weaving together "pagan" elements such as mythological beasts and magic with Christian narrative? A comparison with the reception of the Harry Potter books and movies in certain Christian communities might make for fine discussion.

Magnolia (1999)

This film offers an interesting case of scriptural use at once transgressive and profound, meaningful and meaningless. Two passages from the Hebrew Bible play a part. In one wrenching scene, a depressive, repressed homosexual (played by William H. Macy) vomits into a public toilet while quoting Ezek 18:20: "The son shall not suffer for the iniquity of the father, nor the father suffer for the iniquity of the son; the righteousness of the righteous shall be upon himself, and the wickedness of the wicked shall be upon himself." Seemingly gratuitous, the use of Scripture here actually serves to highlight the film's central *leitmotif*: family dysfunction passed from parent to child through incest and abuse. The second passage, Exod 8:2, forms part of the conceptual background for the film's conclusion. It reveals Yahweh's words to Pharaoh: "And if thou refuse to let them go, behold, I will smite all thy borders with frogs." *Magnolia* ends quite remarkably, with an actual rain of frogs that serves as a redemptive event, altering the path of its characters all caught in a downward spiral of self-destruction because of the sins of their fathers.

P. T. Anderson reports that the rain of frogs in *Magnolia* was not initially taken from the Bible at all, but from Charles Fort, an early nineteenth-century writer on strange natural phenomena, including documented "rains" of frogs. Anderson says that he did not even know there was a plague of frogs in the Bible until he had completed the film's script. When he found it there, it served as a sort of synchronistic confirmation that his story was on the right track.

Since another theme in the film is that events and people are interconnected, Anderson weaves Exod 8:2 into the fabric of the film. He drops the biblical citation, chapter and verse, into tiny details—for example, waving on a placard in the studio audience of a quiz show scene. Like the John 3:16 poster held up at athletic events, Anderson's use of the citation here is less an invitation to viewers to look it up than it is a type of visual icon. It is the director's "deep play." Asked in an interview about the deeper significance of the film's many references to Exod 8:2, Anderson laughs: "I just thought it was a fun directorial, bored-on-the-set thing to do" (ptanderson.com/articlesand-interviews/austin.htm). As a means of illustrating the ease with which readers produce eisegetical readings of Scripture, one might ask students to discuss the significance of these references—before sharing Anderson's comments, of course. Some students will likely try to find answers on the Internet, however, and will come across the Anderson interview. When they share their information, one might respond by suggesting the Anderson is being insincere ("Is it really plausible that an educated American reader would be familiar with arcane literature dealing with raining frogs and *not* with the Exodus story?!"). Whether or not Anderson is sincere in confessing his ignorance of the text, discussion of the use of Scripture in the film alerts students to the difficulty that frequently attends our efforts at discerning authorial intent and also highlights the fact that authors—including biblical authors—sometimes quote other texts out of context or find significance that was not intended by the original author.

Overall, *Magnolia* is about ordinary and tiny moments of grace, points at which people at their most brittle and broken moments of debasement can be profoundly changed. And children can be angels and prophets, speaking out the truth in surprising ways. One theological interpretation of the movie is that the same God of Exodus who brings the Israelites out of slavery (Exod 2:23–25), brings such moments to save people through giving them hope.

For further discussion, see Reinhartz, *Scripture on the Silver Screen*, 24–38.

The Matrix (1999)

The hero of *The Matrix* has two identities. On the "profane" level, he is a mid-level computer programmer named Thomas Anderson. But he is also known to some as Neo, a computer hacker and illegal software dealer. Neo receives his Monomyth-style "Call to Action" from Morpheus (Laurence Fishburne), who gradually reveals to Neo the truth: reality as we know it is actually an elaborate cyber-illusion in which humans are unwittingly caught, believing it to be reality. What appears to be America in the year 1999 is actually, he says, "the world that has been pulled over your eyes to blind you from the Truth." The truth of the situation is much more horrible: Artificial intelligences have taken control of humankind; needing a reliable source of energy, these computers have learned to grow humans to serve as living batteries. While they are drained of their life energies, all humans are kept pacified or "asleep" by being literally plugged into the cyber-world of the Matrix.

Morpheus heads a small group of rebels who have learned to subvert the Matrix to some extent. But as much as they can do, they await The One who can lead them all to salvation. Morpheus—a type of John the Baptist—is convinced that Neo is this person. Neo must come to that recognition on his own before he is able to manipulate the Matrix to serve his own ends—to liberate the world from sleep, ignorance, and bondage. This narrative and its philosophical underpinnings—that humankind is spiritually and conceptually enslaved by malevolent beings and awaiting the awakening of a savior—is classically "gnostic," a point hardly lost on contemporary gnostic groups who have been known to use *The Matrix* as a sort of missionary tool. The film certainly fits the characteristics of Gnosticism (as presented in, e.g., Hans Jonas's seminal study, *The Gnostic Religion*).

One see shades of the film's stark dualism reflected in a few passages of the New Testament such as 1 Thess 5:4–5 ("We are not of night, nor of darkness, so let us not sleep as others do"), Eph 5:14 ("Wake up! O sleeper, rise from the dead"), and 1 Peter 2:1 (where Christians are "now 'aliens' to this fallen world"). And much has been made over the prominent messiah motifs. Christians, in particular, have reveled in the opportunity to read into the film a dizzying array of Christ-parallels, often with little critical reflection—almost certainly with a specificity that the Wachowskis had never intended. (Fanciful readings of the film's purported symbolism can be found online and provide cautionary tales about the pitfalls of reading and interpretation without basic controls in place.) The directors were not setting out to create a parable for Christianity (cf. the interview with Larry Wachowski in *Time Magazine*, April 19, 1999). So while many tout *The Matrix* as a sort of pop-culture scripture ideal for turning a jaded, hyper-stimulated Generation Exile to Christ, *The Matrix* is hardly a Christian movie. There is also little truly "biblical" about it. The Bible is never quoted, beyond the appearances of biblical names (the "promised land" for the rebels is called Zion; the name of Morpheus's ship is the Nebuchadnezzar). The ship's plaque reads Mark III, 11 ("Whenever the evils spirits saw Him, they fell down before him and cried out, 'You are the Son of God!' "), the significance of which is not entirely clear.

The final scenes in which Neo battles Agent Smith, dies, and is resurrected by Trinity's kiss are fun to show in class; students can point out parallels to and diversions from the New Testament resurrection accounts. How is Neo a Christ-type? What sort of powers (or body) does he have after resurrection? What is Trinity a type of in this setting? And what theological function might the ending have, in which Neo flies off to the heavens without immediately redeeming the world? The two subsequent *Matrix* movies answer some of these questions as well as make for a good illustration of different New Testament Christologies. One might show the scenes from *Matrix: Reloaded* in which Neo arrives on Zion and has to do the prosaic, hands-on work of a Jesus-figure rather than that of a majestic redeemer, or the final battle between Neo and Smith in *Matrix: Revolutions* to illustrate *Christus Victor* atonement theories that imagine Christ on the cross as a sort of "bait" which Satan swallows and thereby destroys himself.

Memento (2000)

Memory is a pervasive theological motif in the Passover narrative in Exod 12–14. The Israelites are instructed again and again to recall the mighty acts of God that have resulted in their deliverance (e.g., 12:14; 13:3, 9). This collective act of remembrance in part constitutes Israel as a people. Israel would in some fundamental sense cease to exist without these shared memories, just as the maintenance of any individual's identity becomes problematic without the capacity to recollect the past.

Life would be chaos without memory, and few films make this point more vividly than *Memento*. When Leonard Shelby (Guy Pearce) and his wife are viciously attacked, the woman dies and Leonard is left with Korsakoff's Syndrome, a rare type of retrograde amnesia that prevents him from forming new long-term memories. He remembers the attack and knows that he wants revenge (the *lex talionis* of Lev 24:17–20 in the Gideon's Bible appears fleetingly on the screen: DVD ch. 2). But as he sets out to find the killer, his condition requires him to tattoo key facts onto his skin and write notes on Polaroid pictures to remind himself of what has taken place and how it fits into his overarching objective. To complicate matters further, the movie scenes unfold in reverse chronological order. This device helps the audience to experience something of the disorientation that plagues Leonard. It also shows the ways in which memory is neither a purely linear nor a passive faculty. Leonard's comments on the nature of memory (DVD ch. 6) may spur provocative discussion of biblical genres and authorial intent: "Memory's not perfect. It's not even that good. Ask the police; eyewitness testimony is unreliable.... Memory can change the shape of a room or the color of a car. It's an interpretation, not a record. Memories can be changed or distorted and they're irrelevant if you have the facts." To what extent, if any, is this an accurate way to understand the operating assumptions of the biblical authors or the legacy of their writings?

Certain events are more charged with meaning than others. For Leonard to retain any shred of identity, select memories are absolutely critical. His case illustrates the link between memory and identity in a striking fashion. Less bizarre but equally helpful examples highlighting this link can be drawn from the experience of the students by posing the following question: If you were asked to choose three or four events for which everyone in the room can clearly recall where he or she was when they took place, what would they be? For earlier generations, choices would include Pearl Harbor, the Kennedy assassination, and perhaps the first moon landing. More recent examples might include the 1986 explosion of the space shuttle Challenger, the 1994 police chase involving O. J. Simpson, and the terrorist attacks of September 11, 2001. Subgroups within a larger culture distinguish themselves in part on the basis of the memories that have attained similarly iconic status. For example, Boston Red Sox fans—and relatively few others—will be able to remember where they were for the heart-breaking loss to the New York Yankees in the 2003 playoffs as well as for their miraculous comeback the following year. Memphians are more likely than most Americans to remember where they were when Elvis Presley died. The memories that make such indelible imprints on the collective consciousness of a group make a kind of statement about the peculiar character of that group. (It is probably significant, for instance, that far more Americans remember hearing the news of Princess Diana's death than Mother Teresa's death, even though both occurred on the same day.) The movie and the follow-up exercise reinforce this dynamic one sees in Exodus as well as in such texts as the Last Supper narratives in the Gospels ("do this in remembrance of me").

Monster (2003)

This film is based on the story of Aileen Wuornos, a Florida prostitute who was sentenced to death for murdering seven men. The opening scene helps students understand the male perspective of Prov 1–9, particularly regarding the dangers of the "loose woman" (e.g., 2:16; 5:3, 20; 6:24; 7:5, 10). The biblical text presents advice from a father to a son. The loose woman does not speak; when she does, it is only as quoted by the father. One does not hear her side of the story. More disturbingly, there is no room for her rehabilitation or redemption. Rather, the discourse encourages the reader to flee from the whore whose paths lead to death. Before showing the film clip, students can be asked to provide a voice for the loose woman by writing a paragraph describing what she would say if interviewed. Responses vary widely, but relatively few give her a sympathetic read.

In the two-minute clip, Wuornos (Charlize Theron) tells us in a voice-over about her childhood as we see scenes from her youth. She explains how she was hopeful about the future, but unloved and subjected to horrific abuse, the details of which are easily available in documentaries and on the Internet. She turns to prostitution at a young age, which leads to more abuse. After the flashback to her childhood, we see Wuornos sitting in the rain holding a gun considering suicide. It is a sad story, to say the least, of one particular "loose woman." The biblical text, however, tends to ignore such stories, a fact which the clip sharply underscores. Taking into account these divergent perspectives aids in developing a thicker description of the moral, cultural, psychological, emotional, and even legal circumstances lying behind a text like Proverbs.

Monty Python and the Holy Grail (1975)

This quirky British comedy, which remains quite popular among undergraduates despite its age, can be used to introduce two topics.

(1) The "Holy Hand Grenade" scene (DVD ch. 22) helps to introduce genre criticism, which studies the form, function, and content of smaller literary units. If specific qualities are found with sufficient regularity across texts, then scholars are justified in identifying a discrete genre, which in turn clarifies which questions may be properly posed to the material. The "Holy Hand Grenade of Antioch" is used near the end of the film to destroy a killer rabbit that blocks the path of the knights. Before deploying it, a friar reads a blessing from the (fictional) Book of Armaments 2:9–21: "O Lord, bless this, Thy hand grenade, that with it, Thou mayest blow Thine enemies to tiny bits in Thy mercy." After a prelate asks him to "skip ahead a bit," the friar continues with the instructions:

> "And the Lord spake, saying, 'First shalt thou take out the Holy Pin. Then, shalt thou count to three. No more, no less. Three shall be the number thou shalt count, and the number of the counting shall be three. Four shalt thou not count, neither count thou two, excepting that thou then proceed to three. Five is right out. Once the number three, being the third number, be reached, then lobbest thou thy Holy Hand Grenade of Antioch towards thy foe, who, being naughty in My sight, shall snuff it.' Amen."

A simple way to begin the discussion is to ask why it is a funny scene. As students articulate the reasons (e.g., it "sounds" biblical but really is not; it contains vocabulary that is anachronistic; it deftly apes King James English), they begin to see that they already have a good ear for biblical forms, for how they can be adapted, for what gets repeated, for the probable *Sitz im Leben* of particular locutions, and the like.

(2) The two-minute scene in which the knights receive their quest for the grail (DVD ch. 8) nicely illustrates the typical elements found in Old Testament call narratives. In groups, students can quickly compare the scene with one or more biblical call narratives (Exod 3:1–22; Judg 6:11–24; 1 Kgs 22:19–23; Isa 6:1–8; Jer 1:4–10). Standard components to note include (a) the encounter with God, (b) the call proper, (c) an objection from the one called, and (d) reassurance or sign (See Brad E. Kelle, "Prophetic Call Narratives," in Roncace and Gray, *Teaching the Bible*, 167).

The Omen (1976/2006)

On June 6, at 6 p.m., a son is born to Robert Thorn, American ambassador to Italy. But he is told at the Catholic hospital that his son is stillborn, and—to spare his beloved wife aching grief—is encouraged to take in another orphaned infant born at the same moment as his son. His wife need not know of the switch. And so the Thorns take home a changeling and, after Thorn is appointed as ambassador to Great Britain, they move to the English countryside, where things slowly begin to go terribly wrong.

Comparing the way that the Bible appears in both the original 1976 *Omen* and its 2006 remake makes for fascinating work in the classroom. Both movies are extraordinary cultural artifacts because the movies capture so well some of the latent neuroses of the past thirty years (e.g., the guilt of the professional parent and the nagging suspicion that perhaps we are not as "religious" as we ought to be). The Christianity behind *The Omen* movies is similarly charged. Catholicism comes across as deeply superstitious but nevertheless informed as to the way that the world will come to an end.

The 2006 remake adds to the beginning a scene at the Vatican in which a professional "apocalypse watcher" interprets modern disasters (the 9/11 attacks, Hurricane Katrina, and the tsunami of southeast Asia all flash across the screen). He keys these modern events in to the book of Revelation's "prophecies" of the disasters that will accompany the opening of the seven seals. Although this mode of interpreting Revelation owes far more to American evangelicalism than to Vatican exegesis, the point is made more trenchantly than in the original *Omen* that we are living at the end of times.

Thorn is "enlightened" because he does not know his Bible nor pay much heed to the insane priest who insists that his son Damian is the son of the devil. But at the same time, he is badly mistaken. As in the Gospel of Mark's "Messianic Secret," the only people who recognize Damien for who he really is are women, lunatics, animals, and the audience. Thorn's ignorance of Christian demonology and apocalypticism extends to the Bible. In a key scene in

F
I
L
M

the 1976 *Omen* (DVD ch. 9) the priest who helped arrange Damien's adoption reads to Thorn from the "Book of Revelations" (sic). The verses are completely fictitious, which suggests that the movie's audience also shares Thorn's biblical ignorance. One interesting exercise is to see whether or not students recognize the verses as spurious, and then to ask in what way the verses sound, or do not sound, authentic. A discussion about the melodramatic language of "apocalyptic rhetoric" would be interesting, especially if this scene were paired with other pseudo-scripture readings in movies (e.g., *Pulp Fiction*'s pseudo-Ezekiel or *Lost Souls*'s scrolling text of a fictitious Deut 17). At this point, it would be good to play the same scene from the *Omen* remake (DVD ch. 13). The quoted verses are identical, but the Bible is absent, and the verses are no longer attributed to Revelation. Students might be pressed to discuss: What does this sudden absence of the Bible mean? Could it be that the 2006 movie presumes a more biblically literate audience?

The only actual biblical quotation in the 1976 *Omen* appears as script on a black screen at the movie's closing: "This calls for wisdom, If anyone has insight, let him calculate the number of the beast, for it is man's number, His number is 666" (Rev 13:18 NIV). In the remake, one added scene shows Thorn and the photographer Keith Jennings (David Thewlis) at a refreshment stand near Cerveteri, where they are headed to find more information about Damien's real mother (a jackal!). The photographer flips through a Bible and notes that the verses quoted by the priest are not found there, but appear to be various images and scriptural fragments drawn from various writings in the Hebrew Bible and the New Testament—just as, he says, the antichrist narrative is never really articulated in Revelation. The unexpected appearance of this more sophisticated hermeneutic would make an excellent scene to use in class (DVD ch. 17).

On the Waterfront (1954)

What can we learn when one author alludes to or quotes the words of another? Writers, both consciously and unconsciously, have appropriated the words of the Bible for centuries. This also happens within and throughout the Bible, though with greater frequency in the New Testament. But the biblical writers rarely spell out in detail their purposes in quoting other Scripture, nor do they specify how much of the original context they intend to conjure up for their audiences.

This classic film, which has in turn been quoted quite often in other works, contains a scene that may be used to introduce intertextuality. At the halfway point in the film (DVD chs. 15–16), the scene depicts the "accidental" death of a longshoreman who has cooperated with a police investigation into union corruption. When a priest, Fr. Barry (Karl Malden), is called in to administer the last rites, he delivers a powerful speech indicting the bosses and challenging the dockworkers to do the right thing. "Some people think the Crucifixion only took place on Calvary," he says, but this is a mistake. Every time the mob tries to intimidate a man and keep him from doing his duty as a citizen—that, says Fr. Barry, is a crucifixion. Moreover, whoever stands by idly as this happens is as guilty "as the Roman soldier who pierced the flesh of Our Lord to see if He was dead." The speech ends with a close paraphrase of Matt 25:40: "If you do it to the least of mine, you do it to me!"

After viewing the clip or reading the excerpted transcript, students should analyze the speech in terms of its use of the biblical text. This exercise serves as a warm-up for studying the interpretation of the Hebrew Scriptures in the New Testament. The following questions, formulated for similar exercises dealing with biblical intertextuality, may be adapted for use with the speech from the film: (1) What texts are cited or alluded to in this passage? (2) Does the text of the New Testament citation exactly match the Hebrew Bible passage? Does it appear that the New Testament author has modified the passage in any way? Are there any evident reasons for the changes? (3) What is the context of the passage in its original setting? Does the New Testament author's use of this passage reflect an awareness of the original setting? (4) How does the quoted passage function in the argument or narrative of the New Testament author? For what apparent purpose is the New Testament author using this particular Hebrew Bible text? What can we learn about the audience on the basis of the author's aims and assumptions?

Biblical texts for use with this exercise are legion. Examples include: Mark 1:1–7; John 19:23–30; Acts 2; 28:23–28; Rom 9:13–15; 15:7–13; 1 Cor 10:1–13; Heb 10:26–39; Jas 2:14–26; 1 Pet 2:4–10; Jude 14–16.

One Flew Over the Cuckoo's Nest (1975)

This film is one of many for use in discussions of cinematic Christ-figures. (The background for this exercise is found in the entry for *Fight Club* on pp. 140–42.) In considering various characters who have been hailed as Christ-figures, students come to realize that the factors leading the early church to proclaim Jesus as the Messiah were varied and complex and that even today there is no unanimity when it comes to defining the essential and the merely incidental traits of Jesus.

In what sense, if any, is it appropriate to consider Randall McMurphy (Jack Nicholson) a Christ-figure? What specific traits, deeds, quotations, or plot devices lead the viewer to apply this label? Here, the protagonist is a violent, foul-mouthed, hyper-sexed convict in an asylum. But he also exhibits many qualities that parallel those of Jesus: He attracts disciples, who frequently frustrate him. He takes them fishing. He tries to open their eyes to a reality they could not previously see (the baseball "telecast"). He "cures" the Chief, who had been thought deaf and dumb. He is variously considered a criminal and a lunatic. The powers that be (the nurse, the doctors) shuttle him back and forth and debate who should take responsibility for rehabilitating him. In the end, he is betrayed by a close confidant, who then commits suicide. He endures great physical abuse and is martyred on behalf of others. Legends about his exploits arise when he disappears. His example helps to "liberate" others from the demons that have plagued them. How should we evaluate this character? Are the similarities sufficiently detailed to warrant comparison with Jesus? What differences militate against a serious comparison?

Pi (1998)

Driven by his work on chaos theory, the genius mathematician Max Cohen (Sean Gullette) programs his supercomputer, Euclid, to calculate Pi so as to unlock the mathematical patterns that rule the stock market. Uploading a disk containing the Hebrew alphabet, Euclid seems to malfunction—and spits out a 216-digit number that is, it turns out, the unknowable, unspeakable Name of God. As a human, Max is too limited a being to contain God's fullness, and the knowledge drives the hero—already plagued by crippling migraines—insane.

Pi is not a movie that is easy to watch. It is filmed in grainy black and white, and has relentlessly vivid and gory scenes of Max's migraines. Indeed, the question here (as in *Jacob's Ladder* and *Last Temptation of Christ*) is whether or not Max is crazy or touched by God. He is not a likeable character, and yet he manages to see the world knitted together by some kind of divine order—he just calls it math, not God. It takes a fundamentalist Hasid (Ben Shenkman) to help Max to see that the two are identical: God reveals himself in numbers, in letters, in nature, and all things are interrelated.

The idea of the all-powerful Name of God as a sacred and hidden number (known as the *Schemhamphoras*) derives from kabbalistic Jewish gematria traditions. It is encoded into the Hebrew text of Exod 14:19, 20, and 21, each verse of which has seventy-two letters. Kabbalistic sages noted that if one were to write these three verses one above the other, the first from right to left, the second in reverse order, and the third from right to left again and so on, the result is seventy-two columns of three-letter names for God. These are further subdivided into four columns of eighteen names each, the four columns corresponding to the four letters of the Tetragrammaton.

Pi is useful in the classroom because it is a deeply Jewish movie and offers one type of authentic approach to the Torah never really depicted in film. What emerges from *Pi* is not a sense of the Hebrew Scriptures as literature, but of the Torah as Bible Code, an encapsulation of the entire cosmos. The world is a manifestation of God, governed by immutable mathematical laws. In this way, the film provides an opening to introduce various "modern" and "premodern" methods of interpretation, including rabbinic exegetical principles such as *gezerah shawa*, *binyan ab*, and *qal wa-homer* (cf. the seven Rules of Hillel and the thirteen Rules of R. Ishmael).

Planet of the Apes (2001)

The *Planet of the Apes* movies were a 1960s phenomenon. At their best, they presented American audiences with a parable about racism and intolerance. Director Tim Burton's "remake" adds religion to the mix of elements that can either socialize or destabilize us. Maverick scientist Leo Davidson (Mark Wahlberg) leaves his research vessel to bring back a wayward, genetically altered supermonkey who has escaped in a shuttle. Davidson's shuttle crashes on the Planet of the Apes, where he is imprisoned with other humans by evil apes until set free by Ari, a scientist who finds herself fascinated by Davidson's keen intelligence and ability to speak. Together, the two liberate humankind from the oppression and cruelty of apes. It is a deliverance story, with Leo as a reluctant Moses and the Kingdom of the Apes as Pharaonic Egypt.

The conceit of the film is that humans and apes are separate species, with humans lower down the developmental scale than apes. The evolutionary debate is posed as an ignorant question: Do lower species have souls? The discourse here mirrors nineteenth-century American parlor conversations on whether or not African American slaves had souls. Perhaps one of the most interesting nuances of the latent evolutionary debate is the movie's assertion that apes, like humans, are fundamentally myth-makers, with an innate need to create cosmogonies or creation myths. In this Eliadean world, apes have religion; they worship a Christ-like figure called Semos, who was present at creation and who, they believe, will also return one day. They also have sacred space, even holy writings. One character, Attar, worships at a candle-lit shrine containing the likeness of an ape, which suggests that we, too, worship a god in our own image. Indeed, the language of creation in the Father's image is made explicit in Attar's prayer: "Bless us holy father, who created all apes in his image. Hasten the day of your return when you bring peace to all apes." Less-evolved gorillas enthusiastically embrace Semos as a deity, but by the end of the movie, it becomes clear that their faith is mere folly. More intellectual apes (including the heroine Ari) scorn such beliefs and devotion as silly. As she leads Leo away from the city, Ari explains that their path takes them through the sacred ruins of Calima. According to the holy writings, she tells him, "that is where creation began; where Semos breathed life into us." She quickly undercuts this "religious" view saying, "But most intelligent apes dismiss it as a fairy tale." In fact, the movie's ending in which Semos returns literally as a *deus ex machina* vindicates Ari's position. Religion is seen not so much as deliberately constructed but the result of a garbled understanding of the way things really were—like nineteenth-century theories of religion as a "corruption of language." At the same time, Burton leaves room for faith to re-enchant the logical world of science. Ari's final words are telling, as she ultimately loses her academic distance and waxes poetic: "One day they'll tell a story about a human who came from the stars and changed our world. Some will say it was just a fairy tale; it was never real. But I'll know."

Although biblical studies and introduction to religious studies courses are typically taught separately, there is considerable overlap, and the perspectives one finds in the film will be, variously, embraced or rejected by many students in courses on the Bible. For instructors who want to confront these larger issues, this film serves as a fine touchstone for discussion.

Pleasantville (1998)

Two bored siblings, David and Jennifer (Toby MacGuire and Reese Witherspoon) find themselves mysteriously transported back into the fictitious, black-and-white sitcom *Pleasantville*, circa 1958, where they find themselves playing out the roles of siblings Bud and Mary Sue Parker. Bud, an avid fan of the old television show, at first revels in his chance to live out the episodes he has so eagerly memorized. Mary Sue, however, takes no interest in embodying the limiting role of a late 1950s teenage girl and quickly relishes the opportunity to bring mayhem into this staid universe. She seduces a young basketball player and thereby introduces sexuality into an aseptic, asexual, unreal world. The gradual sexual awakening of Pleasantville's citizens is graphically and strikingly illustrated by the literal (and gradual) colorization of Pleasantville's black-and-white world into brilliant Technicolor. Sexual awakening is portrayed graphically and colorfully; in one scene (likely to embarrass some students) Bud's mother (Joan Allen) masturbates in the bathtub for the first time, at the climax of which a tree outside her window bursts brilliantly and suddenly into flame (DVD ch. 18). It does not take a scholar to recognize this as the tree of knowledge of good and evil. Bud's mother now knows something about herself, about human potential, that powerfully transforms her and her world.

Overall, *Pleasantville* can be read as a thoughtful and creative meditation on Genesis. It addresses questions of what it means to be human, to possess free will, and what is the true nature of sin. Similar to other ancient exegeses of Genesis including texts such as the *Hypostasis of the Archons* from the Nag Hammadi Library in which Eve (and other female characters) bring redemptive knowledge to Adam and other men, it offers a subversive reading of the Christian idea of the "fall" and "original sin." Pleasantville's Lover's Lane is a gorgeously colorized Eden with no ironic danger present, and when Bud's love-interest Margaret plucks a scarlet apple from a black-and-white world and offers it to him, we see clear allusions to Bud's sexual awakening. Margaret becomes an Eve (the film has several Eve figures). But here the act is outrageous only in the eyes of a demiurgical Don Knotts—a minor "god" who controls the Pleasantville cosmos. This can and will upset some conservative students (many Christians were disgusted by the film) while others are likely to be inspired by a liberating reading of the biblical text.

Pleasantville incorporates and subverts traditional Christian interpretations of Eve as the temptress who provokes the fall. It sees women as sexual creatures who nevertheless employ sexuality for positive, even salvific ends. Still, the knowledge that Bud and Mary Sue bring to Pleasantville is not merely sexual knowledge, but something more diffuse—the knowledge of human creative potential. Mary Sue herself cannot be transformed ("colored") until she immerses herself in literature—no amount of raw sexuality will redeem or transform her. Thus Pleasantville makes the point that sexuality is not the only thing that can save humanity; rather, the true key to a transformed life is to live in accordance with one's true inner nature, which each person must discover for herself or himself. To what extent, one may ask students, does this point capture the spirit of the Genesis narrative?

For further discussion, see Reinhartz, Scripture on the Silver Screen, 144–65.

Pulp Fiction (1994)

This Quentin Tarantino film follows the tangled paths of two hit men, the wife of their boss, a washed-up boxer, and a pair of small-time thieves. Many students will be familiar with the final scene of the movie (DVD ch. 26), a speech delivered by Jules, one of the hit men (played by Samuel L. Jackson). Jules has just decided to leave his life of crime after surviving—in his mind, miraculously—an ambush earlier in the day. In this three-minute scene he points a gun at one of the thieves while he recites, and then analyzes, the speech he had been accustomed to delivering just before dispatching his victims. The text, he says, is taken from Ezek 25:17.

Jules's speech, which is readily available on the Internet, provides an opportunity to reflect on the task of interpreting the Bible, critically and otherwise. One might pose a discussion question along these lines: "To what extent is it appropriate to think of this speech as an example of biblical interpretation?" Astute readers will take the trouble of consulting Ezek 25 and will find that it does not say what Jules says it says. (His version is a pastiche of fiery phrases that "feel" like Ezekiel, as well as bits from Gen 4 and Ps 23.) What is the difference between paraphrasing and interpreting? Must we read biblical texts in context? Must we view the rest of the movie in order to understand Jules? Is Jules's application of the text's significance to his own situation a legitimate way of reading? Or is it a form of eisegesis? Is it always incumbent on the interpreter to give the author's intent a privileged place when determining the meaning? Is it ever possible to have a "wrong" interpretation of a text? (Jules's assessment of his own former way of construing the text suggests that the answer is yes.) Students may raise other hermeneutical questions: Is a murderer truly capable of understanding the Bible? What, precisely, is the proper object of the interpreter—the mind of the author, along with the appropriate historical-cultural setting? the text by itself? the "world in front of the text"? For example, should we ask whether it is Jules or Tarantino who is responsible for the misquotation?

For further discussion, see Reinhartz, *Scripture on the Silver Screen*, 97–113.

Raging Bull (1980)

Martin Scorsese's film is based on the life of Jake LaMotta—his rise and fall as a middleweight boxer, his stormy relationships with brother Joey and wife Vicki, his brief imprisonment, and his sad post-ring career as a stand-up comedian and night-club owner. After the closing scene, which shows Jake practicing his stage routine in front of a mirror, the text of John 9:24–26 (NEB) appears on the screen: "So, for the second time, [the Pharisees] summoned the man who had been blind and said: 'Speak the truth before God. We know this fellow is a sinner.' 'Whether or not he is a sinner, I do not know,' the man replied. 'All I know is this: once I was blind and now I can see.'"

Rather than viewing the short clip in class, the scene works best in connection with an out-of-class writing assignment dealing with intertextuality and hermeneutics. Once they have viewed the film, students should respond to the following questions: Why does Scorsese add the postscript from John's Gospel? Since an author has only one chance to leave a final impression, is there some significance in this choice? Does the postscript help the audience to understand the film better? Does the film, conversely, help the audience to understand John (or the passage about the man born blind) better? Do the characters in the biblical text (the man born blind, the Pharisees, Jesus) stand for characters in the film in some allegorical fashion?

It matters little whether students consult secondary sources—commentary on the ending is surprisingly scarce. It is sometimes interpreted as a summing up of Jake's "rebirth" after a tortuous journey through personal and professional failures. Or, it may point at Scorsese himself, who had been struggling with drug addiction just prior to making the film. (His cinematic "recovery" resulted in a film judged by critics to be one of the century's best.) This instance of appropriation of the biblical text is one in which the cliché "there are no wrong answers" seems to apply. The follow-up discussion after students have written on the topic functions as a forum for clarifying what we mean, exactly, when we talk about "biblical interpretation." Most students will notice connections or similarities or parallels between the movie and John. Is this the same thing as observing Scorsese in the act of interpreting the Bible? Could we clarify matters by asking him what he had in mind when he ended the film on this note? Time permitting, the discussion may be broadened by including opposing views regarding authorial intent (e.g., Wimsatt and Beardsley on "the intentional fallacy" and E. D. Hirsch Jr.).

Raging Bull presents an explicit and undeniable case of appropriation. A more devious way to broach the same set of question is to assign a short paper on a film without any such explicit biblical references. For example: "Write a two-page paper on (1) the way in which *Eyes Wide Shut* alludes to the Letter to the Romans; (2) the way in which *The March of the Penguins* reflects on Prov 31; or (3) the way in which *Napoleon Dynamite* (re)interprets Acts 10–11." After they have done the assignment, the instructor can inform students that there are in fact no connections between these randomly chosen movies and the corresponding texts. Students trust—up to this point, at any rate—that their professor would not play a trick on them, and as a result many come up with quite ingenious comparisons. But is it necessarily the case that all the papers must be exercises in eisegesis? Along with many of the basic metacritical questions raised by scholars, a range of differing (and entertaining) viewpoints will emerge in the ensuing debate as students defend or attack the examples of biblical interpretation their classmates have produced.

The Rapture (1991)

This is a controversial, troubling film that is sure to provoke strong reactions from viewers. Sharon (Mimi Rogers) is a young, bored woman who fills the emotional and spiritual holes in her life as a switchboard operator by cruising swingers bars with her boyfriend. An unsettling sexual encounter and an even more unsettling dream provokes Sharon's sudden "born again" conversion to Christianity. The experience transforms Sharon's understanding of the world and its purpose, and she completely renounces her previous life of sin. Few films portray the psychology of conversion as effectively as *The Rapture*, but Sharon's life before conversion is conveyed graphically enough to make this film potentially embarrassing for many viewers.

An enthusiastic new convert, Sharon finds herself drawn to other fundamentalist Christians, particularly those who cluster around a preternaturally wise child prophet. The child warns his community that they must prepare for the Rapture, the final apocalyptic event in which true believers are suddenly caught up into the heavens while unbelievers are left behind on earth.

(The primary text expressing the notion of a "rapture" is 1 Thess 4:16–17 and not, as is commonly thought, the book of Revelation.) He reads portions of the Gospel of Mark's "Little Apocalypse" (Mark 13: "there will be wars and rumor of wars"), a brief scene that might work well shown in the classroom, particularly in discussions of these texts in modern discourse (DVD ch. 9). Some students may be surprised at the bewildering variety of millenialist interpretation, examples of which are plentiful on the Internet.

David Duchovny plays Sharon's lover Randy. Inspired by Sharon, Randy converts and the two marry, have a child, and begin their lives as committed Christians. Randy's tragic death provokes another crisis for Sharon. She sells or gives away all her possessions, packs up her car, and moves with her young daughter out to the desert to await further instructions from God. The movie becomes progressively more difficult to watch as she and her child, starving and freezing, wait fruitlessly for further signs.

It is difficult to know what to make of *The Rapture*'s shocking ending, and perspectives vary on whether or not the film is authentically Christian or anti-Christian. What it means to convert—from the first days of glowing self-assurance, bursting pride, and missionary zeal to the thoroughgoing conviction that one is right and outsiders are wrong, to the intensely personal struggles of faith—are well captured. Certainly, its view of certain strands of fundamentalist Christianity is not essentially incorrect, nor does it get its theology or hermeneutics wrong, at least from a biblical point of view. Still, it presents a disturbing theodicy: What kind of God demands such sacrifices from his children? What kind of God kills his children who fail to believe in him, and rewards only those who believe in him at all costs? It is difficult for many viewers not to sympathize with the strong-willed Sharon, who makes a decision she must deal with for eternity. At the same time, the consequence of this sympathy is that the audience finds itself on the opposite side of a vast divide from God—thus leaving many viewers distressed, bewildered, and even outraged. *The Rapture* works well in the classroom, but should be previewed by the instructor beforehand and used with discretion.

Rosemary's Baby (1968)

Roman Polanski's movie about a woman who unwittingly gives birth to the antichrist stands as a classic of the thriller genre. Unbeknownst to his wife Rosemary (Mia Farrow), Guy Woodhouse (John Cassavetes) has literally made a deal with the devil to aid his struggling career as an actor. Rosemary's growing suspicions that their neighbors make up a coven of witches with whom Guy is conspiring climax with the revelation that the child she has just borne is not her husband's, but Satan's.

The closing scene (DVD ch. 31) is in many ways a fiendish parody of the infancy accounts of Matthew and, especially, Luke. At four minutes, it is short enough to be shown in class to prompt a discussion of the central themes and plot elements of these narratives. Ask students to identify the elements from the Gospels that they detect in some form in the movie's final scene and then to decide whether it is more similar to Luke or Matthew. The point of the exercise is not to praise or to blame Polanski for his fidelity to the Gospels. Rather, it forces students to (1) read the Gospels closely and in context so as to determine which themes are central for the biblical writers and which are incidental, (2) avoid the harmonizing impulse that accompanies much reading of the Gospels, and (3) hone their skills in recognizing the various reconfigurations undergone by biblical motifs in the later tradition.

Among the echoes of the New Testament infancy accounts, the following may be noted: (1) the mother's name is a variant of Mary; (2) those who have come from far and wide to pay their respects to the newborn babe represent a variety of nationalities, similar to the magi in Matt 2; (3) the mother's husband is not the true father of the child; (4) Rosemary's child "shall overthrow the mighty and lay waste their temples" and "shall redeem the despised" (cf. Luke 1:48, 51–52, 71; 2:34); (5) Rosemary is chosen "out of all the women in the whole world" to bear Satan's child (cf. Luke 1:30–33, 42–45, 49); (6) the cries of "Hail!" echo the "Hail, favored one!" of Luke 1:28; (7) the gathered company declares that the birth of the child marks "Year One"; for them, 1966 *Anno Domini* is the true inaugural "year of the Lord"; (8) just before the credits roll, Rosemary appears to accept her role as mother and gently rocks the child to sleep, even as her facial expression suggests that she is full of wonder at what this turn of events will mean; compare this with Mary's reactions in Luke 1:38; 2:19, 51.

Schindler's List (1993)

Is the Bible historically accurate? Films based explicitly on historical events constitute helpful analogies for use in discussions of this important question, which inevitably arises in biblical studies courses. Any number of works lend themselves to this exercise (e.g., *Amistad*, *The Killing Fields*, *Malcolm X*, *Glory*, *Munich*), but this moving Steven Spielberg film about an opportunistic German industrialist who saves more than a thousand Polish Jews from extermination in the Holocaust is perhaps the most familiar.

To set up the discussion, the instructor should present a few historical inaccuracies found in the film. These are easy to locate on the Internet. A few examples: (1) The film downplays Schindler's drinking and womanizing. (2) The "list" was not compiled by Schindler (Liam Neeson) or Itzhak Stern (Ben Kingsley) but by another Jewish subordinate, Marcel Goldberg, who exacted bribes from Jews who realized that the alternative to work in Schindler's factory was almost certain death. (3) Schindler's transformation from cold-hearted businessman to "righteous Gentile" motivated by charity was not the result of seeing an anonymous girl in a red coat during the liquidation of the Krakow ghetto (the only splash of color in the black and white body of the film: DVD ch. 14). (4) Because Schindler was never awarded the Golden Nazi Party Badge, he could not have tearfully regretted not selling it and using the money to save more Jews (DVD ch. 37).

Do such errors matter? On what factors does one's answer depend? Does it still qualify as a "true story" if this is the extent of the artistic license taken by Spielberg or by Thomas Keneally, on whose novel the screenplay is based? Is there a line that, when crossed, marks the boundary between the realms of fiction and nonfiction? For example, would it be true if (1) the film portrays Schindler saving eleven thousand Jews instead of eleven hundred? (2) if "Schindler" were simply a composite of several different Germans who had taken risks in saving Jews? (3) if the film puts into Schindler's mouth words he may have thought but never actually spoke? Can the story qualify as "true" if it is fictional in the ordinary sense? If yes, is it possible to form a precise definition of "truth"? Should tolerance for "white lies" correspond to one's sympathy for a cause—in this instance, reminding the audience of the horrors of Hitler and lauding heroic resistance? Should the film have a disclaimer informing viewers that some liberties have been taken with the historical record? Is the author safe in assuming that the audience is competent at recognizing the genre and understanding its implicit rules? Or is the genre classification not perfectly clear?

This line of questioning can be pursued with several different texts (e.g., the primordial history in Genesis, the Exodus, or the Pentecost narrative in Acts 2) regardless of the stance the instructor or the students take on the particular historical questions involved. The books of Esther and Judith raise these issues and also share the film's thematic focus on the survival of the Jewish people. For many students, however, Jesus' life, death, and resurrection constitute the most obvious parallel. Rudolf Bultmann framed the issue in terms of the related German concepts of *historie* (what actually happened) and *geschichte* (the historic event that becomes significant for human existence). His approach met resistance at several points, most notably in his inclusion of the resurrection among the "mythical" elements of early Christian teaching. Bultmann denies that the resurrection took place as described in the Gospels but that the legitimacy of the kerygma is not thereby undermined. What truly matters, he says, is not the actual events transpiring on Easter but, rather, their ultimate significance, namely, the way in which Jesus has opened up a new self-understanding for human beings. But can an event really become historic (*geschichtlich*) that was not at some point historical (*historisch*)? Is it more important to settle this question for some events than for others? Is it possible to understand the biblical texts without understanding how their authors would have answered this question?

Seven (1995)

Sin is without a doubt among the most ubiquitous concepts students will encounter in their study of the Bible, yet many survey courses dedicate little class time to it. The conceit of this film is helpful for immersing students in the biblical thoughtworld and encouraging reflection on later theological developments of the doctrine of sin. Two detectives are chasing a serial killer who chooses seven victims, egregious examples of each of the seven deadly sins—gluttony, wrath, greed, envy, sloth, pride, and lust. The New Testament alludes to a category of "mortals sins" (1 Jn 5:16–17) but the enumeration belongs to the late patristic and medieval periods.

Instead of a lecture on sin, a variety of writing or research assignments can engage the attention and energy of students: (1) Which of the seven sins appear most often in the Hebrew Bible? in the New Testament? Good answers to the question require facility with concordances, sensitivity to differences between translations, and also alertness to considerations of genre, audience, and purpose. (E.g., is Jesus' silence on a particular sin due to his approval of the deed in question? Or is it explained by his tacit assumption that his audience would automatically understand his views on the matter?) (2) If the class were to compile a list of biblical characters to represent each of the sins, who should be paired with which sin? Popular images of particular characters are occasionally at odds with what the texts actually recount, and so answering this question forces students to attend to what narrators include, what they emphasize, and what they implicitly or explicitly condemn as sinful. (3) Has subsequent tradition successfully identified those offenses deemed the most heinous in the Bible? Are there serious sins which the traditional list of seven omits?

The Seventh Sign (1988)

The *Seventh Sign*—nicknamed "Rosemary's Omen"—is not a great movie, but there is good material to work with in the classroom:

(1) Note the female "savior" in pregnant heroine Abby (Demi Moore). She is a sympathetic character, and a great deal of the narrative tension comes from her need to understand what she and her unborn child have to do with the apocalyptic events unfolding around her.

(2) The role of Judaism here is more fully delineated than in other similar movies. There is a teenage boy, Avi, who knows his Talmud and acts as Abby's

able guide in the world of Judaism. He takes on the role of junior detective and Bible scholar with enthusiasm, and gets a lot of stuff right that many other movies tend to get wrong. There is a lot about something called the Guf, a hall of souls in Jewish kabbalistic teachings, which needs to be empty before the Messiah can return. The idea of the Guf being emptied works well with the idea of the Messiah's return at the end of Revelation; it is therefore one "Jewish" interpretation of Revelation, which some scholars, of course, have argued is a thoroughly Jewish first-century apocalyptic text.

(3) The apocalypticism of this movie, like other movies that interpret current events as the plagues of the book of Revelation (*The Rapture*, *The Omen* [2006], *Omega Code*) works nicely alongside a study of the biblical book. How does the director "read" Revelation? Note that the movie opens with someone wading into the water with a scroll, breaking a seal, and dropping it into the sea which then boils around it. Is this as students imagine the opening of the seven seals?

(4) Jurgen Prochnow plays a fabulously menacing Christ who goes by the name of "David." The neat twist here is that he is not the antichrist come at the end of days, the way we might expect for such a storyline. Instead, as he himself makes clear, he comes not as the Lamb but as the Lion, to pour out his wrath on humankind. A good question for students involves whether or not this Christ is the one they find in Revelation; it might help them to reevaluate their preconceptions of Jesus as being as nice and irenic as they often imagine him to be.

The Shawshank Redemption (1994)

Andy Dufresne (Tim Robbins) is an innocent man, unjustly accused of murdering his wife and her lover. Based on a short story by Stephen King, *The Shawshank Redemption* remains a hugely popular film. Many see in Andy Dufresne a Christ-figure and in the film an inspiring tale of hope and redemption. Dufresne endures his time in prison with dignity, moral fortitude, a willingness selflessly to help others, and a pervasive sense of faith that he will find his deliverance.

And he does find that deliverance: a small rock hammer that he has used, over many years, to chip his way out of his prison cell. Not one to sit around and wait to be saved, Andy cannot help but offer a parting jibe to the evil, hypocritically Christian prison warden who serves as the movie's chief antagonist: he leaves the rock hammer for the warden after his escape tucked into a carved-out Bible—appropriately opened at the book of Exodus. Andy's last note to the warden we see written at the front of the Bible: "You were right: salvation lay within."

Andy Dufresne is undeniably a Jesus-figure, but one with a low Christology. He is Dufresne the Teacher, Dufresne the suffering servant, Dufresne the fisher of men. Only after his symbolic rebirth and resurrection—crawling half a mile through a narrow tunnel, spat out into the rain—does he stand with head upraised, arms extended to the side, in triumphant praise as Dufresne the Christ-figure. Students can easily engage in an analysis of this character-ization: Are the similarities sufficiently detailed to warrant comparison with Jesus? What differences militate against a serious comparison, despite any similarities?

Many Christians bristle at the film's supercilious and self-righteous warden as representatively Christian, but others have read the character differently: if Andy is the Christ of the film, the warden is the Sadducee or Pharisee—nit picking in his interpretation of the law, committed to his Bible, cruel and rigid. His misuse of the Bible is evident from the needlepoint slogan posted on his office wall: "His judgement Cometh and that Right Soon."

Most of all, *The Shawshank Redemption* is about, well, redemption. But it is not Dufresne's escape from Shawshank prison that constitutes redemp-tion; it is his quiet hope and his role as a leader that effects redemption in those around him. In this way, the film's narrative takes its secondary focus in a man Dufresne befriends and mentors in prison, Red (Morgan Freeman), who narrates the film. His experience with Andy transforms him and, at the culmination of the film, leads to his "salvation" in an Eden-like setting where his reunion with Andy mirrors the return of the faithful disciple to heaven. Meanwhile, Andy's presence as an example of hope and steadfast resistance in the face of arbitrarily cruel human authorities lives on in the stories that Shawshank's residents tell about him, long after his departure—not unlike the stories of Jesus that circulated among his first disciples.

For further discussion, see Reinhartz, *Scripture on the Silver Screen*, 129–43.

Signs (2002)

Although the main action involves an invasion by extraterrestrial beings, this film is as much a psychological drama as it is a sci-fi thriller. The story focuses on the family of Graham Hess (Mel Gibson), a former pastor, and like all of M. Night Shyamalan's films, it features an unexpected twist at the end. Scenes from the film may be used in connection with a variety of subjects:

(1) The audience learns that Graham's vocational crisis was a result of his wife's tragic death in an auto accident. As she lay dying, she tells him that it was "meant to be" (DVD ch. 19). This scene concisely introduces the clas-sic problem of theodicy: Why do bad things happen to good people? How can apparently senseless suffering occur if the universe is under the watch of an all-loving, omnipotent deity? How would various biblical writers (e.g., Proverbs, Job, Ecclesiastes, the Deuteronomistic Historian) evaluate Graham's

response (when his son is in grave danger of dying, he cries out, "Don't do this to me again. Not again. I hate you!")?

(2) The death of Graham's wife is told in a flashback, which introduces the final seven-minute scene of the film (DVD ch. 19). The surprise ending, tying together as it does a number of seemingly unrelated plot elements, raises the question of divine providence. When Paul writes in Rom 8:28 that "all things work together for good for those who love God, to those who are called according to his purpose," what exactly does he think this might entail? Would he say that the film's denouement is an example of this theological principle at work? Since Graham is shown returning to the ministry in the closing frame, is it at all appropriate to regard it as a "biblical" or "Christian" film?

(3) Giant crop circles are the "signs" to which the movie's title refers, but their simultaneous appearance around the globe leads to a conversation between Graham and his brother about signs in the Johannine sense, that is, miracles (DVD ch. 10). "People break down into two groups when they experience something lucky," Graham states. "Group number one sees it as … a sign, evidence, that there is someone up there, watching out for them. Group number two sees it as just pure luck.… What you have to ask yourself is what kind of person are you? Are you the kind that sees signs, sees miracles? Or do you believe that people just get lucky?" This dialogue could be connected to the biblical concept of providence, but it also opens a point of entry for other discussions:

(a) What is the nature of faith? Do the New Testament authors present it as something that one either has or does not have? Do they conceive of humanity as being divided into two such groups? Can a person desire or decide to have faith who does not already have it (cf. the cry of the father in Mark 9:24: "Lord, I believe; help thou my unbelief!")? Is faith "belief that" certain propositions are true? Is it a matter of trust or "belief in" God or Jesus? Or is the difference between these two conceptions not so great? When Paul commends the faith of Abraham in Rom 4, on what aspect does he focus? When James asserts the need for works in addition to faith, what understanding of faith is he addressing?

(b) What is a miracle? Is it accurate to characterize a miracle as a violation of the ordinary laws of nature? According to biblical writers, why do they occur? What do they mean? What do they prove in the mind of the authors who record them? Frequently one encounters the tendency to assume that ancient readers were utterly credulous when confronted with reports of the miraculous. The conclusion of Matthew's Gospel contains a detail that problematizes such an assumption. As the disciples are gathered to receive the Great Commission from the resurrected Jesus, Matthew writes that "some doubted" (28:17). Who were "they" and what did they doubt? Did they doubt that this was indeed Jesus, risen from the dead? Did they doubt that the resurrection possessed the significance claimed by the early Christians? It is odd that the author would present some of Jesus' closest followers as doubting even when given such a seemingly clear sign, but that is precisely what Matthew does. If the resurrection had probative value, what did it prove, and to whom?

(c) What is the purpose of the Fourth Gospel? John always uses "signs" (*semeia*) for Jesus' marvelous deeds rather than other available synonyms for "miracle." In John 20:30–31, the author states his purpose for writing, saying that Jesus had done many other signs that have not been recounted, but "these are written so that you may come to believe that Jesus is the Messiah" (NRSV). Some textual variants give a slightly different meaning on the basis of the verb tense: "these are written so that you may continue to believe." So which is it? Does the author anticipate that the recorded miracles will persuade the unbeliever to come into the fold of the faithful? Or is the purpose to strengthen the faith of those already in the fold?

Sling Blade (1996)

This film is one of many for use in discussions of cinematic Christ-figures. (The background for this exercise is found in the entry for *Fight Club* on pp. 140–42.) The question may be put to students this way: In what sense, if any, is it appropriate to consider the protagonist a Christ-figure? What specific traits, deeds, quotations, or plot devices lead the viewer to apply this label? Here, Karl (Billy Bob Thornton) is a mentally retarded man who has spent most of his adult life in a psychiatric hospital after murdering his mother and her lover. But he also exhibits many qualities that parallel those of Jesus: He was born in a shed. He is humble and powerless. He participates in table fellowship with those who have been ostracized by the larger community. He carries with him a Bible and a book on carpentry. He spends a lot of time in quiet contemplation. In the film's climax, he willingly accepts punishment for an act of violent revenge (like the Christ in Rev 14:14–20—thus, Karl is a reminder that, if one takes into account the entire New Testament canon, Jesus is an ambiguous figure). How should we evaluate this character? Are the similarities significant? Are they sufficiently detailed to warrant comparison with Jesus? What differences militate against a serious comparison?

For further discussion, see Mark Roncace, "Paradoxical Protagonists: *Sling Blade*'s Karl and Jesus Christ," in Aichele and Walsh, *Screening Scripture*, 279–300.

Spartacus (1960)

The Roman slave revolt that began in 73 B.C.E. inspired Howard Fast's 1952 novel *Spartacus*, which became the basis for this blockbuster directed by Stanley Kubrick and starring Kirk Douglas. The closing scenes (DVD chs. 38–39, 45) provide an opportunity to highlight two points of intersection between the New Testament and its Roman sociopolitical context: (1) When the revolt is quashed, Spartacus dies by crucifixion, which alerts students to the fact that Jesus' manner of death was not unique to him. It was typically reserved for slaves and for those found guilty of crimes against the state, such as treason. What, if anything, might this suggest about the reasons behind Jesus' death under Pontius Pilate? It was also the most despicable way to die, which makes Paul's summary of his gospel message as "Christ crucified" (1 Cor 1:18–25; cf. Gal 3:13) all the more remarkable. (2) Spartacus is crucified together with six thousand slaves along a 130–mile stretch of the Appian Way between Rome and Capua. (Try to imagine taking a two-hour trip by car, with every second or so bringing a new crucifixion into view.) It is easy to guess that the idea of deterrence lay behind such a spectacle, and, although the inclusion of Spartacus among those executed is likely unhistorical, the harsh punishment accurately suggests the degree to which Roman society could not function without the institution of slavery. These considerations are especially pertinent to Paul's Letter to Philemon concerning a runaway slave. Many readers wonder why Paul refrains from condemning slavery when, apparently, he has an occasion to do so (cf. 1 Cor 7:20–24; and the household codes at Eph 6:5–9; Col 3:22–4:1; 1 Tim 6:1–2; Tit 2:9–10; 1 Pet 2:18–19). It comes as a surprise to hear that opposition to slavery on general moral principle is exceedingly rare in the ancient world—a fact obscured by the anachronistic abolitionist motives the screenwriter puts in Spartacus's mouth. These factors remind students to attend to genre; much of the New Testament consists of occasional writings, and the process of deriving moral or theological norms from its contents is sometimes not as simple as it may appear.

Stigmata (1999)

Stigmata tells the story of a young woman named Frankie (Patricia Arquette) who, though an atheist, becomes possessed by the spirit of a dead priest who wants the existence of a new Gospel—containing the authentic words of Jesus—to be revealed to humankind. Because of the powerful secret she harbors, Frankie is under attack by a demon who oppresses only the holiest and most devout of saints with the stigmata, the five wounds of Christ. With the help of a sympathetic priest sent from Rome to investigate her case (Gabriel Byrne), Frankie learns that there are dozens of ancient Gospels in addition to the four canonical ones, but that the Roman Catholic Church has systematically suppressed them because of their revolutionary implications.

This film is one of several recent Hollywood movies that explore the idea that traditional Christian accounts of God, humanity, and salvation might simply be wrong. According to *Stigmata*, the truth about Jesus is contained not in the church-sanctioned Bible but in a document that has been maligned and censored by cynical religious authorities. Of course, in real life there is a *Gospel of Thomas* that may even contain some authentic sayings of Jesus, but it is hardly considered by most scholars to be the closest of the Gospels to the historical Jesus; nor has it been covered up by the Vatican. Students are quite amused to know, given how dangerous a document is the *Gospel of Thomas* according to the film, that it is readily available online and in stores.

Stigmata can work quite well in the biblical studies classroom because it still cites the text more or less accurately and it presents an authentic struggle in ancient Christianity recast as a modern dilemma. Where does one find the Kingdom of God? The line in the film, repeated at various points, is "The Kingdom of God is inside/within you (and all about you), not in buildings/mansions of wood and stone. (When I am gone) Split a piece of wood and I am there, lift the/a stone and you will find me." The line is a combination of *Gos. Thom.* 3a and 77b. (There are also echoes of Stephen's words in Acts 7:48: "the Most High does not dwell in houses made with hands.")

A fruitful line of discussion in the classroom would be to ask for responses to its female, atheist Christ-figure. It is perhaps the only Hollywood movie to have such a figure, and what is still remarkable is that *Stigmata* generated virtually no controversy at its release. A second line of discussion might be the nature of spirituality asserted by the movie as, well, more "spiritual" than "religious." *Stigmata* hinges upon a paranoid and caricatured interpretation of the Vatican (as does *The Da Vinci Code*). But it also puts forward a version of Christianity fairly well suited to American young people disillusioned by institutionalized religion and seeking an alternative.

Two scenes work particularly well in class: one inside the Vatican where the *Gospel of Thomas* is introduced as a supposedly subversive document (DVD ch. 18), as well as the final scenes where exorcists attempt to free Frankie from her possession, but the words from *Thomas* are repeated again and again. Just showing these scenes in isolation, however, requires some setup for students who have not seen the film, so it is best to assign the movie outside class time and then to follow up with the final scenes. The film ends with the ominous notice:

> In 1945 a scroll was discovered in Nag Hamadi, which is described as "The Secret Sayings of the Living Jesus." This scroll, the *Gospel of St. Thomas*, has been claimed by scholars around the world to be the closest record we have of the words of the historical Jesus. The Vatican refuses to recognize this Gospel and has described it as heresy.

It is baffling how a film could use the *Gospel of Thomas* as its central theme but then get the details of the text so wrong: it was found at Nag Hammadi, not Nag Hamadi, which is in Egypt, not in Israel (where the film places the cave where it was discovered); it formed part of a codex, not a scroll; and it was written in Coptic, not in Aramaic. What is the point of including the Gospel at all if one is going to be careless with the little details? Are the mistakes the result of mere carelessness? Or are the discrepancies intentional? If intentional, what is the desired effect of the changes?

Touch (1997)

Touch's screenplay is by Paul Schrader, a self-confessed Calvinist who also wrote the screenplay for Scorsese's *Last Temptation of Christ*. Juvenal (Skeet Ulrich) is a strange fellow. He is young, cute, disarming—and a miracle worker. He quickly catches the eye of a Christian promoter and impresario, Bill Hill (Christopher Walken). When Hill dispatches his friend Lynn (Bridget Fonda) to capitalize on Juvenal's healing talents, the two fall in love.

Juvenal is a bit like Francis of Assisi—he has that gentle air, and he, too, suffers the stigmata. As a Jesus-figure, Juvenal breaks the mold, if only because he is not celibate. Students have been moderately shocked by this young Jesus who swears and who sleeps with a woman. The scene is not that graphic; it is just that Jesus-figures never get romantically involved because if they do, they lose their superpowers—look at Superman, after all. The same thing happens here: Juvenal loses his ability to work miracles. (For general background to discussions of cinematic Christ-figures, see the entry for *Fight Club* on pp. 140–42.)

Touch is really about the hypocrisy of organized religion versus the more freewheeling, charismatic impulse we see in Juvenal. Like Jesus in the Gospels, Juvenal is surrounded by people who are out to get from him what they can. Hill is a charlatan. Tom Arnold (over)plays August, a goofily militant Catholic fundamentalist who heads up an organization called OUTRAGE, the Organization Unifying Traditional Rites As God Expects. These are caricatures, but nevertheless their shallowness is often grating and the pokes at fundamentalism come off as a series of cheap shots that go on too long. But August and Hill are foils for the sweetness and sincerity of Juvenal, to whom many contemporary college students might relate and to whom the movie points as the ideal of a humane, engaged, and faithful servant of God.

Students are often asked their impressions of Jesus and Christianity in general at the outset of a New Testament course. Many of their impressions of how Jesus "was" tend to be normative (i.e., he was gentle, he worked miracles, he healed, and so on) just as, often, students evince a wariness of "institutionalized" religion or the way in which people, historically, have twisted Jesus' "original" words and actions in a way that is self-serving or removed from Jesus' original intent. Both themes come through loud and clear in *Touch*. Students might then be asked, after viewing the movie, to write a brief reflection piece on the Christology of *Touch*. Do they like this Jesus? Does he resonate with them? Is Juvenal true to the Gospel depiction of Jesus? If so, which one? If not, from where did this image of Jesus come?

Unforgiven (1992)

This dark western contains characters and scenes well suited to the discussion of signature Pauline themes in Romans, albeit with key variations. When a cowboy who has horribly slashed the face of a town prostitute gets off with a slap on the wrist, the victim's friends offer a bounty to anyone who will kill him. Enter William Munny (Clint Eastwood), once an outlaw but now a law-abiding widower and struggling farmer. To pay the bills, he reluctantly agrees to do the job along with his old partner Ned Logan and the Schofield Kid. In a conversation after the job is done, the Kid, visibly shaken, reveals that this killing was his first (DVD ch. 27). "Hell of a thing, killin' a man," says Munny. "Take away all he's got and all he's ever gonna have." "I guess he had it comin'," the Kid replies, echoing a line heard at several points in the film. Munny's response brings to the surface the story's dominant theological undercurrent: "We all got it comin', kid."

Do we, in fact, "all got it comin'"? If so, why, or in what sense? Would the line work as a dynamic equivalent of Rom 3:23: "All have sinned and fall short of the glory of God"? Some see Munny's line as a summary of the doctrine of original sin, more closely associated with Rom 5:12. Is Munny saying that all humans are guilty of some sin? (The sadistic sheriff Little Bill Daggett would concur. When a witness accuses him of beating an innocent man, he responds, "Innocent? Innocent of what?") "It" is punishment for our crimes—but when will "it" come? There appears to be no prospect of postmortem retribution if, as Munny says, death takes it all away now and forever. Is Munny's point, rather, that as sinners we all deserve "it," even if we are never caught for the crimes we have committed? (The film's ending suggests that he is finally able to escape his violent past, while Logan ends up being tortured and killed by Daggett for a crime he did not commit. Daggett later tells Munny that he does not deserve to die, to which Munny replies, "Deserve's got nothin' to do with it.") In some sense, while the protagonist acts like a Stoic, the film's perspective provides a counterpoint to that found in works like Seneca's *De providentia*: Why do bad things happen to good people? They do not, says Seneca, because what we consider bad is not actually bad. Munny likewise suggests that they do not, but for the reason that there are no "good people" to whom bad things happen.

Whereas the film makes no such effort, one of Paul's aims in Romans is to explain how humans have gotten themselves into this existential predicament and how they may escape it. Follow-up discussion or a writing assignment may ask students to examine texts from Paul's Jewish milieu that identify various sources for the human tendency toward sin (e.g., Eve, Satan, or an "evil heart": Sir 25:24; Wis 2:23–24; *4 Ezra* 3:20–27; 4:30; 7:116–118).

F
I
L
M

PART 3:
ART

Gardner, that human beings possess a variety of modes of learning or "intelligences."

The use of art in the classroom also acknowledges the role that the visual plays in our daily lives. We are, perhaps more than ever, surrounded and inundated by images, a reality facilitated by developing technologies. Reflecting the pervasiveness of the image in the larger culture, students increasingly arrive in our classrooms with at least a rudimentary sense of the visual arts. Although some of our students lack an acquaintance with such things, many arrive with a curiosity about art museums and the strange and wonderful objects they hold. Moreover, many students have been exposed to a culture of learning in their secondary education in which images and the visual are used to enhance the learning environment. Our use of the visual in our classrooms responds to these sensibilities and curiosities.

Our students' "visual" inclinations, however, do not necessarily mean they know how to engage the visual within an educational context. Thus, in one sense we are simply meeting our students halfway, that is, starting with the visual and then refining their sense of what it means to "see." Moreover, to return to John's Gospel again, the importance of learning to see cannot be underestimated, for it is the sensory modality most closely associated with knowing, particularly in our own increasingly visual culture. This phenomenon is neither recent nor limited to the twentieth and twenty-first centuries. Indeed, we might say that from time immemorial, seeing and its relationship to knowing has been a central component of human self-consciousness and pedagogy. Simply put, our students live in a world in which the visual is central. If we fail to take account of this reality, we not only miss an opportunity to educate "the whole person," but we also ignore one of the most important avenues through which our students learn.

Thus far we have used the terms "visual," "art," and "image" in an interrelated, almost synonymous manner. It might be helpful to parse these terms a bit more and in the process articulate what we mean when we talk about "art." In using the phrase "visual art" we refer broadly to a work or an object, usually created by a human agent, that is primarily intended to be perceived or experienced through the faculty of sight. This broad definition allows for the inclusion of a range of objects or

Gardner, that attending to multiple intelligences enhances student learning and the retention of ideas and skills.[1]

Second, in an age of biblical fundamentalism (an interpretive perspective adopted by both "conservatives" and "liberals"), students have to be prodded to see the possibility of multiple interpretations in texts, especially texts that many hold as sacred. Most students have been better trained to think that "beauty is in the eye of the beholder," which assumes that an interpreter's perspective shapes her interaction with a piece of art, than to recognize the same phenomenon exists when approaching a written text. One hopes that their recognition that a Picasso or Matisse yields many interpretive possibilities dependent upon the "eye of the beholder" will be translated to the prophets and the Gospels when we address the visual and the textual side by side.

Third, even when we as teachers do not incorporate the visual into our classrooms, it is present in our students' minds. Regardless of their religious upbringings, as products of Western culture, our students carry with them images related to the writings we explore, including mental pictures of Jesus shaped by the memory of Jim Caviezel playing Jesus in Mel Gibson's *The Passion of the Christ* and visions of God colored by Michelangelo's depiction on the ceiling of the Sistine Chapel. Many students come to class "knowing" exactly what these figures look like and how they act in certain situations. Such "knowledge" often negates genuine, open interaction with the text. Intentionally incorporating the visual into our classrooms sheds light on these culturally given images, allowing both students and instructors to be more critical of how we use mental images to fill in textual gaps. The use of images, therefore, can disrupt students' mental images, encourage them to develop more complex mental pictures, and prepare them for the multivocality of the text.

In addition, attention to the visual requires students to think metaphorically, abstractly, and in other nonliteral ways. These ways of "seeing" are similar to the forms of perception employed in religion and religious texts.[2] Religious discourse, including biblical writings, swells with metaphor and imagery. Students, often pressed into a literal reading of textbooks, are sometimes hesitant to engage fully the metaphors and images presented in the Bible. Examining visual art, including abstract art, can help students think in abstract and metaphorical terms.

---

1. For a brief discussion of artistic intelligence in relation to the theory of multiple intelligences, see Howard Gardner, "Artistic Intelligence," *Art Education* 36 (1983): 47–49.

2. Margaret R. Miles, *Image as Insight: Visual Understanding in Western Christianity and Secular Culture* (Boston: Beacon, 1985), 4.

CATEGORIES FOR EMPLOYING ART IN THE CLASSROOM

There are a variety of ways that art can be used in a biblical studies class; here we will outline three general approaches: (1) art as illustration; (2) art as narrative interpretation; (3) art as illumination. These three fluid categories are borrowed from the work of Katharine Martinez on the use of images in the field of American history.[3] This is a subject that, like ours, has been historically beholden to the textual, and so Martinez's categories are easily adaptable to our work.

ART AS ILLUSTRATION

Using visual art as an illustration of a particular point or idea about a text or tradition is the most basic approach to employing the visual in the classroom. An image can be employed to underscore a specific interpretation or to help students recognize something about the text that they might otherwise overlook. For example, if we wanted to have students remember the observation made at the beginning of this chapter—that John's Gospel is as much about the visual as it is about the verbal—we might show students an image of a twelfth-century manuscript in which the words of the first chapter of John are printed in the form of a cross.[4] Similarly, a teacher may want to emphasize that in the nativity stories, especially Luke's annunciation scene, the designation "virgin" implies a young girl. However, students sometimes have difficulty grasping that within Luke's social context an unmarried girl was truly a girl and not a young woman. To help them appreciate this, one might show an image that highlights Mary's youth, such as *The Annunciation*, by Jennifer Linton, which depicts Mary as a pubescent girl lying on the ground with her head propped on her arm.[5] Even though Linton's image places the story of the annunciation in a contemporary context, it allows students to analyze the text in relation to its historical context and invites students to see something about the text that they might have overlooked or misunderstood.

A
R
T

---

3. Katharine Martinez, "Imaging the Past: Historians, Visual Images and the Contested Definition of History," *Visual Resources* 11 (1995): 21–45.

4. "Gospel of St. John," *Gospel Lectionary*, twelfth century. British Library, London. Cited 13 March 2007. Online: www.imagesonline.bl.uk/britishlibrary/controller/textsearch?text=john%20cross&&idx=1&startid=13401.

5. Jennifer Linton, *The Annunciation*, 2002. Collection of the Artist, Toronto. Cited 13 March 2007. Online: www.jenniferlinton.ca.

ART

ART AS NARRATIVE INTERPRETATION

While images can be utilized to illustrate texts, works of visual art often involve more complex relationships between text and image than the illustrative model allows. In fact, simply treating visual art in terms of textual illustration runs the risk of replicating a problematic assumption that has historically plagued textually focused fields of study—that images are somehow easier to comprehend or less complex than written texts. We might describe this as the legacy of Gregory the Great and his infamous claim (in *Ep.* 105 of book 9) that church art was primarily to teach the unlearned masses what they were unable to read in the text.[6] Implied in this assertion is an assumption that images are readily understandable even when an audience has little or no resources for interpreting images. Despite Gregory's claim, images are not necessarily easier to understand than texts and they require their own sort of "reading."[7] In a way similar to how we make sense of a psalm or a Pauline letter, we make sense of images by interpreting the signs within the image in relation to certain concepts and ideas, within a certain contextual frame. This approach can involve having students read images explicitly framed as narrative interpretations of biblical texts or reframing nonbiblical images in relationship to a specific document or pericope.

For example, Marc Chagall's *Creation of Man* is an interpretation of Gen 1:26–27 ("Let us make humankind in our image…").[8] Chagall renders this verse by depicting a winged, human-like creature holding the limp body of a man in its arms. This winged creature occupies the center of the canvas, which is painted primarily in shades of blue, while in the upper right-hand corner rainbow colors spiral out of a red orb. Intermingled with the spiraling colors are various images, including a ram-headed person carrying a scroll, a crucifix, a praying figure, another angelic being, and hands holding tablets.

When presented with an image such as this, students should first describe what they see. What are the elements of art in the image? Lines, colors, composition? Then students may ponder how what they see reads the text: What does it capture from the text? What does it highlight? What does it downplay? Specifically, one might ask students what the red globe might represent. Something from the text? Why does it have these attendant

---

6. While Gregory's claim may appear to be disparaging toward art, it was part of his defense against the destruction of icons or images.

7. Mieke Bal, "Reading Art?" in *Generations and Geographies in the Visual Arts: Feminist Readings* (ed. G. Pollock; London: Routledge, 1996), 25–41, esp. 32.

8. Marc Chagall, *The Creation of Man*, 1956–58. Musée National Message Biblique Marc Chagall, Nice. Cited 27 March 2007. Online: www.musee-chagall.fr.

images—a crucifix, angels, animals? This method of reading the image parallels the method of reading texts in which we look first at its component parts—the words, grammar, syntax, structure, imagery—before addressing its meaning(s).[9]

Chagall's painting shows us, moreover, the complex ways in which an image reads a text. With its allusions to the giving of the Mosaic Law suggested by the tablets, to the crucifixion, and to cultural gender roles (through an image of a bride and groom), Chagall's painting rings with many of the same intertextual allusions and echoes that are often brought by interpreters to the text of Genesis. In this way, the painting does not "solve," but rather highlights, the interpretive challenges. The depiction of an angel holding the body of the man, for example, does little to explain Genesis' use of the plural, "Let us make humankind/Adam in our image." Is this Chagall's depiction of God? Or, could this winged figure be a co-creator implied in the plural pronouns? Chagall's painting, indeed, is as multilayered and complex as Gen 1.

One issue to be aware of is that the language of images, just as the language of biblical texts, is not universal.[10] The meanings of the various elements that comprise a particular piece of visual art may need to be translated into a language understandable by students. For example, in Chagall's painting, students may not recognize the stone tablets as a visual sign of the Decalogue, unless, of course they have seen Charleston Heston in *The Ten Commandments* (to use one image as a cipher for translating another)! Leading students through a piece of art often requires helping them translate the unfamiliar and ambiguous.

With images that are explicitly framed as biblical interpretations, it can be illuminating to show more than one image interpreting the same text as a way of highlighting how texts yield multiple meanings. For instance, alongside Chagall's twentieth-century version of the sixth day of creation, one might have students view a medieval manuscript that illustrates the same text. Juxtaposing different images, especially ones from different time periods, allows students to see the various ways a single text can be imagined and understood. This can also be used to help students see the diachronic development of interpretations in the Western tradition in general.[11] More-

A
R
T

---

9. For a useful guide in thinking about what to look for in a piece of art, see Steven Engler and Irene Naested, "Reading Images in the Religious Studies Classroom," *Teaching Theology and Religion* 5 (2002): 161–68.

10. Miles, *Image as Insight*, 29–34.

11. For a discussion of how art can be used to discuss the history of a biblical text's interpretation, see Robin M. Jensen, *The Substance of Things Seen: Art, Faith, and the Christian Community* (Grand Rapids: Eerdmans, 2004), 34–45.

over, the use of images from different historical, social, and cultural settings demonstrates how textual interpretations are shaped by contextual concerns, issues, and questions. This, in turn, can allow us to talk with students about how their own locations similarly shape the interpretive grids that they bring to the biblical texts.

Besides paintings that explicitly frame themselves as biblical interpretations, we find it particularly enriching to reframe images depicting subjects other than biblical ones, encouraging students to read these images in relation to particular biblical texts.[12] Often images that are explicitly biblical replicate the ideological assumptions communicated through the texts, while images of other subjects, reframed in relation to the Bible, challenge those ideological presuppositions.

For example, read in relationship to 1 Corinthians, Robert Mapplethorpe's 1982 black-and-white photograph of body builder Lisa Lyon, simply entitled *Lisa Lyon*, provides a provocative starting point for a critical discussion of Paul's comments regarding women's roles in worship, specifically his suggestion that women who pray and prophesy in the religious assembly be veiled.[13] The portrait displays the female body builder from the waist up. Her right arm is flexed and her left hand pushes her right wrist for resistance. Lyon wears a black leather bustier and a black hat with a sheer black veil. Through the veil, the audience can see a stoic Lyon. Admittedly, the veil that Lyon wears is different from veils worn in the ancient world; however, the image allows students to think about some of the implications involved with veiling. In particular, Lyon's posture of power, as suggested in her flexed arm, prompts students to read 1 Cor 11:2–16 (concerning the veiling of women who prophesy) as a text about power and limiting power. One might ask them to imagine that this portrait of Lyon represents women in Paul's congregation: Does she represent the women Paul hopes to address in his letter or does Lyon embody the women in the congregation after they have received the letter? If students suggest the former, we might encourage them to use elements from the image to explain why they think Paul felt the need to address these women. If students suggest the latter, then have them imagine how Lyon's image functions as a response to Paul. In particular, what does this portrait suggest about how Paul's audience might have responded to his assertion that women ought to be veiled? Among other things, this image allows students to imagine that Paul's view may have met with various responses among the women in the

---

12. See Bal, "Reading Art?" 27–28, for a discussion of framing and reframing.

13. Robert Mapplethorpe, *Lisa Lyon*, 1982. Reproduced in *Robert Mapplethorpe and the Classical Tradition* (ed. G. Celant et al.; New York: Guggenheim Museum, 2004), pl. 75.

Corinthian community. It suggests the possibility, for instance, that women remained powerful even under the veil.

ART AS ILLUMINATION

Martinez identifies as a final pedagogical approach using art as illumination, which entails making connections between different subjects with and through visual art, employing artistic pieces to make one's way through complex ideas. Abstract art can be a helpful avenue into many of the topics that arise in the examination of biblical texts, including issues of hermeneutics and the creation and function of texts. While abstract art is sometimes understood as nondenotative or nonrepresentational, works of art typically recognized as abstract still show patterns, feelings, and ideas.

Using pieces of abstract art in the biblical studies context involves metaphorical thinking, using the visual experience to consider an idea or feeling. Because these pieces are typically open-ended, they can serve as conversation partners for understanding a variety of difficult concepts.[14] For instance, it can be challenging for students to grasp that their view of a particular writing is filtered through layers of interpretive tradition. It can be even more difficult for them to understand that many of the biblical writings began as oral traditions that have been shaped to fit into written narratives, adding to the interpretive layers surrounding a particular story. An image such as Paul Klee's *Around the Core*, a painting that consists of a spiraling line and layers of color around a small drop-like center, provides a path into these issues with students. Students can be asked to imagine the line as a textual tradition which develops around the "kernel" of an oral tradition or they might be prompted to think about the colors of the painting as overlapping traditions.[15]

In addition, as teachers of biblical subjects, we often find ourselves addressing topics of ethical, political, and social importance. Our subject matter necessarily raises discussions of class, ethnic identity, peace and war, sexuality, and family relationships. Given the cultural importance of the biblical texts in these discussions and students' differing relationships to these texts, at times it is helpful to offer a "neutral" text or image to begin these often polarizing conversations. As Robin Jensen points out, visual art potentially serves a prophetic function, illuminating "individual and communal

A
R
T

---

14. Douglas Adams and Diane Apostolos-Cappadona, "Art as Religious Studies: Insights into the Judeo-Christian Traditions," in *Art as Religious Studies* (ed. D. Adams and D. Apostolos-Cappadona; Eugene: Wipf & Stock, 1987), 3–11, esp. 8.

15. See the discussion of Klee's work in this volume on pp. 230–31.

evil."[16] Art, such as Mary Lovelace O'Neal's abstract lithograph *Racism Is Like Rain, Either It's Raining or It's Gathering*, challenges the viewer to imagine how racism functions and how it might be challenged.[17] Using a piece of art to discuss topics such as racism or poverty, before turning to the biblical texts, helps students see the historical and contemporary reality of such problems and allows them to reflect on their understanding of the issues before considering the way in which they are addressed in biblical texts. Ideally, this has the effect of making some students less defensive when studying the Bible critically and other students more aware of how these ancient texts might have contemporary relevance.

TEACHING STUDENTS TO READ AND THINK THROUGH IMAGES

Successfully employing visual art in the classroom requires teaching students how to read and think through images in a careful and critical fashion. Sometimes we assume that they will be better equipped to interpret images or visual art than texts, since students have been raised in a world in which they are bombarded with images. However, it is problematic to equate exposure to the visual with an ability to navigate critically the complexities inherent in a piece of visual art. In fact, the need to teach students how to read biblical texts is paralleled by the need to teach students how to read visual texts. Furthermore, students must be taught to take time with art, not to just look at a piece, but to really *see* a piece. As Douglas Adams and Diane Apostolos-Cappadona have observed, the learned discipline of seeing means that viewers allows a piece of art to engage, challenge, and even transform them.[18]

There are a variety of ways to encourage students to become more careful readers of images. For example, students can study images outside of class in conjunction with the texts they read for class. Course websites and blogs make this relatively easy, since an instructor can gather images electronically for students to view. It is also interesting to have students find and share relevant images. In our own classrooms, students have submitted images ranging from Adam and Eve for an Altoids advertisement to a *Rolling Stone* photograph of Madonna, taken by David LaChapelle, which can be read as an allusion to Revelation's Great Prostitute. This approach allows students to gather images and analyze them on their own. In addition, it can help instructors build their own image collections.

---

16. Jensen, *The Substance of Things Seen*, 97.
17. See the discussion of this piece in this volume on pp. 233–34.
18. Adams and Apostolos-Cappadona, "Art as Religious Studies," 4–5.

To help students read images, especially ones that involve the interpretation of biblical texts, it can be advantageous to provide a guideline for them to follow. First, encourage students to take time to look carefully at an image. This may seem obvious; however, students tend to turn quickly to the question of what an image means. Second, have students describe the artistic elements within the image. It may be necessary to provide them with the requisite vocabulary (color, line, texture, balance, etc.) and a set of explicit questions to consider: What media are used to create the image? What lines, shapes, textures, colors, and patterns do you see? Do the lines and shapes of the image suggest movement? How does the image use space? Is there negative space? Or, is the piece completely "full"? Is the piece monochromatic?

Third, prompt students to read the image either alone or in relation to a particular text. For instance, ask them to talk about what the text "says" and how it "says" it. If they are reading an image in relation to a text, ask them to describe what parts of the text the image captures and what parts it seems to ignore. Finally, students should be given the opportunity to communicate their own opinions about the piece. Given the deliberate nature of the process, the opinions they articulate are, one hopes, grounded in their observations of the image rather than their initial impressions.

Making art an integral part of the classroom requires a number of commitments on behalf of the teacher. First, it takes time to find pieces that provoke us and speak to us. While images are becoming easier to access through electronic resources, developing a collection of high-quality images still is labor intensive. Image databases, such as ARTstor (a nonprofit digital library sponsored by The Andrew W. Mellon Foundation) and CAMIO (a nonprofit database sustained by OCLC—the Online Computer Library Center), allow instructors and students at subscribing institutions access to thousands of images for instructional purposes.[19] Thankfully, these electronic resources make it possible for instructors to use copyrighted images legally, which is a growing concern in the digital age. Also, we recommend using images that captivate or challenge you as a teacher; this makes it much easier to help students engage with the piece. Second, it takes a certain willingness to consider different types of art. If all of our images are medieval manuscripts or renaissance paintings, they lose their power to provoke students to look for the different ways texts and images function and communicate. We need to look in unexpected places, among the self-taught artists, conceptual artists,

---

19. ARTstor (www.artstor.org) provides access to over 500,000 digital images, including artistic works and images of material culture, and CAMIO (www.oclc.org/camio/default.htm) provides access to over 90,000 images. Most museum websites have online collections that are searchable by artist's last name or by title.

and photographers. Artists, especially modern and contemporary ones, often challenge commonly held ideologies and theological assumptions. Before we bring these types of images into the classroom, we have to consider whether we are ready for those challenges.[20]

BIBLIOGRAPHY

Adams, Douglas, and Diane Apostolos-Cappadona. *Art as Religious Studies.* Eugene: Wipf & Stock, 1987.

Apostolos-Cappadona, Diane. *Dictionary of Christian Art.* New York: Continuum, 1998.

Bal, Mieke. "Reading Art?" Pages 25–41 in *Generations and Geographies in the Visual Arts: Feminist Readings.* Edited by G. Pollock. London: Routledge, 1996.

Blessing, Jennifer. "Cindy Sherman." No pages. Cited 7 March 2007. Online: www.guggenheimcollection.org/site/artist_work_md_146F_3.html.

Boime, Albert. "Henry Ossawa Tanner's Subversion of Genre." *Art Bulletin* 75 (1993): 415–42.

Carey, Frances. *The Apocalypse and the Shape of Things to Come.* London: British Museum Press, 1999.

Cartilidge, David R. *Art and the Christian Apocrypha.* London: Routledge, 2001.

Celant, Germano, et al., eds. *Robert Mapplethorpe and the Classical Tradition.* New York: Guggenheim Museum, 2004.

Crown, Carol, ed. *Coming Home! Self-Taught Artists, the Bible, and the American South.* Jackson: University Press of Mississippi, 2004.

———. *Wonders to Behold: The Visionary Art of Myrtice West.* Memphis: Mustang, 1999.

De Borchgrave, Helen. *A Journey into Christian Art.* Oxford: Lion Hudson, 2001.

De Capoa, Chiara. *Old Testament Figures in Art.* Translated by Thomas Michael Hartmann. Los Angeles: J. Paul Getty Museum, 2003.

Drury, John. *Painting the Word: Christian Pictures and Their Meanings.* New Haven: Yale University Press, 1999.

A
R
T

---

20. In addition to items catalogued in this chapter, Roncace and Gray, *Teaching the Bible*, contains other strategies using art: see Daniel E. Goodman, "*Guernica* and the Art of Biblical Hermeneutics," 5–6; Sandie Gravett, "Genesis 22: Artists' Renderings," 97–98; Lynn R. Huber, "Introducing Revelation through the Visual Arts," 398–400; and Jaime Clark-Soles, "Christology Slideshow," 282–84.

Du Bourguet, Pierre. *Early Christian Painting*. Translated by Simon Watson Taylor. New York: Viking, 1965.

Engler, Steven, and Irene Naested. "Reading Images in the Religious Studies Classroom." *Teaching Theology and Religion* 5 (2002): 161–68.

Fagaly, William A. *Tools of Her Ministry: The Art of Sister Gertrude Morgan*. New York: American Folk Art Museum, 2004.

Ferguson, George. *Signs and Symbols in Christian Art: With Illustrations from the Paintings of the Renaissance*. Oxford: Oxford University Press, 1966.

Fine, Steven. *Art and Judaism in the Greco-Roman World: Toward a New Jewish Archaeology*. Cambridge: Cambridge University Press, 2005.

Gardner, Howard. "Artistic Intelligence." *Art Education* 36 (1983): 47–49.

Giebelhausen, Michaela. *Painting the Bible: Representation and Belief in Mid-Victorian Britain*. London: Ashgate, 2006.

Gitay, Zefira. "Hagar's Expulsion: A Tale Twice-Told in Genesis." Pages 73–91 in *Abraham and Family: New Insights into the Patriarchal Narratives*. Edited by Hershel Shanks. Washington, D.C.: Biblical Archaeology Society, 2000.

Grubb, Nancy. *The Life of Christ in Art*. New York: Abbeville, 1996.

———. *Revelations: Art of the Apocalypse*. New York: Abbeville, 1997.

Holland, Juanita Marie, ed. *Narratives of African American Art and Identity: The David C. Driskell Collection*. San Francisco: Pomegranate, 1998.

Hornik, Heidi J. *Illuminating Luke*. Harrisburg, Pa.: Trinity Press International, 2003.

———, and Mikeal Parsons. "Art." Pages 299–322 in *The Blackwell Companion to the Bible and Culture*. Edited by John F. A. Sawyer. Malden, Mass.: Blackwell, 2006.

Jeansonne, Sharon Pace. *Women of Genesis: From Sarah to Potiphar's Wife*. Minneapolis: Fortress, 1990.

Jensen, Robin M. *Face to Face: Portraits of the Divine in Early Christianity*. Minneapolis: Fortress, 2005.

———. *The Substance of Things Seen: Art, Faith, and the Christian Community*. Grand Rapids: Eerdmans, 2004.

———. *Understanding Early Christian Art*. London: Routledge, 2000.

Kandinsky, Wassily. *Concerning the Spiritual in Art*. Translated by M. T. H. Sadler. London: Tate, 2006.

Kirk-Duggan, Cheryl A. "Let My People Go! Threads of Exodus in African American Narratives." Pages 123–43 in *Yet with a Steady Beat: Contemporary U.S. Afrocentric Biblical Interpretation*. Edited by Randall C. Bailey. Semeia Studies 42. Atlanta: Society of Biblical Literature, 2003.

Lubbock, Jules. *Storytelling in Christian Art from Giotto to Donatello*. New Haven: Yale University Press, 2006.

A
R
T

Martinez, Katharine. "Imaging the Past: Historians, Visual Images and the Contested Definition of History." *Visual Resources* 11 (1995): 21–45.

Mathews, Thomas F. *The Clash of Gods: A Reinterpretation of Early Christian Art*. Princeton: Princeton University Press, 1999.

Meer, Frederik van der. *Apocalypse: Visions from the Book of Revelation in Western Art*. London: Thames & Hudson, 1978.

Meyer, Jerry D. "Profane and Sacred: Religious Imagery and Prophetic Expression in Postmodern Art." *Journal of the American Academy of Religion* 65 (1997): 19–46.

Miles, Margaret. *Image as Insight: Visual Understanding in Western Christianity and Secular Culture*. Boston: Beacon, 1985.

———. *Carnal Knowing: Female Nakedness and Religious Meaning in the Christian West*. Boston: Beacon, 1989.

Milroy, Elizabeth. " 'Consummatum est …': A Reassessment of Thomas Eakins's Crucifixion of 1880." *Art Bulletin* 71 (1989): 269–84.

Morgan, David. *Protestants and Pictures: Religion, Visual Culture, and the Age of American Mass Production*. Oxford: Oxford University Press, 1999.

———. *The Sacred Gaze: Religious Visual Culture in Theory and Practice*. Berkeley and Los Angeles: University of California Press, 2005.

———. *Visual Piety: A History and Theory of Popular Religious Images*. Berkeley and Los Angeles: University of California Press, 1998.

O'Grady, Ron, ed. *Christ for All People: Celebrating a World of Christian Art*. Maryknoll, N.Y.: Orbis, 2001.

Plate, S. Brent, ed. *Religion, Art, and Visual Culture: A Cross Cultural Reader*. New York: Palgrave, 2002.

———. *Walter Benjamin, Religion, and Aesthetics: Rethinking Religion through the Arts*. New York: Routledge, 2005.

Sharper, Philip and Sally, eds. *The Gospel in Art by the Peasants of Solentiname*. Maryknoll, N.Y.: Orbis, 1984.

Sollee, Dorothy, et. al. *Great Women of the Bible in Art and Literature*. Grand Rapids: Eerdmans, 1994.

Steinberg, Leo. *The Sexuality of Christ in Renaissance Art and in Modern Oblivion*. 2nd rev. ed. Chicago: University of Chicago Press, 1997.

Strychasz, Jennifer. "Margo Humphrey, *The Last Bar-B-Que*, 1989." No pages. Cited 14 March 2007. Online: www.artgallery.umd.edu/driskell/index.htm.

Takenaka, Masao, and Ron O'Grady. *The Bible through Asian Eyes*. Auckland: Pace, 1991.

Wright, Susan. *The Bible in Art*. New York: New Line Books, 2005.

Zuffi, Stefano. *Gospel Figures in Art*. Translated by Thomas Michael Hartmann. Los Angeles: The J. Paul Getty Museum, 2003.

BIBLICAL SUBJECTS IN ART

Lynn R. Huber, Dan W. Clanton Jr., and Jane S. Webster

The works discussed in this chapter are organized roughly according to the order in which their subject matter appears in the canon. Due to the impermanent nature of many website addresses, it will frequently be necessary to perform a simple artist or title search at the sites listed with many of these works. The indices may be consulted to find entries with classroom strategies related to particular texts and topics. All secondary literature cited here is included in the preceding bibliography (pp. 184–86).

Domenichino, *Adam and Eve* (1623–25) [Musée des Beaux-Arts, Grenoble; www.artrenewal.org]
This early seventeenth-century oil portrays the encounter between Yahweh and the first humans in Gen 3:8–13. Both humans have eaten of the Tree, and now Yahweh is confronting them about their disobedience. Domenichino renders this scene with a wonderful flourish, as God hovers above the lush landscape with his divine council. On the ground below, we see not only a lion and lamb lying together (perhaps a nod to the idyllic nature of the Garden that is about to be shattered), but also the serpent as it slithers away. The two humans are about to embark on the "blame game" found in 3:11–13. There is obviously a humorous inference here, as Domenichino renders Adam with shrugged shoulders, holding his hands in a gesture of resignation as he motions to Eve as the source of the disobedience. One can almost hear Adam saying, "What am I gonna do with her, eh? Fugedaboutit!" As such, this piece can be used to indicate not only Adam's attempt to blame Eve (which is problematic in light of the Hebrew word *immah* in 3:6), but also to demonstrate the continued attempt to read Gen 2–3 as somehow Eve's fault.

Gustave Doré, *The Deluge* (1865) [www.biblical-art.com]
This image invites students to see the flood story from a different perspective. Many artistic renderings follow the biblical text, which focuses on

the character of Noah and the ark as a vehicle of salvation. Instead of looking at the ark, Doré depicts what one might see looking from the ark out into the rising flood waters. He shows people scrambling up a rock, parents pushing their children to the highest point possible to escape the deluge. A tiger, with a cub in its mouth and others at its feet, is perched atop the rock. The sky is dark, and the crashing waves take the shape of a hand about to swallow the victims. When students are asked what issues this image raises, they typically note that it calls into question God's indiscriminate destruction of the earth. How can the young children, pathetically huddled on the rock before their demise, deserve to die? And what about the animals? Are they also wicked? Indeed, the biblical deity is clear that the flood is intended to destroy animals as well as humans (Gen 6:7). But why? The juxtaposed images of the cubs and the children underscore the death of two groups who seemingly cannot be morally culpable. Moreover, the adults in the image are endeavoring to save the children—that is, they are acting righteously, which, again, raises the question of wholesale annihilation. Can "all flesh" warrant death (6:13)? The image also compels one to imagine the scene awaiting Noah and his family when they exit the ark. There is the rainbow, of course, and a chance at new life, but there would also be the aftermath of the flood—the countless dead bodies of the animals and humans who did not survive. In short, Doré's provision of an alternate point of view invites thought about the image of the deity and the complexity of the flood story.

A
R
T

Guercino, *The Angel Appears to Hagar and Ishmael* (ca. 1652–53) [National Gallery, London; www.nationalgallery.org.uk]

Jean-Baptiste-Camille Corot, *Hagar in the Wilderness* (1835) [Metropolitan Museum of Art, New York; www.metmuseum.org]

Pietro Berrettini da Cortona, *The Return of Hagar* (ca. 1637) [Kunsthistorisches Museum, Vienna; www.khm.at/homeE3.html]

Avi Katz, *The Angel Comforteth Hagar* (late twentieth century) [www.avikatz.net/sf/aliencorn/alienframe.htm]

Guercino, *Abraham Casting Out Hagar and Ishmael* (1657) [Pinacoteca di Brera, Milan; www.wga.hu]

Barent Fabritius, *Hagar and Ishmael* (1658) [Metropolitan Museum of Art, New York; www.metmuseum.org]

Willem Bartsius, *Abraham Pleading with Sarah on Behalf of Hagar* (1631) [J. Paul Getty Museum, Los Angeles; www.biblical-art.com]

The story of Hagar in Gen 16 and 21 is confusing for several reasons. First, readers are not entirely sure how the two chapters relate to one another; that is, should we read them in narrative succession so that chapter 21 follows chapter 16 in the plot, or should we regard chapter 21 as a doublet from a different literary source? Second, the reader is unsure about the identity of Hagar. Is she a slave or a maidservant? Is she Abraham's wife, or merely a surrogate womb for Sarah? Third, it is uncertain how the parties in this triangular relationship and their offspring relate to one another. Is Abraham in love with Hagar? Does he love his son Ishmael? How does Sarah regard Ishmael? Does she treat Hagar brutally or in accordance with the social mores of the time? Alongside these key questions, we can discern the singular importance of Hagar in this narrative: She is the first woman to have a theophanic experience as well as a promise of progeny. She even becomes the only character in the Bible to name God in 16:13 and is the only mother who finds a wife for her son. Even so, ambiguity and perplexity surround Hagar.

Comparatively speaking, there has not been much art with Hagar as its subject. The pieces we do have, though, can serve not only to address the uncertainties of this significant character, but also to help students with them as they see how other biblical interpreters have addressed them in the past.

Regarding the first difficulty, that of the relationship of chapters 16 and 21, artistic renderings of Hagar are admittedly not much help. This is because, as Zefira Gitay has noted, artists have always favored chapter 21 because of the added drama of the danger young Ishmael faces. They can portray the distress of Hagar, the impending death, and timely appearance of the angel. Many of the most famous pieces of Hagar do indeed focus on this peril in the wilderness, such as those by Guercino and Corot. Others, however, focus on chapter 16. In Cortona's work, for example, we see Abraham welcoming Hagar back from the wilderness with open arms while Sarah lurks in the background, looking none too pleased (see the piece by Katz). By juxtaposing these images and asking students to identify the chapter on which the image is based, one can easily begin a conversation addressing narrative and source-critical issues.

Art is far more useful, however, in dealing with the second and third ambiguities. That is, a thoughtful panoply of images can initiate and stimulate fruitful discussions on these matters. A good place to begin is Guercino's 1657 oil. Here we see Abraham facing Hagar and a weeping Ishmael, pointing with his right hand, but holding his left palm up either in a gesture of blessing or one indicating a command of silence. Sarah is shown in the left of the frame, glancing over her right shoulder in what appears to be a dismissive look. The emotion here on Ishmael's part is palpable, but Abraham appears steady as a rock. One can then compare this piece with the one by

Willem Bartsius in which Abraham is tugging at Sarah's robe in an attempt to
persuade her to change her mind about banishing Hagar and Ishmael, while
Isaac looks off of the frame, probably at his brother leaving. Here we see a
much more emotional Abraham who appears to be devastated by the forced
exile of his wife and son. It is crucial for students to understand and identify
with the emotions present in these chapters, because once they become emotionally invested in a narrative, their excitement and advocacy are piqued. In
contrast to the pieces that focus primarily on Abraham, the work of Fabritius
centers on Hagar's reaction to Abraham's decision. She is weeping in his arms,
while a wide-eyed Ishmael looks on. Comparing these images (and others in
this vein) will allow teachers to present variant readings of these characters,
evidence for which can be found in the text. One could then ask students to
identify the passage(s) that could support such a rendering over another, and
once students become involved in working out the mechanics of representation and interpretation, they will be able to formulate their own reading(s) of
the text.

Albrecht Dürer, *Lot and His Daughters* (1496–99) [National Gallery of
Art, Washington, D.C.; www.nga.gov]

Lucas van Leyden, *Lot and His Daughters* (ca. 1520) [The Louvre, Paris;
www.wga.hu]

Albrecht Altdorfer, *Lot and His Daughters* (1537) [Kunsthistorisches
Museum, Vienna; www.artchive.com]

Joachim Wtewael, *Lot and His Daughters* (ca. 1600) [State Hermitage
Museum, St. Petersburg; www.hermitagemuseum.org]

Hendrik Goltzius, *Lot and His Daughters* (1616) [Rijksmuseum, Amsterdam; www.rijksmuseum.nl]

Orazio Gentileschi, *Lot and His Daughters* (ca. 1621–24) [National Gallery of Canada, Ottawa; cybermuse.gallery.ca]

The destruction of Sodom and Gomorrah in Gen 18–19, along with the
story of Lot and his family, has long fascinated interpreters and artists. A
study of various images can help students consider the traits and motivations
of the different characters; it can also help them glimpse how artists pick up
on and perpetuate biblical views on key moral issues, such as sex, alcohol,
and revenge. One can begin with the rather docile treatment of the story by
Albrecht Dürer, which depicts a scene after the destruction of the cities and
the transformation of Lot's wife but prior to the sexual encounter in 19:30–38.
Lot is portrayed as a well-dressed patriarch, and his girls are dutifully fol-

lowing him in their trek. Dürer's work is more interested in the spectacular rendering of the destruction of the cities in the top of the frame than it is in the sexual aspects of the story. In almost all of the pieces that are more focused on the fantastic rain of fire from heaven, one can ask students to play a variant of "Where's Waldo," because Lot's wife is usually present but nearly camouflaged in her new existence as a pillar of salt.

Beginning with Dürer allows instructors to illustrate the near-chronological move away from an interest in the destruction of the cities to a more eroticizing focus on the sexual encounter in later works. A medial position between these two trends is found in the piece by van Leyden, which portrays several events in the story. At the top of the work, we see a colorful burst of devastation, but we also see Lot and his daughters leaving the city with their mother left behind at the right center. Dominating the lower central region is a scene of Lot and his daughters after their journey. One daughter is pouring wine for their father, while the other sits, visibly uncomfortable, with her hands in her lap as Lot begins to embrace her. All the figures are fully clothed, and the viewer may recognize that this is but a preamble to the sexual act not depicted.

After examining the works of Dürer and van Leyden, students can view several pieces that focus almost exclusively on the sexual, alcoholic aspects of the story, beginning with Albrecht Altdorfer's depiction. The frame here is dominated by a horizontal pairing of Lot and one of his daughters, both fully nude, with a quite lecherous smile on Lot's face. We also see the prominence of wine, as well as Lot's other nude daughter either resting up or waiting in the wings, as Sodom and Gomorrah burn in the top right of the frame. In this same vein of images that focus on sex and liquor are the works of Joachim Wtewael and Hendrik Goltzius. Both of these show two naked daughters lounging with Lot as they all drink. Everyone seems to be enjoying themselves, and there is no indication that either daughter has any compunction.

Since students should consider carefully the interests and motivations of the daughters, it is helpful to conclude with Orazio Gentileschi's piece. Here, we see no lecherous sex, no glorification of liquor, and no destruction. Instead, it depicts two women, crouching over the form of their father, incapacitated from liquor, looking and pointing off the frame to, we assume, the destruction of Sodom and Gomorrah. The starkness of the painting allows students to focus on the daughters and what they might be thinking. Obviously they have already made the decision to ply Lot with alcohol, but they have not yet engaged in any sexual activity with him. The off-frame destruction they are witnessing might lead them to believe that they must act. As Sharon Pace Jeansonne (*Women of Genesis: From Sarah to Potiphar's Wife*) notes, the motivation for the actions of the daughters is complicated not only by their belief that their father is the only man left in a world that will need repopulating, but they may also be continuing the cycle of sexual abuse he nearly initiated when he offered them up to the men of Sodom. In other words, there could be a motive of revenge in their drunken exploits with Lot. Gentileschi's work, in short, allows teachers to focus closely on the plight of the daughters and as such is able to elicit more concentrated cogitations from students.

George Segal, *Sacrifice of Isaac* (1979) [Princeton University, Princeton, N.J.; speccoll.library.kent.edu/4may70/exhibit/memorials/segal.html]

Albert J. Winn, *Akedah* (1995) [Jewish Museum, New York; www.jewish museum.org]

When George Segal was commissioned to memorialize the campus riots against the War in Vietnam and the subsequent death of four young people at Kent State University on May 4, 1970, he created a statue that depicted a modernized version of Abraham (see Gen 22), with knife in hand, standing over a kneeling supplicant Isaac, bound at the wrists and wearing only athletic shorts. Kent State declined the statue—it was deemed inappropriate—but Princeton purchased the bronze cast and erected it near its chapel. This statue may facilitate discussion of the sacrifice of children, whether by Abraham, Jephthah, God, or the fathers of soldiers ever since. How does the story of the Akedah justify or challenge the sacrifice made by parents during times of war? Or, more generally, how does this provocative artwork understand the original text? What aspect does it emphasize? What does it miss?

Albert J. Winn's black-and-white photograph *Akedah* encourages students to think about some of the implications of the story of Isaac's binding. In particular, it can be used to highlight the issue of theodicy, which is central in this story, in a contemporary way. Winn captures the image of a male torso, including the left arm, which bears tefillin and which has a bandage, suggesting a blood test recently has been taken. In his explanation of the piece, Winn, who is Jewish and HIV positive, compares the tourniquet used in taking a monthly blood test to the ritual of wearing tefillin. Among other things, Winn's image seems to push the audience to consider the story from the perspective of Isaac, since the only figure in the image is the one who is "bound." Isaac, one might argue, is being metaphorically represented by a modern HIV-positive man. After telling students about Winn's explanation of the piece, one might ask them to discuss why Winn names his piece *Akedah*. What part of the story does Winn seem to capture? What does he leave out? In particular, an instructor might encourage students to explore what Winn's image communicates about the story's notion of sacrifice. How could God ask for the sacrifice of Abraham's precious son? Similarly, how could God allow for the deaths of so many from HIV/AIDS? (For related exercises, see Gravett, "Genesis 22: Artists' Renderings," in Roncace and Gray, *Teaching the Bible*, 97–98.)

Gustave Doré, *Jacob Wrestling with the Angel* (1855) [Granger Collection, New York; www.ibiblio.org]

Doré depicts a winged angel, dressed in white, struggling with Jacob (Gen 32:22–32). The angel is prevailing, as he calmly clasps both of Jacob's wrists and pushes him down off of the rock where they are perched, despite Jacob's strained resistance. This portrayal is what one would expect: the divine being easily forcing the human into submission. But this, of course, is different from the biblical scene, where it is reported that the "man" did not prevail against Jacob (32:25) and the confrontation culminates with Jacob releasing his unidentified opponent (32:26). Students may consider why Doré does not follow the biblical script more closely. Are we to imagine that it is a scene earlier in the contest—before Jacob ultimately triumphs? Or is the artist uncomfortable with the notion that Jacob "wrestled with God ... and prevailed" (32:28)? What are the theological implications of Jacob's victory? Further, the biblical text does not refer to Jacob's adversary as an "angel" (cf. the title). Rather, it says that Jacob wrestled with "a man," but Jacob later interprets the experience as having struggled with the deity (32:30). In light of this ambiguity, how are viewers to interpret Doré's figure? Is it God? If not, then why not simply render the figure as a man (i.e., without wings)? Finally, Jacob's garb is reddish in color. Does this recall his brother Esau/Edom, whose name means "red" (Gen 25:30)? Indeed, the biblical text implies that Jacob, as he is about to meet his brother for the first time in years, is struggling with past issues—hence the themes of blessing (32:26) and the mixing of pronouns in the Hebrew text, suggesting the "likeness" (i.e., twins) of the two combatants.

Avi Katz, *The Alien Corn* Series (late twentieth century): *Judah Meeteth Tamar by the Roadside; Samson and Delilah; The Angel Comforteth Hagar* [www.avikatz.net/sf/aliencorn/alienframe.htm]

If students tire of Baroque and Renaissance paintings, a series of works on biblical characters created by Avi Katz called *The Alien Corn* series can offer fresh perspectives. Since 1990 he has been the staff artist for the *Jerusalem Report*, illustrated over one hundred books, and helped found the Israel Society for Science Fiction and Fantasy. This eclecticism, and especially the interest in science fiction, is obvious in his work for *The Alien Corn* series, which renders all of its subjects in bright, almost neon, colors and in futuristic settings. In so doing, Katz defamiliarizes these figures and allows students to approach them in a very different environment.

For example, in Katz's piece titled, *Judah Meeteth Tamar by the Roadside*, we see a bleak terrain with only two figures in the fore. One is wearing what appears to be armor from Old Spain, driving a vehicle that resembles a Land Speeder from *Star Wars*. This figure, who we know from the title is Judah, is leaning out of the right side of his craft, beckoning the other figure, Tamar, to enter. She is dressed in an outfit reminiscent of the 1980s TV show *Miami Vice*, with her bikini top, large sunglasses, and "pageant hair." Her right hand is lifted, and she seems to be gesturing for Judah to come to her as well. In the top right corner of the piece we see a short snippet—in both Hebrew and English—from Gen 38, so that we can identify easily the scriptural context of the image, even without the accompanying title. Genesis 38 is notoriously difficult to understand, in terms of its place in the surrounding Joseph novella as well as the intentions and possibly scandalous behavior of Tamar. By placing this scene in such a novel context, Katz allows students to come to the story with fresh eyes. Students can ask questions about Tamar's behavior and dress, as well as Judah's role in the incident, so that new stock can be taken of this narrative.

An even more provocative rendering is Katz's *Samson and Delilah*, in which we see the brief narrative of Judg 16 transplanted into a seedy-looking motel. Samson is completely naked on the bed, with a very satisfied look on his face. Delilah is wearing nothing but a negligée, and her position in the frame makes it obvious that she has just finished sexually gratifying Samson. As Samson rests, Delilah signals to a robot standing in the doorway to come in. The robot's torso is shaped and colored like an old barbershop pole, with red and white swirls, so the viewer knows that Samson is about to be sheared. In depicting the scene in this fashion, Katz allows us to ask various questions: What is Delilah's role? Does she cut Samson's hair, or does someone else? In the Masoretic Text, it is clear that even though Delilah "calls to a man," she is the one who does the cutting. However, in the Septuagint and Vulgate, this man is called a barber, and it is he who does the shaving, so the textual evidence is sketchy. Does Delilah seduce Samson? The Masoretic Text (Hebrew Bible) tells us, "She made (or let) him sleep on (or between) her knees," but does not tell us anything about intercourse. In sum, by portraying Delilah in this way, Katz counters the biblical text, and students can be asked to compare and contrast the text and image, as well as be queried as to the history of interpretation of Delilah that may have influenced this depiction.

A final example will suffice. In his work *The Angel Comforteth Hagar*, Katz bucks the dominant depiction of Hagar in Western art by focusing not on Gen 21, but rather on Gen 16 in which a pregnant Hagar runs away from Sarah's rather brutal treatment (16:6). His work depicts Hagar as a runaway, pregnant teen waiting at what appears to be a bus stop. Hagar has removed her roller skates but looks extremely depressed as she sits on the bus bench, fountain drink in hand. Next to her sits what we presume to be the angel, but this angel looks more like a robot, or even a bit player from *Tron*, than the typical angel in Western art. Nevertheless, the angel puts its arm around Hagar in a show of comfort that contrasts with the command in 16:9 to return to Sarah so that she can abuse Hagar more. As such, Katz has provided ample material here for students to return to Gen 16 and 21 and ask newly formed questions about (1) Hagar's status as an unwed, pregnant woman in the ancient world; (2) Sarah's treatment of Hagar; and (3) the fate of this notable, yet often overlooked character in the Torah.

In short, Katz's series—which also depicts Esau as a red Wookie and Ruth as a sexually charged Vulcan—takes familiar biblical characters and resituates them in the far reaches of the galaxy. In so doing, students' imaginations can be fired to (re)approach these figures from alternative vantages with innovative interrogations.

Michelangelo, *Moses* (ca. 1515) [San Pietro Church in Vincoli, Rome; www. wga.hu]

This monumental marble statue, 235 cm in height, was commissioned for the tomb of Julius II, which was never completed. Moses is presented as a towering, powerfully built figure, with unkempt hair and a long beard, certainly not the hesitant, stuttering figure we encounter early on in texts like Exod 4:10. The most noticeable attribute of this figure, though, are the two short, stubby horns Michelangelo has placed on the crown of his head. This iconic feature of Moses is based in a physiognomic description of the great leader in Torah. In Exod 34:29, as Moses descends from Mount Sinai, he is described as "not aware that the skin of his face was radiant, since he had spoken with Him [God]" (JPS). The verb "was radiant" is translated from the Hebrew verb *qāran*, which is a near homonym for *qeren*, the Hebrew word for "horn," as in an animal horn. The conflation of the two words is somewhat understandable; even in Ps 69:32 the verbal form is used as a participle to indicate an animal "being with horns." Jerome, in the Vulgate, renders Exod 34:29 in part, "his face was horned as a result of his speaking with God." All of this may seem but an interesting footnote, but when we add this textual tradition to other literature like John 8:44, in which Jesus tells a group of Jews, "You are from your father the devil, and you choose to do your father's desires" (NRSV), then we see the beginnings of one of the most prevalent anti-Jewish myths in history: that Jews have horns because in some way, they are connected to the devil. As such, Michelangelo's work can be used not only to contrast images of Moses in the Torah, but also to highlight the seemingly trivial origin of an anti-Semitic myth, with the hope of countering it.

Gustave Doré, *Jephthah's Daughter Coming to Meet her Father* (1865) [www.biblical-art.com]

Arnulf Rainer, *Jephthah's Daughter Goes to Greet Her Father* (1995–98) [Museum Freider Burda, Baden-Baden; www.samm lung-frieder-burda. de]

Barry Moser, *The Daughter on the Pyre* (2003) [Illustration in Moser, *The Holy Bible: King James Version: The Pennyroyal Caxton Bible* (New York: Viking Studio, 1999); www.womeninthebible.net/BIBLE-1.9C.htm]

These three paintings relate the story of Judg 11 in dramatic and telling ways. Without disclosing the title, one can show students the woodcut by Gustave Doré. Central to the composition, the daughter leads a crowd of young women in exuberant but modest dance, stepping lightly, almost suspended over the earthen mountain path. The grain of the woodcut rises and falls with the energy of her dance. Does the illustration capture the moment when she celebrates her father's victory or bewails her virginity? Students can make a decision based on evidence they identify, both from the content and the artistry of the work. If they argue, for example, that the moment captured must be before the daughter learns of her fate, they might point to the presence of her timbrels and the fact that she is dancing (cf. Judg 11:34). Alternatively, they may reason that the black and white of the illustration suggests that the daughter knows she has only two choices: to die or to live.

Next, one can consider the revision of Doré's woodcut by Arnulf Rainer. Rainer takes Doré's woodcut and colors it with streams of bright red, blue, yellow, and pink rays emanating from the dancing daughter, as though she were the center of radiant flames of fire. The whole scene is haloed with entwining lines. Students can speculate on the meaning of these lines. Are they brambles of wood, foreshadowing the fuel of her sacrifice and, perhaps evoking the Akedah? Or do they suggest barbed wire, emphasizing her loss of freedom (to live or to choose her own destiny)? Or is Rainer evoking a motif of the Jewish Holocaust, offering a social critique of those who went to their death without resistance? Here, too, students could make arguments one way or another using evidence from Rainer's illustration.

Finally, Barry Moser's engraving captures an anorexic adolescent already half-consumed by the pyre in which she lies. Her resolute face reaches upward, yet her eyes are closed. She goes to her death with intention, to honor her father.

These depictions of Jephthah's daughter may be used to pose a number of questions: (1) Which image best conveys the sense of moral and political chaos that pervades the second half of Judges? (2) Which is the best illustration of the story in Judg 11? (3) What do these images suggest about the value and purpose of women and their sacrifices in the Bible, and how are these sacrifices often expected today in the shaping of young girls?

Jean-Léon Gérôme, *Bathsheba* (1889) [Private collection; www.biblical-art.com]

Most people assume that the story of David and Bathsheba is one of adultery (2 Sam 11:1–12:14). In order to provoke a careful reading of the text and to set the stage for a consideration of the image, students can perform an exercise in which they "put the characters on trial." If this were a modern story, what charges could be laid and what might stick? Is it a seduction, voyeurism, sexual harassment, adultery, or a rape? Teachers can also take the opportunity to define these terms and discuss the possible consequences of the charges. It is sometimes enlightening to ask the men first and then the women what they conclude, which provides a chance to discuss gender perspective and feminist biblical hermeneutics.

Then, when students are presented with this painting, they can describe how Gérôme has interpreted this narrative, and how it is communicated in his painting. Students might say, for example, that Gérôme depicts a seduction. Bathsheba entices David: She is bathing naked on an open rooftop; she is turned to the sun—and to David—and her chest is illumined; her hip is hitched up in a traditionally provocative pose; she stands in the center of the symbol of a fertile woman, a "v" created by the black shadowy woman on the left and the white garment on the right. The black and white come together at her feet and suggest that she has power. Furthermore, the angle of the kneeling woman and the pointed tower direct both Bathsheba's and the observer's gaze to David. She is "inviting his attention." Alternatively, students might suggest that, according to Gérôme, David is a voyeur: David is partially concealed by the balustrade and the altitude of his balcony; he is in the shadowy background; he is alongside a phallic pointed tower. Bathsheba has not noticed him (yet) or she would cover up. Or they might argue that Gérôme is depicting sexual harassment; that is, in David's exalted state (at the top of the painting and in the building) and unreachable position (distant perspective), he can do whatever he likes without consequences. The evening assignation and the outstretched arms of both Bathsheba and David creating mutual union might suggest adultery. Bathsheba has cast her veil of purity (the white garment) to the side. Then again, rape might be implied by the dark and crooked visual line of the wall reaching to David set against the con-

A
R
T

trast of Bathsheba's white skin and garment. In short, placing this open-ended painting of Bathsheba beside 2 Sam 11 demonstrates how biblical interpretation is truly "in the eye of the beholder."

Dieric Bouts the Elder, *Prophet Elijah in the Desert* (1464–68) [Sint-Pieterskerk, Leuven; www.biblical-art.com]

Peter Paul Rubens, *The Prophet Elijah Receiving Bread and Water from an Angel* (1625–28) [Musée Bonnat, Bayonne, France; www.ibiblio.org]

Abraham Bloemaert, *Landscape with the Prophet Elijah in the Desert* (1610) [The State Hermitage Museum, St. Petersburg; www.hermitage museum.org]

Washington Allston, *Elijah in the Desert* (1818) [Museum of Fine Arts, Boston; www.mfa.org]

Among the themes upon which to focus when reading the stories of Elijah (1 Kgs 17:1–19:25; 2 Kgs 1:1–2:12) is that of eating in the wilderness. In the first, Elijah curses Israel with a drought and goes to the Wadi Cherith east of the Jordan where he is fed bread and meat by ravens (1 Kgs 17:6). In the second, fearing Jezebel, Elijah flees to Judah, leaves his servant, and then goes another day's journey into the wilderness. There he sits down under a tree and hopes to die (1 Kgs 19:4). An angel awakens him from sleep with "a cake baked on hot stones" and a jar of water. Again, he falls asleep and is fed by the angel, who says, "Get up and eat, otherwise the journey will be too much for you." Elijah went "in the strength of that food" for forty days (1 Kgs 19:8). With students, brainstorm a list of possibly related themes, such as the exodus, Babylonian exile, Jesus' temptation, or his multiplication of the loaves and fishes. Remind them that the Deuteronomistic Historian was likely writing from the exile and thus experiencing some form of wilderness at that time. How might these feeding miracles of Elijah be received by the Babylonian exiles?

One might continue the discussion by breaking students into groups and giving each group a color copy of one of the paintings listed above. Ask them to work together to identify what the artist emphasizes with composition, color, background, foreground, structures, characters, props, garments, gestures, space, light and dark, and flow lines. By emphasizing these features, what emotions does the artist try to evoke in his contemporary audience? For example, does the painting suggest hope at a time of war, shame for overindulgence during times of peace, or confidence in God's providence during times of famine? Ask them to form guesses based on their observations of the paintings. Each group can then collaborate with each of the other groups, sharing what they have learned and discussed. As they rotate around the room, each group is able to incorporate new insights. In the plenary session that follows, each group can explain what they learned about (1) Elijah, (2) the use of traditional motifs in later biblical texts, and (3) how artists use these motifs rhetorically for their own audiences.

John Singer Sargent, *Frieze of the Prophets* (1895) [Boston Public Library, Boston; sargentmurals.bpl.org]

This frieze, part of Sargent's giant mural *Triumph of Religion*, which he executed (but never completed) for the Boston Public Library between the years 1890 and 1919, is well-known and easily the most famous piece of the larger mural. It depicts an imposing golden and winged Moses holding the Ten Commandments. At his right is Elijah; at his left, Joshua. Spread out on either side of this central triad are sixteen other prophetic figures: the three major prophets, the twelve minor prophets, and Daniel.

The painting has had a rather lively and interesting history of reception in both Jewish and Christian circles and has a number of potential uses in classroom contexts. With a total of nineteen figures represented, the range of possibilities for discussion can at best be only hinted at here.

(1) One may note the individualism at work in Sargent's presentation of the prophets in contrast to the more schematic images represented immediately above (which have to do with the Egyptian oppression). This artistic observation is certainly significant for the mural as a whole: Egypt, despite its power, is ultimately depersonalized, whereas these few lone figures, and the religion they represent, in no small way "triumph" over the glory that was Egypt. But it is also somewhat indicative of earlier approaches to the prophets (e.g., Wellhausen) which saw them as the high point of and *telos* in the development of Israelite religion.

(2) The centrality of Moses to the entire tableau and especially the centerpiece where he appears with Joshua and Elijah might be analyzed. Why these three? Why does Sargent portray Moses with the prophets anyway? Is it a construal of Exod 3 as a prophetic call narrative? And why Joshua and Elijah as opposed to, say, Samuel or Nathan, who are arguably as important?

(3) In addition to the winged (!) Moses with two tablets, there are other distinctive elements of representation: Joshua is appropriately drawing a sword; Amos has a shepherd's crook; Daniel carries a scroll; and Jonah is mostly concealed behind Jeremiah and Isaiah—a reluctant prophet to the end! Equally as intriguing and more interpretively daring is the pathos Sargent captures with a number of the figures, especially Jeremiah, Zephaniah, Joel, and Obadiah. Students could be asked about how and where Sargent's

A
R
T

depictions reflect the biblical text. How are they *interpretations*? Finally, do they cast any light on the text and in what way? Obadiah, for instance, is probably the most poignantly depicted. A comparison with the grief and cry for justice, even vengeance, that pervades this briefest of prophetic books supports Sargent's depiction. But Sargent's depiction, in turn, may cast further light on Obadiah. Perhaps the grief that is captured so poignantly and visually in the painting is two-part: (a) the grief the prophet feels after the destruction of Jerusalem, and (b) the grief the prophet feels for having personally to carry a rather vicious message of retribution. This latter point, if correct, is at least implicitly present in the text but is brought to the fore in a powerful and visual way by Sargent's painting of Obadiah.

Raphael, *The Vision of Ezekiel* (1518) [Galleria Palatina, Palazzo Pitti, Florence; www.wga.hu]

William Blake, *The Whirlwind: Ezekiel's Vision of the Cherubim and Eyed Wheels* (1803–5) [Museum of Fine Arts, Boston; www.mfa.org/collections]

William H. Johnson, *Ezekiel Saw the Wheel* (1944–45) [Smithsonian American Art Museum, Washington, D.C.; americanart.si.edu]

Norbert H. Kox, *Ezekiel's Vision* (contemporary) [Collection of the Artist; www.apocalypsehouse.homestead.com/EZEKIEL.html]

Julius Schnorr von Carolsfeld, *The Glory of God* (1851–60) [Illustration in von Carolsfeld, *Die Bibel in Bildern* (Leipzig: Georg Wigand, 1906); www.pitts.emory.edu/woodcuts/1853BiblD/00011489.jpg]

The vision of the divine in the first chapter of Ezekiel is a particularly powerful text; however, as is the case with other visionary texts, such as the book of Revelation, a literal reading of the vision yields an almost absurd portrait of divine being and power. Reading this text in conjunction with select images can encourage students to think beyond the constraints of literal language and to understand the details of the text as evoking moods and abstract qualities of the divine.

One way of beginning this conversation is to have students sketch the vision as the instructor, or a student, reads aloud the text of Ezekiel. Students should be provided with blank paper and encouraged to capture the details of the text. Of course, this requires that the reader read slowly and deliberately. After they have tried their own sketches, students can discuss what they think Ezekiel's vision is about. Is it about the winged creatures with multiple faces? The wheels that move and spin? Or, is it about communicating characteristics associated with God? If it is about more abstract characteristics, why does the author include such vivid detail? The conversation can encourage students to think about the vision as a rhetorical construction, which aims to persuade its audience to accept a particular view of God and of Ezekiel.

Students may then consider what the various artists capture in the text and how they interpret the purpose of Ezekiel's vision in their illustrations. The images by Raphael and William Blake are the most detailed. In Raphael's painting one is able to see the winged creatures, but one of its most striking aspects is the proximity between God and earth. Even though Raphael does not depict the "wheels" described in the vision, he seemingly captures the text's suggestion that the divine vision is close to the earth (Ezek 1:15). Blake's watercolor rendition utilizes the male body to represent the human form of the living creatures described by Ezekiel (1:5). This muscular body conveys a sense of strength and power. Like Raphael, Blake avoids depicting literal wheels; however, he does allude to a circular form and motion around the body of the living creature. In both images, we see the artists communicating particular themes in the text, by highlighting certain details and disregarding others.

The paintings by Johnson and Kox, both self-taught artists, are simpler than the others. These paintings lend themselves to discussions of the text's function. Johnson's work uses a primitive style to depict Ezekiel experiencing the vision of the wheels. The audience sees a partially clothed prophet, looking up into the sky, with two wheels floating above his head. The prophet's arms and hands are in the air, and he looks as though he has fallen to the ground. Johnson reminds the viewer and the reader that the vision of Ezekiel communicates something about Ezekiel, as a prophet, and is part of a larger story in which the prophet plays a key role. In contrast to Johnson's focus on Ezekiel, Kox uses oranges, reds, and yellows to depict an abstract vision of rotating "wheels" that blaze above a body of water. Above the wheels, which look strikingly similar to depictions of UFOs, is a spot of light, which might be the divine. In some sense, Kox places the viewer in the role of Ezekiel experiencing the fiery vision. What does Kox imply by placing the viewer in this position? Does it suggest, for example, that Ezekiel's vision is meant to reveal the divine nature to the audience?

After showing Julius Schnorr von Carolsfeld's work and inviting students to make sound effects and to move "in any of the four directions without veering," students may contemplate why Ezekiel's vision of God has wheels. Is it meant to imply that God is able to move, in this case, to Babylon? This leads easily to questions of why God might leave Jerusalem (it was defiled) and go with the exiles (the privileged). Kinesthetic learners appreciate acting this out: God sits in Jerusalem, stands up, the temple (chair) is forcefully knocked over, and then God crosses the room, sits down in exile, and chats with Ezekiel. (Perhaps other players can be included: the people left behind who do not have access to God and the exiles in Babylon who do have access to God. The tension of the Reconstruction between the Jews and the people of the land comes into clearer focus.)

For a related exercise, see Johanna Stiebert, "Ezekiel's Inaugural Vision," in Roncace and Gray, *Teaching the Bible*, 179–80.

Albert Pinkham Ryder, *Jonah* (ca. 1885–95) [Smithsonian American Art Museum, Washington, D.C.; americanart.si.edu]

Most images of Jonah focus on either the "great fish" swallowing the recalcitrant prophet or the typological relationship between Jonah and the risen Christ. In fact, Jonah (along with Susanna) is depicted frequently in early Christian art and sarcophagi. In Ryder's oil, we see a chaotic, dark scene in which Jonah has just been tossed overboard by the "pagan" sailors after discovering he is the cause of the storm that plagues them. God is seen hovering above the action, flanked by wing-like spans of gold light, while Jonah is in the choppy waves, holding his arms aloft, helpless and seemingly ready for oblivion. This piece challenges both of the standard *topoi* of Jonah mentioned above; it also raises questions for students about the character of God and Jonah and the nature of the narrative itself. For example, is God controlling all this action? If so, why? If Jonah is a prophet, why is he so ready to accept death? What kind of a prophet would act like this, or, why is Jonah so negative about carrying out God's commission? If he is ready for death, why does God commission the "great fish" to swallow him? Energetic teachers can also ask students to reflect on the technical aspects of Ryder's work, adumbrated nicely on the Smithsonian's webpage, complete with QuickTime movie commentary (see americanart.si.edu/collections/tours/ryder/). Ryder fiddled constantly with his works, and his *Jonah* is no exception. He even reused an older canvas, as a faint image of a female character is visible via an autoradiograph. The technical aspects of Ryder's paintings could also be incorporated into a discussion of Jonah, insofar as God seems to be constantly fiddling with Jonah, attempting to perfect his understanding of treating Gentiles with justice, while Jonah is trying to reuse the traditional understanding of "insider-outsider" categories prevalent in Israelite ideology for so long.

Jean Fouquet, *Job sur le fumier* (1452–60) [Musée Condé, Chantilly; expositions.bnf.fr/fouquet/grand/f093.htm]

In a miniature illustration from the Book of Hours of Étienne Chevalier, Jean Fouquet depicts Job on the ash heap being instructed by his three friends. Job has come to the end of his strength; his ribs and sinews show through his darkened boil-stricken skin, his beard and hair hang unkempt and grey. The ashes cradle his broken body. In contrast, his three pious friends, dressed in rich hues of red, gold, blue, and white and with crowns on their heads, keep their distance from Job, stand over him and "look down their noses" at him. One friend extends his delicate foot in Job's direction, perhaps to check for life or perhaps in disdain that his foot is soiled. A castle stands in the background, and travelers (perhaps Elihu?) approach along the way. All things seem to point heavenward—the trees, the castle, the visual lines of the friends' figures, the clear blue sky—except for Job who has succumbed to despair. Will he curse God now? The Latin subscript ironically appears to cite Ps 95:1, "O come, let us sing to the Lord; let us rejoice in our salvation!"

One can ask students if they can identify one friend from the other by their gestures and stance. Teachers might assign one of the speeches of the various friends to each of several small groups and ask them to match the speech with one of the characters in the painting. Which is the agitated Zophar (20:1–29), Eliphaz the accuser (22:1–30), and Bildad the cynic (8:1–22; 18:1–21)? Can they identify the intent of the friends' accusations: What would be an equivalent contemporary friend's comment? How might they themselves respond to this friendly piece of advice? How does Job respond? Finally, students may reflect on the way the order and the clarity in this small painting challenge the disorder and chaos of Job's reality (cf. Job 2:12). The artistry of the painting suggests that order is more divine.

Marc Chagall, *Ahasuerus Sends Vashti Away* (1960) [Svetlana & Lubos Jelinek, Chrudim, Czech Republic; www.spaightwoodgalleries.com/Pages/Chagall_60Bible_lithos3.html]

Gustave Doré, *The Queen Vashti Refusing to Obey the Command of Ahasuerus* (1865) [www.biblical-art.com]

Edwin Long, *Vashti Refuses the King's Summons* (1879) [Bob Jones University Museum and Gallery, Greenville, S.C.; www.bjumg.org/collections/old_masters/centuries_18_19/long.htm]

When Vashti refuses King Ahasuerus's request to be exhibited, the king and his sages send out an edict to all the provinces so that people know that "every man should be master in his own house." This story obviously supports male domination in the household, but this introductory tale, as well as the greater narrative of Esther, demonstrates that female subversion works. Vashti gets what she wants by refusing to use her sexuality; Esther gets what she wants by using her sexuality. The king never seems to get what he wants, except perhaps Esther.

Art captures both sides of this story as well. In Chagall's color lithograph, Ahasuerus dominates. The royal red of rage in his ornate robe bleeds into the innumerable people close to him, and extends down the stairs. His height and weight—supported by the dark diagonal lines dividing the pair—over-shadow Vashti, who hides crouching under the stairway, face downcast and fading pink and green, seeing darkness. Compare this to Gustave Doré's engraving. Here, Vashti stands straight and proud at the top of stairs, with her arm outstretched in restraint, bathed in light and in layers of white clothes (as innocent), but no crown. She is surrounded by angry men looking and leaning into her; they are in shadow. Finally, in Edwin Long's painting, Vashti looks weak, uncertain, and sad; she clutches her garments in a gesture of modesty. Her servants are pleading for her to go to the king.

This series of paintings can serve to demonstrate how an artist's (and author's) perspectives and commitments may be communicated in the con-struction of a story or an artistic rendering, in this case, the (in)appropriate response of Vashti.

Botticelli, *The Return of Judith* (1470) [Galleria degli Uffizi, Florence; www.arca.net/uffizi1/Uffizi_Pictures.asp?Contatore=112]

Giorgione, *Judith* (1504) [The State Hermitage Museum, St. Petersburg; www.hermitagemuseum.org]

Jan Sanders van Hemessen, *Judith* (ca. 1540) [Art Institute of Chicago; www.artic.edu/aic/collections]

Caravaggio, *Judith Beheading Holofernes* (1598–99) [Galleria Nazionale d'Arte Antica, Rome; www.wga.hu]

Artemisia Gentileschi, *Judith Slaying Holofernes* (ca. 1620) [Galleria degli Uffizi, Florence; www.wga.hu]

Valentin de Boulogne, *Judith and Holofernes* (ca. 1626) [National Museum of Fine Arts in La Valletta, Malta; www.wga.hu]

Johann Liss, *Judith and Holophernes* (1628) [Kunsthistorisches Museum, Vienna; www.wga.hu]

While the apocryphal narrative of Judith has long fascinated interpreters due to its rather gruesome, yet religious heroine, many students are unfamil-iar with this story. Once they engage it, however, they find themselves caught up in the many issues raised by the text, such as divine justice; what makes a Jew a Jew during the Second Temple period; the status of women during this period; and finally, deceit and violence in the name of God. Unfortu-nately, the depiction of Judith in the Western artistic tradition has focused almost exclusively on only one moment in the narrative: Judith's beheading of Holofernes in 13:8. As such, the tradition has siphoned Judith into a singular mode of feminine violence, and usually she is doomed to be presented in one of two ways: as a brutish woman who readily embraces her role in the killing; or as a highly feminized figure who looks as if she could not possibly partake in this murderous act.

Both depictions find support in the narrative. Students can view a sampling of both trends to illustrate how different ideas of "woman" permeate both the apocryphal text and the artistic tradition. Put another way, if, as some scholars claim, Judith is a cipher for "Jews" during the Second Temple period, then how we interpret her character affects not only the way we understand women during that period, but also how we interpret Jewish identity therein. As such, these different trends of interpretation allow us to raise important questions, such as: What could be the ideological motivations for portraying "troublesome" women like Judith in certain ways? Is there a dominant trend in biblical scholarship akin to the trend(s) we see in art? Which one of these pieces resonates with your view of the story, and why? How do these images of Judith address the larger view(s) of and concerns about women within biblical literature?

Botticelli's work portrays a "feminine Judith" in which we see Judith and her maid on their way back from the enemy camp, presumably going to Bethulia. There is no hint here of any urgency, no sense that a hideous beheading has just taken place. Rather, Botticelli has painted a pastoral scene, with Judith in lovely attire, looking as if she and her servant were simply out for an afternoon stroll. Only the small sword in Judith's hand and the severed head of Holofernes in the servant's basket betray what has just happened. Similarly, the piece by Giorgione shows a serene looking Judith with a pious visage standing near a large tree, looking down upon the severed head of Holofernes, upon which she has placed her left foot. Giorgione's Judith displays no trace of the grim determination found in her apocryphal counterpart, and in fact she seems almost too "dainty" to have performed such a grisly task.

On the other hand, there are copious examples of a more macabre trend in portraying Judith. Jan Sanders van Hemessen shows us a totally nude, muscular Judith with Holofernes' sword raised in her right hand and the bag she will use for his severed head in her left. Looking at this Judith, the viewer is left with little doubt that this woman is fully capable of lopping off Holofernes' head. Along these same lines, we must mention the grand tradition of Judiths begun by Caravaggio. We are told in the apocryphal narrative that Judith has to whack Holofernes' head not once but twice in order to decapitate him. Caravaggio and those who follow him, including Artemisia Gentileschi and Valentin de Boulogne, focus on this precise moment in order to depict the action of the beheading itself, complete with what students familiar with the television drama *CSI* would term "arterial spatter." These gruesome renderings allow us to pursue the issue of violence in the name of God and its justification. Finally, concluding with the work by Johann Liss allows students to enter into the psyche created by this line of representation. Liss shows the viewer the massively muscular back of Judith, as well as the freshly decapitated body of Holofernes, as she is loading his head into her basket. The real key to this work, though, is that she is gazing out at the viewer with a look that radiates determination and ruthlessness. It is truly a "Schwarzenegger" moment, and it allows teachers to broach this character in a very different light than many other renderings, focusing as they do on Judith's feminine presence.

In sum, comparing and contrasting these two trends of interpreting Judith permits instructors not only to illustrate divergent renderings of the same narrative, but it also opens up space for questions about women and violence in the Bible.

Ralf Kresin, *Susanna im Bade* (1999) [www.kresin.de/websites/oelbilder/susanna.html]

Sisto Badalocchio, *Susanna and the Elders* (ca. 1609) [Ringling Museum of Art, Sarasota; www.ringling.org/collections.asp. The Ringling Museum attributes this painting to Agostino Carracci]

Rembrandt van Rijn, *Susanna and the Elders* (ca. 1636) [Mauritshuis, The Hague; www.mauritshuis.nl/index.aspx?Contentid=17521&Chapterid=2341&Filterid=988]

Artemisia Gentileschi, *Susanna and the Elders* (1610) [Schonborn Collection, Pommerfelden; www.metmuseum.org]

Allesandro Allori, *Susanna and the Elders* (1561) [Musée Magnin, Dijon; www.musee-magnin.fr/homes/home_id24567_u1l2.htm]

George Pencz, *Susanna and the Elders* (ca. 1532) [Spaightwood Galleries, Upton, Mass.; spaightwoodgalleries.com/Pages/Bible_Susanna.html]

Agostino Carracci, *Susanna and the Elders* (from *The Lascivious Series*, mid-1590s) [Metropolitan Museum of Art, New York; reproduced in Diane De Grazia Bohlin, *Prints and Related Drawings by the Carracci Family* (Washington D.C.: National Gallery of Art, 1979), 291]

The story of Susanna represents one of the narrative gems of the apocryphal corpus and has been rendered in numerous media, including music, literature, and art. Containing as it does a plot that focuses on an attempted rape and cover-up by those in authority, as well as a pious and beautiful heroine, it is no coincidence that artistic renderings of the story have been somewhat schizophrenic in their approach. That is, within the works that treat this theme, one can find scenes of sexual aggression and seduction alongside depictions of righteous refusal and pictorial piety. For this reason, paintings of Susanna can serve to demonstrate several important concepts in the biblical studies classroom, for example, (1) the multiple possibilities of interpretations of narratives about women; (2) the ways in which mostly male interpreters read this story of an embattled woman, which can serve as a springboard to discuss ideologies in interpretation; and (3) the process by which potentially harmful readings of female characters can de dissected to reveal the tentative foundations on which they stand.

Students should pay attention specifically to the two main thematic levels of the story: the sexual level in which we find the attempted rape and the discussion of the elders' lust; and the level of piety, which includes Susanna's refusal and prayer, as well as all of Daniel's presence and dialogue. Even though the latter level appears to dominate within the story, it is the former we find most often in the artistic tradition. Nonetheless, it is helpful for students to view artistic renderings that treat both themes in an attempt to highlight the three concepts mentioned above. In addition to the variety of material from the Renaissance, earlier and later examples exist. The earliest, from the mid-fourth century c.e., is a painting from the Praetextatus Catacomb in Rome, depicting Susanna as a lamb between two wolves (cf. du Bourguet, *Early Christian Painting*, pl. 55). In 1999, Ralf Kresin painted Susanna drying off in a shower, with the elders peering at her through a turned corner in the tiles.

Badalocchio's oil is one of the "Pious Susanna" pieces. She is depicted as both shocked and terrified, grasping her cloak in an attempt to cover herself. Her hand is raised to defend or shield herself from the advances of the elders, and her eyes are fixed skyward to symbolize her reliance on God to save her from this predicament, lyrically stated in her prayer in verses 42–43. Rembrandt's and Gentileschi's famous pieces are similar. In the former, the figure of Susanna dominates the frame as she struggles and contorts her body in order to hide her nakedness from the elders, all the while gazing directly at the viewer, out of the frame. This image is quite discomforting, as this Susanna seems to be imploring the viewer for help in an immediate fashion. No less gripping is Gentileschi's work, which depicts a Susanna in clear emotional turmoil, arms raised to resist the elders, all placed in a cold stone setting. Using these images allows students to empathize with Susanna in her plight to remain true to God, as she is presented in the story. Teachers can also utilize these images to note the ways in which both male and female interpreters focus on the more ethical, less erotic themes in the story and thereby stimulate discussion on the role of background in interpretation.

At the same time pious readings of Susanna are present in Western art, a more sexually aggressive interpretation tends to dominate the tradition. One can turn directly from Gentileschi's stark and painful expression of Susanna's confusion and despair to Allessandro Allori's mid-sixteenth-century oil. Here we see a scene of enjoyed seduction, in which Susanna seems to be caressing the heads of both elders, as one edges his hand up her inner thigh. We get no sense from this work that Susanna is conflicted, scared, or in despair, as the narrative describes her. Instead we see a woman who might be willing to acquiesce to the elders' advances. Other works in this vein heighten the theme of sexual aggression, some depicting an attempted rape. For example, Georg Pencz's engraving depicts Susanna with a leg draped over the knee of one of the elders, while both of them are holding her wrists tightly, and one of them is fondling her left breast. Similarly, Carracci's piece shows a terrified, fully naked Susanna trying to get away from the elders, one of whom is grabbing her *derriere*, and one of whom has pulled his robe up to allow himself to masturbate behind a column on the right side of the piece. Given the level of violence and sexuality exhibited here, it is safe to say that Carracci was interested in Susanna for the opportunity to portray a scene of erotic aggression, not a picture of piety.

These sexually charged, and often lewd, images allow students to interrogate the story as to the sexual elements within it, as well as to discuss larger issues raised by such renderings. For example, was Susanna "asking for it" by bathing nude? How does this portrayal of sexual violence connect with other examples in biblical literature? What effect does viewing scenes of sexual violence have on us and the way we return to the story time and time again? The artistic renderings of this text, both pious and pornographic, are fertile ground for feminist and ideological queries.

A
R
T

Fra Angelico, *The Annunciaton* (ca. 1440–45) [Museo di San Marco, Florence, Italy; www.artstor.org; a number of annunciation paintings are attributed to Fra Angelico and his workshop; one similar to this fresco resides in the Prado in Madrid and is viewable online at museoprado.mcu.es]

Henry Ossawa Tanner, *The Annunciation* (1898) [Philadelphia Museum of Art, Philadelphia; www.philamuseum.org]

Raphael Soyer, *Annunciation* (1980) [Smithsonian Museum of American Art, Washington, D.C.; americanart.si.edu]

Viewing these three markedly different annunciation paintings together provides an opportunity to explore themes introduced in Luke's narrative and to push students to think critically about "truth" and what is represented as real. After reading Luke 1:26–56, students view these images and are asked to describe how each image captures the text.

Fra Angelico's work serves as a beautiful example of a Renaissance annunciation scene: Mary sits indoors on a columned portico as an angel with rainbow-hued wings kneels before her. Mary is haloed and wears a blue robe. In the background and to the left, we see a fence that suggests the garden off of the portico is closed off. Students viewing this image might be encouraged to think about how this depiction of Mary indoors and separated from the world by a fence highlights her virginal or "untouched" nature. For many students, Mary's gesture indicates her faithful acceptance of Gabriel's news.

Painted at the end of the nineteenth century, Henry O. Tanner's oil painting uses realism to render Luke's story of Mary. Tanner's painting captures the moment when Gabriel, represented as a glowing pillar of light, approaches the young, Jewish girl. Mary, clothed in simple robes, sits on a bed and hesitantly looks up at the luminous figure. Her expression is marked neither by fear nor eagerness. Mary's surroundings appear to be earthen or stucco-like, a woven rug is on the floor and a simple blanket hangs behind Mary. As students experience this painting, they can compare its portrayal of Mary's social context to Fra Angelico's portrayal. It might be illuminating to remind students of Luke 1:46–56, since Tanner's painting can be read as highlighting the "lowliness" of Mary.

After viewing Tanner's rendition, Raphael Soyer's 1980 painting might prove quite thought provoking, since it depicts a modern scene of two women in a bath or dressing room. The painting's title frames it as an annunciation scene. A woman, dressed in a pink skirt and black top, leans against a cool blue wall and gazes at a second woman. This second woman is dressed in a slip of pale blue, the traditional blue identifying her with Mary. Mary's hair is tied back, and she carries a towel that indicates she has just washed in the sink basin. Prompting students to read this painting in relation to the annunciation story might involve asking them what washing and water suggests about Mary's character in Luke. One might encourage students to read her tied-back hair as an indication of controlled sexuality, a common trope in visual depictions of women. In addition, students can consider what Soyer communicates by translating this story into a modern context. Is this a way of capturing Mary's claim that "from now on all generations will call me blessed" (Luke 1:48)?

Furthermore, these paintings can serve as entry into a conversation about truth and realism. When viewing these images, students often comment on how Tanner's depiction seems so real. This sense of reality is communicated primarily through the setting, which fits how many modern Westerners imagine the first-century Palestinian setting. The knowledge that Tanner was

A
R
T

the son of an African Methodist Episcopal bishop who often painted religious and biblical scenes and that he even traveled to Palestine to capture better the settings might initially reassure students that Tanner's painting captures "how it must have happened." However, this type of assumption can be troubled by adding that Tanner explicitly sought to "humanize" the characters in his biblical paintings, showing that they were "kin" to everyone. As an African American painter living at the turn of the twentieth century, this had social and political implications. For Tanner, this painting of Mary is not simply about capturing a realistic picture, but it is also about depicting Mary's connectedness to all people, regardless of race. In other words, while Tanner sought to capture some of the reality of ancient Palestine, his painting was shaped by complex social, historical, and political issues (Boime, "Henry Ossawa Tanner's Subversion of Genre," 415–42). What appears real, students learn, is shaped by the artist's political and theological commitments. One might ask students: Does this make Tanner's painting any less true to the text? Once students have thought about how realism functions in Tanner's painting, they can think about how Fra Angelico and Soyer's paintings may be just as true to the text, even though they do not strive for historical realism. This question opens up a conversation about distinctions between realism and truth.

A
R
T

Luc Olivier Merson, *Rest on the Flight into Egypt* (1879) [Museum of Fine Arts, Boston; www.mfa.org]

Matthew's depiction of the holy family's flight into and out of Egypt (Matt 2:13–23) is one of the ways that the author constructs his understanding of Jesus' identity, especially as he portrays Jesus as a new Moses. French artist Luc Olivier Merson provides a way of illustrating this interpretation, as well as providing a way of highlighting the differences between the Matthean and the Lukan birth narratives.

Merson's painting, dominated by the dark colors of a night sky, positions the view at a distance from this desert scene. To the left we see a statute of the sphinx, partially buried in sand. Resting between the front feet of the sphinx is a female figure, presumably Mary, with an infant in her arms. The infant glows, the light reflecting onto Mary's face. To the right of the statue we see a figure laying face down on the ground by a campfire and a lone donkey next to a saddle. The night sky, the sphinx, and the glowing child create a scene of mystery and dramatic importance.

This painting provides an effective way into a conversation about the unique elements of Matthew's birth narrative. Students should make a connection between the sphinx, a symbolic image of Egypt, and the depiction of Jesus as a new Moses. Further, students can discuss whether Merson's focus on Mary and his depiction of Joseph face down faithfully portrays Matthew's narrative or whether this depiction of Mary seems more in line with Luke's Gospel.

Otto Dix, *The Temptation of Jesus* (1960) [Marian Library, Dayton; campus.udayton.edu/mary//gallery/works/temptationofjesus.htm]

Buoninsegna di Duccio, *The Temptation of Christ on the Mountain* (ca. 1308–11) [The Frick Collection, New York; collections.frick.org]

The story of the temptation of Christ links Jesus and humans most profoundly. As Matt 4:1–11 tells it, the Spirit leads Jesus into the wilderness to be tempted by the devil. For forty days and nights, Jesus eats and drinks nothing. Then the devil comes to him and tempts him three times: first with bread, second with protection, and third, "all the kingdoms of the world and their splendor" if Jesus falls down and worships him.

In Otto Dix's lithograph, the kingdoms of the world are represented by the façade of a skyscraper and the hash marks of other undistinguished buildings; they are well lit but too far off to impress. In the foreground, a rather weary looking Jesus is overshadowed by a menacing devil whose four horns and pointed chin form strong visual lines piercing the head of Jesus, extending down his face and back. The seated Jesus raises a weak hand in response, but the slump of his body and hollowed eyes suggest that he is defeated.

The painting raises a variety of questions. Is Jesus calmly responding to a pesky annoyance, or is he overcome? Is Jesus connected to the divine or abandoned? Is this a positive or a negative view of Christ? If Jesus meets humanity most closely in this narrative, what is Dix saying about humanity and the pursuit of power and the wealth of the nations (e.g., the devil controls the cities; humans disappear in the city)? What does Dix imagine for the future? (A continual decline of cities through evil; the good are helpless to stop it?) How does this painting alter the meaning of Matt 4? (Jesus can no longer resist temptation; the cities are too nebulous, the devil too powerful?)

Compare Dix's lithograph with Buoninsegna di Duccio's tempera painting on wood. Here, Jesus is robed in royal red and navy robes, flanked by two angels, with his hand extended in command to the devil to leave. His feet are planted solidly on a rock, and the lines and textures of the painting support him. The devil, in contrast, is old, naked, winged, and possibly only one-armed; he is so dark that his features are obscured. He perches precariously on a precipice ready for a fall or flight. Three superb cities stand in subordination to these four figures; complete with the details of loggias, battlements, towers, Gothic windows, and red-tiled roofs, the bright pink and yellow cities are protected by stout walls and fed with lively running streams of water. Compared to Dix, how does Duccio represent Jesus? Is Jesus more human or divine? What is the relationship between Jesus and the development of cities? It would seem that Jesus is casting the devil out of the cities in order to preserve them for habitation, to "bless them." Does this corrupt the meaning of Matt 4?

Henry Wolf, *Christ Walking on the Sea* (1899) [Smithsonian American Art Museum, Washington D.C.; americanart.si.edu]

Henry Ossawa Tanner, *Christ Walking on the Water* (no date) [Smithsonian American Art Museum, Washington D.C.; americanart.si.edu]

B. J. O. Nordfeldt, *Christ Walking on Water* (1951) [Smithsonian American Art Museum, Washington D.C.; americanart.si.edu]

Each of these pieces literally provides a different angle on the story of Jesus walking on water (Mark 6:45–52; Matt 14:22–33; John 6:16–59). Comparing these different paintings alongside the Gospel accounts opens up conversation about how writers, like artists, shape the elements of a story to communicate a particular idea or to fulfill a specific function.

Henry Wolf highlights the storm at sea, as sea swells dominate the foreground of the picture. The boat filled with the disciples is about to be overcome by the waves. To the upper right, however, we see a haloed Jesus walking on water that is still. Jesus, arms outstretched in a cruciform pose, emerges out of the darkness toward the boat. In this way, Wolf's artwork seemingly suggests peace and salvation in relation to Christ and his crucifixion. Like Wolf, Henry O. Tanner places Jesus toward the upper right hand corner of his illustration, although he is represented through the faintest of sketching. Tanner captures Matthew's and Mark's references to the ghost-like figure of Jesus. In the foreground of this artwork, Tanner depicts a view into the hull of the boat. We see the ribs of the boat's hull as it seems about to tip over. Most of the disciples are huddled at the far end, but one disciple, probably Peter, hangs on to the edge of the vessel. Perhaps, Peter is ready to jump out of the boat toward the apparition, making this artwork a story about Peter's sudden burst of eager faith.

B. J. O. Nordfeldt's modern oil painting is the most distinctive of the three. Nordfeldt does not include a boat, focusing on Jesus instead. The absence of the boat has the effect of placing the viewer in the boat, viewing Jesus as he approaches. The figure of Jesus, which is in the center of the painting, is abstract and surrounded by an abstract outline alluding to the disciples' mistaking Jesus for a ghost. Underneath Jesus' feet are fish, linking this story to the feeding miracle which precedes it in Matthew and Mark and which surrounds the story in John. In the latter account, the story of Jesus walking on the water ties together the feeding of the five thousand with Jesus' teaching about the bread of life, claiming, "I am the bread of life" (John 6:35). Read in relation to John's Gospel, Nordfeldt's painting might be understood as a visual blending of the story of the fish and bread, if we read Jesus as the bread, and the story of Jesus walking on the water.

These three visual depictions of the "same" story, which has three textual versions, allow students to see how artists and authors shape the meaning of an image or a story by selecting and arranging its parts. To make this point, students can identify the focus or significance of each piece (e.g., faith, Jesus, disciples) in relation to the angles from which the viewer approaches various aspects of the images. What, for example, does the view into the boat suggest about the meaning of Tanner's painting? Is this an attempt at having the viewer empathize with the experience of the disciples in the boat? This line of inquiry can be expanded to compare the angles and arrangements of the paintings in relation to the texts. What does Nordfeldt communicate about this story by having the viewer see Jesus in relation to the fish? Does this perspective capture the perspective taken in the Johannine account?

Ian Pollock, *Talents* (2000) [Private collection, Macclesfield, United Kingdom; www.eichgallery.abelgratis.com/p10.html]

Jesus' parable of the talents evokes multiple interpretations (Matt 25:14–30). To illustrate this, students can study Pollock's work which features a large Caucasian male in a black suit juggling three smaller males with different racial features (possibly African American and East Asian). Students may consider some of these questions: What is a talent, according to Pollock: the ability to juggle balls, finances, or slaves? Is the master good? What do the colors and positions of the players suggest? Is a picture worth a thousand words—that is, is the picture as effective as the parable? Gauging effectiveness depends in part on the intended effect. Is it simply to reproduce Jesus' lesson in a different medium? To apply the parable to a different historical setting? Does Pollock depend on a prior familiarity with the Matthean text? How might a viewer without this familiarity respond to this work? The painting may also be used to discuss the role of slavery in America and how the parable has been used to rationalize injustice in the pursuit of multiplying talents, or to discuss problems of translation, as in the word "talent." Students' mixed responses will demonstrate to them the "riddle of parables," the need for interpretation, and the impact of bias on their interpretation.

Pollock has produced forty paintings based on Jesus' parables which may be used in a similar way. For a related exercise dealing with divergent responses to the parables, see Guy D. Nave Jr., "The Social Functions of Parables," in Roncace and Gray, *Teaching the Bible*, 297–98.

Henri Lindegaard, *On the Earth and in Heaven* (2003) [Reproduced in *La Bible des contrastes: Méditations par la plume et le trait* (Lyons: Réveil, 2003); www.biblical-art.com]

Henri Lindegaard, *The Gift for Today* (2003) [Reproduced in *La Bible des contrastes: Méditations par la plume et le trait* (Lyons: Réveil, 2003); www.biblical-art.com]

In John 3, Nicodemus comes to Jesus at night seeking the one who comes from God. Jesus answers, "No one can see the kingdom of God without being born again/from above." (The Greek here can mean either "from above" or "anew.") Nicodemus is confused and asks Jesus how he can be born again; Jesus says that he must be born of "water and of Spirit."

Lindegaard's *On the Earth and in Heaven* can illustrate the complex distinction between the world of Jesus and that of Nicodemus. The "earthly" horizontal blinds on the left reveal Nicodemus's reverse-question-mark shape edged in black, suspended halfway between sitting and seated. One hand holds his chest; the left hand droops pointing to a womb-shaped void. To the right, the vertical "transcendent" lines capture Jesus' figure with predominantly white overlaid on black. He points upwards with his left hand and extends his right to Nicodemus, the line of his hand forming the top of the womb-shape but now suggesting a baptismal font. The vertical and horizontal lines meet in the center in the form a cross, indicating that Jesus brings the spiritual and the earthly together.

Compare the illustration and story of Nicodemus in John 3 to Lindegaard's *The Gift for Today* and the story of the Samaritan Woman in John 4. Whereas Jesus meets Nicodemus at night, he meets the woman at noon. Nicodemus is a male Jewish authority-figure who does not understand Jesus; she is a female Samaritan outcast (possibly) who recognizes Jesus as the Messiah. Lindegaard captures these differences well in his illustrations. The white and black contrast is still sharp, but rather than vertical and horizontal lines separating the two characters, the two characters in *The Gift for Today* are embraced by five bright beams emanating from the sun in the top center of the illustration. Jesus' hand is outstretched to the woman; she cradles her water jug tipped toward him at hip level (perhaps that she is offering herself to him sexually, as the allusions to "living water" might suggest). He leans toward her; she leans away from him. He beseeches her with upturned white face; she is turned to him, her face in the dark. The innocent and modest buttons on her dress challenge our presuppositions of this woman as one who is seductive and "of a certain age."

These two illustrations can be employed to highlight contrasts in these two particular stories in the Gospel of John and as prime examples of other contrasts in this gospel, such as light/dark, earthly/heavenly, us/them, day/ night, and male/female.

Lucas Cranach II, *Christ and the Fallen Woman* (1532) [The State Hermitage Museum, St. Petersburg; hermitagemuseum.org]

Valentin de Boulogne, *Christ and the Adulteress* (1620s) [J. Paul Getty Museum, Los Angeles; www.getty.edu]

Rembrandt, *The Woman Taken in Adultery* (1644) [National Gallery, London; www.nationalgallery.org.uk]

William Blake, *The Woman Taken in Adultery* (1805) [Museum of Fine Arts, Boston; www.mfa.org]

Even though most scholars regard the story of Jesus and the woman caught in adultery in John 8 as a later addition, it has captured the imaginations of visual artists throughout history. Representations of this text are especially interesting because of the diverse ways in which they depict the relation between the woman and her accusers, the scribes and Pharisees, and the relation between these characters and Jesus. These images provide an entry point into conversations about John's characterizations of women and "the Jews" and the ways in which subsequent interpreters have approached these gender and ethnic categories.

Students can analyze how each artist depicts the characters or set of characters from the text, including the accusers, the woman, and Jesus. What types of costumes do the artists use? Are certain characters depicted in particular colors? How are the different characters positioned in the paintings? Encourage them to write down notes as they view each of the paintings.

Lucas Cranach's painting offers the most explicitly negative depiction of the scribes and Pharisees, employing stereotypes, such as crooked noses and scowling faces. In fact, one of the accusers, immediately to the left of Jesus, bears a striking resemblance to a pig. Although Jesus is depicted with neatly tended side curls, these seemingly convey a sense that he is the ideal Jewish rabbi in contrast to those around him. Cranach suggests the judgmental nature of the scribes and Pharisees in contrast to the compassion of Jesus, as the accused woman stands demurely, her head bowed, indicating her probable innocence. In contrast, Valentin de Boulogne's painting depicts a woman whose head hangs apparently in shame, as she is brought before Christ with her blouse falling off. The accusers stand in the darkness behind Jesus, carefully watching him (perhaps judging him) as he bends down to write on the ground. Jesus looks up at the woman, and the light that shines on both of these characters suggests a connection. The woman may be guilty, but she is drawn to and considered by a gentle-looking Jesus.

Rembrandt's painting of this scene offers a unique depiction, as we see the action from afar. The action takes place within or just outside of a large and seemingly opulent structure, although it is depicted in dark and somber tones. The only light in the painting seems to fall upon Jesus and the woman, who kneels before him in a white dress. Even though the scribes and Pharisees are adorned luxuriously, Jesus is clearly the central focus as he stands head and shoulders above those around him. Jesus' simple dress, moreover, sets him apart from the surroundings and the scribes and Pharisees. Again, the scene depicts the woman in positive terms; she kneels before Jesus and her white robe could be mistaken for a baptismal garment.

In contrast to the other paintings, William Blake's watercolor eschews stereotypical depictions of Jewish leaders; we simply see the backs of the accusers as they turn away. Blake focuses instead on the interaction between Jesus and the woman, which is highlighted by their matching pale robes and light hair. The woman watches intently as Jesus is still bent over and writing on the ground.

Additional questions for students: Do they see any patterns in how the characters are portrayed? If they do, what do these patterns say about how people have read and interpreted this text? In particular, what might these patterns say about how people have tended to interpret John's negative depictions of "the Jews" throughout the Gospel?

As students talk about the artists' depiction of the woman, they should note her somewhat sympathetic portrayal. Arguably, in each of the paintings the audience is given the sense that she actually takes Jesus up on his command to "Go and sin no more" (8:11). In other words, through the close connections the artists draw between Jesus and the woman we are given the sense that she repents or converts. However, students can discuss how this repentant woman is characterized: Is she depicted as strong and active or weak and passive? What does this say about the understandings of gender that each artist brings to the text? Does this understanding of gender cohere with this particular text or even John's Gospel as a whole?

Margo Humphrey, *The Last Bar-B-Que* (1989) [David C. Driskell Collection, University of Maryland Art Gallery, College Park; www.artgallery. umd.edu/exhibit/02–03/driskell2003/humphrey_bbq.html. The print reproduction does a better job of capturing the color and detail of this art work; see Juanita Marie Holland, ed., *Narratives of African American Art and Identity: The David C. Driskell Collection* (San Francisco: Pomegranate, 1998), pl. 76]

Albrecht Dürer, *The Last Supper* (1523) [Museum of Fine Arts, Boston; www.mfa.org]

While there are countless depictions of the Last Supper, this lithograph by Margo Humphrey is unique because of the artist's explicit attempt at reinterpreting traditional portrayals of the scene. Specifically, Humphrey draws upon African and African American imagery and culture. Most notably, she depicts Jesus and the disciples as African or African American, using brown and blue pigments for their skin. She also clothes the traditional characters in patterns that echo traditional African prints. The context of a bar-b-que itself, which includes chicken along with wine and bread, places the story of the Last Supper in the context of southern African American traditions. It is important that students realize that this recontextualization of the Gospel story is not a parody or a piece of humor. Humphrey explains, "*The Last Bar-B-Que* is a serious piece: a rewriting of history through the eyes of my ancestry, a portrayal of a savior who looks like my people" (Strychasz, "Margo Humphrey, *The Last Bar-B-Que*, 1989").

This image can be used to highlight both the Last Supper as a Passover meal, at least in the Synoptic Gospels, and African American hermeneutical traditions. Specifically, the allusion to the Exodus narrative in the story of the Last Supper allows us to think about the Gospels' appropriations of the narrative in relation to traditional African American appropriations of the narrative. We might encourage students to think about how these more recent interpretive strategies resemble ancient strategies. In order to accomplish this, students can read one or more of the Synoptic accounts of the Last Supper, as well as a reading which discusses African American interpretations of the Exodus narratives (such as Kirk-Duggan, "Let My People Go! Threads of Exodus in African American Narratives," 123–43). One might ask students to consider whether or how the Exodus narrative and African American appropriations of this narrative relate to other themes within the Synoptic Gospels. It is also possible to compare Humphrey's lithograph with another more famous depiction of the Last Supper, such as one of Albrecht Dürer's woodcut versions, asking students to compare the images in relation to the text or texts.

El Greco, *The Disrobing of Christ* (*El Espolio*) (1579) [Toledo Cathedral, Toledo, Spain; www.wga.hu]

One of El Greco's most famous works, *The Disrobing of Christ*, hangs in the sacristy (priests' change room) in the Cathedral in Toledo. Students can compare the accuracy of the content in this painting to the account in Mark 15:16–24 and its parallels. What does El Greco change or add (e.g., the number of people present, the unlikely scarlet robe, the Spanish gentle-man)?

What does El Greco emphasize? Consider the elongated figures, the off-balance focus on Jesus, his red robe and his eyes pointing upward rein-forced by the ascending clouds in the background, the press of people, and the unnatural lighting. With these types of emphases, what Christology is El Greco communicating? (Jesus is central but oppressed by evil; he transcends the physical; he wears royal signs of wealth in spite of the description of his undignified death in the Gospels, etc.) Students should be alerted to the fact that the details in a painting help us to identify what is central to the artist's interpretation of the narrative.

Finally, what response was El Greco trying to evoke from his primary audience, that is, the religious authorities who change their clothes to prepare for or to conclude worship? (The scarlet robe might suggest cardinals.) On the one hand, the religious authorities will discard their regal clothes of status and power to enter worship; on the other hand, they also put on these clothes of status and power! How does this image align with Jesus' status and power during his crucifixion? Might this suggest anything about El Greco's attitude toward the religious authorities of his day? This painting demonstrates how artists use biblical art to both affirm and to challenge the religious authorities and social conventions of their contemporaries.

A
R
T

Macha Chmakoff, *J'ai soi* (*I Am Thirsty*) (twentieth century) [From *Les 7 dernières paroles du Christ*; arts-cultures.cef.fr/artists/chmakoff/mchma34.htm]

According to the Gospel of John, Jesus states that he is thirsty while he hangs on the cross. After a drink of wine, he says, "It is finished," and "gives up his spirit" (John 19:28–30). Given the abundance of water themes in the Gospel of John (see 2:6; 3:23; 4:7–15; 5:7; 7:38; 13:5; 19:34), and especially the claim that Jesus is the source for living water (4:10; 7:38), his words on the cross come as a surprise. Macha Chmakoff's image can help one to con-sider the irony of this phrase in John. The painting is awash in aqua, blue, greens, and yellows swirling out from Jesus in a fluid cross; he seems about to drown in the color, but he reaches—with his arm attached to the beam of the cross—upward into the light. He is both the source and the victim of water.

Matthias Grünewald, *The Small Crucifixion* (ca. 1511–20) [National Gal-lery of Art, Washington, D.C.; www.nga.gov. This is a less famous but more easily accessible version of the Isenheim Altarpiece (Musée d' Unterlinden, Colmar; www.wga.hu)]

El Greco, *Christ on the Cross Adored by Donors* (ca. 1590) [The Louvre, Paris; www.louvre.fr]

Thomas Eakins, *The Crucifixion* (1880) [Philadelphia Museum of Art, Philadelphia; www.philamuseum.org]

Marc Chagall, *The Crucifixion* (1940) [Philadelphia Museum of Art, Philadelphia; www.philamuseum.org]

Arnulf Rainer, *Wine Crucifix* (1957/1978) [Tate Britain, London; www.tate.org.uk]

These paintings represent a variety of ways of understanding the Gospel accounts of the crucifixion and of Jesus' crucified body. An effective method of incorporating these into the New Testament classroom is to show these images after students have explored in some detail the Gospel accounts of Jesus on the cross. The images bring into relief different emphases in the Gospel stories. Students can note—perhaps on a handout containing the titles and artists—which images capture which aspects of the Gospel accounts.

El Greco's panting depicts the body of Jesus as a beautiful thing; the elongated and pale body hanging on the cross suggests a fine line between the erotic and the violent. Jesus turns his head upwards, which can be read as a questioning, pleading, or even longing. The troubled sky in the background alludes to the Gospel accounts of a darkened sky, as well as to the turmoil preceding and following the crucifixion event in the Gospels. Matthias Grünewald's painting, in stark contrast, famously depicts the tortured and seemingly decaying body of Jesus on the cross. Another version of the crucifixion by Grünewald, the Isenheim altarpiece, hung in a hospital offering perhaps solace or meaning to those whose bodies were also decaying (Jensen, *The Substance of Things Seen*, 139–42). Among other things, Grünewald's piece raises the question of the purpose of depictions of the crucifixion, an issue to be examined with students in relation to the Gospels as well. For instance, are depictions of the crucifixion intended to comfort or to challenge, to engender devotion or to prompt action?

Thomas Eakins's painting, which originally was received with much criticism for its realism, suggests the humanity of Jesus (cf. Milroy, "'Consummatum est...': A Reassessment of Thomas Eakins' Crucifixion of 1880," 269–84). The expression of Jesus, his head hanging in darkness, evokes the abandonment of Jesus' expression in Mark 15:34, "My God, my God, why have you forsaken me?" Arnulf Rainer's painting offers only the sense of a body on the cross, alluding to a body in the contours of his abstract cross. Rainer's use of dark red splattering and staining, however, clearly connotes blood and, thus, the violence of the crucifixion. (It may be possible to connect discussion of this aspect of the piece to the various reactions to the violence Mel Gibson incorporates in his interpretation of the cross in *The Passion of the Christ*.) The title of this piece, *Wine Crucifix*, points to Christian tradition's association of the Eucharist with the crucifixion. In this way, the piece can be utilized to discuss theological and christological interpretations of the crucified body. Rainer originally produced it as an altarpiece for the Student Chapel of the Catholic University in Graz, Austria. After the work was removed from this setting, he bought it back and decided to rework it, explaining that he "realised that the quality and truth of the picture only grew as it became darker and darker." The history of the piece thus provides an analogy for the way in which the meaning of a work can sometimes change over time, even for the author.

On first glance, one might think that Marc Chagall's painting is the least focused upon the body of Jesus. To be sure, it lacks the bloodiness of Rainer's painting and the realistic depiction of the body seen in Eakins's version of the event. Chagall's painting, however, highlights the ethnic and religious orientation of this body by suggesting Jesus' Jewish identity by clothing him with a Tallit or Jewish prayer shawl. Instead of the plain white loincloth employed by other artists seemingly to preserve Jesus' modesty, Chagall covers Jesus' genitals with an emblem of Jewish identity. Chagall's painting provides an important reminder for many students who might read the Passion narratives as "the Jews" crucifying Jesus, as though Jesus were not himself Jewish (let alone the fact that his crucifixion is carried out by the Romans!).

Matthias Grünewald, *Crucifixion* (1501–2) [Staatliche Kunsthalle, Karlsrhe; www.wga.hu]

O. A. Stemler and Bess Bruce Cleaveland, *Consider the Lilies* (1928) [Illustration from Lillie A. Faris, *Standard Bible Story Readers, Book One* (Cincinnati: Standard, 1928); www.lavistachurchofchrist.org/Picture.htm]

Anonymous, *Worship the Lamb* (1702) [Illustration from Martin Luther, *Biblia: Das ist die gantze Heilige Schrift, Alten und Neuen Testaments*; www.pitts.emory.edu/woodcuts/1702BiblD/00012955.pdf]

To emphasize the unique perspective of Jesus presented in each New Testament text, to reinforce these differences, and to encourage students to bridge the gap between verbal and visual learning, one might cut and paste three portraits of Jesus and give the following instructions: "Describe how three New Testament texts emphasize the role and significance of Jesus in different ways, linking each text to one of the paintings below. Support your answer with details from both the paintings and the text." The portraits of

Jesus should highlight various aspects of his character or function (e.g., as teacher, crucified one, exalted one, wonder worker, or prophet). There are myriad examples from which to choose in addition to these three (see www. biblical-art.com). Thus, for example, Grünewald's black chalk drawing on grey paper emphasizes Jesus' suffering and death; alone, Jesus' face is downcast and hollow, his head wrapped in heavy thorns, and his crooked body strains against the pull of gravity. This drawing might be used to illustrate the central characteristics of the Gospel of Mark with its extended passion narrative. In contrast, Lillie Faris's children's book illustration depicts Jesus in a garden of lilies surrounded by several women, one child, and a solitary man, all listening in rapt attention. Jesus is sitting on a rock in a white robe with his arms out in explanatory gesture. Birds feed at his feet. The mountain in the background suggests that this is a scene from the Sermon on the Mount, or more explicitly, Matt 6:28–29. Students might conclude that this painting represents the teaching Jesus of the Gospel of Matthew with its five major blocks of sayings. Alternatively, *Worship the Lamb*, by the unknown illustrator of Martin Luther's *Biblia*, presents Jesus as a lamb before God on the heavenly throne surrounded by angels and witnesses. Students would likely identify this representation of Jesus as coming from Revelation (5:8) or the Gospel of John (1:29). This summative evaluation can help students see the "larger picture" of the Gospels, their diversity, and their emphases.

For other images, see Jaime Clark-Soles, "Christology Slideshow," in Roncace and Gray, *Teaching the Bible*, 282–84.

A
R
T

The Arch of Titus [Many websites contain images of this Roman landmark; www.bluffton.edu/~sullivanm/titus/titus.html]

After the Maccabean revolt, the Jews governed themselves for about a century until Pompey established Roman supervision of Judea. Many Jews actively resisted this occupation. According to Josephus, this "Fourth Philosophy" persisted in challenging Rome, leading to a devastating war from 66 to 70 C.E. During the Roman siege led by Titus, Jerusalem and the temple were destroyed and many Jews were killed; some were taken to Rome as slaves. (Book 6 of Josephus's *Jewish War* provides the best account of the revolt and its aftermath.) When Titus died in 81 C.E., the city of Rome commemorated the conquest of Judea by erecting the Arch of Titus. On the inside of this arch is a carved relief depicting the Romans taking some of the treasures out of the temple, specifically a very large seven-branched candelabra (menorah) and several silver trumpets.

The triumph depicted in this arch has an accompanying sorrow. For the Jews, the destruction of the temple as the center of their sacrificial worship required a reformation of their sense of the sacred. Students can imagine themselves as one of the slaves being marched into Rome on that day and can make a list of questions they might have had about God and their own identity.

The class can then read Acts 6:8–15 (cf. Luke 19:41–44) and check their list with the complaints made against Stephen and the followers of Jesus. Then one can examine Acts 7 to identify ways that the book of Acts—and the early Christians—responded to these allegations. In brief, the Jews blamed the Christians for the destruction of the temple because they believed that Jesus was God; the Christians blamed the Jews for the destruction of the temple because they did not believe that Jesus was God. This provides background for some of the Jewish-Christian polemic found in the New Testament.

At the conclusion of the discussion, students may be apprised of the fact that Jews have refused to walk under the Arch of Titus, with one notable exception: On the day when Israel was given independence in 1948, a contingent of Roman Jews marched under the arch in the opposite direction from the original triumphal entry. As their own sign of triumph, Israel used the image of the menorah from the Arch of Titus in their coat of arms, an image seen on all Israeli passports.

Michelangelo, *The Conversion of St. Paul* (1542–45) [Capella Paolina, Palazzi Pontifici, Vatican City; www.wga.hu]

ART

After students have read and carefully compared the third-person accounts of Paul's conversion (Acts 9:1–19; 22:6–21; 26:12–18) with Paul's own accounts (Gal 1:11–24; 1 Cor 15:1–11), they can consider Michelangelo's Vatican fresco *The Conversion of St. Paul*. This painting facilitates discussion of composition in terms of both the content (what part of the narrative is captured, the characters, the gestures, etc.) and the form of the painting (background, foreground, focal lines, use of color, shadow, light, etc.). Students may be asked to make a list of what they see in the painting. In the ensuing discussion, one should outline the focal line from the top left corner, through the figure of Christ and his outstretched arm, through the uplifted arms of the soldiers, the bright face and arm of the man bent over Paul, into the upturned white face of Paul. The line continues through Paul's right leg, through the valley of people, to the city in the distance (Damascus? Jerusalem? Rome?). The message is clear: Paul is inspired to carry the light to all people and, as some would have it because the sight line is in the shape of a shepherd/bishop's hook, oversee the church. This fresco can open conversation about the nuances of storytelling and art. Other queries to pose: Which of the specific conversion accounts does Michelangelo represent, or does he harmonize them? What does he add to the basic biblical account?

Caravaggio, *The Conversion of St. Paul* (1600–1601) [Cerasi Chapel, S. Maria del Popolo, Rome; www.artstor.org]

Raphael, *St. Paul Preaching in Athens* (1515–16) [Victoria and Albert Museum, London; www.vam.ac.uk]

Valentin de Boulogne (?), *Saint Paul Writing His Epistles* (ca. 1618–20) [Museum of Fine Arts, Houston; www.mfah.org]

Rembrandt, *The Apostle Paul* (ca. 1657) [National Gallery of Art, Washington, D.C.; www.nga.gov]

Rembrandt, *St. Paul in Prison* (1627) [Staatsgalerie, Stuttgart; www.staats galerie.de/gemaeldeundskulpturen/nl_matrix.php]

Having students interact with a variety of portraits of Paul provides a creative way of discussing the life of Paul as it is seen in Acts and the Pauline letters (e.g., Acts 9:1–31; 1 Cor 15:3–10; Gal 1:11–24; Phil 3:4–6). Each of the above paintings depicts a different aspect of Paul's life. For example, Caravaggio shows the conversion of Paul in a dramatic fashion. Dressed in Roman garb, Paul lies flat on the ground after having fallen off his horse. Pointing out Paul's clothing in this image provides an opportunity to remind students of Paul's Roman citizenship. While Caravaggio captures the beginning of Paul's Christian life, as depicted in Acts, Rembrandt paints an elderly Paul. He sits in prison with a sword (a traditional indication of his death), a number of leather-bound books perhaps alluding to his familiarity with the Scriptures, and a stylus suggesting he has written or is about to write.

It is possible to have students interact with these images in a number of ways. One approach is to show students the images before they have read the texts that describe Paul's life. Students can think about what the images "say" about Paul, his life, and his significance; they can also record their impressions of Paul in the portraits. Is the Paul they see the same as or different from the Paul described in the texts? Since certain images directly relate to Acts, namely, the paintings by Caravaggio and Raphael, and others seem to capture Paul's letter writing activity, this can lead into a discussion of how Paul's life is portrayed in Acts (which never mentions his letters) in contrast to how Paul describes his own life.

Teachers can print out color copies of the images for small group use in class. Each group describes how its image relates to the assigned readings (from both Acts and the Letters) about Paul. Which text or texts does the image best capture? What parts of Paul's story does the image neglect? This might lead to a conversation about the different portraits of Paul in the New Testament.

Wisnu Sasongko, *The Ceremony of Resurrection* (2003) [Asian Christian Art Association, Yogyakarta, Indonesia; www.asianchristianart.org]

This abstract acrylic painting depicts resurrection in relation to the crucifixion, thereby linking the general resurrection of the faithful to Christ's resurrection. As such Sasongko's painting provides a visual context for discussing 1 Cor 15.

Sasongko's painting consists of dark background with abstract patches of color, which provides a contrast to the light, off-center cross shape in the foreground. The cross shape is made up of tiny human figures wearing white. The human figures are abstract and featureless, although they appear linked together by thin arms. The amorphous nature of the figures prompts one to ask if they are bodies or souls and how this relates to 1 Cor 15. The off-centered position of the cross, specifically the horizontal beam close to the top edge of the painting, creates the effect of it being raised or moving upwards. In this way, Sasongko suggests that the cross, composed of human bodies or souls, is being resurrected. To the right side of the cross on a patch of yellow, it is possible to see faint hash marks, presumably marking off those who are being raised or resurrected. Interestingly, the piece offers no indication as to where these figures have come from or where they are headed. This would be something an instructor might want to ask students about, encouraging them to use the Pauline text to help "fill in the gaps."

Students can consider how the image captures or fails to capture Paul's understanding of the resurrection. For example, if Paul understands the church as "the body of Christ"—a body that has been crucified as well as raised—is this an image that Paul would endorse? Or, if Paul had been an eyewitness to the moment of resurrection, what would he have expected to see (e.g., something like the giant talking cross of the *Gospel of Peter*?)? Or would he say that resurrection is not something that can be depicted? Students should use details from the text and from the image to support their interpretation. In particular, they can study Sasongko's use of color, light and dark contrasts, and abstraction (in reference to the small bodies or souls) in relation to Paul's text.

Rembrandt van Rijn, *St. Paul in Prison* (1627) [Staatsgalerie, Stuttgart; www.staatsgalerie-stuttgart.de/gemaeldeundskulpturen/nl_rundg.php?id=7]

Paul Klee, *The Captive* (1940) [Collection of Mr. and Mrs. Frederick Zimmerman, New York; www.sai.msu.su/wm/paint/auth/klee/klee.captive.jpg]

Students soon learn that when they are reading Paul's letters, they are reading over his audience's shoulder, just as one overhears one side of a phone conversation. They have to figure out what is happening in the background to understand the letter. Several of the Pauline letters are written from prison (e.g., Ephesians, Philippians, Colossians, 2 Timothy, and Philemon), and this setting frequently influences the tone and content of the correspondence. After reading 2 Timothy or other letters from prison, students are assigned to write a detailed description of a painting that would capture the essence of Paul in prison. In class, they share their responses. Then, one after the other, these two paintings are displayed without identifying the title of the works.

Rembrandt presents Paul as an old man pausing in thought while in the midst of writing. One arm rests on a large open book, probably the Scriptures; his elbow rests on loose pages, perhaps one of his letters, and his hand is pensively raised to his chin. His eyes are unfocused and tired. His foot is on a discarded sandal; does it indicate that he has "finished the race" (2 Tim 4:7), or that he is ready to put on "whatever will make him ready to proclaim the gospel of peace" (Eph 6:15), or that he is not really "bound" after all? Beside him on the cot lie other large tomes, some personal belongings, and a leather bag. Leaning against the bed is a sword with its tip buried in the floor. Its cross-shape hilt evokes both the crucifixion and the metaphor for the word of God, the "sword of the spirit" (Eph 6:17). The sword also foreshadows his impending death. On the far left, the edge of a barred window permits light to halo Paul's face and lift him upwards, transcending the dark prison and this "earthly life." In chiaroscuro fashion, the extension of light suggests the reality of a greater presence around Paul. The prison is filled with this presence. Paul is neither overcome by the darkness nor the prison walls. He suffers hardship, "even to the point of being chained like a criminal. But the word of God is not chained" (2 Tim 2:9). Rembrandt's painting suggests freedom rather than imprisonment.

In an abstract self-portrait from the end of his own life, Paul Klee captures the torment of prison. The flattening of three-dimensional features provides two facial expressions: one perhaps identified as contentment, the other as alertness. Both are the "stand up expressions" of someone in pain. But the head-shaped body gives another facial expression, that of peaceful death. The strong black crosshatches over a red background might evoke the debilitating connective tissue disease that crippled Klee; they might also represent the swastikas of Nazi Germany and the pain of Klee's exile to Switzerland. The central pale blue light connects his prison walls to his heart and mind and "holds him together," in spite of the forces that fragment him.

As students compare and contrast these two paintings, they might note that the common elements—the bars, light, death images—are used to convey two very different messages. In one, prison has no power even if it is physical;

in the other, prison is overwhelmingly powerful even if it is metaphorical. This comparison will help students to pay attention to the details of both the texts and the visual arts in order to construct meaning. It will also challenge their understanding of metaphor and reality in language.

Alternatively, these images may be used to discuss various uses of the "prison" metaphor (e.g., Pss 68:6; 79:11; 107:10–16; Eccl 7:26; Isa 42:7; 58:6; 61:1; Luke 4:18–19; Rom 7:23; Gal 3:22; Rev 1:18), texts written to or by prisoners, or narratives that take place in captivity (e.g., the stories of Joseph, Jeremiah, Daniel, and the apostles in Acts).

Bamberg Apocalypse (ca. 1000) [Staatsbibliothek, Bamberg, Germany; www.bamberger-apokalypse.de]

Albrecht Dürer, *The Apocalypse* (ca. 1496) [Wetmore Print Collection, Connecticut College, New London; camel.conncoll.edu/visual/Durer-prints/index.html]

William Blake, *The Four and Twenty Elders Casting Their Crowns before the Divine Throne* (ca. 1803–5) [Tate Britain, London; www.tate.org.uk]

Grace Cossington Smith, *'I Looked, and Behold, a Door Was Opened in Heaven'* (1953) [National Gallery of Art, Canberra; nga.gov.au]

Myrtice West, *Thou Art Worthy …* (1985) [Reproduced in Carol Crown, ed., *Wonders to Behold: The Visionary Art of Myrtice West* (Memphis: Mustang, 1999), 59]

Robert Roberg, *John Sees God* (1992) [Reproduced in Nancy Grubb, *Revelations: Art of the Apocalypse* (New York: Abbeville, 1997), 40]

Students often associate the book of Revelation with violence and destruction, even though the book includes an extended scene of heavenly worship (Rev 4–5) and seven subsequent visions of worship. These scenes of worship reflect one of Revelation's main rhetorical aims, to assert divine authority over and against earthly or political authorities. It is possible to draw upon the rich tradition of artistic renderings of Revelation as a means of highlighting this aspect of the text.

It is also possible to use these images as a way of showing students how interpreters' imaginations—the ways that interpreters visualize the text—engage in theological interpretation. Since the visual nature of Revelation's narrative itself encourages students to imagine their own vision of the text and the heavenly throne room, teachers might begin by reading chapter four aloud and having students do a quick sketch of what they imagine as they hear John's description of the heavenly throne room. The class can then compare their own visual interpretations to various artistic renderings of the throne-room scene. Students can reflect on how the text describes the divine presence and how the visual depictions, including their own, try to make sense of the text's abstract description of God. Do they, like Blake's watercolor or Dürer's woodcut, depict God in human form? Or, do they take a more literal approach, such as Robert Roberg in his multimedia depiction of a hot pink (his rendering of carnelian) abstraction sitting upon a throne, or Myrtice West with her abstract figure? Do the depictions of the divine replicate or challenge cultural assumptions about God? Concerning the depiction of the elders that surround the throne, do they, like the illumination from the *Bamberg Apocalypse*, highlight the political nature of the elders by including crown imagery? Or do they interpret the crowns as halos, making the elders religious figures? How do these interpretive moves reveal the artist's assumptions about the nature of God's influence? In addition, what meanings are implied by the various locations of the heavenly throne room in relation to earth or in relation to John? What does Dürer suggest about heaven and God by showing the throne room just above the horizon of the earth? Does this communicate something about the relationship between heaven and earth that is found in Revelation? Or, what does Grace Cossington Smith's painting imply by John looking up through the door of heaven only to see the seats of the elders on their thrones? Does this suggest some distance between the divine and the earthly?

A
R
T

Beatus of La Seu d'Urgell (tenth century) [Museu diocesà d'Urgell, Spain; casal.upc.es/~ramon25/beatus/beat_65.jpg]

Bamberg Apocalypse (ca. 1000) [Staatsbibliothek, Bamberg, Germany; www.bamberger-apokalypse.de]

Albrecht Dürer, *The Apocalypse* (ca. 1496) [Wetmore Print Collection, Connecticut College, New London; camel.conncoll.edu/visual/Durer-prints/index.html]

William Blake, *The Whore of Babylon* (ca. 1800–9) [The British Museum, London. Frances Carey, ed., *The Apocalypse and the Shape of Things to Come* (London: British Museum Press, 1999)]

Robert Roberg, *The Whore of Babylon Riding of a Beast with Seven Heads* (1991) [Collection of the artist; www.robertroberg.com/art.php]

Norbert Kox, *Mother of Harlots: The Pie-Eyed Piper* (1996) [Collection of the artist; www.nkox.homestead.com/writings_west.html; also available in Carol Crown, ed., *Wonders to Behold: The Visionary Art of Myrtice West* (Memphis: Mustang, 1999), 120]

The image of Babylon, the great prostitute, in Rev 17 has captured the imaginations of artists over the centuries. The text's depiction of Babylon combines gendered, sexual, and political references to build a critique of the Roman Empire. These pieces of art emphasize different aspects of Revelation's imagery in unique ways, reflecting six distinct interpretations of the chapter. The two manuscript illustrations, from the *Beatus of La Seu d'Urgell* and the *Bamberg Apocalypse*, downplay the sexualized aspect of Revelation's depiction in favor of the religious and political nature of the imagery. The latter depicts a somewhat regal looking prostitute, clothed in purple robes. One has the sense that this prostitute is a medieval European queen or noblewoman. The illustration from the former, however, appears to connect the prostitute to Muslim influences in medieval Spain, as she wears a crown with a crescent moon and sits in a position that echoes the depiction of princesses in medieval Islamic manuscripts. Dürer's woodcut also captures the religious and political elements of the imagery by highlighting the complicity of the "kings of the earth" in the activities of the prostitute. This detailed image shows the prostitute on a beast as a variety of figures representing different social roles come before the prostitute, including a kneeling monk!

In contrast to the medieval images, William Blake's watercolor, which depicts a bare-breasted Babylon, and Robert Roberg's mixed-media, in which a bleached blonde Babylon rides a hot pink beast, emphasize the sexuality of Revelation's imagery. This approach communicates Revelation's assertion that the prostitute, or the political power that the imagery symbolizes, is seductive. Even John is "greatly amazed" by the prostitute's appearance (Rev 17:6). In addition, Blake's painting captures the text's suggestion that the prostitute is drunk on the blood of the saints, as he portrays faint soul-like figures flowing out of (or in to) the large goblet held by the prostitute.

The painting by Norbert Kox is certainly the most provocative as it depicts the prostitute as a cross-dressing Jesus-figure riding the beast onto the island of Manhattan. The prostitute's face resembles traditional images of Jesus and her left arm is taken from the Statue of Liberty, including the torch. Kox depicts Manhattan on the verge of destruction under the feet of the beast, creating an image that evokes 1950s monster movies. Given the criticism of traditional American Christianity (the Jesus-prostitute wears a flaming sacred heart) and civic religion (the Statue of Liberty) inherent in Kox's depiction, the painting provides an entry into conversations about whether or not the U.S. might be indicted by Rev 17. While some students might find this image extremely offensive, it reflects a salient modern interpretation of Revelation's imagery.

A final idea: students can look at the images prior to reading Rev 17 and develop a portrait of Babylon based on the artwork, which can then be compared to the text itself.

Abstract and Nonbiblical Art

Lynn R. Huber

The possible ways that abstract and reframed nonbiblical art might be used to explore biblical studies themes and topics with students are limited only by the instructor's imagination. The works discussed in this chapter are organized alphabetically according to the name of the artist. Due to the impermanent nature of many website addresses, it will frequently be necessary to perform a simple artist or title search at the sites listed with many of these works. The indices may be consulted to find entries with classroom strategies related to particular texts or topics. All secondary literature cited here is included in the preceding bibliography (pp. 184–86).

Marcel Duchamp, *Fountain* (1917/1964) [Museum of Modern Art, San Francisco; www.sfmoma.org]

Fountain (originally exhibited in 1917, although later copies were exhibited in 1964) is one example of the "ready-made" genre of art made famous by Marcel Duchamp. Similar to art made of "found objects," Duchamp's ready-mades were functional objects that the artist transformed into art works by renaming them and placing them within artistic contexts. One of the most famous examples of this genre, *Fountain* consists of a ceramic urinal, signed "R. Mutt, 1917." *Fountain* provides a way of talking about a number of topics related to biblical studies, including how context shapes perception and interpretation and how things and ideas can be redefined. For example, an image of *Fountain* can be used to facilitate student discussion about how the biblical texts are approached and understood differently in different contexts. A writing that is treated as sacred in a religious context is approached differently in an academic context. The writing, like the ready-made object, does not change; but how the piece is perceived and interpreted changes. Presenting a urinal as a fountain is sufficiently jarring to drive this point home.

In a specifically New Testament context, *Fountain* can assist discussion about how the Gospels portray Jesus' approach toward those traditionally understood as undesirable (e.g., sinners and tax collectors). In a way similar to Duchamp's redefinition of a urinal into a piece of art, Jesus redefines or renames these cultural outsiders, naming them as followers and participants in the kingdom of God. For instance, Jesus' invitation to Levi (Matthew) effectively redefines the tax collector, traditionally unacceptable as the follower of a Jewish religious leader, as a disciple (Matt 9:9–12; Mark 2:13–17; Luke 5:27–32). In some sense, Jesus places these culturally unacceptable people into a new context—the kingdom of God.

Paul Klee, *Around the Core* (1935) [Dallas Museum of Art, Dallas; camio. oclc.org]

This work by Swiss expressionist Paul Klee provides a tool for discussing the complex ways that textual interpretations accrue and develop. The center of this mixed-media painting is a bright red teardrop shape with an open center. The image evokes a blood drop or a kernel, although it is possible to "see through" the open center in the drop. The drop is surrounded by what at first glance appears to be overlapping ovals; however, a closer inspection reveals that the ovals are formed by a single line. The overlapping layers are created by a unified "thread." Further, the largest of the ovals reaches past the edge of the canvas, effectively leaving the multiple layers open and unbounded.

It can be difficult for students to grasp that their view of a particular writing is filtered through layers of interpretive tradition. It can be even more challenging for them to understand that many of the biblical writings began as oral traditions that have been shaped to fit into written narratives, adding to the interpretive layers surrounding a particular story. *Around the Core* can be used as a visual aid for addressing these concepts. As the image is shown to the students, ask them to imagine the drop or the kernel as a story. If this small drop is the creation story, then how do we understand the rest of the image? It is helpful to have students first describe what they see and then describe what the ovals, layers, and lines might represent in this scenario, namely, the layers of meaning that develop around an oral tradition or a text. The line around the oval might be understood as suggesting that there is some unity to these layers of interpretation, although this would be something one may question. Are the layers of interpretation around a text bound together or unified in some way?

Furthermore, students may contemplate and discuss where, if the drop represents a text or a story, they as textual interpreters are located in relation to the text. Are they, like the viewer of the painting, looking at the whole picture, able to see how the layers move out from the drop? Are we able to see a narrative's interpretive layers as we read it? Or, are they standing in the ovals, their view of the drop colored by the earth-toned pigments of the ovals? One may, moreover, press students to consider the "hole" in the drop. Why does it have a hole? If we imagine the drop as a text or a story, does this suggest that the story is, even in its original form, somehow incomplete? This can lead to discussions about how even supposedly original versions of stories involve interpretive decisions that leave out possible elements.

Barbara Kruger, *You Invest in the Divinity of the Masterpiece* (1982) [Museum of Modern Art, New York; www.moma.org]

This piece prompts the viewer to question how individuals and communities "invest" in particular visions of the divine. The composition of the piece is similar to many of Kruger's works: black-and-white photographic prints (here of the Sistine Chapel ceiling) are framed in a red border, while black bands across the work bear the text of the piece's title. In this case, the word "divinity" is the focal point, as it is on a black band in the middle of the image and its font is much larger than the rest of the title. The images that Kruger employs in this artwork are taken from Michelangelo's painting of God creating Adam on the Sistine Chapel ceiling. However, these images are only portions of the creation scene; the iconic "fingers touching" scene comprises the top portion of her work.

This artwork can be used as entryway into conversations about how cultures and individuals imagine and construct, especially through images and texts, notions of the divine. In particular, the artwork encourages a feminist analysis of the Judeo-Christian theological imagination, as Kruger, a feminist artist, specifically uses images of the creation of man by a God depicted in male terms. To engage these issues, students can consider Kruger's choice of words or images. For example, what does the word "invest" imply? Why does Kruger utilize these images and not, for instance, images of Eve in the garden?

Robert Mapplethorpe, *Ken, Lydia, and Tyler* (1985) [Robert Mapplethorpe Foundation, New York; www.guggenheim.org/exhibitions/mapplethorpe; also in the catalog *Robert Mapplethorpe and the Classical Tradition* (ed. Germano Celant et al.; New York: Guggenheim Museum, 2004), pl. 100]

In this black-and-white photograph, Mapplethorpe draws upon the classical artistic tradition of depicting nude bodies in highly formal poses. In this image Mapplethorpe presents his subjects, all three nude, from the shoulders down. The sculpted bodies of Ken and Tyler are turned toward the similarly sculpted body of Lydia, who stands between them and facing the camera. The arms of Ken and Tyler mirror each other: they each have one arm behind Lydia and their other arms in front of Lydia, hands clasping in front of her pubic area. Lydia is encircled by Ken and Tyler's arms, although their bodies remain somewhat distant from hers.

This image provides a tool for reflection on biblical constructions of gender and sexuality. More specifically, it can be used to introduce elements of the gender ideology underlying the Levitical regulations about menstruation and childbirth and about acceptable and unacceptable sexual practices (Lev 12; 15:19–33; 18; 20:10–21). For instance, after reading aloud Lev 12 or 15:19–33, students may comment upon how the photography visually represents ideas in the text. Students should observe the way in which Mapplethorpe depicts the female body as circumscribed by the males' arms. This is analogous to the separation of the female from the community after giving birth and during menstruation, which similarly is being circumscribed by male boundaries. Given that the center of this image is the handclasp of Ken and Tyler over Lydia's pubic area, students likely will also note that the image suggests masculine control over feminine sexuality and reproduction. Notably, it is the priest who makes atonement to God on the woman's behalf (e.g., Lev 12:7). The handclasp also can be used as a way of explaining the Levitical use of "uncovering nakedness" to describe sexual intercourse (Lev 18).

Further, the calm mood of *Ken, Lydia, and Tyler* allows students to think about how gender ideologies function in a culture. Ideologies are not often enforced through coercion; rather, power relationships and dynamics are commonly accepted unthinkingly by those living within them, even those who benefit least. Likewise, Lydia seemingly allows her body to be hemmed in by the arms of Ken and Tyler.

Barbara Morgan, *Martha Graham-Letter to the World-(Swirl)* (1940, printed ca. 1980) [Smithsonian American Art Museum, Washington D.C.; americanart.si.edu]

This photograph captures dancer and choreographer Martha Graham "mid-swirl" in one of her most famous dance compositions, *Letter to the World*, which was inspired by the writings of Emily Dickinson. In the photograph we see Graham stepping forward, in the direction of the camera, in an exaggerated fashion while her arms seem to pull backwards. This image, especially with its title, evokes the biblical instances of women communicating a message of prophetic or divine significance. It can be used, for example, as an illustration of the Samaritan woman who tells her village about the stranger at the well (John 4) or the story of the women who are entrusted with the news of the empty tomb in the Gospel accounts. The image of Graham, which conveys a simultaneous urge to move forward and a hesitation, seemingly captures the women's mood as described in Matt 28:8: "So they left the tomb quickly with fear and great joy, and ran to tell his disciples" (NRSV). An instructor might project this image in order to help students imagine the text and ponder how it fits with the narrative's mood and message.

Mary Lovelace O'Neal, *Racism Is Like Rain, Either It's Raining or It's Gathering Somewhere* (1993) [David C. Driskell Collection, University of Maryland Art Gallery, College Park; www.artgallery.umd.edu/exhibit/02-03/driskell2003/oneal_racism.html. The print reproduction captures better the detail of this artwork; see Juanita Marie Holland, ed., *Narratives of African American Art and Identity: The David C. Driskell Collection* (San Francisco: Pomegranate, 1998), pl. 87]

This lithograph by American artist Mary Lovelace O'Neal evokes a sense of imminent crisis and change, a mood that permeates the biblical canon, including Jesus' warnings of coming judgment and strife in the Gospels (e.g., Luke 12:49–59). The layout of the piece, the left half of the image a stark dark gray and the right side a mass of competing colors and abstract shapes, creates this sense of tension. The colors and shapes on the right, including bright orange-reds, pinks, purples, blues, and black, run down the painting, suggesting movement and disorder. The dripping effect contributes to the sense that the mass of color is in the foreground of the artwork and is about to move over the stark gray space. Viewed in relation to the title, the color mass appears as a storm ready to overtake the gray. A curved line of black stretches from a black mass in "the storm" across the gray to the edge of the piece.

The title of O'Neal's piece and its inclusion in an exhibit that served as response to the Rodney King verdict, the "No Justice, No Peace? Resolutions" exhibit at the California Afro-American Museum, indicates its political nature and power. The chaos of the colors, which push against and begin to overtake the gray, might be read either as racism itself or as various reactions and responses to the gray of racism and oppression. In terms of the later reading, these responses are neither neat nor unified; rather, they are jumbled and bleed into one another.

While the evocative nature of this piece would allow it to be used in a number of ways, one option is to view it in relation to Jesus' announcements of the division his presence will bring to the earth. In Luke, Jesus proclaims,

> I came to bring fire to the earth, and how I wish it were already kindled! I have a baptism with which to be baptized, and what stress I am under until it is completed! Do you think I have come to bring peace to the earth? No, I tell you but rather division! … When you see a cloud rising in the west, you immediately say, "It is going to rain"; and so it happens. And when you see the south wind blowing, you say, "There will be scorching heat"; and it happens. You hypocrites! You know how to interpret the appearance of the

earth and sky, but why do you not know how to interpret the present time? (Luke 13:49–51, 54–56 NRSV)

Students may view the image as they hear the text being read aloud. After describing the details of the image, they may consider how it could be understood in relation to the text. Could the cloud of colors be interpreted as the division that Jesus brings? If so, what kind of division is this? Is it solely those who follow Jesus in opposition to those who do not follow? Or, is it something more complex? If colors are the division brought by Jesus, what is the dark gray? Could this be the kingdom of the world in contrast to the kingdom of God?

Pablo Picasso, *Guernica* (1937) [Museo Nacional Centro de Arte Reina Sofía, Madrid; Carsten-Peter Warncke, *Pablo Picasso, 1881–1973* (Cologne: Borders, 1998), 148–49]

Arguably Pablo Picasso's most famous painting, *Guernica* depicts the terrors of war in powerful fashion. The painting, as is well known, depicts the destruction of the Basque town of Guernica during the Spanish civil war in 1937. The painting lends itself to discussions of destruction and war in biblical texts, especially since the painting includes a sun-like eye of God (positioned in the upper left half of the painting and somewhat near the center) or some other all-seeing entity watching the destruction unfold. The action occurring beneath the eye includes a number of images that can be related to violent biblical texts: a writhing horse, a fallen statue, humans (especially women) crying out in horror. Students should consider the eye's relation to the violence. Is there anything in the biblical text that corresponds to the eye? *Guernica* truly captures the feel of texts such as Lamentations or Ezek 7:4, in which God says to Israel, "My eye will not spare you, I will have no pity. I will punish you for your ways, while your abominations are among you" (NRSV).

Picasso's inclusion of four explicitly female figures, including a mother and child, make this image a helpful resource for engaging biblical texts from a critical feminist perspective (although Picasso himself was not known to espouse a feminist attitude). For instance, the image provides a compelling counterpart to prophetic texts, such as Isa 1, which depicts Israel's destruction using feminine imagery. In particular, viewing the image of the mother wailing over her dead child highlights the irony in the prophetic explanation of Israel's misfortune because the people "did not defend the orphan" (Isa 1:23). The inclusion of primarily female figures highlights that women are often the victims of war and violence, a fact often hidden in the biblical depictions of the destruction of an unfaithful Israel. God's willingness to let Israel, his whore-of-a-wife, be destroyed at the hands of other nations stands in contrast to the image of women wailing in the midst of war. Picasso poignantly reminds the viewer that it is women and children who typically suffer most during war.

At the lower edge of the painting is a fallen statue of a man. This element, along with the depictions of women fleeing from destruction, also makes *Guernica* a compelling illustration of apocalyptic texts. Students can view this image alongside Mark 13, for example, which describes the desolating sacrilege in the temple and which laments over those who are pregnant and nursing during the coming destruction.

Guernica is such an important piece of modern art that it is easily found in a variety of print sources, and photographs of the painting can be found in art databases such as ARTstor. The original painting is quite large (349.3 x 776.6 cm), which contributes to its power; thus it is ideal for students to view it in a large format.

Edward Rauscha, *The End #1* (1993) [Tate Modern, London; www.tate. org.uk]

The *End #1* is an acrylic and pencil piece done in shades of gray, black, and white. It appears as if Rauscha has captured a moment between two frames from an early black-and-white movie: the top frame cut off at the top of the painting and the bottom frame cut off at the bottom of the painting. The piece takes it name from the text that appears, cut off of course, in each of the frames. Printed at the top and the bottom of the image in gothic text is "The End." "Scratch marks" on the painting contribute to the illusion that these are movie frames.

Rauscha's work provides an illustrative tool for discussions about biblical eschatologies. Is the "end" as described by Revelation, for example, really an end or is it also a beginning? How might Rauscha's capturing of the moment between two "The End" frames be similar to the eschatological thinking in the writings of Paul? Are Paul's audiences, like Rauscha's viewer, experiencing a suspension of the end (it is here, but not quite)? One might simply ask students to assay how this image captures or does not capture the sense of "the end" described in a given text.

Robert Rauschenberg, *Yellow Body* (1968) [Guggenheim Museum, New York; www.guggenheim.org]

Yellow Body is made by a process of solvent transfer, in which images from print sources, such as newspaper and magazine pictures, are burnished onto the canvas. Bound together by the square of yellow color, these appropriated images appear as traces and blurred memories. The piece of art is complex, yet the process of solvent transfer means the images are subtle.

Students can ponder how this piece might be understood like a text such as the biblical writings. How does Rauschenberg's work relate to its historical and social context? How is its use of sources similar to or different from that of the writings of the Hebrew Bible or the New Testament? If we imagine this piece of art as a biblical text, what does the square of yellow represent? Is it a concept or story around which the author of the text anchors the pieces that are combined to make his or her own story? For instance, is it the story of the historical Jesus around which prophetic images, ideas about the Messiah, and Greco-Roman conventions about miracle workers are arranged? How we should interpret and assess the appropriation of images, whether by Rauschenberg, Paul the Apostle, or John the Seer? Do we interpret them in relation to their original contexts, in relation to their new contexts, or both? Further, students may contemplate the overall effect of appropriated images on the viewer or audience. For example, does appropriation primarily serve to make the innovative seem familiar?

Cindy Sherman, *Untitled Film Stills* (1977–80) [*Untitled Film Still #21*, 1978. Museum of Modern Art, New York; www.moma.org; *Untitled Film Still #15*, 1978. Guggenheim Museum, New York; www.guggenheimcollection.org]

The sixty-nine black-and-white photographs that make up Cindy Sherman's *Untitled Film Stills* series can be used to introduce conversations about topics such as genre and traditional feminine imagery. In these images, Sherman creates self-portraits that mimic typical film scenes of the 1950–60s. In one of the most famous ones, *Untitled Film Still # 21*, Sherman depicts a young woman in a business suit and a dress hat. The camera angle allows the viewer to see the skyscrapers towering above Sherman. She looks off camera, and her expression is one of hesitation. The scene is reminiscent of films in which a young heroine is off to her first job in the "big city." In contrast to this "innocent" young woman, the young woman in *Untitled Film Still # 15* appears provocative and sexually alluring. Her long legs, hot-pants, and high heels worn with anklet socks suggest the woman might be a dancer. Her pose, sitting in a windowsill looking down into a street, could suggest regret, sadness, or loneliness. Jennifer Blessing's commentary on the image for the Guggenheim Museum describes the image as "the tough girl with the heart of gold" (Jennifer Blessing, "Cindy Sherman").

Sherman's photographs use visual cues, such as angle, setting, and costume, to allude to generic films. These scenes, as the above two images suggest, often revolve around stereotyped female roles. "Reading" these visual cues in Sherman's images can help students appreciate how even the most subtle detail in an image or text can prompt an audience to interpret it according to a particular set of criteria. Something as simple as Sherman's hat in *Untitled Film Still #21*, for example, instructs the viewer to read the image as a young woman's first job or her first trip to the city. Similarly, certain words and phrases (e.g., "begat," "verily," "behold!") direct a reader to interpret a biblical text according to a certain genre or a set of interpretive criteria.

Since the film stills focus on feminine imagery, they also can be used as analogies to the biblical depictions of the feminine according to certain types, such as the prostitute with a heart of gold (Rahab), or the virgin and the whore of Revelation. One might employ Sherman's photographs as a way of elucidating how biblical depictions of the feminine similarly draw upon cultural conventions, rather than depicting the lives of actual women. In addition, the film stills can facilitate conversation of how biblical texts have contributed to the construction of feminine stereotypes.

A
R
T

PART 4:
LITERATURE

Introduction: Teaching the Bible with Literature

Jaime Clark-Soles

In his introduction to *The Vintage Book of American Short Stories*, Tobias Wolff writes:

> That sense of kinship is what makes stories important to us. The pleasure we take in cleverness and technical virtuosity soon exhausts itself in the absence of any recognizable human landscape. We need to feel ourselves acted upon by a story, outraged, exposed, in danger of heartbreak and change. Those are the stories that endure in our memories, to the point where they take on the nature of memory itself. In this way the experience of something read can form us no less than the experience of something lived through.[1]

If this is true, then surely fiction, poetry, and Scripture have much in common. All literature aims to act upon readers to shape them somehow, to suggest something about realities and possibilities. This introduction will suggest reasons to use fiction and poetry in teaching the Bible and address some of the practical considerations.[2]

Why Use Poetry and Fiction?

Spiritual Formation

Literature has the power to form, deform, or transform individual readers and communities of readers. Anyone who has read Wayne Booth's *The Company We Keep: The Ethics of Reading Fiction* or Azar Nafisi's *Reading Lolita in*

---

1. Tobias Wolff, ed., *The Vintage Book of Contemporary American Short Stories* (New York: Vintage, 1994), xiii.

2. Let me state from the outset that I teach in a Christian, Protestant seminary in the Bible Belt and this context profoundly influences my thinking and practices. While I share many concerns and goals with those who teach in other contexts and with other commitments, I do not presume to speak for everyone who teaches the Bible.

Tehran needs no convincing on this point. Witness the appeal of ubiquitous book clubs. Reading texts can create, destroy, and re-create. Both the Bible and other literature engage the great themes: truth, beauty, despair, sacrifice, hate, love, fear, questing, death, birth, rebirth, redemption, citizenship, good, evil, deceit, pain, joy, missed opportunities, second chances, human motivations. Even if one is reading for mere entertainment or information, all reading contributes to formation. Some reading deforms. (For instance, Booth relates an experience in which an African American colleague protested including *Huckleberry Finn* on the reading list, given its portrayal of African American people.[3]) Some reading has the power to transform us; I put the Bible in that category. Simply put, reading good fiction and poetry can help us become better, deeper people.

COMMUNITY FORMATION

Reading literature can, and frequently does, create community. This has a number of important implications. First, in class I have the students respond to the assigned story: What was it about? What response did it evoke from you? Did you see yourself in the story? There are, of course, no right answers to these questions. Sometimes, however, students are reluctant to respond in this way to the biblical text for fear that they are showing that they do not know the "right" answer. I use literature to form community in my own classrooms, and I encourage my students to do this in their churches to get people "unfrozen" and speaking and learning about one another and what makes them tick, to investigate the human situation and how various characters address it. These practices raise questions about how texts function in groups, questions closely tied to topics such as form criticism, canon formation, and the like.

BETTER READERS

Reading good poetry and fiction makes students better exegetes and hermeneutes. I want students to develop certain skills and habits. They learn to attend to themes, metaphor, character development, plot, diction, patterns, structure, rhetoric, and tone. Many students have not been taught to read *anything* in a detailed, nuanced fashion. Add to this the fact that some already think that they know "the" meaning of a given biblical text, and the teaching project may be stymied from the outset. Working with poetry and fiction

---

3. Wayne Booth, *The Company We Keep* (Berkeley and Los Angeles: University of California Press, 1988), 3–8, 26–27.

provides a way through the impasse as the students, in effect, sight-read non-biblical material and may then bring those sensibilities to their engagement with the biblical texts.

A familiar job description of the Bible teacher says that the task is to make the strange familiar and the familiar strange. In the first instance, there are people for whom reading fiction (and, less so, poetry) is customary but they do not read or cannot seem to find enthusiasm for the Bible, perhaps because it seems antiquated, hopelessly oblique and obscure, or requires a special code to crack it. They are at home with fiction but not with the Bible. When they begin to see that they already have skills to bring to the biblical text, the text begins to have a more familiar look to them. ("Oh, this is a story, this is a character, this is a plot, this is an ironic tone, this is symbolic," and so on.) It gives them a sense of connection with the biblical text and a confidence that they can derive something from it.

On the other hand, I have students who are very comfortable with the Bible but who do not read fiction or poetry on any regular basis. Inviting them to read other materials can provide for them new eyes and ears and, therefore, new experiences with the Bible. The familiar becomes strange again and thereby regains the power to scandalize, intrigue, encourage, infuriate, or transform them. As Nathan the prophet knew, sometimes the indirect route is just what is needed for a person to encounter truth, especially hard truths about oneself.

The ability to interact with story or metaphor opens up possibilities for reflection (With what do I identify or not identify? Why or why not?). In this process students learn how multivalent, polysemous texts can be opened up or closed down for an audience; they understand how the audience is distanced as an outsider or invited in to make the story their own in some way. It teaches them to entertain endlessly provocative possibilities and revel in that rather than insisting upon a single signification. Indeed, they feel freer to do so with the nonsacred texts because there is nothing "transgressive" about it since it is "just literature."

Better Communicators

Reading good fiction and poetry makes students better communicators. In my context, that means that they write and preach better. Like the poet and short-story writer, preachers need to have maximum effect with a minimum of words. Poetry and fiction train them in allegory and metaphor, forms of communication that are simultaneously less direct than prosaic propositions explicated pedantically and more direct in that they produce a feeling, an experience, not necessarily mediated through reasoned arguments. Students are then ready to understand the punch of a parable or sublimity of a psalm, to listen for cadence, meter, and rhythm. They get in the habit of asking, "How does language actually *work*?"

BETTER LEADERS

Reading good fiction and poetry can make my students better community or congregational leaders insofar as they come to know more fully (1) themselves, (2) others who are truly unlike them, and (3) others who are ostensibly unlike them. Students learn to honor the stories of others—to let people tell their stories the way they actually see them and to have the listener respect that story as it is with its plot, characters, and so on. It teaches them to be better pastors by sitting quietly and patiently while people narrate their stories in their own way, without editing. (Think of Job and his friends, who sought to explain Job's story, to correct it, or to talk him out of it.) Moreover, they will gain skills in helping individuals and groups articulate their own stories; from there, community can form around individual and shared narratives.

TRUTH, BELIEF, REALITY, AND HISTORY

Reading good fiction and poetry broadens our notions of truth, belief, reality, and history. For every class I teach, I assign the incisive chapters from Dostoevsky's *The Brother Karamazov* entitled "Rebellion" and "The Legend of the Grand Inquisitor." Is the Legend of the Grand Inquisitor "true"? Well, what do you mean by true—that it happened at some point in history and was properly recorded and notarized? No. Is it true? Of course. Is Ivan "real"? Should we conduct a quest for the historical Ivan? Do we have to dig behind the text to discover whether Dostoevsky knew a historical man named Ivan Karamazov? Do we have to discern which part of Ivan, if any, is really a projection of Dostoevsky's own personality and then discard Dostoevsky's influence, or can we simply read Ivan as "real" just as he stands in the text—conveying shattering truths about the human situation? Is fiction "true"? Are the biblical stories "true"? Whether the subject is the Akedah, the exodus, or the life of Jesus, these kinds of questions and concerns will never be far from the surface.

Practical Considerations

Choosing the Material

How tight should the connection be between the biblical and nonbiblical material? There are three options. First, one can set them up to be in direct connection (e.g., present a poem about the Samaritan woman when studying John 4). There are a number of books that provide literature coded to specific passages this way.[4] Second, one can take a thematic approach. For instance, when we study Luke, who is rather keen on forgiveness, I have students read Simon Wiesenthal's *The Sunflower: On the Limits and Possibilities of Forgiveness*. Third, one can simply have students read good poetry and short stories quite apart from forcing a direct connection. I like this approach because it allows for more play and creative, revelatory imagining in a way that making one-to-one correlations does not, because the latter approach tends to predetermine and overdetermine their reading rather than allowing for the mystical, explosive, subtle, and unpredictable.

Processing the Material

Deciding how and where to process the material is the next consideration. I take a varied approach on this. Options include: (1) discuss the material during class time; (2) have students post their responses to an online discussion forum (providing them with some basic guidelines), as well as responses to a certain number of classmates; (3) let it lie, like the seed that grows automatically in Mark 4, or allow students to start their own thread on the course website; (4) have them keep a journal about it; and (5) allow them to decide how to incorporate readings into other work for the course (e.g., creative project, research paper, church project).

Challenges

Two main challenges confront teachers who want to incorporate literature into biblical studies courses:

(1) Students do not necessarily know how to read fiction and poetry. How

---

4. E.g., Robert Atwan and Laurance Wieder, eds., *Chapters into Verse: Poetry in English Inspired by the Bible* (New York: Oxford University Press, 1993); David Curzon, ed., *Modern Poems on the Bible: An Anthology* (Philadelphia: Jewish Publication Society, 1994); and David Jasper and Stephen Prickett, eds., *The Bible and Literature: A Reader* (Oxford: Blackwell, 1999).

much time should be invested in that larger project? Some students do not get the point and complain that "this is not a literature class."

(2) Given heightened concerns about race, gender, ethnicity, and sexual orientation, how does one factor this into choosing what to read? Much good literature is good precisely because it tackles rather than avoids these issues, which also loom large in biblical texts. On the other hand, I once assigned Flannery O'Connor's "The Artificial Nigger," and it became problematic as people were offended by having to read the word "nigger" repeatedly. The point was lost on them that O'Connor was critiquing the social relationships between blacks and whites in the south, not condoning them. Add to that fact that I am a white, heterosexual female, and it can make choosing some of the texts a heavy task. How sanitized do I want things to be?[5]

BIBLIOGRAPHY

Atwan, Robert, George Dardess, and Peggy Rosenthal, eds. *Divine Inspiration: The Life of Jesus in World Poetry.* New York: Oxford University Press, 1998.

———, and Laurance Wieder, eds. *Chapters into Verse: Poetry in English Inspired by the Bible.* New York: Oxford University Press, 1993.

Bartel, Roland, ed. *Biblical Images in Literature.* Nashville: Abingdon, 1975.

Bennett, J. A. W. *Poetry of the Passion: Studies in Twelve Centuries of English Verse.* Oxford: Clarendon, 1982.

Birney, A. L. *The Literary Lives of Jesus: An International Bibliography.* New York: Oxford University Press, 1989.

Booth, Wayne. *The Company We Keep: The Ethics of Reading Fiction.* Berkeley and Los Angeles: University of California Press, 1988.

Carlson, Paula, and Peter Hawkins, eds. *Listening for God: Contemporary Literature and the Life of Faith.* Vols. 1–4. Minneapolis: Augsburg Fortress, 1994–2003.

Cavill, Paul, and Heather Ward. *Christian Tradition in English Literature: Poetry, Plays, and Shorter Prose.* Grand Rapids: Zondervan, 2007.

Cunningham, David S. *Reading is Believing: The Christian Faith through Literature and Film.* Grand Rapids: Brazos, 2002.

---

5. In addition to items catalogued in this chapter, Roncace and Gray, *Teaching the Bible*, contains other strategies using poetry: Jaime Clark-Soles, "Poetry and Exegesis," 8–9; Brent A. Strawn, "Poetry and History," 38–39; F. V. Greifenhagen, "Lot's Wife: Bringing Minor Biblical Characters Out of the Shadows," 91–92; Roy L. Heller, "Modern Poetry and Prophetic Form Criticism," 169–70; and L. J. M. Claassens, "Ezra, Nehemiah, and the Foreign Women," 236–38.

Curtis, C. M., ed. *God: Stories*. Boston: Houghton Mifflin, 1998.

Curzon, David, ed. *The Gospels in Our Image: An Anthology of Twentieth-Century Poetry Based on Biblical Texts*. New York: Harcourt Brace & Company, 1995.

———, ed. *Modern Poems on the Bible: An Anthology*. Philadelphia: Jewish Publication Society, 1994.

Davie, Donald, ed. *The New Oxford Book of Christian Verse*. Oxford: Oxford University Press, 1981.

Detweiler, Robert. "Christ and the Christ Figure in American Fiction." *The Christian Scholar* 47 (1964): 111–24.

———, and David Jasper, eds. *Religion and Literature: A Reader*. Louisville: Westminster John Knox, 2000.

Ditsky, John. *The Onstage Christ: Studies in the Persistence of a Theme*. Lanham, Md.: Rowman and Littlefield, 1980.

Duriez, Colin, ed. *The Poetic Bible A Selection of Classic and Contemporary Poetry Inspired by the Bible from Genesis to Revelation*. Peabody, Mass.: Hendrickson, 2001.

Ficken, Carl. *God's Story and Modern Literature: Reading Fiction in Community*. Philadelphia: Fortress, 1985.

Gallagher, Susan, and Roger Lundin. *Literature Through the Eyes of Faith*. New York: Harper San Francisco, 1989.

Gros Louis, K. R. R., James S. Ackerman, and Thayer S. Warshaw, eds. *Literary Interpretations of Biblical Narratives*. Nashville: Abingdon, 1978.

Hass, Andrew W. "Literature, World." Pages 535–48 in *Jesus: The Complete Guide*. Edited by Leslie Houlden. London and New York: Continuum, 2003.

Impastato, David, ed. *Upholding Mystery: An Anthology of Contemporary Christian Poetry*. New York: Oxford University Press, 1997.

Jasper, David. "Literature, English." Pages 525–35 in *Jesus: The Complete Guide*. Edited by Leslie Houlden. London and New York: Continuum, 2003.

———, and Stephen Prickett, eds. *The Bible and Literature: A Reader*. Oxford: Blackwell, 1999.

Jeffrey, David Lyle, ed. *A Dictionary of Biblical Tradition in English Literature*. Grand Rapids: Eerdmans, 1992.

Kreitzer, Larry J. *The New Testament in Fiction and Film: On Reversing the Hermeneutical Flow*. Sheffield: JSOT Press, 1993.

———. *Pauline Images in Fiction and Film: On Reversing the Hermeneutical Flow*. Sheffield: Sheffield Academic Press, 1999.

Liptzin, Solomon. *Biblical Themes in World Literature*. Hoboken, N.J.: Ktav, 1985.

L
I
T
E
R
A
T
U
R
E

Maney, J. P., and T. Hazuka, eds. *A Celestial Omnibus: Short Fiction on Faith.* Boston: Beacon, 1997.

Maus, Cynthia Pearl. *The Old Testament and the Fine Arts: An Anthology of Pictures, Poetry, Music, and Stories Covering the Old Testament.* New York: Harper, 1954.

Milward, Peter. *Biblical Influences in Shakespeare's Great Tragedies.* Bloomington: Indiana University Press, 1987.

Moseley, Edwin M. *Pseudonyms of Christ in the Modern Novel.* Pittsburgh: University of Pittsburgh Press, 1962.

Murphy, Daniel. *Christianity and Modern European Literature.* Dublin: Four Courts Press, 1997.

Nafisi, Azar. *Reading Lolita in Tehran.* New York: Random House, 2003.

Olshen, Barry N., and Yael S. Feldman, eds. *Approaches to Teaching the Hebrew Bible as Literature in Translation.* New York: Modern Language Association, 1989.

Paschen, Elise, and Rebekah Presson Mosby. *Poetry Speaks: Hear Great Poets Read Their Work from Tennyson to Plath.* Naperville, Ill.: Sourcebooks Mediafusion, 2001.

Pollock, Constance, and Daniel Pollock, eds. *Visions of the Afterlife.* Nashville: Word, 1999.

Porter, Stanley E., Michael A. Hayes, and David Tombs, eds. *Images of Christ: Ancient and Modern.* Sheffield: Sheffield Academic Press, 1997.

Prickett, Stephen. "The Bible in Literature and Art." Pages 160–78 in *The Cambridge Companion to Biblical Interpretation.* Edited by John Barton. Cambridge: Cambridge University Press, 1998.

Rosenberg, David, ed. *Congregation: Contemporary Writers Read the Jewish Bible.* San Diego: Harcourt, 1987.

Rosenthal, Peggy. *The Poets' Jesus: Representations at the End of a Millennium.* Oxford: Oxford University Press, 2000.

Shaheen, Naseeb. *Biblical References in Shakespeare's Comedies.* Newark, Del.: University of Delaware Press, 1993.

———. *Biblical References in Shakespeare's Tragedies.* Newark, Del.: University of Delaware Press, 1987.

Sims, James H. *Dramatic Uses of Biblical Allusions in Marlowe and Shakespeare.* Gainesville: University of Florida Press, 1966.

Steiner, George. "Night Words: High Pornography and Human Privacy." Pages 68–77 in *Languages and Silence: Essays on Language.* New Haven: Yale University Press, 1998.

Tennyson, G. B., and Edward Ericson. *Religion and Modern Literature.* Grand Rapids: Eerdmans, 1975.

Trott, James H., ed. *A Sacrifice of Praise: An Anthology of Christian Poetry in English from Caedmon to the Mid-Twentieth Century*. Nashville: Cumberland House, 1999.

Wagenknecht, Edward, ed. *The Story of Jesus in the World's Literature*. New York: Creative Age, 1946.

Warshaw, Thayer. *Handbook for Teaching the Bible in Literature Class*. Nashville: Abingdon, 1978.

———, Betty Lou Miller, and James S. Ackerman. *Bible-Related Curriculum Materials: A Bibliography*. Nashville: Abingdon, 1976.

Wieder, Laurance. *King Solomon's Garden: Poems and Art Inspired by the Old Testament*. New York: Abrams, 1994.

———, ed. *The Poets' Book of Psalms: The Complete Psalter as Rendered by Twenty-Five Poets from the Sixteenth to the Twentieth Centuries*. Oxford: Oxford University Press, 1995.

Wiesenthal, Simon. *The Sunflower: On the Limits and Possibilities of Forgiveness*. New York: Schocken, 1997.

Willimon, William H. *Reading With Deeper Eyes: The Love of Literature and the Life of Faith*. Nashville: Upper Room, 1998.

Wolff, Tobias, ed. *The Vintage Book of Contemporary American Short Stories*. New York: Vintage, 1994.

Ziolkowski, Theodore. *Fictional Transfigurations of Jesus*. Princeton: Princeton University Press, 1972.

Poetry

Ira Brent Driggers and Brent A. Strawn

Poems in English inspired by, responding to, reinterpreting, or simply sharing thematic concerns with the Bible number into the thousands. In the space available here, it will be possible to discuss only a small, selective sample of this gargantuan body of literature. (Discussion of pedagogical strategies in connection with specific texts begins on p. 256.) The list of works below is provided as a resource for instructors desiring to broach specific biblical texts through poetry. Most of these works are readily available online or in easy-to-find anthologies:

TORAH

Joseph Addison, "The Spacious Firmament on High" [Gen 1]
D. H. Lawrence, "Let There Be Light!" [Gen 1]
Geoffrey Hill, "Genesis" [Gen 1]
A. E. Housman, "When Adam Walked in Eden Young" [Gen 2]
Thomas Traherne, "Eden" [Gen 2]
e. e. cummings, "Sonnet IV" [Gen 2]
Anthony Hecht, "Naming the Animals" [Gen 2]
Karl Shapiro, "The Recognition of Eve" [Gen 2]
Theodore Roethke, "The Follies of Adam" [Gen 2]
Walt Whitman, "As Adam Early in the Morning" [Gen 2]
Ralph Hodgson, "Eve" [Gen 3]
Abraham Cowley, "The Tree of Knowledge" [Gen 3]
John Keats, "Sharing Eve's Apple" [Gen 3]
William Blake, "Earth's Answer" [Gen 3]
Derek Walcott, "The Cloud" [Gen 3]
Emily Dickinson, "Eden Is That Old-Fasioned House" [Gen 3]
W. H. Auden, "They Wondered Why the Fruit Had Been Forbidden" [Gen 3]
Christina Rossetti, "Eve" [Gen 3–4]

Sigfried Sassoon, "Ancient History" [Gen 4–5]
Francis Quarles, "On the Two Great Floods" [Gen 6–9; 19]
W. S. Merwin, "Noah's Raven" [Gen 8]
Robert Herrick, "The Rainbow: or Curious Covenant" [Gen 9]
Laurance Wieder, "The Tower of Babel" [Gen 11]
Delmore Schwartz, "Sarah" [Gen 17–18]
Daryl Hine, "The Destruction of Sodom" [Gen 18–19]
A. D. Hope, "Lot and His Daughters I" [Gen 19]
A. D. Hope, "Lot and His Daughters II" [Gen 19]
Emily Dickinson, "Abraham to Kill Him" [Gen 22]
Wilfred Owen, "The Parable of the Old Man and the Young" [Gen 22]
Henry Vaughan, "Isaac's Marriage" [Gen 24]
John Donne, *Holy Sonnets*, No. 11 [Gen 27]
Francis Quarles, "On Jacob's Purchase" [Gen 27]
Jones Very, "Jacob Wrestling with the Angel" [Gen 32]
George Herbert, "Joseph's Coat" [Gen 37]
Diana Hume George, "Asenath" [Gen 40]
Celia Gilbert, "The Midwives" [Exod 1]
Robert Frost, "Sitting by a Bush in Broad Daylight" [Exod 3]
Weldon Kees, "The Coming of the Plague" [Exod 9]
Isaac Rosenberg, "The Jew" [Exod 26–27]
Arthur Hugh Clough, "The Latest Decalogue" [Exod 34]
Robert Herrick, "The Chewing the Cud" [Lev 11]
Charles Reznikoff, "Day of Atonement" [Lev 16]
Norman MacCaig, "Golden Calf" [Num 14]
Robert Herrick, "To His Conscience" [Deut 16]

PROPHETS

Alicia Ostriker, "The Story of Joshua" [Josh 3]
Phyllis McGinley, "Women of Jericho" [Josh 6]
X. J. Kennedy, "Joshua" [Josh 10]
Charles Reznikoff, "Joshua at Shechem" [Josh 24]
Henry Vaughan, "The Stone" [Josh 24]
Lord Byron, "Jephtha's Daughter" [Judg 11]
Robert Graves, "Angry Samson" [Judg 13–16]
Robert Crashaw, "Samson to His Delilah" [Judg 16]
Henry Wadsworth Longfellow, "The Warning" [Judg 16]
P. Hately Waddell, "David and Goliath" [1 Sam 17]
Charles Reznikoff, "I Do Not Believe That David Killed Goliath" [1 Sam
    17–18]

Lord Byron, "Song of Saul before His Last Battle" [1 Sam 31]
Philip Levine, "The Death of Saul" [1 Sam 31]
John Berryman, "King David Dances" [2 Sam 6]
Charles Lamb, "David in the Cave of Adullam" [2 Sam 23]
John Greenleaf Whittier, "King Solomon and the Ants" [1 Kgs 10]
G. K. Chesterton, "The Surrender of a Cockney" [1 Kgs 19]
Rudyard Kipling, "Naaman's Song" [2 Kgs 5–6]
Lord Byron, "The Destruction of Sennacherib" [2 Kgs 19]
George Meredith, "Lucifer in Starlight" [Isa 14]
Robert Harris, "Isaiah by Kerosene Lantern Light" [Isa 29]
William Meredith, "On Falling Asleep by Firelight" [Isa 65]
Francis Quarles, "Isaiah 66:11" [Isa 66]
Carl Rakosi, "Israel" [Jer 3]
Gerard Manley Hopkins, "Thou Art Indeed Just, Lord" [Jer 12]
John Wheelwright, "Live, Evil Veil" [Ezek 1]
Algernon Charles Swinburne, "Aholibah" [Ezek 23]
Wilfred Owen, "The End" [Ezek 37]
Jones Very, "My People Are Destroyed for Lack of Knowledge" [Hos 4]
Herman Melville, "The Ribs and Terrors..." [Jonah 1–2]
Randall Jarrell, "Jonah" [Jonah 3–4]
Thomas Hardy, "A Dream Question" [Mic 3]
Jonathan Swift, "The Day of Judgement" [Zeph 1]
William Blake, "In a Myrtle Shade" [Zech 1]
George Herbert, "Easter Wings" [Mal 4]

WRITINGS

John Hollander, "Psalms" [Ps 23]
Henry Williams Baker, "Psalm 23" [Ps 23]
Allen Ginsberg, "Psalm III" [Ps 27]
Denise Levertov, "O Taste and See" [Ps 34]
Thomas Stanley, "A Paraphrase upon Part of the CXXXIX Psalm" [Ps 139]
David Curzon, "Proverbs 6:6" [Prov 6]
Delmore Schwartz, "Do the Others Speak of Me Mockingly, Maliciously?" [Prov 27]
Hart Crane, "To Brooklyn Bridge" [Job 1]
Elizabeth Sewell, "Job" [Job 1–2]
Jones Very, "Hath the Rain a Father?" [Job 38]
Jay MacPherson, "The Beauty of Job's Daughters" [Job 42]
Robert Lowell, "The Book of Wisdom" [Song of Solomon 8]

Derek Mahon, "Ecclesiastes" [Eccl 1]
Robert Southwell, "Times Go by Turns" [Eccl 3]
J. P. White, "In Ecclesiastes I Read" [Eccl 7]
Francis Thompson, "Past Thinking of Solomon" [Eccl 12]
Christopher Smart, "The Conclusion of the Matter" [Eccl 12]
Elinor Wylie, "Nebuchadnezzar" [Dan 2]
John Keats, "Nebuchadnezzar's Dream" [Dan 2]
Emily Dickinson, "Belshazzar had a Letter" [Dan 5]
David Rowbotham, "Nebuchadnezzar's Kingdom-Come" [Dan 6]
Carl Rakosi, "Services" [Neh 8–9]

GOSPELS AND ACTS

G. K. Chesterton, "Joseph" [Matt 1]
Samuel Taylor Coleridge, "A Christmas Carol" [Matt 2; Luke 2]
William Butler Yeats, "The Magi" [Matt 2]
William Everson, "The Flight in the Desert" [Matt 2]
T. S. Eliot, "Journey of the Magi" [Matt 2]
Sylvia Plath, "Magi" [Matt 2]
Robert Graves, "In the Wilderness" [Matt 4; Luke 4]
Jorge Luis Borges, "From an Apocryphal Gospel" [Matt 5]
Yusef Iman, "Love Your Enemy" [Matt 5]
Countee Cullen, "For Daughters of Magdalen" [Matt 6]
Theodore Roethke, "Judge Not" [Matt 7]
Karl Kirchwey, "He Considers the Birds of the Air" [Matt 8]
Anthony Hecht, "Pig" [Matt 8]
Vachel Lindsay, "The Unpardonable Sin" [Matt 12]
Henry Vaughan, "The Daughter of Herodias" [Matt 14]
James Dickey, "Walking on Water" [Matt 14]
Vassar Miller, "Judas" [Matt 27]
Countee Cullen, "Simon the Cyrenian Speaks" [Matt 27]
James Wright, "Saint Judas" [Matt 27]
Judith Wright, "Eli, Eli" [Matt 27]
Sylvia Plath, "Mary's Song" [Matt 28]
William Cowper, "The Sower" [Mark 4]
Allen Ginsberg, "Galilee Shore" [Mark 6]
Geoffrey Hill, "Canticle for Good Friday" [Mark 15]
Edna St. Vincent Millay, "To Jesus on His Birthday" [Mark 16]
Rupert Brooke, "Mary and Gabriel" [Luke 1]
Primo Levi, "Annunciation" [Luke 1]
C. S. Lewis, "The Nativity" [Luke 2]

Henry Vaughan, "The Shepherds" [Luke 2]
William Butler Yeats, "The Mother of God" [Luke 2]
T. S. Eliot, "A Song for Simeon" [Luke 2]
Jones Very, "John" [Luke 7]
e. e. cummings, "A Man Who Had Fallen among Thieves" [Luke 10]
Christina Rossetti, "A Prodigal Son" [Luke 15]
Elizabeth Bishop, "The Prodigal" [Luke 15]
Robert Bly, "The Prodigal Son" [Luke 15]
Hilaire Belloc, "To Dives" [Luke 16]
Paul Kane, "Asleep at Gethsemane" [Luke 22]
Eric Pankey, "The Confession of Cleopas" [Luke 24]
Denis Devlin, "Ascension" [Luke 24]
Emily Dickinson, "A Word Made Flesh Is Seldom" [John 1]
D. H. Lawrence, "The Body of God" [John 1]
Dylan Thomas, "In the Beginning Was the Three-Pointed Star" [John 1]
Edgar Lee Masters, "The Wedding Feast" [John 2]
Seamus Heaney, "Cana Revisited" [John 2]
Howard Nemerov, "Nicodemus" [John 3]
Emily Dickinson, "I Know Where Wells Grow—Droughtless Wells" [John 4]
Henry Colman, "On Lazarus Raised from Death" [John 11]
A. R. Ammons, "The Foot-Washing" [John 13]
Nina Kossman, "Judas' Reproach" [John 13]
Lawrence Ferlinghetti, "Christ Climbed Down" [John 19]
James Joyce, "The Ballad of Joking Jesus" [Acts 1]
Dylan Thomas, "There Was a Saviour" [Acts 5]
Thomas Merton, "St. Paul" [Acts 9]
Rosemary Dobson, "Eutychus" [Acts 20]

LETTERS

Dylan Thomas, "And Death Shall Have No Dominion" [Rom 6]
Peter Kocan, "AIDS, among Other Things" [Rom 6]
Francis Quarles, "On a Feast" [1 Cor 5]
Samuel Taylor Coleridge, "Forbearance" [1 Cor 13]
Robert Frost, "Revelation" [1 Cor 14]
John Milton, "Sonnet XIV" [2 Cor 5]
William Cowper, "Contentment" [Phil 4]
William E. Brooks, "Pilate Remembers" [1 Tim 6]
George Herbert, "Hope" [Heb 6]

REVELATION

> William Cowper, "Sardis" [Rev 3]
> Charlotte Mew, "The Trees Are Down" [Rev 7]
> John Crowe Ransom, "Armageddon" [Rev 16]
> Victor Daley, "A Vision of Sunday in Heaven" [Rev 21]
> W. H. Auden, "Victor" [Rev 21]

The works discussed in this chapter, many of which are related to multiple texts and topics, are organized alphabetically according to the author's name. The indices may be consulted to find entries with classroom strategies related to particular texts. All secondary literature cited here is included in the preceding bibliography (pp. 246–49).

Todd Alcott, "Television" (*The Spoken Word Revolution: Slam, Hip Hop and the Poetry of a New Generation* [ed. M. Eleveld; Naperville, Ill.: Sourcebooks, 2004])

This is a hysterical prose poem that purports to be the words of a television to any and all who watch it. As one might expect it is dominated by a series of repeated demands: "Look at me." The television knows, however, that those who watch it need to do other things, such as eat or sleep or go to the bathroom. The television is willing to let those things occur, but it repeatedly insists "I am here for you" at all times.

While students find the poem quite funny, it is also pedagogically useful on at least two fronts: (1) It is a good example of poetic personification where something that does not normally speak or have a voice is given both, along with a personality which evokes either sympathy and identification or disgust and distance. One might compare personification strategies in a number of places in Scripture; for example, in the personification of destroyed Zion in Lamentations, Wisdom in Prov 8–9, Balaam's ass in Num 22, or the trees and the bramble in Jotham's fable (Judg 9:7–15). (2) The poem is a wonderful example of how literary texts must be interpreted, especially in an oral/aural environment. The poem is funny enough when read silently, but it can be even funnier if it is read aloud—that is, if it is interpreted *orally*. The volume that contains the poem, *The Spoken Word Revolution*, contains a CD that has a track of Alcott himself reading his poem. His rendition makes this funny poem even funnier. More to the point, however, is the fact that poems (and other literary compositions) sound and mean differently when they are interpreted performatively. That can be well done or poorly done, of course, but the point is that oral (i.e., public) performance (i.e., interpretation) of literature often brings out nuances and aspects that are not apparent in a flat, eyes-only, mouth-closed, "traditional" reading. This raises all kinds of interesting questions for students to ponder, for example, the purported oral origins of much that is found in Scripture, the public performance of the Psalms, or the oral aspects of Jesus' teachings underlying the Gospel accounts. The insights into the differences between written text and oral performance could be achieved by any number of poems where recordings of readings done by the author exist and can be played alongside the text for comparative purposes (again, some good, some bad). Many such readings are available online or in poetry anthologies (e.g., Elise Paschen and Rebekah Presson Mosby, eds., *Poetry Speaks*).

Matthew Arnold, "Progress" (*The Poems of Matthew Arnold* [ed. M. Allott; 2nd ed.; London: Longman, 1979]; www.bartleby.com/236/125. html)

In this twelve-line poem Arnold begins with a re-enactment of Matt 5:17–20 (stanzas 1–3) and then reflects upon the significance of Jesus' words for a modern world consumed with antireligious notions of progress (stanzas 4–12).

The instructor can use the poem to reinforce fundamental Matthean concerns, namely, the purpose of the Mosaic law and the relationship between the church and Judaism. To this end, students should already be somewhat familiar with the message of Matt 5:17–20: Jesus does not represent a break with the Torah but rather its fulfillment, so that Jesus' disciples must follow it more deeply, looking to Jesus as its ultimate authority and thereby surpassing the scribes and Pharisees in their obedience (thus the famous "antitheses" of 5:21–48). It would also help if students knew what was at stake in this claim: that the community of believers represents the true Israel and is not some bastard offshoot.

With these pieces in place students are better equipped to evaluate Arnold's poem vis-à-vis its biblical source. Initial questions should include: How well do the words of Arnold's Jesus follow the Matthean script? What prompts Arnold's Jesus to stress the importance of the Mosaic law? What, according to the poem, is the relevance of Jesus' message today? Careful examination should reveal that while the words of Arnold's Jesus (stanzas 1–3) follow Matt 5:17–20 rather closely, the message is put toward radically different ends. In the poem Jesus scolds his disciples for *wanting* to break from Torah, while Matthew's Jesus (according to the scholarly consensus) seeks to *assure* an audience of its *continuity* with Torah and thus its identity as the people of God.

The rest of the poem (stanzas 4–12) criticizes the modern pursuit of progress at the expense of spiritual health—as the soul "perishes of the cold"

258 TEACHING THE BIBLE

(line 32). Thus Jesus urges fidelity to the law as a way of checking this dangerous tendency. There is therefore also a general lesson for exegesis here: What difference does attention to historical and narrative contexts make in the interpretation of the text? What other interpretations of Matt 5:17–20 might we arrive at if we did not have those contexts to set parameters?

Despite these discontinuities, students may very well sympathize with the poem's overall message. If that is the case, instructors could bring to their attention the warning against "earthly treasures" in Matt 6:19–34, a passage (in the same sermon) that anticipates the poem's chief anxiety: "No one can serve two masters" (6:24). Finally, the poem's concluding acceptance of all religions (stanzas 10–12) raises interesting questions to which students often gravitate naturally. Although this is another instance of the poem standing at odds with Matthew, intrepid instructors may want to move the discussion in this direction, particularly since the Sermon on the Mount asserts the *absolute* authority of Jesus. Indeed, Matthew's Gospel contains some of the more polemically harsh passages in the New Testament (e.g., 23:1–39; 25:31–46).

Wendell Berry, "Whatever Happens" (*Given: Poems* [Emeryville, Calif.: Shoemaker and Hoard, 2005])

This very short poem (only seven lines) from Berry's celebrated "Sabbaths" collection (poems he wrote on Sabbath days over the years) could be instructively used to discuss realized/realizing eschatology or the present presence of eternal life as found in the Gospel of John, where one "has" eternal life, even now (cf. 3:36; 5:24; 6:47; 17:3). The poem describes how those who have learned to love one another (another Johannine theme) have found their way to "the lasting world" and will not leave it, no matter what. The poem begins and ends with the same phrase, "whatever happens," showing the similarity of *Urzeit* and *Endzeit*, or at least how the *Endzeit* presses in upon the present.

William Blake, "The Lamb" (*William Blake: The Complete Poems* [ed. A. Ostriker; Harmondsworth: Penguin, 1977])

This famous little poem by William Blake opens with the simple question: "Little Lamb, who made thee? / Dost thou know who made thee?" (lines 1–2). While the first stanza (lines 1–10) fosters a sense of thanksgiving with its stress on the idyllic comforts of the lamb's life (food, stream and mead, wooly clothing), the second stanza (lines 11–20) fosters a sense of identification between the lamb and its creator who "calls himself a Lamb" (line 14).

Although the poem does not engage any specific biblical texts, instructors can use it to engage thematically related passages. For instance, the opening emphasis on the sheer gift of the lamb's life and the seemingly "natural" provision it finds in the world (stanza 1) finds an interesting parallel with Matt 6:19–34, where Jesus assuages human anxiety over possessions through the analogy of birds: "They neither sow nor reap nor gather into barns, and yet your heavenly Father feeds them. Are you not of more value than they?" The connection between provision and creation is easier to see in the poem, where the refrain "made thee" (lines 1, 2) is followed by the refrain "gave thee" (lines 3, 5, 7, 9, 10). Thus instructors may wish to introduce the poem before the biblical text, asking students to find and explain the connection ("How does the poem, and especially stanza 1, shape the lamb's view of his own life and its provisions?"). Then, with this connection in mind, the students will be better equipped to see it in the biblical text, where humans "store up treasures" (Matt 6:19) because they forget what the birds know, namely, that all of life is a gift from God. Theologically minded instructors could also segue into a discussion of the Christian life as defined by dependency on God and the connection between that dependency and thanksgiving (see Ps 23; 1 Cor 4:7;).

The poem also finds interesting parallels with the Gospel of John, which identifies Jesus not only as "the Lamb of God" (1:29, 36) through whom all of creation came into existence (1:1–5) but also as the "gate" and "shepherd" who provides for his own sheep (10:1–18). In this case attention to differences will better illuminate the biblical text: What do the sheep of John's Gospel receive that the lamb of Blake's poem does not? How is the lamb-provider depicted differently in each work (see also the Lamb of Rev 5:6–13; 7:9–17)? How does John's focus on the collective sheep differ rhetorically from Blake's focus on the individual lamb?

Robert Bly, "Warning to the Reader" (*Eating the Honey of Words: New and Selected Poems* [New York: HarperCollins, 1999])

This prose poem is a wonderful text to use with students when they find the Bible difficult to understand or too hard to take. It describes the beauty of a swept-clean granary with shafts of light against the walls coming in through slats between the wallboards: "So in a poem about imprisonment, one sees a little light." But this is a dangerous situation—birds can get trapped in these granaries and never get out because they insist on flying against the walls, thinking the bands of light are windows. Instead, "The way out is where the rats enter and leave; but the rat's hole is low to the floor." Bly ends by warning writers not to promise too much in poems by showing (only? mostly?) the sunlight on the walls, and by warning readers not to love "poems of light" too much lest they end up "as a mound of feathers and a skull on the open boardwood floor...."

The poem is useful in discussing the necessity of sticking with difficult texts; perhaps it is only with them that a way out (low to the floor?) is found.

Similarly, the poem works well with students' inherent penchant to favor "nice" texts and "positive" messages, both in Scripture and, perhaps even more poignantly, in interpretation and proclamation.

Robert Bly, "St. George and the Dragon" (*Eating the Honey of Words: New and Selected Poems* [New York: HarperCollins, 1999])

This is an interesting poem to discuss with reference to the relationship of the testaments—or even their competition. In it, Bly describes a sculpture made by Bernt Notke in 1489 for Stockholm Cathedral (images are available on the Internet). The dragon is, as Bly notes, losing, but he goes on to say that "As children, we knew ... / ... our part / Lay with the dragon." As for the knight, Bly associates him with the New Testament, which he read as an immature boy. True, the "solar knight" is victorious, but the dragon remains "the great spirit / The alchemists knew of. / He is Joseph, sent down / To the well. Grendel, / What we have forgotten, / Without whom is nothing." The Joseph story is evoked here, as is the monstrous demon of Beowulf. Bly asserts there is something raw and truthful about these figures and their *sine qua non* status. They may have been forgotten, but they must, in the articulation of the poem, be remembered and resaid. They constitute what Bly calls our "muddy greatness" which stands in contrast with the victorious "solar knight" (= the New Testament). Students might discuss the different images in the poem, their association with different parts (and testaments) in the canon, and see with which they identify and why. Moreover, perhaps it is possible for one to identify with several images and both testaments simultaneously. After all, Bly states that, as children, he knew his part lay with the dragon (= the Old Testament?) but that he also read the New Testament as a boy. Perhaps the contrast in the poem, then, is finally just an apparent one, yielding to a more subtle canonical synthesis in the last analysis.

Robert Bly, "The Yellow Dot" (*Eating the Honey of Words: New and Selected Poems* [New York: HarperCollins, 1999])

This poem is dedicated to the memory of poet Jane Kenyon (see below for the discussion of her poem "Otherwise"). It is a fascinating take on theodicy. To put it bluntly, the poem offers no complex theodicy, perhaps because none is ultimately satisfying. Instead, the poem begins with a simple assertion: "God does what she wants. She has very large / Tractors." God can do whatever she wants with those tractors; nothing can stop them (or her). Bly then likens God to a seamstress whose needlework is life. God is working on a larger pattern, and those of us who live on the quilt, as it were, are of no matter. So, the husband of a sick wife (Kenyon's?) cries, " 'Don't let her die!' But God says, 'I / Need a yellow dot here, near the mailbox.' " A yellow dot by the mailbox makes no sense, but then again, the death of the wife at forty-eight years of age does not make much sense either. One can be angry, as the husband is in the poem, but as Bly says, the turbulent ocean (a new metaphor for God) "doesn't / Mean anything" and a chicken's claws (another metaphor for God's ways) "will tear / A Rembrandt drawing if you put it down."

The poem is useful to facilitate class discussions on gendered (especially feminine) God-language, the meaning of suffering, and God and the problem of evil. Its particular theodicy has obvious resonances with certain emphases in the Reformed tradition of systematic theology, but it might also be profitably compared with the speeches at the end of Job (38:1–41:34).

Robert Bly, "A Home in Dark Grass" (*Eating the Honey of Words: New and Selected Poems* [New York: HarperCollins, 1999])

This is brief poem that, like many of Bly's poems, deals with death. In this particular case, death is both inevitable and natural: "We did not come to remain whole. / We came to lose our leaves like the trees." Moreover, death is even a good, as Bly ends the poem with the wish that we might find "A home in dark grass, / And nourishment in death." The poem might be compared, then, with some of Jesus' statements about his own death that similarly portray it as a good (e.g., John 12:24). The poem might also be used as a foil to texts that think of death as an enemy that must be defeated (e.g., Rom 7–8; 1 Cor 15) or as an inevitable evil (e.g., Ecclesiastes).

Billy Collins, "The Trouble with Poetry" (*The Trouble with Poetry and Other Poems* [New York: Random House, 2005])

This short poem identifies the problem with poetry as the fact that poetry encourages the writing of more poetry and the cycle will never end, Collins avers, until perhaps the day comes when "we have compared everything in the world / to everything else in the world." The poem is useful in addressing the issue of literary productivity leading to more literary productivity, and the sense in which subsequent interpretation of texts like Scripture is, in a way, little more than the urge to write more poetry based on the inspiration given by the primal poem. In his clever way, Collins also highlights the nature of much poetry (or at least poetic metaphor) as comparison and imitation, the latter of which he discusses in the end of the poem as the urge to "steal" from other poems. This stealing might be more acceptably presented as "influence" or "inspiration," but it, too, underscores the power of foundational literature that leaves its imprint on all subsequent interpretations, retellings, even—to some degree—antiversions. Finally, Collins ends with a reference to the book of poetry he carried inside his uniform "up and down the treacherous halls of high school"—a wonderful image showing how important literature (just literature!) can help people survive.

Billy Collins, "Introduction to Poetry" (*The Apple That Astonished Paris* [Fayetteville: University of Arkansas Press, 1996]; www.loc.gov/poetry/180/001.html)

This is a good poem to use for a class session devoted to hermeneutical theory or one that discusses the difference between author-centered approaches, such as historical criticism, and text-centered ones, such as various types of literary criticism. Collins uses a number of interesting metaphors describing how he wants his students to treat a poem, culminating in an image of having them water ski across the surface of the poem "waving at the author's name on the shore." But, instead, the students want to torture a confession out of the poem. They strap it to a chair and beat it with a hose "to find out what it really means."

At least two things are clear in the poem: Collins's own stance on how best to interpret poetry, which is one that is not overly beholden (if at all) to author-centered approaches, and his students' approach which is more firmly entrenched in the quest for a singular meaning, which Collins clearly presents as a bad approach (likened unto torture). A third item is also clear, however: namely, that interpreting different genres of texts may require different approaches, such that it may not be the nature of poetry to contain something that could be described as "what it really means"—or, at least, not in such a way that that meaning emerges from tying the composition to a chair and beating a confession out of it!

Richard Crashaw, "Two Went Up into the Temple to Pray" (*Complete Poetry of Richard Crashaw* [ed. G. W. Williams; New York: Norton, 1974]); www.luminarium.org/sevenlit/crashaw/twowent.htm)

This poem by Richard Crashaw offers a concise and penetrating commentary on Luke 18:9–14, a story unique to the Third Gospel. Directed by Jesus to "some who trusted in themselves that they were righteous and regarded others with contempt" (Luke 18:9), the story contrasts the prayers of a contemptuous Pharisee and humble tax collector, thus illustrating what might be called true and false prayer. The poem itself is short and rather straightforward, so that instructors may introduce it to students in class without sacrificing much time. In fact, given the brevity of Luke 18:9–14, students need not be familiar with this before class, either.

In courses that aim to teach exegesis, the poem can be read alongside the biblical passage as a way of practicing basic interpretive skills. Once students are familiar with both texts, instructors should ask: What in the biblical text supports Crashaw's interpretation? What in the biblical text challenges it? What important elements of the text does the poem leave out (e.g., the narrative audience, the stigma of the tax collector, other Lukan teachings on prayer)? What difference do these omissions make to our understanding Luke 18:9–14? Here the point is simply to emphasize the nature of exegesis as an argument about the text using evidence from the text.

In courses that either introduce or focus on the narrative elements of the Gospels, instructors may use the poem as an aid for illustrating the power of irony (in this case situational irony). So Crashaw draws the implications for Jesus' claim that only the humble tax collector, in recognizing his need for divine mercy, went home "justified" (Luke 18:14): The very man who "dares not send his eye" (line 4) toward God is the one who actually treads closer to God, while the one who "stands up close" (line 3) to "brag" (line 2) draws closer only to "God's *altar*" (line 5, emphasis added). In this way the poem can spark a conversation on the function of irony as a way of accentuating the literary and artistic nature of the Gospels: What irony does the poem capture? What other ironies can be identified in the biblical passage (e.g., the differences between a Pharisee and tax collector, the audience to which Jesus directs the story)? From here the instructor can point to other instances of situational irony within the Gospel of Luke: for example, the implied contrasts between lowly Galilean Jews (from whom Jesus comes) and powerful political rulers (Luke 1:5; 2:1–4; 3:1–2), or the contrasted fates of the rich man and Lazarus (Luke 16:19–31). Depending on the goals of the course, the instructor could set these examples of situational irony alongside cases of *dramatic* irony—for instance, Nicodemus's confusion over "rebirth" in John 3—thus accentuating the literary richness of the Gospels. (What difference does it make whether we understand the Gospels as works of art and the Evangelists as relatively skilled writers? How might the use of literary irony affect or "involve" an audience differently than, say, a simple treatise or letter?)

If the topic of discussion is restricted to the Gospel of Luke, one could tie the above examples of situational irony to the larger theme of reversal, particularly as it pertains to the social status quo (e.g., Luke 1:46–55; 4:16–30; 6:20–21, 24–25; 14:7–24; 16:19–31): What aspects of the Lukan reversal theme does the poem capture? What aspects does it fail to capture? In addition, one could place the poem and Luke 18:9–14 alongside other important references to prayer within Luke, both in the immediate narrative context and elsewhere (Luke 6:28; 11:1–4; 20:4–7; 22:40–46): What aspects of the Lukan view of prayer does the poem capture? What aspects does it fail to capture? Regardless of the trajectory, the instructor will want to emphasize how, in the case of Gospel narratives, particular themes can rarely be reduced to a single passage. Rather, gauging a Gospel's perspective on an issue involves attention to multiple passages, each falling within its own narrative context.

Countee Cullen, "The Litany of the Dark People" (*Chapters into Verse: Poetry in English Inspired by the Bible* [ed. R. Atwan and L. Wieder; Oxford University, 2000]; http://grace-ed.org/blog/archives/101)

The speaker of this three-stanza "litany" is a collective people who have turned from "ancient deities" (line 3) to the "Christ of Bethlehem" (line 8). As a result of this conversion, they experience peace and hope in Christ's solidarity with their sufferings and a love for their persecutors. Instructors will find this piece a helpful means of elucidating (whether by comparison or contrast) New Testament passages that coalesce some or all of the same themes (e.g., Matt 5:38–48; Mark 13:9–13; Rom 7–8; Phil 3:2–21; 1 Thess 1:6–10; 2:13–16; Heb 2:1–18; 1 Pet 2:18–25; 3:8–22; 4:12–19; Rev 11:15–19; 19:1–21). Depending on course objectives, the poem may also be placed in conversation with early Christian martyrdom literature as the same themes are often at work there (e.g., *The Martyrdom of Polycarp* or *The Passion of Perpetua and Felicitas*).

Of all of these potential parallels, perhaps the closest is Paul's letter to the Philippians. Like the community speaking in the poem, the Philippian Christians have "left behind" their pagan past (line 4; Phil 3:7–8), seek a oneness with the "mind" of Christ (line 7; Phil 2:5), find solidarity with the sufferings of Christ (lines 9–12; Phil 1:29–30; 2:5–8; 3:10), and journey unswervingly to their spiritual destination (lines 13–16; Phil 3:12–16). The similarities to Phil 3:2–21 are particularly striking (leaving the past behind, pressing on toward the goal, knowing Christ's sufferings), although the poem's loving attitude toward the community's opponents sounds more Matthean (Matt 5:38–48) than Pauline. If instructors choose to introduce the poem before turning to Philippians, they will want to direct the conversation toward those basic themes. For example, "How do the speakers describe their collective past, present, and future? What is their relationship to Christ in each?" Conversely, instructors may use the poem by way of conclusion: "What parallels (and differences) do you find between the poem and Philippians?"

Because the poem's title brings an obvious ethnic dimension to its meaning (Cullen was a nineteenth-century African American) instructors may also use it as an exercise in cultural hermeneutics. Reading the first stanza in isolation from the title and subsequent lines, for instance, students will likely assume a strictly spiritual significance to the conversion of the speaking community. Taken as a whole, however, the poem illustrates how the meaning of Christian conversion—and the way the converted community defines itself— will vary depending on the status of that community within the larger society.

Here important questions include: How does the title affect our understanding of the poem? What difference do stanzas 2–3 make in our interpretation of stanza 1? How might an American slaveholder or segregationist interpret the meaning of Christian conversion differently?

Emily Dickinson, Poem #1735 ("One Crown That No One Seeks") (*The Complete Poems of Emily Dickinson* [ed. T. H. Johnson; 3 vols.; Boston: Little, Brown, 1960]; famouspoetsandpoems.com/poets/emily_dickinson/poems/9402)

Although consisting of only eight short lines, Emily Dickinson's poem captures well the irony of both the crucified Messiah and the complicity of Pontius Pilate in the Messiah's death. Without actually naming him, the first stanza (lines 1–4) contrasts Christ's godly status with his seeking, and even "coveting," the shameful alienation of the cross. The result of this ironic scenario, according to line 4, is the equally ironic "deification" of the cross' "stigma." The second stanza (lines 5–8) proceeds to contrast the irony of Christ with the irony of the powerful Pontius Pilate who, as the agent of Christ's "coronation," must perpetually remember his complicity while living in hell. Thus the irony comes full circle, as the earthly ruler is now made low, "pierced" by his own transgression.

This poem draws most directly from the canonical accounts of Jesus' trial before Pilate and his subsequent "coronation" with a crown of thorns— the "crown that no one seeks" (Matt 27:29; Mark 15:17). Because the poem captures so much irony in so few lines, it can bring to light what is easily missed in these accounts, particularly since students are not normally trained to look for irony in the Bible ("What examples of irony do you find in the poem, and what are these ironies saying about Jesus and Pilate?"). Along these lines, Mark's Gospel will probably work better than Matthew's since it so emphasizes the kingly dimensions of the term "Christ" and thus the irony of a crucified king (Mark 15:2, 9, 12, 18, 26, 32). Students may also glean one or both accounts for evidence of what the poem calls "stigma," reinforcing the element of shame that is often new to introductory-level students.

Looking to the larger narratives, the instructor may ask whether, or to what degree, Matthew and Mark really do depict Christ seeking out or "coveting" his own shameful death (as the poem claims). Also, do they reveal an interest in Pilate's fate after the crucifixion? These questions will help students zero in on the Evangelists' main emphases by using the poem as a foil. The first question may also serve as a segue to a larger discussion on the differences between the Gospels, since it is John's Gospel that most mirrors the poem in its depiction of Christ as a deity who seeks out his own death.

Looking to different New Testament texts, certain passages in Paul's letters can speak to Christ's reversal of the cross' stigma (e.g., 1 Cor 1:18–25; Phil 2:5–11), while Luke's emphasis on reversal can speak to the bringing low of the powerful (e.g., Luke 2:51–52). Particularly if the course is organized thematically, rather than book by book, the instructor can use these passages alongside the poem to accentuate other dimensions of the crucifixion's significance.

W. S. Dipiero, "Near Damascus" (*Restorers* [Chicago: University of Chicago Press, 1992])

This poem gives the perspective of Saul of Tarsus as he lies on the ground, having just fallen from his horse on the way to Damascus, "[his] mouth / plugged with road grit and surprise" (lines 6–7). From this perspective Saul sees the smallness of the world up close—red ants bulldozing, a wasp dragging a grasshopper, and heat-crusted mud slots that seem as big as lunar craters.

As the poem attempts to describe an unnarrated moment within Acts 9:1–9 (cf. Acts 22:6–11; 26:12–18), instructors may wish to use it as an entry point into Luke's characterization of Saul/Paul and his conversion in particular. To this end, students should be asked to name the ways the poem accentuates Saul's (1) denigration and (2) recalcitrance. In the former case one easily sees Saul's lowly state among the bugs, with even his horse looking upon him with contempt (line 23). In the latter case one notes Saul's resistance to the lightning flash that knocks him from his perch (line 8–9) and his willingness to eat nearby larvae "if it would have saved [his] sight" (line 15).

This approach to the poem can prime students for questions of Lukan literary design and theology: How fitting is the dynamic of being knocked off of a horse in the case of this particular character, especially given Saul's history in the narrative (Acts 7:58–8:3) and the purpose of his journey to Damascus (Acts 9:1–2)? How is this dynamic more appropriate (if not also more necessary) than, for instance, a "normal" resurrection appearance such as the apostles experienced (Luke 24:13–49; note also the theme of reversal forecast as early as Luke 1:51–53)? Why does Luke choose not to pursue the themes of denigration and recalcitrance to the degree that Dipiero does? What themes does Luke pursue instead, and what difference does this make theologically?

Another helpful discussion may stem from the question, "Where does the poem anticipate Saul's salvation?" Dipiero's single reference to Saul's future is subtle but significant given its location at the end of the poem (lines 25–27). That he subtly likens Saul's fall from the horse to Christ's crucifixion—"the light shaft ... nails me down" (lines 24–25)—provides instructors with an opportunity to explore Paul-Christ parallels both in Acts and in Paul's own letters. The poem's emphasis on Saul's recalcitrance—even after his fall—can also lead into an exploration of Paul's own view of justification as predicated upon divine grace.

John Donne, "Nativity" (*John Donne's Poetry* [ed. A. L. Clemens; 2nd ed.; New York: Norton, 1991]; www.sonnets.org/donne.htm#002)

John Donne offers in this sonnet a subtle harmonization of the Matthean and Lukan nativity stories, presenting the instructor with several avenues to explore. First, if the class is somewhat familiar with these accounts, the instructor might read the poem aloud and then ask students to list the poem's biblical references as precisely as possible. Depending on the size of the class, the instructor may also wish to break students into small groups, thereby encouraging peer interaction, the culling of knowledge, and friendly competition. Although some of the poem's more theologically abstract lines might remind students of any number of biblical verses, the two obvious Synoptic references are Luke 2:7 (the inn having no room; line 5) and Matt 2:1–23 (the magi, Herod, and the flight to Egypt; lines 6–8, 13). There are also a few more Johannine references to God entering the world as a human (lines 1–4, 9–10). In addition to being a simple test of Bible content, this exercise gives the class an opportunity to explore the birth of Jesus as systematic theologians, engaging multiple biblical texts over a single issue.

Another important issue raised by the poem is that of harmonizing disparate Gospel accounts. In fact, introductory textbooks frequently cite the harmonization of Matthean and Lukan nativities stories to illustrate this traditional approach to the Gospels. As part of the above exercise, then, instructors may wish to include a question that forces students to think in those terms; for example, what Gospel passages does the poem combine? The introduction of Tatian's *Diatessaron* or Augustine's *Harmony* may prove helpful here as ancient examples of the tendency to read the Gospels as a single account rather than as four distinct narratives with their own theological-rhetorical interests. The poem's more Johannine references to Jesus' divinity may also contribute to this discussion, particularly if the instructor wants to discourage students from reading the Synoptic Jesus as altogether divine or (in less polemical terms) to bring attention to John's distinctively "high" Christology. Here the poem serves less as an object of interpretation than as a segue to the introduction of critical approaches to the Gospels.

Finally, as an exercise in theological reflection, the instructor might use the poem to explore the traditional doctrine of the Incarnation. Donne addresses the radical claim of God being born from a woman's womb (lines 1–2) as a weak child subject to human powers (line 3–8), the divine condescending implied by this claim (line 9–12), and the role of faith in discerning the infant Jesus' identity (line 10). With respect to this issue the poem can be placed in conversation with John's prologue (John 1:1–18, esp. vv. 1–13) or the "Christ hymn" of Philippians (Phil 2:5–12), as both passages treat God's movement toward humanity and the ironic vulnerability such movement includes.

William Drummond of Hawthornden, "For the Baptist" (*Dr. W. H. Drummond's Complete Poems* [Whitefish, Mont.: Kessinger, 2005]; rpo.library. utoronto.ca/poem/726.html)

This fourteen-line work by the Scottish writer William Drummond pays homage to the character of John the Baptist in his unique role as final prophetic precursor to Christ. The spare nature of the poem brings it most closely into line with Mark 1:1–8. For reasons discussed below, however, instructors will find it helpful to incorporate Synoptic parallels (Matt 3:1–12; Luke 3:1–17), if not also the somewhat different Johannine version (John 1:6–9, 15, 19–42).

Placing the poem in conversation with Mark's account can help students better appreciate the terse Markan style and the way that style often contributes to Mark's rhetorical objectives. Although it is common to find instructors explaining Mark as a source upon which Matthew and Luke elaborate (which is most likely the case historically), Mark's rhetorical effect is often better experienced *after* students have read the more extensive Synoptic parallels. To this end, instructors may wish to assign those parallels (as well as John's account) for homework, and then begin the next class with a reading of Drummond's poem. Initial questions should include: What does the poem omit from the biblical stories about John's desert ministry? What does it choose to focus on instead? This will inevitably lead students to note Drummond's emphasis on John's ascetic, animal-like existence and habitat (lines 2–8), his very simple message of repentance (lines 9–11), and his isolation from mainstream civilization (lines 8, 12–14). From there the instructor can pose the more fundamental question: Is the poem in any way deficient for its omission of so many details we have come to associate with John? The purpose of the ensuing discussion should help students see that it is obviously *not* deficient but rather, as a work of art, it forwards its own distinctive interpretation of John. It is only deficient if we hold it to strictly (modern) historical standards, that is, if we require it merely to record data rather than shape an audience (as ancient writers intended, and as ancient audiences expected).

The point here is obviously to help students understand that, like Drummond, Mark is not to be disparaged but rather appreciated for his very brief account of John's desert ministry (he too is a kind of artist). Thus the instructor should be sure to follow the discussion of Drummond with a discussion of Mark. Drummond's emphases are closely parallel to Mark, not only in the details mentioned above but also in his opening line, which in many respects captures the essence of Mark's simple view of John: "The last and greatest herald of heaven's king."

Instructors may also wish to require students to identify the major differences between the poem and Mark 1:1–8, if only to accentuate certain dimensions of the biblical account. Most notably, Drummond casts the human landscape in much more negative terms (lines 4, 12–14; cf. Mark 1:5), so that John no longer leads a peripheral ministry of renewal but stands in utter solitude, with his call to repentance echoing "from the marble caves" (line 14).

Stephen Dunn, "At the Smithville Methodist Church" (*New and Selected Poems 1974–1994* [New York: Norton, 1995])

This delightful poem is about a daughter of "post-Christian" parents who goes off to Vacation Bible School and gets a dose of religion at the local Methodist church. The poem helps one to consider the power of biblical texts and the competition they offer to other, rival narratives, and vice versa. At one point Dunn compares Jesus with Lincoln and Jefferson and the stories about Jesus with those about evolution. "Soon it became clear to us: you can't teach disbelief / to a child, / only wonderful stories, and we hadn't a story nearly as good," and "Evolution is magical but devoid of heroes. / You can't say to your child / 'Evolution loves you.' The story stinks / of extinction and nothing / exciting happens for centuries." The poem ends on a note of contrast: the child singing about Jesus in the back seat of the car with the adult parents driving, "rid[ing] it out, sing[ing] along / in silence." In fact, a close study of the poem's lineation suggests that the parents may be more inclined toward the child's (and church's) perspective than the content itself suggests. The poem is thus a complex illustration of the power of narratives (and poems!) and the energy that is created by their interface.

George Eliot, "The Death of Moses" (*Chapters into Verse: Poetry in English Inspired by the Bible* [ed. R. Atwan and L. Wieder; New York: Oxford University Press, 2000])

This poem is profitably used in a class on Deuteronomy, especially after completing the book, or in any lecture dealing with the powerful figure of Moses in the Pentateuch. Eliot, who is best known for her novels, proves to be an insightful reader of Deuteronomy as she describes the last moments of Moses' life. The poem is about what the title purports—in the poetic case, God attempts to send an angel to take Moses' life. First, Gabriel, "the messenger / Of mildest death," who refuses since Moses is one of a kind (cf. Deut

34:10). Next, Michael, who declines since he taught Moses wisdom and so Moses is a part of him. Finally, the angel of death, "Zamaël, the terrible," who accepts but is twice rebuffed: first by the radiance gleaming from Moses' brow, which leads the angel to state, "An angel this, deathless to angel's stroke"; and, second, by Moses' own address, which instructs him to reap "fruitless plant and common herb" but "Not him who from the womb was sanctified / To teach the law of purity and love." The last rebuff sends Zamaël fleeing, baffled.

So God himself must come to take Moses. God commands Moses to close his eyes, put his feet together, and place his hand over his heart. Moses obeys with perfect obedience, a detail echoed in much of what is said of Moses in the Torah, but which is nevertheless in contrast to the need for his death in Moab in the first place: because of his *disobedience* (see 32:48–52). But when the Lord commands Moses' spirit to leave his body, it cannot. "I love this body with a clinging love: / The courage fails me, Lord, to part from it." This detail, too, resonates with aspects of the presentation of Moses in Deuteronomy, including his repeated insistence that he wishes to see the Land (3:23–29) or even the fact that his last words to Israel are ones of blessing (33:1–29). In the face of this resistance, the Lord comes down and kisses Moses, and this carries him to heaven. Even this detail finds a curious echo in Deut 34:5, which says that Moses died "at the LORD's command," but which could be (certainly too) literally translated "at the mouth of the LORD." After Moses' death, heaven and earth mourn his loss because "No prophet like him lives or shall arise / In Israel or the world forevermore" (see 34:10). The fact that no one knows Moses' burial place (34:6) is discussed in the poem, and the last lines are spot on when it comes to Moses' death in Deuteronomy: "He has no tomb. / He dwells not with you dead, but lives as Law." Throughout the book, that is, Moses is at pains to set the words of Deuteronomy before the people precisely because he will not accompany them into the Land and because these words are especially oriented toward that Land (12:1). Moses must die, but the Law will continue on. Eliot's poem thus nicely captures a number of smaller details and larger movements in Deuteronomy and in the presentation of Moses in the Pentateuch.

J. W. von Goethe, *Faust* (*Faust I and II* [trans. S. Atkins; Goethe: The Collected Works 2; Princeton: Princeton University Press, 1994])

The literary unity of the book of Job is a thorny problem. There are at least four major issues that must be addressed in a discussion of the book's composition: (1) the relation of the prose prologue (which mentions "the *satan*" and the divine council) to the prose epilogue (which does not); (2) the relation of the prose framework to the internal, poetic material; (3) the structure of the third cycle (Job 22:1–27:23; Bildad's speech is unexpectedly short;

Zophar is nowhere to be found; and Job's speech seems long and unlike his previous speeches); and (4) the "fit" of the Elihu speeches (32:1–37:24) since this figure emerges out of thin air, as it were, and is not referred to again by name thereafter.

Many possible solutions, of course, have been raised to explain one of these problems or the other, or even several at a time. For instance, perhaps the structure of the third cycle is a literary device to show that the argument has completely broken down among the interlocutors and they are completely "talking past" one another. An interesting idea derived from Goethe's *Faust* by J. J. M. Roberts draws an analogy between the complicated compositional history of that work and the book of Job. *Faust* already bears some thematic connections to Job (e.g., Mephistopheles is given permission by God to test Faust, making this testing of cosmic significance like Job's), but in this particular comparison it is the history of the literary piece's composition that bears evaluation. Goethe's *Faust* had a very long and complex composition (see Goethe, *Faust I and II*, 306–307). It began with "Urfaust," composed between 1773–75 and first published (in part) in 1782. After this came *Faust: A Fragment*, written during 1778–90 and published in 1790. *Faust I*, composed in the years 1797–1801, was not published until 1808. Finally, *Faust II* was begun 1800–1801 but was not completed until 1831, when it was sealed for posthumous publication which took place finally in 1833.

This history indicates that Faust as we now have it was written over a protracted period of time—indeed over a period of sixty-one years. Goethe did not write it all at one sitting, nor even in one extended period. There were long gaps of time when he did not work on Faust actively (at least *in writing*, as far as we know), and much of it was written out of order. Note, for example, that he completed act 5 (1830–31) of *Faust II* before he completed act 4 (1831), the last to be finished. Act 4 was begun, however, in 1827–28, before the opening scenes of act 2 were written (1828). Note also that the first two scenes of act 1 and Faust's death in the middle of act 5 were the first things written in *Faust II*, already back in 1800–1801. What is perhaps equally as striking is that *Faust II* was begun before *Faust I* was completed and some eight years before *Faust I* was published.

While none of this is perfectly analogous to the book of Job, it does present a fascinating example of a masterpiece of dramatic literature (certainly Job fits that description!) with a remarkably rich and complicated compositional history. That process can be teased apart, analyzed, divided. About 1,600 verses of "Urfaust" (1773–75/82), that is, can be found to correspond to verses in *Faust: A Fragment* (1790). The latter, in turn, lends some of its material—some rewritten, some borrowed entirely—to *Faust I* (1808). Nevertheless, Goethe's *Faust I and II* can be read and appreciated as a holistic piece of work. So, too, Job, despite all its problems of literary unity (or lack thereof).

Janet Ruth Heller, "Devorah" (*Modern Poems on the Bible: An Anthology* [ed. David Curzon; Philadelphia: Jewish Publication Society, 1994])

This four-line poem simply observes that the biblical text does not report that, after the events of Judg 4, Deborah settled down with Barak, raised a family, and ceased her duties as judge over Israel. The poem, of course, underscores the taciturnity of the biblical narrative. One may use the poem to point out the ambiguity around the phrase, "wife of Lappidoth" (4:4), which could alternatively mean that Deborah was a "fiery" individual. Whether or not Deborah was married, she is not depicted as a domestic figure. Rather, she is clearly called a prophetess and is said to have "judged" Israel (4:5), not to mention being a singer and songwriter (Judg 5). Heller, thus, has good reason to suggest that Deborah continued to exercise leadership during the forty years in which the land rested (5:31). One can ask students to comment on the purpose of the poem, as well as its own reticence. Is there a reason it is so brief? How might one extend the poem? What did Deborah—and Barak and Jael, for that matter—do after delivering the Israelites?

George Herbert, "The Holy Scriptures (1)" and "The Holy Scriptures (2)" (*The Complete English Poems* [ed. J. Tobin; London: Penguin, 2004])

These two poems from the central section, "The Church," of Herbert's extensive collection *The Temple* are beautiful paeans to Scripture that might be profitably explored at the beginning or end of a semester on the Bible, or even both. Is it easier to praise the Bible, as Herbert does, prior to knowing its unsightly details? Is it possible to praise the Bible, as Herbert does, after knowing those details? How and in what way? There might be something of Ricoeur's second naïvete at work here. Herbert ends the first poem by writing of Scripture: "heav'n lies flat in thee, / Subject to ev'ry mounter's bended knee." Is a dispositional stance of "submission" or a hermeneutics of trust necessary for interpretation of Scripture? For positive interpretation of Scripture? For interpretation of the Bible *as Scripture*? The second poem plays with the interconnections of Scripture and is interesting to contemplate with reference to intertextuality or the Reformation practice of letting Scripture interpret Scripture: "This verse marks that, and both do make a motion / Unto a third, that ten leaves off doth lie." The conclusion admits that there are other "books" one might live life by, but these are no less (or, rather, in Herbert's opinion, are far more) problematic than Scripture: "Stars are poor books, and oftentimes do miss: / This book of stars lights to eternal bliss." At this point, one could introduce Wayne C. Booth's notion of coduction and the ongoing process of evaluating new literary works on the basis of works with which we are already familiar so as to determine which books are our true friends, whose company we would like to keep long term (see his *The Company We Keep*).

George Herbert, "The Pulley" (*The Complete English Poems* [ed. J. Tobin; London: Penguin, 2004])

This poem is an intriguing conversation partner with Ecclesiastes insofar as it takes up the issue of rest. In four short stanzas the poem describes how God gave humanity every blessing and all of God's treasures save one: rest. God decides not to give rest to humanity lest humans adore the gifts and not God, or rest in nature, not the God of nature. In the last stanza, God is content to let humans have all "the rest" (of the blessings) but to have them with "restlessness" so that "If goodness lead him not, yet weariness / May toss him to my breast."

In its brief compass the poem builds an entire metaphysic that is remarkably dense and extensive. God gives all good gifts (Eccl 2:24), but they are not sufficient in themselves—a point with which Qoheleth is painfully familiar (e.g., 2:1–19)—in part because they do not provide rest, another point Qoheleth laments (2:23; 8:16). But insofar as Herbert's poem argues that rest and restlessness remain as the final (perhaps even decisive) path to God, it accounts for most of Qoheleth's problems. Of course, the poem's perspective avers, the things Qoheleth recounts do not satisfy or lead to rest (or God), for those good things are not invariably designed to do so; rest is restrained by the Divine. But Herbert's poem goes even further—evoking the possibility that Qoheleth's frustrated (restless?) search may, in the end, "toss him to my breast." This language is probably far too intimate for Qoheleth, but the book does end with a rather orthodox-sounding epilogue that speaks of the "fear of God" (12:13)—a point that is also mentioned in the body of the book (5:7; 8:12–13). At the very least, Herbert's poem provides an alternative metaphysic from that recounted in Qoheleth. In a sense these two perspectives are in contrast and competition. What is perhaps most remarkable about Herbert's is how in such brief compass it accounts for Qoheleth's and ties it firmly to an explanation rooted in God's own purposes, a point that Qoheleth would certainly challenge, at least on some levels (see, e.g., 3:11). Students might want to debate whether Qoheleth's metaphysic, in turn, can account for Herbert's. (Since the poem deals with the creation of humans and the issue of rest, it could also be used with the opening chapters of Genesis.)

George Herbert, "Death" (*The Complete English Poems* [ed. J. Tobin; London: Penguin, 2004])

This twenty-four-line poem might be used in any number of teaching sessions where death is the topic. It describes the transformation of a personified Death from a once "uncouth hideous thing, / Nothing but bones," to something "Much in request, much sought for, as a good." The cause of this remarkable transformation? Christ's death, of course, which "put some blood" into Death's face! Subsequently, the poem indicates, Christians view Death now as at the final judgment, at which point all Death's bones "with beauty shall be clad." The final stanza indicates, then, that believers can die as easily as they sleep; it matters little whether their pillows are down or dust.

The poem's connection of sleep and death is instructive insofar as this metaphorical connection is also found in the Bible (see Ps 13:3; Sir 30:17; Matt 9:24; Mark 5:39; Luke 8:52; John 11:13). The poem could also be used to describe the difference Christ's death makes in Christian understandings of death in the New Testament (e.g., Mark 10:45; Rom 6:1–4; Heb 2:14–18; 5:7–10). Finally, the poem could be used as a foil or dialogue partner with other, less positive understandings of death found in the Bible, especially in the lament psalms which want release from the realm of death (e.g., Pss 3; 4; 5; 7; 9; 12; 44; 58; 60; 74; 141; 142) or in the book of Ecclesiastes. Are the problems with death found in the latter book "solved" by Herbert's poem, or at least its referent? Qoheleth might say "no," noting the irony that, in fact, Death's "conversion"—if it be so—comes only via the *death* of Christ.

A. E. Housman, "The Carpenter's Son" (*The Poems of A. E. Housman* [Oxford: Clarendon, 1997])

A. E. Housman offers a quasi-parody of the crucifixion in this work, in which Jesus, the unnamed speaker, reflects on the meaninglessness of his death for the benefit of witnessing friends. His reflections begin at the moment "the hangman stops his cart" (line 1), but by the poem's midway point (line 13) it is clear he is already hanging. Generally speaking, the first half of the poem emphasizes Jesus' regret ("Oh, at home had I but stayed," line 5), while the second half emphasizes Jesus' warnings to his friends ("See my neck and save your own," line 23). Interestingly, the poem's only refrain ends with an encouragement to avoid Jesus' fate: "Live, lads, and I will die" (lines 4, 28).

The parodic nature of the poem makes it an easy foil to the New Testament's perspective on the crucifixion, regardless of whether the instructor chooses to focus on the Gospels, a particular Gospel, a Pauline letter, or the larger topic of New Testament Christology. In the case of the Gospels, for instance, instructors can use the poem to elucidate, by way of contrast, the interpretations of the passion provided by one or more of the Evangelists: How does the poem differ from the Gospel(s) on the question of why Jesus died? On the question of how and why Jesus anticipated, accepted, or resisted his death? On the question of how we understand the meaning of Jesus' death? On the question of how Jesus' death should shape our own actions? In the case of each disagreement, what is at stake for a particular Evangelist in depicting Jesus precisely this way? Conversely, what seems to be at stake for Housman in his own depiction?

This kind of discussion will prove particularly helpful if students are encouraged to cite specific biblical passages and frame their answers in theological-rhetorical, and not simply historical, terms (avoiding answers like, "Mark depicts it this way because that's the way it really happened"). If the format of the course allows for the inclusion of all four Gospels, the discussion can also bring to light interesting differences between them; for example, the lack of a Gethsemane prayer in John's account. Indeed, Jesus' fleeting resistance to suffering and death in Gethsemane (Matt 26:39; Mark 14:36; Luke 22:42) constitutes an interesting parallel to the poem.

Since the poem so forcefully asserts the meaninglessness of Jesus' death, and the futility of his life because of that death, students may benefit from an exploration of biblical passages that acknowledge the possibility (though not the validity) of that perspective (e.g., Mark 8:31–33; 1 Cor 1:18–25). In each case, why does it happen that some perceive the crucifixion as meaningless but others as meaningful? Given the insistence of Housman's Jesus that friends *avoid* his fate, instructors may also include certain questions raised by liberation theologies: How can an overemphasis on Jesus' death potentially lead to un-Christian expressions of faith? What biblical passages can contribute to this? Are such passages genuinely at fault or simply misinterpreted? Finally, there is the question of canonical versus noncanonical versions of the Jesus story: What cultural and religious factors stand behind our infatuation with alternative versions—whether contemporary (literature and movies) or ancient (apocryphal Gospels)? What role should those alternatives versions play in our study of the Bible, whether for academic or religious purposes?

Langston Hughes, "Harlem" (*Montage of a Dream Deferred* [New York: Holt, 1951])

This is a powerful and brief poem that could be profitably used in a class on the prophets. It begins with a simple, prose question: "What happens to a dream deferred?" It then explores possible answers: A deferred dream can dry up, fester, stink, crust over like a piece of candy, or sag under a heavy load. These are quite different options and are worth exploring in the classroom in greater detail with reference to specific dreams. Then comes the final climactic line set off by itself and in italics for emphasis: "*Or does it explode?*"

The fact that the poem is entitled "Harlem," an important location in African American history in the United States and a place where racial tensions often ran hot, is noteworthy. In fact, in 1964, an explosion of sorts took place in the riot following the fatal shooting of a fifteen-year-old African American boy, James Powell, by a white police officer.

Hughes's poem does not urge rioting, but it does observe that explosive results can occur when dreams are deferred. The poem might be instructively compared to the explosive rhetoric of the prophets who often speak in violent images and metaphors, apparently in part to arrest their audience and command their attention, and perhaps because the prophetic dream—Yahweh's dream—has been deferred too long. In Hughes's case, as often in the prophets' and Yahweh's, the dream that must not be deferred is one of justice and equity (see, e.g., Isa 1:10–17; 5:1–7; Amos 2:6–8; 5:21–24; Micah 6:1–8).

Ben Jonson, "A Hymn on the Nativity of My Savior" (*Ben Jonson* [Oxford: Oxford University Press, 1985]; www.poets.org/viewmedia. php/prmMID/19312)

In this twenty-four-line "hymn" Ben Jonson uses the nativity story as a way of reflecting upon Christ's theological significance for humankind. As a summary of numerous christological themes it is perhaps best used to help students understand the relationships between biblical interpretation, canonization, and the formulation of doctrine. This use of the poem will be most effective at the end of a New Testament survey course, after students have learned the basic contents of the canonical documents, and after they have learned to see each document as a distinctive theological voice arising from its own historical context (i.e., after they have learned to honor the rhetorical integrity of each document and to accept the tensions between them).

If these elements are in place, students can analyze the poem as a creative articulation of the doctrine of the Incarnation through the blending of biblical passages. A helpful way to begin such an analysis would be by identifying Jonson's possible biblical allusions, either through a small group exercise or a homework assignment that uses an English concordance. General references to Christ's birth (line 1), infancy (line 22), and the searching shepherds (lines 3–6) obviously draw on the Matthean and Lukan nativity accounts. Possible Johannine references include connections between life and light (line 2), the Word rejected by the very world it created (lines 10–11), that same Word taking on human nature (lines 17–18), and the identification of wills between Father and Son (13–16). However, some Johannine references could just as easily draw from passages like Phil 2:6–11 and Col 1:15–20. Finally, the poem's references to salvation (lines 8–9) and atonement (lines 19–23) could draw on any number of passages, so that part of the fun for students will be sharing and collecting insights.

During this first phase of the exercise instructors should, when necessary, push students to articulate their reasons for seeing specific scriptural allusions. They may also wish to poll the class on how convincing those arguments are. (This could easily lead to a lesson on identifying implicit Hebrew Bible allusions in the New Testament, since the same type of argumentation is at work.) When a sufficient number of allusions have been discussed, the instructor should pose questions that force the students to ponder the role of canon and exegesis in theological reflection: How many different dimensions of Christ's significance does Jonson cover? To how many documents does he (potentially) allude, and do you see any tension between those documents when they are read on their own terms (e.g., the question of Christ's divinity or the reason for his earthly existence)? If so, does the poem's combining of various passages compromise the rhetorical integrity of those documents? How does the canonization of multiple documents benefit the task of theological reflection?

Although instructors should make the connection in a way best suited for their classes, students should arrive at a better appreciation for the sticky issue of appropriating the Bible for the formulation of doctrine (an appropriation that "critical" approaches are not entirely equipped to perform but which religious communities nonetheless must). Approaching this issue through a poem, as opposed to a traditional creed or doctrine, may prove more comfortable for some students (at least initially). It will also exemplify how the "uncritical" or "precritical" appropriation of biblical passages pervades Christian culture, leaving the class to debate the consequences (both positive and negative) of that reality.

Instructors might also use this poem in the ways suggested for John Donne, "The Nativity" (see above).

Anna Kamienska, "The Weariness of the Prophet Elijah" (*Modern Poems on the Bible: An Anthology* [ed. David Curzon; Philadelphia: Jewish Publication Society, 1994])

This short poem is a rendition of the scene in 1 Kgs 19:1–8 in which Elijah, fatigued and harried by Jezebel, asks to die (19:4). As students compare the two texts, they can debate whether the Elijah of the poem, while certainly depressed, goes so far as to wish for death. Or is he asking for "release" from his dismal circumstances and for a good night's rest? Either way, the poem highlights the utter despair of the biblical account, which can open up discussion about the difficult nature of the lives of prophets (cf. Moses, Samuel, Jonah). In particular, this poem and biblical text are natural conversation partners with the laments of Jeremiah (Jer 11–20). Indeed, characteristic of Jeremiah, Kamienska's Elijah expresses both anguish and hope—hope that the deity understands his weariness, because, after all, prophets only hear whispers of the divine (a reference to the "sound of silence," 1 Kgs 19:12 NRSV) and they are awakened with a "jolt of new hurt" and called to cross new deserts. Furthermore, the poem invites closer consideration of the overall portrayal of Elijah. Is one to feel sympathetic or skeptical? While the former seems an obvious response, the latter may be appropriate as well. For instance, a careful reading of the remainder of 1 Kgs 19 suggests that God and the prophet are on different pages: God asks Elijah what he is doing at Horeb (19:9); God does not address Elijah's fear of death (19:10); God disagrees with Elijah's assertion that he alone is faithful (cf. 19:10, 18); and Elijah appears unaffected by God's appearance (19:11–13), giving the same answer as the one before the theophany (cf. 19:10, 14). The poem, in short, helps students see that prophetic biographies can be quite pathetic and ambiguous.

John Keble, "Hezekiah's Display" (*Chapters into Verse: Poetry in English Inspired by the Bible* [ed. R. Atwan and L. Wieder; New York: Oxford University Press, 2000])

This poem takes its cue from 2 Kgs 20:12–19, the account of the Babylonian envoys received by Hezekiah (cf. Isa 29:1–8). The biblical text is puzzling. It is out of place chronologically; the reason for the Babylonian visit is unclear, as is the reason for Hezekiah's revealing his wealth; the motivation for Isaiah's reaction is nebulous, and so is the literary/rhetorical purpose of the passage. The poem, indirectly, addresses some of these uncertainties, thereby opening exploration of the issues. For example, the poem exhorts Hezekiah not to show his wealth because God will manifest it in due time. The king should be humble and grateful for the riches that God has given. Is this the "message" of the biblical text? Is Isaiah's judgment oracle (2 Kgs 20:18–19) a response to the king's pretentiousness? The poem here evokes a connection with postexilic texts such as Haggai and Third Isaiah in which God does display Israel's wealth—in fact, the wealth of the nations is brought to Israel. Keble is also suspicious of the Babylonian motives for the visit, and he depicts them in an unflattering light. Like Isaiah, then, the poet is leery of foreign alliances of any kind. Keble's piece is also reminiscent of a number of anti-Babylonian biblical texts (e.g., Ps 137; Jer 51). The poem makes no mention of Hezekiah's response to Isaiah's prediction of defeat (2 Kgs 20:19). One might ask students how they would incorporate this enigmatic line into the poem? Lastly, the final lines of the poem refer to (without naming) the four Judean kings who follow Hezekiah before the fifth sees the temple looted. The poem can prompt study of basic historical content, namely, students can identify the kings: Manasseh, Amon, Josiah, Jehoiakim, and Jehoiachin. Apparently, then, Keble understands Isaiah's prophecy as foreshadowing the events of 598 B.C.E. rather than 586 B.C.E. Teachers can use this opportunity to discuss the exilic or postexilic editing of the Deuteronomistic History—that is, how one might understand Isaiah's "prophecy."

Jane Kenyon, "Otherwise" (*Otherwise: New and Selected Poems* [St. Paul: Gray Wolf, 1996])

As a way of reiterating or introducing what William P. Brown, in his commentary, has called Qoheleth's emphasis on the "glory of the ordinary," one could easily use this beautiful poem by Jane Kenyon. In twenty-six lines, Kenyon describes the beauty of a day in her life, a beauty that is poignantly underscored by the repeated refrain "It might have been otherwise." She recounts waking up in the morning, being in good health, eating a delicious breakfast, taking a walk with the dog, work she loves, lying with her mate, having dinner together, sleeping in a decorated bedroom. All of these things "might have been otherwise." As she lies in bed, she plans on another day just like the day she has just had but then, in the climactic final lines, she writes: "But one day, I know, / it will be otherwise."

The poem nicely captures the "glory of the ordinary" and also how the ordinary is made that much more glorious by the inevitability of chance, decay, death. There are, of course, any number of pieces in various media that make the same point (e.g., U2's song "Beautiful Day" or Sheryl Crow's "Soak Up the Sun"). But Kenyon's poem is especially powerful given its concision and perfect rhythm that lead inevitably to the final lines that reframe her "beautiful day" in an inimitably poignant way. Moreover, this poem was almost prophetic for Kenyon: "Otherwise" was first published in a collection (*Constance: Poems*), which appeared on July 1, 1993. In January 1994, she was diagnosed with a virulent form of leukemia and died only fifteen months later at forty-eight years of age. See the "Afterword" in *Otherwise* by her husband, the poet Donald Hall, along with her final poem, "The Sick Wife," which she dictated a month before her death. Setting "Otherwise" next to "The Sick Wife" further underscores the poignant truth of "But one day, I know, / it will be otherwise."

D. H. Lawrence, "The Hands of God" (*Complete Poems of D. H. Lawrence* [ed. V. de Sola Pinto and W. Roberts. London: Heinemann, 1972])

In the opening line of this short poem, Lawrence quotes Heb 10:31 (RSV) verbatim, only to follow it with a second line suggestive of the sometimes ambivalent reactions to the prospect of becoming a part of God's people: "It is a fearful thing to fall into the hands of the living God / But it is a much more fearful thing to fall out of them." The poem concludes with a cry for salvation from "ungodly knowledge": "Let me never know myself apart from the living God!" A primary aim of the author of Hebrews is to assist his audience in experiencing "confidence" by showing them how Jesus has neutralized the most persistent causes of fear, namely, judgment by God and persecution by humans (e.g., 2:15–18; 3:6; 4:16; 10:35; 13:6). But in order to help them see themselves as God sees them, he draws on a register of language in some respects expressive, even evocative, of fear (5:7; 12:18–29).

This poem provides a point of departure for discussing the motif of fear as it appears in a wide range of biblical texts. Analyses of fear language present in microcosm many of the broader debates about "God-talk" and its implications for contemporary Jews and Christians. (Among the responses to this biblical imagery is the simple omission from lectionary readings of such "hard" texts as the so-called imprecatory psalms [e.g., 83, 109, 137, 139] in which the author calls down the wrath of a decidedly fearsome God on his enemies.) Especially in the Old Testament, "fear of God" is mentioned so frequently that it functions as a virtual synonym for "faith" or "true religion" or "the beginning of wisdom" (Prov 1:7; 9:10). Proselytes to Judaism are often termed "God-fearers." Paul tells the Philippians to work out their salvation "with fear and trembling" (2:12–13). And Jesus himself, in Heb 5:7, is said to have his prayers heard "on account of his godly fear." Is it possible to tell when biblical authors use "fear" to denote something like "reverence" and when they mean something like "terror"? Are these different aspects mutually exclusive? (A concordance search will quickly turn up dozens of texts for consideration.) An examination of how various authors negotiate this question also highlights the ways in which early Judaism and Christianity resembled or differed from Stoics, Epicureans, and other intellectual systems that emphasized the importance of emotional tranquility for a life of virtue.

D. H. Lawrence, "The Hills" (*Complete Poems of D. H. Lawrence* [ed. V. de Sola Pinto and W. Roberts. London: Heinemann, 1972])

This six-line poem is a dark parody of Ps 121. When Lawrence lifts up his eyes to the hills, "there they are." But that is it. Indeed, he states that no strength comes to him from them; only from darkness and blindness does he receive strength. The poem is an alternative perspective to that offered in Ps 121, which celebrates the Lord, the maker of heaven and earth, who keeps Israel and "you," who does not sleep or slumber, but is restless in protecting the psalmist (and the reader) from all evil, now and forever (121:2, 3–5, 7–8). Psalm 121 is an expansive psalm, to be sure, promising too much—more than can be reasonably expected. Is it disappointment in the face of Ps 121's unfulfilled promises that leads Lawrence to write his poem (and others to read it now)? Or is there something *beyond* mere disappointment at work in Lawrence's poem? Does it, like so many of the biblical laments, attest to a connection between darkness and the Lord of Life (cf. César Vallejo, "I Am Going to Speak of Hope" below)? If so, then it becomes an example, like the lament psalms and other similar texts (e.g., portions of the book of Lamentations), that poetry *about* suffering and *from* suffering is profoundly humane insofar as it gives transformative voice to the sufferer, allowing the victim to speak. Moreover, in many of these types of grief-poems, the listener is compelled to feel addressed by and even to identify with those in pain. Poems like Lawrence's, that is, may prove to be salves to the injured and an impetus to compassion for the reader. All this, in six lines!

Similar exercises might be carried out with other "revisions" of the Psalter. (Dozens of examples may be found in Wieder, *The Poets' Book of Psalms: The Complete Psalter as Rendered by Twenty-Five Poets from the Sixteenth to the Twentieth Centuries*.)

C. S. Lewis, "Stephen to Lazarus" (*Poems* [New York: Harvest Books, 1964])

In this short poem the martyr Stephen (Acts 7:54–8:1) expresses amazement over the raising of Lazarus from the dead (John 11:1–44). Surprisingly, however, Stephen's amazement stems from his pity over the plight of his biblical counterpart who, being "already free among the dead" (line 3), surrenders such freedom to return to the "fetters" (line 4) of life. The poem will help instructors elucidate some of the main features of both episodes, both of which are crucial moments in their respective narratives.

Students need not have a thorough knowledge of the entire Stephen episode (Acts 6:1–8:1), or even his death (Acts 7:54–8:1), to understand his perspective in the poem (line 1 clarifies that he is the "first martyr"). They will, however, need to know that Lazarus (mentioned only in the title) is raised by Jesus from the dead in the Fourth Gospel. With that knowledge in place, instructors can begin with basic interpretive questions: What is Stephen's perspective on the raising of Lazarus? How does he view the relationship between death and life? What kinds of metaphors does he use to make his point? After exploring the poem, instructors may then turn to the text of Acts, whether the entire Stephen episode (which will require more preparation on the part of students) or the death scene specifically (which takes little time to read in class): What is it about the Stephen episode that justifies his perspective in the poem? What details in the biblical text reinforce Stephen's perspective in the poem, particularly the notion that death is liberation from life? What episodes in the larger narrative of Acts support this idea? What is the danger of understanding death only in these terms? What episodes or themes in Acts counterbalance this perspective?

The poem will prove equally helpful in elucidating the Johannine views of life and death as depicted in the Lazarus episode and related passages in the Fourth Gospel. A bit more preparation is required in this case, however, insofar as the Johannine views of life and death cannot be captured in a single episode. Thus instructors may wish to begin with a discussion of John's distinctively "realized" eschatology and the implications this has for issues of life and death: Because Jesus is the very incarnation of God (John 1:1–18) through whom believers come to abide in God's love (John 14:1–15:11), death and life are necessarily cast in terms of such abiding—or not abiding. True life is thus *eternal* life (e.g., John 17:3), abiding in the Father through the Son, quite apart from one's biological "life." The raising of Lazarus, though technically less a resurrection than resuscitation, nonetheless points towards Jesus' significance in bringing such eternal life (John 11:21–26). Thus Lewis's poem here serves as a foil: How would the *Johannine* Jesus respond to Stephen? To what extent would he acknowledge Stephen's antipathy toward the struggles of life (see John 15:18–25; 17:11–19)? On what grounds would he oppose Stephen's understanding of life and death? To get more mileage out of the poem instructors may ask students to assess it both before and after discussing the Fourth Gospel, thus allowing students to experience the difference John's perspective makes to such issues.

Henry Wadsworth Longfellow, "The Three Kings" (*The Complete Poetical Works of Henry Wadsworth Longfellow* [Laurel, N.Y.: Lightyear, 1993]; www.hwlongfellow.org/poems_poem.php?pid=243)

Henry Wadsworth Longfellow retells, in this fourteen-stanza work, the story of the three kings (Greek: *magi*) traveling from the east in search of the king of the Jews. Because it is a rather elaborate retelling (more elaborate than, for example, T. S. Eliot's "The Journey of the Magi"), the poem can be used to familiarize students with the biblical account, found only in Matt 2:1–12.

The instructor may begin by asking students to list points of convergence and divergence between the poem and the Matthean account: Where does the poem correspond most precisely with Matthew? Where does the poem elaborate upon Matthew? Which of these elaborations do you find to be faithful interpretations of Matthew's story? Which do you find unfaithful? Where can you find Longfellow drawing upon the Lukan nativity story? What do you think motivated Longfellow to elaborate in each (or some) of these cases?

To make this exercise more efficient instructors could ask students to read the Matthean account closely before class, in which case analyzing the poem will reinforce for them what is contained, and not contained, there. It may prove more interesting, however, to introduce the poem and questions first, with Bibles closed, and with the instructor writing students' answers on the blackboard. This approach will likely spark more debate about, or at least more immediate interest in, what exactly Matthew says. Students may then read Matthew in order to verify, or disprove, specific claims made during the class discussion. If teachers wish to guide students more directly in documenting differences, they may pose specific questions about, for example, how the poem describes the number of kings/wise men (three, not specified in the biblical text), or how it foreshadows the death of the baby Jesus.

Because the poem includes so many nonbiblical details (e.g., conversations while traveling, the response of Mary to the gifts), instructors may also wish to engage students on the nature of "gap filling" in the reading of Gospel narrative: To what extent is it inevitable? How, and under what circumstances, is it beneficial and/or detrimental to exegesis? In what other artistic genres does one encounter it? In what other circumstances is it common?

Thomas Babington Macaulay, "Deus Iræ" (*The Miscellaneous Writings, Speeches and Poems of Lord Macaulay* [London: Longmans, Green, 1880]; rpo.library.utoronto.ca/poem/1357.html)

This poem is one of several modern translations of a famous medieval Latin requiem sequence, the title of which is taken from its opening line, *Deus Iræ* ("God of wrath"). With a plethora of scriptural allusions the speaker anticipates the coming day of judgment, beginning with an ominous tone of divine wrath but concluding with a plea for divine mercy, forgiveness, and salvation (lines 59–62).

Instructors may place various biblical documents in conversation with the poem: for example, prophetic promises of "the day of the Lord" (Joel 2; Amos 5; Zeph 1); psalms celebrating God's judgment (Pss 9; 82); the apocalyptic visions of Dan 7–12; the parables of judgment in Matt 25; the expectation of Christ's return in Paul (1 Thess 4:13–5:11; 2 Thess 2); or any number of similar passages in the book of Revelation. Depending on the instructor's objectives in using the poem, the following questions will prove helpful: What makes the anticipated day both "great" and "awful" (line 1)? How does the poem depict God? How does the poem describe the relationship between divine judgment and creation (lines 17–20, 60)? The relationship between divine judgment and death (lines 9–18, 55–58)? How does it depict Jesus in relation to God's coming judgment (lines 35–44)? What difference does it make that the speaker professes faith in God, as opposed to being an enemy of God (and how is that difference at work in designated biblical texts)?

As the poem is replete with references to both the Hebrew Bible and the

New Testament, it would work quite well on the final day of a Bible introduction course, especially if the course ends with a lesson on the book of Revelation. Instructors could challenge small groups to identify as many scriptural allusions as possible, whether in class or (for better results) using various concordances outside of class. As the theme of divine judgment can be seen in virtually every major section of the biblical canon, this exercise gives students the opportunity to engage the whole spectrum of canonical writings in a single exercise. Having experienced the dominance of this theme, students may also begin to understand how it is almost inevitable for the book of Revelation to be equally replete with scriptural references.

Edgar Lee Masters, "Business Reverses" (*Chapters into Verse: Poetry in English Inspired by the Bible* [ed. R. Atwan and L. Wieder; New York: Oxford University Press, 1993])

This humorous poem by Edgar Lee Masters tells the story of two businessmen who set out with bread and fish to "follow the crowds who follow / The prophet of Galilee" (lines 7–8). They aim to profit from the hunger of the crowds, but Jesus (who remains unnamed) squanders their economic hopes through the miraculous feeding of five thousand people (Matt 14:13–21; Mark 6:30–44; Luke 9:10–17; John 6:1–15). The story ends, ironically, in financial loss for the two fortune seekers: "what was there to do / But dump our stock on the sand?" (lines 53–54).

Masters's approach to the feeding of the five thousand (the only miracle common to all four Evangelists) offers an amusing and readable entryway into the social world of the Gospels and the liberating dimensions of Jesus' miracles. Instructors can use the poem as a conversation starter, leading students to a better understanding of the very serious social implications of Jesus' miracles. Initial questions should focus on the poem itself: What are the financial consequences of Jesus' miracle for the fortune-seeking businessmen? What are the financial consequences for the crowds who follow Jesus? Students who protest that the poem fabricates the two businessmen might nonetheless learn from the conversation. Thus the instructor might ask: Despite such fabrications, does Masters nonetheless capture the economic dimensions of Jesus' miracle (in all four Gospels someone is spared from *buying* provisions)? In a world of limited supply, how do the "haves" tend to benefit from the desperate need of the "have-nots," and is the scenario of the poem nonetheless realistic in this sense? What does the leftover surplus of food (lines 49–52, also noted by all four Evangelists) mean for a world accustomed to limited supply? In what ways might we overlook the economic dimensions of this or any miracle in favor of an overly spiritualized interpretation or interest in the historicity of the miracle itself?

This kind of conversation can easily lead into an exploration of other social dimensions of the Gospel narratives, if not an outright introduction to social-science criticism. Guiding questions might focus on the element of oppression: Where in the Gospels do we find people like Masters's two fortune seekers, that is, characters motivated by the prospect of personal gain at the expense of others; here instructors should point out how even the disciples fit this description (Mark 10:35–45)? How does the ministry of Jesus effect the "reversal" of such business (following the title of the poem)? Conversely, one might focus on the communal or material dimensions of Jesus ministry: How does a particular healing address the issue of social exclusion? How many kinds of physical needs does the ministry of Jesus address? Along these lines, it is interesting to note that the poem, although focused on the miraculous pro- vision of food, makes a passing reference to the *loss* of swine (Matt 8:32; Mark 5:13; Luke 8:33). Regardless of the particular line of questioning, the poem can help students see Jesus' ministry as a material phenomenon just as much as a spiritual one, and a social phenomenon just as much as a personal one.

Pablo Neruda, "Ode to a Beautiful Nude" (*The Wadsworth Anthology of Poetry* [ed. J. Parini; Boston: Thomson Wadsworth, 2006])

Feminists and others have worried about the problem of the male gaze that objectifies women and sees them as little more than sexual objects. So it is that feminist biblical scholars have worried about the male gaze in the Song of Songs, which contains a number of *wasf*s—a descriptive poem-form that celebrates the body of the beloved. The Song also contains two *wasf*s where the woman celebrates the man's body, but, regardless of the referent, Neruda's poem might be used as a kind of modern-day *wasf*. Neruda's ode is espe- cially interesting in how it begins: "With a chaste heart, / with pure eyes, / I celebrate your beauty." He then proceeds to describe the "beautiful nude" in poetic detail, beginning with her feet and moving to the ears and then to other parts of the woman's body—breasts, eyelids, shoulders, spinal line, and other regions—each described with allusive and erotic metaphors like those found in the Song of Songs. Here too, then (cf. Sharon Olds's poem "Topog- raphy" below), one sees the art of poetic reticence. Neruda tells just enough, not too much. The beautiful nude dressed in poetic metaphor turns out to be as seductive—better: more seductive—than one shown starkly in a room with all the lights on. Moreover, by means of his poetic skill and his capac- ity to conceal even while revealing, Neruda shows that he does, in fact, have a chaste heart and pure eyes. His "gaze," that is, is a true celebration of the woman's beauty, not one that objectifies the woman solely for sexual grati- fication. Students might benefit from contrasting poetic technique like that found in the Song of Songs and Neruda (and others) with less allusive and

L
I
T
E
R
A
T
U
R
E

reticent techniques of pornographic art or writing (cf. George Steiner, "Night Words," 68–77).

Sharon Olds, "The Signs" (*The Gold Cell* [New York: Knopf, 2004])

The poet of the Song of Songs says that love is stronger than death (8:6). What does that mean? This short poem by Sharon Olds suggests a connection between death and love but does so by means of a different metaphor than that used in the Song. Instead of erotic love between a man and a woman, Olds's poem concerns parental (specifically, maternal) love for children. This shift in metaphorical referent may help students think of the love in the Song as much more (and less than) sexual activity proper, which in common idiom has been ciphered as "love" (e.g., "making love," "we are lovers").

In the poem, the children are getting ready to depart for camp, and they are loaded on the bus. The bus is described in terms of death: Its windows are tinted black so that the children are only seen "as / figures ... through a dark haze, like the dead." But even with this haze and tint, Olds can pick out her son with the barest of clues: a tuft of hair, a curve of the chin. The same is true for all the other mothers. Finally, the bus departs, still in its deathly mode: "in a Stygian stink of exhaust." But now Olds can pick out this bus as easily as she could pick out her son within it. And even when it turns the corner and goes into the world, Olds would "know this world anywhere / as my son's world, I would love it any time in his name." The fierce maternal love Olds feels for her son makes his departure a death. And yet, her maternal love is stronger than death. By confronting a different but related love metaphor, students come to see with more specificity the distinctive aspects of the metaphor used in the Song of Songs.

Sharon Olds, "The Twin" (*The Gold Cell* [New York: Knopf, 2004])

The poem is written for Lazarus Colloredo, a famous seventeenth-century conjoined twin. Details of Lazarus and his conjoined twin brother named Joannes Baptista ("John the Baptist") are available on the Internet along with an etching done by a contemporary artist. The etching that is available on the Wikipedia website must have been what Olds was writing about, given the close correspondence between the poem and the image (this is an instance of *ekphrasis*: art commenting on art). There are differences of opinion and conflicting reports regarding whether or not Joannes was alive. Olds's poem, for its part, implies not. Olds consistently refers to the malformed twin that extended from Lazarus's chest as an "it." The poem states that the twins were given only one name, but that Lazarus, after he was grown, had the conjoined twin baptized and named. She notes that Lazarus looks at the observer with eyes "full of weariness ... / across his brother, the one he named / John the

Baptist, who goes before him / into the wilderness." The last line is quite evocative, especially if Joannes was "dead." The poem might be used in a class on John the Baptist in the New Testament, especially the way his life and death prefigures that of Jesus. It could also be used to generate discussion and insight into Jesus' sense of things upon hearing of John's death (Matt 14:12–13). Does he too, like Lazarus, look at us, across John the Baptist, with a direct gaze, "without expectation, [with] heavy-lidded eyes / full of weariness"?

Sharon Olds, "Topography" (*The Gold Cell* [New York: Knopf, 2004])

This poem is a useful example to discuss the allusive (and elusive) nature of poetic metaphor and the poetic device of understatement. In this case, the poem's content concerns love and sexuality and thus is an appropriate text to use with the Song of Songs which contains similar themes. "Topography" describes the two lovers' bodies as if they were folded into each other like two sides of a map of the continental United States. The parts of the body are evoked but not precisely delineated ("my / New Orleans deep in your Texas, your Idaho / bright on my Great Lakes, my Kansas / burning against your Kansas your Kansas / burning against my Kansas"). There is sexuality here, of course, but of an understated or reticent sort. And there is poetic (and erotic) climax with "all our cities twin cities, / all our states united, one" but in a way that is as concealing as it is revealing. One need only contrast a recent movie with full frontal nudity or various top-40 songs that are increasingly graphic about the sex act. Once students are alert to the sexuality and eroticism at work in the Song of Songs, it is easy to find it everywhere and to miss the fact that, while it is there, it is there in an allusive way. Olds's poem illustrates this phenomenon and begins to suggest reasons for why this is so in the last line where she describes the lovers' union as one "with liberty and justice for all." One wonders, that is, if Olds's reticence is not from prudery (indeed, many of the poems on sex in *The Gold Cell* are far from allusive!) but from a concern with human decency or privacy. The reader is allowed to participate with the imagination, that is, but not with the eyes, as it were. Perhaps the Song of Songs is similarly oriented toward decency and justice.

Linda Pastan, "Why Are Your Poems So Dark?" (*Poetry Magazine* [August 2003]: 249)

This short but powerful poem answers the question posed in the title by alluding to the poet's sadness. When that question is asked directly, however, the poet refers the inquirer to "Ask the moon. / Ask what it has witnessed." Earlier the poet had pointed out that the moon is dark, too, most of the time. The poem is a powerful piece to use with regard to the importance, even necessity, of sadness and grief as part of the human predicament and condition. The darkness of the moon is just the way it is, and it is that way most of the time. That is as it should be. But in the twist that connects the darkness of the poet's poetry to her sadness, the poet suggests that this darkness is also rooted in what has been seen and witnessed.

One could easily use the poem in conjunction with particularly dark, painful, or terrifying portions of Scripture—for instance, Judges, Ecclesiastes, and Revelation—as a kind of response to or anticipation of students asking: "Why is this story so dark?" Or one might even use it with reference to larger canonical units, testaments, or the entirety of Scripture. "Why is the Scripture so dark so often?" Ask the moon, ask what it has witnessed, which is to say, the Scripture has *seen* quite a bit in its day throughout its long history of composition and reception. It is a book of sorrows, deeply acquainted with grief. It does not tell "dark" stories or poems to depress its readers but because it must do so, because it must witness, because it must tell the truth about what it has seen and what it knows to be true.

Marge Piercy, "The Book of Ruth and Naomi" (*Modern Poems on the Bible: An Anthology* [ed. David Curzon; Philadelphia: Jewish Publication Society, 1994])

This poem nicely illustrates the various foci of the book of Ruth. The first stanza correctly notes that in many ways it is a peculiar and arcane story dealing with land inheritance, gleaning, threshing floor décor, marriage customs, and exchanging sandals. Historical, social-scientific, and literary critics thus have plenty to study, on the one hand. But, on the other hand, as the second stanza articulates, female readers enjoy it as a delightful story of the solidarity and love between two women. The poem focuses on this aspect of the story, suggesting that all women desire the close companionship of one other woman.

Although the poem highlights the friendship of Ruth and Naomi, commentators have detected a contrasting strand in the biblical version, which students might be asked to find. For example, Naomi is not particularly enthused that Ruth has decided to return with her. In fact, after Ruth's well known "where you go, I will go" speech (1:16–17), the text reports: "When Naomi saw that she was determined to go with her, she said no more to her" (1:18). Likewise, when the two reach Bethlehem, Naomi instructs the people to call her Mara ("Bitter") saying that the Lord has dealt harshly with her and brought her back empty (1:20–21). Does Ruth's companionship mean nothing? One might ask, then, if the poem's depiction of the Ruth-Naomi relationship is faithful to the biblical story or if it is embellished. If it is a love story, which is more salient in the biblical account: the love between Ruth and Naomi or between Ruth and Boaz? In addressing this question, one should notice, as the poem does, that Ruth, rather strikingly, brings the baby produced with Boaz as a "gift" to Naomi (4:14–17). What is the significance of the child for Naomi? For Ruth? For Israelite history (4:18–22)? Finally, one might consider the title of the poem: Is it more fitting than simply "Ruth"? Or perhaps simply "Naomi" would be more appropriate—after all, the book begins and ends with her (cf. 4:17)?

Francis Quarles, "David's Epitaph on Jonathan" (*Chapters into Verse: Poetry in English Inspired by the Bible* [ed. R. Atwan and L. Wieder; New York: Oxford University Press, 2000])

Quarles's work provides an opportunity to reflect on the relationship between David and Jonathan. Students can compare the poem with the text on which it is based (2 Sam 1). The biblical version is a lament over Saul and Jonathan, though the poem does not mention the former. Based on the events in 1 Samuel, why would David mourn Saul's death? Does it spring from genuine sorrow, or is it part of David's political machinations? Why does Quarles omit any reference to Saul? The poem, in general, helps students consider the complex relationships among Saul (king; rejected and tormented by God; father), David (outlaw; king's son-in-law; king-to-be), and Jonathan (prince; son; friend). In 2 Sam 1:26, furthermore, David refers to Jonathan as a brother, but also proclaims that Jonathan's love was better than the love of women. Does this imply a homosexual relationship (cf. 1 Sam 18:1; 20:17)? Class discussions can be interesting. Typically some students simply assume that David and Jonathan are lovers—that is, they think the text makes it obvious—while others assert that the idea never occurred to them. Does the poem suggest a sexual relationship? Any double entendres or innuendos? Here students may note, among others, the flower/garden imagery and the idea that Jonathan was the joy of David's heart. Finally, the poem can lead to a comparative discussion of other fraternal affiliations (e.g., Jacob and Esau) or close friendships (e.g., Ruth and Naomi) as portrayed in the Bible.

Rainer Maria Rilke, "Abishag" (*Modern Poems on the Bible: An Anthology* [ed. David Curzon; Philadelphia: Jewish Publication Society, 1994])

Many poems give a voice to silent biblical characters. Such is the case with the first stanza of this piece, which provides a glimpse into the mind of Abishag: She is uncomfortable and frightened, glancing nervously about the room as she keeps David warm. Not surprisingly, perhaps, the poem focuses exclusively on this aspect of her duties, omitting any reference to her serving the king (cf. 1 Kgs 1:2). The biblical world, indeed, is foreign to contemporary audiences in this scene—a fact which the poem underscores by noting that her "childlike arms" were "bound by servants" around the aging king. Did the biblical Abishag also undertake her duties reluctantly? Is this story reminiscent of Esther—a beautiful virgin brought to a needy king? Might Abishag, like Esther, stand to gain from this experience?

The poem also imagines the thoughts of David. What, based on previous stories, may be referenced by David's reflections on "deeds accomplished" and "unfelt pleasures." Similarly, the poem refers to David's "tangled life," which can prompt a review of the complicated nature of the king's reign (2 Sam 9–20). In the final stanza, David acknowledges, with regret, his sexual impotency. Is this symbolic of his decline (compare his earlier actions with Bathsheba)? Other questions to consider include: How would Bathsheba have felt about Abishag's presence? Based on 1 Kgs 2:19–22, how do other characters understand Abishag's status? Students might extend the poem and imagine what ultimately happened to Abishag—an issue on which the biblical text is silent.

John Savoie, "Trimmed and Burning" (*Poetry Magazine* [July 2003]: 207)

This poem is a wonderful example of the power of the final line to transform expectations and meanings. The poet begins by confessing that he has sheltered a flame and goes on to say that, while it would have been better to let it die or snuff it himself, he has nurtured it because it is holy. The poem proceeds to describe that flame with imagery drawn from pilgrims and devotees in a cathedral full of candles, which underscores the holiness of the flame and offers hints into its nature. The poem ends with the following two lines: "Yes, that is the kind of flame I have / sheltered, only that mine burns black." With the final line, the reader is disoriented. What seems to have been a "good" thing, even if it is a flame of lost or unrequited love, turns out to be something that burns black. What does that mean? Why "black"? The final line causes the reader to go back and reread the entire poem, wondering about this flame that is like the candles burning in the cathedral "only" (= "but for the fact that"?) the poet's flame burns black.

Many poems have final lines that produce this sort of rereading process. They can be put to good use in thinking about any number of biblical texts that end in unusual ways which lead to a reconsideration of prior materials. For example, Ps 137, with its violent ending about children being dashed against the rock; the rather enigmatic ending of Lamentations (esp. 5:22); the end of Solomon's reign as recounted in 1 Kgs 11, which raises serious questions about preceding chapters and his legendary "wisdom"; the shift in Commandment 10 to internal affect states ("coveting"), which leads to wondering about the role of Commandments 1–9 in similar, interior ways; the complete deterioration that occurs at the end of the book of Judges (17–21); the ending of Amos, which seems to move from complete darkness to simplistic sweetness;

the epilogue(s) to Ecclesiastes; the odd and virtually mid-sentence ending of Jonah; or the enigmatic conclusion to the Gospel of Mark.

William Stafford, "With Kit, Age 7, at the Beach" (*Allegiances* [New York: Harper & Row, 1970]; www.poemhunter.com/i/ebooks/pdf/william_stafford_2004_9.pdf)

This poem is useful in introducing speech-act theory, which has been applied to various aspects of biblical literature (God's creative word), ancient thought (nominal realism and divine/personal names), and biblical theology (Scripture as illocutionary address with perlocutionary response expected; see Dale Patrick's work on the rhetoric of revelation in the Hebrew Bible).

The poem's *locutionary* content is the poem itself—the words of the poem—which describe the poet and his daughter's trek up a beach dune to watch a sea-storm. The *illocutionary* force "what words do when they are said" is found in the poet's response to Kit's question: "How far could you swim, Daddy, / in such a storm?" / "As far as was needed," I said, / and as I talked, I swam." The storm apparently raises questions for the daughter, questions that pertain to her daddy's efficacy, at least that is how the father takes them (see below). So she asks about his abilities vis-à-vis a storm of such magnitude. In saying that he could swim as far as was necessary he is, in fact, swimming—the words *do* something. In this case, they promise that the father has what it takes, is sufficient to the challenge and task that might be posed by the daughter and a storm that she (or they together) might encounter in the future. The *perlocutionary* force—what readers are supposed to do on the basis of the words—is found in two places: First, in the poem itself, the daughter's question has perlocutionary content that evokes a response from her father. Second, the poem might have perlocutionary force on contemporary readers, who might think to parent, mentor, or "swim" differently in light of it.

An audio file of Stafford reading a slightly different version of the poem in 1974 is available online (www.poets.org/viewmedia.php/prmMID/15922). The difference in aural/oral and written/published versions of this poem could also be instructive in at least two ways: (1) discussion of change and variation in compositions over time; (2) the difference in effect when poetry is read silently or spoken aloud (see the discussion of Todd Alcott, "Television" above).

César Vallejo, "I Am Going to Speak of Hope" (*The Rage and Bone Shop of the Heart: Poems for Men* [ed. R. Bly, J. Hillman, and M. Meade; New York: HarperCollins, 1992])

This striking prose poem of four brief paragraphs is useful for two pedagogical purposes: probing (1) the universality of pain and suffering and (2) the tension between the title of the poem and the content itself, which might say something of the relationship of pain and hope. In contrast to the title, the poem itself never once mentions hope. Instead, it speaks exclusively about pain and ache—consistently, repeatedly, and insistently. The suffering Vallejo describes is profound in the deepest sense for three reasons. First, it is of a transcendent sort: The pain is not simply Vallejo's, nor does it inhere with his status as an artist, a man, a human being, or a member of a particular religious or even nonreligious group. Instead, "Today I am simply in pain." Moreover, the ache is without explanation. It is too deep to have a cause and is in a sense undifferentiated: It is as bad as if his bride were dead or his throat were slashed or if his life were different. "Today I am simply in pain." Lastly, the pain is completely inefficacious. This pain is not the result ("a son") of anything, nor is it a progenitor ("a parent") of anything good. And yet, the tension between the content and the title of the poem emerges at this point and is worthy of reflection. What does Vallejo mean by the title, "I am *going to* speak of hope"? Is it that he believes—hopes—he will eventually get to speak of hope but that now, today, when he is simply in pain, he cannot? Or is it that speaking of pain is the necessary prerequisite before one can speak of hope? If it is the latter, the poem bears comparison to a number of places in the Hebrew Bible where lament and articulation of pain apparently precede any expression of hope, as in the lament psalms.

The tension between the title and the content may also foster discussion of the titles of biblical works, many of which were added to the compositions by someone other than the author. Are there examples of titles which seem to fit their texts particularly well or particularly poorly? (Examples include Genesis, Numbers, Deuteronomy, 1–2 Samuel, the superscriptions of many of the Psalms, Lamentations, any of the Gospels, Acts, Hebrews, Revelation.) In what way does a title predispose readers to approach a text in a certain frame of mind?

Reed Whittemore, "Psalm" (*Good Poems* [ed. G. Keillor; London: Penguin, 2002])

This brief poem is a wonderful text to use with any lament psalm or similar grief-filled passage of Scripture. The opening line is immediately arresting: "The Lord feeds some of His prisoners better than others." This is just the beginning of a series of images that Whittemore calls "the dark images of our Lord." In this way, the poem could be employed with any number of difficult texts found in the Bible. In some ways Whittemore's poem is like the canon of Scripture, however, insofar as both press through and beyond—but not around—these dark images. As Whittemore says, the dark images "make it seem needful for us to pray not unto Him / But ourselves." But when that happens—and the poem ends with this—"we are truly lost / And we rush back into the safer fold, impressed by His care for us." One could easily have students ponder the end, which seems like a non sequitur in light of the poem's beginning. How does one (*can* one?) go from the "dark images" to the "safer fold"?

Oscar Wilde, "Ave Maria Gratias Plena" (*The Complete Works of Oscar Wilde* [New York: Harper Perennial, 1989]; www.englishverse.com/poems/ave_maria_gratia_plena)

This work by the Irish poet Oscar Wilde takes its title from the traditional Roman Catholic *Ave Maria* prayer, which is an adaptation of various verses in Luke 2:26–45. Although the poem does not cite specific verses from Luke's Gospel, it does focus on the key Lukan interest in Christ's humble birth to a young Jewish peasant woman, contrasting these origins with Zeus's more "wondrous" possession of human women in Greek mythology (lines 1–8).

This poem gives two counterexamples to Mary: Danae, upon whom Zeus fell "in a rain of gold" (line 3), and Semele, whose "dread vision" (line 5) of Zeus resulted in her own death. Instructors may wish to explore these myths in more detail so that students can better appreciate their appropriation by Wilde and more clearly see the continuities and discontinuities vis-à-vis Luke's account of Mary and the birth of Jesus. This will raise important questions regarding the New Testament's cultural background: How might an ancient audience familiar with Greek mythology have experienced the story of Christ's birth, coming as it does from a divine-human encounter? How might that experience have differed between believing audiences (the likely recipients of the Gospels) and nonbelieving audiences (who would have learned of Christ's birth indirectly)? Depending on course objectives one may also wish to pose the more fundamental question of how present-day Christians should deal with such mythological precedents in articulating a notion of biblical authority, a question often raised with reference to the Gilgamesh epic in Old Testament courses. (For a list of liaisons of Zeus, see www.csun.edu/~hcfll004/zeusgirl.html.)

Along these lines the basic theme of Wilde's poem is worth noting. The rather undramatic story of Mary, "some kneeling girl with a passionless pale face" (line 12), defies the speaker's expectations for how divinity encounters humanity. The instructor may therefore pose questions about the particular ways Wilde captures this surprise: What in the poem (especially lines 9–14) speaks to the humble, unspectacular nature of Jesus' birth, and how does Wilde's treatment of the Zeus stories accentuate the differences? How does the

L
I
T
E
R
A
T
U
R
E

poem's title ("Hail Mary, full of grace") contribute to this ironic theme? What details in Luke's nativity account affirm Wilde's interpretation?

This discussion may then lead to more directly exegetical questions about Luke's first two chapters. How does even the *preparation* of Jesus' birth, most notably the stories of Elizabeth and Zechariah, speak to his humble origins? What is the effect of Luke's repeated and seemingly fleeting references to the powerful Roman Empire in this regard (1:5; 2:1–2; 3:1–2)? With all of this in mind, what kind of God does Luke's Gospel describe, and what is the implicit theological message for hearers who, like Wilde's speaker, expect to encounter more spectacular and powerful tales of the divine? In answering these questions students might also envision an early Christian community struggling to articulate a view of the suffering, human Jesus as the full revelation of God.

William Butler Yeats, "The Second Coming" (*The Collected Poems of W. B. Yeats* [ed. R. J. Finneran; New York: Collier, 1989]; www.online-literature.com/yeats/780)

This very famous poem works well introducing students to apocalyptic eschatology and the specific theme of Christ's second coming. In typical apocalyptic sequence, the first stanza depicts a bloody "anarchy...loosed upon the world" (line 4), while the second stanza ominously anticipates the arrival of a lion/human beast (Rev 4:7; 5:5)—"its hour come round at last" (line 21)—an allusion to Christ's final judgment.

The most obvious biblical parallel here is probably the book of Revelation. However, instructors may just as easily use the poem in teaching the "little apocalypse" shared by the Synoptic Gospels (Matt 24:1–25:46; Mark 13:1–37; Luke 21:3–36), certain Pauline passages that speak of the Parousia (1 Cor 15:20–28; 1 Thess 4:13–5:11; 2 Thess 2:1–12), or even the visions of Dan 7–12. In all of these passages one sees a dramatic divine intervention into history that brings vindication for the suffering innocent through the conquering of God's reign over the powers of chaos/evil. Students should therefore read the poem with the following questions in mind: How does the first stanza depict the human situation, and where can these things be seen in the world today? Why does the speaker believe "some revelation is at hand" (line 9)? What form will this revelation take, and what seems to be its purpose? How is its true identity revealed in the final line, and what is ironic about this "birth"?

The surprise of Yeats's poem—particularly given its title—is that it does not actually depict the "second coming" but simply anticipates it in the nativity story: "what rough beast, its hour come round at last, / Slouches towards Bethlehem to be born?" (lines 21–22). For courses with overtly theological objectives, this gives instructors a helpful illustration of the connection between incarnation and Parousia (the "deeper" meaning of Advent). Instructors should know, however, that Yeats's appeal to the *Spiritus Mundi* ("spirit of the world," line 12) suggests that knowledge of the second coming is inherent in all people—a subtle but significant difference from Jewish/Christian apocalyptic eschatology, the highlighting of which will help instructors accentuate the distinctiveness of the biblical perspective.

PROSE: FICTION AND NONFICTION

Jaime Clark-Soles, Patrick Gray, and Brent A. Strawn

The works discussed in this chapter, many of which deal with multiple texts and topics, are organized alphabetically according to the name of the author rather than canonically. The indices may be consulted to find entries with classroom strategies related to particular texts. All secondary literature cited here is included in the preceding bibliography (pp. 246–49).

Mikhail Bulgakov, *The Master and Margarita* (trans. M. Ginsburg; New York: Grove, 1967)

With the exception of John, Jesus' encounters with Pontius Pilate in the Gospels are remarkably brief and short on dialogue (Matt 27:11–14; Mark 15:2–5; Luke 23:1–5; John 18:28–19:12). What happened and what words were exchanged at this meeting, perhaps the most significant legal proceeding in recorded history? Literary retellings of the story provide a platform on which to discuss the issues that arise when scholars assess various reconstructions of the encounter.

Bulgakov's surrealistic satire on life in the Soviet Union—complete with flying witches, talking cats, and a visit from Satan—was first published nearly 30 years after his death. The plot alternates between early twentieth-century Moscow and first-century Jerusalem. The second chapter (18–43) concerns Pilate and his interaction with Jesus, here called Yeshua Ha-Nozri. (Chapters 16, 25, and 26 also focus on Pilate as well as on Matthew and Judas.) This twenty-five-page retelling corresponds with the canonical versions at several points but obviously includes much material not found elsewhere. Bulgakov makes no claim that his story is a true or historically accurate rendering of the trial. (In fact, the story is first told by Satan and later appears in the Master's novel, which he burns when the manuscript is rejected.) To provoke spirited discussion of the key issues, however, one may shift the burden of proof to the students and ask, "What in this account *cannot* be accurate?" Elements to be subjected to scrutiny include: Bulgakov's general characterizations of Pilate (Was he fond of his dog? Did he suffer from migraines?)

and of Jesus (Was he twenty-seven years old at the time? How many languages could he speak?); the authenticity of particular sayings attributed to Jesus (e.g., 27: "There are no bad people in the world"); the identity of the other criminals executed; the context and tone of Pilate's famous question ("What is truth?"); the likelihood of a secretary being present to preserve a record of the trial; the plausibility of their discussion about the nature of the power of the state (30); and the nature of Jesus' relationship with Matthew and other followers. Another way to frame the question is: Where does this narrative take elements that are only implicit in the canonical versions and make them explicit?

Sorting through the possible answers to these questions provides an opportunity to introduce the basic principles of the historical method formulated by Ernst Troeltsch (methodological doubt, analogy, correlation) and the criteria for assessing the authenticity of dominical sayings formulated by Norman Perrin and others (multiple attestation, dissimilarity, coherence).

One outcome of this exercise is that students as well as teachers come to realize how much we *do not* know about the events portrayed in the Bible. Extrabiblical sources sometimes support biblical portraits of events and characters, sometimes they undermine biblical portraits, and sometimes they do both, as is the case with Pontius Pilate. His character, it is often argued, is drawn sympathetically and is let off the hook by the Gospel writers. Josephus (e.g., *B.J.* 2.175–177) depicts a Pilate who was not weak or indecisive or concerned to mollify the Jews under his rule but was rather a fairly nasty guy. On the other hand, Josephus reports an earlier incident in which Pilate actually backs down for fear of unduly antagonizing the Jewish populace and causing an uproar (*Ant.* 18.55–59; Philo, *Legat.* 299–305, also reports that he is admonished by the emperor for offending the Jews' sensitivities). In this manner, students may see that determining "What would Pilate do?" is perhaps no less tricky than determining "What would Jesus do?"

Shusaku Endo, *Silence* (trans. W. Johnston; New York: Taplinger, 1969)

One way to plunge students into the study of the New Testament is to expose them to its perennial concerns as they arise when the Christian faith is introduced into new settings. *Silence* is a particularly vivid example. Endo's novel is based on historical figures and events during the early Christian mission in Japan, before and after the country was closed to foreigners in 1603 (all missionaries were expelled in 1614) and intense persecution by the Tokugawa shogunate had begun. The story focuses on Rodrigues, a Portuguese Jesuit, who has come to Japan to minister to the clandestine community and to learn the truth about his mentor Ferreira, who has apostatized under threat of torture. Rodrigues is betrayed by another apostate, Kichijiro, and spends more than half of the story in hiding or in prison before a climactic encounter with Ferreira.

The wrenching story provides a touchstone for discussing several texts and topics in a New Testament survey:

(1) To what extent is Rodrigues a kind of Paul figure? A very effective method of creating apostates among the missionaries was to torture Japanese Christians until the priests agreed to deny their faith. While this method is not attested in the New Testament, Paul's evangelizing activities in Asia Minor not only resulted in his frequent incarceration but also exposed his converts to unwelcome attention from their non-Christian neighbors and the Roman authorities on occasion. Are there any signs that Paul has qualms about this? Does he address the hardships his followers will meet as a consequence of their conversion? (Perhaps have students take on the persona of one of Paul's addressees who write him a letter on this question or the persona of one of the persecutors. What sorts of rationales might they have for wanting to stamp out this new, foreign religion?)

(2) Rodrigues faces the almost certain alternatives of martyrdom or apostasy throughout the novel. Early on, he almost seems to long for the death of a martyr though he has been instructed not to seek it actively. Do any New Testament writings address this issue? A comparative text may be found in Phil 1. Some interpreters believe that the imprisoned Paul in Phil 1:20–30 is contemplating suicide. At the very least, he is contemplating the possibility that he will soon die for the faith. Is it plausible that he is considering suicide as an option? Do other texts suggest that entertaining this course of action should be off limits?

(3) Christianity grew very quickly after its introduction to Japan by Francis Xavier. Christian expansion in the first century, though modest in sheer numbers, was similarly rapid. What factors might account in part for this rapid spread (a captivating message? social benefits accompanying conversion? good roads?)? Tertullian's dictum that "the blood of martyrs is the seed of the church" is now something of a truism, but it is hardly self-evident that persecution might actually be reason for the success of the movement.

(4) To what extent is Kichijiro a kind of Judas figure?

(5) In his preface and in other writings, Endo is captivated by what happens when foreign ideas such as the Christian faith come into Japan. He refers to Japanese culture as a swamp which sucks up and smothers various ideologies it encounters, transforming and even denaturing them in the process. When and where does this happen in early Christianity?

(6) Endo tests the logic of martyrdom by posing a question: If sacrificing the body is good, is sacrificing one's very soul (e.g., by apostatizing) even better? Is this syllogistic reasoning attested in the Bible? Compare this atti-

tude with that of the Letter to the Hebrews toward apostasy (6:4–6; 10:26–31) or Matt 12:32 on the sin against the Holy Spirit as unforgivable.

(7) The novel's title refers to the silence of God in the face of unspeakable evil and thus evokes the classic problem of theodicy, especially as it is manifested in apocalyptic literature. Ask students to imagine a dialogue between Endo and the author of Revelation. Where might they have similar ideas about God? Where might they diverge?

If the instructor prefers a shorter work, Endo's play *The Golden Country* (trans. F. Mathy; Tokyo: Tuttle, 1970) focuses on Ferreira and touches on many of the same themes as the novel.

Harry G. Frankfort, "On Bullshit" (*The Raritan Review* [Fall 1986]: 81–100)

Despite the humorous and slightly off-color title, Frankfort, a retired moral philosopher from Princeton University, sets himself a serious (if somewhat tongue-in-cheek) task: to define "bullshit," in particular to distinguish it from lying. Building on the prior work of such figures as Max Black and Ludwig Wittgenstein, Frankfort concludes that bullshit is different from lying and that it is, ultimately, a more serious enemy to truth than is lying. Liars, he argues, at least care somewhat about the truth even if only to (and because they) willfully misrepresent it. Bullshitters, however, could not care less about the truth; what is said may or may not correspond to the truth/facts. They only care how they appear, especially before others (just like, one might argue, the Pharisees excoriated by Jesus in the Gospels).

Students greatly enjoy the essay because, although at times the discussion is somewhat theoretical, the subject matter is entertaining and the writing enjoyable. It can be used as a way to invite students to think about interpretive dispositions. It is better to try to tell the truth in interpretation—even if that is difficult—than to just look good doing it. Likewise, seeking after truth—again, even if difficult—is better than not trying at all. It also helps students to reflect on the nature of Scripture as truth-telling literature. Finally, it facilitates contemplation of the importance of truth-telling in public speech, in preaching, teaching, commentaries, and classroom discussion—platforms where bullshit is often in oversupply. Students might think of this essay as an extended analysis of the dangers of the faculty of speech so frequently mentioned in the Bible (e.g., in Proverbs and the Letter of James).

Susan Glaspell, "A Jury of Her Peers" (*The Best American Short Stories of the Century* [ed. J. Updike and K. Kenison; Boston: Houghton Mifflin, 1999]; www.learner.org/exhibits/literature/story/fulltext.html)

In this suspenseful story set in rural Iowa, Mrs. Peters (the sheriff's wife) and Mrs. Hale (the wife of the man who discovers the murdered John Wright) accompany their husbands to the home of Minnie Foster Wright. What could drive a wife to murder? Throughout this brilliantly crafted story, the reader watches and listens as the men conduct their investigation but come up with no hard evidence, while the women actually piece together how the murder occurred and remember Minnie as a vivacious young woman. Twenty years with John Wright destroys her as he kills everything she loves, including the canary she had to keep her company as she toiled. As the women piece together what must have happened, they draw upon their own knowledge of women's experience and assess their own lives. The author repeatedly describes the sheriff's wife in the same terms as she describes Minnie. The effect is heightened by the fact that none of the men in the story take any women seriously. When the men come into the kitchen to look for evidence, they do not stay long: "'Nothing here but kitchen things,' he said, with a little laugh for the insignificance of kitchen things."

Notice how the author chooses to designate the characters. Sometimes Mr. Hale is "Mrs. Hale's husband" or Mrs. Peters is "the sheriff's wife, married to the law." Gendered experience and knowledge, power relations between the sexes, the nature of justice, the gendering of evil, solidarity between those who suffer—all of these themes and others that regularly arise in a biblical studies course receive attention. This story allows readers to discuss such themes with a story about which they have no preconceived ideas before dealing with the biblical narratives. This story is also useful to read alongside the New Testament *Haustafeln* (Col 3:18–4:1; Eph 5:21–33; 1 Tim 2:8–15; 1 Pet 2:18–3:8), especially 1 Peter as it valorizes silent suffering and calls for the submission of women and slaves. Glaspell's story is also well suited for teaching exegesis because she is so careful with her diction and literary technique. When one is trying to show that language such as "hour," "abide," "see," "light," and "darkness" are terms intentionally used by the author of the Fourth Gospel, for example, a story such as this can help make the point that authors can be very deliberate in their choice of language. Finally, the use of irony is on brilliant display in this story, much as it is in a text like the Fourth Gospel, among others.

Stephen Greenblatt, *Will in the World: How Shakespeare Became Shakespeare* (New York: Norton, 2004)

How does one reconstruct the ancient world, ancient peoples, even ancient individuals? This is a serious problem for biblical studies in the historical mode, but the problem is not confined solely to historicism. Greenblatt's popular book on Shakespeare demonstrates that many of the same problems bedeviling biblical studies also obtain for almost any study concerned with literary texts from the past. Insofar as some students (and scholars!) are overly dubious about reconstruction of whatever sort, while others are overly excited about it, Greenblatt's work is a fascinating, oblique approach to the problems involved, demonstrating that one must be dubious, but there is a good bit to be excited about. And, in turn, while one can get excited, it is quite reasonable to maintain a good bit of doubt. Reading the preface (12–14), the opening "Note to the Reader" (17–19), or the first chapter (23–53) will be sufficient to introduce the problem.

(1) Greenblatt's book is itself eminently reasonable and judicious but it is not without imagination. He has searched the vast sea of Shakespeare studies including the wealth of data that has been culled on the playwright's life, influences, and so forth. And there is a lot to be known on this score. In this way Greenblatt's approach resembles that of any good biblical scholar who amasses historical data of various sorts to investigate, say, the Deuteronomist or the apostle Paul.

Despite the large amount of data available for Shakespeare's life, career, and legacy, the picture is far from complete. "Even with this relative abundance of information," he writes, "there are huge gaps in knowledge that makes any biographical study of Shakespeare an exercise in speculation" (18). As an example, consider the chronology of the plays. The relative chronology which is so crucial for any biography inevitably requires speculation. Or, as another example, the exact date of Shakespeare's birth (April 23 or April 26, 1564) has been debated, though, according to a parish register, the baptism of "Gulielmus filius Johannes Shakspere" took place on the later date. While this would seem definitive, Greenblatt points out that some scholars have argued for a three-day interval between the birth and baptism. Even "hard evidence," that is, can be debated and interpreted differently. So too in biblical studies! When the evidence is even softer, it should come as no surprise that the degree of certainty is still less and the range of opinion still broader. Greenblatt discusses the difficulties surrounding identifying with certainty the Stratford grammar school teacher, Simon Hunt, who presumably would have taught Shakespeare. Is it the Simon Hunt who matriculated to the University of Douai in 1575 and became a Jesuit in 1578? But there is another Simon Hunt who died in Stratford ca. 1598, and maybe he is the one who was Shakespeare's teacher. Even more to the point, records for the school do not survive, so there is no solid proof that Shakespeare even attended the school. But where else would he have gone and where else would he have been educated? These kinds of questions and ambiguous evidence are cognate with the kinds of problems and issues that beset biblical scholars.

(2) It is at this point that the use of imagination comes in. The sources regarding Shakespeare's life are fragmentary. "What matters most are the

works" themselves (18), but how these relate to his life is an exercise in imagination. But it is not solely an exercise in *historical imagination*; instead, it is an exercise in the *interpretive imagination*, or, in a word, hermeneutics. Greenblatt "aims to discover the actual person who wrote the most important body of imaginative literature of the last thousand years. Or rather, since the actual person is a matter of well-documented public record, it aims to tread the shadowy paths that lead from the life he lived into the literature he created" (12). What clues might "unravel the great mystery of such immense creative power" (ibid.)? What links are there "between the timeless work with its universal appeal and a particular life that left its many scratches in the humdrum bureaucratic records of the age" (13)? Given the problems surrounding the interpretation of the "scratches" Shakespeare's life left, the works are given preeminence in the interpretive process. They are not, however, given sole proprietary rights because the scratches do exist and do have a role to play in the interpretive process. Relating the two is the problem and promise; and imagination helps.

Framed in these ways, the connections to certain conundrums in biblical study are rather obvious. Greenblatt's book thus casts important light on: (a) how the hermeneutical problems faced in biblical studies extend to other disciplines; (b) the importance of the artifactual and historical record; (c) the preeminence of the literary remains themselves when dealing with the past; (d) the role of imagination in relating the historical and the literary, as well as in the interpretive process as a whole. It might be used profitably in a class on hermeneutics or as a comparative exercise with regard to how biblical scholars traffic in similar discussions. One might compare, for example, the roles archaeology and epigraphy have played in understandings of Israelite religion, attempts at dating Paul's letters, debates between the minimalists of the Copenhagen school and the maximalists, or note a particularly robust reconstruction of a Christian community on the basis of writings in the New Testament (e.g., Raymond E. Brown's work on the Johannine community or various attempts to describe a "Q community").

Jack Handey, *Deep Thoughts* (New York: Berkeley, 1992)

Students often think that Jesus' parables are clear-cut stories with a lesson that is easy to discern. It is difficult for them to appreciate the radical twist that characterizes many of the Gospel parables. The absurdist "Deep Thoughts" of comedian Jack Handey, familiar to many students from their appearance on the television program *Saturday Night Live*, can be very useful in helping students to think about the nature and function of parabolic discourse. Many of these are available on the Internet. For example:

Maybe in order to understand mankind, we have to look at the word itself: "Mankind." Basically, it's made up of two separate words—"mank" and "ind." What do these words mean? It's a mystery, and that's why so is mankind.

We tend to scoff at the beliefs of the ancients. But we can't scoff at them personally, to their faces, and this is what annoys me.

If trees could scream, would we be so cavalier about cutting them down? We might, if they screamed all the time, for no good reason.

If you're in a war, instead of throwing a hand grenade at the enemy, throw one of those small pumpkins. Maybe it'll make everyone think how stupid war is, and while they are thinking, you can throw a real grenade at them.

In each of these instances, Handey's thoughts take an unexpected twist, which is what makes them amusing. One anticipates that he will say "mankind" is made up of "man" and "kind," that we should not scoff at the beliefs of the ancients, or cut down trees, or throw grenades. But Handey pulls the rug out from under us. This element of surprise can be compared to Jesus' parables, particularly many of those in Luke. The first hearers would have been shocked, for instance, when the Samaritan stops to help (10:25–37), when the poor and lame are invited to the dinner (14:15–24), when the prodigal son is given a banquet (15:11–32), when the manager is commended for being dishonest (16:1–9), or when the kingdom of God is likened to a mustard seed and yeast (13:18–20). Like Handey's one-liners, Jesus' parables take unexpected turns that jar the hearer or reader into thought. They may also have been met with laughter. Jesus and Handey provide short, entertaining, memorable sayings which "work" because of the unexpected. Thus, Handey helps students rethink what parables are and how the genre functions.

Ron Hansen, *Atticus* (San Francisco: HarperCollins, 1996)

This novel is a modern version of Luke's Prodigal Son parable (15:11–32). Atticus Cody has two sons. Frank is successful, with a good career, a great wife, and wonderful children. On the other hand, Scott and disaster are never separated for long. Scott drives the car recklessly with his mother in it. When they crash, she dies and he lives. His father continues to love him, even though Scott is shiftless and cannot (or will not) keep a job. He spends time in a mental hospital where he falls in love with another patient. He follows her when she moves to Mexico, where he lives off the trust fund set up by his father, squandering it on riotous living.

When Scott is found dead, Atticus is told that it is suicide. Atticus starts sleuthing and begins to suspect murder. It appears to be nothing more than a murder mystery until the story takes an astonishing twist: It turns out that Scott is alive and in trouble. The story moves from third-person to first-person narration, as Scott poignantly watches (and relates to the reader) his father's search for clues to his son's murder. Scott is too ashamed for all he has done to let his father know that he is alive. Eventually, they are reunited and find redemption.

What is the point of this story? In what ways is this story similar to or different from Luke's parable? What does it bring to life or what gaps does it fill in the original parable? For example, there is an "explanation" as to why no mother is mentioned in Luke 15. (Sometimes students do not notice the absence of women.) Also, the son does not set out intending to become prodigal or profligate. His sin is not willfulness, but a complete lack of any will or intention. In this way, the novel's more "realistic" character development throws into relief certain conventions of the parable genre.

The story would nicely accompany a study of the parables of Jesus. Insofar as parables represent Jesus' preferred mode of teaching, it is important to understand how the genre functions. An analytic paper treating a well-known parable alongside a literary retelling of that parable serves as a helpful heuristic device for addressing the hermeneutical questions pertaining to genre, purpose, and meaning. Time permitting, the ensuing discussion may be integrated with a broader study of the history of the interpretation of parables, touching on the different approaches of, for example, Jülicher, Jeremias, Dodd, and Crossan. (For other exercises on the parables, see Roncace and Gray, *Teaching the Bible*, 297–304, 326–28.) More generally, the story would also serve the study of form criticism. The form of the story up to a certain point is simply a fictional novel that starts to look like a murder mystery. But the second part of the novel moves away from third-person to first-person narrative with the protagonist assuming the role of narrator. This authorial strategy constitutes a point of contact with the Gospels. Where, if at all, do the Evangelists shift from third-person to first-person? Is the narrator omniscient? Does a first-person perspective always signal to the reader the unfolding of an essentially historical narrative?

Robert Heinlein, *Stranger in a Strange Land* (New York: Putnam, 1991; originally published in 1961)

This Robert Heinlein novel about a human raised by Martians and later brought back to earth as an adult, arguably the most significant work of science fiction written in the twentieth century, is one of many for use in discussions of literary Christ-figures. In considering various characters who have been hailed as Christ-figures, students come to realize that the factors leading the early church to proclaim Jesus as the Messiah were varied and complex and that even today there is no unanimity when it comes to defining the essential and the merely incidental traits of Jesus, among neither Christian theologians nor secular audiences. For this exercise, which may take the form of an essay where class time is not available for plenary discussion, the whole class could read the same work or the instructor may give a limited number of choices.

The question may be put this way: In what sense, if any, is it appropriate to consider Valentine Michael Smith a Christ-figure? What specific traits, deeds, quotations, or plot devices support such a label? Smith exhibits many qualities that parallel those of Jesus: He comes into the world "from above." He says, "I am God" (though he also greets others with the phrase "Thou art God"). His name, Michael, means "who is like God." He has twelve close associates and a mentor, whom he calls "Father." He can perform miracles, such as levitation and making objects and people disappear. He makes the governmental authorities nervous. He preaches a message of love and nonviolence and acquires a following as leader of the Church of All Worlds (which later spawned a real-life group that used the name and organization described in the novel). When he dies—willingly, it seems, as if it were a sacrificial act—he cries out, "I am son of Man" and arranges himself in such a way that the light hitting him will give the appearance of an angel's halo. How should we evaluate Smith? Are the similarities significant? Are they sufficiently detailed to warrant comparison with Jesus? What differences militate against a serious comparison, despite any similarities?

A similar exercise could be performed with the following works, among others: Aslan in C. S. Lewis's *Chronicles of Narnia*; Ransom in C. S. Lewis's Space Trilogy; Gandalf, Frodo Baggins, and Aragorn in J. R. R. Tolkien's *Lord of the Rings*; the eponymous hero of the *Harry Potter* novels of J. K. Rowling; Simon in William Golding's *Lord of the Flies*; Billy Budd in Herman Melville's *Billy Budd*; Jim Casey in John Steinbeck's *The Grapes of Wrath*; Santiago in Ernest Hemingway's *The Old Man and the Sea*; Benjy in William Faulkner's *The Sound and the Fury*; Prince Myshkin in Fyodor Dostoevsky's *The Idiot*.

William Hoffman, "The Question of Rain" (*God: Stories* [ed. C. M. Curtis; Boston: Houghton Mifflin, 1998], 95–107)

One "dusty, choking summer," thirty-seven-year-old Pastor Wayland receives a visit at the parsonage from a parishioner, Alex Bradner. When Bradner's textile business is suffering from the drought, he comes to ask Wayland to pray for rain. Now Alex "had little spiritual depth. He was generous with his pocketbook, but not himself." It turns out that Alex wants a community-wide Sunday service, a "Special Prayer Day for Rain." Wayland is not inclined to devote a special service to the topic. More members of the congregation join to voice the request. Again, he puts them off trying to explain that a distinction should be maintained between "asking for grateful hearts" rather than "putting in a special order." The distinction is lost on the congregants who begin to lose their jobs as plants close down due to lack of rain. As the week moves toward Sunday, Wayland is, ironically, working on a sermon about baptism. The story chronicles the struggle Wayland endures all week, the conversations he has, the counsel he seeks, his prayers, what he sees and hears around him in the community and church. In the end, he holds a prayer service and it rains.

This story might be used in conjunction with the contest between Elijah and the priests of Baal (1 Kgs 18). It also correlates well with the Gospel of John and its concern over "signs faith," that is, faith that is based upon seeing a miracle. Do moderns believe in miracles? At one point Wayland interacts with an educated doctor who derides the blue-collar parishioners for believing in miracles, at which point Wayland becomes defensive on their behalf: "Miracles happen," he says, even today. "He did believe that, didn't he?" The doctor replies, "But you wouldn't want to put your chips on the line, would you? ... I mean right up there in front of everybody in church, to put your chips on the line for a miracle?"

The story helps seminary students reflect upon their role as pastors of congregations. (Would they pray for rain upon a request from a congregant? Would they devote a special service to it or does the regular liturgy already cover all human problems? Would it matter which congregant or how many congregants made the request? Would the rich businessman's request be treated in the same way as the poor homeless woman's?) In nonseminary settings, the story is well-suited to a more general study of prayer as it appears in Scripture. What is the point of prayer? Is it as Wayland describes it? ("We don't pray to ask favors as if [God] is a rich uncle, but to have fellowship with Him, to achieve a feeling that we are close and in His care.") When the Letter of James says that "The effective, fervent prayer of a righteous man avails much" (Jas 5:17), is it appropriate to ask, "How much?" When Paul says that we should "pray without ceasing" (1 Thess 5:17), does he mean it literally? What is in the "small print" that goes with the claim (in 1 John 5:14–15) that "if we ask any thing according to his will, he hears us. And if we know that he hears us in whatever we ask, we know that we have obtained the requests made of him"?

Soren Kierkegaard, *Fear and Trembling* ([trans. A. Hannay; London: Penguin, 1985; originally published in 1843], 44–48)

The story of the binding of Isaac in Gen 22 (the Akedah) stands as one of the most enigmatic narratives in Scripture. Kierkegaard's philosophical reflection on the mystery of faith as manifested by Abraham begins with a four-page exordium consisting of four different retellings of the story. Each version emphasizes a different aspect of the "gaps" in the canonical text (e.g., Abraham's state of mind, Isaac's awareness, the aftermath of the near sacrifice). In one version Abraham feigns madness as he raises the knife so that Isaac will blame his father for the horrible act instead of God. Abraham begs God to forgive him for his willingness to kill his son and Isaac loses his own faith in God in other versions. Kierkegaard concludes by affirming that "no one was as great as Abraham," and at the same time wondering, "who is able to understand him?"

Biblical narrative tends to be quite sparse, and nowhere is this truer than here. One might ask students whether Kierkegaard's attempts at retelling the story make it more understandable. In some ways they do, but in other ways they raise key interpretive questions that highlight the utter strangeness of the narrative as well as the difficulty of extracting a simple, straightforward lesson: Does Abraham know that the voice is God's? If he does, is he also aware that it is a test? If he does not know that it is a test, why does he go through with the sacrifice and what does he think about God? If he does know that it is a test, does he also know what would constitute "passing" the test? (When commanded by God to kill, it might be natural to assume that the proper response is, in fact, to kill.) How old is Isaac, and how would his age influence the dynamic between father, son, and deity? Does Isaac hear the angel's voice in verse 11? What is Sarah's role? Is it appropriate to think of this as a test of Sarah? (Note her prior treatment of Hagar and Ishmael.) What is life like for the family after this incident? (Interestingly, Abraham goes to Beersheba, and the next mention of Sarah is when she dies—at Hebron.) Is Abraham meant to be an example to the reader, or is he unique? Of all the stories one might tell about "the father of the faithful," why tell this one?

Such questions provide helpful reminders that what is not said can sometimes be as important as what is said in a story. While it is possible to inject into the narrative concerns that were not present for the author or original readers, it is difficult to deny that many of these considerations are crucial for assessing the character of Abraham and for hearing the "message" conveyed.

Similar analyses might be conducted with other retellings of this story, such as Philo (*Abr.* 168–183); Josephus (*Ant.* 1. 222–236); Qur'an 37:99–113; *The Brome Play of Abraham and Isaac* (a fifteenth-century English mystery play); and Woody Allen's retelling contained in his essay "The Scrolls." For other exercises on the Akedah, see Roncace and Gray, *Teaching the Bible*, 92–100.

Ursula Le Guin, "The Ones Who Walk Away from Omelas" (*The Wind's Twelve Quarters* [London: Orion Group, 2000; originally published in 1973], 278–83)

This stunning story is set in a town called Omelas as its residents prepare for the great Festival of Summer. "The people in Omelas are happy people. Happiness is based on a just discrimination of what is necessary, what is neither necessary or destructive, and what is destructive." They have religion there, but no clergy. Of utmost importance is this: There is no guilt in Omelas. The town has the veneer of utopia, but it holds a dark secret. The narrator proceeds to explain that in a squalid basement of one of the gorgeous buildings, there is a locked room with no windows and a damp, dirt floor. She describes the room in depressing detail and then indicates that in the room, a child is sitting: "It could be a boy or a girl. It looks about six, but actually is nearly ten." She goes on to describe this "it"—naked and covered with festering sores—which "lives on a half-bowl of corn meal and grease a day." The child has not always lived there; it has memories of its mother and sunlight. Sometimes it speaks: "Please let me out. I will be good."

All the people in Omelas know the child is there and some have come to see it: "They all understand that their happiness, the beauty of their city, the tenderness of their friendships, the health of their children, the wisdom of their scholars, the skill of their makers, even the abundance of their harvest and the kindly weathers of their skies, depend wholly on this child's abominable misery." Usually those who come to see the child are young people. When they see the child, they are shocked and want to bring it out into the sunlight, clean it, feed it, but at that moment, if they chose to do so, Omelas would be destroyed. "Those are the terms," says the narrator. "To exchange all the goodness and grace of every life in Omelas for that single, small improvement: to throw away the happiness of thousands for the chance of happiness of one: that would be to let guilt within the walls indeed."

Most of the citizens of Omelas have come to accept these conditions. Some people, however, after seeing the child, walk away from Omelas, but when they do, each does so alone. "The place they go towards is a place even less imaginable to most of us than the city of happiness. I cannot describe it at all. It is possible that it does not exist. But they seem to know where they are going, the ones who walk away from Omelas."

This story can be used in conjunction with 1 Peter to discuss concepts of atonement, the suffering of the innocent, scapegoating, and evil. What is evil? Who is to blame for it? How might the problem of various kinds of evil be solved? Additional questions to pose might include: What constitutes happiness or joy? Upon what is it predicated? How do various biblical texts attempt to answer these questions? How is joy related to suffering? What is guilt—a subjective feeling, an objective state before God, or something else? What is its purpose and how, exactly, does guilt work for individuals and societies? How may it be eradicated? What are its consequences? Fruitful texts for dialogue include Lev 4 (on unintentional guilt); Josh 7 (on collective responsibility); and Rom 7 (on internal struggle with awareness of guilt).

Finally one might ask, "How does this story intersect with our own society?" Where is the church or synagogue in this town and, if it existed, what would you expect it to do? This generates vigorous discussion that can be correlated with a variety of Bible-related topics, for example, economic systems, child abuse, liberation theology, doctrines of atonement, issues of individual conscience, mindless adoption of cultures and systems into which one is born, and the nature of hope.

Malcolm X and Alex Haley, *The Autobiography of Malcolm X* ([New York: Ballantine, 1965], 185)

Students in biblical studies courses encounter any number of scholarly theories formulated to answer questions about authorship, provenance, dating, and so forth. They also encounter somewhat less scholarly theories outside of class (such as those of John Allegro and Dan Brown). Almost anything is possible, but not everything is equally plausible or probable. A brief anecdote from Malcolm X gives students an intriguing but improbable example for which to articulate standards for evaluating hypothetical reconstructions of the world in, behind, and before the text.

Malcolm tells of his participation in weekly debates when he was incarcerated for robbery at the Norfolk Prison Colony. In one debate, he argues that "William Shakespeare" was the pen name of King James (of the King James Version). He reasons as follows: The kjv represents the finest literature in the English language, and its language is the same as Shakespeare's. King James, he says, recruited the best writers of the time to translate the Bible. Shakespeare should have been included, but he is nowhere reported to have been part of the translation committee. Why not? Because "Shakespeare" existed only as the alter ego of the king.

A related theory has Shakespeare as one of the translators of the Psalms in the kjv (shakespeare.about.com/b/a/027673.htm). Counting forty-six words from the beginning of Ps 46, one finds the word "shake," and counting forty-six words backwards from the end, one finds the word "spear." The Bard, moreover, was forty-six years of age when the kjv was translated. Just a coincidence? Yes, probably. (Earlier translations, such as the 1551 edition of the Matthews Bible and the Geneva Bible of 1599, feature the same coincidence.)

What kinds of assumptions are made in these theories? What kinds of evidence would support or undermine the hypotheses put forward? Upon whom does the burden of proof rest? Where is technical expertise required to adjudicate the question and where does logic or common sense suffice?

Flannery O'Connor, *The Violent Bear It Away* (*Collected Works* [New York: Library of America, 1988; originally published in 1960], 329–479)

This Gothic novel about a dysfunctional Tennessee family can serve as an alternative approach to a unit or an entire course on Old Testament prophetic literature. Where class time is not available for plenary discussion, student work may take the form of an essay. The title is a reference to the Douay Version of Matt 11:12.

As the novel opens, Old Tarwater has just died. Through flashbacks and through the main character, his fourteen-year-old grand-nephew Francis Tarwater, the reader is presented with a vivid portrait of a backwoods prophet. Old Tarwater has unsuccessfully attempted to raise his nephew Rayber as a prophet and is subsequently placed in a psychiatric hospital for four years. Rayber refuses to baptize his mentally retarded son Bishop as a form of rebellion against his strict religious upbringing. Baptizing the child is the primary mission with which Francis is charged as Old Tarwater again tries to pass on the mantle to his grand-nephew. Spurred on in part by voices he hears, Francis, too, tries—ultimately in vain—to avoid his "calling" as a prophet. He gets drunk, burns down a farmhouse, drowns a child, and is a victim of assault while hitchhiking on the way to his awakening.

To what extent is it appropriate to think of Old Tarwater or Francis as prophets? Students react quite strongly to this grotesque narrative and its bizarre characters, and reading with this basic question in mind helps them to identify what constitutes prophecy as it appears in the Bible. Quite frequently students see the prophets as nothing more nor less than predictors of the future. And because they are enshrined in the canon, it may be difficult for students to appreciate the impression made by many of the prophets on their original audiences. The dialogue generated by O'Connor's story leads to a more nuanced understanding of the phenomenon. References to specific prophets are scattered throughout the novel. Much of the opening chapter depicts Francis's reflections on and doubts about his own calling as a prophet. It also contains Old Tarwater's own "call narrative" (332) and Rayber's psychologizing interpretation of his uncle's experience (341–42). Are the confirming signs of one's prophetic vocation always recognized by the one called? Is it possible to escape one's destiny as a prophet when called by God? Is it necessary for the recipient of revelation to acquiesce to or cooperate in mediating the experience? These are recurring questions as Francis struggles to discern God's will (cf. 430–31).

LITERATURE

Biblical texts with which the novel may be read in tandem include Isa 6:1–13; Jer 1:4–10; 20:7–12; Ezek 2–5; Hos 1:1–8; Joel 1:13–20; and Jonah. For related exercises on the prophets, see Roncace and Gray, *Teaching the Bible*, 162–69.

Peggy Payne, "The Pure in Heart" (*God: Stories* [ed. C. M. Curtis; Boston: Houghton Mifflin, 1998], 222–35)

What would happen if you were a Yale-trained Presbyterian pastor and one ordinary night, while grilling kebabs with your wife, you actually heard the voice of God? Such is the struggle that besets Swain Hammand. Swain, the ever-rational, respectable leader must decide whether or not to tell his equally rational, respectable congregation that he has heard the unbidden but certain voice of God say, "Know that there is truth. Know this." He knows that his parishioners will ascribe this to "stress." He discusses the situation with his wife who feels that, as a minister, it is his job to testify when God speaks. Certainly his choice will affect their marriage. Either he tells the story from the pulpit, which may lead to his dismissal, or he does not, at which point he will lose his wife's respect and his own integrity. In the end, he tells the story. Phone calls are made between worried parishioners and, finally, the church operations committee votes to recommend that the pastor seek professional counseling. The congregants take sides, but not a single parishioner is curious enough to approach Swain to learn more about his experience.

Swain Hammond approximates those characters in Scripture who are set apart, looked on with suspicion, and even persecuted for having profound personal encounters with the voice of God. Moses repeatedly encounters the voice of God firsthand from a burning bush (one of Swain's experiences finds God's voice coming from shrubs), and after his close encounter on Sinai he must veil his face. Moses is called a friend of God, sees God, hears God, and is now incomprehensible to his fellow Jews. And where does it get him? Not into the Promised Land, as one might expect.

The story works well with biblical texts that deal with people hearing God. Hearing the voice of Jesus or God comprises a primary theme in the Fourth Gospel. In the Lazarus story (John 11:1–44) Jesus calls out to Lazarus who then moves from death to life. For Swain, too, "The voice is unmistakable. At the first intonation, the first rolling syllable, Swain wakes, feeling the murmuring life of each of a million cells" (223). This story also fits nicely with a study of the biblical prophets (esp. Jeremiah, Hosea, or Ezekiel) or of the Akedah. The story can also be assigned alongside a study of Paul, who was at the time of his call a success within the Jewish religious establishment (Phil 3). Then he encountered God in a profoundly immediate, revelatory, physically taxing way, and everything changed. He became persecuted, beaten, shipwrecked, arrested, despised by Jews and Gentiles alike.

For seminary students, it is well worth the time in class or in writing to ask, "What would you do in Swain's situation and why?" It helps them think about the nature of their churches and their pastoral role, as well as the role of personal experience in shaping encounters with the stories one reads in Scripture.

Iain Pears, *An Instance of the Fingerpost* (New York: Riverhead, 1998)

The length of this erudite murder mystery precludes its candidacy for a complete read by students taking a semester-long course, but one could still easily use portions of it effectively. Divided into four parts, the novel narrates the "same" story set in seventeenth-century England from the perspective of four different characters. This has obvious connections with the four Gospels. All of the delights and difficulties of hearing a story from multiple perspectives apply. Whom to believe? Upon what basis? How do their own perspectives and agenda color what they include and omit and shape that which is included?

The book elegantly displays *prosopopoeia* as each of the four narrators truly speaks within character, exhibiting a style distinct from each of the other narrators. Having students read part 1, chapter 1, and part 4, chapter 1, and then examining the claims of the narrators makes for good discussion relevant to biblical studies. What reasons do the narrators give for recounting their stories? Are they convincing? What is their relationship to the events which they narrate?

Especially useful for courses on the Gospels is the beginning of the last part told by Anthony Wood (559–62). Wood begins his version of the events by noting, "Two men, it seems, can see the same event, yet both remember it falsely." According to Wood, one narrator, Prescott, is insane and another, Cola, is a liar. Of Wallis, another narrator, Wood writes, "Wallis himself was so used to living in the dark and sinister world of his own devising that he could no longer tell truth from invention, or honesty from falsehood. But how can I tell which assertion to believe, and which to reject?" (561). He cites his own personal familiarity with the concerned parties and his own "disinterested state" as reasons to trust his own ability to tell the story correctly.

The questions one might pose about Wood's qualifications might also be posed to Luke, for example, who begins his own Gospel with a prologue commenting on the reliability of previous accounts of the Jesus story (1:1–4). All things considered, would it be better to have an outsider tell the story of the early church or an insider? What are the advantages and disadvantages in each case, assuming that accuracy is a desideratum?

L
I
T
E
R
A
T
U
R
E

J. K. Rowling, *Harry Potter and the Sorcerer's Stone* (1st American ed.; New York: A. A. Levine, 1998)

Due to their phenomenal popularity, one need not assign students to read any of the *Harry Potter* novels as a prerequisite for using them in a biblical studies course. An instructor may also rely on familiarity with one of the controversies surrounding the series, namely, its alleged celebration of sorcery. A number of Christian groups in the U.S. and elsewhere have criticized what they regard as positive messages about witchcraft. Others, referring to the distinction between "black" and "white" magic, insist that the novels are harmless on this score and that, besides, they are fantasies and not how-to manuals for the occult arts.

This debate is not entirely unlike the debate that took place at Corinth between those who thought Christian faith was incompatible with the consumption of meat that had been sacrificed to idols and those who saw no problem with the custom (1 Cor 8–10). In his response Paul initially sides with "the strong," claiming that the meat has not in fact been offered to strange gods since the idols are not gods at all. But he comes down on the side of "the weak" when he says that a sense of community solidarity should guide their actions and that they should not create stumbling blocks for those who feel pangs of conscience at the thought of eating. One way to get students to pay close attention to Paul's arguments and the social dynamics at work in Corinth is to ask them to assess the aptness of the parallel to the Harry Potter controversy. On the basis of the principles Paul lays out in 1 Cor 8–10, how would he address this contemporary question? One possible hitch to anticipate—perhaps by arbitrarily dividing the class into two teams—is that very few students will be sympathetic to the view that Harry Potter is an agent of demonic influence or to any analogous principle that would bolster the "fundamentalist" perspective. (It has been argued, in fact, that the novels function as a sort of Christian theological allegory, sometimes with the wrinkle that the main character is a Christ-figure.)

One variation of this approach is to connect the black magic–white magic distinction to Hebrew Bible texts referring to, and usually condemning, sorcery (Deut 18:10–14; Lev 19:26, 31; 20:1–6; 1 Sam 28; 2 Kgs 21:6; Mal 3:5). Is it possible to discern a logic to the system whereby certain practices are permitted and others are proscribed? Do these texts lend themselves to fine distinctions between different types of magic? Would the miraculous deeds of the prophets or of Jesus qualify as magic by the terms of modern definitions? (For a related exercise, see Kenneth L. Cukrowski, "Just Like Magic: The Acts of the Apostles," in Roncace and Gray, *Teaching the Bible*, 338–39.)

Dorothy Sayers, *He That Should Come* (*Four Sacred Plays* [London: Victor Gollancz, 1957; originally published in 1939], 215–74)

Judaism in the Roman period was anything but uniform, and few works make this clearer than this one-act drama intended originally for performance as a radio play. Sayers writes that her primary aim is to depict the birth of Jesus against its "crowded social and historical background." Indeed, the nativity occupies only a small portion of the play. The characters—including magi, shepherds, Pharisees, Jewish merchants, and Roman soldiers—come together for one night in a small town inn, and their conversations reflect different aspects of Roman administrative policy (such as taxation), social tensions between different classes of Jews, travel conditions in the empire, Jewish attitudes towards Rome, various degrees and kinds of Hellenization, and widely divergent forms of messianic expectation among Jews. Pertinent to the reception of the Christian message among Gentiles, the dialogue also explores the ways in which pagans might have made sense of the title "Messiah."

A reading of this entertaining work takes less than an hour and can be easily staged inside or outside of class. There are fifteen speaking parts, plus a handful of minor parts with only a few lines. Although British turns of phrase may throw American students off balance, little or no rehearsal is needed for a successful "performance." As preparation or as follow-up, students can be assigned short papers or presentations detailing what is known about the stock characters who appear in the play. This will help familiarize them with useful reference works on the sociocultural contexts of the biblical world and will serve as a vivid reminder that there is a vibrant "world behind the text" that is assumed and built upon by the New Testament authors.

Similar exercises might involve one installment in Sayers's twelve-play cycle focusing on specific events or periods in the life of Jesus, *The Man Born to be King*, written also for radio broadcast in England during World War II.

Amy Tan, "Fish Cheeks" (*The Bedford Reader* [6th ed.; ed. X. J. Kennedy, D. Kennedy, and J. E. Aaron. Boston: Bedford/St. Martin's, 1997], 54–55)

In this story, the Chinese American adolescent protagonist falls in love with the minister's son who is "not Chinese, but as white as Mary in the manger." The girl's family invites the minister's family over for Christmas Eve dinner, one which includes not turkey, dressing, and cranberry sauce, but rather squid and tofu. While her relatives "licked the ends of their chopsticks and reached across the table, dipping them into the dozen or so plates of food, Robert and his family waited patiently for platters to be passed to them." Her shame increases when the whole meal is finished off with a loud belch by her father, who does so as a polite Chinese custom. Many years later, the girl-turned-woman realizes the full meaning of her mother's words spoken to her on that day: "You must be proud you are different. Your only shame is to have shame." Only as an adult does she see that her mother was teaching her to exult in her identity and to find an anchor in the love of her community regardless of the reactions of the dominant culture.

This 492-word story is a goldmine for anyone attempting to deal with issues of biculturalism and levels of accommodation and assimilation to one's host culture. Its use would help students better understand the experience of Paul's own life situation as a Hellenistic Jew turned Christian and the experience of Gentile pagans now turned Christian by analogously treating issues raised in a more familiar landscape than the first-century Mediterranean. It might also be used in connection with the issues raised in Ruth and Ezra concerning intermarriage in ancient Israel. The story poignantly highlights the intersections of religion, culture, ethnicity, and family ties, all matters overtly relevant to characters in both the Hebrew Bible and New Testament. It is particularly well-suited to Gal 2 and, in the place of the fourteen-year-old Chinese girl who is the protagonist in "Fish Cheeks," one might picture Cephas when the "ones from James" arrive.

In addition to fleshing out the lived experience of first-century Christians, students can also engage in conversations about modern analogues, especially since one class will often contain both students who live bicultural lives and those who do not. Students can move from there to a larger discussion of identity formation and the ways that even those who do not live biculturally also inhabit various identities, some of which inevitably conflict. (For a related exercise, see Timothy J. Sandoval, "Diaspora and Identity," in Roncace and Gray, *Teaching the Bible*, 242–44.)

J. R. R. Tolkien, *The Lord of the Rings* (3 vols.; Boston: Houghton Mifflin, 2002; originally published in 1954–55)

The connections between Tolkien's life's work, *The Lord of the Rings*, and Scripture are fairly numerous and well-known (websites discussing the parallels as well as Tolkien's Christian background are plentiful). One thinks, for example, of Gandalf the Gray's role as Christ-figure in the trilogy, giving his life for his companions in the first book, only to be "resurrected," as it were, as Gandalf the White in the second. The connections between Tolkien's work and Scripture only multiply when one takes into consideration the elaborate mythology he envisioned as lying *behind* the trilogy, which he published only later in *The Silmarillion*. So, either the trilogy (or the movies based on them) or *The Silmarillion* could work well for any number of purposes; for instance, they could introduce students to a particular biblical theme from the stories with which they are already familiar or open discussion on the influence of Scripture on other media.

Another, perhaps less obvious connection between the trilogy and portions of Scripture is the role of the tragic. (Warning: this paragraph reveals the ending of the trilogy.) Students typically have problems understanding tragedy. They are often irredeemably and existentially optimistic and this tendency is both reinforced and created by a never-ending wave of happy-ending movies and stories. Life, however, is seldom *that* happy. So it is that students might dislike the fact that Frodo, when finally at Mount Doom where the Ring of Power must be destroyed, is unable to do it, despite the fact that he alone has been able to bear its weight and resist its temptation. At the critical moment, he succumbs to the Ring's power and desires it for himself. It is only destroyed when Gollum/Smeagól takes the Ring back and, in the struggle that results, falls, with the Ring, to destruction. What happens then is something of a "happy ending" as Sam and Frodo are rescued and all recover, but thereafter the tragic reemerges. Frodo's wound from the Nazgûl never fully heals, and, in the end, the burden and grief of being the Ring-bearer means that he must leave Middle Earth. While this is something of an honor—only he and Bilbo (another Ring-bearer) of all the hobbits are allowed to accompany the elves to the West—it is also clearly the result of the pain caused by bearing the Ring.

Other tragic elements might be highlighted, especially the fact that it is the race of humans that is most frail vis-à-vis the temptations of the One Ring and the other rings of power. They are unable to resist their power, and this is repeatedly emphasized in a number of vignettes, perhaps most poignantly by Ilsidor, who failed in an earlier attempt to destroy the Ring. Whatever the case, student (dis)comfort with the tragic element in Tolkien could be discussed via the place of the tragic in a number of places in Scripture. Of note here are the ending to the garden story in Gen 2–3; the fact that one of the first two brothers ends up murdering the other (Gen 4); the devolution at the end of the book of Judges; the doomed kingship of Saul; or the ongoing struggle with sin evident in Paul.

Students might also be asked about the significance of the Ring itself: Is there some biblical analogue for the Ring? If so, what is it? Is there any way, short of asking Tolkien himself, to adjudicate between interpretations of this element? (Here, one might play a trick on students by fabricating a biblical construal of the Ring and then having them argue for or against its propriety; for example, the Ring symbolizes sin, Satan, free will, or the Holy Spirit. The process nicely illustrates the difference between exegesis and eisegesis.)

L
I
T
E
R
A
T
U
R
E

Leo Tolstoy, *War and Peace* (trans. A. Briggs; New York: Penguin, 2005; originally published in 1865–69)

Who is the antichrist? Throughout history people have offered various answers to this question, such as Nero, Adolf Hitler, Mikhail Gorbachev, Ronald Reagan, or one of the popes. Pierre Bezukhov, a central character in Tolstoy's magnum opus, would reject all of these identifications. A friend suggests to Pierre that, if one assigns a number to each letter of the alphabet, "L'Empereur Napoleon" adds up to 666, the "number of the beast" mentioned in Rev 13:18. Napoleon has invaded Russia, and Pierre has come to believe that he is destined to be the French general's assassin. Chapter 19 of book 8 contains his brief ruminations on this insight (the passage in Anthony Briggs's translation is less than five pages). Pierre attempts to write his own name so that it also adds up to 666, and after several unsuccessful tries he "discovers" that "L'russe Besuhof" ("the Russian Bezukhov" in improper French) adds up perfectly. By what means he was connected with the events foretold in Revelation he did not know, but "he did not doubt that connection for a moment."

This short narrative nicely dramatizes much of the history of interpretation of John's Apocalypse as well as portions of the book of Daniel, with its "creative math" and inconsistently applied principles. As Tolstoy describes it, Bezukhov's method for reading the text and for forecasting history is absurd. Having students dissect his hermeneutical decisions helps to make explicit what responsible interpretation of the Bible does and does not permit. By viewing contemporary examples of reading Revelation through the prism of current events—and vice versa—students may see that some caution may be in order when approaching such a complex document.

For a related exercise, see Mark Roncace, "Symbolism in Revelation," in Roncace and Gray, *Teaching the Bible*, 391.

Mark Twain, "Letters from the Earth" (*The Bible According to Mark Twain* [ed. H. G. Baetzhold and J. B. McCullough; New York: Simon & Schuster, 1995; originally published in 1909])

Silence sometimes speaks louder than words. Biblical texts are frequently so familiar that students have great difficulty imagining the narratives they contain taking any other form, yet an alertness to the specific details and questions *not* included or addressed can be the key to understanding the author's aims, the genre of the work, or its theological implications. To help students appreciate the possible significance of what is not said in a text (but might have been), one could do much worse than assigning Mark Twain's various "supplements" to the Bible at the beginning of a course. His "Letters from the Earth" is the longest—nearly fifty pages—and best known of these writings (www.sacred-texts.com/aor/twain/letearth.htm), but many others are available online and in print. Among the titles typically anthologized with "Letters" are such shorter works as "Extracts from Adam's Diary," "Adam's Expulsion," "Eve's Diary," "Autobiography of Eve and Diaries Antedating the Flood," "Passages from Methuselah's Diary," "Passages from Shem's Diary," and "God of the Bible vs. God of the Present Day." Most of these texts are five to ten pages long and may easily be broken into smaller passages for in-class discussion.

The simplest way to use these texts is to assign students to read excerpts and then respond in writing: In what ways do these "supplements" help you to notice features of the biblical narratives that you did not notice the first time you read them? Where do they raise significant historical, literary, or philosophical questions, and where do they simply function as entertainment? Intriguing examples abound, including the following:

(1) Were Adam and Eve psychologically similar to humans today or were they "blank slates" when they were created? Adam's diary contains amusing descriptions of Eve's concern for the fish, which have to live in the cold water (19–20; she gets them out and puts them in bed with her to keep them warm). Adam recounts his confusion at the water trickling from Eve's eyes when he tells her to leave him alone (8). Together they are perplexed at a new creature that appears—is it a bear or a kangaroo (12–16; they end up naming it Cain once they realize it is of their kind)? In attempting to take the Genesis narratives at face value and bracket anything outside the text, any number of questions naturally arise: Did Adam and Eve love each other? Did they understand the concept of "love"? Did their relationship evolve over time? That the author seems totally uninterested in answering such questions suggests that to read Genesis as one would modern fiction or biography would be a category mistake.

(2) "Letters" largely consists of correspondence between the archangels Satan and Gabriel reflecting on the peculiar features and foibles of humankind. One topic of discussion is the creation of the universe—including differences between human and heavenly experiences of the passage of time—and the instituting of unchanging physical laws of nature (219–21). Were Gen 1–11 a scientific treatise on the origins of the universe, these are subjects one might expect to see addressed.

(3) The opening passage of "Letters" (218–21) takes place in the "heavenly council" that many scholars posit as the background for the plural form *elohim* in Gen 1:26 (cf. 3:22; 11:7). Twain also explains Satan's alienation from this council and his relationship with the serpent in Eden. Were Genesis a treatise of systematic theology, one might expect some sort of reflection on such weighty matters as the origin of evil and the population of the supernatural realm. The Genesis account of the fall likewise receives much less attention than a modern writer like Twain (cf. 229–32) would devote to it.

(4) An abiding concern in "Letters" is the Bible's internal (in)consistency. This concern is unavoidable in an academic approach to the study of the Bible. The last sections address this topic generally by considering the different images of God in the Hebrew Bible and the New Testament (250–60). Some of the points will coincide with those made by most critical scholars; other points are caricatures or examples of inattentiveness to genre or context. This section provides ample material with which to begin a discussion of what, precisely, constitutes a contradiction and what strategies are available for making sense of such problematic texts.

Mark Twain, "The Story of the Good Little Boy" (*The Complete Short Stories of Mark Twain* [ed. C. Neider; New York: Bantam, 1984], 66–70)

This very short story (available online) tells of Jacob Blivens, a boy who is well behaved in every way but seems to have all the bad luck. Jacob believes the stories that he reads in the Sunday school books in which the good boys are happy and prosperous and the bad boys suffer with broken legs and the like. But it never turns out like this for Jacob in his own life. The bad boys have fun being mischievous and Jacob suffers terribly before dying a meaningless (nonheroic) death. The story nicely illustrates the view of the Teacher in Ecclesiastes. Jacob's life experiences do not match up with the neat worldview expressed in the book of Proverbs: Good people are blessed and wicked ones are punished. Jacob tries valiantly to reconcile his life with the one described in the religious books, but he never can. Similarly, Job and the Teacher expect the perspective of Proverbs to "work": Job protests mightily when he suffers for "no reason" (cf. Job 2:3), and the Teacher claims that he pursued a life of wisdom (Eccl 1:16–17). Job and the Teacher, however, have different approaches to coping with the incongruity. How would Job, Job's wife, Job's friends, and the writer of the epilogue of Ecclesiastes (12:13–14) respond to Jacob's plight? Students may also be asked if they identify with Jacob and what advice they would give to Jacob based on their own experiences and wisdom.

Garry Wills, *Lincoln at Gettysburg: The Words That Remade America* (New York: Simon & Schuster, 1992)

Wills's thesis in this Pulitzer prize winning book is that in the ultra-short Gettysburg Address—it is only 272 words and took a maximum of three minutes to deliver—Lincoln remade America by remaking the U.S. Constitution. Ten to twenty thousand people were in attendance at the cemetery in Gettysburg on November 19, 1863. But, according to Wills:

> Lincoln is here not…to sweeten the air of Gettysburg, but to clear the infected atmosphere of American history itself, tainted with official sins

and inherited guilt. He would cleanse the Constitution—not, as William Lloyd Garrison had, by burning an instrument that countenanced slavery. He *altered* the document *from within*, by appeal from its letter to the spirit, *subtly changing* the recalcitrant stuff of that legal compromise, *bringing it to its own indictment*. By implicitly doing this, he performed one of the most daring acts of open-air sleight-of-hand ever witnessed by the unsuspecting. Everyone in that vast throng of thousands was having his or her intellectual pocket picked. The crowd departed with a new thing in its ideological luggage, *that new constitution Lincoln had substituted for the one they brought there with them*. They walked off, from those curving graves on the hillside, under a changed sky, into a different America. Lincoln had revolutionized the Revolution, giving people *a new past to live with* that would *change their future* indefinitely. (38, emphasis added)

Stated this way, Wills's interpretation of the Gettysburg address bears marked similarity to what Moses (better: the Deuteronomists) does in the plains of Moab in Deuteronomy. Moses/Deuteronomy, too, performs a daring sleight-of-hand, subtly altering a constitutive (in many ways *the* constitutive) document/event: Sinai. Israel walked away with a new constitution—Deuteronomy—that gave them a new past to live by and one that would guide them in the future and change that future fundamentally, forever. It is in Deuteronomy that Moses/the Deuteronomists win the ideological Civil War that was waged at many points in Israelite history, but perhaps at no time more seriously than in the seventh century B.C.E. Wills continues:

> Both North and South strove to win the battle for *interpreting* Gettysburg as soon as the physical battle had ended. Lincoln is after even larger game—he means to "win" the whole Civil War in ideological terms as well as military ones. And he will succeed: the Civil War *is*, to most Americans, what Lincoln wanted it to *mean*. Words had to complete the work of the guns. (37–38, emphasis original)

In many ways this is true for Deuteronomy as well, which has left its indelible stamp across the Hebrew Bible, most notably in the Deuteronomistic History. Moreover, people tend to think that Sinai/covenant means what Deuteronomy wanted it to mean. This is apparent even in the New Testament when Jesus says the greatest commandment in all the law is precisely Deut 6:5.

Wills's remarks also raise interesting questions regarding the genre of Deuteronomy as a polity or constitution (as suggested by S. Dean McBride) or a revision of said constitution (through amendments or through an interpretive address such as Lincoln's).

L
I
T
E
R
A
T
U
R
E

Tom Wolfe, *A Man in Full* (New York: Farrar, Straus, Giroux, 1998)

One subplot in this sprawling novel set in the 1990s centers on Conrad Hensley, a working-class Californian who loses his job and, through an incredibly unfortunate series of events, ends up in prison though he is guilty of no crime. While incarcerated, he receives a copy of the writings of Epictetus by mistake, which proves indirectly to be his salvation. The Stoic insights of Epictetus, who had also spent time in prison, help Conrad to conquer his fears and to withstand the horrors of prison life until a timely earthquake leads to his escape. Portions of chapters fifteen, seventeen, and nineteen chronicle Conrad's prison experience in gruesome detail and contain several excerpts from Epictetus (352–69, 395–418, 441–65; the first excerpt may be omitted if length is a concern). Instructors should be aware that the realistic descriptions of jailhouse activity and inmate dialogue are quite graphic.

Stoic philosophy was a major component of the intellectual milieu in which much of the New Testament was written. The author of the Acts of the Apostles mentions Stoics by name (17:22–31), and scholars frequently detect their influence in Paul's letters (e.g., Rom 1:19–21; 2:14–15; 1 Cor 7:29–31). It is sometimes argued that in Phil 1:19–26 the imprisoned Paul is contemplating suicide in accordance with Stoic ideas about a proper death (cf. also his reflections on contentment in Phil 4:11). In addition, the martyrs in 4 Maccabees are clearly characterized as heroes of Stoic self-control. Wolfe's narrative can serve as an engaging introduction to Stoic thought, in tandem with secondary reading or class lecture. Questions for discussion may include: Does Wolfe accurately and adequately represent Stoic teachings? Is the way in which Epictetus helps Conrad to cope with his situation plausible? (Most likely, few students will have firsthand knowledge of prison life.) Do Stoic teachings address any of the same questions and concerns addressed in New Testament texts (e.g., fear of death in Heb 2:14–15)?

PART 5:
OTHER MEDIA

INTRODUCTION

Music, film, art, and literature are by no means the only materials that can be productively employed in the biblical studies classroom. This final section orients the reader to a number of media that can enhance teaching and learning and outlines representative strategies for use with examples drawn from various categories (Cartoons and Comics; Youth Literature, Programming, and Entertainment; Animated Television; Television Dramas and Documentaries; and Internet Websites). As with each of the previous sections, this survey is certainly not exhaustive. Teachers are encouraged to use the material presented here as a stimulus for designing creative and engaging class sessions and assignments.

The indices may be consulted to find entries with classroom strategies related to particular texts. All secondary literature cited in the following chapters is included in the following bibliography.

BIBLIOGRAPHY

Arp, Robert, ed. *South Park and Philosophy*. Boston: Blackwell, 2006.

Barnhart, David. "The Collaborative Comic Strip." Pages 318–20 in *Teaching the Bible: Practical Strategies for Classroom Instruction*. Edited by Mark Roncace and Patrick Gray. Atlanta: Society of Biblical Literature, 2005.

Boer, Roland. *Knockin' on Heaven's Door: The Hebrew Bible and Cultural Criticism*. London: Routledge, 1999.

Bottigheimer, Ruth. *The Bible for Children: From the Age of Gutenberg to the Present*. New Haven: Yale University Press, 1996.

Brown, Alan, and Chris Logan, eds. *The Psychology of The Simpsons*. Dallas: Benbella, 2006.

Burke, David G., and Lydia Lebrón-Rivera. "Transferring Biblical Narrative to Graphic Novel." *SBL Forum* (2004). Cited 21 May 2007. Online: www.sbl-site.org/Article.aspx?ArticleId=249.

Clanton, Dan W., Jr. "The Bible and Graphic Novels: A Review and Interview with the Authors of *Marked* and *Megillat Esther*." *SBL Forum* (2006). Cited 21 May 2007. Online: www.sbl-site.org/Article.aspx?ArticleId=477.

Clark, Terry Ray. "Biblical Graphic Novels: Adaptation, Interpretation, and 'Faithful Transfer.'" *SBL Forum* (2007). Cited 21 May 2007. Online: www.sbl-site.org/Article.aspx?ArticleId=641.

Cohen, Norman J. *The Way into Torah*. Woodstock, Vt.: Jewish Lights, 2000.

Eisner, Will. *Comics and Sequential Art: Principles and Practice of the World's Most Popular Art Form*. Tamarac, Fla.: Poorhouse, 1985.

Garrett, Greg. *Holy Superheroes! Exploring Faith and Spirituality in Comic Books*. Colorado Springs: Piñon Press, 2005.

Heitzmann, William Ray. "The Political Cartoon as a Teaching Device." Pages 50–62 in *Cartoons and Comics in the Classroom: A Reference for Teachers and Librarians*. Edited by James L. Thomas. Littleton, Colo.: Libraries Unlimited, 1983.

Inge, M. Thomas. *Comics as Culture*. Jackson: University Press of Mississippi, 1990.

Irwin, William, Mark T. Conrad, and Aeon J. Skoble, eds. *The Simpsons and Philosophy*. Chicago: Open Court, 2001.

Kemp, James. *The Gospel according to Dr. Seuss*. Valley Forge, Pa.: Judson, 2004.

Keslowitz, Steven. *The Simpsons and Society*. Tucson: Hats Off, 2003.

Mazur, Eric Michael, and Kate McCarthy, eds. *God in the Details: American Religion in Popular Culture*. New York: Routledge, 2001.

McCloud, Scott. *Understanding Comics*. New York: HarperCollins, 1993.

McKee, Gabriel. *The Gospel according to Science Fiction*. Louisville: Westminster John Knox, 2007.

Morris, Tom, and Matt Morris, eds. *Superheroes and Philosophy: Truth, Justice, and the Socratic Way*. Chicago: Open Court, 2005.

Neal, Connie. *The Gospel according to Harry Potter*. Louisville: Westminster John Knox, 2002.

Oropeza, B. J., ed. *The Gospel according to Superheroes: Religion and Popular Culture*. New York: Lang, 2005.

Pinsky, Mark I. *The Gospel according to the Simpsons*. Louisville: Westminster John Knox, 2001.

———. *The Gospel according to Disney*. Louisville: Westminster John Knox, 2004.

Short, Robert. *The Gospel according to "Peanuts."* Louisville: Westminster John Knox, 1979.

———. *The Parables of Peanuts*. San Francisco: Harper, 2002.

Szesnat, Holger. "Who Knows? Wikipedia, Teaching and Research." *SBL Forum* (2006). Cited 21 May 2007. Online: www.sbl-site.org/Article.aspx?ArticleId=603.

Tooze, G. Andrew. "Do Superheroes Read Scripture? Finding the Bible in Comic Books." *SBL Forum* (2007). Cited 9 May 2007. Online: www.sbl-site.org/Article.aspx?ArticleId=614.

Umphlett, Wiley Lee. *Mythmakers of the American Dream: The Nostalgic Vision in Popular Culture*. New York: Cornwall, 1983.

Weinstein, Simcha. *Up, Up, and Oy Vey! How Jewish History, Culture, and Values Shaped the Comic Book Superhero*. Baltimore: Leviathan, 2006.

Work, Telford. "Veggie Ethics: What 'America's Favorite Vegetables' Say about Evangelicalism." *Theology Today* 57 (2001): 473–83.

OTHER MEDIA

images and conventions, such as stereotypes, to convey its message (e.g., Gary Larson's *The Far Side*). As such, a cartoon is different from a comic strip, which is usually characterized as "sequential art," that is, a piece containing several panels that tells a more intricate story or joke. Furthermore, the "comic book" is a term that usually refers to a serialized piece of sequential art, often with more detail and depth of plot than a newspaper comic strip. Finally, there is the graphic novel, which can be a collection of comic books or simply a novel told in the form of text and images.

Long thought by many within academia to be a childish pursuit, scholars are now taking serious stock of the contribution comics and comic art have made to the culture, as is evinced by the instructional materials and programs of study listed by the National Association of Comics Art Educators (www.teachingcomics.org). In this vein, M. Thomas Inge notes that comics "deal with the larger aesthetic and philosophical issues mainstream culture has always defined in its arts and humanities. The comics are another form of legitimate culture quite capable of confronting the major questions of mankind" (*Comics as Culture*, xxi). Others have focused on the technical acumen needed to create such art. Will Eisner notes "an average comic book story would reveal the involvement of a range of diverse disciplines that would surprise a pedagogue" (*Comics and Sequential Art*, 147). How, then, does one employ comic art profitably in the classroom? The following discussion sketches some examples using material that relates to the book of Genesis.

Comic art can assist in the teaching of biblical content because in the process of rendering a biblical text for the purposes of humor, a cartoonist will often either reinforce or subtly change the text's content. For example, in a 2005 *Natural Selection* cartoon, Russ Wallace creates a humorous play on God's command in Gen 1:28. The comic depicts Adam and Eve covered in fruit, performing multiplication problems on a blackboard. Adam remarks, "I'm not sure why He told us to do this, but I think we should do what He says." Obviously, Wallace is playing with double meanings here, but his portrayal allows us to approach important content-related questions: Who is being addressed in 1:28? What does this command mean? What is its importance, given that it is repeated three times in the first nine chapters of Genesis? And, more abstractly, did these first humans have the conceptual ability to distinguish God's intended meaning from the one shown in the cartoon? That is, were they created with fully functioning cognitive abilities? Similarly, Wiley Miller's 1998 *Non Sequitur* cartoon allows one to examine the character of the serpent. It depicts both Adam and Eve eating apples, while the serpent remarks, "My long-term goal is to become a tobacco lobbyist." By drawing the connection between the serpent and a lobbyist for tobacco companies, Miller implies that the former is morally questionable by linking it to the latter. Similarly, in Tom Toles's 2001 *Randolph Itch* cartoon the serpent is held responsible for Cain's killing Abel by slyly suggesting that Abel let Cain shoot an apple off his head. Not only does Toles's work allow for the relatively simple matter of distinguishing between his depiction and the narrative in Gen 4, but it also permits students to continue the discussion of the serpent's character because it both furthers the inherited understanding of the serpent—which many students demonize, literally—as essentially evil and at the same time lends credence to the view of the serpent as trickster.

Once content has been taught, other pedagogic goals can be pursued, such as introducing method, history of interpretation, and instigating discussion of contemporary issues. As one might guess, newspaper comics are not an arena in which issues of biblical critical method come up frequently, but there are some examples one might use. A *Peanuts* strip features Charlie Brown being insulted by Violet. Linus asks Charlie Brown, "She really took you apart, didn't she?" to which Charlie Brown replies, "Uh-huh ... Step by step, verse by verse, and line by line." Linus then makes the connection between her approach to the insulting and biblical studies by noting, "You sound like a victim of higher criticism." This gentle comparison can easily serve as a transition into a discussion of method. Another strip shows Linus discussing the prologue to the Gospel of Luke. Linus dispenses biblical-critical advice to Charlie Brown, such as "Note the role of Gabriel.... He also appears in Revelations [sic] and Daniel.... Ask yourself what 'finding favor' really meant to Mary.... Check out Hosea 11:1." After this lesson, Chuck looks depressed at his lack of knowledge and says sadly, "All I ever knew about was the star and the sheep on the hillside," to which Linus responds, "Merry Christmas, Charlie Brown!" Indeed, many students share this sentiment when it comes to critical approaches to the Bible, and this strip could be a way to open up conversation about certain hesitations or outright mistrust. Analyzing the strip on a much deeper level, one might suggests that Linus here is—perhaps unintentionally—engaging in a hermeneutical act of serious religious significance. Summarizing a point made by Daniel Boyarin, Norman Cohen writes, "Interpreting texts by means of connecting one text to another, or by revealing the link between texts and the historical context in which they are produced, the student of Torah *re-cites* ... the word of God, and so recreates the original moment of revelation" (*The Way into Torah*, 20).

One of the most useful areas comic art can address is the history of biblical interpretation. For example, in Rick Detorie's 2003 strip *One Big Happy*, young Ruthie asks a simpleminded question about what Noah and his family did for food on the ark. Her grandfather replies that they probably fished, to which Ruthie replies in a childlike fashion, "No, no, no! They only had two worms!" Questions such as Ruthie's—which are not addressed by the biblical

O
T
H
E
R

M
E
D
I
A

narrative—can stimulate the imaginations of students and send them scur-rying to find out what other interpreters have conjectured in the past. Once these interests have been piqued, one can then turn students' attention to the history of interpretation on a specific issue. Another question not addressed by the biblical narrative, but one that has occupied interpreters, is why exactly Noah was chosen to build the ark. In one of Johnny Hart's *B.C.* cartoons from 2006, a young ant poses this query to his father, who replies laconically, "He was the only holy man on earth. That—plus he was the only one familiar with the cubit system." Or, finally, one can explore the comic views of what became of the ark after the flood, as Mike Peters does in a 2005 *Mother Goose and Grimm* comic that shows the ark being used as a casino, while Noah wist-fully reflects, "Well, after the flood it was just sitting here." In sum, there are a variety of ways in which comic art can be used to broach the history of inter-pretation of a given passage.

Comic art can also be used profitably to stimulate discussion on a par-ticular topic. Editorial comics and comic books tend to work better in this regard than one-frame cartoons or an isolated comic strip. For example, the comic on evolution and creationism by David Horsey from 2005 depicts a dinosaur eating Adam in the Garden of Eden. The 2004 cartoon on gay mar-riage by Larry Wright shows the ark being boarded by same-sex couples, two-by-two, while a man (presumably one of Noah's sons) asks Noah, "Are you sure God suggested stopping in Massachusetts?" Another example is the more serious 2005 hurricane Katrina-based cartoon by Mike Luckovich which pictures numerous dead animals in the midst of the flood, with Noah telling the viewer, "Cut me some slack! I'm a Bush crony who's never built a boat before!" In each of these cases, one can easily stimulate discussion through an examination of the cartoon's use of Genesis to make a statement about current events.

A more involved use of comic art to stimulate discussion about Gene-sis can be found in two recent comic book series. In December 2006, Viper Comics released the first issue of *The Lost Books of Eve*, written by Josh Howard, whose credits include the fan favorite *Dead @ 17*. The comic's offi-cial website (vipercomics.com/features/the_lost_books_of_eve.asp) invites the reader to:

> Journey back to a time when magic still thrived, dragons and fallen gods roamed the earth, and man was just a myth. The Garden of Eden was a place of perfect peace and tranquility. That is, until its keeper, Adam, went missing. Now, his newly created wife, Eve, must venture outside the safety of the Garden for the first time to go in search of her husband, all the while battling monsters, beast men, wizards, demons, and even the gods them-selves.

Howard's work opens with a quotation from Gen 2:15–18, 21–23, and follows with a quotation from "The Lost Books of Eve 1:1," which details Eve's "insatiable curiosity" and Adam's decision to build a raft so that Eve could see the oceans. Evidently, Adam is lost at sea, and Eve is now left alone in the Garden. One of the most interesting devices Howard uses is to portray God physically, so that God and Eve can converse. God is drawn as a male figure, outlined completely in white, with three eyes on its face, eyes on its palms, and a larger eye on its chest. Eve finally decides to journey out of Eden to find Adam, and she is accompanied by Asherah, one of the guardians of the gate. In its compact narrative, Howard's comic not only introduces key Edenic concepts like free will, but also presents the reader with an enlarged palette of the Garden so that it comes alive. Finally, Eve's character is fleshed out nicely (in more ways than one, given Howard's propensity for scantily clad heroines) so that her motivations and experiences become the touchstone for the story. As such, Howard's work can be employed to explore the character of Eve, the Garden, issues raised by the situation(s) of the first humans, and the ways in which other interpreters have rendered Eve.

A much more intricate example is the ongoing comic book series *Testament*, written by Douglas Rushkoff. Published by Vertigo Books, the "mature readers" imprint of DC Comics, this series contains one of the most sophisticated uses of biblical materials within the field of comic art. Rushkoff's website (rushkoff.com) describes *Testament* this way: "What if the Bible were happening right now? In the world of *Testament*, the archetypal struggle for dominion over humanity is being fought by the revolutionaries of two eras against the would-be tyrants of their ages." That is, Rushkoff identifies various themes within biblical literature and writes complex narratives that take place simultaneously in three different time periods: one in the setting of the biblical story, one in a more totalitarian and dangerous future, and one in sacred time, which is inhabited by deities. Space restraints do not permit adequate summary of the series, but a few words can be said about the first issue.

Rushkoff's first volume, entitled *Akedah*, is a retelling of Gen 22. Juxtaposed with the biblical narrative is the story of Jake Stern and his father Alan, who has developed a tracking chip to assist in locating soldiers. The draft has been reinstated and all potential candidates are required to be implanted with these chips. After much deliberation, Alan decides to implant his son's chip into their family dog and as such does not sacrifice his son to a government he mistrusts, just as Abraham does not sacrifice Isaac, an act Rushkoff links with the deity Moloch. In the succeeding issues, Jake discovers that his father's identification chip is being used to quell dissent against the new government and that all of these evils have been orchestrated by three gods: Astarte, Atum-Ra, and Moloch. They are being opposed, then as now, by Mel-

OTHER MEDIA

chezidek, Elijah, and Krishna, acting on behalf of God. Rushkoff is trying to alert his readers to the power of the Bible as human story. In the introduction to the graphic novel collection of the first five issues of *Testament*, Rushkoff writes, "We could all use the kind of wake-up call that a good dose of Bible could provide. ... For by 'insisting' that the Bible happened at some moment in distant history, the keepers of religion prevent us from realizing that the Bible is happening right now, in every moment" (6). In 2007, Vertigo released the second graphic novel collection, comprising issues six through ten, as *Testament: West of Eden*. Teachers can be thankful for this second volume, as it contains a section titled "Mysteries and Meanings: Notes on the Biblical History behind *Testament*." Written by Rushkoff, these annotations to the first ten issues of *Testament* are extremely helpful in connecting the comic with the biblical stories behind them. DC Comics has also posted the notes to *Akedah* online (www.dccomics.com/media/special/Testament_Vol_1_Notes.pdf).

Beyond Genesis, there are several useful graphic novels that can be mentioned. The oldest, and one of the most influential, is Will Eisner's seminal *A Contract with God* (1978), reprinted in *The Contract with God Trilogy* in 2006. Long considered the first graphic novel in America, Eisner's title story is rich in Joban allusions, yet set in modern New York. The past few years have seen a flowering of biblical graphic novels. A partial list includes Jim Krueger and Mario Ruiz, *Testament* (2003); A. David Lewis, with M. P. Mann and Jennifer Rodgers, *The Lone and Level Sands* (2005); Steve Ross, *Marked* (2005); and J. T. Waldman, *Megillat Esther* (2005).

Two final suggestions on ways to implement learning-by-comics. First, students can draw their own cartoons/comics. As David Barnhart ("The Collaborative Comic Strip") has noted, when students—alone or in groups—participate in the creative process of selecting the perspective and fashioning the focus of a particular story or event, they not only perform exegesis but also become more aware of the choices made by later painters, writers, musicians, and filmmakers in their renderings and perhaps even of how those choices have influenced what they understand about the text. Second, in the grand tradition of *The New Yorker* and, subsequently, *Biblical Archaeology Review*, the teacher can ask students to fill in the thought bubbles found in preexisting cartoons and then justify or explain their choices. Students often have as much fun creating dialogue for this assignment as they do creating their own cartoons, and the less artistically inclined students can participate in a more substantial way.

Youth Literature, Programming, and Entertainment

Mark Roncace

This chapter offers teaching strategies related to children's Bibles, the *VeggieTales* video series, and computer video games.

Children's Bibles

Children's Bibles offer an easy and enjoyable way to engage biblical texts. They have two particular advantages. First, they are readily available in a wide variety of approaches and styles. Books vary depending on the age, gender, and religious affiliation (e.g., Catholic or Jewish) of the intended reader. Used children's Bibles can be purchased very cheaply on the Internet, and the local public library should have plenty on hand. Secondly, many students are familiar with the genre; in fact, students have confessed to reading their children's Bible as a "Cliffs Notes" version. Students also appreciate the opportunity to reflect on what they read and were taught as a child in comparison to the "real" Bible. A study of the differences can prove invigorating and enlightening.

When employing children's Bibles in class, it is helpful to break students into groups and have one person in each group act as the "teacher" by reading the story aloud as the others listen; the teachers must be sure to show the accompanying sketches to their "class." It is very easy to gather a collection of children's Bibles so that different ones can be distributed to different groups. Of course, if only one children's Bible is available, it could simply be read to the class as a whole. Students are then asked to discuss the following types of questions, which could be modified, or made more specific, based on the text: How does the children's version compare to the canonical text? What elements does the children's version omit, add, or change? How do the deletions or additions influence the overall story? What motivates the changes in the children's version? Is there an explicit "lesson" for children to learn? How do the accompanying illustrations help readers interpret the story? Is the children's version a responsible and helpful way to render the story? In general, and not surprisingly, children's versions simplify matters, which underscores and facilitates reflection on the complexities of the biblical text.

Many different biblical passages, particularly from the Hebrew Bible, could be studied via children's Bibles. The tales of Jacob, Joseph, Moses, Joshua, Elijah, Saul, David, and Esther come immediately to mind. Sometimes it is instructive to point out which stories are virtually absent from children's Bibles, such as many of the narratives in Judges or the story of Job. Other stories are found in most children's Bibles, such as Jonah, which can be analyzed here for the purposes of illustrating how a class discussion might unfold.

While commentators debate the meaning and purpose of the canonical book of Jonah, in many children's Bibles the meaning and purpose are clear: It is a story of disobedience, punishment, repentance, and forgiveness. This is accomplished in several ways. First, as students immediately recognize, children's Bibles generally omit the fourth and final chapter in which Jonah becomes angry that God does not destroy Nineveh. In the last verse of the book, God poses a question to Jonah, thus concluding the story in a wonderfully open-ended fashion. In contrast, numerous children's stories end with the Ninevites heeding Jonah's message and repenting to avoid God's wrath. There is no bush, no worm, and no irate prophet. This simpler ending rewrites a complex story and ambiguous protagonist into a tidy tale of forgiveness and "second chances"—for both Jonah and Nineveh. Even some of the children's accounts that do include elements of the canonical ending mold it into a lesson for Jonah and the reader. For instance, *My First Study Bible* has Jonah say in conclusion, "God reminded me that He loves everyone. I learned that I should love people like that, too." Similarly, *Bible Stories for Children* concludes with, "So Jonah came to understand God's ways and how much he loved his people, and Jonah was glad that Nineveh was saved." This "moral of the story" serves to interpret the biblical text, and whether or not one approves of the lesson, it is important to see that no such moralizing occurs in the biblical text. (It is a common feature of children's Bibles to have a moral point to the stories. Asking students if they deem this appropriate often leads to lively discussions.)

Children's versions typically contain more subtle differences that significantly alter the story. For example, in the canonical version, Jonah's prayer from the belly of the fish is rather peculiar (Jonah 2). He never repents, and he is eager to return to the temple, which does not accord with God's commands to go to Nineveh. In children's versions, by contrast, Jonah clearly repents. For example, Jonah says, "I'm sorry I ran away. Next time I'll do as you tell me" (*My First Bible*). Or Jonah "had plenty of time to think about how he had behaved, and now he was sorry for disobeying God (*Children's Everyday Bible*). Or finally, "Jonah thought about how he disobeyed God. He felt bad, 'I'm sorry, God. I should have obeyed you. If you still want me to go to Nineveh, I'll go' " (*Little Boys Bible Storybook*). Telling the story in this fashion also suggests, incorrectly, that the big fish is a vehicle of punishment (akin to being put in "time-out") rather than of salvation.

Further, Jonah's message to the Ninevites in the canonical version is a terse declaration of coming destruction: "Forty days more and Nineveh shall be overthrown" (3:4). Children's Bibles expand Jonah's message considerably in order to include explicitly the call for repentance. For example, Jonah "told both the king and people about the God of earth and heaven, who would no longer let their cruelty and wickedness continue. They must admit how wrong they had been, tell God they were sorry and then change their ways, or else God would punish them and their proud city" (*Children's Bible in 365 Stories*). In short, these changes serve to simplify the story's ambiguities; thus students are able to see more clearly the interpretive challenges that confront readers of the canonical version.

Another feature of children's Bibles that lends itself to use in the classroom is the tendency toward harmonization. Two examples can be offered. First, rather than presenting separately both creation stories found in Gen 1–3, nearly all contemporary children's Bibles rewrite the two stories into one. The most common way to unite them is to move the account of the creation of the man from dust and the woman from the man's rib in the Garden of Eden to the sixth day of the first story. This rewriting omits any reference to Gen 1:26–27 where male and female are created simultaneously and in God's image. Further, some children's Bibles depict only the man created on the sixth day. For instance, the *Good News Bible Stories for Children* says: "When all this was done, God made man from the dust of the earth and called the man Adam. God looked at everything He had made and saw that it was very good. Then God took a rest!" Similarly, the *New Catholic Picture Bible* reads: "God said, 'I shall make man in My image. I shall make him to rule over all the things that I have created.' God formed man out of the dust of the earth." The text then proceeds directly to the seventh day of rest. Yet another example is *The Bible Story*, which reads, "Last of all, God said, 'I will make man. I will make him in my likeness and after my image.' So out of the dust of the earth God formed the first man." God then sets the man in the Garden. In many of these harmonized versions, the woman, remarkably, does not appear during the seven days of creation. She is not created in God's image; she is not part of the creation that is pronounced good. This observation typically evokes animated responses from students.

Secondly, rather than providing two separate accounts of Jesus' birth, children's versions typically combine the stories found in Matthew and Luke into one narrative. Students can be asked to identify the elements of the children's story that come from each Gospel. They can also note the elements that are omitted as a result of the harmonization. Children's versions usually follow Luke's story through the shepherd's visit before switching to Matthew's account for the visit by the wise men and the subsequent flight to Egypt. As a result, the most commonly excised material is Luke's scene of Jesus' presentation in the temple where his parents offer a sacrifice of two turtledoves and two pigeons "according to what is stated in the law of the Lord" (Luke 2:24). By rewriting the story in this fashion, the fact that Jesus was Jewish, and that events surrounding his birth followed Jewish customs, is easily overlooked. The genealogies in both Matthew and Luke also establish Jesus' Jewish lineage, but, of course, these do not appear in children's Bibles. Students, in short, are able to appreciate more fully the distinctive elements of the canonical accounts by comparing them to the blended children's stories.

Finally, it can be a fun and productive exercise for students to write—and perhaps even illustrate—their own children's version.

VEGGIETALES

Co-created by Phil Vischer and Mike Nawrocki, *VeggieTales* is a series of children's computer-animated films. The popular series features comical anthropomorphic vegetables as characters. Most of the episodes are fairly short (thirty to forty minutes), and biblical studies instructors should have no difficulty selecting specific scenes to play in class. The films are explicitly didactic and draw on a variety of biblical stories. Series titles include:

> *Where's God When I'm S-Scared?* (Daniel and the Lion's Den)
> *Dave and the Giant Pickle* (David and Goliath)
> *Are You My Neighbor?* (Parable of the Good Samaritan)
> *Rack, Shack, and Benny* (Daniel in the Furnace)
> *Josh and the Big Wall!* (Battle at Jericho)
> *King George and the Ducky* (David and Bathsheba)
> *The Ballad of Little Joe* (Joseph and his Brothers)
> *Duke and the Great Pie War* (Ruth; Moses and Miriam)

Three additional episodes illustrate how class discussion might unfold:

Esther: The Girl Who Became Queen (2000)

It would be possible to view this entire thirty-minute video and use it as a basis to launch discussion of the biblical text. Three scenes are particularly helpfully as they highlight the sexual and violent nature of the biblical story—material that is inappropriate for children. First, the drunken king demanding that the beautiful queen Vashti display herself for the viewing pleasure of the men at the feast (1:10) is certainly a scene with adult themes. Before showing the parallel film clip, students might be asked to imagine how they would rewrite that scene for a children's audience. In the *VeggieTales* version Vashti refuses to make the king a sandwich at three in the morning, resulting in her being expelled from the palace (DVD ch. 1). Similarly, the sexually suggestive nature of Esth 2 in which the girls vying for the position of the new queen spend a night with the king (2:12–14) is altered as Esther wins a singing contest (DVD ch. 2). Here students can pay special attention to the words of Esther's song since it refers to God. This mention of the deity provides a chance to mention the Greek version of Esther, which also includes the divine element. Finally, the violent and vengeful conclusion of the biblical story (Esth 9) can be contrasted with Haman's fate in the film: banished to the island of perpetual tickling (DVD ch. 8). These film clips not only introduce an element of humor into the class; more importantly, they help students consider the "mature themes" in the biblical story: Is Esther an innocent girl who does what she must to save her people, or does she use her sexuality to bring about the bloody destruction of those who oppose her? As a concluding exercise, students can attempt to identify the "lesson" of the biblical book. Very few of them indicate "courage," which is the moral of the *VeggieTales* film ("you never need to be afraid to do what's right"). This can lead to a discussion of (1) the didactic nature (or lack thereof) of biblical narrative, (2) Purim and the significance of the book in Jewish tradition, or (3) the "lesson" that Esther might have taught to its original audience—how to live successfully under foreign rule (cf. Daniel and Joseph).

Jonah: A VeggieTales Movie (2002)

This movie-length (eighty-three minutes) version of Jonah features several scenes that could be used to study the biblical book. Perhaps the best is the six-minute concluding scene (DVD ch. 21) which can be compared to Jonah 4. How is the film interpreting the canonical account? What does it change, retain, or omit? And how do the differences alter the overall significance and purpose of the story? Among a variety of possible topics one could pursue, the following may be noted: (1) In the Bible, Jonah and God have a more direct relationship than in the film where the deity (or a divine voice) is absent; this changes the literary and theological texture of the story. (2) In the biblical text, God plays a much more adversarial role as he appoints a worm to destroy the plant and sends a sultry wind to torment Jonah (4:7–8). By contrast, in the film, we are told only that God's compassion provided a plant to shade Jonah. The plant is eaten by Khalil—Jonah's traveling companion—and no wind is mentioned. (3) In the film, Khalil explains that God spared Nineveh because the Ninevites repented, so God gave them a "second chance." This is not unlike the biblical text (3:10). However, God's final questions to Jonah (4:10–11) focus on God's sovereignty and love for all creation, not Nineveh's repentance and "second chance." That is, God cares for the people (and animals!) of Nineveh even though they "do not know their right hand from their left."

(4) Like the biblical version, the story of Jonah in the film ends without any resolution—Jonah is still on the hillside confused and frustrated. The characters in the film to whom the Jonah story is being told (it is a story within a story) object to this open ending until the storyteller observes (DVD ch. 22): "It's not what Jonah learned; it's what you learned." Just as the biblical text summons the reader to a response by concluding the book with a question, so too the film calls the reader to wrestle with the issues raised in the story.

(5) The film ends with a song, in line with the biblical account, that explains, "Jonah was a prophet, but he never really got it." The point, according to the song, is that God wants people to be merciful and compassionate. To develop this idea, teachers can shows students a picture of a T-shirt which reads in large letters, "Jesus loves you!" and in smaller letters underneath, "Then again, he loves everybody" (www.cafepress.com/larknews.23099704). If "Jesus" is replaced with "God," then this shirt illustrates one of the central theological issues that the book of Jonah invites its readers to ponder: How can God show mercy and compassion to everyone? Aren't we more special? Surely God loves us more than our enemies? The students who dislike the sarcastic tone of the T-shirt can perhaps begin to understand Jonah's bitterness—his difficulty in "getting it"—in response to God's compassion for Nineveh.

Gideon: Tuba Warrior (2006)

Only about half (12–15 minutes) of this episode is a retelling of the Gideon story (Judg 6–8). If the *VeggieTales* version of Jonah includes the complex ending, it omits it altogether with Gideon (Judg 8). There is, as one might suspect, no mention of Gideon's vengeance on the people of Succoth for failing to assist him in his pursuit of the Midianite leaders (Judg 8:1–17) or of Gideon's ephod which led to false worship and problems for Gideon (8:22–28). Obviously these omissions change the overall portrayal of Gideon, thus prompting students to consider the rhetorical and theological function of Judg 8. What is the point for including those dubious elements? Is there any significance to the deity's absence during this part of the narrative? Similar omissions at the beginning of the story also change the animated version. In it the Midianites are simply presented as the enemy—no reason is supplied as to why they plan to attack the Israelites. In the Bible, of course, God designed the Midianite oppression as punishment for Israel's sins, and God seems initially reluctant to deliver them (6:6–10), which yields a different image of God from the one in the film. In both versions Gideon is depicted as initially fearful and reluctant, but the *VeggieTales* Gideon overcomes his fear more quickly and with fewer protestations. For instance, in the canonical account, Gideon is shown as fearful right up until the eve of the battle when he journeys to the Midianite camp for one last sign of victory, the hearing of a dream presaging Israelite victory (7:7–15). In the *VeggieTales* retelling, Gideon accidentally overhears the dream and tells God: "I did not need that [sign], but thanks anyway." In general, students can discuss the differences between Gideon's image and role in the two accounts. The subtitle of the film is "a lesson in trusting God." What subtitle would students supply for the biblical story?

Video Games

Bible-related video games offer the opportunity to think about important issues, including the violent nature of biblical texts, how texts are reinterpreted for modern audiences, and the effect, intended or otherwise, such games might have on those who play them. Teachers can derive pedagogical benefit simply by showing the video game's website in class rather than actually purchasing the product and attempting to demonstrate the game.

There are relatively few Bible-based video games (excluding trivia oriented ones), though the number is growing. Not surprisingly, the books of Joshua and Revelation are the two texts featured most prominently. For example "Joshua and the Battle of Jericho" (Wisdom Tree Games) is described this way:

> You, as Joshua, must lead God's people into the land of promise. But watch out! There are falling rocks, soldiers, battering rams and elite forces that will try to block your every move. But God has given you the power. Weapons like the horn of Jericho, God Speed, power-ups, secret exits and other armor will help you in your quest. Conquer the Canaanites, Amorites and Hittites as you collect silver and gold, race through deadly mazes, and defeat the enemies of God!

Obviously the game reflects the violent rhetoric found in Joshua; the cover depicts a strong-armed man wielding a sword. Joshua, of course, can lose the game, which can open the door for discussion of the Canaanites perspective (e.g., what if Joshua had lost?). Interestingly, Wisdom Tree's slogan is "family friendly learning that excites the mind." Whether or not killing Canaanites is "family friendly" is something that students enjoy discussing.

The recently released "Left Behind: Eternal Forces" is adapted from the best-selling *Left Behind* book series by Tim LaHaye and Jerry Jenkins. Like the novels, the game is loosely based on the book of Revelation, focused on the so-called "Rapture" of believers. The game has been criticized for encouraging the killing or converting of non-Christians ("convert or die"), but Tyndale House, the publisher, denies the accusation. They do, however, admit, "The game is a good versus evil story, which in turn results in conflict." Players lead the Tribulation force against the antichrist in a battle of "physical and spiritual warfare." Like the book of Revelation, the game is a violent battle between good and evil. Similarly, in "Catechumen," a game by N'Lightning Software, players are told: "Your mentor and brethren have been captured by the demon-possessed Roman soldiers. It is your job to work your way through the catacombs to free them. Satan has a powerful hand in the Roman Empire and has powerful foes to block your every effort." In the process, players will "encounter Satan's minions and banish them back to their evil realm. Evil lurks everywhere you turn. With your Sword of the Spirit in hand, you must confront the demons head on and show them nothing can overcome the power of the Holy Spirit."

In general, these Bible-based video games are relatively tame when it comes to the depiction of violence. For instance, one reviewer writes of "Catechumen": "It's a joy to know my son can immerse himself in such an interactive game without the threat of any blood, guts or gore." Several observations and questions emerge here: Presumably, few people would be able to say the same thing about certain biblical texts—"I am glad my children can read them without the threat of blood, guts, or gore." How, then, does that affect their attitude toward the Bible? While the Bible-based games may be relatively innocuous, they still clearly have a violent theme. Do people fail to recognize video game violence because it is not "real," that is, only on a screen? Likewise, do people overlook the violence in the biblical text because it is "only a text"? What is the relationship between graphic violence and "real" violence? Further, do people tend to excuse violence as long as the "bad guys" are the ones being killed? Does this make Joshua's or Revelation's violence somewhat palatable? What makes someone a "bad guy"—that is, what is the heart of the conflict (moral/religious values; land possession; etc.)?

In short, students are invited to see the biblical text in a different light when they witness it translated into a video game. How does the new medium affect one's reading of the text? Showing students these video games provides an excellent visual contrast to, say, the books of Ruth or Jonah or Jesus' words in the Sermon on the Mount, which present a much different view of outsiders/enemies. If there are, indeed, many different perspectives in the canon, students can be invited to reflect on why the particularly violent ones are adapted to video games. What would a video game based, for example, on Jonah look like? Why do the video games opt for the texts that present a black-and-white (i.e., dualistic) worldview? What are the implications of using biblical imagery, themes, and language to promote such a worldview?

Animated Television

Dan W. Clanton Jr. and Mark Roncace

This chapter discusses several episodes from each of three prime time animated television shows—*The Simpsons*, *South Park*, and *Family Guy*.

The Simpsons

The popular Fox television cartoon *The Simpsons* has attracted not only countless admirers, but also the attention of scholars (e.g., Keslowitz, *The Simpsons and Society*; Brown and Logan, *The Psychology of The Simpsons*; and Pinsky, *The Gospel according to the Simpsons*). The best source for information on the show is The Simpsons Archive (snpp.com), which contains synopses and transcripts of all episodes, except the most recent ones. It also has a list of the show's references to religious issues, including a list of biblical references arranged by book (www.snpp.com/guides/religion.html). Teachers might simply glance through the list to glean something to mention in class without showing the clip. For instance, when discussing the book of James and how his views of works and salvation relate to Paul's views, one can quote Homer: "Wow. God does so much for me and he doesn't ask anything in return." Or if the issue of the trinity emerges in discussions of the Spirit in Acts, one can cite, with sympathy, Ned Flanders (the conservative Christian neighbor of the Simpsons), who is clearly having trouble understanding the concept when he says: "Homer, please don't tempt the Gods." Then, looking upward and stuttering, says, "I mean, mean God. There's one God. Only one. Well, sometimes there's three." Similarly, Bart raises some of the same questions as those found in 1 Cor 15 concerning bodily resurrection when he asks his Sunday school teacher: "What if you're a really good person, but you get into a really, really bad fight and your leg gets gangrene and it has to be amputated. Will it be waiting for you in heaven?"

In addition to numerous one-liners, the show also has featured entire episodes which explore themes related to the Bible. What follows is a brief sketch of how a few episodes might be employed in the classroom. Note that only the first nine seasons are currently available on DVD; the rest will presumably be released in the future. Each episode is about twenty-two minutes, so it could be shown in its entirety; in many cases, however, teachers could select a representative clip. In addition to the specific suggestions provided below, simply asking students what questions the episode raises about the biblical text or topic can be a helpful, if risky, strategy. Students often connect the cartoon and text in insightful ways. Note: Some students will occasionally find the humor offensive to their personal values and beliefs; teachers should proceed with due sensitivity and caution.

"Homer vs. Lisa and the 8th Commandment" (Second Season, 1991)

In this episode, Lisa (the daughter) fears that the family might go to hell because Homer steals cable TV by getting an illegal hookup. First, the title of this episode can help students note that the Commandments are not numbered in either Exod 20 or Deut 5 and as a result they are counted differently in different traditions. If students are asked to number the Commandments, they will come up with different lists, in part because there are more than ten imperative verbs. Those students who focus on Deut 5:6–21 typically end up numbering according to the Catholic tradition in which the law prohibiting theft is the seventh, not the eighth commandment (i.e., the title of the episode reflects only one tradition of numbering the commands).

The first half of this episode can underscore certain features of the biblical laws, for instance, their simplicity. The biblical text does not list penalties for breaking the Commandments, which raises the question of what the penalty might be—perhaps exclusion from the covenant community, which of course is quite different from contemporary penalties for theft. By contrast, in *The Simpsons* the consequence for breaking the law is clear: eternal punishment in hell (a concept that students are surprised to learn is not in the Hebrew Bible). This can lead to discussion of how the specific punishments were added (or changed) as biblical laws developed. Similarly, the Decalogue does not define stealing with any specificity or give any regulations to govern various scenarios. Homer calls attention to this issue when in a conversation with Lisa he agrees that stealing is wrong but then goes on to ask Lisa, "When you had breakfast this morning, did you pay for it? And did you pay for those clothes you're wearing?" As an eight-year-old, Lisa did not. Later Lisa probes the issue much more deeply than Homer when she asks the minister, "So even if a man takes bread to feed his starving family, that would be stealing?" The minister says it would not be, unless the man puts anything on the bread, such as jelly. This exchange can set up a discussion of the development of biblical laws to deal with more complex societal situations. Further, just as getting a free cable hookup might be seen by some (i.e., Homer) as a victimless crime, or even no crime at all, so too the Israelites evidently had difficulty in determining cases of disputed ownership (see Exod 22:1–12, especially v. 9).

Bart and Lisa's Sunday school teacher asserts one must obey the Ten Commandments in order to avoid eternal damnation. Here one can ask students what Jesus would think about this view. After they typically say that Jesus would disagree, one can have them consult passages such as Matt 5:17–20 or the text in which Jesus answers the rich man's questions about how to inherit eternal life by enjoining him to keep the commandments (Matt 19:16–30; Mark 10:17–31; Luke 18:18–30). This often enlivens the discussion and helps Christian students take a more active interest in the laws.

"Simpsons Bible Stories" (Tenth Season, 1999)

Bored in church, the Simpsons doze off, dreaming of themselves in the Garden of Eden, making the Exodus from Egypt, and as David fighting Goliath. Thus this episode conveniently breaks roughly into three six-minute vignettes. In the Adam and Eve sequence, one can simply ask students to point out the differences between cartoon and biblical version, such as: Who is present when the deity forbids eating the fruit (both Adam/Homer and Eve/Marge in the cartoon vs. only Adam in the Bible)? What punishment is stipulated for eating the fruit (nothing specific vs. death)? Who eats the fruit first (Adam vs. Eve)? Why does Eve eat the fruit (because she does not want to waste the fruit vs. to gain knowledge to be like God)? Who does God approach first after they have eaten (Eve vs. Adam)? There are similarities as well, such as the man names the animals and both the man and woman are present when the snake appears. One can ask about the overall portrayal of the characters. Like the biblical story, the cartoon depicts Eve as the more intelligent, cerebral creature. She, for instance, wants to call one of the animals "groundhog," but Adam has already named it "land monster." Adam eats the fruit compulsively, but Eve tries to convince him to stop (an obvious difference from the canonical account) and then reasons that "it's a sin to waste food" before she eats. She confesses her failure when confronted by the deity, but the man tries nonchalantly to push the apple cores out of sight and then fails to intercede on her behalf when God expels her from the garden. The cartoon also helps students contemplate the image of God. In the biblical version, the deity is more anthropomorphic than in the cartoon, where God is represented as a hand reaching out of heaven. The biblical God might be seen as more merciful since the humans are not punished by death for eating the fruit (Gen 2:17). But neither deity is particularly forgiving, as seen in Adam's protests in the cartoon just prior to being expelled, "God is love, right?"

Two other thoughts: Adam, surmising that God will let them back in the garden, asks "How long can God hold a grudge?" The answer is "forever and ever" (which is the preacher reading from the Bible as Homer emerges from his dream). This gives students a chance to reflect on the Pauline concept of original sin as an interpretation of the Garden story. Secondly, when Adam is hungry for some bacon, the pig simply pulls some out of its own flesh and gives it to him. This prompts students to inquire about the nature of life as God intended it (i.e., "should we be vegetarians?"), and to reflect on how this text might be brought to bear on general environmental issues.

The second and third vignettes stray a bit farther from the biblical account than the first one, but they still offer some talking points. In the cartoon, Moses, played by Milhouse, is depicted as timid and fearful and needs the help of Lisa (Miriam?) to accomplish his mission. When Lisa first urges Moses to confront Pharaoh about the Israelites, Moses resists identification with the slaves saying, "Oh, now they're my people?" This captures nicely Moses' "identity crisis" seen in the biblical text (e.g., Exod 3:11, 13–15); it also reminds students that Moses was raised as an Egyptian. The cartoon underscores the violent nature of the biblical story by omitting the killing of the firstborn (although there is a reference to it) and the death of the Egyptians in the Red Sea. Instead, after the water washes over them, the Egyptians play like children in a pool, splashing one another. After the Israelites cross the Sea, one of them asks, "What's next? Land of milk and honey?" to which Lisa, looking at a scroll says, "Actually it looks like we're in for forty years of wandering in the desert." Although this does not quite follow the biblical plot line, it does highlight the fact that the story of ancient Israel is one of constant suffering and oppression.

The third vignette, featuring Bart as David and Nelson as Goliath, may be more difficult to employ pedagogically. The most impressive aspect is that it plays off the idea that there are two different names associated with the killing of Goliath in the biblical text (David in 1 Sam 17, and Elhanan in 2 Sam 21:19). One can also take this opportunity to discuss the textual problems with 1 Sam 17. This last sketch could be shown as part of a review at the end of the semester, asking students how many Hebrew Bible allusions they can find and how they "work." There are references to Solomon's judgment regarding the baby, Jezebel, Sodom and Gomorrah, the Canaanites, Methuselah, Samson, the Tower of Babel, and Jonah (and perhaps David's womanizing and his friendship with Jonathan).

"Thank God It's Doomsday" (Sixteenth Season, 2005)

This episode, a spoof of the *Left Behind* series, introduces students to certain aspects of apocalyptic literature and its interpretation. Homer sees a movie about the rapture entitled "Left Below" and becomes worried that he will not be among the righteous on judgment day—illustrative of the dualistic nature of apocalyptic thinking. Marge, however, assures him not to worry because signs will precede the end, a notion that has biblical parallels. When Homer interprets several odd events as signs, even though they have perfectly natural explanations, he decides to do some research on the rapture. He discovers a book entitled "1989: The Year of Armageddon," and later Lisa apprises him that seers have been predicting the end for centuries and have all been wrong, both of which challenge a prophetic reading of biblical books. By factoring in the number of verses in Revelation and the number of people present at the Last Supper, among other peculiar numbers, Homer calculates that the apocalypse will begin in one week. This illustrates how the symbolic nature of apocalyptic discourse lends itself to a wide range of interpretations. Numbers can be easily manipulated.

Nobody listens to Homer until he makes a prediction, citing Rev 6:13, that "the stars will fall to the earth," which is what happens when a celebrity-filled blimp crashes—again demonstrating how signs can be variously interpreted. Soon Homer has a large group of followers who believe the end is nigh. If students are asked to read Rev 6, they will immediately notice many other "signs" that should precede the end—ones not cited by Homer. This helps students to appreciate the selective nature of interpretation, as does the fact that when Homer's prediction proves incorrect, he revises it based on a new calculation. Students might also be invited to consider how Homer's statement, "God loves you. He's gonna kill you," reflects the violent nature of apocalyptic literature and the image of Jesus in Revelation as it compares to his portrayal in the Gospels (e.g., in the Sermon on the Mount).

South Park

South Park is Peabody Award-winning animated comedy series about four elementary-age boys who reside in the small town of South Park, Colorado. Created and written by Trey Parker and Matt Stone, it has aired on Comedy Central since 1997. It is well known for its parody and satire, often in crude and vulgar form, as it addresses a variety of political, religious, and social issues. Many of the *South Park* episodes are available for individual purchase ($1.99) on iTunes, including the three discussed here. Note: *South Park* is much more potentially offensive than *The Simpsons*, so again, teachers should exercise due discretion.

"Cartmanland" (Fifth Season, 2001)

This episode deals with the issue of theodicy through the rising and declining fortunes of two characters: Cartman (a foul-mouthed, racist, and devious little boy) and Kyle (a basically good-natured Jewish character). As the episode opens, Cartman's grandmother has died and leaves him a million dollars with which he plans to buy an amusement park in order to have all the rides to himself. This good fortune for Cartman leads to a crisis of faith for Kyle. Furthermore, Kyle is afflicted with a hemorrhoid. He tells his friend Stan, "All my life I was raised to believe in Jehovah, to believe that we should all behave a certain way and good things will come to us. I make mistakes, but every week I try to better myself.... And what does this so-called God give me in return? A hemorrhoid! It doesn't make sense!" He then looks upward and asks God, "What is your logic?" Kyle eventually decides, "There is no justice! There is no God!" and renounces his Jewish faith. In order to help him through this existential crisis, his parents tell him the story of Job, which is simultaneously animated. Curiously, they end the story prior to Job's confrontation with God and the restoration of his family and fortunes. This causes Kyle to exclaim, "That's the most horrible story I've ever heard. Why would God do such horrible things to such a good person just to prove a point to Satan?" His father replies, "Uh, I don't know," to which Kyle says, "Then I was right ... there isn't a God." Meanwhile, Cartman is in the process of losing the park. Once Cartman's fortune has vanished and Kyle sees him humiliated, he instantly recovers from his hemorrhoid-related illness. The show ends with Kyle once again looking to heaven, saying "You *are* up there."

This show can be used in the classroom to illustrate not only the issue of theodicy, but also a modern adaptation of the Job story (albeit very different from, e.g., Archibald MacLeish's *J.B.*). Students may consider why the retelling of Job's story in the cartoon omits the divine speeches and Job's restoration. How would Kyle have reacted to God's response to Job? To the epilogue? Unlike Kyle, Job never doubts God's existence, only God's justice (cf. Holocaust survival literature). Did Job go too far, or not far enough? Other questions to consider: Why do Kyle's parents tell him the story of Job—is the book appropriate (cathartic or helpful) literature for someone who is suffering? How do Job's friends function in the plot of the book in comparison to the way in which Cartman functions in the cartoon? How does Deuteronomistic theology (reward for righteousness and punishment for sin) play out for the various characters?

"Are You There God? It's Me, Jesus" (Third Season, 1999)

In this show the people approach Jesus and ask that God appear to mark the millennium celebration. Jesus is excited about the renewed interest in him because of the millennium and asks that God grant the people's request. God, however, warns Jesus about his pride and refuses to appear. Like a number of Jesus films, the show depicts a Jesus who is struggling to come to terms with his own identity and mission; thus it can be employed in tandem with conversations about various Christologies present in the Gospels. When God does not show up at the celebration, the people become upset and prepare to crucify Jesus, leading him to conclude that God hates him (cf. Jesus' cry of dereliction on the cross in Mark 15:34 and parallels). The show can also invite reflection on the theology of the cross: What is the purpose of Jesus' death according to the Gospels and to Paul (and subsequent Christian tradition)? When Jesus realizes that his own pride clouded his judgment and that sometimes God must not grant requests in order to allow people to work through problems, God appears. The theophany is neither frightening nor awe-inspiring in the classic sense, but God looks nothing like the people expect. This could be used in conjunction with discussions of *imago Dei*, the face of God in the Hebrew Bible, the incarnation, or more general theological discussions about the nature of the deity as it relates to human understanding.

"Super Best Friends" (Fifth Season, 2001)

The boys discover David Blaine, magician and cult leader, performing miracles in the streets. Stan realizes that Blaine and his cronies are interested in the power and wealth that can accrue with a large following. Stan tries to convince the other boys that they have been brainwashed, but it appears to be too late as they have forsaken their friends and families to follow Blaine. Stan calls on Jesus and other religious figures (Buddha, Mohammed, Krishna, Joseph Smith, and Moses) to destroy Blaine and thwart the suicide pact he has instituted. The episode could be employed as part of a discussion of miracles and magic and how, if at all, to distinguish between the two. Students might also consider the way in which people respond to such demonstrations of special powers. In the show, people find Jesus' miracles much less impressive than Blaine's and are thus inclined to follow Blaine's teaching. To what extent does Jesus' authority in the Gospels derive from his miraculous power? How do miracles function in the Gospel narratives in comparison to the cartoon? The show could also open discussion about the social and psychological dynamics of religious movements, from the early Christian church to the contemporary. Stan observes that cults are dangerous because they promise hope, happiness, and an afterlife, but they require you to pay money and any religion that asks you to pay money is wrong. Viewers are invited to consider how the major world religions may or may not fall into the same category. How might one compare Blaine's movement to the early Jesus movement or churches founded by Paul? How did each attract converts? Did the early Christian community as described in Acts function like the cartoon's cult?

Family Guy

Created by Seth MacFarlane, *Family Guy* is an animated Fox television series about an American family in Rhode Island. The comedy has run from 1999 to the present, with a few brief interruptions. In comparison to *The Simpsons* and *South Park*, the show is not nearly as rife with religious themes, but a few episodes do offer teaching possibilities. Most of the episodes, including the two discussed here, are available on DVD.

"If I'm Dyin' I'm Lyin'" (Second Season, 2000)

In order to revive their favorite television show, Peter tells the "Grant a Dream Foundation" that his son Chris is dying and that his last wish is for the show to return to the air. Their deception is successful, but problems ensue as people find out that Chris is supposedly dying. In order to stay out of legal trouble for defrauding the Foundation, Peter claims that he has healed Chris through some sort of divine power. Now, however, people begin to flock to Peter and view him as a charismatic faith healer and, eventually, as God. Lois, Peter's wife, tells him, "These people are worshiping you. Don't you think there's someone who might resent that? A being who's all-knowing and all-powerful?" Always the dense one, Peter responds, "Someone's got a pretty high opinion of herself." Once Lois points out that God could be displeased by the idolatry of Peter's followers, Peter retorts, "When did God ever say he didn't want someone else being worshiped like him?" Lois rightly responds that it is one of the Ten Commandments, but Peter dismisses her claim, saying, "Oh, come on Lois, those were written like two hundred years ago. Times have changed." Immediately following this claim, the Griffin family begins to experience phenomena that parallel the plagues delineated in Exod 7–11. The light bulbs in the house go out (darkness); the family dog Brian gets fleas (flies); and Chris gets zit-like boils all over his face. Peter insists there must be a rational explanation for these occurrences but begins to demur when the baby's bath water turns to blood. As Peter tries to find a natural reason for these events, Brian slaps him, exclaiming, "God is pissed!" As frogs erupt out of Peter's clothing, the family runs outside, only to see Peter's followers dancing around a massive golden statue they have made of Peter (an obvious parallel to the golden calf). Peter finally admits that he is a fake, and lightning strikes the statue, toppling it over onto Chris. Brian excitedly points out that this is the final plague—the death of the firstborn—and Peter realizes the error of his ways. He apologizes to God, and the plagues stop. Peter says, "Thank God. I mean, thank me," at which point a frog jumps into his face and the episode ends.

This episode, obviously, weaves together several themes and texts from the book of Exodus. In the biblical story the giving of the laws follows the plagues, whereas here it precedes it. This might lead students to reflect on why God is opposed to the Egyptians—what have they done to rouse divine wrath? Peter's idea that the Ten Commandments are outdated can open discussion about the meaning and significance of the laws for contemporary people of faith. Further, the show can illustrate the humanity of Pharaoh, since it is evident that Peter is a metaphorical Pharaoh. The end of the Exodus story finds a parallel in the cartoon in that both Pharaoh and Peter have not quite changed their thinking—Peter hangs on to the notion that he is God, while Pharaoh sends his army after the fleeing Israelites. Have neither Peter nor Pharaoh ultimately been that impressed with the plagues? The episode may also help students to reflect on the golden calf. In the biblical text, unlike the cartoon, those who have witnessed the plagues and been saved by God are the ones who, nonetheless, construct the false god; in the cartoon, as expected, those who worship the false deity are the ones who commit the idolatry. Finally, one can consider the portrayal of God in Exodus as opposed to the God rendered here. Is the God of Exodus a deity who, as Lois says, is "all-knowing and all-powerful"? What motivates God to send the plagues in the biblical text as compared to the cartoon? Is God "pissed" or not?

"The Father, the Son, and the Holy Fonz" (Fourth Season, 2005)

After a family crisis about whether or not to baptize their son, Peter begins to search for a religion that appeals to him in a series of scenes reminiscent of Woody Allen's *Hannah and Her Sisters*. He tries to be a Latter-Day Saint (but gives up because of the restrictions on alcohol), a Jehovah's Witness (but in witnessing, he confuses the story of Jesus with the plot of the TV series *Quantum Leap*), and a Hindu, but all to no avail. Finally, Peter's father, Francis, tells him, "You want to find religion? All you've got to do is look in your heart. Who's always been there for you, offering wisdom and truth? You've known him all along, son. Now, worship him!" Peter, of course, misunderstands his father's advice and founds the First United Church of the Fonz, based on the 1950s nostalgia TV show *Happy Days* (1974–84). In the scenes of worship from Peter's new church, the writers humorously incorporate catch-phrases and references from the show into what appears to be a rather normal Protestant liturgy. Peter even offers a reading from "the Letters of Potsie to the Tuscaderos." Ironically, Peter's growing following and the success of his new religion upset Francis, who manages to sabotage his accomplishments by recruiting Sherman Hensley (George Jefferson of *The Jeffersons*) and Gavin MacLeod (Captain Stubbing of *The Love Boat*) to start their own churches. Peter feels like a failure, but Lois tells him that the values he preached were worthwhile; even if only one person was improved through his church, it was worth it. The show ends with Francis praying to the Fonz to the sounds of Bill Haley and the Comets' "Rock around the Clock."

This episode, even though it includes no stories or substantial references to the Bible, can still be used rewardingly in the classroom. Given the resurgence in social-scientific approaches to the Bible and especially to nascent Christianity in the first century, Peter's founding of a new church can provide a humorous and satiric example of a similar movement in our time. Most scholars agree that early Jewish followers of Jesus were caught unprepared by his execution and had to recover from that blow to their movement if it were to survive. They searched their scriptures, the font of their worldview, for a way to understand and explain not only what had happened but also why it was important. In sections of Scripture such as Isa 52:13–53:12 they found texts that resonated with their experience and allowed them to tell their faith-story in such a way that other Jews and even Gentiles listened. In this episode, we find Peter performing a similar action. Disillusioned with his inherited tradition, he develops a new one based on the main source of his worldview: popular culture, and specifically television. He does not abandon his Christian tradition completely, however, as the worship scenes show; rather, he adapts it to his new way of viewing the world. As such, this episode can be used to illustrate the formation of new, scripturally based religions and can specifically serve as an analogue to the formation of Christianity in the first century.

O
T
H
E
R

M
E
D
I
A

Television Dramas and Documentaries

Dan W. Clanton Jr. and Mark Roncace

This chapter addresses episodes from two TV dramas—*NYPD Blue* and *Criminal Minds*—as well as three documentaries.

NYPD Blue

NYPD Blue was a critically acclaimed television police drama set in New York City. It was created by Steven Bocho and David Milch and aired on ABC from 1993 to 2005. The episodes discussed here are scheduled to be released on DVD in 2007.

"Lost Israel," Parts 1 and 2 (Sixth Season, 1998)

These are generally considered among the best episodes the series has produced. In part 1, Steve and Sherrie Egan report the disappearance of their son Brian. Detectives Bobby Simone and Andy Sipowicz are assigned to the case. Mr. Egan suggests that a homeless mute named Israel, who communicates mainly by pointing to seemingly obscure biblical passages, might have something to do with Brian's disappearance. At the beginning of the second episode, Israel commits suicide, leaving his Bible open to Ps 119, which Andy interprets as a secret message. Most of Andy's time in part 2 is spent trying to decipher this hidden message. As the investigation continues, it becomes clear that Mr. Egan is involved in his son's murder.

The last few scenes in part 2 are the most intense and probably the best for showing in class. The encounter between Bobby and Mr. Egan in the observation room is reminiscent of a confessional. Mr. Egan, the penitent, is looking for forgiveness, and Bobby can offer it to him. Mr. Egan questions the existence of God and asks why God would not want someone who was suffering to be taken away. He then asks Bobby to shoot him, and when Bobby refuses, he asks for help in confessing. It is unclear whether or not Mr. Egan experiences any remorse over murdering his son, but the subsequent confession (not shown in the episode) implies that he does. Bobby, like most people, does not think there is forgiveness for Mr. Egan's murder and implies that Mr. Egan himself does not think there is either. The most emotional moment in the entire episode comes when Andy recites Ps 119:81–88 to comfort Mrs. Egan after she learns that her husband has confessed to killing their child. The section that Andy reads represents a supplication to God for protection because of the speaker's adherence to the law. It is a moving piece of poetry, and Andy's reading of it seems to bring about catharsis after the episode has brought all the characters into a state of emotional turmoil. Andy has finally realized Israel's message, and Mrs. Egan seems to be consoled after the murder of her son.

These episodes, particularly the final scenes of part 2, illustrate the theological purposes and functions of the psalms. Perhaps Ps 119 could serve to explore the ways in which the composer(s) of the psalms viewed them; that is, unlike other texts in the Hebrew Bible, these pieces are *direct discourse* aimed at God. The immediacy of the language as well as the variety of discourses (laments; praises; psalms ruminating on creation and wisdom; and liturgical psalms for specific purposes) point to a range of experiences captured in language so direct that it is as though one is eavesdropping on some of the most intimately relational God-language ever composed. The function of these poems, then, would be to tie the reader (either visually or orally) to God through the experience of first-person narration of petitions, praises, and pleas. This scene might also prompt closer analysis of Ps 119:81–88. Do these verses function like a lament psalm? What genre of psalm would be most appropriate to recite to Mrs. Egan at this point? How might she identify with the speaker in Ps 119:81–88? Are there ways in which her situation is different or not applicable? Does that matter? How are psalms most effectively employed today in the lives of individuals and communities? More generally, the episode prompts thought about the nature of forgiveness. Bobby claims that "forgiveness doesn't depend on us" and that remorse and understanding are necessary for forgiveness. Is this true? Who can offer forgiveness and how should it be sought? One could also consider Andy's initial struggle to interpret Israel's "message." Must one be a "believer" to "get" the psalms? How might psalms speak differently to a person depending on their dispositions? Finally, showing the concluding scenes could serve as a prelude to asking students to compose their own psalm in response to a public or private traumatic event.

CRIMINAL MINDS

This television crime drama debuted on CBS in 2005. It follows a team of FBI profilers; its unique focus is, as the title indicates, on the criminal, rather than the crime. The team builds a psychological profile of criminals so as to anticipate acts of violence in hopes of stopping them. The episodes discussed here are scheduled to be released on DVD in 2007.

"The Big Game" and "Revelations" (Second Season, 2007)

These two episodes contain a complex set of biblical allusions and references. "The Big Game" opens with a team of FBI profilers investigating a murder at which the criminal(s) have left a page from the book of Revelation, with 6:8 highlighted ("I looked and there was a pale green horse! Its rider's name was Death, and Hades followed with him"). The profilers slowly realize that the killer(s) understand their activities as both justified by and the carrying out of Scripture. A video of the murder, posted on the Internet, mentions Lev 26:18 as a warning ("And if in spite of this you will not obey me, I will continue to punish you sevenfold for your sins"). When they capture a second victim, the killer(s) engage in a scriptural argument over the woman once they have tied her up. As the woman begs for her life and apologizes for her behavior, one quotes Rev 2:22–23, a passage dealing with the punishment of the adulterous Jezebel, and the other quotes Luke 15:10 ("Just so, I tell you, there is joy in the presence of the angels of God over one sinner who repents"). The former killer wins out, and in the second videotaped message distributed over the Internet, the prophecy regarding the canine complicity in the death of Jezebel in 2 Kgs 9 is read prior to releasing a pack of dogs that maul and kill the victim. Over the course of this and the next episode, we realize that there is only one killer: a young man named Tobias. His father Charles was compulsively literal about the Bible and had branded a cross on Tobias's forehead so that he would have "the mark of the Lord" on him. The profilers hypothesize that Tobias's brutal treatment at the hands of his father resulted in a psychopathic condition in which he developed a split personality: one as Tobias and the other as Raphael, an angel of God.

In "Revelations," the profilers are searching Tobias's house and make three important discoveries: They find the phrase "Honor thy Father" scrawled all over his walls; they recover his father's frozen dead body in the basement; and they discover that his father was very ill and asked his son to euthanize him. Tobias responded with "Thou shall not kill," but his father retorted, "Honor thy father." Based on these three discoveries, the agents surmise that this gray area in Tobias's otherwise strictly religious, dualistic upbringing triggered the onset of a split personality in order to keep his father alive through adopting his personality. So, there are now three personalities within Tobias's psyche. As they begin to understand Tobias better, another murder is committed, this time with Isa 59:4 left at the scene ("No one brings suit justly; no one goes to law honestly; they rely on empty pleas; they speak lies, conceiving mischief and begetting iniquity"). The remainder of the plot continues to interweave biblical references (Rev 8; Gen 23:4; Job 15:31; Exod 21:17).

Given the length and complexity of these episodes, it could be time-prohibitive to show them in their entirety in a class session. Instructors could show a clip that uses a certain image, such as the Jezebel murder by dogs in "The Big Game," as a prelude to a discussion of women in Revelation. Or, one could discuss the use of Scripture in ethical decision-making, based on the debates between Tobias and his father Charles. There are also larger issues addressed by these shows, such as the intersection of religion and violence. Students could be asked to reflect on the ways in which the Bible has been used to justify violent actions. Alternatively, students might identify the various ways in which the Bible is treated in these shows: object of religious devotion or font of violence? One might also analyze the hermeneutical approach of the show, namely, treating the Bible as a code of sorts; unlocking its mystery is the key to finding the answer. This can be compared and contrasted to the interpretive approaches taken by religious and academic communities.

DOCUMENTARIES

There is no shortage of documentaries that deal with Bible-related matters. Indeed, professors' mailboxes are often stuffed with catalogues full of them. Many of these—too many to mention—are potentially useful in the classroom, but they are usually prohibitively expensive for individual teachers to purchase. Instructors should be aware that there are a number of documentaries and TV specials that are becoming available on the Internet for just a couple of dollars. Such is the case with the following three from iTunes.

"The Real Sin City: Sodom and Gomorrah" (*Digging for the Truth*, The History Channel, Season 2, 2006)

This forty-five-minute program asks whether the biblical story is "just a parable" or if there is "evidence that such a thing actually happened." Teachers could use this show to open discussion about a number of technical aspects of biblical archaeology. In fact, the very title of the show—*Digging for the Truth*—could lead to conversation about the nature of truth that digging can, and cannot, yield. In its desire to attract an audience, the show takes a misguided approach by setting the question in a dramatic black-and-white manner: either the biblical story is just a made-up tale or it actually happened (i.e., it is true). Instructors can explain that if archaeologists find evidence that Sodom and Gomorrah were destroyed, it does not make the biblical account "true." Analogously, if several millennia from now, archaeologists discover evidence that New Orleans suffered major water damage in the early twenty-first century, it would not "prove" a belief that God sent Katrina to destroy the city. What kind of truth is the biblical narrative interested in conveying? And how does that compare to the work of an archaeologist?

"The First Christians" (*Lost Worlds*, The History Channel, Season 1, 2007)

This program provides background on the life of Saul/Paul, sketching the history of the port city Tarsus and explaining how the Roman and Jewish culture there would have shaped him. It follows Paul's journeys to Ephesus and, through computer-enhanced imaging, reconstructs the temple of Artemis that Paul would have found there. This, of course, can connect with study of the religious and philosophical traditions of the first-century Roman world, an important context for understanding Paul and his writings. Teachers might discuss the show's claim that Paul and Christianity triggered the decline of "pagan" worship in Ephesus and the destruction of the Artemis temple. How and why was Christianity influential in cities such as Ephesus? What other factors may have contributed to the decline of certain Roman traditions? The show also examines the theatre, "brothel," and bath houses at Ephesus, all of which factor into understanding Paul, his message, and the spread of Christianity (cf. Acts 19–20). The exploration then moves to Cappadocia, where archaeological remains of some of the earliest Christian communities and churches are examined. As with many documentaries, the value of this one may lie primarily in the fact that it gives students concrete visual images—if only tentatively reconstructed ones—to connect with the content of the biblical text.

"Resurrection: A Search for Answers" (ABC News, 2006)

This *20/20* special, approximately forty minutes long, opens up opportunity for discussion about a variety of questions concerning Paul, the early Christian community, the nature of the Gospel accounts of the resurrection, as well as larger theological and philosophical issues. Elizabeth Vargas interviews a variety of scholars, theologians, and archaeologists, including, among others, John Shelby Spong, Paul Maier, Karen King, Arthur Dewey, Luke Timothy Johnson, Ben Witherington III, Daniel Schwartz, and Kathleen Corley.

The show could be connected to specific biblical texts. For instance, it begins by asking how a religion could start with a man crucified, the issue that Paul addresses in his discussion of the foolishness of the cross (1 Cor 1:18–25). The program traces the crucifixion and resurrection story from the Gospels but does not make any effort to distinguish among the four accounts, a task students could undertake. Is it possible to talk about "the" Gospel story, or are

OTHER MEDIA

there too many discrepancies among the canonical accounts? One wonders why the apocalyptic signs reported in Matthew are so infrequently mentioned in these types of conversations about the historicity of the resurrection—the tearing of the temple curtain, the earthquake, and mass resurrections in Jerusalem (Matt 27:51–53). Should these reports be taken into account when attempting to reconstruct events? Further, the program explores the question of bodily versus spiritual resurrection, with views presented on both sides. Students might be assigned to weigh in on the conversation based on various New Testament texts (e.g., 1 Cor 15).

The program can also be used to facilitate reflection on broader topics. The show raises some of the standard pieces of evidence for the historicity of the resurrection, such as that the earliest disciples must have been truly convinced of its veracity since they were willing to die for the cause. This might lead to a discussion of how to weigh and assess evidence. If a group of people whole-heartedly believe something to be true, does this make it so? What are the philosophical merits of Lee Strobel's notion that millions of Christians cannot be wrong? How does one evaluate and respond to the assertion that the "resurrection is a fact" in contrast to the idea that "it requires faith"? The program is fairly balanced, presenting a variety of views on the subject, although it may be a worthwhile exercise to ask students if it is an evenhanded report. Are there important topics or perspectives omitted? What bias does this reveal? Finally, the program features scenes from a variety of contemporary Christian celebrations of Easter—from Catholic Mass, to African American Protestant churches, to Christians in Jerusalem. This may aid students in reflecting on the diversity of the tradition; it may also help Christian students gain an "objective" perspective on their own cultic practices.

Internet Websites

Mark Roncace

There are countless websites that teachers might successfully employ in the classroom; this chapter discusses four possibilities.

Cyberhymnal.org

In addition to the variety of popular and classical musical pieces that can be employed in the classroom, many Christian hymns can also be utilized to prompt study of biblical texts. One particularly good resource is Cyberhymnal, a website that features over 6,100 hymns and gospel songs from various Christian traditions. The site enables one to search by title, Scripture allusions, tunes by meter, tunes by name, or by topic. Hence teachers can locate potentially useful items quite easily. As with Youtube (see below), Cyberhymnal can be employed to find material related to less popular biblical texts. For example, by clicking on "scriptural allusions" and then "Habakkuk," one finds the titles of seven hymns listed according to the verse references in Habakkuk to which they allude. When one clicks on the title, the lyrics are displayed, a piano rendition of the hymn plays, and the verse from Habakkuk streams across the top of the screen. Many of the hymns make interesting hermeneutical moves which students can observe by noting which parts of a biblical text are omitted and which are highlighted or how the biblical text is recontextualized to give it a new meaning. So for instance, students might be asked to speculate why no hymns reference Hab 1, a theologically rich text in which the prophet, in typical lament language, challenges the justice of God. One hymn refers to Hab 2:14 ("The earth will be filled with the knowledge of the glory of the Lord, as the waters cover the sea"), and two other hymns allude to Hab 2:20 ("Let all the earth keep silent before the Lord"). In the biblical text, both of these verses appear in a series of five woe oracles, which serve as a warning for evildoers (Hab 2:5–20). The hymns, however, use them for a rather different purpose. For example, the line "to keep silent before the Lord" becomes a call to worship on "the Lord's day" (i.e., Sunday), a striking reversal of the prophetic "day of the Lord."

The number of hymns related to less-studied New Testament texts is equally impressive. For example, the link to hymns for 1 Peter features over fifty pieces, many of which could lead to fruitful discussions of the biblical text. To take but one example: A song entitled "Do Not Be Surprised," written by Susan Peterson in 1998, reinscribes the rhetoric of 1 Pet 4:12–15, namely, that one should embrace suffering by identifying with Christ. This can facilitate a discussion of the historical setting of 1 Peter, how the passage may have been understood by its first audience, its relevance or lack thereof for contemporary faith communities, and its social and political implications. Similarly, the link to 2 Thessalonians reveals a number of songs, one of which is entitled "What a Gathering," based on 2 Thess 2:1 ("Concerning the Lord Jesus Christ and our being gathered together to him..."). The tone of the song, not surprisingly, is hopeful as it anticipates the gathering of the saints when the Son of Man returns, which is "drawing nigh." By contrast, the biblical passage appears to be rejecting the notion that the return is near. Instead, it warns that the "the man of lawlessness" must come first and then be annihilated by Jesus. The biblical text, quite unlike the song, is meant to assuage the fears of those believers who thought the gathering of the saints had already taken place. Thus, the song is much more akin to 1 Thessalonians, which expects the imminent Parousia, than it is to 2 Thessalonians from which it draws its lyrics.

Hymns, in short, are compelling intertexts for those studying the Bible. And there is no shortage of hymns relating to both well-known and more obscure texts. Simply presenting the hymns and asking students how the piece interprets the biblical text can prompt thoughtful dialogue. Finally, students may be invited to write their own hymn based on a given text.

Wikipedia.com

Wikipedia.com is a free online encyclopedia that is collaboratively written by its readers. Anyone can write, edit, and add articles. The very nature of Wikipedia as a multiauthored, continuously edited document is wonderfully analogous to the development of biblical literature. Wikipedia does not, however, always provide the best information about biblical texts and topics. Thus, teachers, understandably, have expressed concern over the fact that many students use the site as a source of information. However, rather than steering students away from Wikipedia because of potential errors or bias in its articles, it can be employed as a teaching tool in a number of ways. One approach is simply to have students read and evaluate a given article. While students may be reluctant to criticize or challenge a traditional biblical commentary because it is written by an expert scholar, they understand that Wikipedia articles can be written by anyone and so they read it expecting to find errors, misinformation, significant omissions, or evident bias. That is, Wikipedia is an excellent opportunity for students to practice being suspicious readers, a skill that can then be applied more broadly.

Another strategy, which flows naturally from the first, is to have students revise and expand articles. Students, especially those in upper-level or advanced classes, will feel, and in fact are, qualified to edit the material, which is quite easily done. So, for instance, students could be asked to supplement the section entitled "The Syro-Ephraimite War" in the article on Isaiah. (As of January 15, 2007, it was only three sentences long.) In some places Wikipedia explicitly requests a supplement; such is the case with the section labeled "Songs of the Suffering Servant," which currently features only one short paragraph. Given the nature of Wikipedia, there is very little uniformity among the articles. For example, the entries on Isaiah, Jeremiah, and Ezekiel vary in length and topics addressed, so students could supplement the articles in a way that would give all three of them a more consistent format. Sometimes there are glaring omissions, such as no mention whatsoever of Jeremiah's laments/confessions. Indeed, just about any article can be supplemented in some fashion.

A third strategy is for students to generate their own new articles (ones not listed anywhere on the site). These may be short entries related to specific biblical texts or topics. Possible articles relating to the so-called Major Prophets might include "Valley of Dry Bones," "Oracles Against the Nations," or even "Third Isaiah." Students are often inspired by the thought of authoring something that will be available for the whole world (in theory), rather than writing a paper that only the instructor or a few peers will evaluate. This "real world" experience is invigorating and is perhaps the most valuable aspect of employing Wikipedia in one's pedagogical repertoire.

Wikipedia has a wealth of information for instructors, including ways to use the website as an instructional tool and a list of student projects that have been developed in conjunction with Wikipedia (Wikipedia.org/wiki/Wikipedia: School_and_University_projects). See also Holger Szesnat, "Who Knows? Wikipedia, Teaching and Research."

Youtube.com

Youtube.com is a popular free video-sharing website which enables users to upload, view, and share video clips. It features a wide variety of content, including movie and TV clips, music videos, and amateur content such as videoblogging. The site may be helpful to biblical studies instructors because users (anyone can access the site) can simply employ the search command to find videos related to any topic. If one searches for the phrase "Adam and Eve," one will find over four hundred videos, ranging from puppet shows, stage productions, sermon clips, music and home videos, cartoons, and others which relate to Gen 2–3. Indeed, some of these videos (certainly not all or even most!) could prove to be valuable teaching tools, though it would take some time to identify which ones best engage students. But rather than using You-tube to locate resources for popular texts, one can find a surprising number of videos for more obscure passages. For instance, a search for "Haggai" yields eleven videos (though that could change as more are uploaded), two of which are potentially useful. One of them is a four-minute, light-hearted video by three teenage boys who discuss how few people have even heard of Haggai, much less know its content. They then give a fairly decent overview, albeit brief, of the historical setting and theological significance of the biblical book. While it is true that the content of the video is basic, one imagines that students are more likely to remember an introduction to Haggai given by three quirky teenagers with a hand-held camera than by the course instructor. The second video relating to Haggai is a seventeen-minute sermon on the topic of stewardship in Hag 1:3–11 and Luke 2:7–11; it could be used to launch a variety of discussions relating not only to the text, but also to the use and interpretation of the text.

Similarly, a search for "Galatians" produces thirty-two hits. Among those one finds a four-minute music video based directly on Gal 5, Paul's discussion of "freedom in Christ" and its implications. Another three-minute video presents a summary, with instrumental background music, of Paul's confrontation with the so-called Judaizers. A third offers a reading of Gal 5:16–26 with corresponding images from contemporary American life. A fourth is an explicitly anti-Muslim commentary on the allegory of Sarah and Hagar in Gal 4. The best way in which each of these videos could be employed depends on the instructor and the educational context.

A search for "The Ten Commandments" produces over two hundred videos, but if the search is refined by adding, say, the word "comedy," the list is reduced to a more manageable nineteen. (Note: Simply adding the word "Bible" is often an effective way to limit searches.) Here one finds a variety of clips that raise serious and important issues, though in funny ways. A six-minute clip of comedian George Carlin's take on the Commandments is certainly vulgar (and no doubt offensive to some), but it raises fundamental questions about who makes laws, the power dynamics involved in maintaining them, the rhetorical nature of the laws, and their practical application (Should parents always be honored? What about people who kill in the name of God? And isn't coveting what drives the economy?). In addition, one can find a clip of an interview with Georgia congressman Lynn Westmoreland, who co-sponsored a bill to place the Ten Commandments in the House of Representatives and the Senate. He is unable to name the Commandments.

Another video shows people who are "caught on tape" breaking the commandments—a person who "steals" a pen by forgetting to return it, a woman raking leaves in her yard on the Sabbath, and a woman "coveting" some items in a catalogue. Again, videos such as these can prompt students to think about a variety of questions, depending on the instructor's agenda. In short, there is a remarkable breadth of material that can be found on Youtube.

One final issue: it is very easy to go directly to the website and play the videos in class—and "favorite videos" can be collected in one's Youtube account. However, Youtube does not make it easy to download and save videos for offline viewing, so if teachers wish to save videos as part of their permanent resources, they will need to employ certain browser extensions or websites that offer free software designed for that purpose.

Thebricktestament.com

The Rev. Brendan Powell Smith, who is not ordained but is rather an atheist, has built thousands of scenes from Hebrew Bible and New Testament texts with Legos and then photographed them for display on the website. They are quite compelling and adhere closely to the biblical plotlines; many illustrations are accompanied by the corresponding biblical verse. The images can be useful in the classroom in a number of ways, but they may be especially facilitative as a means for students to ponder the lurid nature of many Hebrew Bible stories. Smith's depictions of incest, gang rapes, beheadings, and genocide are tolerable only because they are done with Legos. Most other media would render them too (porno)graphic for many viewers. According to the press releases listed on the website, one Catholic publication, reviewing the coffee-table book of Lego illustrations, observed that children will "love ... examining what figures from which sets [of Lego Bricks] were used to create the scenes" and that the book "is guaranteed to be passed around the living room." Either the book does not include many of the scenes available on the website or this reviewer has not looked carefully at the illustrations. They are not fit for children. To give one example: Genesis 34—the account of Dinah and Shechem—is clearly rife with adult themes, but pause and imagine what would be required to depict the details of that story visually. This is what Thebricktestament does, thereby providing students an opportunity to contemplate the specific content of the narrative. On a more theoretical level, students can reflect on the ramifications of translating the biblical text into this unique medium.

INDEX OF BIBLICAL TEXTS

OLD TESTAMENT/HEBREW BIBLE

APOCRYPHA/DEUTEROCANONICAL BOOKS

New Testament

INDEX OF NONCANONICAL TEXTS

Music Index

M
U
S
I
C

I
N
D
E
X

M
U
S
I
C

I
N
D
E
X

Film Index

F
I
L
M

I
N
D
E
X

ART INDEX

A
R
T

I
N
D
E
X

A
R
T

I
N
D
E
X

Literature Index

Crashaw, Robert, "Samson to His Delilah," 252; "Two Went Up into the Temple to Pray," 262–64

Cullen, Countee, "For Daughters of Magdalen," 254; "The Litany of the Dark People," 264–65; "Simon the Cyrenian Speaks," 254

cummings, e. e., "A Man Who Had Fallen among Thieves," 255; "Sonnet IV," 251

Curzon, David "Proverbs 6:6," 253

Daley, Victor, "A Vision of Sunday in Heaven," 256

Devlin, Denis, "Ascension," 255

Dickey, James, "Walking on Water," 254

Dickinson, Emily, "Abraham to Kill Him," 252; "Belshazzar had a Letter," 254; "Eden Is That Old-Fasioned House," 251; "I Know Where Wells Grow—Droughtless Wells," 255; "One Crown That No One Seeks," 265–66; "A Word Made Flesh Is Seldom," 255

Dipiero, W. S., "Near Damascus," 266–67

Dobson, Rosemary, "Eutychus," 255

Donne, John, *Holy Sonnets*, No. 11, 252; "Nativity," 267–68, 277

Dostoevsky, Fyodor, *The Brothers Karamazov*, 244; *The Idiot*, 306

Drummond, William, "For the Baptist," 268–69

Dunn, Stephen, "At the Smithville Methodist Church," 269

Eliot, George, "The Death of Moses," 269–70

Eliot, T. S., "Journey of the Magi," 254; "The Lovesong of J. Alfred Prufrock," 48; "A Song for Simeon," 255

Emmerich, Anne Catherine, *The Dolorous Passion of Our Lord Jesus Christ*, 113

Endo, Shusaku, *The Golden Country*, 300; *Silence*, 298–300

Everson, William, "The Flight in the Desert," 254

Faulkner, William, *The Sound and the Fury*, 306

Ferlinghetti, Lawrence, "Christ Climbed Down," 255

Frankfort, Harry G., "On Bullshit," 300

Frost, Robert, "Revelation," 255; "Sitting by a Bush in Broad Daylight," 252

George, Diana Hume, "Asenath," 252

Gilbert, Celia, "The Midwives," 252

Ginsberg, Allen, "Galilee Shore," 254; "Psalm III," 253

Glaspell, Susan, "A Jury of Her Peers," 300–301

Goethe, J. W., *Faust*, 270–72

Golding, William, *Lord of the Flies*, 306

Graves, Robert, "Angry Samson," 252; "In the Wilderness," 254

Greenblatt, Stephen, *Will in the World: How Shakespeare Became Shakespeare*, 301–3

Handey, Jack, *Deep Thoughts*, 303–4

Hansen, Ron, *Atticus*, 304–5

Hardy, Thomas, "A Dream Question," 253

Harris, Robert, "Isaiah by Kerosene Lantern Light," 253

Heaney, Seamus, "Cana Revisited," 255

Hecht, Anthony, "Naming the Animals," 251; "Pig," 254

Heinlein, Robert, *Stranger in a Strange Land*, 305–6

Heller, Janet Ruth, "Devorah," 272

L
I
T
E
R
A
T
U
R
E

I
N
D
E
X

MEDIATING RELIGION

Conversations in Media, Religion and Culture

Edited by

JOLYON MITCHELL
and
SOPHIA MARRIAGE

T & T CLARK
A Continuum imprint
LONDON • NEW YORK

T&T CLARK LTD

A Continuum imprint

The Tower Building
11 York Road
London
SE1 7NX, UK

370 Lexington Avenue
New York 10017–6503
USA

www.continuumbooks.com

First published 2003

ISBN 0 567 08867 7 HB
ISBN 0567 08807 3 PB

Excerpts from *Tales from Ovid* by Ted Hughes. Copyright © 1997 by Ted Hughes.
Reprinted by permission of Farrar, Straus and Giroux, LLC. (*United States of America*)
Reproduced with permission from Faber and Faber Ltd. (*Rest of World*).

British Library Cataloguing-in-Publication Data
A catalogue record for this book is available from the British Library

Typeset by Fakenham Photosetting Ltd, Fakenham
Printed and bound in Great Britain by MPG Books, Bodmin

Contents

List of Figures and Tables

Figures

Tables

Contributors

Jeremy Begbie is Associate Principal of Ridley Hall, Cambridge. He teaches systematic theology there and in the University of Cambridge. He is also Honorary Reader at the University of St Andrews, where he directs 'Theology Through the Arts' at the Institute for Theology, Imagination and the Arts. He has written several books, including *Theology, Music and Time* (Cambridge University Press, 2000).

Heidi Campbell is a Research Assistant with the Media and Theology Project at the University of Edinburgh, where she completed her PhD in computer-mediated communications and practical theology. She is also an Adjunct Professor of Communications at Spring Arbor University (USA). Her research in religion and cyberculture has been presented at numerous conferences in the USA and Europe.

Clifford G. Christians is a Research Professor of Communications in the Institute of Communications Research at the University of Illinois, Urbana. His teaching and research interests include communication ethics, the philosophy of technology, and the philosophy of social science. He is co-author of *Media Ethics: Cases and Moral Reasoning* (Longman, 6th ed., 2001) and *Good News: Social Ethics and the Press* (Oxford University Press, 1993).

Lynn Schofield Clark is a Post-Doctoral Fellow and Research Associate on the faculty of the School of Journalism and Mass Communication at the University of Colorado. She is Director of the Teens and the New Media @ Home research project. She has written and co-edited several books, including *From Angels to Aliens: Teens, the Media, and Beliefs in the Supernatural* (Columbia University Press, 2001) and *Practising Religion in the Age of the Media: Readings on Media, Religion and Culture* (Oxford University Press, 2001).

Christopher Deacy is a lecturer in Religious Studies at Trinity College, Carmarthen. From 1999 to 2001 Chris was a Leverhulme Research Fellow in Religion and Film at the University of Wales, Lampeter, from where he also gained his PhD in July 1999. His books include *Screen Christologies: Redemption and the Medium of Film* (University of Wales Press, 2001).

Franz-Josef Eilers, svd, is Professor for Social Communication and Missiology at the Divine Word School of Theology in Tagaytay City, Philippines. He also teaches at the University of Santo Tomas, Manila, and is Executive Secretary for the 'Office of Social Communication' (OSC) of the 'Federation of Asian Bishops' Conferences' (FABC) in Manila. He is author and editor of several books, including *Church and Social Communication* (Logos, 2nd ed., 1997).

Mediating Religion

Mark Fackler is Professor of Communications at Calvin College, in Grand Rapids, Michigan. He is co-author of *Media Ethics: Cases and Moral Reasoning* (Longman, 6th ed., 2001) and *Good News: Social Ethics and the Press* (Oxford University Press, 1993). He has taught and lectured in East Africa.

John P. Ferré is a Professor of Communication at the University of Louisville. In addition to numerous articles and reviews, he has written several books, including *Good News: Social Ethics and the Press* with Clifford G. Christians and Mark Fackler (Oxford University Press, 1993).

Myrna R. Grant is Associate Professor of Communications Emerita at Wheaton College, Illinois, and Associate Professor of Speech, Communications and Theatre at North Central College, Naperville, Illinois. She wrote her doctoral dissertation on aspects of the early radio career of her friend Malcolm Muggeridge. She is an expert on Russian religion and the author of several books and scholarly articles.

Gregor Goethals is Professor Emeritus at Rhode Island School of Design and a graphic designer at Sundial Studio, Sonoma, California. Her books include *The TV Ritual* (Beacon Press, 1981) and *The Electronic Golden Calf* (Cowley, 1991).

Rosalind I. J. Hackett is Professor of Religious Studies and Adjunct in Anthropology at the University of Tennessee, Knoxville. She has published widely on religion in Africa. Her current research is focused on religious conflict in Africa, especially Nigeria.

Cees Hamelink is Professor of International Communication at the University of Amsterdam, and Professor of Media, Religion and Culture at the Free University in Amsterdam, The Netherlands. He is also Visiting Professor at the Catholic University of Leuven, Belgium, and the City University of London. He is the editor-in-chief of the International Journal for Communication Studies: *Gazette*. Among the fifteen books he has authored are *Cultural Autonomy in Global Communications* (Longman Group, 1983), *The Politics of World Communication* (Sage, 1994), *World Communication* (Zed, 1995), *The Ethics of Cyberspace* (Sage, 2000) and *Human Rights for Communicators* (forthcoming).

Jörg Herrmann, is a scientific collaborator at the department of Practical Theology of the Humboldt-University/Berlin working on a Habilitation about the influence of media experiences on religious worldviews. He has published in film and religion, art, multimedia, aesthetics and culture.

Mary E. Hess is Assistant Professor of Educational Leadership at Luther Seminary, the largest ELCA Lutheran Seminary in North America. Her areas of research and teaching include transformative adult education, media literacy and its relation to religious education, and the integration of digital technologies into theological education. She is a core member of the International Study Commission on Media, Religion and Culture.

Richard Holloway was Bishop of Edinburgh and Primus of the Scottish Episcopal Church till his retirement at the end of 2000. He was Gresham Professor of Divinity in London till October 2001 and is a Fellow of the Royal Society of Edinburgh. His recent books include *Doubts and Loves: What is Left of Christianity* (Canongate, 2001) and *On Forgiveness* (Canongate, 2002).

Stewart M. Hoover is Professor in the School of Journalism and Mass Communication at the University of Colorado. He is joint Professor in the Department of Religious Studies and in the Program in American Studies. His books include *Mass Media Religion: The Social Sources of the Electronic Church* (Sage, 1988), *Rethinking Media, Religion, and Culture* co-edited with Knut Lundby (Sage, 1997), and *Religion in the News: Faith and Journalism in American Public Discourse* (Sage, 1998).

Peter Horsfield teaches in the School of Applied Communication at RMIT University in Melbourne, Australia. He was previously engaged in the Electronic Culture Research Project for the Commission for Mission of the Uniting Church in Australia, Victoria. He is a core group member of the International Study Commission on Media, Religion and Culture and author of two books and numerous chapters and articles in the area of media, religion and culture.

Alf Linderman is the Director of Studies at the Faculty of Theology at Uppsala University. He is the author of *The Reception of Religious Television* (Coronet, 1996) and has published several articles on media, religion and culture. Linderman is currently involved in research projects focusing on computer-mediated communication and religion, on religion in television, and on the mediation of interreligious dialogue.

Mia Lövheim is a doctoral candidate in the sociology of religion at the Faculty of Theology at Uppsala University. Her research focuses on young men and women and the construction of religious identities on the Internet. She is currently involved in a research project on computer-mediated communication, religion, community and identity headed by Alf Linderman.

Jim McDonnell founded the Catholic Communications Centre (CCC) in 1990 and has been its Director ever since. He is currently exploring the implications of digital media and wrote a chapter on Internet communities, 'Casting the Net: Virtual and Real' in *Street Credo: Churches in the Community* (Lemos and Crane, 2000).

Sophia Marriage is Communications Officer for the University of Edinburgh. She was Project Officer of the Media and Theology Project and was assistant director of the Third International Conference on Media, Religion and Culture. Prior to her current job, she was Press and Information Officer for the Scottish Refugee Council. Her own research concentrated on the Roman Catholic Church in Malawi and the Philippines. Since her PhD, her focus has been on changes in the church in contemporary society.

Jolyon Mitchell is Senior Lecturer at New College, Edinburgh University. He is director of the Media and Theology Project, and directed the Third International Conference on Media, Religion and Culture. Prior to this he worked for BBC World Service and Radio 4 as a producer and journalist, for whom he continues occasionally to make programmes. He is author of *Visually Speaking: Radio and the Renaissance of Preaching* (T&T Clark, 1999) and a range of articles in the field of communications and theology. He is currently working on *Media and Christian Ethics* (Cambridge University Press, forthcoming).

David Morgan is the Phyllis and Richard Duesenberg Chair in Christianity and the Arts at Valparaiso University. He is author of several books including *Visual Piety* (University of California, 1998) and *Protestants and Pictures* (Oxford University Press, 1999).

Hamid Mowlana is Professor of International Relations and the founding director of the International Communication programme at the School of International Service, American University, Washington, DC. He is author and editor of numerous books on international communication and international relations. He was president of the International Association for Media and Communication Research (IAMCR) from 1994 to 1998.

Steve Nolan is a research student at the Centre for Religion, Culture and Gender at the University of Manchester and a working Baptist minister in London. His doctoral research uses psychoanalytic (Lacanian) film theory to explore how liturgical representation contributes to the construction of religious identity. He has published articles on religion and film in several journals, including the *Bulletin of the John Rylands University Library of Manchester, Literature and Theology* and *Worship*.

Gaye Ortiz is Senior Lecturer in Theology and Religious Studies, and Head of Cultural Studies at York St John College. She is also president of the European section of OCIC (International Catholic Organisation for Cinema) and co-author with Clive Marsh (Blackwell, 1997) of *Explorations in Theology and Film*.

Frances Ford Plude is Professor of Communications, Notre Dame College, Cleveland, Ohio. With a doctorate from Harvard she has written numerous articles and several chapters on issues related to communication and communication theology. She is a core group member of the International Study Commission on Media, Religion and Culture.

Rubina Ramji is at the University of Ottawa researching the portrayal of religion, and especially Muslim women, in mass media. She is co-chair of the Religion, Film and Visual Culture Group for the American Academy of Religion. She is author of articles included in *God in the Details: American Religion in Popular Culture* (Routledge, 2000), *Identity Politics in the Women's Movement* (New York University, 2001) and *Islam in America* (Columbia University, 2000).

David W. Scott is Assistant Professor at the University of South Carolina. He earned his PhD at the University of Georgia. Scott writes about Mormon culture with particular attention to the role of mass media in Mormon life. His chapter, 'Mormons, Mass Media, and the Interpretive Audience' co-authored with Daniel Stout and Dennis Martin, appeared in the book *Religion and Mass Media: Audiences and Adaptations* (Sage, 1996).

Mark Silk is Director of The Leonard E. Greenberg Center for the Study of Religion in Public Life at Trinity College, Hartford, Connecticut. He is the author of *Spiritual Politics: Religion and America since World War II* (Simon & Schuster, 1998) and *Unsecular Media: Making News of Religion in America* (University of Illinois, 1998), and edits the magazine *Religion in the News*.

Daniel A. Stout is Associate Professor in the Department of Communications at Brigham Young University. He co-edited with Judith Buddenbaum *Religion and Mass Media: Audiences and Adaptations* (Sage, 1996) and *Religion and Popular Culture: Studies on the Interaction of Worldviews* (Iowa State University Press, 2001). He is author of numerous journal articles and is the founding co-editor of *The Journal of Media and Religion*.

Robert A. White is Director of the Centre for Interdisciplinary Studies in Communication of the Gregorian University, Rome. He is editor of the book series *Communication and Human Values*, and Chairman of the Publications Committee of the International Association for Mass Communication Research. He is a member of the Society of Jesus. He initiated the book series *Comunicación* in Latin America and is Series Editor of *Communication, Culture and Theology* published by Sheed & Ward.

1

Introduction

Sophia Marriage and Jolyon Mitchell

> Never has there been more need for conversation between civilisa-
> tions, because never have they been able to inflict so much damage on
> each other.
> (Theodore Zeldin)[1]

Conversation lies at the heart of our human existence, at the heart of our
cultural understanding and at the heart of our religious experience. It is
fundamental to our being and allows us to express our thoughts, reach new
depths of understanding and promote human growth. Conversation is also
an art, a craft and a science. The best conversations reflect careful listening
to what the other has to say. They require attentiveness to enable a listener
to move towards somebody else's viewpoint and so to understand the world
from the other's perspective. In the words of the German philosopher
Hans-Georg Gadamer, 'a conversation is the process of two people
understanding each other'.[2]

In a world where global communications are easing discussions across
time and space, new forms of media are facilitating conversations. The
media have come to play an ever greater role in our religious and cultural
understanding. In addition, it is now recognised that the audience plays a
central role in this interaction. One of the themes which this book explores
is to what extent different media and audiences reshape identity, traditions
and means of expression. It is this balance between audience and producer
which brings the conversations to life. Through these discussions views of
the other and communication can be transformed.

Real understanding of the other does not come easily in conversations.
All too often it is not until the breakdown of communication that any
serious thought is invested in repairing and enhancing conversation
between different groups. The tragic damage caused by the spiral of violence in cities such as Jerusalem points to the dangers of failing to listen to
the other, however alien. The conversations that Zeldin particularly values

---

[1] Theodore Zeldin, *Conversation* (London: Harvill Press, 1998), p. 91. Zeldin's ruminations upon conversation began as six radio talks on BBC Radio 4, and only later were turned
into a book.

[2] Hans-Georg Gadamer, *Truth and Method*, trans. by Garrett Barden and John Cumming
(New York: Crossroad, 1982), p. 347.

are 'meetings on the borderline of what I understand and what I don't, with people who are different from myself'.[3] Borders can often be places of tension, conflict and even creative change. The following essays come from a variety of disciplines, many of the authors standing on the borderline between different fields of research.

This book emerged from conversations at the Third International Conference on Media, Religion and Culture, hosted by the Media and Theology Project of the University of Edinburgh in July 1999. Over two hundred participants attended the conference, representing thirty-five countries. Broadcasters, journalists, communication scholars, theologians, religious studies specialists, research students, pastors, priests, nuns, film producers and video makers engaged in lively discussion during the three days. It is often said that you can experience four seasons in one day in Edinburgh. Like the changeable weather the discussions blew in many thought-provoking directions over those three days. Some of the essays in this book began their life as presentations at the conference. Other essays are the outcome of innovative research and responses to recent world events. They have all been adapted in the light of careful listening and ongoing discussions about the interaction between media, religion and culture, and together they show the wide range of topics in this rapidly expanding area of study.

Not only does this volume emerge from concrete conversations at the conference, but it also aims to contribute to a set of current discussions on related topics. In the same way that the exchange of ideas at the meeting in Uppsala (1993) led to the publication of *Rethinking Media, Religion and Culture*,[4] and dialogue at the Boulder public conference (1996) was the catalyst for *Practising Religion in the Age of the Media*,[5] so the discussions at the Edinburgh conference (1999) provide the foundation for *Conversations in Media, Religion and Culture*. This book seeks both to reflect some of the highlights of the Edinburgh international conference and to bring new perspectives into a vigorous ongoing conversation. It therefore fits into a growing body of published work, as well as offering several original features.

Previous discussions around the relationship of media, religion and culture have tended to ignore work in the more established fields of film and religion; media ethics; media literacy; and religion and conflict. Each of these interdisciplinary areas of research has been given a part of its own, with a range of original essays included. This book cannot, and does not, aim to encompass all the possible areas of study. It does, however, include representatives from different cultural and religious backgrounds. All the articles give expression to the wider conversations now held in many

---

[3] Gadamer, *Truth and Method*, p. 88.
[4] Stewart Hoover and Knut Lundby, *Rethinking Media, Religion and Culture* (London: Sage, 1997).
[5] Stewart Hoover and Lynn Schofield Clark, *Practising Religion in the Age of Media* (New York: Columbia University Press, 2002).

universities, institutions for religious education, and media organisations throughout the world.

Many of these discussions highlight real differences of opinion and approach. One event at the Edinburgh conference provoked passionate reactions: the presentation of *Terminal Time*. This was an interactive television computer programme that told the story of the past 1000 years in the form of a television documentary. Audience response played a role in determining the course of the programme, which then unfolded to reflect the audience's ideological bias. Some people found this provocative, but raw and lacking in the artistic craft of traditional communication technologies. Others, in spite of the rough edges of the production at the time, thought it was the way of the future and were fascinated. Edinburgh University's neo-classical nineteenth-century Old College Library, where *Terminal Time* was screened, contrasts strikingly with the state of the art computer, powerful projector and large cinema screen required for the screening. The diverse responses to this world première are a valuable reminder of the tension between those who embrace the traditional and those who delight in new communication technologies.

Two other underlying tensions in the conversations provide further background for interpreting the essays in this book. The first is the divergence in research focus between those who primarily investigate points of reception and those who mainly examine the content of media texts. Some essays concentrate on how audiences receive and make use of the media, whilst others focus on how media messages are created, produced, and disseminated. The second, closely related to the first, is the difference of research method. Some contributors employ what could be described as a religious studies phenomenological approach, and others draw on a theological and/or historical approach. These underlying tensions in the conversation can be detected through a careful reading and comparison of the essays in each of the seven sections of *Mediating Religion*.

One of the central points of cultural and religious understanding is the search for identity, and a discussion of this theme provides a valuable starting-point for the book. The first part explores empirically how religious identity is formed in a world of media growth. Examples are used from the USA and Britain to assess the perceived influence of media on identity creation.

Asserting identity can create borderlines and lead to conflict. Part 2 therefore concentrates on the role that certain media have in the creation and sustenance of conflict. Hackett's essay, written before the events of September 11, investigates how religious and cultural identity is used by the Nigerian media in managing and manipulating conflict. Ramji sets out a critical case against North American news and film media for their stereotyping of Muslims. Silk's analysis of American newspaper coverage of Islam after September 11 provides a more positive interpretation of the communicative situation.

The conflict so prevalent in media representations today clearly influences aspects and expressions of popular piety. This is analysed in Part 3 where visual and musical media in relation to our religious and cultural identity, come under scrutiny. Grant and Ferré investigate the uses and influences of various forms of media on that piety, and the responses of religious and media practitioners to such media use.

Part 4 wrestles with the responses of faith groups to some of the questions raised in the previous three parts. These questions are considered through the eyes of the audience, through a specific faith group, and through the eyes of faith leaders. The essays investigate how religious groups can educate themselves to develop media literacy skills that will ensure the media is not solely responsible for the formation of cultural or religious identity.

The book then moves into investigations of more specific forms of media, and their religious and cultural implications. Film and more recently new media play a significant role in the structuring and patterns of everyday conversations. This affects the way that business relationships are formed, personal relationships sustained and our interactions with the wider world conducted. Parts 5 and 6 consider these different forms of media and the responses of faith communities to them, examining some of the questions raised by both film and new media for identity creation, religious expression and cultural meanings.

Many of the preceding parts have implicitly tackled ethical issues at both production and reception points. The final part in the book brings together writers in the field of media ethics. Essays from a number of different perspectives provide distinct insights into new ways of approaching this subject. For example, several of the authors question the dominance of Western approaches in the ethics of communication and provide complementary ways of examining the media.

The final chapter revisits the conversations of the book, places them in context and points towards new areas for research. It identifies seven emerging strands in the ongoing discussions. Four annotated bibliographies, specifically connected with the issues raised in the last four parts, then provide a useful research tool, and a good starting-point for future research and conversation.

The seven parts in *Conversations in Media, Religion and Culture* demonstrate how this area of study reaches across a variety of different disciplines and uses a wide range of research techniques and practices. It is a field of research influenced and in many cases led by both media practitioners and academics. Through conversations in both university seminar room and recording studio, we face the borderlines in the contemporary world. For Zeldin some conversations have the potential to change us:

> Mere personal advancement or respectability can no longer be the main purpose of conversation. What is missing from the world is a sense of direction, because we are overwhelmed by the conflicts which surround us, as though we are marching through a jungle that never

ends. I should like some of us to start conversations to dispel that darkness, using them to create equality, to give ourselves courage, to open ourselves to strangers...[6]

Mediating Religion: Conversations in Media, Religion and Culture could not have come to fruition without the invaluable assistance of many colleagues. As editors we are extremely grateful to all the contributors for participating in this project and providing fascinating material based on their research. We would like to have included numerous other discussions from the conference and research projects emanating from it, but the constraints of space limited us from going beyond the twenty-nine essays included here.

We wish to acknowledge the invaluable help of Heidi Campbell, Angie Inchley, Eliza Getman and Sarah King Head for their work on the manuscript. We are thankful to Sheena Carlyle for her hard work prior to, during and after the conference itself. Without the vision of Adán Medrano, and the International Study Commission for Media, Religion and Culture, generously sponsored by Stichting Porticus, the conference could never have happened. Stewart Hoover and David Morgan, as chairs of that commission, provided great encouragement and assistance with the conference and then with the production of this book. We are also grateful to colleagues of the Uppsala group, including Knut Lundby and Alf Linderman, as well as the members of the International Study Commission for Media, Religion and Culture who are sources of inspiration. We are indebted to the British Academy and to what was the Faculty of Arts, Divinity and Music at Edinburgh University for their generous support of the editorial process; as well as to the Jerusalem Trust for supporting the Media and Theology Project and the trustees of the Henry Scott Holland Trust for the opportunity to test out the ideas of the conclusion in a public setting. We very much appreciate the help and encouragement offered by colleagues at New College, the Faculty of Divinity, including Nick Adams, Duncan Forrester, David Kerr, Elizabeth Koepping and Michael Northcott. Colleagues from other universities have also provided valuable assistance as anonymous readers.

On a personal note Jolyon Mitchell would like to thank CARTS and Clare Hall in Cambridge and Peter Mitchell, Catharine Beck, Fiona and Richard Parsons, Anna King, F. Ellis Leigh, John Eldridge, Kenneth and Mary Habershon, and Mark and Iona Birchall for their direct and indirect help with this volume. He is indebted to Clare, his wife, who helped make this book happen in more ways than she can imagine, as well as Sebastian and more recently Jasmine Mitchell for keeping him laughing throughout the editorial process.

Sophia Marriage acknowledges the huge support of her family, Alwyn, Hugh and Zoë, and especially thanks Jonathon, for his encouragement, love and understanding as she juggled different commitments, priorities and preoccupations and for providing light relief and distraction along the way.

---

[6] Zeldin, *Conversation*, p. 97.

This book is dedicated to three outstanding teachers, Peter Mitchell, Catharine Beck and Alwyn Sherratt whose conversations through life have inspired us.

PART 1

Identity, Media and Religion

2

Religion, Media and Identity: Theory and Method in Audience Research on Religion and Media

Stewart M. Hoover

This chapter reviews recent work at the intersection of media, religion and culture, and makes the argument for a specific approach to that intersection: audience- and reception-centred study of identity and meaning. This argument is both conceptual and based on field experience in qualitative reception research. The conceptual turf is that of evolving theory and phenomena both in religion scholarship and in media scholarship. The empirical argument is based on ongoing qualitative field research in media households.

The place of religion in mass communication research and media studies has been the subject of a consistent, if quiet, debate for several decades. A landmark work on the effects of religious content emerged in the 1950s[1] but was followed by relatively little serious or sustained research or scholarship. The emergence of the phenomenon we now know as 'Televangelism' in the 1970s stirred a flurry of research and publications[2] but the focus was limited to the terms of reference of that type of broadcasting. Some good historical work has been done on religious radio over the years, as well as small discourses on religious publishing and religion and the press. However, these disparate approaches did not until recently stimulate a serious scholarly consideration of the extent, limits, critical issues and significance of looking at religion and media.

Related scholarly discourses particularly in the area of 'media ritual' did emerge, and have been helpful to the cause. Following Carey's germinal essay on 'Communication as Ritual',[3] a number of scholars from a variety of perspectives have considered questions of the non-rational, organically cultural ritual, and deeply meaningful aspects of public communication, the media, commodity culture and popular

---

[1] Parker, Barry, and Smythe, *The Television-Radio Audience and Religion* (New York: Basic, 1954).

[2] For a complete discussion of this literature see Lynn Clark, 'The Protestantization of Research on Media and Religion', S. Hoover and L. S. Clark (eds.), *Practicing Religion in the Age of the Media* (New York: Columbia University Press, 2002).

[3] James Carey, *Communication as Culture* (Boston Unwin-Hyman, 1989).

culture.[4] Still, media scholarship has tended not to foreground or center questions of religion, for a number of reasons.[5]

This situation has begun to change. It is beyond the scope of this paper to detail all the reasons for this change. However, the most fundamental explanation lies in real historical developments in the worlds of religion and the media, and the scholarships that contemplate them. Media studies have been somewhat slower to recognise something that has been seen for longer in religion studies – that increasingly the worlds of religion and media are coming together in the context of lived lives and practices.

This chapter will review part of this turf and move to the description of one stream of research and theory-building that addresses the way religion is finding its way into and out of what we think of as 'secular' media. In sum, audience practices of reception are subverting the bright line that we once thought existed between 'religion' and 'the media'. It is my argument here that this distinction is no longer a realistic or relevant one, and that we can learn a great deal about both religion and the media by understanding how and where they occupy the same conceptual and practical spaces.

While there are a variety of ways that the intersection between religion and the media might be and is being studied, I will discuss here a particular and focused area of work: questions of symbolism, identity and meaning, and the way that media and religion interact and intersect in the construction of meaning and identity in contemporary culture. This chapter, and my broader research on the topic, is based on collaborative work under way with a talented group of colleagues.[6]

The direction we take is one that recognises this convergence between the worlds of religion and the media, and between the scholarships that contemplate them. The motive force in these matters is the contemporary project of the reflexive self[7] and its trajectory through culture and history. To ask questions about what we used to call 'religion', however, necessarily implies that what we are actually interested in is one dimension of the task of shaping self-identity. That is the one identified by Weber in his classic work on Protestantism, described by one scholar of Weber as 'the need human beings have to invest their lives with larger meaning and purpose than the routines of mundane existence provide ...'[8] Put another way,

---

[4] See in particular Eric Rothebuhler, *Ritual Communication* (Newbury Park: Sage, 1999); Daniel Dayan and Elihu Katz, *Media Events* (Cambridge: Harvard University Press, 1993); and Tamar Liebes and James Curran (eds.) *Media, Ritual and Identity* (London: Routledge, 2000).

[5] For a more complete discussion, see Stewart Hoover and Shalini Venturelli, 'Religion: The Blindspot of American Media Theory', *Critical Studies in Mass Communication* (Summer 1993) and Clark, 'The Protestantization of Research'.

[6] For more information, see www.colorado.edu/Journalism/MEDIALYF. Also, see Hoover and Clark, and Hoover, Clark, Alters, Champ, and Hood, forthcoming.

[7] Anthony Giddens, *Modernity and Self-Identity* (Stanford: Stanford University Press, 1993).

[8] Bruce Douglass, 'Weber and the Making of the Modern Individual', lecture to the faculty seminar, University of Edinburgh, April, 2001.

there seems to be a human tendency to invest concrete activity in the material sphere with a cloak of significance and importance. And, more significantly, to do this in a way that is conscious of needing to make this investment appear socially plausible.

Weber obviously felt that this was a task with religious implications and outcomes, and it is still possible to make such an argument today, though today what is changing is the form and boundaries of what we think of as 'religion' or 'the religious'. This transformation is an essential element of the convergence that is occurring between the worlds of 'religion' and the 'the media'. Where once we could think of these as separate, even as competing spheres of influence, this is no longer the case. Instead, I think it is most helpful to think of religious practice inhabiting an emerging 'religious-symbolic marketplace' constructed at the confluence of religion and the media.

The most important trend in religion is 'personal autonomy' in matters of faith. Increasingly today, religion is seen as a project of the autonomous, reflexive self. Much research and theory has emerged on this, most notably by Wade Clark Roof,[9] but this theme surfaces across contemporary religion research. Roof describes the dominant mode of contemporary religious practice as 'seeking' or 'questing'. History, institution, and doctrine mean less than voluble symbols that are meaningful to autonomous selves in the here and now. On a recent BBC Radio 4 program devoted to religion in Britain, Linda Woodhead of Lancaster University was interviewed about her in-depth studies of religion in the small town of Kendal, Cumbria, UK. She described the landscape there very much in terms of these trends:

> Woodhead: We find what we call a turn to life – people want to get something out of religion in their personal lives, they don't want to just sit quietly and be told what to do. They want to have more in the way of experience and participation.
>
> Interviewer: Well, they want their lives improved *now*, they're not as concerned in the future, in heaven – if it exists.
>
> Woodhead: They want their lives improved now, and they may be therefore less willing to just sit and be disciplined as it were. They want to see, they want their lives *resourced* and they want to feel that this is making a difference to them in the here and now. So far we've found more than one hundred outlets of the new spiritual movements, even in a small town like Kendal, so this is clearly a growth area.

Three trends in religion that are most significant to my argument are present here. First, the fact of the seeking, questing, autonomous self; second,

[9] Wade Clark Roof, *Spiritual Marketplace* (Princeton: Princeton University Press, 1999) and *Generation of Seekers* (Berkeley: University of California Press, 1994).

the re-articulation of what we used to call 'religion' into something else, something less problematic – most commonly 'spirituality', or 'the spiritual'; and third, the fact that a marketplace of supply exists, even in this small town, outside the bounds of traditional religion. Sociologists such as Robert Wuthnow have called these trends a 'restructuring' of religion, away from a situation where religious institutions and histories are definitive to a situation where individual practice, according to its own logic, becomes more definitive.

At the same time, the world of the media is also changing, in part in response to these trends in autonomous seeking. As the self and its quest come more into play, the prerogatives of religious institutions to legitimate certain symbolic forms and practices fades, opening the way for a wider range of symbolic resources to be brought to bear. It almost goes without saying that among those resources will be, increasingly, cultural commodities of the media sphere. The range of symbolic resources relevant to spiritual questing, available through all media, is wide and ever-expanding. In a sense, what is happening is that the media marketplace is acting *like* a marketplace. As demand for such things has grown, supply has also grown.

The best and most convincing examples of this exist in American television. The expanding diversity of television channels in the US has led to more and more specialisation in genre and content. In part due to this, we have experienced over the past six years an unprecedented explosion in program content dealing with religion (again, as broadly defined, to include spirituality, mysticism, transcendence). For one example, the series *Touched by an Angel* has been one of the ten most popular prime-time programs in the US for the past five years. Significantly, it is a program that is both conventional and unconventional in its religion. It does include angels and talk of God, but carefully avoids reference to the specificity of Christianity, for example, so as to be more broadly accessible to spiritually autonomous audiences.

It is possible to lay out a highly condensed argument about the nature of the religious quest of the self, drawn from a number of sources, but relying most heavily on Roof's work. Religious identity is today oriented toward the 'self'. It is not *absolutely* any of these, but tends to be more *private, subjective, implicit* and *reflexive* than in the past. It is increasingly oriented toward symbols. Autonomous selves tend to pick and choose from among traditions, and this has the effect of making the symbols of those traditions more *horizontal*, less embedded in their received histories, and it makes the symbols the most prominent aspect. Religious *identities* are then increasingly mapped with reference to these symbols. Moreover, this deserves much more discussion than I am able to give it here, and the sensibility is one which seeks simultaneously to be '*fluid*' and '*grounded*'. It must be fluid in order to be true to the task of a kind of continuous re-making and perfecting of the self and identity, but the whole point, after all, is some kind of 'grounding'.

Another way of representing the underlying restructuring here is through the set of 'religious subcultures', laid out by Roof in his book *Spiritual Marketplace*[10]:

(1) Born-again Christians (2) Mainstream Believers (3) Metaphysical Believers and Seekers (4) Dogmatists (5) Secularists.

His contemporary religious 'types' are really self-explanatory, but I will highlight a couple of points. First, there are great differences between different national contexts in the relative proportions of these. In the US, of course, we have many more born-again believers than in Europe or elsewhere. Second – and this is most important – it is clear that the category Roof calls 'metaphysical believers and seekers' is really the voluble front of these trends.

As this religious sensibility has moved ahead, it has further tended to find articulation in modes of practice that have traditionally been repressed in formal, institutional Christianity in the West. These modes are *the body, objects, the visual, rituals,* and *experience.* One of the most interesting and productive areas of contemporary religious scholarship in fact is the phenomenological study of new religious movements and sensibilities as they engage these various modes. Neo-pagan and Wiccan spirituality, for example, are in part defined by their contemporary adherents in terms of their modulation of these repressed modes. What is most important to my argument here, though, is that these modes of expression and experience are present in an unproblematic way, in the realm we call 'the media'. Thus, both in terms of the implicit challenge the media context poses to institutional authority, and in terms of its aesthetic and experiential characteristics, the media sphere must be seen as a place where the contemporary religious or spiritual quest of the self can be worked out.

Mid-century mass communication research attempted some rudimentary understanding of religion, but these efforts proved unsatisfactory for two important reasons. First, those earlier paradigms in media studies were deeply rooted in the view that religion was a residual and fading feature of the social landscape, worthy of study only in the most cursory way. Second, the objectivist-quantitative methods preferred particularly in the United States proved woefully inadequate to the study of something so subtle, complex and nuanced as religion, much less the emerging quasi-religions, spiritualities and meaning explorations of the contemporary era.

Fortunately, media studies has moved forward from those times, and now provides some helpful conceptual and theoretical tools appropriate to the study of these phenomena. The turns toward critical, interpretivist, and culturalist theory, and toward qualitative methods, have opened the possibility of accounting for a wide range of motivations, meanings and sensibilities, including those within the realm we might broadly call 'the religious'. Through our qualitative investigations we have discovered that religion is both a very particular and at the same time more broadly significant field of inquiry within media studies. On our way to understanding

[10] Roof, *Spiritual Marketplace*, pp. 180–216

religiously-modulated meaning-making in the media sphere, we have explored media reception practice in some depth and detail, and have developed a way of interpreting it that we find helpful to the task of understanding the subtle and nuanced practices of identity and the self in which we are most interested.

In our analysis and interpretation of our field material (interviews and observations) we have found ourselves looking at three different *modes of engagement* with the media. First is what we call *experiences **in** the media*. This is quite familiar to media scholarship. It is the range of informant accounts that speak to their involvement with media texts and objects, their understanding of them, their identification with them, their interpretation and articulation of them on their own terms. Second is what we call *interactions **about** the media*. These are accounts that speak to media as a currency of exchange in social relations, a point of social solidarity or a means of resistance, for a few examples. This category is familiar from the work of James Lull, Henry Jenkins, Hall and Jefferson, John Thompson and many others.

The third mode is the one that intrigues us the most, and the one that is more unique to our approach. We call it *accounts **of** the media*. These are informant accounts wherein they reflexively position themselves historically, socially and culturally in relation to media practice. We first began thinking about this mode when we encountered in our field material evidence that informants were telling us one thing and doing quite another. For one example, in a family interview a father was talking about how in his family great care is exercised to control the children's access to material the parents deem offensive. 'So', he said, 'that means that when we watch films on video, I have the controller and I fast-forward through violent or sexual content'. The children would have none of it. A twelve-year-old son jumped in, 'What are you talking about? You *never* fast-forward'. After a good deal of interchange back and forth, finally the father sheepishly admitted, 'Well, I did *one time*'. This is familiar to everyone who has ever studied media audiences. In the old days we called it the problem of 'demand characteristics'. We could not trust our objective data because we know people talk about their media behaviors in socially conformist ways. In the US, everyone watches public television and no children ever have access to violent cartoons.

We began thinking harder about this issue, though. We became convinced we needed to move beyond a kind of 'gotcha' reaction to these things, where we've '*caught them out*' and instead begin theorising why it is the case that it is socially and culturally appropriate to give such accounts, what the accounts are, and what kind of purpose such accounts serve. Why is a certain self-presentation regarding media behavior appropriate on the part of certain informants in certain contexts? How and why do these become systematic (for example, the general social desirability of public television viewing, the taste preference for film over television, the derogation of the daytime serial, etc.)? What overall project is being worked on through these accounts? To the latter, I have a rudimentary answer, one I hope to explore in greater detail in the future. I suspect (and I must refer in particular to the important work Roger Silverstone[11] has done on this) that media technology is still imperfectly and incompletely integrated into the context of contemporary domestic space. Our nascent desire for the dimly remembered past of *Gemeinschaft* has us struggling to resolve what we see to be an inherent contradiction between *these* technologies and *that* life. In any case, this mode of engagement with media is one we find more and more obvious in our field material as we look at it and for it.

So, how do we begin to grasp the meanings that emerge from such experiences? Amidst the social and interpretive complexity that emerges from field material, we have seen informants' own accounts as a point of 'interpretive stability'. Specifically, we have begun to see that our central project is the gathering of what I call '*plausible narratives of the self self*' through which we can see and understand the complex interplay of symbols and practices contributing to the making of meaningful identities. This is another area which deserves a good deal more explanation than I can give here. This idea is clearly rooted in pragmatist traditions in social theory and social psychology, and owes much to recent restatements of symbolic interactionism[12] and the new 'positive psychology' of Martin Seligman and Mihaly Csikszentmihalyi. It assumes that the process of construction of the self and identity is a reflexive process and one that is conscious of its contexts, histories, interactions and web of social relations. These narratives further contain elements that are for us both documentary and also articulations of cultural exchange around presentations of the self. We do know something from these accounts about what they do as well as how they make a meaningful account (Charles Taylor's notion of 'accountability' is similar) of what they do. This is rich material.

I want to conclude with examples from our field transcripts that illustrate the range of material that can be brought to bear in pursuance of these ideas. The first illustrates the complexity and subtlety I spoke of earlier. It also demonstrates the nuanced nature of meaning-making around the category of 'the religious'. It begins with our interviewer raising the question of religion in relation to media behaviour.

> I: When you're renting videos – or any of the videos that you won – do they relate to spirituality or religion?
> J: We had one.
> U: The 'island' thing?
> I: The what?
> U: The Ireland thing.
> J: There was one...
> W: Oh, the Secret of Irish Rum [*The Secret of Roan Inish*]
> J: Yeah, that was a good one.

[11] Roger Silverstone and Eric Hirsch, *Consuming Technologies* (London: Routledge, 1992).

[12] Norman Denzin, *Symbolic Interactionism and Cultural Studies* (New York: Routledge, 1992); Kenneth Gergen, *The Saturated Self* (New York: Basic Books, 1991).

W: It's kind of a folk tale.

I: What about *Jesus Christ Superstar* [it was on a nearby shelf in plain sight]?

(everyone responds at once; general shouting, discussion, laughter.)

W: Before we started going to church. That [*Jesus Christ Superstar*] was our religious thing. At Easter we'd watch that.

U: That's another movie we memorised. We also made up songs from it.

W: We started watching that in Florida.

J: Plus we tape movies. Like *Monty Python's Holy Grail.*

W: I'd say that's their all-time favourite.

U: I think in an attempt to imitate parts of the Holy Scripture...

I: That's the family's all-time favourite – *The Holy Grail?*

W: I guess it might be considered sacrilegious by some people...

There is no doubt that *Monty Python and The Holy Grail* would be considered sacrilegious in some quarters, particularly traditionally religious ones. This excerpt illustrates some important learnings we have gained from the field. First, that there is a kind of ubiquity and inevitability about mediated cultural resources in the home. This household is now a conservative Christian one where the mother (the 'W' in the transcript) has banned broadcast and cable television so as to be more selective about what the family sees and uses videos as a way of programming their access to culture. Nonetheless the family is deeply embedded in media culture. Before their most recent foray into formal religious identification, they used a video of the film *Jesus Christ Superstar* as a sort of family religious ritual, even viewing it on one of the most important and formal Christian holidays.

There is, then, a second learning here. These sorts of mediated materials and objects are quite unproblematically integrated into everyday practices of spiritual and religious meaning-making. Whereas religious authorities of various kinds might wish to lay out a bright demarcation between legitimate and illegitimate religious symbols and practices, this household makes its own judgments about the legitimacy and authenticity of such things.

The third learning here relates to the earlier discussion about religious 'seeking' and the self. In order to understand the practices described in this excerpt we must see the self and the autonomy of the self as the point. This woman, and her daughters, are engaged in a process around cultural meanings, around particular religious meanings in this case, that is oriented to their own reflexive sense of themselves and their place in the web of social relations. They feel no need to look outside themselves for authority or confirmation; they make those judgements by themselves, in their own time and place. This is the new religiosity described and predicted by Roof and others. At the same time, this passage illustrates the extent to which media practice is and can be integrated into this type of consciousness. It plays a subtle, nuanced and complex role, but one that is increasingly essential in the media age.

The next example moves a bit more into the realm of the 'plausible narratives of the self', and its relationship to the levels of media engagement introduced earlier. The complexity and subtlety of interactions with and use of media materials provide the basis for negotiation of an account of the self. This informant, whom we call Barbara, presents a narrative of the interrelationship of media, religion, identity and family interaction.

Barbara watched *Days of Our Lives* every day with her strict Methodist grandmother during summer vacation when she was growing up. Barbara's aunt objected, but Barbara continued to watch soap operas, even scheduling her classes around them in college. Her favorite is *General Hospital*. Eventually, after the grandmother died, the aunt had a change of heart, and became devoted to *The Young and Restless*.

> Barbara: Yeah, but you know I hate to admit it, but I love soap operas, and I probably, sometimes though when they're being really vicious and mean, I think, 'Oh, this is probably not a good thing to be watching'.
>
> Interviewer: Do you apply to soap operas what you were telling me before, that you like the way the characters mesh together? [She had said this about 'Seinfeld' and 'Thirtysomething'.] That's certainly what soap operas do.
>
> B: I think it's probably just entertainment. [Laughs.] You kind of get caught up in the characters' lives, I guess, probably. I don't watch them on a regular basis, just when I'm home I'll kind of flip one on. [Laughs.] ...[*General Hospital*] was one I watched all through college. I would schedule my classes around it.
>
> I: Oh, so you were a serious watcher then.
>
> B: I was back then. My mother just hated it, too. But my grandmother who I used to spend summers with, that was her big thing, was she had her soap operas and she would catch me up every summer when I'd go down.... It was kind of like it was naughty. [Laughs.] It was like I was doing something naughty.

Barbara goes on to describe how she would watch it, along with other girl-friends in the college commons area. They would often talk and make fun of it. She explains that her husband Tim now thinks that it's horrible. [He says] 'I can't believe you still watch that junk!' Barbara goes on to reflect: 'I think I probably shouldn't watch that kind of stuff, because it's not real wholesome or uplifting. Most of the characters are a big mess!'

> I: That didn't bother your grandmother.
>
> B: Oh, no. She was from the South. She grew up, her father was a Baptist minister, very strict. So she was kind of rebelling. [Laughs.] She grew up in the Methodist church. She was my dad's mother. She was

like one of the leaders in the Methodist church. She helped start one
of the churches down there.

Several issues are notable here. First of all, the interpretive framework
received from her religious faith (an account *of*) has receded almost
entirely into the background here. It is still there, conditioning her discussions with the interviewer, but also mixed with a second *account* *of* a
broader social opprobrium attached to soap opera viewing. In other words,
while she might relate her religious background to her sense that soap
opera viewing is undesirable, that doesn't seem to be the main point that
guides either her practices or how she describes them to the interviewer.

Two or three other levels of salience or meaning stand out instead. First,
there is the simple level of pleasure, both in the text itself and in the naugh-
tiness of viewing it in resistance to received proscription. Second, there is a
level of ritual social connectedness. This co-viewing experience comes to
define her relationship with her grandmother. And the grandmother's own
negotiation of the various discursive and salience levels is interesting, too.
From a much older generation, she nonetheless was a regular viewer of a
type of television frowned upon by legitimating authorities from two
different directions.

There is also connectedness, an *interaction* *about*, that integrates her practice with classmates in college, and a continuing *account* *of* discussion with
her husband, who now acts in the role of derogator of her guilty pleasure.

Examples such as this illustrate the complex and nuanced nature of the
relationship between religious and social values and viewing practices of
the media sphere. It is not really possible to see a clear line of demarcation
between 'religion' and 'television' here. It is further not only a question of
how people find religious meaning in television. Distinctions do exist, in
the form of received scripts (from secular as well as religious sources) about
the soap opera genre (and viewing of television in general). But Barbara is
integrated into the audience for *General Hospital* in a rather transparent way.
She exhibits two of the levels of salience introduced earlier. There is pleasure in the text/object itself and a further pleasure in the resistance represented by viewing it. There is also social/cultural currency in her
co-viewing, first with her grandmother (pleasure here, too, of course) and
then with her cohorts at university.

There is a kind of grounding here, but of a complicated sort. On the one
hand, her awareness of *accounts* *of* which derogate the soap opera from various perspectives is meaningful, and she must negotiate a place for herself
with regard to them. She does this by describing her involvement as 'in the
past' and only incidental today. She is, in effect, saying, 'Who am I? I am **not**
a soap opera viewer', an important definitional task. But, she is also aware
that, at one point in her life, she was positioned in a more naturalised way
within the ritual of soap opera viewing, and specifically within a broad ritual
of a particular story arc within the program, the famous 'Luke and Laura'
cycle.

Barbara's experience with *General Hospital* illustrates the extent to which meaning-construction in the media sphere can be both a *negotiation* and a *struggle.* It is not a straightforward, manifest process, but one that derives from inter-related accounts, discourses, behaviors, saliencies and practices.

This is a very complex map. To fully understand it, we must understand how these various symbolic resources are grounded referentially in social history, and how Barbara herself negotiates a meaningful place within them. It is a narrative of resistance, of solidarity, of autonomy and of social location. It is a subtle and quiet narrative. There is no epiphany here, no *axis mundi*, no numinous, no pilgrimage. Instead there is a playful, reflexive, self-aware mapping of herself in social and cultural space and time, using found and experienced symbolic resources located in media content and practice as well as in religious self-understanding, history and positionality.

And it is also complex and contradictory. David Morley has suggested that we need to move beyond the proposition that audiences act in often complex and contradictory ways:

> It is what we do with that action that makes the difference. From my own point of view it is the lack of a sufficiently sociological or materialist basis that is the key problem. Certainly if all one could say is that 'it's always complex and contradictory', it would hardly seem fair to the trees to bother to do so. The point, however, is in my view an empirical one: The question is one of understanding (and here I continue to believe that Bordieu has much to offer in this respect) just how 'complex' or 'contradictory' it is, for *which* type of consumers, in which social positions, in relation to *which* types of texts or objects. The 'distinctions' are all, in this respect they are what we need to look for.[13]

It is my position, at the moment anyway, that these 'plausible narratives of the self' provide important interpretive purchase on the questions of the making of meaning and identity in contemporary life. Religion, or practices, symbols and meanings in the realm we used to think of as 'religion', comes into play in certain of these constructions, and the media sphere is both an important context and a provider of voluble symbols to this project.

---

[13] David Morley, 'The geography of television: Ethnography, communications, and community', James Hay, Lawrence Grossberg and Ellen Wartella (eds.), *The Audience and its Landscape* (Boulder, Co: Westview, 1996), p. 323.

3

The 'Funky' Side of Religion: An Ethnographic Study of Adolescent Religious Identity and the Media[1]

Lynn Schofield Clark

'I watch a lot of extraterrestrial stuff,' Jodie, a young Anglo-American woman from an impoverished economic background, told me as she puffed her cigarette. 'They're different. It's a new outlook on what could be happening, rather than on what already is happening, or what in the past has happened.' Sceptical about the God she associated with organised religion, Jodie was fascinated instead by other forms of the supernatural such as the paranormal, ghosts and aliens. When I asked her which television program was most like her religious beliefs, she offered this intriguing answer: 'It would have to be *X-Files*. Because, no matter what anybody says ... I've seen everything that everyone's compiled together about aliens. There's no doubt in my mind that we are not the only intelligent life ... God was a higher being. How do we know he wasn't an alien? On *X-Files*, Mulder, he would say something like that: how do we know God's not an alien?'

How, indeed? Some scholars in the studies of contemporary religion have questioned whether the entertainment media are to blame for what they might call the distorted beliefs of young people like Jodie.[2] In this era of irregular attendance at religious organisations, stories like Jodie's suggest that while the local synagogue, mosque or church may be sources of information about the realm beyond, so are television programs like *The X-Files*.

While few young people might declare that they 'believe' God to be an alien, Jodie's statement raises intriguing questions about religious beliefs among US teens and the relationship of the media to those beliefs. Jodie, for instance, never said she wasn't a religious or spiritual person. She simply made it very clear that her religious beliefs were unconventional, to say the least. She was interested, as another teen termed the mediated depictions of the supernatural, the afterlife and the paranormal, in the 'funky' side of religion. Based on my previous experiences as a mentor of young people in

[1] This chapter is drawn from Lynn Schofield Clark, *From Angels to Aliens: Teens, the Media, and Beliefs in the Supernatural* (Oxford: Oxford University Press, 2003).

[2] W. Fore, *Television and religion: The shaping of faith, values, and culture* (Minneapolis: Augsburg, 1987); and Q. Schultze, R. Anker, et al, *Dancing in the Dark: Youth, popular culture and the electronic media* (Grand Rapids: Eerdmans, 1991).

various civic, educational and religious settings, I suspected that even as her particular statements of belief might be somewhat idiosyncratic, her interests in the realm beyond were not unique. Moreover, while previous research had assumed that such interests in the 'funky' side of religion were more or less related to deviant behavior, I wondered how such beliefs might be related to both self-presentation of a religious identity and to larger ideological themes of the culture that are reflected in and shaped by the media.

It is the goal of this chapter, therefore, to explore the ways in which popular television programs and films such as *The X-Files*, *Buffy the Vampire Slayer* or *The Sixth Sense* have served as a resource in how contemporary US teens understand religion, the realm beyond this world, and their own relationship to these things. I focused on programs like these because teen audiences prefer them to more explicitly religious programs, and because they were identified by teens as programs that offer intriguing stories of the realm beyond this world – a realm of concern for monotheistic religions. Thus, my primary research question was: what is the role of the media in religious identity-construction, particularly when the media's tales of the supernatural may seem to be compelling and in direct contrast with those of historic institutions of religion? I found that tales of the supernatural in the entertainment media are an important context for how teens understand beliefs more traditionally understood as related to the historical institutions of religion. In this chapter, I explore five different ways in which this context of supernatural stories in teen media interacts with traditional religion in the identity narratives of adolescents.

An important related question for the specific case of religious identity quickly emerges. Why would teens like Jodie, who have little connection with organised religion and a great deal of interest in the media depictions of the realm beyond, still claim a religious or spiritual identity for themselves at all? In other words, why don't teens like her identify themselves as secularists, the label sociologists might prefer for persons holding such unconventional beliefs who have no affiliation with religious organisations?

US teens and religious identity

Much of contemporary research into the religious formation of young people is based on the assumption that teens learn of and form their beliefs about angels, God or Allah, and the devil – the more traditionally 'religious' supernatural beings – in the context of church, the synagogue or mosque, and that their religious identity is thus formed in relation to these organisations.[3] Yet while the majority of teens claim that they identify with the traditions of organised religion, mounting data suggest that actual

---

[3] F. J. Beeck, *Catholic identity after Vatican II: Three types of faith in one church* (Chicago: Loyola University Press, 1985); D. Gustafson, *Lutherans in crisis: The question of identity in the American republic* (Minneapolis: Fortress, 1993); and C. Lynch, 'Choosing faith across generations: A qualitative study of church-affiliated high school seniors and their parents', Unpublished dissertation, Emory University (2000).

participation is much less widespread.[4] The lack of attendance at religious services may be particularly pronounced among teens. As Stolzenberg, Blair-Loy and Waite[5] demonstrated, family attendance declines once the child reaches the age of ten, and attendance for individual young people does not rise again until they join the ranks of parenthood themselves. This suggests that a great number of young people in the US, despite their claim of a 'religious' identity, might be classified, using Marler and Hadaway's[6] phrase, as 'marginal members': those people who attend services several times a year or less, yet are not hostile toward the organisation.[7]

Relatively little research has been conducted into the relationship of the media to religious identity among young people. Following in the tradition of 'effects' research, Martinez-de-Toda and Tomkinson[8] have argued that representations of religion in the popular entertainment media cause some young people to form negative perceptions about religion. Others, embracing 'uses and gratifications' and 'cultural studies' approaches, have explored how the religious attitudes of adult individuals influence the use and interpretation of television, print journalism or other media.[9] Yet as Raymond Williams has pointed out, we cannot understand culture if we limit ourselves only to the study of the individual's relationship to particular mass communication forms. We must view those particular forms, as

[4] C. K. Hadaway and P. L. Marler, 'Did you really go to church this week? Behind the poll data', *The Christian Century* (6 May 1998), pp. 472–5; W. C. Roof and W. McKinney, *American mainline religion: Its changing shape and future* (New Brunswick, NJ: Rutgers University Press, 1987); S. Warner, 'Work in progress toward a "new paradigm" for the sociological study of religion in the United States', *American Journal of Sociology* 98 (5) (1993), pp. 1044–93.

[5] R. M. Stolzenberg, Blair-Loy, M., and Waite, L. J., 'Religious participation in early adulthood: Age and family life cycle effects on church membership', *American Sociological Review* 60 (1995), pp. 84–103.

[6] P. L. Marler, and C. K. Hadaway, 'Toward a typology of Protestant "marginal members"', *Review of Religious Research* 35(1) (1993).

[7] See also A. Argue, D. R. Johnson, and L. K. White, 'Age and religiosity: Evidence from a three-wave panel analysis', *Journal for the Scientific Study of Religion* 38(3) (1999), pp. 423–35.

[8] J. Martinez-de-Toda, 'Youth, media and spirituality', Paper presented to the third international conference on media, religion and culture, Edinburgh, Scotland (July 1999) and A. Tomkinson, 'Adolescent perceptions of religious identity and popular broadcasting', Paper presented to the third international conference on media, religion, culture, Edinburgh, Scotland (July 1999).

[9] J. Buddenbaum, 'The media, religion, and public opinion: Toward a unified theory of cultural influence', D. Stout and J. Buddenbaum (eds.), *Religion and Popular Culture: Studies on the interaction of worldviews* (Ames: Iowa State University Press, 2001), pp. 19–38; N. F. Hamilton, and A. M. Rubin, 'The influence of religiosity on television viewing', *Journalism Quarterly* 69(3) (1992), pp. 667–78; S. Hoover, *Mass media religion: The social sources of the electronic church* (Thousand Oaks, CA: Sage, 1988); A. Linderman, *The reception of religious television: Social semeiology applied to an empirical case study*, Unpublished dissertation, Department of Theology, Uppsala University, Sweden (1996); T. Rendleman, '"Evil" images in *At Play in the Fields of the Lord*: Evangelicals and representations of sexuality in contemporary film', *Velvet Light Trap: A Critical Journal of Film and Television* 46 (2000), pp. 26–39; C. L. Roberts, 'Attitudes and media use of the moral majority', *Journal of Broadcasting* 27(4) (1983), pp. 403–410; and D. Stout, and J. Buddenbaum, *Religion and mass media: Audiences and adaptations* (Thousand Oaks, CA: Sage, 1996).

well as particular articulations of identity by individuals, in relation to socially and historically situated discourses.[10] Critical/cultural studies approaches to identity therefore attempt to address the individual subject in relation to his or her larger context.[11] This is where stories of the supernatural become especially important in a consideration of teen religious identity.

Among today's US teens, religious beliefs are not a regular subject of conversation,[12] except in the discussions that take place around tragic events, such as the Columbine school shooting incident.[13] Stories of supernatural occurrences, on the other hand, occur much more frequently. In fact, they are the raw material of such longstanding traditions as horror films, sleepovers, campouts and legend trips, all important features on the landscape of adolescent life.[14] They are an important cultural context that informs how teens evaluate stories of the afterlife, both those that are introduced in the media as well as those introduced in formal religious settings. How these stories interact with the narratives of faith groups among young people with varying commitments to formal religion, however, has not been explored in previous research.

To explore this question, in-depth interviews were conducted as part of a larger multiple stage audience research project on families with young people in their homes. Data was collected between March 1996 and January 2000, involving a total of 269 individuals, 102 of whom were teens.[15]

[10] J. Carey *Communication as culture: Essays on media and society* (Boston: Unwin Hyman, 1989).

[11] See D. Buckingham, *The making of citizens: Young people, news and politics* (London: Routledge, 2000); D. Buckingham (ed.), *Reading audiences: Young people and the media* (Manchester and New York: Manchester University Press, 1990); M. Gillespie, *Television, ethnicity and cultural change* (New York: Routledge, 1995); K. Lowney, 'Teenage satanism as oppositional youth subculture', *Journal of Contemporary Ethnography* 23(4) (1995) 453–84; D. Morley and K. Robins, *Spaces of identity* (London: Routledge, 1995); H. Naficy, *The making of exile cultures: Iranian television in Los Angeles* (Minneapolis: University of Minnesota Press, 1993); and K. Woodward (ed.), *Identity and Difference* (London: Sage, 1997).

[12] R. Wuthnow, *Growing up Religious* (Boston: Beacon Press, 1999); P. Benson, 'Young adolescents and their parents project' [No pagination]. Data provided courtesy of the Lilly Endowment and the Search Institute (1984). Retrieved from www.arda.com (February 2000).

[13] See, e.g., W. M. Zoba, 'Do you believe in God? Columbine and the stirring of America's soul', *Christianity Today* (4 October 1999), pp. 33–43.

[14] E. Bird, 'Playing with fear: Interpreting the adolescent legend trip', *Western Folklore* 53 (1994), pp. 191-209; and B. Ellis 'Legend-tripping in Ohio: A behavioral survey', *Papers in Comparative Studies* 3 (2) (1982), pp. 61–73.

[15] As Associate Investigator of the Symbolism, Media and the Lifecourse project at the University of Colorado's Center for Mass Media Research, I conducted interviews and observations with ninety-four persons (fifty-five of whom were teens) and supervised other interviewers, focusing on the media and supernatural beliefs among young people. Stewart M. Hoover was Principal Investigator of this project, and its members included then-doctoral students Diane Alters, Joseph Champ and Lee Hood.

Traditionalists: affirming the boundary between religion and media

The first pattern that emerged in the analysis of the data was this: those young people most committed to conservative religious organisations were the most interested in preserving a strict separation between their religious beliefs and the stories of the supernatural presented in popular media. Teachings of religion and the content of the media were seen to occupy very different places, believed by these teens to be in contradiction with one another. Some evangelical Christian teens, as Hood[16] has noted, talk about the relationship between religious and fictional legends in terms of the popular moralistic question of evangelical Christianity, 'What Would Jesus Do?' When asked whether or not she thought about God when watching television, for example, Sara Hansen, a Euro-American upper middle class teen from an affluent suburb, replied:

> Sara: Yeah, like Jesus wouldn't want you to be watching this. Jesus wouldn't want you to be watching this cause it's not very Christian-like.
> Interviewer: What specifically?
> Sara: Just like bad language and stuff, and sex stuff, all that stuff.[17]

Sara described the problems of fictional television in terms of what she understood to be its moral message. This approach was not limited to evangelical Christian teens, however. A similar statement was made by Zeke Schwoch, a Mormon Euro-American middle class young man from a small city. He explained that he tried not to watch much television because 'you do your best to stay out of the world'.[18] Equating media with 'worldly', and hence non-religious or 'secular' values, he noted that he believed the media 'would make me forget a little bit what I was supposed to be doing' because the messages there can be 'spiritually distracting'. This distinction between religion and morality on one hand, and the media and immorality or distraction on the other, was also echoed in the statements of a conservative bi-racial Arab-African/Euro-American Muslim teen. Responding to my question of whether or not he saw a relationship between his family's strict rules limiting media consumption and Muslim teachings, Hasan Ahmed affirmed that he did:

> Because you're supposed to follow whatever your parents say and respect your parents. And you're supposed to read the Qur'an, which

---

[16] L. Hood, 'Ghosts, spirits, and Schwartzenegger: Children's connections to God in mediated culture', Paper presented to the third international conference on media, religion, and culture, Edinburgh, Scotland (July 1999).

[17] Interview with Sara Hansen, conducted by Lee Hood on 2 November 1997 as a part of the Symbolism, Media and the Lifecourse Project.

[18] Interview with Zeke Schwoch, conducted by Joseph Champ on 26 February 1998 as a part of the Symbolism, Media and the Lifecourse Project.

is like the Bible to us, so if you stay away from Nintendo, you'll read the Qur'an more.

While this distinction seemed common among those young people associated with traditional religion, a number of teens who identified themselves as 'religious' had more difficulty articulating what they believed was a difference between their religious beliefs and those the conservative teens would describe as those 'of the world'. These and the following stories, I believe, are less clearly explained by either statistical reports on teen beliefs or by prior qualitative research.

The intrigued teens: wishing to separate religion and legend, but having trouble doing so

Not all young people were as comfortable with a blurring between religious and fictional legends as was Jodie, the young woman introduced earlier who proposed that God might be an alien. Young people whose parents stressed the importance of religion learned that there *should* be a distinction between religion and folklore, and I was, on several occasions, given by teens the 'official' stance of their synagogue, mosque or church toward the 'fictional' representations of the supernatural in the media. For instance, Elizabeth Farley, a young Euro-American suburban woman of lower socioeconomic status who was actively involved in an aging Lutheran congregation, was puzzled when I told her that some people had mentioned *The X-Files* to me when asked which television program was most like what they believed in. As one of my peer interpreters, I had asked her to reflect on this strange phenomenon with me. Elizabeth hesitated, seeking the right words, then said:

> *The X-Files*, it's kind of, not really what you believe *religiously*, but what you *believe*, just, what you believe in, like ghosts and stuff. If you really believe that there's ghosts, or extraterrestrials.

Elizabeth attempted to draw a firm boundary between *religion* as it is related to the historic institutions of Christianity, and beliefs that might fall outside of those traditions, such as belief in extraterrestrials or ghosts. Because she placed herself *inside* the traditions of established religion, these alternative beliefs were *outside* the realm of possibility. At least, she believed that they *should* be, as illustrated in the following comments. I had asked her whether or not her own beliefs were similar to what she had seen on *The X-Files*:

> Not really. Like, when they were saying there was a sighting of an alien. I can *sort of* believe it, but there's also something that could've been written off. 'Oh well, somebody could've been faking it,' or whatever. And same thing with ghosts. They're saying, 'there's ghosts haunting my house.' That could be anything, or it could just be in their mind. But when it gets into a thing like *The Exorcist,* which was this thing on

television last week, about *The Exorcist,* about people being possessed and stuff. That kinda weirded me out, because I have a ouija board, and that's how the girl got possessed, it was through using the ouija board by herself. And I was like, 'Okay, put *that* away under my bed and never use it again!'

Recognising that such things as aliens and ghosts are outside of the realm of the beliefs associated with the historic institutions of religion, Elizabeth would go so far as to say that these phenomena *probably* do not exist. But she thought she'd get rid of the ouija board, just in case. Elizabeth voiced an expectation that an alignment would exist between religious institutions and certain 'legitimate' beliefs represented in the media, yet her comments also demonstrated that such representations in fictional media (such as exorcisms) are at least vaguely recognised as in some way related to 'legitimate' religion. This seemed to throw open the possibility, for Elizabeth, that the phenomena outside legitimate religion might possibly be true, but probably were not. Maintaining a boundary between legitimate religious beliefs and those depicted in fiction, therefore, seemed more difficult than at first might be expected.

The mystical teens: religion informs teen culture experience

The practice of visiting dark, deserted and isolated areas to tell scary stories and to sometimes engage in illicit activities has been a part of youth culture for a long time. Nancy Donahue, a Euro-American young woman from an underprivileged background, talked of her experiences with these practices. Nancy had been raised in a nondenominational evangelical church with which she was still affiliated, although she had rarely attended since her pre-teen years. She said she never talked about religion with anyone, in fact, despite her mother's interest in a church with some similarities to Scientology. She scoffed when I asked her about religious institutions, noting that her aunt had become an evangelical and that had turned her off to organised religion. Yet her experiences in teen culture were not limited to ghosts, demons, and spirits, as she noted:

Nancy: I've seen an angel.
Interviewer: You've seen an angel? What was that like?
Nancy: Down by Deer Valley, at the creek. Oh my God, she was BEAU-TIFUL.
Interviewer: Did she say something to you?
Nancy: She was too far away to say anything.
Interviewer: Wow. How could you tell she was an angel?
Nancy: Well, cause, we were sitting there, and I don't know, Casey was saying something about there were demons there, you know. I could feel an evil presence. And I turned around and looked, and I just stood there and stared. (Laughs.) I had no breath!

Interviewer: So, have you seen demons, too?

Nancy: Uh-unh. Never. I've felt an evil presence, though ... I got that weird feeling when we were at the park one night, that really weird feeling. Seen a kid's shoe, like way up in a tree. But I felt like, 'let's go. I don't feel right here, let's go.' [...]

Interviewer: Is that something your friends talk about, I mean, obviously when you were down at the creek, you did.

Nancy: I did with Casey, he was my boyfriend at the time, one of my ex-boyfriends. And Naomi. Naomi turned around and saw a totally different one, I guess. Casey told me it was probably my guardian angel. Cause he's hard-core Christian.

Interviewer: Oh. So, he wouldn't've seen the demons, then? He'd see the angels instead?

Nancy: He didn't see 'em (the angels). But he knew they were there.

Interviewer: Wow. What were you all doing before that?

Nancy: (long pause) We were at the Pancake House.

There's no telling what was happening just before Nancy and her friends arrived at the creekside, but based on similar legend trips that center on encountering fear, we could guess that Nancy's hesitation might suggest drinking, drugs or some rebellious activity. What is interesting here is that Nancy, a young person with few positive experiences with traditional religion, found her fears dispelled with the appearance of a being that her 'hard-core Christian' friend interpreted as a guardian angel. Nancy drew upon a religious category, that of a guardian angel, to explain and provide comfort in the context of the 'secular' experience of a legend trip. When asked in a survey form whether or not she believed in angels, Nancy would have probably responded that she did. Given the beliefs she expressed, she might even identify herself as a Christian, although clearly she harbored many hesitations about the institutions of religion. Nancy's case demonstrates the difficulties in equating religious identity with that of religious institutions, while also highlighting the appeal of certain representations of the supernatural that are deemed legitimate in mediated culture and elsewhere.

While Nancy's story illustrates the importance of the interpretation of personal experience in the context of peers with regard to beliefs about the supernatural, we found that her story and those of others like her also have connections to the mass-mediated realm. The media may not be the first place these young women learned about the supernatural, nor is it the only place in which their views are reinforced. Yet it shouldn't be surprising that they enjoyed movies, television programs and video games that invoked fear or provided 'facts' about supernatural experiences – most teens do, after all. Such 'facts' are not limited to the documentaries or news reports on such phenomena, but often surface in popular programs of prime time or as plots or subplots in blockbuster movies, as we will see in the next cases.

The experimenters: appreciating both legitimate and delegitimated religion

The next teens I highlight, as interviewed and analysed by Alters,[19] are interesting for their stated identifications which are at some distance from Christianity, yet in somewhat surprising ways draw upon media representations of the supernatural in their identity-construction. Annae and Katie Gardner were two sisters who at fourteen and twelve were Euro-American middle class members of a family of committed and articulate Wiccans, a religious system increasingly seen as legitimate, yet whose adherents still comprise a small and often marginalised group.[20] In the family's interview, the young women and their parents expressed frustration that their religion was so frequently represented as folklore, such as in the popular teen film about witchcraft, *The Craft*. Their criticism that such films portray 'witches' as commanding evil powers and casting spells (rather than portraying the Wiccan respect for the free will of others and not willfully committing evil, the preferred definitions offered by their parents) suggested the wish for clearer boundaries between religion and the fictional representations of legend in popular culture. At the time of the group interview, the girls explained that they liked the film *The Craft* primarily for the fashion and glamour of its central teen characters. In her individual interview, however, Katie revealed that she saw more commonalities than differences regarding her Wiccan identity and practices and those she saw in the popular film:

> Interviewer: Last time, we were talking about *The Craft*. You and Annae really liked it, and your mom was saying, 'it's not real.' What do you like about *the Craft*?
> Katie: I just like the fact that some of it is actually real. They took some stuff that actually you can do.
> Interviewer: What's an example?
> Katie: In *The Craft*, they change their appearance, like hair color or eye color. When my friends were over, we were down in the basement and ... we got Becky's hair to be about this long [chest-length] and black ... Pretty much what happened is, while we were watching *The Craft*, we wrote down stuff which we might want to try later. And then we did.
> Interviewer: And it actually worked. Did you tell your mom?
> Katie: No, because we didn't know whether she would approve or be mad at us for trying that stuff.

Based on previous conversations with Katie's mother, it was clear that she would not be pleased that Katie embraced more of the practices she saw in

---

[19] D. Alters, 'Identity and meaning: The project of self-reflexivity in a family', Paper presented to the annual meeting of the Society for the Scientific Study of Religion, Montreal, Quebec (November 1998).

[20] Interview with the Gardner family, conducted by Diane Alters on 26 September and 10 October 1997 as a part of the Symbolism, Media and the Lifecourse Project.

the popular movie than those she witnessed in her parents' group. Katie's older sister Annae, too, bent the family's religious tradition, although in her case it was to draw connections between Wicca, *The Craft*, and the long-standing popular teen practices of the ouija board. Annae, being a Wiccan, seemed to be consulted as an 'expert' on these rituals by her friends:

> Interviewer: Do you see the stuff you've learned in Wicca in *The Craft*, or are those two separate things?
> Annae: Yeah. Like when they call the quarters [although, as she notes, in the movie they get the phrase wrong and instead 'cull the corners']. And a lot of the ritual stuff they do is the same . . . like burning incense, putting up a circle, lots of other stuff. It's pretty interesting.
> Interviewer: And you've done that too, in your ritual?
> Annae: Uh-huh. I do it whenever I'm with my friends, and do like the ouija board, we always put up a circle, like smudge the room and everything.
> Interviewer: Why do you do that?
> Annae: Because sometimes the ouija board attracts negative energy. And it can get spirits like to tell you whatever you want to hear, or they'll tell you stuff just to hurt you.

Katie and Annae's parents struggled to assert their religious identity as distinct from that which they see in teen media culture. Yet in this case, as their religion itself has often been represented as folklore and has been delegitimated historically, such distinctions are even more difficult to maintain. In fact, the alignment of the teens with the identity ascribed to them by their peers – that of Others, experts in the 'dark arts' of the ouija board – serves as an obviously appealing aspect of Wiccan identity-construction for the Gardner teens.

The resisters: loving the supernatural and hating organised religion

Finally, there were teens who, rather than at least nominally voicing respect for certain institutions of organised religion, verbally thumbed their noses at what they took to be the collusion between organised religion and its relation to legitimate, middle- and upper-middle class culture. In some cases, this took the form of challenging the beliefs deemed 'acceptable' by voicing an identification with those that were delegitimated, as Jodie, the teen in the introduction, had done by alluding to a connection between God and alien life. Eric Day, a Euro-American teen from an underprivileged background who was a friend of Jodie's, was equally explicit in drawing connections between his beliefs and his media preferences. Eric described his mother as 'orthodox Christian' and his father as nonpractising, and noted that he had not attended church regularly since his pre-teen years. His favorite television programs and films echoed his interests in views that he seemed to see as challenging to the status quo. On the one hand, he expressed great scepticism about organised religion and what it had to say about the supernatural realm in particular, yet on the other, he was very interested in considering the possibilities of what might be out there in the realm beyond:

> Eric: People go with this, 'I ain't gonna believe it unless I see it'. I'm sorry, but I'm not gonna believe it unless I see it, touch it, and taste it.
> Interviewer: Okay, so when you see stuff in television or in the movies that's about angels or ghosts, or the devil, do you sometimes feel like what they're portraying in television is authentic?
> Eric: It depends ... anything that's really fake like the *Nightmare on Elm Street* movies, or these dreams about the psychos who blow their head off and then the next year they're back, I don't believe it. No, it's fake. But there were a few – Stephen King, H.P. Lovecraft. The reason I like them so much is because things they write about could actually happen.
> Interviewer: Could, or do you think they did?
> Eric: There's a possibility, I mean, it's possible. Theologically, scientifically, and everything else, it's possible.

Eric later echoed Jodie's comment that it might be interesting to think of God as an extraterrestrial, but also, like Jodie, he noted that certain tenets normally associated with Judeo-Christian beliefs, such as angels, hell, and the afterlife, were also possible. Yet Eric also evaluated his own experiences as a 'hell' that he felt traditional religion had not addressed, making an alternate explanation all the more attractive.

Conclusion

This chapter has examined the role of the media in religious identity-construction among US teens. I have identified five different ways in which teens either affirm or blur the supposed boundaries between the beliefs about the realm beyond and religion and similar beliefs popularised in the media. The teens divided into Traditionalists who were highly committed to their religious traditions and interested in separating religion and media, Intrigued teens who wished to affirm such a separation but were still drawn to supernatural experiences and events outside of their traditions, Mystical teens who had marginal ties to traditional religion but a great deal of interest in the supernatural realm, Experimenters who actively sought resources on the supernatural realm from the media, and Resisters who challenged organised religion while embracing unorthodox views of the supernatural realm.

My study results in three findings that suggest further research. First, in its discussion of unorthodox beliefs and experiences among self-identified religious teens, the study has demonstrated that religious identity and religious beliefs cannot be assumed to be directly related to one's religious affiliation or lack thereof. I have demonstrated that there is, in fact, more than one type of religious identity. This, I hope, may encourage scholars in cultural studies to explore the multifaceted and pluralistic nature of religion in US society today, particularly as it extends beyond the Traditionalist variation that is the most frequent subject for analysis and critique.

On a related note, this study relates to the discussions in the sociology of religion that explore the topic and definition of secularisation. The study demonstrates that ideological reasons for self-identifying as 'religious' or 'spiritual' may be quite important, and they thus complicate the study of secularisation. While an increasing number of young people seem to be only marginally related to organised religion, we must question whether or not supernatural experiences, and the generalised New Age spirituality that is at some distance from organised religion, are both distinct from either definitions of religion or of secularism, regardless of how young people self-identify with religion. Much work remains to be done on supernatural beliefs and their relationship with more 'official' beliefs advocated by religious organisations.

Second, this study relates teens' interests in the supernatural realm to their perceived position of powerlessness relative to the larger society. While this position may change as teens mature, the approach taken to religion and the supernatural in the teen years may prove to influence the shape of religious beliefs in generations to come. Future research is needed to explore both the issue of the generalisability of the five patterns outlined here, and the question of religious change over time.

Third, from this study it is possible to infer that the media, as an element of culture, echo cultural ideologies about religion, specifically the equation of religion with morality. Within this ideological framework, the media may also serve as a resource for teens who wish to experiment with various forms of supernatural or spiritual practices. Or, the media may serve simply as an unacknowledged background that unconsciously frames understandings and identity narratives, such as in the case of teens with more marginal interests or relationships to religion. Thus, the media, in their ability to frame and reinforce ideas about religion as moral, mystical, powerful and a source of critique of the wider culture, give definition to the ways in which contemporary US teens construct identities of themselves as 'religious'.

4

Desperately Seeking Credibility: English Catholics, the News Media and the Church

Jim McDonnell

Introduction

Since the late 1970s there has been a decline of trust in and a questioning of the credibility of social institutions generally. This decline is partly attributable to a growing generalised awareness of the weaknesses of hitherto sacrosanct bodies. In Britain, the Monarchy, Parliament and the Established Church have all obviously suffered from this growth in public scepticism. Indeed, one of the major reasons for the defeat of the Conservative government in 1997 was the so-called 'sleaze' factor, the perception that too many politicians were guilty of sexual peccadillos and financial improprieties. Institutions and their representatives now find themselves living in the 'x-ray environment' created by the modern news media, an environment in which they are constantly subject to intense and often hostile scrutiny.

Under such a persistent media gaze institutions have had to face up to the fact that they can no longer take their authority or credibility for granted. For an institution like the Catholic Church this realisation has come slowly and been particularly hard to bear. As Andreas Schedler has written:

> Credibility represents a key component of any institutional arrangement worth its name. Our everyday language contains a whole array of distinctions that express the difference between credible and noncredible institutions. Most of them follow the theatrical, or should we say, Platonian imagery of reality versus façade. They contrapose real, substantive, and effective institutions against hollow, apparent, formal, fictitious ones, in essence, genuine institutions against shadow institutions, institutional caricatures, empty shells.[1]

The gap between appearance and reality is, of course, the crack which the news media are constantly striving to widen so that they might expose the

---

[1] Andreas Schedler, 'Credibility: Exploring the Bases of Institutional Reform in New Democracies'. Paper prepared for presentation at the XIXth International Congress of the Latin American Studies Association (LASA), Washington, DC, 28–30 September 1995.

internal conflicts behind the façade of unity or the failings and misdemeanours of an institution's representatives.

Institutions like the Catholic Church which claim moral and spiritual authority and the right to offer guidance not only to individuals but to society generally are particularly vulnerable in such an environment. The mass media are irresistibly drawn to look for its flaws and failings. For the Church it is crucially important that the gap between the ideal and the actual, the appearance and reality, should be as narrow as possible. Credibility is easily lost and hardly won.

Over the past two decades the Church has had to endure increasing revelations of just how far some of its representatives have fallen from grace. The emergence into the public eye of the whole sad topic of child sexual abuse has been particularly difficult for the Church. Even though most child abuse takes place within families, it has been the exposure of child abuse by clergy that has often captured the news headlines and which has seemed especially shocking. In modern society the most damaging allegation that can be made about an institution or its representatives is that it connived at and covered up sexual abuse.

One can assume that media coverage of scandals involving child abuse or the sexual misdemeanours of clergy has had a deleterious effect on the credibility of the Church in general. However, until 1998 no research had been done in Britain to examine the extent of this assumed effect or to find out what differences there might be between Catholics and non-Catholics in their perceptions of the Church. Moreover, no effort had been made to investigate if there was any difference between the ways Catholics and non-Catholics might be affected by media coverage of the Church. Indeed almost no research had been done into how Catholics actually obtained information on religious matters and Church affairs and the role of the media in this process. In 1997, therefore, the Catholic Communications Centre on behalf of the Catholic Media Trust commissioned two research projects: the first, a large scale quantitative and qualitative study by NOP, a British polling organisation, that profiled the Catholic population of England and Wales and investigated how Catholics obtained secular and religious information and the relative importance of different information sources,[2] and the second, a smaller scale qualitative study that examined perceptions of the Catholic Church in England by Catholics and non-Catholics, conducted by J. M. Cross.[3]

---

[2] NOP Research Group, *Catholics and Their Use of Information Sources* (London: NOP Research Group, 1998). NOP conducted an omnibus survey of 4,965 people in England and Wales in November 1997, nine focus groups in January and February 1998 and 400 telephone interviews with practising Catholics (weekly or monthly Mass attendance) in February 1998.

[3] James M. Cross, *Perceptions of the Catholic Church in England and Wales: Qualitative Research Report* (1998). Cross conducted in-depth interviews with ten Catholics and ten non-Catholics and five Catholic and five non-Catholic focus groups.

Perceptions of the Catholic Church

As might be expected, both studies confirmed the importance of personal experience in shaping people's perceptions of the Catholic Church as an institution. The Catholics drew upon their experiences of being brought up as Catholics and participating in Church life; the non-Catholics referred to their experience of Catholic friends and acquaintances and in many cases to more direct personal involvement with Catholic schools.[4]

The NOP study found that the image of the Church held by Catholics was a complex one. Younger Catholics (sixteen- to twenty-five-year-olds) were inclined to hold more negative images ('old fashioned', 'restrictive', 'sexist', 'hypocritical', 'dictatorial') and to stress the Church's power and wealth, while older age groups were more inclined to balance the good and bad ('faith', 'comforting', 'solid', 'world-wide', 'well established', 'traditional' but also 'changing', 'in turmoil', 'irritating', 'authoritarian' and 'patriarchal'). Those images which Catholics held of the Church were, as J. M. Cross discovered, often quite close to those held by non-Catholics.

Cross found that non-Catholic awareness of the Catholic Church as an institution was vague. Non-Catholics were often not very clear about the distinctions between different churches but they had quite definite views about Catholics as individuals. There was a perception that Catholic faith can be a valuable *personal* spiritual resource and a genuine respect for the religious commitment of individual Catholics. The highly laudatory media coverage of the death and funeral of both Cardinal Hume, and later, of Cardinal Winning in Scotland are good illustrations of this point.

On the other hand, in the Cross study, there was a prevalent assumption that Catholics are characterised by sheep-like obedience and passivity, especially in the realm of sexual morality: 'If you're a Catholic you have to believe that abortion is a bad thing, you can't look at both sides and decide whether you're for or against contraception or abortion or whatever it is. Therefore if you are a Catholic you have to be against abortion. It stops you from thinking'.[5]

As far as many people are concerned this obedience is reinforced by guilt: 'In Catholicism the emphasis on suffering and guilt is totally alien to me . . . Anglicanism and Catholicism are different on the question of suffering and guilt. The Church of England has no real concept of suffering and guilt'.[6]

---

[4] 'Experience of Catholic schools extended well beyond those who were, or who had been, Catholics. A number of those we spoke to had attended Catholic schools because their parents had judged that these were good schools in a very general sense, not because they or their parents had any intention of converting. Further, the experience of Catholic schooling proved to be, almost without exception, a positive one. Evidence of considerable good-will toward the schools, as caring and capable organisations, suggests that they are effective ambassadors for the Church itself: those they educate are not only more aware of the Church, but are more disposed to think well of it.' Cross, *Perceptions* pp. 16–17.

[5] See James M. Cross, *Perceptions*, p. 25.

[6] Cross, *Perceptions* p. 26.

In addition, even when the Catholic Church is seen as attractive there is a sense that there is an underlying hypocrisy. As one non-Catholic expressed it:

> The Catholic Church as an idea I think is very beautiful and I think it gives you a lot of food for your imagination and there's a lot of literature and art and everything. Also the spiritual side of it is very enriching. But as an organisation and as a group of people, I think they're very moral about what other people do, whereas there is the feeling with Catholicism that whatever I do wrong I can just go to Church, say sorry, and it's alright and I don't have to feel guilty about it. So they are very very good at making you feel guilty because they can come from a very very high moral standpoint but not actually necessarily live by that themselves.[7]

The role of the media

This view of Catholics as controlled by guilt, focussed on matters of sexual morality and more or less hypocritical is strongly linked to the way Catholic issues tend to be covered in the news media. For both Catholics and non-Catholics the media played an important secondary role in reinforcing existing perceptions and in highlighting perceived inconsistencies between Church teaching and practice. One non-Catholic put it this way: 'I think that most of the things which I associate with the Catholic Church, for example, the fact that it is strongly anti-abortion, are to do with the media. Nobody goes out and writes a story on the good aspects of the Catholic Church, but you often get articles on abortion or contraception in which the Catholic Church's position on the matter is brought into it. This doesn't portray it in a very good light.'[8]

One thoughtful respondent in the NOP study put his finger on the tendency of the news media to identify specifically 'Catholic' stories: 'There are a greater number of column inches given to the Church of England because it is the Established Church, and therefore if there is a voice required on a moral issue then it tends to be that. The issues for the journalists who ask for a Catholic opinion would be on abortion, married priests, divorce, ... the ones that are seen as classic Catholic issues.'

On the whole, most practising Catholics are remarkably sanguine about media coverage of the Church.[9] Some 44 per cent of them believe that the Catholic Church is treated quite fairly, and 3 per cent 'very fairly' by the media.[10] On the other side, however, 24 per cent believe that it is treated

---

[7] Cross, *Perceptions* pp. 40–41.

[8] Cross, *Perceptions* p. 18.

[9] Nine group discussions were conducted with sixty-eight Catholics from a mix of social classes, ages and patterns of church attendance from different parts of England and Wales.

[10] Practising Catholics are defined as those who regularly attend Mass weekly or at least once a month.

TABLE 1:   **Main reasons for churches being treated unfairly**

	Catholic Church %	**Church of England** %
Media does not publicise positive aspects/ only publicise negatives/ scandal	29	24
Sensationalism/exaggeration	19	10
Misrepresentation/ criticise without knowledge/ not treated seriously	17	26
Anti-Catholic/ anti Church of England	11	9
Not enough media coverage	6	0
Stereotyped image of people/Church	4	4

'quite unfairly' and 8 per cent 'very unfairly'. As Hoover points out, there is a general sentiment that 'religious people and groups are misunderstood by the press and that they themselves have reason to feel that they have been particularly misunderstood by some coverage ... There was also the common sentiment that *other* groups are sometimes *advantaged* when they are not'.[11]

Catholics think that the Church of England gets a better press: 49 per cent regard it as being treated 'quite fairly', and 9 per cent 'very fairly'. Only 15 per cent think it is treated unfairly (13 per cent quite, 2 per cent very). When asked why the churches might be treated unfairly the reasons given were not dissimilar for the two bodies.

Interestingly the Catholics felt that the press was more likely to sensationalise Catholic stories and more prone not to take the Church of England seriously. Typical comments from Catholics were: 'It's [the Church] seen as very high and mighty and strict, with quite a lot of tradition.' 'They only highlight the bad incidents and negative publicity.' 'They don't give it a lot of publicity one way or the other unless there is a scandal.'

The media and scandal

Though Catholics expressed considerable annoyance at the narrowing down of media coverage to a few 'classic Catholic issues', when they were asked to recall specifically 'Catholic' stories in the media they spontaneously highlighted various 'scandal stories'. The single biggest category, cited by 43 per cent of practising Catholics, was 'priests abusing children'.

---

[11] Stewart M. Hoover, *Religion in the News* (Thousand Oaks, CA, London: Sage, 1998), p. 103.

Other more specific responses recalled the then recent (February 1998) case of a priest in Wales convicted of child abuse (2 per cent), and the story of the disgraced Scottish Bishop Roderick Wright (7 per cent) which had taken place in September 1996.[12] A variety of more positive news stories about the Pope's visit to Cuba (12 per cent), Cardinal Hume (7 per cent) and Mother Theresa's death and funeral (4 per cent) were also mentioned. Just 3 per cent of the sample mentioned abortion issues.

Initially Catholics were inclined to give little credibility to the media as a source of news about Church matters, but further discussions made it clear that television and newspapers played the major role in conveying information and that their coverage was generally believed. Even though both groups had a clear sense of the media's tendency to focus on bad news stories, this awareness did not lead the Catholics to dismiss such stories as necessarily unreliable. Virtually all respondents in the NOP groups, for example, were aware of the Bishop Wright story, though there was less detailed knowledge among the younger members. The aspects of the story which had stuck in people's minds were his disappearance, the emergence of his teenage child (some thought there were more children), the involvement of (at least) two women and his move to the Lake District to live. This information came from television, newspapers and radio as well as Church publications. Respondents specifically mentioned television chat shows and newspaper feature articles as well as news bulletins as sources of information.

For some Catholics the Wright story aroused compassion: 'It reminds you that priests are human, that they can fail in the same way as the rest of us. They shouldn't be put on a pedestal.' Other Catholics were angry and appalled by what Bishop Wright had done: 'I was ashamed. I felt that he had let our Church down. Later there was talk of him coming back into the area to be reconciled as a priest, and that gave more scandal to me, and I was absolutely appalled.'

That reaction, with its concern that the Church has been 'let down', finds an echo in the comment of an American Catholic who thought that press coverage of scandals might undermine the institutional authority of the Church: 'I think of all the dirty laundry on the lawn, the scandal and the horrible things . . . I think they have taken away some of the security of people's lives, the reverence for the church, the respect for religious people. I feel sometimes they have a tendency to identify [that] this is what is happening to all religions and they don't highlight enough those who have been extraordinarily good and have been models of greatness in their lives.'[13]

Younger Catholics, however, were more inclined to focus on the credibility issue, perceiving scandals in terms of the hypocrisy of the clergy: 'The

---

[12] Roderick Wright, Bishop of Argyll and the Isles, disappeared with his lover and announced that he would marry her. A few days later his former lover and her son appeared on television to denounce his actions. Bishop Wright then sold his story to the *News of the World*. The story was national headline news for two weeks in September 1996.

[13] Hoover, *Religion* p. 102.

more you hear about Catholic priests having affairs with women or young boys, you think, they are telling us to live such a righteous life. They are being hypocrites, aren't they?'

The charge of hypocrisy may be especially significant for many younger people because they are also the group which often feels most at odds with Church teachings. As Cross puts it, 'The Church's teachings on abortion and contraception are particularly salient for people in their late teens and early twenties, whether Catholic or not. Media coverage of these topics is picked up on and discussed. What seems to be communicated by such coverage is a sense of prescriptive authoritarianism, backed up by guilt.'[14] This presentation of Catholic views may well be reinforced by the tendency of the news media to contrast the perceived certainties of the Catholic Church with the perceived liberalism of the Church of England.

Young people who are practising Catholics may also feel that it is difficult enough holding unfashionable views without having to contend with charges that the Church is not only out-of-touch but also hypocritical. One girl explained that when she told people she was a Catholic they assumed that she could not even have a boyfriend!

These events have forced even the most complacent of Church leaders to recognise that allegations of abuse and 'cover up' have reinforced the widespread notion that the Church is deeply hypocritical. At the least, such allegations have been demoralising among the Church's own members and tended to undermine their confidence in their leaders. As one young Catholic commented: 'I would give them [priests] very little credibility. They give us double standards. They have got an angle on everything. I don't trust them.'

Even if this is not a majority view, such comments serve to underline the extent to which the Catholic Church, like other institutions, has to come to terms with the degree to which scandals:

> are contexts for significant, if sometimes imperfect, moral reflection. They 'work to shift and reform the common sense of what is permissive and what is transgressive in societies'. They cause vigorous debate about an issue and speculation about moral right and wrong. Scandals encourage speculation and moral thinking perhaps not in an ideal way but in a nonetheless useful way. Shifts in public opinion and the dominant moral code occur because of such thinking.[15]

From the point of view of the credibility of Church teaching, this process of 'moral reflection' has called into question the requirement that priests be celibate. No matter how illogical or unfair it might be, there is no doubt that there is a firm link in the public mind between the celibacy rule and sexual misconduct by the clergy. This link is promoted and reinforced by

[14] Cross, *Perceptions* pp, 18–19.
[15] John Dardis, 'Speaking of Scandal', *Studies: An Irish Quarterly Review* 89 (2000), p. 313.

media coverage that seeks to give some straightforward explanation as to why those who are supposed to be guardians of morality have acted so badly. The one explanation that seems to have become accepted by Catholics and non-Catholics alike is that celibacy is an unnatural condition and requiring celibacy is bound to create problems. As respondents in the NOP study put it: 'The Catholics I have met as a result of those stories all come back to the same solution: that priests should be married.' 'Maybe they should let a priest get married . . . if this is going on then why not make it public and change the rules and say that priests can get married and have children?'

Thus because of its rule on priestly celibacy the Catholic Church finds itself attracting more institutional blame for the personal misdeeds of the clergy than might otherwise be the case. Non-Catholics in the Cross study seemed inclined to see scandals involving the clergy as *individual* rather than *institutional* failings and thus are not inclined to be unduly shocked by them. However, in the public mind the rule of celibacy is seen as an unreasonable expectation on priests, and therefore the Church must share some of the responsibility for their lapses:

> It is an individual thing but it is brought about by stupid rules. It's not natural for priests not to be married, but the Church won't let them. To lead a celibate life – I don't think they can do it. Why are they being put into that situation? Because of a stupid rule.

This attitude is the one that most closely mirrors that expressed in the media. The broadcast and press coverage of the Bishop Wright affair, for example, carried numerous stories which assumed that celibacy was outdated and the Church's position absurd. Within three days the focus of the national press headlines was celibacy. As the story ran on and became more complicated other issues were taken up, but the underlying hostility to the Church's position on celibacy did not change. Only one or two articles tried to put the question of celibacy into perspective.

Unfortunately since then a number of major stories involving allegations of child sexual abuse and the Church's failure to take the appropriate actions in such situations have made the problem of credibility even harder. The Archdiocese of Cardiff has found itself particularly exposed to public and media scrutiny. Its former Communications Officer was convicted of abuse and eventually given a prison sentence; the Archbishop himself was arrested and accused of assaulting a girl when he was a priest (though this accusation was dropped when no supporting evidence could be produced); and a recently ordained priest (who, while a student for the priesthood, had persuaded the Archbishop to accept his transfer from another diocese) was convicted of abuse and imprisoned. Moreover, the prevalence of such incidents eventually led to the making of an investigative television documentary by BBC Wales which was aired on national television and which effectively accused the Archbishop of being incompetent, uncaring and unfit to govern the diocese. And these events unfolded against a further series of accusations that the new Archbishop of Westminster had failed to act properly in the case of a convicted child abuser some years before. In the end, Archbishop Ward of Cardiff resigned in ill-health in November 2001 still asserting that he had acted at all times in good faith and claiming that he had been treated unfairly by the media. The difficulties have been exacerbated by general public hysteria about the prevalence of child abuse and by the tendency of the media to use pictures of priests convicted of abuse as symbols of a wider malaise.

In his article on media coverage of scandals in Ireland, Michael Breen comments:

> One notable feature of media coverage of these scandals has been the use of Brendan Smyth as a symbol for the demise of Irish Catholicism. Smyth was initially jailed in 1994 in Northern Ireland for abuse and subsequently in the Republic of Ireland on similar charges. He died in prison. One now infamous photograph is used with great frequency ... It was taken on the occasion of a court hearing, with Smyth allegedly reacting angrily to the taunts of a photographer ... [I]t has become the most frequently used icon of abuse in the Irish Church. In July 2000, the *Evening Herald* used this photo, superimposed over a playground full of toys, in a general article dealing with paedophilia in Ireland.[16]

In Britain, a similar fate has befallen the convicted abuser John Lloyd, formerly the Communications Officer of the Cardiff Archdiocese. His photograph is frequently re-used when allegations of abuse are made about others or the topic of sexual abuse is discussed. Moreover, the growing popularity of the Internet and the emergence of news sites such as that run by the BBC means that his case is continually being recalled. A news story on the Internet is inevitably accompanied by links to past similar stories and incidents.

The scale of criticism of the Church about these matters in 2000 eventually led the Archbishop of Westminster to set up an independent inquiry under Lord Nolan, a senior judge, into how the Church's own guidelines on dealing with allegations of abuse were being implemented. That inquiry was due to make an interim report at Easter 2001 and published its final report in September. The Church moved swiftly to accept the report's findings and committed itself to implementing all its recommendations, including the establishment of a national office for child protection.

The Nolan inquiry marked a significant step forward for the Church. It was, at least implicitly, recognition that it had to take concrete and public action to begin to earn credibility from the media and the general public (including many of its own members). Accepting this is perhaps the most

---

[16] Michael Breen, 'The Good, the Bad and the Ugly: The Media and the Scandals', *Studies: An Irish Quarterly Review* 89 (2000), p. 335.

difficult culture shift facing the Church. The Catholic Church has for so long taken for granted its right to spiritual and moral authority that it is extremely difficult for it to adjust to a milieu in which that right is constantly being questioned.

The Bishop Wright story as well as subsequent scandals forced the Catholic Church in England and Wales to take more seriously the way in which it presents itself in the media arena. There is within the Church leadership a much greater appreciation that good public relations and proper crisis management are not black arts reserved for politicians and commercial companies. On the whole, the Church's past tendency to deal with difficult stories by concealment and silence has largely been abandoned. Church leaders have publicly apologised for the damage and hurt caused by poor or insensitive handling of past allegations.

However, the adjustment to a new way of thinking that recognises in media scandals an opportunity to improve the Church's credibility as well as a moment of danger, is still in its infancy. For that change to take place the Church will have to accept fully the extent to which its actions and beliefs are inevitably subject to media interest and scrutiny. It will have to accept that it cannot, and indeed must not, be absent from the public discourse of the media even when that discourse is experienced as threatening and hostile.[17] Above all, it will have to ensure that its actions, particularly at moments of crisis, are as congruent as possible with its aspirations and beliefs.

How that engagement with the public discourse might occur is suggested by the career of the late Cardinal Hume. His enormous public credibility was due to the fact that he was able to speak authoritatively without seeming authoritarian, that he was transparently honest and sincere and a man of real holiness. His personal communication style was highly appropriate to the age of television, but no one accused him of being a mere media performer. He survived the media spotlight because he was perceived to embody the values he professed. So the Church as an institution has to recognise and accept that its credibility will have to be won and re-won in the media every day and among the public. It has to bear in mind that it is most credible, both to its own adherents and to a wider public, when it is truly able to give its message 'not only in words but in the whole manner of its life'.[18]

---

[17] Dardis, 'Speaking of Scandal', p. 316.
[18] Pope Paul VI, *Communio et Progressio: The Pastoral Instruction ... on the Means of Social Communication, No. 11* (London: Catholic Truth Society, 1971).

Further Reading

C. Arthur (ed.), *Religion and the Media* (Cardiff: University of Wales Press, 1993).

J. Fulton, et al., *Young Catholics at the New Millennium* (Dublin: University College Dublin Press, 2000).

S. M. Hoover, *Religion in the News* (Thousand Oaks, CA, London: Sage, 1998).

'Scandals in the Church: The Irish Response', *Studies: An Irish Quarterly Review* 89 (2000).

P. A. Soukup, 'Church Media and Scandal' in James Lull and Stephen Hinerman, (eds.), *Media Scandals* (Cambridge, England: Polity Press, 1997).

D. A. Stout and J. M. Buddenbaum. *Religion and Mass Media: Audiences and Adaptations* (Thousand Oaks, CA., London: Sage, 1996).

PART 2

Conflict, Media and Religion

5

Managing or Manipulating Religious Conflict in the Nigerian Media

Rosalind I. J. Hackett

Islam continues to make inroads even though Jihad is no longer waged by sword. It doesn't have to. Those agents of the devil compound people's misery by using electronic and print media to heap insults on Christians.[1]

Most Muslims believe that unjustified attacks on Islam are not restricted to the Nigerian press alone. The ignoble role of the international press ably controlled by western imperialists, who are all out to silence Islam, cannot be ignored.[2]

In the course of writing a book on religious conflict in Nigeria (*Nigeria: Religion in the Balance*, Washington, DC: US Institute of Peace, forthcoming) I have become interested in the various sites where intolerance is generated or suppressed.[3] Educational institutions have long been one of the principal sites for defending religious identity and contesting religious rights in black Africa's most populous state.[4] Officially, Nigeria is a secular state with

---

[1] Jolly Tanko Yusuf, *That We May Be One: the Autobiography of Ambassador Jolly Tanko Yusuf* (Grand Rapids, MI, 1995), p. 108.

[2] Lakin Akintola, 'Who is a Fanatic?', *Al-Madinah* (September 1995), pp. 10–18.

[3] A version of this paper was presented at the Society for the Scientific Study of Religion Annual Meeting, Boston (7 November 1999).

[4] Nigeria, known to many as the 'giant of Africa', has a population of over 110 million. (In fact, one in six Africans is a Nigerian.) It is a multi-religious state, with fairly equally balanced proportions of Muslims and Christians (it is often said that the former may be slightly larger), with a small minority still adhering to localised, indigenous forms of religious practice, claiming no religious affiliation, or belonging to one of the Eastern-related or spiritual science religious organisations which have become part of the religious landscape in the last few decades. (See, for example, Rosalind I. J. Hackett, *Religion in Calabar: the Religious Life and History of a Nigerian Town* [The Hague and New York: Mouton de Gruyter, 1989].) Statistics on the breakdown of religious groups are unavailable, unreliable or out of date, and hence highly contested. Religious affiliation was excluded from the last census in 1991 for fear of political manipulation. Some earlier statistics are available (Toyin Falola, *Violence in Nigeria: The Crisis of Religious Politics and Secular Ideologies* [Rochester, NY: University of Rochester Press, 1998], Appendix, pp. 305–16). Basing his statistics on the 1963 census in which the Christian population was enumerated at 19.1 million (34.5%) out of 56.6 million, and the Muslims at about 40%, Matthews Ojo estimates the present Christian population to have grown to around 52 million – in part because of significant evangelism in the North. Personal communication, London, 14 July 1999.

freedom of religion guaranteed in the 1999 Constitution. There has been a
history of clashes between students, parents, teachers and government officials from missionary and colonial times up until the present day.[5] Now the
mass media constitute one of the principal locations for the propagation
and (self-)representation of religious groups. The growth of Nigeria's
media institutions and industries has paralleled the expansion and diversi-
fication of the religious landscape. There has been an attendant increase in
competition between religious groups. Apart from sporadic government
(federal and state) clampdowns on religious broadcasting at the height of
some of the riots, as well as the harassments of the press that come from the
several military governments that Nigeria has had to endure since independence in 1960,[6] Nigeria could be said to possess a virulent and diverse
media scene. It is arguably one of the most lively and developed on the
African continent.[7]

What I explore in this chapter is the role the modern media have played
in the interreligious tensions and conflict that have characterised Nigeria
since the late 1970s.[8] I examine how both the print and broadcast media
have served to initiate, exacerbate or reduce the tensions and cleavages
between the two principal religious constituencies of Muslims and
Christians. The different forms of media I am including in my purview
range from government broadcasts, radio/television news items, public
broadcast information, privately circulating video and audio cassettes, independently produced news magazines, religious publications and inspirational literature. I am not including here computer-mediated forms of
communication, as they are a recent phenomenon in Nigeria with still
limited use. However, it is worth noting the growing influence of electronic
discursive communities in diaspora.[9]

Given my lengthy experience as a researcher on and in Nigeria, I have
witnessed many of the developments described in this chapter at first hand.[10]

---

[5] Rosalind I. J. Hackett, 'Conflict in the Classroom: Educational Institutions as Sites of
Religious Tolerance/Intolerance in Nigeria', *Brigham Young University Law Review* (1999).

[6] Babatunde Olugboji, *Suppression of Press Freedom in Nigeria* (Lagos: Constitutional
Rights Project, 1997).

[7] According to Matthews, Ojo, the first newspaper was produced in Nigeria in 1859.
There are now twelve national dailies, six news weeklies, three regular weekly tabloids and
about five evening papers all publishing in English. (See, Matthews Ojo, 'Religious Reportage
in the Contemporary Nigerian Press', Paper read at Religion and Media in Nigeria, at SOAS,
London [1999].) For the origins of Nigerian journalism in religious (Christian) publications,
see R. Akinfeleye, 'Religious Publications: Pioneers of Nigeria Journalism', Onuora E. Nwuneli
(ed.), *Mass Communication in Nigeria: A Book of Reading* (Enugu: Fourth Dimension, 1985).

[8] The literature (academic, popular, and government) on the subject is vast, and therefore impossible to list here, revealing how much this is a matter of profound public concern.
The most recent and comprehensive treatment of the topic to date is Toyin Falola's *Violence
in Nigeria* (1998).

[9] Misty Bastian, 'Nationalism in a Virtual Space: Immigrant Nigerians on the Internet',
West Africa Review 1 (1), (1999).

[10] For example, in my study of the religious life and history of the town of Calabar in
south-eastern Nigeria from 1979–1983, I included a survey of religion in the print and broadcast media, as part of my discussion of popular religion (Hackett, *Religion in Calabar*, ch. 9).

But I have also been influenced by the observations of others, when, in their writings or as personal communications, they have implicated the media in the heightening of religious tensions. For example, in the words of Father Matthew Hassan Kukah, an astute and experienced analyst of, and commentator on, Nigeria's religious and political scene, 'the media has helped in fanning and sustaining the embers of bigotry'. He is here referring to the larger media institutions, but how often have I heard it said that something as small as a public address system or an offensive banner was at the root of an altercation between Christians and Muslims!

It is important, therefore, to consider not only the content of these mediated discourses in terms of religious intolerance, but also the potency of the modern media to increase the impact of a message and the scale of its reception. Furthermore, they have the capacity to construct new geographies both real and imaginative, and to (re)shape perceptions of social reality and para-social contact.[11] This is linked to the pressing question of the representation and mediation of otherness by the Nigerian media, which can receive only brief treatment in the present essay. Similarly, how might globally circulating materials be appropriated and transformed by local actors? Issues of timing and access/exclusion, as well as relations of power within, and institutional control of, the media, also bear consideration. All of this needs to be seen against an historical background of mutual fears of domination and repression among both Muslims and Christians.[12]

Conceiving of religion more generally, I support Bruce Lincoln's advocacy of the need to have a model of religion which is not based on beliefs and moral injunctions (and by functionalist association, peace and stability), but rather 'multiple components that can relate to one another in a variety of ways, including disjuncture and contradiction'.[13] He describes these components as:

> (a) a discourse that claims its concerns transcend the realm of the human, temporal, and contingent, while claiming for itself a similarly transcendent status; (b) a set of practices (ethical, ritual, and sometimes also aesthetic) informed and structured by that discourse; (c) a community organized around the discourse and its attendant practices, whose members define their identity with reference to them; and (d) an institutional system that regulates discourse, practices, and community, reproducing and modifying them over time, while still asserting their eternal validity and transcendent value.[14]

---

[11] David Morley and Kevin Robins, 'Cultural Imperialism and the Mediation of Otherness', Akbar Ahmed and Cris Shore (eds.), *The Future of Anthropology: Its Relevance to the Contemporary World* (London: Athlone, 1995); cf. John Thompson, 'The Theory of the Public Sphere: A Critical Appraisal', *The Polity Reader in Cultural Theory* (Cambridge: Polity Press, 1994).

[12] Pat Williams and Toyin Falola, *Religious Impact on the Nation State* (Aldershot, UK: Avebury, 1995).

[13] Bruce Lincoln, 'Conflict', M. Taylor (ed.), *Critical Terms for Religious Studies* (Chicago: University of Chicago Press, 1997), p. 65.

[14] Bruce Lincoln, 'Conflict', p. 65.

He further argues that whenever one of these components (and it is often that of community – entirely apposite in the Nigerian context) plays a role of 'some seriousness' within any given conflict, it should be acknowledged that the conflict has a religious dimension. The heuristic value of this model in analysing the complex interplay of religious, political, economic and ethnic factors in what gets generally labeled as 'religious conflict' in Nigeria will become apparent in the course of this paper.[15] It further tallies with the 'manipulationist' theory (i.e., manipulation of religion by selfish, unscrupulous politicians) held by many Nigerian observers.[16]

In terms of our focus on media in Nigeria's religious public sphere, it is important to emphasise at the outset that studies of religion, media and culture are rare in/on Africa. Existing media studies on Africa pay little or no attention to religion.[17] The same goes for Nigeria.[18] Scholars of religion in Africa seem to find the leap from texts and institutions to popular culture and mass mediated forms of religion too problematic. Fortunately there are

---

[15] cf. Peter B. Clarke and Ian Linden, *Islam in Modern Nigeria: A Study of a Muslim Community in a Post-Independence State 1960–1983* (Mainz: Grünewald, 1984), p. 42.

[16] cf. Sa'idu Adamu, 'The Press and Nigerian Unity', A. Mahadi (ed.), *Nigeria: the State of the Nation and the Way Forward* (Kaduna: Arewa House, 1994), p. 471; Jibrin Ibrahim, 'The Politics of Religion in Nigeria: the Parameters of the 1987 Crisis in Kaduna State', *Review of African Political Economy* 45 (6) (1989), pp. 65–82; and Usufu Bala Usman, *The Manipulation of Religion in Nigeria: 1977–1987* (Kaduna: Vanguard, 1987).

[17] L. Bourgault, *Media in Sub-Saharan Africa* (Philadelphia: University of Pennsylvania Press, 1995); D. Spitulnik, 'Anthropology and Mass Media', *Annual Review of Anthropology* 22 (1993), pp. 293–315; and G. Walsh, *The Media in Africa and Africa in the Media: An Annotated Bibliography* (London: Hans Zell, 1996). There are a few exceptions. See the work of Keyan G. Tomaselli, who directs the Graduate Programme on Cultural and Media Studies at the University of Natal, Durban: Keyan Tomaselli, *Appropriating Images: The Semiotics of Visual Representation* (Hojbjerg, Denmark: Intervention, 1996); and Keyan Tomaselli and Fr. N. Nkosi, 'Political Economy of Televangelism: Ecumenical Broadcasting vs Teleministries', *Communicare* 14 (1) (1995), pp. 65–79. He tends to write more on the political economy of (religious) broadcasting in South Africa, and on theoretical issues. Knut Lundby has done work on Zimbabwe (Knut Lundby, 'Media, Religion and Democratic Participation: Community Communication in Zimbabwe and Norway', *Media, Culture, and Society* 19 [1997], pp. 29–45); Ben Soares has written on Mali (Ben Soares, 'Muslim Proselytization as Purification: Religious Pluralism and Conflict in Contemporary Mali', A. A. An-Na'im [ed.], *Proselytization and Communal Self-Determination in Africa* [Maryknoll, NY: Orbis, 1999])' and Andrew and Harriet Lyons did some important early research on religious broadcasting in Benin City, Nigeria, and more specifically on the late Benson Idahosa's media-oriented Pentecostal ministry, the Church of God International (Andrew and Harriet Lyons, 'Magical Medicine on Television: Benin City, Nigeria', *Journal of Ritual Studies* 1 [1987]; and 'Religion and the Mass Media', J. K. Olupona and Toyin Falola [eds.], *Religion and Society in Nigeria: Historical and Sociological Perspectives* [Ibadan: Spectrum, 1991]). In preparing this paper for publication, I was happy to come across the work of Bala Musa on religious broadcasting policy and praxis in Nigeria (Bala Musa, 'Pluralism and Prior Restraint on Religious Communication in Nigeria: Policy versus Praxis', J. Thierstein and Y. R. Kamalipour [eds.], *Religion, Law, and Freedom: A Global Perspective* [Westport, CT: Praeger, 2999]).

[18] See, for example, Onuora E. Nwuneli (ed.), *Mass Communication in Nigeria: A Book of Readings* (Enugu: Fourth Dimension, 1985); and Luke Uka Uche, *Mass Media, People and Politics in Nigeria* (New Delhi: Concept, 1989).

cultural anthropologists who have an eye for these newer developments, even if the religious dimension is not always their principal focus.[19]

I am, of course, interested in the ways in which the Nigerian case may challenge or complement the diverse taxonomies and narratives of current media scholarship as it has developed in the West.[20] To what extent is Western-derived theory regarding information and communications technologies, and their impact on social structure, political communications and religious activities, valid for talking about Africa? However, my primary orientation here is more empirical, in that I want to examine the significance of media representations of religious identities and interests from the end of the 1970s onwards. It was during this period, notably the 1980s, that Nigeria experienced a number of serious religious riots, chiefly in the North of the country. I intend to show how public discourse on religious conflict has been elevated to a national level by the expanding mass media sector. I shall also examine how, in some cases, irresponsible and unbalanced public media coverage of events served to exacerbate tensions at the local, national and international levels.

Along similar lines I explore briefly the impact of the growing production and circulation of privately produced religious texts, particularly those which propagate distorted and demonising messages about competing religious groups. The media arguably now constitute an important interface/discursive site for the negotiation of difference and representations of the Other.[21] There is plentiful evidence that Nigeria's religious public sphere is increasingly competitive, not least because of the rapid growth of Christian and Muslim revivalist (primarily youth) groups.[22] I have argued, along with others, that this resurgence of revivalism has been one of the key factors in explaining the stormier religious climate of Nigeria since the 1970s.[23]

Closely linked to this growth of revivalist activity is the appropriation of new media technologies by the Christian charismatic and Pentecostal

[19] See Karin Barber (ed.), *Readings in African Popular Culture* (Oxford: James Currey; Bloomington, IN: Indiana University Press, 1997); Misty Bastian, 'Fires, Tricksters and Poisoned Medicines: Popular Cultures of Rumor in Onitsha, Nigeria and Its Markets', *Etnofoor* 11 (2) (1998), pp. 111–32; Brian Larkin, 'Hausa Dramas and the Rise of Video Culture in Nigera', J. Haynes (ed.), *Nigerian Video Films* (Jos: Nigerian Film Corporation, 1997); and Birgit Meyer, '"Delivered from the Powers of Darkness": Confessions about Satanic Riches in Christian Ghana', *Africa* 65 (2) (1995), pp. 236–55.

[20] Rosalind I. J. Hackett, 'Hot/Cool Media: Variations on the Theme of Religious Communication', Paper read at Religion and Media in Nigeria Seminar, at SOAS, London (1999).

[21] Rosalind I. J. Hackett, 'Charismatic/Pentecostal Appropriation of Media Technologies in Nigeria and Ghana', *Journal of Religion in Africa* 26 (4) (1998), pp. 1–19; and Morley and Robins, 'Cultural Imperialism'.

[22] Rosalind I. J. Hackett, 'The Symbolics of Power Discourse among Contemporary Religious Groups in West Africa', L. Martin (ed.), *Religious Transformations and Socio-Political Change* (Berlin: Mouton de Gruyter, 1993).

[23] Rosalind I. J. Hackett, 'Radical Christian Revivalism in Nigeria and Ghana: Recent Patterns of Conflict and Intolerance', A. A. An-Na'im (ed.), *Proselytization and Communal Self-Determination in Africa* (Maryknoll, NY: Orbis, 1999); and Ibrahim, 'The Politics of Religion', p. 66.

organizations.[24] Not only do the new media facilitate their evangelistic and expansionist goals and efforts to Christianise popular culture for the safe consumption of 'born-again' Christians, but as symbols of modernity they enhance the status of aspiring church founders. The primary case in point would be Archbishop Professor Benson Idahosa, known to many as the Apostle of Africa, who was one of the earliest African Pentecostal evangelists to establish connections with American counterparts. He equipped his Church of God International in Benin City with a television studio (funded by the former PTL Club) and made sure that graduates from his Bible college (and they came from many parts of Africa) were trained in mass communications.[25] In the 1980s, Idahosa and one of his former associates, Rev. Ayo Oritsejafor, were dominating religious programming in the region.[26]

Some analysts of the new generation Pentecostal churches in Africa have favored an interpretation that sees them as the products of Western (notably US) religious imperialism.[27] While there is concern in many African countries over the unidirectional flow of information from North to South, this chapter is not about the imperialism of Western media in a non-Western setting.[28] I am not insensitive, however, to the hegemonic interests of state- and federally-controlled media. Yet, as cogently argued and illustrated by Brian Larkin in his study of the burgeoning Hausa video culture in Northern Nigeria over the last two decades, the privatised, decentering and grassroots forms of media production and consumption offered by video technology (notably video dramas) are creating new public spheres and cultural worlds without state sponsorship or control.[29] So he rightly emphasises, as I wish to also, that our analysis must take into account the macro and micro levels and the synergy between them. In his words, 'What is seemingly a local phenomenon, is part of a worldwide change in the political economy of contemporary media'.[30] We need to be attentive to how local values and conditions mediate the reception and uses of media technology. Larkin sees this latter, post-oil-boom phase as being 'mapped onto' the earlier colonial and independence phases, with their respective media technologies (cinema and radio, followed by television[31]) and particular structures of economic organisation, political regulation and popular spec-

---

[24] Paul Gifford notes, in contrast, that the mainline churches do not even bother to compete in this regard. They spend their money in other areas (medicine, education, development) but not on mass-mediated literature or communication (Paul Gifford, *The New Crusaders: Christianity and the New Right in Southern Africa* [London: Pluto, 1991], p. 101).

[25] Lyons and Lyons, 'Religion and the Mass Media', pp. 112–13.

[26] Lyons and Lyons, 'Religion and the Mass Media', p. 111.

[27] See Paul Gifford, *The New Crusaders*.

[28] cf. Nwabu Mgbemena and Onuora Nzekwu, 'Africa and the New World Information Order', O. E. Nwuneli (ed.), *Mass Communication in Nigeria: A Book of Reading* (Enugu: Fourth Dimension, 1985).

[29] Brian Larkin, 'Indian Films and Nigerian Lovers: Media and the Creation of Parallel Modernities', *Africa* 68 (3) (1997), pp. 105–7.

[30] Larkin, 'Indian Films', p. 106.

[31] Regional television networks were established in the closing moments of colonial rule (up to 1960).

tatorship. The present study is more focused on actual local events; although, as we shall see, the international origins and connections of Christianity and Islam are ever constructed, experienced and imagined through transnational agents, symbols, literature and music all against the backdrop of the cultural and economic flows of the new global economy.

Historical background

Any discussion of religion in the Nigerian media has to begin with some reference to the history of Christian-Muslim relations. Many would agree that the Nigerian political scene is not dominated by religion but still very much influenced by it.[32] Nigeria, like many other African nation-states that have emerged from under the cloak of colonialism, has sought to negotiate equitably its extensive ethnic and religious pluralism, and channel such diversity into national integration.[33] Many changes were required to divest the country of its colonial heritage, not least in the areas of educational and media development. The much talked about imbalance in the country, then as now, stems from the advantages gained by those who received Western education.[34] It was in the South that Christian missionaries were most active in establishing schools. Because of the British policy of non-intervention towards the Muslims in the North, the latter did not gain the benefits of Western education. This resulted in a lasting and destabilising dichotomy and is firmly imprinted on the historical memory of Muslims. Nigerian Christians, for their part, still harbor fears of political domination by the northern Muslim Hausa-Fulani peoples. They remember the *jihad* movements of the nineteenth century that promoted a new exclusive, intolerant and militant Islamic orientation.[35] Nor have they forgotten the Islamisation policy of 'One North, One Islam' of northern Muslim leaders

[32] See J. A. Atanda, Garba Shiwaju and Yaya Abubaka (eds.), *Nigeria Since Independence: The First 25 Years.* (Jericho: Heinemann Educational Books [Nigeria] Ltd, 1989); and Simeon O. Ilesanmi, *Religious Pluralism and the Nigerian State* (Athens, OH: Ohio University Press, 1997).

[33] The population of Nigeria is generally held to be over 110 million, with between 250 and 400 ethnic groups. The three main peoples are the Igbo, Yoruba and Hausa. Islam was introduced into the country in the fourteenth century and by the nineteenth century had become the religion of the Hausa, Fulani and Kanuri. Christianity was introduced into the South of the country by mainly British missionaries in the mid-nineteenth century, but it was not until the twentieth century that it established itself with the aid of British colonial rule (Don Ohadike, 'Muslim-Christian Conflict and Political Instability in Nigeria', J. O. Hunwick [ed.], *The Role of Religion in National Life: Reflections on Recent Experiences in Nigeria* [Evanston, IL: Northwestern University Press, 1991], pp. 102–3).

[34] A. E. Ekoko and L. O. Amadi, 'Religion and Stability in Nigeria', Atanda et al., (eds.), *Nigeria Since Independence*; and E.U.M. Igbo, 'Towards Distributive and Social Justice in Nigeria', F. U. Okafor (ed.), *New Strategies for Curbing Ethnic and Religious Conflicts in Nigeria* (Enugu: Fourth Dimension, 1997).

[35] Abdullahi A. An-Na'im, 'Islam and Human Rights in Sahelian Africa', David Westerlund and Eva Evers Rosander (eds.), *African Islam and Islam in Africa*, (London: C. Hurst, 1997), p. 83; and Elizabeth Isichei, *A History of Nigeria* (New York: Longman, 1983), p. 202–3.

during the First Republic of the early 1960s.[36] The majority of the country's political leaders have been from the North (although not always Muslim). While successive governments have employed various quota strategies to try to reflect the 'federal character', Nigerians have every reason to be doubtful of the concept of fair play, with nepotism and corruption rife at so many levels.

Turning to the media more specifically, both sides cite discriminatory practices. Take, for example, the comments of former Ambassador Jolly Tanku Yusuf, an outspoken Christian leader from the northern part of the country:

> Christians have been denied access to electronic media in 16 Northern states, while Islam monopolizes 24 hours for its broadcast in the same area. Agents of the devil compound the misery by using the media to heap insults on Christians. Every hour the Muslims broadcast provocative statements about Christianity. It means nothing, they proclaim, that people attend church on Sunday only to dance and to listen to songs! Authorities merely wink.[37]

He goes on to set this within the context of his overall (conspiracy) theory that Muslims are seeking to take over Nigeria and turn it into a Muslim state.[38] Muslims were, in fact, initially reluctant to utilise the media for the propagation of their religion since they viewed the majority of the media outlets as Western-influenced. The avid appropriation of modern media technologies by Christian charismatic groups with their 'American' styles of worship further confirmed these fears.[39] Yet some Muslim leaders saw the need for and advantages of mass-mediated religious communication. Sheikh Abubakar Gumi, a radical, anti-Sufi Muslim leader, who rose to become the most influential Muslim in Northern Nigeria in the 1970s, was one of the first Nigerian Muslims to recognise the potency of the mass media. He founded the powerful 'return to source' group known as Izala, which was active in proselytising through the use of campaigns and recorded cassettes.[40] He was successful in gaining influence at two powerful media organs: the Federal Radio Corporation of Nigeria (FRCN), Kaduna, and the *New Nigerian* newspaper.[41] Sheikh Gumi received the King Faisal

---

[36] Ohadike, 'Muslim-Christian Conflict', p. 104.

[37] Yusuf, *That We May Be One*, p. 84.

[38] The type of restriction on Christian access to the media in Kano State, as well as other northern states, was reported to me by Rev. Dr. Isaac Laudarji. Even at festival time he claimed that their 'constitutional rights' were denied. Interview, Kano, 2 July 1997.

[39] cf. Jubril Bala Mohammed, 'Ideological Parameters of Nigerian Journalism', O. Dare and Adidi Uyo (eds.), *Journalism in Nigeria: Issues and Perspectives* (Lagos: National Union of Journalists, Lagos State Council, 1996).

[40] Matthew Hassan Kukah, *Religion, Politics and Power in Northern Nigeria* (Ibadan: Spectrum, 1993).

[41] In his autobiography, Gumi makes the interesting reflection about the advantages of the print over the broadcast media in terms of feedback: 'My hope was that I could use the print media to exchange ideas with them [the Tariqa brotherhoods] and at the same time

International Award for distinguished service to Islam in 1987, and in particular for the translation of the Qur'an into Hausa. There were complaints from a number of Muslims that the foreign media paid more attention to the award than the Nigerian media. The latter were still celebrating the Nobel Prize for Literature to Wole Soyinka.[42] They may have also been reticent to give high profile to such a controversial figure who did not preach a message of national unity. The underreporting of Muslim-related events is commonly attributed by Muslims to Christian domination of the media in Nigeria.[43] Sunday Dare, a leading Nigerian journalist, rather attributes it to public misunderstandings about the 'objectivity' of the media and the ideological orientations of the various leading newspaper owners. He points to the presence of several 'free-thinkers' within the journalistic community, who would nevertheless be included in the 'secularist' category perceived by many Muslims as Western and Christian. He also notes that it is easier for journalists to work in the 'space' created by Christian or secular paradigms of religion-state separation.[44]

It has been Muslims in the South who have been more receptive to the benefits of modern media in promoting and defending their religion. In his study of media use by Muslims in south western Nigeria, H. O. Danmole describes the diverse ways in which southern Muslims availed themselves of first print media, then radio and television.[45] The early efforts of the various Muslim missionary societies (such as Ansar-ud-deen and Anwar-ul-Islam) to promote and defend Islam were later followed by the influential Muslim Students' Society of Nigeria (founded at the end of the colonial period) and other youth groups. In particular, the National Council of Youth Organisations (NACMOYO) has been active in promoting the cause of Islam through the media. There has also been a tradition of mosque-based organisations, such as the Islamic Brotherhood Group, the Young Muslim Gospelers Association of Nigeria and Young Muslim Light of Truth, using the media to proselytise, albeit within their limited means. Danmole

---

educate the people further. I was aware that the newspaper had certain advantages which the radio did not provide' (Sheikh Abubakar Gumi with I. A. Tsiga, *Where I Stand* [Ibadan: Spectrum, 1992], p. 136). Late in 1970 he began a series of articles on the 'correct Islamic perspective' in the only Hausa weekly newspaper, *Gaskiya ta fi Kwabo*. For detailed discussion of the way the FRCN and the *New Nigerian* are seen by many as instruments of Northern hegemony see Kukah, *Religion, Politics and Power*, ch. 3.

[42] Pat Williams and Toyin Falola, *Religious Impact*, p. 176.

[43] In fact, it is generally accepted by most people to be the case at a national level (although Northern-based media do report more on Islam). Ojo ascribes this to the greater number of newspaper proprietors and editors who are Christians. He even notes that the *National Concord*, under Muslim ownership, devotes more columns to Christian sermons than Muslim ones (Ojo, 'Religious Reportage'). For early complaints from Muslims in Western Nigeria to the colonial government in 1954 about discrimination against Muslims in the Nigerian Broadcasting Service, see Matthew Hassan Kukah and Toyin Falola, *Religious Militancy and Self-Assertion: Islam and Politics in Nigeria* (Aldershot, UK: Avebury, 1996), pp. 83–4; and Ilesanmi *Religious Pluralism*.

[44] Personal communication, Cambridge, MA, 9 May 2001.

[45] H. O. Danmole, 'Media Use of Muslims in South-western Nigeria: Parallels and Comparisons', Paper read at Religion and Media in Africa, at SOAS, London (1999).

emphasises the significant role now being played by the newer Islamic organisations based on professional calling, such as the Muslim Bankers Association, and especially the Muslim Media Practitioners of Nigeria. Muslim women's groups are also given to purchasing airtime on radio and television. Islamic programs, notably in connection with Ramadan – the month of fasting – which are sponsored by individuals or organisations, have now become commonplace due to the need for revenue by the radio and television stations. Indeed, honorary titles may be conferred on those who are active and generous sponsors by local religious communities.

I now want to examine the different types of media both separately and comparatively. I shall then consider the landmark 1987 riots in Kaduna State for the way in which they evoked important questions about the role of the media in religious conflict.

Broadcast media

The broadcast media have always been more subject to government control and by extension, (self-)censorship, than the print media.[46] Even the recent emergence of independent radio and television stations in Nigeria has not considerably altered the picture.[47] There are strict government guidelines from the Nigerian Television Authority (NTA) about religious broadcasting. Programs are previewed for content which may be provocative or critical of other religious groups. NTA staff are very aware of their responsibilities in promoting religious tolerance and the power of their medium to inflame negative sentiments. However, the censorship factor has led, according to Danmole, to a regrettable state of non-reporting of crucial and sensitive matters of public interest.[48] For example, he cites the 'OIC incident', as it is known, when the federal government secretly made a move to become a member of the Organisation of Islamic Conference in 1986, (and similarly in January 1997, when there were plans for Nigeria to join the Islamic economic group, the D-8). This important national issue was avoided by the broadcast media, yet hotly debated in the newspapers.

It is significant to note that at the height of religious troubles, it is the broadcast media which are first subjected to regulation. State governments often respond by banning open-air preaching, religious broadcasting and the playing of religious cassettes in public.[49] But, interestingly, they also use the broadcast media to try to reassert control over the situation. As the Kaduna State riots in 1987 escalated and spread, the Emir of Kano made radio appeals reminding people that Islam was a religion of peace. The

---

[46] Danmole, 'Media Use'.

[47] Musa suggests that this stricter control, and reluctance to grant licences to religious broadcasting stations is in part linked to the ways in which the broadcast media have been used to heighten religious tensions. (Musa, 'Pluralism and Prior Restraint', p. 107).

[48] Danmole, 'Media Use', pp. 8–9.

[49] *West Africa*, 27 March 1987, p. 551.

Kano State governor quoted passages from the Bible and the Qur'an claiming that neither religion advocates violence against those of other beliefs. President Ibrahim Babangida used his nationwide television broadcast to downplay the religious aspects of the riots and give them a political spin.[50]

In terms of programming, the earlier BBC-style model of according equal time-slots to recorded worship services of the main denominations (i.e., a variety of mainline Christian, as well as Islam) has persisted on most of the regional networks but has been superseded by privately purchased airtime (chiefly on Fridays and Sundays). The revenue has become essential to the stations, and it is one of the reasons given for the repeal of the ban on religious broadcasting in 1987.

Space does not permit me to discuss in detail the vast and ubiquitous cassette and video culture that now pervades Nigeria.[51] These emergent and ephemeral forms of 'small media' are perhaps even more instrumental in circulating religious propaganda than the independent media institutions. Selling or sharing these is not subject to any form of censorship – except perhaps an occasional ban on their being played on public streets, which can be considered a form of provocation. Alternatively, some religious groups may discourage the use of the controversial 'conversion' tapes, where Muslim converts, for example, recount their conversion to Christianity.

Some reference needs to be made to perceptions of the capacities of the modern media to actually 'shut out' the Other. A telling example of the use of these technologies as 'weapons' against the enemy comes from the renowned German Pentecostal evangelist Reinhard Bonnke, who has a campaign to Christianise Africa, from the Cape to Cairo. Here he is talking about his crusade site in Kigali, Rwanda (before the genocide) and about the need to mobilise as his team spreads toward Africa's Muslim North:

> [o]ur crusade site was next to a golden-domed, Libyan built mosque, and even during our meetings the 'call for prayer' came from its minaret loud-speakers. Our powerful PA system of course allowed no interference and the Holy Spirit moved 'like a mighty wind', but we need to close ranks with those whom God has ordained to stand with us when the actual crunch comes.[52]

Print media

The high profile of the print media in Nigeria means that under-, over- or mis-reporting of events can have significant social effects. Even if

---

[50] *West Africa*, 27 March 1987, p. 552.

[51] See Brian Larkin, 'Hausa Dramas'; for Mali see Dorothea Schulz, 'Praise Without Enchantment: *Griots*, Broadcast Media, and the Politics of Tradition in Mali', *Africa Today* 44 (4) 1997), pp. 443–64.

[52] *Revival Report* D/90E, 2. Cited in Gifford, *The New Crusaders*, pp. 114–15, n. 12.

people cannot afford to buy a paper they will generally read them at the newsstand or borrow other people's. In the words of Bidmos, an Islamic scholar, '[m]ore often than not the actions or reactions of the Muslim to the Christian's actions or vice versa are determined by the mass media reports'.[53] He could have also added the influence of deviance reporting.[54] The predilection of many newspapers for such descriptive labels as 'fundamentalists', 'Shi'ites', 'fanatics', etc., notably when referring to Muslims, is, I would suggest, extremely instrumental in shaping attitudes.[55]

The political economy of the print media looks different from that of the mainstream broadcast media. They are far less beholden to government authorities when it comes to self-censorship due to predominantly private ownership. This explains in part why there has been an upsurge in what Falola calls 'hate literature' between Muslims and Christian literature marked by stereotypical and negative images.[56] This is particularly the case with the second type of publication considered here, the more ephemeral (independent) publications such as tracts, inspirational literature, etc., rather than the secular media.

Newspapers/news magazines

In a chapter on religious conflict in Nigeria, Anani Seriki includes a section on the provocative nature of some publications.[57] He suggests that it is primarily those that malign or ridicule the Prophet Muhammad that cause the most trouble. For instance, he cites an article which appeared in the *Sunday Standard* of 28 February 1988, where he (the Prophet Muhammad) is described as an 'epileptic prophet'. The Katsina riots in March/April 1991 stemmed from the actions of some enraged Muslims in connection with a newspaper report. Yakubu Yahaya, follower of Ibrahim El-Zakzaky, the national Shi'ite religious leader, led thousands of supporters to burn down the *Daily Times* office after an article appeared in *Fun Times* (a publication of the government-run *Daily Times*) in December 1990 suggesting that the Prophet Muhammad had an 'affair with a woman of easy virtue' and then married her. The newspaper later apologised.

---

[53] M. A. Bidmos, *Inter-Religious Dialogue: the Nigerian Experience* (Akoka-Yaba, Nigeria: Faculty of Education, University of Lagos, 1993), p. 21.

[54] Michael J. Breen, 'When Size Does Matter: How Church Size Determines Media Coverage of Religion', J. Thierstein and Y. R. Kamalipour (eds.), *Religion, Law, and Freedom: A Global Perspective*, (Westport, CT: Praeger, 2000), pp. 163–4.

[55] See, for example, the series of reports in the *National Concord* on the riots in Abule Taylor, Lagos in late May 1998, when a branch of the Maitatsine movement was involved in clashes with the security forces.

[56] Toyin Falola, *Violence in Nigeria*, ch. 9.

[57] Alani A. Seriki, 'The Nigerian Society and Religious Conflicts: A Retrospective View', R. D. Abubakre et al. (eds.), *Religion and Service to Humanity* (Ilorin: Nigerian Association for the Study of Religion, 1993).

Inaccurate media reports can have a catalytic function with regard to pre-existing tensions. Bidmos cites three examples of this. The first, in his words, 'stormed the whole nation like a thunderbolt'.[58] It was a press report in the early 1980s concerning the alleged government subvention of ten million Naira to build the central mosque in Abuja, the new federal capital. It sounded as though the Christians were being snubbed, whereas in reality they had received an equivalent sum but were still in negotiations about how to build such an ecumenical centre.[59] The press, according to Bidmos, was reluctant to publish government explanations of the matter as compared to their earlier damaging speculations. Second, Bidmos points to the uneven reporting of the Kaduna State riots of 1987. He claims that there was too much emphasis on the Muslim backlash rather than on the initial provocation by Christians in Kafanchan.[60] The third example cited by Bidmos was a case of fictitious reporting involving a purported crash-landing of a plane in Jeddah in 1990 and a Nigerian drug-smuggling ring in Saudi Arabia. Kukah makes reference to a report put out by a Kaduna-based magazine in December 1987 that all Christians had been released from jail following the riots, supporting the view that the release was a miscarriage of justice. These 'spurious allegations' were, he argues, 'determined to mislead the Tribunal or create confusion'.[61]

Bidmos also bemoans the failure of the press to report events that serve to promote religious harmony. He describes them as 'being poised for action whenever a seemingly uncomplimentary statement was made by a Muslim leader expressing a personal opinion' (such as expressed by Sheikh Abubakar Gumi, the controversial Muslim leader who said that Muslims would never accept a Christian president in Nigeria).[62]

Even very local stories and rumors can take on interreligious implications of greater import when reported irresponsibly by the media. For example, in 1995 in the city of Jos in Northern Nigeria, there were Muslim reports of Arabic script appearing on a rock and then on the newborn baby of a pastor. According to a Jos resident, by rushing to print these unfounded stories, the newspapers inflamed the situation which had already resulted in fighting between Muslim and Christian youths.[63]

---

[58] Bidmos, *Inter-Religious Dialogue*, p. 21–2.

[59] Another reading of the incident is that then President Shagari initially gave money to the Muslim community and only followed up with an equivalent donation to the Christians when the Christian Association of Nigeria protested. Personal communication, Matthews A. Ojo, London, 14 July 1999.

[60] Falola, *Violence in Nigeria*, pp. 179–80.

[61] Kukah, *Religion, Politics and Power*, p. 197.

[62] See the interviews in *Hotline*, 11–24 January 1988, for example. But for an excellent example of positive reporting, see A. Adegbamigbe, 'Friends after Wars', *The NEWS* (22 January 2001).

[63] Story reported by Hannah Danfulani, Bayreuth, 25 February 1997.

Religious publications

Denominationally-based publications or author-funded publications are common in Nigeria because of the proliferation of small-scale printers and publishing houses. These are less subject to monitoring or control by government officials or religious leaders. At times they publish extremely defamatory materials. For example, the Sword of the Spirit Ministries of Ibadan conducted a crusade in the Northern Nigerian city of Sokoto, the historic seat of Nigeria's caliphate. In the Ministries' magazine (available only to subscribers, but this is a large and influential church with UK connections), the operation in 'this formerly renowned Islamic stronghold' was 'directed at destroying the enemy's strongholds and deceits in Sokoto'. The preaching was described as unveiling 'the enemy's oppressive weapon of deceit in the lives of the people', and by the end 'well over 4,500 adults had been delivered from the devil's clutch'.[64] The widely circulating *Who is This Allah?* (whose author, G. Moshay, actually claims that Allah is Satan) went into a second printing four months after its first run in 1990.[65] Additional examples could include *Today's Challenge* (published in Jos and renowned for its anti-Muslim sentiments)[66] and *The Pen* (a Muslim magazine published from Kano and known for its anti-Christian rhetoric).

Incidents

The now historic Kaduna State riots of 1987, already referred to above, began in the small town of Kafanchan at the College of Education after purported derogatory remarks by a Christian (former Muslim) preacher about the Prophet Muhammad at a campus crusade. This enraged Muslim students, who then attacked Christians and their places of worship. The Christians retaliated. Before long the fighting between the students spread to the town and thence to other parts of the state, as well as neighboring states. Many hundreds of people were killed, and in addition property was extensively damaged.

It is easy to come across complaints leveled at the media for having played a negative role in this particular situation. Jibrin Ibrahim unequivocally states that 'the role played by the media in fuelling the crisis [in Kaduna State] cannot be overemphasised'.[67] Ibrahim singles out in particular the

---

[64] *The Sword of the Spirit*, No. 47, 1991, pp. 8–9. Cited in S. Brouwer, Paul Gifford and Susan D. Rose, *Exporting the American Gospel: Global Christian Fundamentalism* (New York: Routledge, 1996), pp. 174–5.

[65] G. J. O. Moshay, *Who Is This Allah?* (Ibadan: Fireliners International, 1990). Cited in Brouwer et al., p. 174.

[66] See Musa A. B. Gaiya, 'The Press and Religious Politics in Nigeria: The Role of *Today's Challenge*', *Jos Studies* 7 (1) (1997), pp. 50–8.

[67] Ibrahim, 'The Politics of Religion', p. 68. Both Ibrahim and Adamu ('The Press and Nigerian Unity', p. 470) point to the roots of this type of divisive reporting in the late 1970s national debate about the inclusion of Sharia provisions in the Nigerian Constitution.

New Nigerian newspaper and the Federal Radio Corporation (FRCN) of Kaduna, both known for their 'pro-Northern establishment and pro-orthodox Islamic views', for having emphasized a reign of terror in Kafanchan and the need to defend Islam.[68] From 9–11 March the FRCN is reported to have broadcast regular bulletins (in both Hausa and English) concerning the massacre of Muslims and burning of mosques in Kafanchan, while they failed to report details of the counter-attack on Christians.[69] Based on his interviews with senior media figures in these institutions, Kukah reveals a different interpretation that in fact the so-called sensationalist reports had been verified for accuracy at the *New Nigerian* and that the FRCN editorial staff had actually refused to publish inflammatory materials submitted by both Muslims and Christians.[70]

The pro-Southern and pro-Christian press were not innocent in this affair, aggravating the situation by writing about the 'Mullahs of easy violence' in *The Guardian* of 14 March. *The Standard* of 13 March and *The Punch* of 14 March reported damage to the Christian communities while ignoring that of the Muslims.[71] Ibrahim also notes the possible significance of a series of thirteen programs broadcast on City Television Kano (CTV), originating in South Africa, which discussed whether the Bible was the Word of God, and whether Jesus was the Son of God, and had been crucified, etc.

Conclusion

As stated at the outset, we are hampered by the fact that media issues, notably in connection with religion, are under-researched when it comes to Nigeria or indeed Africa as a whole.[72] It would therefore be foolhardy in writing about such a complex and vast country as Nigeria to attempt easy generalisations implicating the media in interreligious conflicts. A more adequate theory of the relationship of religion and media in Nigeria awaits. It should at least include the issues of sponsorship and ownership, local/global interactions and agency, media use, access, etc. So it is not possible to conclude this brief overview by declaring the media to be either guilty or innocent of heightening Nigeria's religious tensions, despite the

[68] Adamu, 'The Press and Nigerian Unity', pp. 470–1.
[69] Panta O. J. Umechukwu, *The Press Coverage of Religious Violence in Nigeria* (Enugu: Ugovin, 1995), p. 33.
[70] Matthew Hassan Kukah, 'Public Perceptions of the Press in Nigeria', O. Dare and U. Adidi (eds.), *Journalism in Nigeria: Issues and Perspectives* (Lagos: National Union of Journalists, Lagos State Council, 1996), p. 175.
[71] Ibrahim, 'The Politics of Religion', p. 69.
[72] For example, in Falola's recently published book on religious violence in Nigeria, there are no media-related entries in the index even though there are incidental references to mediated messages of political consequence, and religious 'hate' literature features in a chapter on symbolic violence (Falola, *Violence in Nigeria*).

tendencies of some scholars to do so.[73] I am prepared, however, to postulate the following:

1 The *growth of media coverage and production* at the local and national levels, and in ever more varied forms, has accentuated the (perceived or real) religious fault lines by projecting them to a wider public. It has raised fears about religious conflict and the spread of it to a national, even international, level.[74]

2 The *rise of religious revivalism* has been influential in generating attitudes of intolerance between Muslims and Christians.[75] It is these groups in particular that have availed themselves of modern media technologies.

3 The gradual *deregulation of the media* has heralded an upsurge in virtually uncensorable material.

4 Difficult economic conditions since the 1980s have meant that the *need for revenue*, rather than considerations of balance, has dominated religious programming.

5 *Effective and fair coverage* of the complexities of a multi-religious state such as Nigeria is a daunting task compounded by the lack of adequate resources and trained journalists in this area.

6 There continues to be *disagreement about coverage and analysis of religious conflict.* Most people agree it should not be played up, but there are those who believe that it should be played down in the interests of public safety and peace, rather than prominently reported and analysed.[76]

There is every indication that Nigeria's media culture will become ever more influential in shaping intra- and interreligious relations, and the overall health of the Nigerian nation. Power relations between Muslims and Christians will continue to be delicately balanced as long as national resources are not shared equitably, and competing for space in the religious

[73] Imo, for example, sees the media as offering an important discursive site for issues of religious pluralism to be considered by a wider public than the scholarly community, and for 'negative effects to be checked', (C. O. Imo, *Religion and the Unity of the Nigerian Nation* [Uppsala: Almqvist & Wiksell, 1995], p. 37).

[74] The hollow pronouncements of many government leaders about the merits of religious tolerance do not always alleviate these fears. Yet the media do provide an outlet for public criticism of inequitable government alliances with regard to religion. The heated public debate on the Sharia issue has received extensive press coverage (see Matthews Ojo, 'The *Sharia* Controversy, Public Discourse and the Nigerian Press', Paper read at Consultation on Media and Religion in Africa, at Legon, Ghana (2000).

[75] For example, Ilesanmi notes that the emergence of 'fundamentalist' religious groups has stunted efforts toward much-needed political innovation with a more positive and creative role for religion in public life (Ilesanmi, *Religious Pluralism*, p. 147).

[76] The Islamic scholar, M. A. Bidmos feels that too much was made of the religious riots in the dailies, and radio and television programs, thus escalating fears about the spread of interreligious conflict (Bidmos, *Inter-Religious Dialogue*, p. 22). See also Baofo, who relates responsible media coverage to human rights and development issues (S. T. Kwame Boafo, 'Mass Media: Constraints and Possible Solutions', R. N. Kizito (ed.), *Communication and Human Rights in Africa: Implications for Development* (Nairobi: World Association for Christian Communication – Africa Region, 1992).

public sphere has, or is perceived to have, political overtones.[77] Questions of media access and representation are increasingly being articulated by the respective religious constituencies in the language of domestic, constitutional and international human rights. To understand these new forces, notably in light of Nigeria's history, scholars of religion and politics are going to have to turn their critical lenses onto the rapidly expanding media sector or be out of the picture themselves.

---

[77] Declarations by several Northern states beginning in late 1999 and continuing up to most recently, that of Borno State in June 2001, that they were Islamic states, and were instituting Sharia law not just as personal but also as public law, have engendered fierce criticisms from Christians and journalists. There was extensive rioting over this issue in Kaduna in February and May 2000, as well as protests, law suits, and mass migrations more generally.

6

Representations of Islam in American News and Film: Becoming the 'Other'

Rubina Ramji

The tragic events that occurred on September 11 2001 with the attacks in New York and Washington confirmed one of America's biggest fears. Several American policymakers had already concluded that militant Islamic fundamentalists were poised to become the next most serious threat to Western interests with the disintegration of the Soviet Union and the end of the Cold War. Although fundamentalists of any religious affiliation can threaten both individual well-being and national security, many people in North America have a special fear of Muslims which is rooted in historical experiences with, and cultural and geographic distance from, countries in which Islam predominates. This fear of Islam, traced through historical conflict between Christians and Muslims, has been transmitted through generations by literature, folklore and Orientalist writings.[1] This fear of Muslims has created negative stereotypes of Islam in general and Arabs specifically, which are then perpetuated by the news media and Hollywood.

Unfortunately, many elements of the news media and an increasing number of Hollywood films represent *all* Muslims as Islamic fundamentalists. I believe that these forms of stereotypes have helped influence American and Canadian policy on foreign issues, such as the Palestinian-Israeli conflict and the Gulf War, and in Afghanistan and the abolition of Taliban rule. As Edward Said claims, anti-Muslim sentiment constitutes the last sanctioned racism, and regrettably, this racism in the Western world has only increased dramatically.[2]

The terrorist activities carried out by some Palestinians against Israel in the late 1960s and the Arab oil embargo of the early 1970s heightened North America's awareness of Arabs and Islam and has helped to breed hostility toward, and a sense of dependence on, people to whom many Americans cannot relate culturally. This chapter will explore the coverage of events that have led to this hostility in the news media and through stereotypical depictions of Muslims in Hollywood films in order to show that

[1] Richard Payne, *The Clash with Distant Cultures: Values, Interests, and Force in American Foreign Policy* (Albany: State University of New York Press, 1995).

[2] Edward W. Said, *Covering Islam: How the Media and the Experts Determine How We See the Rest of the World*, Rev. ed. (New York: Vintage, 1997).

the racism in these representations has created a feeling of separateness from Muslims and Islamic culture.

The majority of Americans are unaware of the cultural values of the Middle East or its distinctiveness. Isolated from the Arab world, they largely view its culture as alien. Many Americans perceive Arab Muslims as dangerous, barbaric and primitive. Prominent American avenues of visual culture, including news stories, television cartoons and popular films, often perpetuate these negative stereotypes. Although the United States claims to be generally tolerant of different religions, an extensive number of Americans believe that the Islamic religion, particularly Islamic fundamentalism, still poses a threat to American interests and cultural values. The American Muslim Council conducted a national poll and found that out of those surveyed, 43 per cent of Americans regarded Muslims as religious fanatics, while only 24 per cent disagreed with this image.[3]

During the Gulf War the media played a large role in controlling the information provided to Western countries and their allies. Given that 65 per cent of all the world's news emanates from America, it is not surprising that it often has a 'Western' slant.[4] Critics challenged the Western domination of Gulf War news coverage and the demonising of the 'enemy'. In India, some journalists voiced specific concerns about the nature of the material emanating from Western media and the almost exclusive pro-war news coverage from Western news agencies and syndicated services. They voiced four major concerns. First, technologies of death were romanticised by the use of such terms such as 'precision bombing', 'surgical strike' and 'smart bombs', which were dehumanising and desensitising. Secondly, there was a lack of context to the war rather than a historical understanding of the events leading up to it. Thirdly, the coverage included the malicious demonisation of Arabs and Muslims in general and Iraqis in particular. And fourthly, the Western media often used double standards regarding the UN sanctions: the twelve resolutions against Iraq were frequently cited as justification, while hundreds of resolutions on the Arab territories occupied illegally were often disregarded.[5] Many were appalled by

---

[3] Pejorative stereotypes of Muslims in the United States have been documented in various other sources. See, for example, Yvonne Yazbeck Haddad, *The Muslims of America* (Oxford: Oxford University Press, 1991); Richard Payne, *The Clash with Distant Cultures: Values, Interests, and Force in American Foreign Policy* (Albany: State University of New York Press, 1995); Mehdi Bozorgmehr, Claudia Der-Martirosian and Georges Sabagh, 'Middle Easterners: A New Kind of Immigrants', R. Waldinger and M. Bozorgmehr (eds.), *Ethnic Los Angeles* (New York: Russell Sage Foundation, 1996); and Yvonne Yazbeck Haddad and John L. Esposito, *Muslims on the Americanization Path?* (Oxford: Oxford University Press, 2000).

[4] Hamid Mowlana, George Gerbner and Herbert Schiller (eds.), *Triumph of the Image: The Media's War in the Persian Gulf – A Global Perspective* (Boulder, CO: Westview, 1992).

[5] P. Sainath, 'The New World *Odour*: The Indian Experience', Mowlana, Gerbner and Schiller (eds.), *Triumph of the Image*, p. 72. See Margaret Miles, *Seeing and Believing: Religion and Values in the Movies* (Boston: Beacon, 1996) also for discussion about news media descriptions of American involvement in the war.

the rampant racism running through the coverage, but this reporting continued in the news more or less unquestioned.

American cultural values and beliefs also played a significant role in determining much of the coverage of the Balkan conflict. For example, the cultural distance between Bosnia, especially its Muslim population, and the United States may partly explain why the atrocities in Bosnia-Hercegovina carried out by the Serbs against the Muslims initially received so little attention in the news media. Richard Payne argues that culturally, Croatia is considered the most closely related to Western Europe and the United States, while Serbia is presumed to be in the middle, and Muslim-controlled Bosnia the most foreign and alien. The Croats are the most integrated into European civilization. The Serbs have identified with Eastern Orthodox countries such as Greece and Russia, and the Muslims, though European and Slavic, are perceived to be associated with Middle Eastern civilisation.[6]

A significant part of the news coverage of the Bosnian conflict illustrates an immense significance placed on the cultural, if not geographical, closeness between the Croats and Western civilisation. Croats were characterised as 'Catholic, westernised, technologically advanced and sophisticated, and practicing western-style democracy'. The Serbs, on the other hand, were routinely categorised as 'Eastern Orthodox, Byzantine, and "primitive remnants of the Ottoman [read: Iraqi] empire"'.[7] Although the Serbs could be considered separate from European civilisation, the Muslims, on the other hand, remain completely outside of the West's cultural domain, therefore alien and 'other'.

Taking into consideration the United States' vast military power and its victory in Operation Desert Storm, leading American scholars and foreign policy experts, including many Muslims, have come to the conclusion that 'religious differences' have facilitated the predominant apathetic Western news coverage and subsequent foreign policy approach towards Bosnia. Samuel P. Huntington of Harvard University observed that initially 'relatively little Western concern was expressed over Croatian attacks on Muslims and participation in the dismemberment of Bosnia-Hercegovina'.[8] Likewise, Richard Holbrooke, Assistant Secretary of State in the Carter administration and advisor to the then presidential candidate Bill Clinton, proclaimed that 'if the situation were reversed and the Christians and Jews were being attacked in Bosnia, there would be a lot more [Western] concern'.[9]

Is it possible that the coverage of the conflicts in Kuwait, Bosnia and Afghanistan have partly been shaped by an underlying fear that Islam threatens the West and its democratic values? Certain dramatic events have provided more news stories to bolster this latent fear. For example, Muslim

---

[6] Richard Payne, *The Clash with Distant Cultures.*

[7] Richard Payne, *The Clash with Distant Cultures.* p. 168. (emphasis added).

[8] Samuel P. Huntington, 'The Clash of Civilizations?', *Foreign Affairs* 72 (3) (Summer 1993), p. 37.

[9] Roy Gutman, *A Witness to Genocide* (New York: Macmillan, 1993), p. 83.

extremist attacks on the United States, such as the bombing of the World
Trade Center in New York in 1993, and increased 'terrorist' attacks against
Israel and other pro-Western states by Islamic groups opposed to the
American-based process of peace in the Middle East, as well as international
Islamic support for Bosnian Muslims, increased American concerns about
radical Islamic fundamentalism and gave more credibility to the belief that
there truly is an Islamic conspiracy. In another example, the Oklahoma
bombing (19 April 1995) resulted in Arab-owned businesses being targeted
for attack, and police investigated various Middle-Eastern individuals, only
to find that those responsible were in fact right-wing American citizens.
Unfortunately the destruction of the World Trade Center and attacks in
Washington in 2001 have only confirmed that Islamic fundamentalism is
indeed a larger conspiracy than first believed. In fact, leaders of the estimated 3.5 million Arab Americans in the United States warned members of
their community 'against wearing distinctively Islamic dress in public until
the wave of anger against American Arabs and other Muslims' in the wake
of the attack on September 11 2001 had died down.[10] While many Western
newspaper commentators were claiming that America's attack on
Afghanistan was being done for the right reasons, much of the reporting in
Middle Eastern countries cried out for restraint and fairness. *The Gulf News*,
in the UAE, stated, 'Bush's intention to "punish" should not disintegrate
into plain revenge, but should incorporate justice as well'.[11] *The Jordanian
Times* demanded that US decision makers 'evaluate whether they have
steered the world's only superpower to dominate under the insignia of justice and international legitimacy' or whether they had already 'succumbed
to short-term interests, shortsighted considerations and the power of arrogance'[12] regarding its policies towards Iraq, the Palestinian-Israeli conflict
and its behaviour towards Afghanistan.

Not only are perceptions assimilated from television news and the newspaper industry, but they are also strengthened through popular film. The
commercial film industry creates cultural products that often reflect societal norms. Film scripts are frequently informed by the news, and the resulting movies can reinforce the images portrayed through news media outlets.
In short, stereotypes can be recycled through different media. On the basis
of this recycling, could it be that for many viewers cinematic representations
are taken for granted as rooted in reality? Do such portrayals, often pure
fantasy, reinforce stereotypes and manufacture consensus? These are controversial points and more research is needed to answer conclusively these
questions, but on the basis of my own work I believe that viewers frequently
accept many of the images on screen as somehow truly reflective of the
world in which they live. This is problematic as 'most movies involving

[10] Martin Kettle, 'Arab Americans Stress Loyalty in Face of Backlash', *The Guardian* (13
September 2001).
[11] 'What the Papers Say in the Middle East', *The Guardian* (13 September 2001).
[12] 'What the Papers Say'.

terrorism look at the subject from a US perspective'.[13] Therefore, in movies depicting Islam, Muslims are often played as backward, exotic, fanatic and extremely dangerous. Meanwhile, the West is too often portrayed as civilised, Christian and advanced.

The movie *Navy Seals*[14] was released in 1990 and was one of the first instances in popular film in which Islamic 'terrorists' were shown to endanger the 'civilised world'. Viewed with hindsight, this movie can be seen as the beginning of the portrayal in American films of the Islamic threat extending into the Westernised world. In the movie, the US flexes its power by stepping in to deal with the threat as it spreads into allied countries (in this instance Spain). A special élite force known as the Navy Seals, created to deal with acts of terrorism and guerilla wars, is sent in to halt the Islamic terrorist group, in order to protect the defenceless, innocent civilians. An Islamic 'anti-American' terrorist, Ben Shaheed, is the leader of a group called Al-Shahoudah, which has stolen stinger missiles and then begins to attack civilian aircraft in Spain. The Navy Seals are sent in to destroy the missiles. This movie illustrates the looming threat of Islam and the terror and death they inflict in their own city, Beirut. In the credits, one of the Muslims is listed only as 'terrorist', with no recognition of the character portrayed. This movie, in effect, links terrorists specifically to Islam.

The threat of Islam to American citizens is felt directly in the film *Not Without My Daughter*.[15] The movie began filming in the summer of 1990 and was released in January 1991 while tension was mounting in the Middle East. The movie's highest box office ranking was the week in which the war in the Persian Gulf started. Although movie reviews denounced it for exploiting the stereotype of the demonic Iranian, it made over 14 million dollars. In the absence of other film representations of Iran and Islamic culture at the time, it was able to gain control of a broad audience in order to disseminate its particular perspective on Islam and Muslims. The movie was granted authenticity and was accepted as characteristic of all Islamic, as well as Middle Eastern, culture, even though it was based on the story of one woman's experience.[16]

In the movie *Not Without My Daughter*, the Islamic threat is now felt directly by an American woman, although not on American soil. Claiming to be a story based on fact, this film depicts women, especially American women, as victims of the savage, violent Islamic religion in Iran, in need of American protection. The religion of Islam is equated with ignorance: Moody (Alfred Molina), in trying to explain his family's behaviour since the revolution, states that they are a very religious people and basically uneducated. And Betty Mahmoody (Sally Fields) constantly reiterates throughout

[13] Christopher Read, 'Terror Movies Surging in Popularity: Viewers Seeking Insight', *National Post* (19 September 2001).

[14] *Navy Seals*, Director: Lewis Teague (USA: 1990).

[15] *Not Without My Daughter*, Director: Brian Gilbert (USA: 1991).

[16] Miles, *Seeing and Believing*.

the film how primitive this Persian and Muslim nation truly is. The only like-able Muslims in the film are those who have had exposure to the West or been influenced by it.

The curiosity of Muslims, who had been viewed from a distance by North Americans, now became viewed with anxiety because Muslim nations were seen as military adversaries. Religious rhetoric became a significant point to sell the Gulf War to North Americans. Islam came to be seen as the embod-iment of evil, tyranny and oppression, in comparison to the good, righteous and democratic United States. The culmination of this stereotype can be seen in the movie *Executive Decision*.[17] Directed by Stuart Baird, *Executive Decision* is about a US 747 airliner being held hostage by Muslim terrorist Nagi Hassan, who is intent on destroying the plane and all of Washington, DC (the heart of America) in a suicidal mission as a form of revenge for the death of his family. This movie takes us one step closer to visualising the 'Islamic threat' attempting to invade US airspace, and therefore heightens American anxiety.

The power of Islam in this movie is displayed through the violence and aggression of men who represent the 'primitive', fundamental and fanatical aspects of Islam, which threatens the innocent, as they continually encroach on US space. Although we may wish to think that these stereotypical depic-tions of Islam subsided with the Gulf War, they do in fact continue to per-sist. *Executive Decision* was made in 1996. *The Siege*,[18] released in 1998, is loosely based on the bombing of the World Trade Center. It continues to perpetuate this primitive, violent and aggressive Islam by finally developing the Islamic threat into a direct attack on the United States and threatening some of its greatest icons, the FBI building (One Federal Place) and New York City, in order to gain the release of an imprisoned sheikh. In fact, all Arab-Americans have become suspects and are persecuted for information regarding the 'homogenous' threat of Islam. American Arabs felt vulner-able and discriminated against by *The Siege*. They went so far as to ask the director to change the plot by substituting 'militiamen' for 'Islamic funda-mentalists'; it was released in its original form. They wanted it to be recog-nised that religious fundamentalism does not equate with terrorism. Other films that continue this discrimination include *Three Kings*[19] (1999) and *Rules of Engagement*[20] (2000).

These stereotypical images have also manufactured themselves into family-oriented animation; popular visual culture intended to fascinate the minds of children. Unfortunately, the message conveyed through this medium continues to strengthen the violent image of Islam as well as the

---

[17] *Executive Decision*, Director: Stuart Baird (USA: 1996).

[18] *The Siege*, Director: Edward Zwick (USA: 1998).

[19] *Three Kings*, Director: David O. Russell (USA: 1999). A more complex movie, that never-theless perpetuates the belief that the only helpful Muslims are those who have had exposure to the West. An Iraqi who is American-schooled helps the three American soldiers in this film.

[20] *Rules of Engagement*, Director: William Friedkin (USA: 2000). Portrays the demon-strators in Yemen as fanatics.

perceived injustice that Muslim women face.[21] Many North American children have come to understand the 'cultural' laws of Islam through Jasmine, a young girl who is forced to follow the rules of her religion against her will, in the movie *Aladdin*.[22] In the film, Princess Jasmine is forced by 'Islamic' law and her father to wed against her wishes. She escapes the palace only to find that the 'threat' of Islam is even greater outside the palace walls. Jasmine is caught for stealing and the penalty is the amputation of her hand: Aladdin comes to her rescue. If children thought that their parents were strict, they realise that they are much better off than Jasmine. This popular Disney film constructs the protagonist Jasmine as the subject of the viewer's pity. The barbaric rules of Islam can only be seen as her jailor, imprisoning her through primitive demands she herself cannot escape. If it were not for Aladdin, Jasmine would be an unhappily married woman with one arm, all accomplished in the name of Islam.

Muslims constitute nearly a quarter of the world's people. They comprise a majority of the population in forty-four countries and over 435 million live in the Commonwealth. Yet this vast and varied group is too often portrayed by significant elements of the film industry and news media as a standardised, homogenous mass: barbaric people who suffer at the hands of a religion that is an 'unfathomable menace of medieval cruelty'[23] or religious fanatics who terrorise the innocent. The news media and the film industry contribute to sustaining such stereotypical images as representative of the whole culture of Islam. Select usage of words by the media (an example of semiotic warfare) in describing Islam plays a large part in the sensationalising and stereotyping of Islam: the word 'terrorist' is used eight times to describe the Muslims in the movie *The Siege*. Rarely do popular films such as those discussed above distinguish between religion and politics in Islamic countries. Furthermore, the acts of terrorists are too frequently inextricably linked with the views and beliefs of most Muslims.

Therefore all we encounter in depictions of Islam is a primitive, backward religion, associated with so-called Muslim fundamentalism, being militant, terrorist and violent. This increases the fear of this 'other' religion. Many Muslims feel that they are not in fact the terrorists but rather the ones being terrorised. Many Muslims entering Western societies often do so with ambivalent feelings of frustration at the attitudes fostered towards them and of fear of Western retaliation based on these racial suppositions. In fact, anti-Islamic sentiment escalated into violence in many parts of the world after the tragic events on September 11 2001, even though no groups had yet claimed responsibility or been officially blamed. For instance, in Chicago a Molotov cocktail was thrown at an Arab-American community

---

[21] Caricatures that portray Islamic women as weak and oppressed have become more pervasive in recent years. See Leila Ahmed, *Women and Gender in Islam: Historical Roots of a Modern Debate* (New Haven: Yale University Press, 1992).

[22] *Aladdin*, Directors: John Musker and Ron Clemens (USA: 1992).

[23] Shermatova, 'It's Not the Qur'an That Kills', *Moscow News* (14 April 1993).

centre, a firebomb was thrown at a mosque in Montreal, in Australia a school bus filled with Muslim schoolchildren was attacked, a Lebanese church was covered in swastikas and an attempt made to burn it down, and 300 protestors in Illinois marching on a mosque kept people from worship. Mosques and Islamic centres in various American and Canadian cities were placed under constant police protection based on a series of threats and anti-Muslim incidents.[24] Not only do elements of the news and film industries too often fail to portray Islam accurately, but they fail to show how Muslim people around the world perceive their own fate and faith in the new world order.[25]

The diversity of Islam is muted or ignored in many of the films discussed above. In spite of the fact that these movies are by no means truly reflective of all, if any, Muslims, they have become increasingly popular. For example, Canadian video stores recorded a large surge in rentals of movies featuring violent terrorist attacks on Americans after the tragic incidents occurring in New York and Washington. *The Siege* was ranked number 3 on the list of top selling DVDs, *True Lies* (a 1994 movie starring Arnold Schwarzenegger as a US agent battling Islamic terrorism) was ranked number 5, and *Air Force One*, a 1997 movie about an Islamic terrorist hijacking of the American president's plane, was renting ten times more frequently than before the attacks. The official spokesperson for Rogers Video, one of the largest video chains in Canada, claimed that people were perhaps trying to gain insight into the events and the minds of the terrorists, looking for similarities and even wondering if the attackers had received their ideas from a Hollywood plot.[26]

This is deeply problematic as, from the films discussed, it is clear that Hollywood frequently paints a distorted picture that equates terrorism with all Islam. This has reinforced other negative stereotypes of Islam. The news media also too often describe conflicts with Islamic countries without genuine empathy or understanding. In both news and film Islam is regularly depicted as 'other', separate from values of Western democracy and society. One consequence of these portrayals is that sadly many Muslims now have to battle against the label of 'Islamic terrorist'. One hope from the ashes and fallout of September 11 is that it will, in the words of Jolyon Mitchell, 'encourage both journalists and popular filmmakers to provide more informed descriptions, nuanced accounts and rich narratives of the complex world of Islam'.[27] The challenge for the creators of news and popular film worldwide is to look beyond the stereotypes reinforced by fears of difference and step into the world of the 'other'.

[24] Staff and Agencies, 'Anti-Islamic Violence Breaks Out Around World', *The Guardian* (13 September 2001).

[25] Answer Hassan, 'Invitation to Islam: Islamic Stereotypes in Western Mass Media', www.psirus.sfsu.edu/intrel/irjournal/sp95/hassan.html

[26] Journalists were also speculating in a similar fashion. See, for example, Christopher Read, 'Terror Movies Surging In Popularity', *National Post* (19 September 2001).

[27] From private correspondence between the author and Jolyon P. Mitchell (January 2002).

7

Islam and the American News Media post September 11

Mark Silk

After the attacks of September 11 2001 the American news media struggled to avoid vilifying Islam while providing coverage of Muslims who, by their own religious lights, viewed the United States with attitudes ranging from ambivalent to bloody-minded. The result was a body of reportage and commentary that managed to achieve considerable balance and complexity in an atmosphere of intense patriotism and war fever.

Hardly had the World Trade Center towers collapsed than American journalists began working on Muslim 'reaction' stories. 'American Muslims joined a stunned nation Tuesday in denouncing the attacks in New York and Washington – and then braced themselves for an anti-Islamic backlash,' wrote *Los Angeles Times* religion reporters Larry Stammer and Teresa Watanabe 12 September. Across the country, similar stories were produced by newspapers of all sizes. Here's a small collection of 12 September headlines: 'Local Islamic leader disavows acts' (*Poughkeepsie* [NY] *Journal*); 'Island's Arabs fear backlash' (*Staten Island* [NY] *Advance*); 'Muslims on Defensive' (Newark [NJ] *Star-Ledger*); 'Muslims fear attacks may cause backlash' (Hagerstown, Maryland *Herald-Mail*); 'Bloomington Muslim community "in shock"' (Bloomington, Indiana *Herald Times*); 'Alabama Muslims angered, concerned by attacks in New York, DC' (*Birmingham News*); 'Islamic residents voice their horror of Tuesday's attacks' (*Plano* [Tex.] *Star Courier*); 'Arab, Muslim communities fear backlash' (Portland *Oregonian*); '[Muslim] Groups express sorrow and fear' (*Boston Globe*); 'Muslims in the US Are Scared of Backlash' (*Wall Street Journal*).[1]

The dominant impulse was to show American Muslims as loyal, law-abiding people who should not be blamed for terrorist acts apparently committed by a few of their co-religionists. In the 13 September *Jackson* (Mich.) *Citizen Patriot*, columnist Brad Flory told of his own German-American forebears, who bought German war bonds up to the point the

---

[1] The danger of vigilante attacks on American Muslims after an incident of domestic terror had been evident in the wake of the bombing of the Alfred P. Murrah Federal Building in Oklahoma City in April of 1995. For anti-Muslim reaction to Oklahoma City, see Edward T. Linenthal, *The Unfinished Bombing: Oklahoma City in American Memory* (New York: Oxford University Press, 2001), pp. 17–22.

United States entered World War I on the other side. 'Dirty Hun' is what they had called his grandfather during the war:

> The grandfather I knew was a rock-ribbed Republican farmer who could have held the pitchfork in 'American Gothic'. He sang beautifully in church, was director of the country school and served on the board of the grain elevator. He sent two sons and one daughter, an Army nurse, in the service during the second big war against Germany. All this is my roundabout way of saying that Americans of Arab descent are not our enemy today.

When it came to this latest suspect alien group, however, there was an additional consideration. Like the vast majority of Americans, Flory's honey-voiced grandfather was a Christian. Americans of Arab descent – at least the ones now under scrutiny – belonged to a religion that was largely unknown and possibly ominous to their fellow citizens. So it was also important to show that Islam was a religion that did not condone such attacks – that it in fact opposed suicide and the killing of innocents.

'Terrorist plot contradicts faith', ran the headline on a 12 September *Bakersfield Californian* story that quoted the imam of the local Islamic Center. 'Tuesday's attacks were not the result of fundamental teachings, but the work of mentally deranged people, according to local Muslim leaders,' wrote Juanita Westaby and Andrew Debraber in the *Grand Rapids* [Mich.] *Press* of 13 September. 'Leading American scholars and practitioners of Islam said yesterday that Osama bin Laden had twisted and debased Muslim theology in a videotaped statement in which he called on "every Muslim" to "rush to make his religion victorious" by emulating those who attacked the United States on Sept. 11,' began Jacques Steinberg's 8 October story in the *New York Times*. Even America's sensationalist supermarket tabloids were on board. The cover of the *Globe*'s 9 October issue pictured bin Laden amid such revelations as 'How he tortures women', 'His secret addiction', and 'How he shames his faith'. Inside, a 200-word 'Quick Guide to Islam' began, 'Osama bin Laden may say he practices Islam, but the terrorist leader is in fact a traitor to his faith – which is a religion of peace.'

This pattern of coverage was more than two decades in the making. After the takeover of the US embassy in Tehran by Iranian radicals in 1979, the American news media were filled with supercharged accounts of 'Islamic fundamentalism' and the 'arc of crisis' in the Middle East. Criticism from both ordinary Muslims and scholars of Islam persuaded journalists to be more careful in their treatment of the religion, particularly when it came to local Muslim communities. In the 1980s, newspapers began to include Islam in their regular religion coverage – for example, by adding an annual Ramadan story to the round of annual Christmas and Easter and Hanukah and Passover stories. And when something bad was done in the name of Islam at home or abroad, a reporter would hasten to solicit reactions from the local imam, affording him the opportunity to condemn whatever had occurred. Anti-Muslim backlash – actual or anticipated – became an important element of the story.[2] Encouragement for such coverage also began to come from Muslim umbrella groups, which, like other religious lobbies, learned the importance of media relations. After September 11, the Islamic Circle of America posted on its web site a 'sample letter to Media' stressing the anguish and sorrow of American Muslims, their fear of backlash, and the un-Islamic nature of the attacks. Along with the letter was a contact list of national media organisations.

Not that there wasn't reason for concern. In one of many articles filed from the heavily Muslim city of Dearborn, Michigan, the *New Yorker*'s Mark Singer wrote sympathetically of Mohammed Esa, a Yemeni immigrant who after September 11 was fired from his job at the small welding company where he had worked for fifteen years. The attacks on the World Trade Center, said Esa's erstwhile boss, made 'their religion – you might as well write it as I say it – the scum of the earth'. The efforts of the media to counter such sentiments were of a piece with the scores of post-September 11 interfaith services that made sure to include Muslim religious leaders among the presiding clergy. Meanwhile, politicians from President Bush on down emphasised that Islam was not the enemy. (President Clinton had done the same in 1998, when announcing US air strikes against supposed terrorist targets in the Sudan and Afghanistan after the bombing of American embassies in Kenya and Tanzania.[3])

How long this period of good feelings would last was, to be sure, open to question. Sixty years earlier the attack on Pearl Harbor initially elicited a similar reaction. In the first weeks after the attack, expressions of faith in the loyalty of resident Japanese came from political, religious and educational leaders. In California, where most of the Nisei lived, the press all but unanimously proclaimed their loyalty and good citizenship. As the *Contra Costa Gazette* editorialised a week after Pearl Harbor, Japanese Americans 'are as indignant as their fairer brothers over the cowardly assault of the Japanese warlords on American possessions'. But within a couple of months fears of Japanese sabotage and espionage took hold. Western congressmen started beating the drums for removing the Nisei from the West Coast, and citizens berated US Attorney General Francis Biddle for opposing it. After a briefing from California attorney general Earl Warren, the dean of American newspaper columnists, Walter

---

[2] For a more detailed discussion of the treatment of Islam in the American media prior to September 11, see Mark Silk, *Unsecular Media* (Urbana and Chicago: University of Illinois Press, 1998), pp. 111–16.

[3] The media made its own form of disclaimer in 1998 as well. A minor zoning dispute over an Islamic school in suburban Washington received national attention in order to call attention to the danger posed to Muslims in America by tensions between the United States and Muslim countries. As ABC News put it in its 16 February broadcast, 'In times of crisis in the Middle East or the Persian Gulf, the Muslim community in this country comes under increased, and often unwarranted scrutiny. And passions are running particularly high right now in a Northern Virginia community over something as seemingly innocent as a school.' For an account of media coverage of this story, see Christian Jacobson, 'Islam in Virginia', *Religion in the News* I, 1 (June 1998), p. 11. Available online at www.trincoll.edu/depts/csrpl

Lippmann, weighed in on the side of evacuation, and he was soon being echoed by more rabble-rousing scribblers like Westbrook Pegler. In California, newspaper editorials shifted 180 degrees. 'Occasionally some misguided but well-intentioned individual will make the statement there are some loyal Japanese,' opined the aforementioned *Gazette* after President Roosevelt's 19 February 1942 evacuation order. 'But there are none such.'[4]

Two months after the September 11 attacks, no such turnaround had come close to occurring. Vigilante assaults on Muslims and people mistaken for Muslims (Sikhs in particular) seemed to be on the wane, as if Americans had taken to heart the kind of condemnation leveled by the *Denver Post* of 18 September: 'As Americans bristle with patriotism in the wake of terrorist assaults, we also must shoulder some shame over ignorant, vengeful attacks on Muslims and others who simply appear to be Muslims.' Timothy Egan's 18 October *New York Times* report on the handful of Muslim families living in Laramie, Wyoming (emblem of anti-gay violence), featured more evidence of supportive neighbors than hostile ones. Ditto the *Hartford Courant*'s story about non-Muslim women at the University of Connecticut wearing headscarfs as an act of solidarity with Muslim women. 'Benevolence Prevails Over Backlash' and 'Neighbors rally behind Muslim school' ran headlines in the 6 October *Washington Post* and 14 October New Orleans *Times-Picayune* respectively.

Yet the news from abroad about Islam was not so positive, especially after the bombing of Afghanistan commenced. '[F]rom Iran to Jordan, Afghanistan to Egypt, a unifying thread within much of the Arab world is anti-American sentiment,' wrote the *Buffalo News*' Nikki Cervantes on 7 October. By mid-October, newspapers from San Francisco (*Chronicle*, 14 October) to Boston (*Herald*, 15 October) were paying critical attention to America's longtime ally Saudi Arabia as the home of Wahhabism, a form of Islam both puritanical and xenophobic. From Riyadh, the *New York Times*' Neil MacFarquhar reported that tenth-graders in Saudi public high schools were being taught to be loyal to fellow Muslims and 'to consider the infidels their enemy'. The Saudis, wrote MacFarquhar, had tirelessly sought to export Wahhabism around the globe. The primary export market for Wahhabism seemed to be Pakistan, where the Saudis had over the years helped set up many madrasas – Islamic schools whose curriculum blended traditional Qur'anic study with radical Islamic politics. First-hand reports on the madrasas (whose numbers were variously estimated at between 7,500 and 39,000) could be found from 4 October to 22 October in the *Boston Globe*, the *New York Times*, *USA Today*, the *Baltimore Sun*, and on ABC's Nightline.

Reporting for the *New Yorker* from Cairo, Jeffrey Goldberg portrayed a flood tide of anti-American and anti-Israeli feelings among Egyptian clerics

---

[4] For an account of the press's treatment of Japanese-Americans after Pearl Harbor, see Morton Grodzins, *Americans Betrayed: Politics and the Japanese Evacuation* (Chicago: University of Chicago Press, 1949), especially pp. 377–99.

and intellectuals. An article by Mark Baxler of the *Atlanta Journal-Constitution*, also datelined Cairo, designated Egypt as a 'seedbed of terror'. The *Pittsburgh Post-Gazette*'s Brian O'Neill devoted his 21 October column to an e-mail from his cousin, an English teacher in the United Arab Emirates, lamenting the prevalence of anti-Semitism in the Arab world. In the introduction to *Newsweek*'s 15 October cover story, 'Why They Hate Us', lead author Fareed Zakaria waved away the image of the Qur'an as manifesto of peace. 'Quotations from it usually tell us more about the person who selected the passages than about Islam,' Zakaria wrote. 'Every religion is compatible with the best and worst of humankind.' 'Fundamentalist Islam is flexing its muscle in traditionally moderate Southeast Asia,' began Paul Wiseman's 30 October *USA Today* dispatch from Kota Bharu, Malaysia. On 1 November the *New York Times* published a lengthy report from correspondent Norimitsu Onishi headlined, 'Rising Muslim Power in Africa Causes Unrest in Nigeria and Elsewhere'. The arc of crisis was back.

At the same time, the comfortable contrast between the good patriotic Muslims at home and the bad ones over there was becoming less black and white. Closer scrutiny of American Muslims disclosed more ambivalence about the United States and its policies than wartime patriotism might seem to require. 'They are Americans who feel duty-bound by Islam to obey American laws,' began a 7 October *New York Times* story by Susan Sachs on high school students at a private Islamic school in Brooklyn. 'But some of them say that if their country called them to war against a Muslim army, they might refuse to fight. They cannot be shaken from the conviction that America is intrinsically anti-Muslim. Yet they see it as the one place where Muslims are free to be themselves.' After a visit to the Muslim Community School in Potomac, the *Washington Post*'s Marc Fisher reported, 'Almost no matter what they were asked, the students' answers often included something about how the United States should focus not just on bin Laden's terror network but on "the real terrorists", which is their code name for Israel, which they refer to as "the illegitimate Zionist regime".' At the same time, Fisher noted that, according to a Zogby International poll, 69 per cent of Arab Americans 'favor an all-out war against countries which harbor or aid terrorists', as compared with 61 per cent of all Americans.

A few reporters took note of *The Mosque in America*, a comprehensive survey of the American Muslim community undertaken by the Council on American-Islamic Relations as part of a larger congregational study project of the Hartford Institute for Religious Research. It showed (among many other things) that while 77 per cent of mosque spokespersons 'strongly' or 'somewhat' agreed that America was 'an example of freedom and democracy we can learn from', 67 per cent 'strongly' or 'somewhat' agreed that America was 'an immoral, corrupt society'. 'With American Muslims, there is this feeling of being torn between our nation and our solidarity with Muslims around the world', the imam of a large mosque in Falls Church, Virginia, told Jean Marbella in the 28 October *Baltimore Sun*.

Ambivalence was one thing. Speaking out of both sides of your mouth was another. At the end of September, Cleveland was roiled by the discovery that Fawaz Damra, an imam prominent in local interfaith efforts, had previously helped found a militant group linked to bin Laden's network. A 1991 videotape of Damra calling Jews 'the sons of monkeys and pigs' was aired on Cleveland television, and Damra's subsequent apology was widely deemed inadequate. Similar discoveries were made about several other leading Muslim clerics – including two among a group invited to the White House to meet with President Bush. 'Publicly, mosque leaders stay on message: Islam is peace, and we are Americans,' wrote the *Washington Post*'s Hannah Rosin 29 October. 'But contradictory statements have leaked out … What if peaceful and radical co-exist within the same community? Or within the same mosque? Or within the same person?' Lamenting that the crypto-radicals had been protected from FBI scrutiny by their religious status, the conservative syndicated columnist Linda Chavez declared, 'Nothing requires us to tolerate those who would kill in the name of religion, or encourage or assist others to do so.' To be sure, there was no shortage of moderate Muslim voices. 'It is time for Muslim scholars and intellectuals throughout the world to participate actively in the campaign against religious extremism,' wrote physician Izaj A. Jatala in a *St. Louis Post-Dispatch* op-ed 23 October. American Muslims 'need to realise there are really extremist elements that need to be countered openly', Harvard graduate student Aisha Y. Musa told the *New York Times* in a 29 October story headlined 'Moderates Start Speaking Out'. 'We have let a vocal minority hijack Islam,' Chicago Muslim leader Umar Faruq Abdallah told Don Lattin of the *San Francisco Chronicle* of 7 October. In a 30 October story, *Newsday*'s Carol Eisenberg described Muqtedar Khan, a political science professor at Adrian College in Michigan, as 'one of a growing number of young, moderate Muslim thinkers who believe themselves engaged in a battle for the soul of Islam'. Needless to say, such moderation hardly lessened concerns about Islamic extremism.

Meeting in Boston in late September, the Religion Newswriters Association issued a warning against using the phrase 'Islamic terrorist' and similar terms – on the grounds that they 'seem to associate an entire religion with the actions of a few'. But by the middle of October a number of commentators had began to suggest that Islam itself was the problem. 'The problem is that Islam has a quarrel with us, and the antagonists are not simply a few extremists trained in the use of a box cutter,' sometime *Atlanta Journal Constitution* columnist Michael Skube contended in the *Washington Post* Outlook section 21 October. 'By now, the elephant – or camel, if you will – in the room can no longer be ignored: Islam not only exhibits a frightful intolerant streak at times, but its very nature seems to be one of intolerance.' Similar opinions were expressed in the *New York Times* by Andrew Sullivan ('This Is a Religion War') and Salman Rushdie ('Yes, This Is About Islam'), by Paris-based Iranian journalist Amir Taheri in the *Wall Street Journal* ('Islam Can't Escape Blame for Sept. 11'), and by UCLA Law School acting professor Khaled Abou El Fadl in the *Los Angeles Times* ('What Became of Tolerance in Islam?'). 'The politically incorrect view of Islam seems to be gaining momentum,' Robert Wright noted in the online magazine *Slate* on 24 October. Indeed, although there were prominent dissenters (notably Cleveland State University law professor David Forte, the president's informal adviser on things Islamic), a slightly hysterical feeling of Western Civilization Under Assault began to take hold. Daniel Pipes, the director of an independent Middle Eastern think tank who became the media's go-to assailant of Islamic militancy, insisted that the enemy was not Islam but 'Islamism' – the current academic term of choice for the political ideology of those eager to bring about the rule of Islamic law. For Pipes, it didn't matter that most Islamists were not terrorists. Islamism was the equivalent of fascism. Writing in the *New York Post* of 13 November, Pipes contended that many American Muslims are Islamists who would like to turn the United States into an Islamic state. 'It means that the existing order – religious freedom, secularism, women's rights – can no longer be taken for granted. It now needs to be fought for.'

The enthusiasm with which ordinary Afghans greeted the collapse of the Taliban regime in mid-November chilled some of the anxiety about the Islamist Menace. Yet there was little prospect of a quick end to the campaign against terrorists acting in the name of Islam or to the anti-Americanism of many Muslims around the world. On 13 November, a visit to Peshawar's foremost madrasa inspired *New York Times* columnist Thomas L. Friedman to urge Pakistan to get down to work melding 'modernity, Islam and pluralism'. As for the United States, it should get its military operation over quickly and return at a later date with up-to-date books and schools. 'Until then', wrote Friedman, 'nothing pro-American will grow here.'

But if the project of making Islam safe for America looked as if it was going to be long and difficult, the project of making America safe for Islam was well on its way. According to surveys conducted by the Pew Research Center for the People & the Press, the proportion of Americans with a favorable view of US Muslims increased from 45 per cent six months before the September 11 attacks to 59 per cent two months afterwards. Among conservative Republicans – that portion of the electorate most likely to be fundamentalist Christians – the increase was most dramatic, with a jump from 35 per cent to 64 per cent. Whatever one's view of the Bush administration's war on terrorism, it is a remarkable thing to mobilise a society against an enemy defined largely in religious terms while enhancing the reputation of the domestic adherents of the religion in question. For this the American news media deserve a good portion of the credit.

PART 3

Popular Piety, Media and Religion

8

The Media of Popular Piety

John P. Ferré

Like many ministers who preceded him, Charles M. Sheldon (1857-1946) faced a daunting challenge: empty pews in his Sunday evening services. Sheldon himself was not to blame. The Topeka, Kansas, neighborhood where his Central Church was located was sparsely populated, and his congregation had already filled Sunday school classes, morning worship and the afternoon Christian Endeavor meeting; it was reasonable for them to want to stay home Sunday evening. Sheldon's choices seemed to be either to muddle along or to cancel vespers altogether.

The resolute Sheldon created a third choice. He would write a 'sermon story' to be read in twelve weekly installments. Each installment would end with a cliffhanger so that people would want to return the following week to find out how the crisis was resolved. Sheldon's first sermon story, *Richard Bruce, or The Life That Now Is*, filled the church after only three weeks. For the next three decades of his ministry, Sheldon would pack his vespers services by writing one or two sermon stories every year. All were simple tales of social commitment that included a happy love story and, of course, dramatic chapter endings. All were subsequently published as novels. Sheldon's seventh sermon story, *In His Steps*, has been in print since 1897, and is still available today in paperback and audiocassette.[1]

Sheldon's remarkable accomplishments were made possible in part by a change in the way Protestant ministers in America judged novels. As late as 1843, the Methodist magazine *Ladies' Repository* could claim that 'nothing can be more killing to devotion than the perusal of a book of fiction'.[2] This blanket condemnation followed in the tradition of Puritans, who opposed fiction for being false, frivolous and sensuous. 'God's altar needs not our polishings,' admonished John Cotton in his preface to *The Bay Psalm Book* (1640). In his *Manuductio ad Ministarium* of 1726 Cotton Mather warned that the powers of darkness had a 'cursed library' comprised of 'romances and novels and fictions'. And exactly one century before Sheldon wrote *In His Steps*, Yale College President Timothy Dwight declared, 'Between the

----

[1] Timothy Miller, *Following In His Steps: A Biography of Charles M. Sheldon* (Knoxville: University of Tennessee Press, 1987), pp. 66–102.

[2] Nina Baym, *Novels, Readers, and Reviewers: Responses to Fiction in Antebellum America* (Ithaca, NY: Cornell University Press, 1984), p. 32.

Bible and novels there is a gulph fixed which few readers are willing to pass.' Despite the rise of the religious novel in the last half of the nineteenth century, Sheldon was cognisant enough of the suspected gulf between the Bible and novels to avoid raising religious objections to his own writings by calling them 'sermon stories'.[3]

The shift from the Puritan rejection of the novel to the Rev. Sheldon's spectacular use of it illustrates a paradigmatic transformation in how a particular communication medium was understood. Unlike the Puritans, who saw the novel as a mode of knowing, a media form with intrinsic traits that channel people's perceptions, Sheldon and other social gospel fiction writers saw the novel as a neutral conduit capable of faithfully communicating the author's intent. Indeed, these are two of the three distinct ways that religious media have been understood. Historically, religious media, like their secular counterparts, have been understood as conduits, modes of knowing, or social institutions, three conceptions that have shaped the way individuals and religious groups have used the media.

Media as conduits

Like Sheldon, who felt free to use whatever medium of communication he had at his disposal, many religious individuals and organisations commandeer communications technologies without the faintest qualm that the medium might alter the message in any way other than to amplify it. Their approach to communication is common sense – say what you mean and mean what you say – and their model, if they actually have a model, is Shannon & Weaver's model of telephone communication, sender – transmission – receiver, where the primary issue is eliminating noise so that the message can be transmitted with fidelity. The media are neutral instruments with the power for good or evil; what matters most is who controls them and what they say. For many evangelists and others who embrace communications technologies as value-free gifts from God, the major issues with which they are concerned are ones of capacity and cost.

The Billy Graham Evangelistic Association exemplifies a missionary organisation that accepts all sorts of media, particularly electronic media, as heaven-sent tools for evangelism. Without even a trace of ambivalence, *Christianity Today*, the popular magazine that Graham himself founded, reported a recent more-bangs-for-the-bucks television crusade. The news was the new look: an MTV-style program targeted at a global audience, most under the age of thirty. The broadcast interspersed Graham's preaching from an earlier crusade in alternating color and black-and-white images with contemporary music, interviews and drama. It ended with an electronic altar call from Graham's son Franklin. Transmitted by satellite to 160

---

[3] David S. Reynolds, *Faith in Fiction: The Emergence of Religious Literature in America* (Cambridge, MA: Harvard University Press, 1981), pp. 2–3.

countries in 48 languages, the program would reach 1.5 billion viewers at a cost of $7.5 million, or about ½ cent per head, a good deal depending upon the rate of return. 'This is not replacing crusades,' said Bob Williams, director of BGEA's international ministries. 'It is expanding them.' In other words, the substance was the same; only the style had changed.[4]

The common-sense view that electronic media simply amplify one's messages underlies recent documentaries that examine the impact of televangelism throughout the continent of South America. In the video *Onward Christian Soldiers*, Gaston Ancelovici and Jaime Barrios trace the inroads that North American-inspired fundamentalism has made in Roman Catholic South America. The evangelists see only the advance of the gospel as they saturate the swollen slums in the cities of South America with their radio and television programs. Here, for instance, is how Jimmy Swaggart Ministries depicts its international broadcasting:

> The gospel presented over television is the single most effective means of bringing the message of Christ to millions of people. With television you can reach more people per dollar spent than by any other means . . . . Every week thousands of letters are received in our offices that testify to the tremendous impact this program has for the work of God.[5]

A convert interviewed in the documentary agreed. 'Everywhere in the world there is television, even in the slums,' she said. 'People at home can listen to a message from God, a message from heaven, and that is very important because we know that the gospel is being spread all over the world.'

But the gospel of individual salvation and moral purity that is being broadcast undermines the democratic work of those who profess a theology of liberation in support of poor, landless and indigenous peoples. In perhaps the most disturbing moments of the documentary, we see Jimmy Swaggart introduce his wife to Augusto Pinochet, the brutal, fascist leader of Chile. The problem of South American televangelism, according to *Onward Christian Soldiers*, is not that television has warped the gospel or that television favors a message that accepts the political status quo. The problem is the conservative message, not the medium.[6]

The 'television war' in Brazil between Roman Catholics and conservative Protestants is depicted similarly by Australia's ABC-TV in its *Seasons of Change* series. In this documentary, the aggression is no longer from the north; it is from the Universal Church of the Kingdom of God, the fastest growing church in Brazil, with millions of followers converted through its television network, the second largest in the country. Many of Brazil's Catholics may have been shocked when a pastor of the church belittled Brazil's patron saint, Our Lady of Aparecida, and then broke a statue of her

---

[4] Ted Olsen, 'Graham Reaches Largest Television Audience', *Christianity Today*, 29 April 1996, p. 66.

[5] www.jimmyswaggart.com/html/world_evangelism_fellowship.htm [6 April 2001].

[6] Gaston Ancelovici and Jaime Barrios, *Onward Christian Soldiers* (New York: First Run/Icarus Films, 1989).

during a broadcast, but the growth of the Universal Church, especially among the urban poor, has been phenomenal.

Partly in response to the surge of Pentecostalism, the Catholic church in Brazil has turned away from the social and political emphases of liberation theology in favor of the individualistic, market-friendly charismatic movement. Catholic charismatics are showcased in programming produced by the Association of Our Lord Jesus in Campinas. The rhetoric of this programming, as expressed by Fr. Edward J. Dougherty, is worthy of advertising apologist Bruce Barton:

> I personally am convinced that the Church has to study marketing so that the customers will be enchanted and really be satisfied.... We do our homework in marketing and we'd like very much to please our customers. We have the best product, which is God; the best price, which is for free; and we have to spread this out. I have no doubt that if Jesus Christ were to be here like we're here he would be on the television.

Brazilian theologian Leonardo Boff observed, 'I think that today there's a vast religious marketplace. The biggest challenge for the charismatic Catholic Church comes from other types of charismatic movements. The Church fears losing followers so it copies the rites and gestures of those movements.'[7]

Although those who see the media as neutral conduits tend to be conservatives who embrace free enterprise in matters of business as well as religion, this viewpoint has adherents across the ideological spectrum. After all, the allure of unalloyed opportunity for religious expression is great. It allows for evangelism and counter-evangelism, and it helps fill pews and coffers.

Media as modes of knowing

Nothing could be further from evangelical technophilia than the thought of Neil Postman, who argues that messages cannot be separated from the media in which they appear. In a statement that should give all religious communicators pause for thought, Postman writes, 'The form in which ideas are expressed affects what those ideas will be.'[8] Postman laments the decline of print as the preferred medium of communication, because print is the home for ideas that are complex, linear, historical and contextual. Not so television, which individuals in industrialised countries watch for an average of three hours every day. Television favors content that is simple,

---

[7] ABC-TV Religious Unit, *Televangelism in Brazil* (Princeton: Films for the Humanities & Sciences, 1998).

[8] Neil Postman, *Amusing Ourselves to Death: Public Discourse in the Age of Show Business* (New York: Viking, 1985), p. 123.

nonsequential, ahistorical and fragmented. Unlike print, which is biased towards education, television is essentially an entertainment medium, and as the preferred medium of our age, has dire consequences for religious faith.

Television converts religion into entertainment. Indeed, for Postman, religion on television is the enemy of authentic religious experience. Unlike worship in a temple or a synagogue, people do not watch television in a consecrated space. They experience religious shows the same way they experience game shows or thrillers – in the bedroom or recreation room or kitchen. And they're likely to experience religious shows with the same semi-attentiveness that accompanies television viewing in general, watching as they ride an exercise bike, perhaps, or eat. The producers of religious programs know the viewing habits of the audience, including the fact that with a quick press of a button the religion could be gone and a soap opera could appear, so they compete for viewers with upbeat programs that exude health, wealth and beauty. They promote values that have everything to do with audience share, but nothing to do with the rigorous demands of true religious devotion. Furthermore, on religious television shows God is subordinate to the evangelist:

> Television's strongest point is that it brings personalities into our hearts, not abstractions into our heads. . . . Jimmy Swaggart plays better than God. For God exists only in our minds, whereas Swaggart is there, to be seen, admired, adored. Which is why he is the star of the show. And why Billy Graham is a celebrity, and why Oral Roberts has his own university, and why Robert Schuller has a crystal cathedral all to himself. If I am not mistaken, the word for this is blasphemy.[9]

For Postman, the television's entertaining characteristics conspire to make it antithetical to authentic spirituality.

Jeff Zaleski argues in the same vein, although less vehemently, in *The Soul of Cyberspace*. The question that weaves through this book of reflections and interviews with Christians, Jews, Moslems, Buddhists and Hindus is, in the words of John Perry Barlow, co-founder of the Electronic Frontier Foundation, 'Can you put *prana* [breath/vital force] through the wire?'[10] The answer for most of the people he interviews is no. The Internet does have religious uses, however. As a voluminous medium with interactive capacities, the Internet can be effective as a source of information, even proselytising, and sometimes social support. But cyberspace, as Zaleski says, tugs the mind from the body; it is a cerebral medium that falls short of presence. Sheikh Helminski, the chief representative of the Islamic Mevlevi order in North America, said, 'I've been reflecting on whether I should have some kind of disclaimer right at the beginning of our web page that

[9] Postman, *Amusing Ourselves to Death*, p. 123.
[10] Jeff Zaleski, *The Soul of Cyberspace: How New Technology is Changing Our Spiritual Lives* (San Francisco: HarperEdge, 1997), p. 34.

says, "Please do not confuse this with spirituality. If it's spirituality you're looking for, go inside, look within."'[11] The Internet can augment spiritual practices, but because its messages are disembodied, it cannot substitute for them. As the director of a Lubavitch site said, 'You can't have a kosher meal on the Net. There are some things that depend on the body. That's part of our religion.'[12] Or in the words of Bob Y, host of the Twelve-Step Web site 'Recovery is Good for You':

> I don't think you can replace the sense of intimacy that is possible in a live situation. And I believe that a sense of intimacy and complete trust are required for successful sponsorship. You can't get a hug via e-mail, you can't get taken out for a cup of coffee. As a sponsor, you can't say, 'I can tell by the look in your eyes that something is wrong. Why don't you tell me what it is?'[13]

To the extent that spiritual practices and experiences are intimately connected with the body, cyberspace cannot accommodate them.

Clifford Christians makes a similar point about the necessity of personal presence to authentic Christian spirituality. He points out that communication throughout most of human history was exclusively oral. Because oral communication requires human presence, personal involvement and dialogue, it enhances the community and promotes emotional closeness and mutual celebration. But these attributes became disengaged from the communication process as history underwent two revolutions, first with the printing press and more recently with electronic media. Now we live in an information age that still has the capacity for rich, intimate understanding, but that more commonly depersonalises people by segmenting them into socio-economic audiences and treating them as markets to be exploited. Style counts more than substance, efficiency more than dignity. 'Oral life must remain our focus, our basic priority, the *sine qua non*,' Christians says. 'I insist that we do not recommend aggressive use of print or electronic style, *unless* our commitment to orality is absolute, categorical, total.'[14] There is plenty of room for print and electronic media in Christians's spiritual world, but only as secondary channels of information and expression. Zaleski and perhaps Postman would say 'Amen'.

Media as social institutions

Somewhere between the contrasting views of media as conduits and media as modes of knowing is the approach that sees that media are indices of social values. The focus of this approach is on systems of production,

---

[11] Zaleski, *The Soul of Cyberspace*, pp. 76–77.
[12] Zaleski, *The Soul of Cyberspace*, pp. 154–5.
[13] Zaleski, *The Soul of Cyberspace*, pp. 246.
[14] Clifford G. Christians, 'Communications and the Church's Outreach: An Historical Perspective', *The Reformed Journal*, March 1977, p. 11.

distribution and reception. Content and technology matter, but neither is determinative. Rather, what media mean is determined in the processes of social construction.

Sharon Iorio's study of how acculturated Mennonites of northwest Oklahoma produce and use media exemplifies the approach to media as social institutions. She interviewed more than 40 acculturated Mennonites, those who conduct themselves as a mainstream denomination rather than as a cloistered or semi-cloistered community, to determine what they believe about media and how they actually use them. Iorio shows, first, that Mennonite use of media is purposeful. For their daily devotions, Mennonites supplement Bible reading with pamphlets, magazines and other denominational publications that they believe nurture their faith. In gatherings at church, they use an array of media, especially visual media, to teach them about their history, inform them of the work of their denomination, and – in videos on marriage, say, or estate planning – to explore applications of their morality. Mennonite use of media is also critical. Iorio points out that while Mennonites do not attempt to regulate the flow of media into individual homes, criticism of media content is common, diminishing the possibility of uncritical media consumption. And, in perhaps her study's most poignant quotation, she shows that Mennonites appreciate the various media they have at their disposal. This quotation is from a minister of an urban church who created a darkroom to produce slides to accompany his Sunday sermons:

> I love the Bible and am thoroughly convinced that it's God's word to us, as old as it is. The principles are still the truth. I desperately wanted to communicate it. And I just realized the traditional sermon of a half-hour monologue wasn't doing it. I felt that having some kind of visual effect would help. That's basically my motivation and I really ought to think about other ways, you know.[15]

This quotation illustrates the purposeful and critical, yet appreciative, approach to media that characterises the Mennonites Iorio studied.

Iorio's summary observation that Mennonite media use 'is an important means through which individuals in the group express self-identification to the group, sustain beliefs and values, shore up frames of reference, and maintain group boundaries' sees the media as neither neutral nor determinative.[16] For Iorio, as well as the Mennonites she studied, media use is a set of rituals that unifies the community in common belief and activity.

Another scholar who approaches media as social institutions is Horace Newcomb. Because of his focus on the creation and production of television, Newcomb is interested in how the values of aesthetics interact with

[15] Sharon Hartin Iorio, 'How Mennonites Use Media in Everyday Life: Preserving Identity in a Changing World', Daniel A. Stout and Judith M. Buddenbaum (eds.), *Religion and Mass Media: Audiences and Adaptations* (Thousand Oaks, CA: Sage, 1996), p. 222.

[16] Iorio, 'How Mennonites Use Media', p. 225.

the demands of the marketplace. The programs that ultimately appear on the broadcast schedule are, to be sure, products that broadcasters believe will attract a large and demographically desirable audience, but typically they are also narratives that follow conventions of the genre, often with just enough variation to make them somewhat distinctive.

Newcomb illustrates the aesthetics and business demands of American television by describing the pitch he made to the producers of the detective series *Magnum, P. I.* for an episode about an evangelist. The evangelist, Newcomb proposed, would have just arrived in Hawaii to recover from a scandal that had led to death threats that he took seriously enough to hire Magnum to protect him. The evangelist and Magnum would become friends, partly on the basis of their shared history as American soldiers in the Vietnam War. When the evangelist is assaulted – ironically, by some of his own supporters who are after the fortunes he has made from contributions – Magnum prevents the evangelist from killing someone in a rage. The evangelist confronts his own violent streak, confesses his need for God's help, and reveals that this need is his motivation to lead others to salvation. He returns home chastened, but renewed in his determination to preach the gospel.

'I was pitching it because I thought it completely in keeping with the character and the fictional world of the series', Newcomb recalls, 'and because I thought we could keep well within the bounds of taste and convention while stretching audience perceptions a bit.' In this case, tweaking television's aesthetic conventions was unsuccessful. 'Religion is so hard to deal with,' one of the producers said. 'You're always going to offend someone.'[17]

For Newcomb, as for Iorio, the characteristics of television technology play an important role. Television's small screen, for instance, makes TV an ideal medium for close-ups. As Newcomb says, 'Television is at its best when it offers us faces, reactions, explorations of emotions registered by human beings.'[18] But the role that the media technology plays is not determinitive. Newcomb points out the importance of the episodic and the serial forms to television writing and viewing, as well as the constant draw upon history, mythical and otherwise, to television content. Television content is shaped not just by technological constraints, but by conventions of business, society and art.

---

[17] Horace M. Newcomb, 'Religion on Television', John P. Ferré (ed.), *Channels of Belief: Religion and American Commercial Television* (Ames: Iowa State University Press, 1990), p. 31.

[18] Horace Newcomb, 'Toward a Television Aesthetic', Horace Newcomb (ed.), *Television: The Critical View*, 3rd ed. (New York: Oxford University Press, 1982), p. 480.

Conclusion

What people believe about the media has everything to do with how they use them. Those who believe that the media are neutral conduits will be likely to adopt them early and use them fully. Those who believe that the media shape expression and perception will exercise more caution, looking for determining characteristics that will reveal appropriate uses for different media. Those who see the media foremost as social institutions will negotiate the processes of production, always mindful of the ways people interpret the media they use.

There are lessons in this classification of the media of public piety. At the risk of appearing syncretistic, something can be gleaned from each approach. The first lesson, this one from those who believe that the media are neutral conduits, is to see the media more in terms of opportunities than limitations. Optimism encourages the willingness to experiment with new forms of communication and can lead to creative solutions to today's communication problems. The second lesson is from those who see the media as modes of knowing: discover the biases of different media, and use different media according to purposes that best suit them. Using media appropriately encourages discernment and sophistication. The final lesson, from those who see the media as social institutions, is to take seriously the human actors in the process of communication, from producers to users. For religious communicators, this lesson requires savvy on the one hand and compassion on the other. Taken together, all three approaches to the media of public piety would promote clear-sightedness and creativity in the service of religious devotion.

Further Reading

C. Arthur (ed.), *Religion and the Media: An Introductory Reader* (Cardiff: University of Wales Press, 1993).

L. A. Babb and S. S. Wadley (eds.), *Media and the Transformation of Religion in South Asia* (Philadelphia: University of Pennsylvania Press, 1995).

M. Budde, *The (Magic) Kingdom of God: Christianity and Global Culture Industries* (Boulder, CO: Westview, 1997).

B. D. Forbes and J. H. Mahan, *Religion and Popular Culture in America* (Berkeley: University of California Press, 2000).

G. T. Goethals, *The Electronic Golden Calf: Images, Religion, and the Making of Meaning* (Cambridge, MA: Cowley, 1990).

S. M. Hoover and K. Lundby (eds.), *Rethinking Media, Religion, and Culture* (Thousand Oaks, CA: Sage, 1997).

J. McDonnell and F. Trampiets, *Communicating Faith in a Technological Age* (Middlegreen: St. Paul, 1989).

W. D. Sloan (ed.), *Media and Religion in American History* (Northport, AL: Vision, 2000).

D. A. Stout and J. M. Buddenbaum (eds), *Religion and Popular Culture: Studies on the Interaction of Worldviews* (Ames: Iowa State University Press, 2001).

9

Unexplored Eloquencies: Music, Media, Religion and Culture[1]

Jeremy Begbie

A few years ago, the Hilliard Ensemble and jazz saxophonist Jan Garbarek collaborated to produce one of the best-selling CDs of the 1990s, *Officium*. A striking combination of ancient medieval vocal music and jazz improvisation, it is at once original and winsome. Whatever the reasons for its huge success, and there are probably many, it can certainly serve very well to highlight some of the principal features of music's involvement with that trio which forms the focus of this book, media, religion and culture.

To begin with, it can remind us that *the media deploy music extensively*. TV, film, documentaries, advertisers and marketers have harnessed this music and its sound-a-likes. Indeed, the media have not hesitated to draw on music of virtually every type and in virtually every context, from 'jingles' to film previews, news bulletins to soap operas.

Conversely, *the media have had a considerable impact on the way music is heard and theorised*. Take, for example, the impact of the recording industry. The pieces on *Officium* were composed at a time when the only way you could hear such music was to gather a singing group or travel some distance to hear others sing. Now you can buy medieval music round the corner and play it as often as you like. The music of virtually all times and places is usually no further away than the nearest CD shop, or (via the Internet) your computer. We can hear Puccini from our armchair, a Balinese Ketchak dance in the kitchen, Brian Eno driving to work, rave on a lunchtime jog. Indeed, music does not have to be pursued; it pursues us, in every conceivable place, from restaurants to airports, shopping centres to taxis.

Recording and digital sound transformation have also meant that most music we hear today is not live. Some will have heard Garbarek and the Hilliards in the flesh, but most will know them through their recordings. In any case, at many so-called 'live' performances, the music is multiply processed – at a typical rock concert, for example. The very phrase 'live recording' is a postmodern oxymoron if ever there were one.

Further, the machinery of marketing has had a massive influence on the

---

[1] The material for this chapter is expanded in much more detail in *Unexplored Eloquencies* (forthcoming).

way music is consumed. *Officium* has been skilfully and carefully marketed, like a vast range of music today, including 'classical' music. David Helfgott, Wynton Marsalis, Kiri Te Kanawa and Nigel Kennedy have all been promoted in ways akin to rock stars. Classical music is not dead, not even dying, but arguably its social role is changing, and this is largely due to the marketing media. One effect has been the shaking up of stylistic boundaries and hierarchies. What kind of music is *Officium?* Some will slot it into 'fusion', others into 'classical', or 'ambient Jazz', or 'cross-over'. The standard categories seem to be less and less applicable: one only need think of the Medieval Babes and similar unclassifiables.[2]

To go to the second member of the trio, *the media use music extensively with respect to religious concerns.* The music of *Officium* will almost certainly be associated with the 'spiritual' or 'religious', not so much because of the words but because of the four-part vocal harmony, the relative slowness of the music, and the reverberation of the monastery in which it was recorded – 'coding' widely used by the media in religious contexts. But whether these particular devices are used or not, when the media engage in religious matters, music is never far away.

And to move to the third member of the triad, in *engaging with religion, the media inevitably engage with culture,* that is, with the manifold ways in which meaning is articulated, negotiated and lived out by social groups. No doubt, some of the appeal of *Officium* depends on the association of an instrument from jazz culture with sounds from a church culture. To the extent that postmodern culture is defined by pick'n'mix bricolage, part of this CD's success might turn on its collage-like juxtaposition of divergent styles. Music's enormous potential for cultural formation is well documented, including the formation of religious cultures. Hymn-singing is an obvious example: it is not only a means through which individuals express themselves, it can be a vehicle through which a group's identity is changed, established, renewed. (One need only recall the history of Methodism.)

In any case, we have said enough to remind ourselves that music has been deeply implicated in the development of the media, not least the media's engagement with religion and culture. If we needed an especially concentrated and relatively recent example of this, then the funeral service of Princess Diana stands out dramatically, surely one of the most potent interactions of music, media, religion and culture ever witnessed.

Without attempting any kind of overview, in this essay, I want to explore some of the dynamics involved when the media enlist music in their engagement with religion and culture. To clear the ground, three comments are in order.

First, where the media have expanded most rapidly, by far the commonest kind of music deployed is 'tonal music', more accurately, *Western tonal*

---

[2] For readable overviews of music in today's consumerist society, see Nicholas Cook's *Music: A Very Short Introduction* (Oxford: Oxford University Press, 1998); and Tia DeNora, *Music in Everyday Life* (Cambridge: Cambridge University Press, 2000).

music. This music came to fruition towards the end of the seventeenth century. It encompasses not only a vast amount of 'classical' music, but almost
all Western 'popular' music. It is the music of REM and Rachmaninov,
Sibelius and the Spice Girls. I shall limit myself to this kind of music, since
it has dominated the contemporary media and since it is the kind of music
readers of this book will probably know best. (This is not to claim, of course,
that is necessarily superior to, or more valuable than others.)

Second, *if we are to speak about the relation between music and religion, a little
precision goes a long way*. The conviction that there is some special affiliation
between music and religion (or 'the spiritual') is ancient and persistent;
even in contemporary music criticism and commentary, we can often find
phrases like 'a spiritual performance', 'transcendent sound', 'sacred
moment'. But if we want to gain insight into the character of this affiliation,
a degree of specificity is necessary. An album was recently released entitled
The Prayer Cycle, described on the cover notes as 'a multi-lingual choral symphony aimed at exploring the nature of spiritual supplication', and featuring, among others, Alanis Morissette, James Taylor and John Williams.
Judging by the music, one could be forgiven for supposing that 'spiritual
supplication' must be serene, meditative and beautiful. In some respects
(though not all), the music resembles that of John Tavener, which is often
described as profoundly 'spiritual'. Without for a moment denying that this
type of music may serve to deepen some people's religious sensibilities, a
few questions are worth posing. Why assume, as many seem to, that spiritual
music has to be slow? Why assume that being close to God necessarily entails
suppressing change and movement? Why assume that simplicity is necessarily more spiritual than complexity? Why assume that true spirituality is
marked by the evasion of conflict? Even a glance at the pages of the
Christian Bible will challenge all of these assumptions, which goes to show
that we are unlikely to gain an intelligent grasp of the connections between
music and religion until we are prepared to acquire some clarity about
which religious traditions we might be addressing. Here I speak from out of
my own tradition, the Christian faith, grounded supremely in the Christian
scriptures. I do this not to close down any conversation about music and
religion more widely, but out of a concern that such a conversation is
carried out accurately and with appropriate respect for pivotal truth claims.

The third comment in effect sets the stage for the rest of this essay. It
can be summed up in the phrase: *music interacts . . . bringing its own distinctive powers to bear*. To take the first part of that to begin with, it is easy to be
bewitched by the notion of a 'pure' music, unsullied by anything extra-
musical. In modern times, it has sometimes been thought that music
reaches its highest forms when it seeks to sever its ties with everything 'outside' itself. But this is highly dubious.[3] Music always comes with a context,

---

[3] cf. Daniel K. L. Chua, *Absolute Music and the Construction of Meaning* (Cambridge:
Cambridge University Press, 1999); and Carl Dalhaus, *Idea of Absolute Music*, trans. R. Lustig
(Chicago: University of Chicago Press, 1989).

which often dramatically affects our reception of it. It comes with other media: we hear U2 *along with* images on a giant screen; we hear a string quartet *along with* the gestures of the players. When Pavarotti sings Puccini's 'Nessun Dorma' in an opera house, a Prince is singing of his beloved; the same notes introduce coverage of the World Cup on TV. What we receive from music depends to a very large extent on the way it engages with other media, and other contingencies in which it is embedded when heard. And, of course, our experience of music is mediated through an extensive range of personal and socio-cultural determinants – upbringing, conventions, education, etc. – all of which the media can exploit. In a TV documentary about Jesus, when we are told the church has smothered the simple teaching of the Galilean Rabbi, shots of the Sea of Galilee might well be accompanied by a lone flute or pipe to bring out the rustic directness of Jesus' message. When the conservative Catholic theologian is interviewed, he is heard against the background of a thick-textured Palestrina four-part Mass.

Music interacts. The idea of 'pure music' is a fiction. The real thing is a 'promiscuous signifier'; it makes close friends with whatever happens to be around. Therefore, to employ music in film, TV, radio or whatever is not to do anything essentially new or strange; music has always been interacting with other media.

Does this mean 'context is everything'? No. Certain patterns of notes lend themselves more readily to some uses than others. For instance, one of the commonest forms of music worldwide is the lullaby, and lullabies generally have slow, smooth descending melodic lines. Their structure is relatively simple, and they involve much repetition. People do not use this kind of music to call people to battle. Patterns of notes have their own properties, and we are physiologically and psychologically 'wired' to appropriate them in some ways and not others. Hence, although there can be a wide range of responses to any given piece of music, it will not be an unlimited range. Nevertheless, context will contribute a vast amount to the way music is heard; it is simply naive to think otherwise. *Music interacts.*

At the same time, music *brings its own distinctive powers.* It has its own capacities, it operates in its own particular ways. Here, reductionism is the hazard – treating music as if it were merely a variety of something else, the commonest form being to regard music as a type of verbal language. Indeed, many have wanted to give music a kind of semantic respectability by trying to show it is at root a subset of speech. Some post-structuralists are fond of construing music as a kind of pre-language, one that depends on language's arbitrary signifying processes but lacks language's ability to denote. But here great caution is needed. The commonalities between music and spoken language are striking, but just as striking are the dissimilarities. To subsume music too quickly under linguistic categories, or any other, will likely cloud its distinctive competencies.[4] We shall look at some of these competencies in due course.

---

[4] For discussion of this see Jeremy Begbie, *Theology, Music and Time* (Cambridge: Cambridge University Press, 2000), esp. pp. 26ff.

Three models of engagement

To explicate at least part of what is happening when the media mobilise music in their engagement with religion and culture, we can usefully draw on Nicholas Cook's *Analysing Musical Multimedia*,[5] one of the most rigorous attempts to systematise music's relations to other media. Cook's discussion ranges widely. With limited space, I shall pay special attention to music/word relations, and in particular to what music brings to words. Much of my discussion will refer to Christian worship, principally because this is clearly a crucial arena (some would say *the* crucial arena) for the con-junction of music and words in the Christian faith. From Cook's work, we can delineate three types of musical multimedia engagement: contest, conformance and complementation.[6]

Contest

The first possibility is that one medium vies for the same terrain as the other, dominating or imposing its own characteristics on the other. So, for example – and we concentrate here on music contesting words – the rhythm and metre of music in a song may interfere with the rhythm and metre of the words. Or the pitch-patterns of the music may conflict with those of the words. In some languages, intonation is especially critical for determining meaning, such that setting words to inappropriate music can obscure or distort their meaning. When early missionaries to South Africa ignored the characteristic falling-rising-falling sentence-tones of Xhosa and Zulu, they were puzzled as to why people could not understand their own language when it was allied to Victorian hymn tunes. Another example is when unsuitable harmony can so distract us that the words are effectively obscured. Organists can be especially fond of embellishing the last verses of hymns to quite ridiculous effect. Or again, music can invoke inappropriate associations. In Northern Ireland, fife and drum marches are part of what defines Protestantism and its territory; Catholic culture and space is in part defined by so-called 'Irish traditional' music, widely played in clubs and bars. To set theologically uncontroversial words to a Protestant style may cause Catholics deep offence.

In the postmodern climate, conflict between music and other media has frequently been deployed, sometimes with ironic intent. To shift to music's conjunction with images for a moment – in Madonna's 'Material Girl', the song's words are effectively subverted by the imagery, changing its central topic;[7] in the American rock band REM's video 'Losing my Religion',

---

[5] (Oxford: Clarendon, 1998).
[6] The terms are introduced and defended in chapter 3 of *Analysing Musical Multimedia*.
[7] See Cook, *Analysing Musical Multimedia*, pp. 147–73.

religious imagery is imposed on lyrics and music which have next to no religious reference at all. In a Christian context, such conflict, especially in worship (and certainly between music and words) has understandably been seen as something to minimise. Traditionally, it is thought that words, answerable ultimately to the words of scripture, should be accorded both respect and primacy.

But two qualifications are needed. First, contest between words and music need not be destructive, nor merely ironic. In a fascinating essay, the musicologist Ellen Rosand outlines the way in which madness is depicted in opera. Monteverdi attaches music to the sounds of words, but ignores the words' meanings. Handel lets his musical devices run riot, virtually free of words and their meaning altogether. Rosand argues that opera is 'generically mad', for its double media provides a perfect model for the splitting or fragmentation of character.[8] It may well be that the disorienting effects of sin on the psyche could be tellingly drawn out by deploying the remarkable effects of radical discrepancy between music and word. Or to use another example, such discrepancy could provide an impressive vehicle for exploring situations in the biblical narrative where words become alienated from their setting. One might think here of the words of Jesus amidst the increasing incomprehension of all those who send him to his death.

Second, as Cook points out, to some extent, at some level, there usually is friction between different media,[9] simply because each medium has its own irreducible ways of operating. When cloudy harmonies obscure the words of a hymn, it is music's distinctive ability to combine sounds which is responsible. The contest model serves to remind us that at some level, translation between the media is impossible and liable to cause conflict. Hence, when music and other media are brought together, the question is not 'Is there contest?' but 'Where is it occurring?', and 'To what use, if any, is it being put?'

Conformance

Cook's second model is 'conformance', and by far the commonest version of this is where one medium is seen as primary, and the other conforms to it (what Cook calls 'unitary conformance').[10] There is space here only to look at the conformance of music to words. This itself comes in two forms, conformance as *assumed* and conformance as *prescribed*.

Sometimes conformance is simply *assumed,* and often quite unconsciously. When music and words are combined, it is presumed, music will

---

[8] Rosand, Ellen, 'Operatic Madness: A Challenge to Convention', S. P. Scher (ed.), *Music and Text* (Cambridge: Cambridge University Press, 1992), pp. 241–87.

[9] Cook, *Analysing Musical Media*, pp. 120ff.

[10] In 'dyadic' conformance, one medium corresponds directly to another; in unitary conformance, one medium dominates, the other conforms. Cook, *Analysing Musical Multimedia*, pp. 101f.

naturally fall into line with the words – if not lexically, then at least semantically. Our reception of the words will not be substantially altered by the music.

Take histories of Christian worship, which have often, in effect, been histories of texts: written prayers, liturgical formats, and so forth: the overriding tendency is for music, along with other non-verbal media, to be treated (at least theoretically) as incidental to worship's substance. Another example is the evaluation of popular music, which until relatively recently was dominated by examination of the lyrics: so-called 'content analysis'. The assumption was that popular music makes its social mark primarily through its lyrics, the music buckling down in conformity.[11] Christian assessments of rock music and rock video have often followed suit. Or take the growing literature available on theology and film: the silent supposition often seems to be that music cannot be seriously implicated as a bearer of theological meaning, since words and images have the lion's share of the attention.[12]

The inadequacies of this are fairly obvious. As anyone who attends a service of worship knows, music can radically affect the received 'content' of the words. How could one write an effective history of, say, black Pentecostal worship, or the significance of the medieval Mass for its participants, while ignoring the role of music? In popular music studies, 'content analysis' has been subject to an avalanche of criticism.[13] In some cases, the straightforward sense of the lyrics may indeed be highly significant for the consumer, as in much folk music. But numerous studies have shown that lyrics are often valued more for their sound than for their obvious verbal reference: they are part of a total sound mix of which music is a determinative element, and that sound mix is itself part of a composite multi-media experience. And regarding film, could we discuss the theological dimensions of a film like *Chariots of Fire*, without taking account of the way a large part of its impact depends on its music? (Could we fully analyse the shower scene from *Psycho* with the sound turned off?)

It is at this point that some respond and say: quite so. We cannot assume conformity, and that is just the problem. Music needs to be made to conform to words.

And so a second form of the conformity model appears: conformity as *prescribed*. This view has a long history, stretching at least as far back as Plato. John Calvin is often cited in this connection. He was deeply concerned that music's enormous emotional and moral power did not distract worshippers from comprehending the theological force of the words. In this respect he stood firmly in the humanist tradition, with its strong respect for Plato's

[11] cf. Richard Middleton, *Studying Popular Music* (Milton Keynes: Open University Press, 1990), pp. 227ff.

[12] cf. e.g, Clive Marsh and Gaye Ortiz, *Explorations in Theology and Film* (Oxford: Blackwell, 1997). This substantial collection is to be welcomed, but one would hope that similar subsequent studies will contain some sustained reflection on music.

[13] Simon Frith, 'Why do songs have words?' A. L. White (ed.), *Lost in Music: Culture, Style and the Musical Event* (London: Routledge & Kegan Paul, 1987), pp. 105–28.

philosophy of music. Augustine (whose anxieties about music were similar to Calvin's) is also quoted with approval. Music must be held in check by the words it sets, and for Calvin that meant the words of the Psalms (for they are God-given), sung in strict unison without instruments. Fuelling this was an intense suspicion of any kind of idolatry, anything that would distract the worshipper from attention to the one true God, made known through his Word, written and preached.[14]

At the very least, the supporters of conformity urge, music should conform at the level of the words themselves (the lexical level). Musical rhythm and metre should match those of the words. This can be an outstanding way of memorising words, as in songs designed to drum multiplication tables into children's heads. Advertisers often rely on the rhythmic and metrical equation of music and words: 'O Lord, won't you buy me a Mercedes Benz?'. And, as we might expect, the device has been used for centuries to enable Christian communities to carry foundational texts in the corporate memory.

But many are keen that there is a suitable 'fit' at the semantic level as well, the level of meaning. What could be more fitting, one might ask, than the 'Cavatina' in *The Deer Hunter* to accompany the poignant return of the Vietnam soldier to his smoky home town? What could be more fitting than the liquidity of Mahler's woodwind writing for an advertisement for motor oil? What could be more fitting to convey the words 'Lord, have mercy' than the Argentinean Ramirez's setting, a choir in low, sultry, slowly shifting harmony, hard-edged percussion evoking the beating of a breast?

'Fitting' – the word crops up regularly among the advocates of conformance. Fitting like a glove to a hand. The language of service is likewise common. Classic Hollywood film theory speaks of music serving word and image.[15] Or the metaphor of amplification may be used, as when Goethe praised a setting of the song 'The Erlking' as superior to Schubert's because the music helped 'the words to *shout out* their own sounds'.[16]

But how adequate is this model, even in its recommended form? The plain fact is that conformance of one medium to another, in the strict sense of one-to-one correspondence, is virtually impossible to achieve and stultifyingly dull when attempted. And the basic reason is simply that music has

---

[14] cf. Jean Calvin, 'Foreword to the Geneva Psalter', Oliver Strunk (ed.), *Source Readings in Music History. From Classical Antiquity through the Romantic Era* (New York: W. W. Norton, 1950), pp. 345–8; *Institutes of the Christian Religion, Vol. 2*, ed. John T. McNeill, trans. Ford Lewis Battles, (Philadelphia: Westminster, 1960), pp. 894–7. For discussion, see Charles Garside, *The Origins of Calvin's Theology of Music: 1536-1543* (Philadelphia: The American Philosophical Society, 1979); and Carlos M. N. Eire, *War against the Idols: The Reformation of Worship from Erasmus to Calvin* (Cambridge: Cambridge University Press, 1986).

[15] Cook, *Analysing Musical Multimedia*, pp. 105.

[16] Quoted in Cook, *Analysing Musical Multimedia*, pp. 101f.

some characteristics that cannot be pressed into linguistic forms. Music always brings something of its own; *otherwise, why would anyone bother setting words to music at all?*[17]

Complementation

This pushes us on to a third model, what Cook calls 'complementation',[18] which can be exemplified in two main ways. First, music can fill *the gaps* left by another medium. So music does things which words could do but do not do. This is common in TV advertising: when time is money, music creates links which would take far too long with words. Another interesting example, which brings together music with media, religion and culture, is that form of multimedia worship known as 'alternative worship' which draws on contemporary 'rave' music. Words typically come in short pithy phrases, the sermon (if there is one) is frequently broken up, and the images are fleeting and diverse. Understandably, such worship often comes under fire for capitulating to the fragmentation of the postmodern screen culture. But the music itself is anything but fragmented – rapid and crackling perhaps, but tied to a cohesive and highly stable harmonic and rhythmic structure. (When more 'ambient' styles are used, much the same applies.) The music seems to be contributing continuity largely absent in the other media: it is 'filling the gaps'.[19] Second, there is another form of the complementation model, in which the *distinctive powers* of each medium work together, each medium doing its own work in its own ways. In fact, this nearly always happens to some extent in multimedia contexts.

An important caveat, however, needs to be registered. The word 'complementation' might misleadingly suggest that music and words sit alongside each other, like patches on a quilt. In fact, the process is much richer: I believe the shape of this dynamic is basically metaphorical, something I have written about elsewhere.[20] The point to stress here is that the media *interact,* bearing upon each other, so that we receive, as it were, a joint production. So for example, in a great hymn, or in the examples I discuss below, music is eliciting dimensions of the meaning of words which are

[17] We should note that even Calvin came to realise this. According to Garside, it was the influence of Martin Bucer and Calvin's experience of hearing the refugee congregation in Strasbourg sing that firmly convinced Calvin of the *importance* of music in intensifying the congregation's praise. Garside, *The Origins of Calvin's Theology of Music*, pp. 18f.

[18] Cook, *Analysing Musical Multimedia*, pp. 103ff.

[19] It is worth remembering that of the artificial images bombarding young people today – a bombardment which provokes much concern among many – a large proportion comes with music, and *the music is usually the very opposite of fragmented.* As Mitchell Stephens puts it in his book, *The Rise of the Image; The Fall of the Word*, in new forms of video, '[The music] is there to order and coordinate, to hold everything together'. (Oxford: Oxford University Press, 1998), p. 190.

[20] Jeremy Begbie, *Voicing Creation's Praise* (Edinburgh: T&T Clark, 1991), pp. 233f. cf. Cook, *Analysing Musical Multimedia*, pp. 57ff.

often not explicit and enabling us to participate in these and other dimensions in ways not always possible through words alone. Music is interacting with words, bringing its own particular capacities to bear.

Interaction in action

To stand back from the models for a moment, we are struck by an intriguing paradox. Conformance between music and words in its strictest form, though often thought to be the 'ideal' model, is in fact extremely rare, in worship as much as anywhere else. Contest and complementation are always present, and there is inevitably interaction between music and words. This is not to say that similarity between words and music is unimportant, only that it is, as it were, a first step towards the generation of fresh meanings, or (we might prefer) of fresh dimensions of meaning in each of the constituent media.

To see a little more clearly what is involved in the words/music interaction, we can highlight two especially distinctive features of music and indicate something of what happens when these are brought to bear upon words in a theological or Christian environment.[21]

The first is perhaps the most obvious of all: *music's ability to mix sounds*. When a painter puts red and yellow in the same space on a canvas, the colours will either hide each other, or merge into each other to make orange. Or that at least is what we see. Objects in our visual field occupy discrete locations which cannot overlap without threatening their integrity as distinct objects. Visually, one cannot have two things in the same place at the same time. In contrast, when we hear two notes played simultaneously on a piano, they do not occupy discrete spaces; each fills the whole of our aural space, yet we hear them as distinct. They neither exclude nor hide each other. Of course this *can* happen, if one sound 'drowns' out the other, but this need not be the case. They can sound *in* and *through* each other.

Music exploits this simple feature of sound perception more than any other art form, giving it considerable theological potential.[22] Think, for example, of the way in which freedom has typically been construed in modernity: human freedom and God's action pitted against each other as inherently antagonistic. The more of God, the less authentically free we can be. By contrast: when one string sets off another on a piano, it is freeing the other to be distinctively itself. During a recent visit to South Africa, on a number of occasions I sang the national anthem, 'Nkosi Sikelel' iAfrika' – God bless Africa. It evoked in me an extraordinary sense of togetherness. A large part of the reason, I suspect, was its four-part harmony, in which no

---

[21] In *Theology, Music and Time*, I speak much more extensively about music's distinctive powers, especially in relation to time.
[22] cf. Jeremy Begbie, 'Through Music: Sound Mix', Jeremy Begbie (ed.), *Beholding the Glory* (London: Darton, Longman & Todd, 2000), pp. 138–54.

vocal line predominates over the others. One's voice and all the others fill the same heard 'space', a space not of many voices each with their mutually exclusive place, but a space of overlapping sounds, where different voices mutually establish each other. Why was solidarity in South Africa so often expressed in harmonious song during the years of oppression? Among the many reasons, I suggest, is that the music provided a taste of authentic freedom for the singers, when in virtually every other sense they were *not* free. Music enabled often unremarkable words to be appropriated in far greater depth because it was bringing its own powers to bear in interaction with them.

For a telling example in film, where words, image and music combine, we can go to the very end of Hitchcock's classic, *Psycho*. The last chord of the film is a superimposition of the chord of A flat minor on D (and the implication from what we have just heard is that the D implies the key of D minor). The two keys, spanning the most dissonant and controversial interval in Western music, the 'tritone', are played together without resolution, a technique known as 'bitonality'. Just before that, on the screen we see Mother's mummified face superimposed on Norman's, a visual depiction of the duality of his personality, but arguably represented more effectively in sound because we do not flip attention from one chord to the other but hear each through the other, so the lack of resolution is all the more striking. Music here is interacting with image (and of course, remembered words). We receive a joint production, music exercising its own distinctive powers.

In this context, it is perhaps hard not to think of all the superimpositions in the Christian scriptures which are not readily resolved – Psalms that resist our attempts to foreclose and synthesise, the eighth chapter of Paul's letter to the Romans, which combines irrepressible confidence with a heavy sense that creation groans as it awaits the liberation of the children of God. Techniques of superimposition have been the bread and butter of much contemporary music. It is perhaps regrettable that those working in the media at the intersection of Christianity and music have not always seen the massive potential of such techniques to elicit the character of some of its most central texts.

A second very obvious feature of music is *its enormous emotional power*. Theories abound about how music might mirror our emotions, or resemble them, or give vent to them, and so on. While there is probably truth in all of these, I believe that critical to music's emotional power is its ability to purify and *concentrate* our emotional life.

In day to day living our emotions are typically transient and confused – they are cloudy; they 'jump out' at us unexpectedly; they are caught up in tangles of competing desires. Music offers us sound patterns of intensified, purified emotion. When a Scottish piper winds a poignant lament over a windswept graveside, he can take our muddled and confused emotional states, refine and concentrate them in sound, giving them a new intensity and vitality, so that we can identify with what is played and, in a sense, discover how we really feel.

When music is drawn intensively into engagement with other media, the process can be immensely rich. As Cook points out, the commonest role for music in contemporary media is to nuance the emotions provided by words and images. When you see a picture of someone fearful, and hear their frightened words, music defines this fear more clearly, inflects the emotion.[23] Here, music can concentrate emotions provided by the other media and in the process, concentrate our own emotional life.

Something of this extraordinary momentum is generated for many by a piece like J. S. Bach's aria 'Erbarme Dich' (together with its preceding recitative) from his *St Matthew Passion*. Peter has denied Jesus, despite pledges of unswerving loyalty. His despair is rendered in a twisted tortuous vocal line. At the words, 'And he [Peter] went out', the Evangelist's voice leaves its comfortable register, reaching a top B, the highest note he sings in the whole work. Bach, through music, links the literal 'going out' to the spiritual exclusion which Peter's guilt brings. With the words ringing in the memory, the aria begins. A muted violin solo spins a melody with repeated appoggiaturas, laden with sighs of grief. When the vocalist enters with the words 'Have mercy, Lord, on me' she begins the violin melody, but at the second phrase, does not reach for the high notes of the original, but dips down, as if she does not have the resources to attain that level. Sorrow's exhaustion in an unfulfilled melody.

Here, the emotions indicated by words are inflected and refined in ways which render them more potent, more lucid, more accessible. And accessibility is just what Bach wants to make possible – because it belongs to the centre of his theological purpose to help the hearer identify with Peter, so that his grief at spurning Christ becomes ours, and in becoming ours, becomes concentrated, intensified.[24]

Wider implications

I have sketched a very broad typology of music's interaction with words. If anything is clear it is that if we are to gain wisdom about the media's enlisting of music in their engagement with religion and culture, we need to recognise that music *interacts, bringing its own distinctive powers to bear.*

It has been possible only to allude briefly to examples of this process

---

[23] Cook, *Analysing Musical Multimedia*, pp. 94ff.

[24] Interestingly, music from the *Passion* has been used in a number of films either about Jesus, or about Christ-like figures: Pasolini's *Accatone*, Tarkovsky's *The Sacrifice,* for example. In Pasolini's *The Gospel According to St Matthew*, 'Erbarme Dich' is used in the Gethsemane sequence as well as earlier in the film. Bach stands at a pivotal point in musical history, when many Lutherans were anxious lest music's emotional powers would devalue words. It is to Bach's credit that he extended music's emotional vocabulary dramatically, while at the same time demonstrating that such music could be faithful to, and massively enrich, our appropriation of words.

which directly involve the media. It is for others to pick up the strands here and apply them further. However, in closing I want to point to three of the wider implications of what we have found.

First, and most obvious, any future study of media, culture and religion will need to take music seriously, especially if such a study is concerned with fostering a responsible use of music in contemporary society.[25] Music cannot be ignored, for the simple reason that the media, culture and religion are not ignoring it.

Second, we need to develop modes of thinking about music which do justice *both* to its interactions *and* to its distinctive features. Part of the reason for the relative neglect of music in media studies is that much academic music theory has inherited patterns of enquiry which default on the notion of a supposedly autonomous musical 'work' to be considered (ideally) in abstraction from any social or cultural practices. This is being repeatedly and forthrightly challenged by music theorists.[26] Unfortunately, much of this writing vastly overplays the 'constructivist' agenda, often construing music purely in terms of the social and cultural forces in which it is embedded. Arguably, the notions of musical autonomy and social reductionism need to be recognised for what they are – as sterile as each other.[27]

Third, if a re-conceptualising of music is under way, I see no reason why those committed to the study of religion should be excluded from the discussion, especially when we bear in mind the close ties between religion and music in history. The frequent absence of any mention of religious belief (Christian or otherwise) in the treatment of music in contemporary cultural studies tells us more, I believe, about an outmoded secularism than responsible, culturally alert scholarship. Engaging with music today necessarily entails engaging with a huge ferment of religious activity (in many forms) worldwide. Every day, religious belief is interacting with music, bringing its own distinctive capacities to bear. Neither academic nor intellectual integrity will be sacrificed by acknowledging this. Quite the opposite.

[25] At the end of an essay in *Rethinking Media, Religion and Culture* (Thousand Oaks, CA: Sage Publications, 1997), Lynn Schofield Clark and Stewart Hoover helpfully outline six possible priorities for future research at the 'intersection' of religion, culture and media (pp. 30–3). It would not be hard to show that music is integrally bound up with all six.

[26] The literature is vast, but cf. e.g. Daniel K. L. Chua, *Absolute Music and the Construction of Meaning*; Nicholas Cook and Mark Everest (eds.), *Rethinking Music* (Oxford: Oxford University Press, 1999); Kathleen Marie Higgins, *The Music of Our Lives* (Philadelphia: Temple University Press, 1991); and Christopher Norris, *Music and the Politics of Culture* (London: Lawrence and Wishart, 1989).

[27] Begbie, *Theology, Music and Time*, pp. 12ff.

Further Reading

N. Cook, *Analysing Musical Multimedia* (Oxford: Clarendon, 1998).

_____ *Music: A Very Short Introduction* (Oxford: Oxford University Press, 1998).

J. Begbie, *Theology, Music and Time* (Cambridge: Cambridge University Press, 2000).

Daniel K. L. Chua, *Absolute Music and the Construction of Meaning* (Cambridge: Cambridge University Press, 1999).

N. Cook and Mark Everest (eds.), *Rethinking Music* (Oxford: Oxford University Press, 1999).

T. DeNora, *Music in Everyday Life* (Cambridge: Cambridge University Press, 2000).

10

Protestant Visual Piety and the Aesthetics of American Mass Culture

David Morgan

In an eloquent study published some years ago, James Carey suggested that communication consists of two rudimentary aspects that remain in tension with one another: the transmission of information and the ritualistic joining of communion. Both draw, he noted, from religious contexts.[1] This observation illuminates American religious mass media, as I will show. In the case of the United States, from the early days of the American republic to the present, religious themes and didactic and devotional uses of imagery have remained a significant part of visual mass culture. Tracts, Bibles, prayer cards, broadsides and millennial charts (Figures 1 and 2), all increasingly illustrated by new technologies of image-making such as lithography and half-tone engraving, served as the means of transmitting religious messages to a vast modern society. At the same time, these images were more than messages. They were the places in a nascent mass culture where many evangelical Christians encountered the impetus for spiritual renewal and personal revelation about what their God expected from them.

Watching videos, films and television or looking at paintings or photographs are not only instances of downloading information. They are also visual experiences whose character, physical structure and social features merit careful aesthetic analysis. By 'aesthetic' I mean the sensuous, imagined, or, more broadly speaking, the embodied experience of meaning, whose significance is measured in feeling no less than in intellectual content. There are several ways in which aestheticians have studied aesthetic experience. For the purpose of this chapter, I will define the aesthetic dimensions of religious media in terms of any media artifact (film, television, video, mass-produced print or image) that evokes one or more of the following responses:

(1) an emotion that is religiously compelling;
(2) the experience of a personal address and the need for response;
(3) a sense of presence or relatedness to another person, a community, or God;

[1] James W. Carey, *Communication as Culture: Essays on Media and Society* (Boston: Unwin Hyman, 1989), pp. 13–36.

(4) a special mindfulness of or attention to a sacred moment, place, or
    object.

In every case, the aesthetic dimension of religious media is the contribution
that the medium's physical structure makes to a common as well as an individual experience of sacred purpose. It is important, therefore, to avoid
either purely formal analysis of the artifact or any manner of reducing it to
political or economic circumstances. To this end, the procedure employed
here is to couple analysis of the artifact to its reception. In every case, the
physical characteristics of the medium are an integral part of the experience and must be scrutinised if the scholar is to account for the felt or
sensuous dimension of religious meaning-making.

Investigation of the aesthetic dimensions of religious media and its reception does not seek to transform religious into artistic experience, but to discern the role of the felt-quality of media reception in the experience of
meaning among religious believers. My principal contention is that the
mass-mediated visual practices of believers are often constitutive of religious
experience and not merely adjunct to it. Scholars may begin to understand
the significance of this fact by examining the aesthetic character of mass
culture's many visual pieties.

Protestantism and the imbrication of media

In theory, Protestantism often privileges verbal or textual discourse as the
principal medium for conveying the central religious message, the gospel.
Written words (and declaimed) are the medium of holy Scripture, God's
chosen means of self-revelation. Because they regard Scripture as God's
speech, or God's Word, many conservative Protestants conflate speech and
script as if the two were identical media. Most of the Bible is not, in fact,
direct or indirect discourse, yet the belief persists among some Protestants
that Scripture is an untrammelled and unparalleled record or transcription
of divine thought and will. Thus, to read or recite passages of the Bible is to
enter into the very medium of divine revelation. Captured in the written
text is the voice of God, the clarity and authority of which do not suffer in
the translation to written text. Because the Bible, according to conservative
Protestant belief, transcribes God's speech by God's own agency (by means
of the 'inerrant inspiration' of the human writers), textuality is a medium
that preserves the actual intention of the speaker.

In practice, however, Protestants almost never rely solely on the spoken
and written word. Teachers, clergy, evangelists, moralists and parents have
modelled other forms of representation such as music, imagery, ritual or
drama on the underlying forms of verbal and scripted discourse. Doing so
has allowed Protestants to augment the appeal and effect of their message. The assumption is that the word can be translated to other media
without compromising its accuracy and authority. A neat distinction of

medium and message (or form and content) enables this assumption. By regarding an image as the medium for transmitting a scriptural message, Protestants make the textual medium of words the content of the non-textual, subordinate medium of an image or a song. Protestants are typically at pains to stress the distinction between, say, word and image, since this allows the image to remain subordinate and therefore to deliver its content (the word) without corrupting it in the translation. Captives of textuality, images are compelled to refer only to the textual content they bear.

Yet as one media theorist has stated, 'Media are not simply channels for conveying information between two or more environments, but rather shapers of new social environments themselves.'[2] Moreover, telling is never the same as showing, so the process of translation from word to image (or any other medium) is something that widens the opportunity for interpretation or aesthetic response. A medium is never without influence on the message. In the domain of spoken words, for example, what one says depends fundamentally on how one says it, and the manner of utterance is inseparable from the medium of utterance: the pitch, timbre or volume of the voice, or the accenting, velocity or repetition of words. Diction shapes meaning no less (though much more subtly) than the mere contents of speech. Indeed, form and content are deftly interwoven in any given speech act. This contribution of a medium to the experience of a media artifact is the aesthetic dimension of meaning-making. And when translation from one medium to another occurs, as in the imbrication of image and word in Protestant uses of mass media, the aesthetic dimension expands even further.

Protestant visual piety and mass culture: the case of religious tracts

Producers may broadcast an evangelical message in what appears to be a strictly instrumental form of information such as a humble tract (see Figures 1 and 2). But if we are to believe what nineteenth-century tract producers and readers reported, the flimsy, inexpensive paper covered with dense print was a medium that did not bear an indifferent relation to its message and the meaning that readers discovered in it. A collection of anecdotes published by the American Tract Society in the 1820s states that 'divinely inspired' truths were 'stamped in bold relief on the face of religious Tracts, and extended to every city, and town, and village, and family, and soul'. Tracts were not simply messages conveniently recorded in an inexpensive format, but objects 'blazing with the effulgence of the truths which God has revealed, in the aspect and connection in which he has

[2] Joshua Meyrowitz, 'Medium Theory', David Crowley and David Mitchell (eds.), *Communication Theory Today* (Stanford: Stanford University Press, 1994), p. 51.

revealed them, and attended, in answer to the prayers of God's people, by the Holy Ghost sent down from heaven'.[3] Far from diminishing the religious aura of sacred artifacts, as Walter Benjamin asserted of modern technologies of reproduction, mechanically-produced texts such as tracts enhanced the production and distribution of sacredness attached to objects in mass culture.[4]

The Tract Society encouraged the devout to select from its stock of several hundred tracts those which addressed the particular situation of the potential convert and then to leave the tract in the person's daily path. The results reported in the Tract Society's literature were most encouraging. One New York resident on the brink of suicide discovered a tract someone had placed in his hat. When he removed the tract and examined it, his attention was 'arrested ... He perused it – it struck conviction to his heart – he instantly fell on his knees, and cried to God to have mercy on him.' Another convert kept a tract near him always, even on his pillow at night in order that it might direct 'his earliest thoughts when he awakes'.[5] The Tract Society even regarded the tract as a talisman at work in the cause of moral reform. One of the Society's annual reports claimed that 'there is a sacredness in the very name and character of Tracts, by which the very sight of them often strikes the profane man dumb, stops the Sabbath-breaker in his course, and disperses those who have companied for purposes of sinful amusement and vice'.[6] So these meagre things exerted a disproportionate power. They enjoyed a meaning or an effect that greatly exceeded their ephemeral encoding of evangelical information.

Of course, it is not surprising to hear the executives of an organisation committed to distributing tracts estimate their power so highly. But these reports came from clergy, educators, colporteurs and readers in the field. A later annual report included an account gathered by a travelling salesman who took tracts and books door to door. A woman in Pennsylvania related to the salesman that one of her neighbours 'had become a confirmed inebriate':

> Calling at his house one day, she read him the tract, 'We Must Live' [which addressed the issue of selling liquor]. After reading it, she showed him the picture [illustrating the tract (Figure 1)], and told him of the wretched condition of his family, who were really in want;

---

[3] 'Usefulness of Tracts,' No. 104, Tracts of the American Tract Society Vol. 3 (New York: American Tract Society, n.d. [ca. 1826]), pp. 3, 14–15.

[4] Walter Benjamin, 'The Work of Art in the Age of Mechanical Reproduction', Hannah Arendt (ed.), *Illuminations*, trans. Harry Zohn (New York: Schocken, 1968), pp. 217–51. I have further discussed the contradiction of Benjamin's celebrated thesis in *Protestants and Pictures: Religion, Visual Culture, and the Age of American Mass Production* (New York: Oxford University Press, 1999), pp. 6–8.

[5] 'Usefulness of Tracts,' pp. 19, 23.

[6] *Third Annual Report of the American Tract Society* (New York: American Tract Society, 1828), p. 22.

No. 474.

"WE MUST LIVE."

PUBLISHED BY THE
AMERICAN TRACT SOCIETY,
150 NASSAU-STREET, NEW YORK.

Figure 1   Robert Roberts, illustration for 'We Must Live,' No. 474, in *Tracts of the American Tract Society*, vol. 12. New York: American Tract Society, n.d., The Library Company of Philadelphia. [1849].

after which he promised that he would drink no more. This promise he has been able to keep several years, maintaining his family, and living respectably.[7]

Showing the man the tract's image bolstered the impact of its message. The illustration referred to (Figure 1) appears to have intensified the effect of the tract's text by turning its printed message into a concrete talisman that compelled the drunkard to repent. The image portrays a tavern interior in which three idle men smoke. Through the window appears a line of people filing into a church. The inebriate in question may have recognized himself in this slothful fellowship, violating Sabbath and wasting away in the grip of many vices (note the spittoon on the floor and the poster advertising horse races). The title of the tract, 'We Must Live,' was the proprietor's reply to an evangelical who objected to sales on Sabbath. But by visualizing the dissipating life of the tavern in contrast to the life of the devout, the image helped bestow an auratic quality on the tract, augmenting its consequence, making the reader into a viewer, that is, making the experience of being told the truth into the experience of seeing it. The effect of this act of visual piety was to transform the evangelical message of repentance and contrition into a personal encounter that demanded a heartfelt response.

The tract was a powerful agency in the evangelical enterprise, since it adapted a face-to-face form of evangelism to mass society.[8] In fact, tracts were among the first instances in modern mass culture in which a mass-produced religious medium was intended to work in the place of oral, face-to-face encounter to generate religious experience such as conviction and conversion. Another tract illustration (Figure 2) shows the manual distribution of tracts. But this was not the only way it happened. The tracts were mailed, left in public places, stacked in dispensaries, stashed in books, shipped around the world by steamboat and rail. But the tract was supposed to evoke a personal encounter, so the image of such an exchange illustrated the Tract Society's first official communication, the announcement of its foundation in 1825 and its intentions for the Christian public nationwide. Tract producers wanted a medium that could make religion happen – the authentic religion of evangelical revival. The tract was deployed as an instrument to this end. It took the place of the evangelist, substituting the reception of the tract for the face-to-face encounter. Written words were imbricated or patterned on spoken words, and the tract's text evoked an encounter between reader and writer that paralleled the ersatz relation of giver and receiver. Likewise, image was modelled on the direct discourse of spoken words. The use of first- and second-person address in the text of many tracts was intended to suggest the co-presence of the tract's author/speaker and the reader/listener, as in the oral mode of homily or conversation.

[7] 'Colporteur Reports, Pennsylvania Branch,' *Thirty-Sixth Annual Report* (New York: American Tract Society, 1861), p. 94.

[8] Morgan, *Protestants and Pictures*, ch. 1.

THE ADDRESS

OF THE

EXECUTIVE COMMITTEE

OF THE

AMERICAN TRACT SOCIETY,

TO THE

CHRISTIAN PUBLIC.

Figure 2   The distribution of tracts, cover illustration to 'The Address of the Executive Committee of the American Tract Society to the Christian Public,' No. 1. New York: American Tract Society, n.d. [originally published in 1825].

The American Tract Society's Address to the Christian public of 1825 identified its audience as 'those whose stations or whose character give them influence over the destiny of their fellow men'.[9] 'We feel justified in soliciting', the authors announced, 'for the object we pursue, your fixed and steady attention, your strong and ardent affections, your hearty and vigorous co-operation.'[10] Next to the Bible and the preacher, 'short, plain, striking, entertaining, and instructive Tracts, exhibiting in writing some of the great and glorious truths of the Gospel', were the instrument of choice. '"The Word of Truth"', the Address insisted, 'is the great instrument of moral renovation.'[11] The cover of the tract (Figure 2) displayed a genteel family delivering a tract, which was probably the very Address, to another well-placed family. The image, in other words, visualised the act of communication undertaken by the tract's authors. The imbrication of image on text underscored both the continuity of the evangelical tract with the 'Word of Truth' and the closed ranks of the bourgeois 'Christian public'.

The use of illustrated tracts shows a careful attempt to ground the mass-produced tract in oral culture. Accordingly, the image that sparked the drunkard's repentance (Figure 1) places the viewer in the room with the drunkard and his debauched company, all of whom appear unaware of the sabbath-keeping apparent to the viewer through the window. The image positions the viewer in a face-to-face encounter with the errant. Other tract illustrations, such as Figure 2, often portray face-to-face exchange as the paradigmatic medium of tract distribution and consumption. The arch medium of personal encounter becomes the content of the secondary or ersatz medium of the tract in order to secure the substitutes's authority, accuracy and reliability. In similar fashion, latter-day versions of the printed tract – religious videos, television programming and cyber-tracts – often encapsulate such oral utterances as direct discourse, prayer, chant, preaching and reading Scripture as well as such traditional material culture and ritual as the Mass, pilgrimage, and worship. This quoting of oral culture presumes that there is no loss or change of meaning in the relay from old medium to new. Another familiar instance is Oral Roberts, Jr., who holds his hand to the camera and asks viewers to touch their television screens in order to establish virtual contact for praying together. The task is to render the new medium faithful to the old, adjusting and translating the differences in order to achieve an equivalence that viewers can accept.

In the history of Christian communication, imbrication, or the patterning of one medium on another, almost always takes place on the model of face-to-face orality. The shift from one medium to another can provide the occasion for experiencing the novel properties of the new medium as both an amplified pronunciation of a message and a moving experience. Even

---

[9] 'The Address of the Executive Committee of the American Tract Society to the Christian Public' No. 1 (New York: American Tract Society, 1825); reprinted, *The American Tract Society Documents 1824–1925* (New York: Arno, 1972), p. 3.
[10] American Tract Society Documents, p. 14.
[11] American Tract Society Documents, p. 4.

something as seemingly instrumental and one-dimensional as an evangelical tract can configure a communion beyond communication. That which appears to be no more than a straightforward transmission of information can also become a place for the revelation of the holy by engaging faces and bodies as the embodied encounter with another. In the setting of mass culture, imbrication has the capacity to help make the indirect into the immediate, mass culture into local, the impersonal into the personal, and communication into communion.

Mass-mediated religion and the public sphere

American Protestants continued to use visual print media to exert a religious influence in the twentieth century. In fact, mass-produced images of Jesus became visual tracts in and of themselves. Among conservative American Protestants the social task of faith has always been to secure a countervailing moral force. Although the last of the state legislatures ratified by the 1830s the Bill of Rights, which entailed the separation of church and state, many Protestants from before the Civil War (1861–65) to the present have used mass-produced images to compensate for the First Amendment's disestablishment of religion, either by enhancing voluntary campaigns to disseminate Protestant influence, by appealing to a unifying symbol for Christians, or even, in the case of one noteworthy image in the twentieth century (Figure 3), by infiltrating public spaces in order to 'reclaim' them as evidence of a Christian nation. Mass-produced images offered one attractive means of influence toward each of these ends.

A fascinating history of visual piety among American Protestants in the second half of the twentieth century shows how a very common mass-produced image of Jesus operated as the mediated site of religious practice (Figure 3). Regarded by millions of mid-twentieth-century American Christians as an authentic likeness of Jesus Christ, the image displayed a radiance that visually approximated the effulgence formerly attributed to evangelical tracts. It also offered a literal transposition of the biblical Word or *Logos* into a portrait-image of Christ that recommended its use as a kind of visual tract. During the 1940s and 1950s the image came to blur the distinction between secular and church interests and thus pursued the nineteenth-century crusade to make the United States a Christian (read: Protestant) nation. Following World War II, when wallet-sized reproductions of Warner Sallman's *Head of Christ* (Figure 3) were distributed in the manner of a tract among American servicemen in Europe and Asia by the YMCA and the Salvation Army, a Lutheran businessman in Indiana undertook a project called 'Christ in Every Purse'. His aim was to distribute the same pocket-sized version of the *Head of Christ* as widely as possible. The businessman contrasted the need for 'card-carrying Christians' to the threat of 'card-carrying Communists'. His campaign

Figure 3   Warner Sallman, *Head of Christ*, 1940. Courtesy Jessie C. Wilson
Galleries, Anderson University, Anderson, Indiana.

continued through the 1950s and into the 1960s as Cold War anti-communism gripped America.[12]

Around 1965 a copy of Sallman's ubiquitous picture of Jesus was placed in the hallway of a Michigan public high school to commemorate a beloved secretary. It remained there without comment until 1992, when a student objected to its presence and the American Civil Liberties Union (ACLU) filed suit on the student's behalf in federal court, charging violation of the constitutional separation of church and state since the local schoolboard supported the superintendent's refusal to remove the picture. After receiving an offer of assistance from Pat Robertson's 700 Club, the schoolboard agreed to accept legal defence free-of-charge from the conservative Rutherford Institute of Charlottesville, Virginia, an evangelically sympathetic, private legal foundation committed to promoting freedom of religion.[13] The school's lawyer argued that the image did not endorse a particular religion but represented Jesus as a historical figure, and therefore served a secular rather than a religious purpose in the public school. Frequent editorials in local newspapers contended that removing the image contradicted the principles enshrined in the Constitution by the 'founding fathers'. 'Our country', as one editorialist wrote, 'is founded on the principles of God and the morals He teaches through the Bible, his recorded word.'[14] The ACLU maintained that the image offended the agnostic student by promoting Christianity.

In a nineteen-page decision, District Court Judge Benjamin Gibson rejected the school's argument and ruled in favour of the plaintiff, stating that 'the true objective [of the image's display] is to promote religion ... in general and Christianity in particular'. Gibson also found that the defendants' 'declaration that the picture is displayed as an artistic work or that it is a depiction of a historical figure does not blind this Court to the religious message necessarily conveyed by the portrayal of one who is the object of veneration and worship by the Christian faith'.[15]

Supporters of the school board ritualistically cloaked the image and cheered successive attempts at appeal all the way to the United States Supreme Court, which, on 1 May 1995, announced its decision not to hear

[12] See David Morgan, '"Would Jesus Have Sat for a Portrait?" The Likeness of Christ in the Popular Reception of Sallman's Art', David Morgan (ed.), *Icons of American Protestantism: The Art of Warner Sallman* (New Haven: Yale University Press, 1996), pp. 192–93.

[13] See the Associated Press report, 'Pat Robertson offers to join Bloomingdale High fray', *The Herald-Palladium* 4 November 1992. For an articulation of the Rutherford Institute's interests, see Steve Dennison, 'Rutherford for the defense in Bloomingdale', *The Herald-Palladium* 13 December 1992. The institute, the article indicates, was named after Samuel Rutherford, a seventeenth-century Scottish clergyman who opposed the divine right of kings.

[14] Vera Stafford, 'Christians need to speak up about Christ's picture', Letters to the Editor, South Haven *Tribune* 4 December 1992.

[15] Hon. Benjamin F. Gibson, Washegesic vs. Bloomingdale Public Schools 3 February 1993, United States District Court, Western District of Michigan, Southern Division, File No. 4:92-CV-146, pp. 9–10.

Figure 4   Jay Drowns, photographer, removal of Sallman's *Head of Christ* picture from Bloomingdale High School, from Kalamazoo Gazette, February 2, 1995, p1. Courtesy Kalamazoo Gazette.

the case, letting stand the appellate decision to support Gibson's ruling. When the image was finally removed (Figure 4), local clergy led prayer as supporters wept. Local papers were peppered with sympathetic editorials that expressed outrage and sadness regarding the fate of the image. Visitations to and gatherings before the image were frequent and carefully covered by local and regional radio, television and print media. A local folk singer recorded a ballad about the episode, entitled 'A Picture Graced the Wall'. School officials left in place of the image the red shroud that had covered it. In following days students pinned picture buttons of Jesus to the shroud, but these were removed later after the ACLU threatened to take the school district back to court.[16]

The entire affair demonstrates how an inexpensive, mass-produced artifact became the celebrated (or embattled) site for the public expression of broadly shared religious sentiment. Scholars risk missing a great deal if they interpret the media artifact in strictly political or economic terms. To wit, editorials by area residents often stressed the iconic significance of the image, asserting that disrespect toward the image was nothing less than contempt for Christ himself. 'If you do not want to look at the picture of Jesus', one woman wrote, 'and give him the recognition he deserves, you do not have to look at the picture'. Another writer warned that the student who brought suit against the school system 'someday shall face this same Jesus and account for his actions'. And another: 'Pity the person who tries to remove Jesus from a hallway or from his life'.[17] Supporters of the image saw in it the very features of the person it represented. A woman from Kalamazoo lamented the end of the era where one entered and was 'greeted by the face of a man whose expression conveyed incredible warmth and kindness'.[18] It is clear that local reception of the picture involved each of the four aesthetic modes of response outlined at the outset of this essay. The appeal of this image in the Bloomingdale controversy relied on its ability to visualise the personal address of the biblical message (as evangelical Christians understood it) and to lend the intensely felt relationship between believer and saviour a public visibility with a political significance. The controversy, in other words, offered a public occasion for a ritualised display of mutual sentiment that promoted the status of a group which felt slighted or even threatened.

Such sentiment confirmed the fears of opponents that the image clearly signified Christian belief. Judicial opinion certainly concurred: an appellate

---

[16] For local response to the court ruling and accounts of ritualised gatherings before the image, see Cris Robins, 'Cover hung over Jesus after vigil', *The Herald-Palladium* 1 March 1993, pp. 1, 4; Rod Smith, 'Jesus painting controversy inspires a ballad', Kalamazoo *Gazette* 10 January 1994, p. C3; Rod Smith, 'Jesus portrait down, not necessarily out', Kalamazoo *Gazette* 2 February 1995, pp. 1, 2; and 'Bloomingdale must remove Jesus portrait', Kalamazoo *Gazette* 9 February 1995, p. 1.

[17] 'Let picture remain', Kalamazoo *Gazette* 28 September 1994; 'Christians need to speak up about Christ's picture', South Haven *Tribune* 4 December 1992; 'Lauds Bloomingdale stand', Kalamazoo *Gazette* 3 December 1992.

[18] 'Jesus portrait symbolized love,' Kalamazoo *Gazette* 5 March 1995.

court judge ruled that the 'portrait has a proselytising, affirming effect'.[19]
This was, of course, the very aim behind distributing evangelical tracts in
the nineteenth century, and it was the exact intention of Christians who distributed Sallman's picture as a visual tract in the twentieth century. But
mass media artifacts can do more for religious belief than deliver information. They inspire intense feeling, offer a call that invites a personal
response, provide a shared or communal experience, and focus attention
on common symbols of belief. This aesthetic dimension is powerfully at
work among Protestants in the material culture of belief, even among
ephemeral, mass-media artifacts, where images visualise texts in the attempt
to give them a presence that will engage a mass audience of believers.

---

[19] Quoted in Charlotte Channing, 'Jesus portrait ruled illegal', Kalamazoo *Gazette* 7
September 1994, p. A2.

11

Christ and the Media: Considerations on the Negotiation of Meaning in Religious Television

Myrna R. Grant

This chapter seeks to explore three questions: what are the origins of Malcolm Muggeridge's objections to the use of television to communicate the gospel,[1] what factors affect the negotiation of meaning in religious television, and why metaphor and story continue to be particularly effective in the transfer of religious meaning in contemporary culture.

Muggeridge and the media

For many academics and media practitioners, Malcolm Muggeridge, the British journalist, broadcaster, social critic and latterly Christian, has come to typify the view that the gospel should not and cannot be communicated on television.[2] The gist of Muggeridge's argument is that the technology of television inevitably is a medium of fantasy, in stark contradiction to the reality of the Christian message. If Christ could have been invited to appear on television, Muggeridge asserts, he would have resisted the temptation because Christ was concerned with truth; television's modus operandi is illusion:[3]

> We have created a Frankenstein-like monster, an enormous apparatus of persuasion such as has never before been known on earth. I've spent the last 40 years working in this apparatus and I know exactly how it works. The effect of it is simply that it says to those whom it influences, and its power is fantastic, 'satisfy your greed, satisfy your sensuality, that is the purpose of life'.[4]

---

[1] M. Muggeridge, *Christ and the Media* (Grand Rapids: Eerdmans, 1977).
[2] T. Boomershine, 'Christian community and technologies of the word', J. McDonnell and F. Trampiets (eds.), *Communicating Faith in a Technological Age* (Slough, UK: St Paul, 1989), p. 96.
[3] Muggeridge, *Christ and the Media*, p. 41.
[4] M. Muggeridge, 'Am I a Christian?', *Vintage Muggeridge* (Grand Rapids: Eerdmans, 1985), p. 13.

His apocalyptic vision

One explanation for Muggeridge's antipathy is his deeply rooted icono-clasm. Muggeridge had an intractable and indiscriminate distrust of estab-lished institutions and authority, including business, educational, religious, political systems and the media. He saw their remedial formulations of progress as comically bogus. His view was that Western civilisation was in its last days. So convinced was he that, as a young writer, he and his family left England for Moscow to start life again in what he thought would be the egalitarian society of communist Russia. His winter in Moscow cruelly shat-tered his illusions and convinced him of the futility of any ideology to create a better world. At a time when many influential writers of his era, George Orwell for example, were sympathetic 'fellow travelers' on the communist path and were anticipating a social Utopia, Muggeridge repudiated both communist and democratic ideologies, returning to England even though he was convinced that modern Britain was a broken-down civilisation. He regularly predicted the disintegration of Western society and saw the inven-tion of television as playing a major role in its collapse.[5] In 1957, on BBC's *London Forum*, he expanded his prediction to argue that the idea of progress anywhere in the world was a disintegrating fallacy.[6]

His historical epoch

As much as Muggeridge liked to view himself as an independent thinker and nonconformist, he was a man shaped by his dramatic times. Beginning in the thirties, as Europe was entering the unsettled decade that would end in war, the Frankfurt School in Germany identified popular media as a tool of government and industry. Asa Berger suggests that a deep distrust of modern media was formed in this era. 'It is probable that the members of the Frankfurt school were nostalgic for a different period ... what might be described as an imaginary golden era ... before the development of capi-talist mass society.'[7] Muggeridge expressed similar longings for a better 'world elsewhere'. In a radio *Critics* review,[8] in reference to *Coriolanus*, he said, 'But surely ... when [Shakespeare] says that there is a world elsewhere, isn't that an intensely poignant moment?'

This early apprehension about the power of media was more than con-firmed in World War II as Goebbels' Third Reich propaganda machine used media with powerful effect to further Nazi aims. By use of every poss-ible educational and communication media, Goebbels instilled in the German people the concept of Hitler as a veritable god, inflaming public

[5] Muggeridge, *Christ and the Media*, p. 23.
[6] BBC Radio, *London Forum*, 2 February 1957.
[7] A. Berger, *Cultural Criticism* (Thousand Oaks, CA: Sage, 1995), p. 45.
[8] BBC Radio, *The Critics*, 4 April 1948.

opinion against the Jews, and convincing Germans of their destiny as the Master Race and thus the legitimate rulers of the world. Three years after Goebbels' suicide on 1 May 1945, Muggeridge wrote and presented a radio talk on Goebbels for BBC's *Third Programme*, in which he called Goebbels 'a fearful object lesson'.[9]

Anxiety about media effects continues to have rigorous modern advocates. Gregor Goethals observes, 'Today, as in earlier centuries, there are modern iconoclasts who warn us of the dangers of society's most recent visual language, television. While there may be genuine disagreement about the appropriateness of technological media for the communication of visual Christian experience, there is a reconciling metaphor: Christ the transformer of culture.'[10]

Meaning and the media

Scholars of differing academic traditions disavowed the view that the media *ipso facto* exert direct persuasive power over audiences. A plethora of research demonstrates that people variously reject media texts, make differing meanings of the same texts, interpret texts literally, ironically or in startlingly idiosyncratic ways. This view has a certain resonance with Judeo-Christian scripture, which indicates that the human will retains a critical capacity to make choices.[11] Psychologist R. Grant reflects, 'It seems endemic to self-consciousness that it should always overshoot its own (notionally) causal explanations and revert to the inexplicable, uncaused autonomy of the first-person perspective which ... we invariably experience as freedom.'[12] This propensity of audiences to read texts in widely varying ways, negotiating their own meaning, is not encouraging news to Christian broadcasters that use the media for evangelism. Although broadcasters may take pains to communicate as clearly as possible to mass audiences, the assumption that the message will be as unambiguous to audiences as it is to them is dubious.

William Biernatzki cites an interesting study of Hmong refugees in Chicago undertaken by Dwight Conquergood of Northwestern University.[13] The Hmong believe that life on earth is controlled by malicious evil spirits who must be appeased. Newly arrived Hmong refugees were assured that such spirits do not exist. As he studied the media choices of this immigrant group, Conquergood observed a very strong preference among the Hmong

[9] BBC Radio. *Third Programme*, 8 May 1948.

[10] G. Goethals, 'The Church and the Mass Media: Competing Architects of Our Dominant Symbols, Rituals and Myths', McDonnell and and Trampiets (eds.), *Communicating Faith*, p. 77.

[11] Gen. 4:6–10, Deut. 5:29, John 7:17.

[12] R. Grant, 'No Conjuring Tricks', *Times Literary Supplement*, 14 November 1997, p. 3.

[13] W. Biernatzki, *Roots of Acceptance: The Intercultural Communication of Religious Meaning* (Rome: Center for Cultures and Religion, Pontifical Gregorian University, 1991), p. 130.

for horror films, which they watched with appreciation and pleasure. In investigating this predilection, Conquergood discovered that the films greatly reassured the Hmong that evil specters do indeed flourish in America.[14]

Not only do people select, organise and interpret messages in differing ways, increasingly audiences resist linear communication. Corporate media has moved away from the hierarchical model of creating products for consumers in a top-down fashion after which advertising campaigns are devised to persuade people to buy the new product. The modern business model is interactive: communicate with and from customers, and audience is key. Messages such as 'Telephone our 800 number and leave a message,' 'E-mail us,' 'Visit us on the Internet,' have become ubiquitous.

Nowhere is this dynamic more dominant than on the Internet, which provides a powerful means of communication between sellers (even of ideas) and consumers.[15] Users are no longer limited to accepting truth claims from a single source. With a click of a mouse they can research and compare information from countless web sites on any topic, including religion, or converse with real people in chat rooms to challenge, question or discuss anything. The *Cluetrain Manifesto* calls this 'the end of business as we know it'. Interactivity is also the end of old media as we knew them.

Meaning in the words themselves

Nevertheless there are still religious broadcasters who maintain the conviction that their very words as they preach the gospel on television are divinely appointed in a unique way. The Holy Spirit, they maintain, overrides cultural considerations and personal variables and predilections. Quoted in this context are scripture verses like, 'As the rain and the snow come down from heaven and do not return to it without watering the earth . . . so is my word that goes out from my mouth: it will not return to me empty, but will accomplish what I desire.'[16]

Mark Noll, in his book *The Scandal of the Evangelical Mind*, calls this attitude toward Scripture 'bible-onlyism', citing the assertion of the Restorationist leader Tolbert Fanning that 'the Scriptures fairly translated need no explanation'.[17] This mechanistic view is disinterested in considering 'appreciation for the ambiguities of language, the limits of [human] understanding, the uniqueness of each individual, and the social nature of language'.[18]

[14] Biernatzki, *Roots of Acceptance*, p. 133.

[15] R. Levin, C. Locke, C. Searles and D. Weinberger, *The Cluetrain Manifesto: The End of Business As Usual* (Cambridge, MA, Perseus, 2000).

[16] Isa. 55:10, 11.

[17] M. Noll, *The Scandal of the Evangelical Mind* (Grand Rapids, MI: Eerdmans, 1994), p. 98.

[18] D. Carson, *The Gagging of God* (Leicester: Apollos, 1996), p. 102.

Meaning in the affective experience

Pierre Babin directs his attention away from the variables that influence how people interpret texts and their desire for interactivity to suggest that it is the *emotions* that are a central dynamic in the creation of meaning.[19] This echoes Aristotle's observation that 'there is nothing in the mind that has not been first in the senses'.[20] This is a helpful insight, because an emotional reaction both individualises communication and is a personal response to the message.

Historically the church has been wary of communication that deliberately rouses people's feelings and imaginations. 'Much suspicion of the arts by the Churches has undoubtedly been engendered by the fear that the arts are essentially about the expression of emotion rather than the more serious business of truth-telling.'[21] Christian evangelism, teaching and preaching are traditionally conducted via a cognitive teaching model. After all, the Great Commission directs the disciples to *teach*.[22]

Television often resists pedagogy and loves narrative. The medium favors open-endedness, ambiguity and emotion, the very qualities that the church disavows as frivolous, dangerous and of fleeting value. Theology, the Queen of the Sciences, has been wary of both emotion and story. Its language is often explanatory and abstract. In contrast, religious language is rich in metaphor and symbol[23] and is able to enliven the human imagination.

Victor Turner uses the term 'liminoid' to refer to a person's fragile state of changed consciousness when an individual becomes engrossed in a film, a piece of music, a play or a television narrative.[24] In this dynamic, the everyday world fades away, and the person is inwardly focused in 'another world'. In the case of television and film, spectators are comfortably seated in dim lighting or the dark. The everyday world fades as the screen comes to life and the sound wraps around them. They are absorbed by the shadows, lights, rhythm, actions and the passions presented. Emotion and sensibility are sharpened. According to Marty,[25] viewers are as though hypnotised, in a sort of second state between waking and dreaming.

Janet Murray describes the psychology of a child's attachment to a teddy bear and relates this dynamic to story:

---

[19] P. Babin, *The New Era in Religious Communication* (Minneapolis: Fortress, 1991).

[20] J. Marty, 'Toward a Theological Interpretation and Reading of Film', J. May (ed.), *New Images of Religious Film* (Minneapolis: Fortress, 1991), p. 135.

[21] J. Begbie, *Voicing Creation's Praise, Toward a Theology of the Arts* (Edinburgh: T&T Clark, 1991), p. 249.

[22] Matt. 28:20.

[23] S. TeSelle, *Speaking in Parables: A Study in Metaphor and Theology* (Philadelphia: Fortress, 1975), p. 193.

[24] V. Turner, *From Ritual to Theater* (New York: Performing Arts, 1993).

[25] J. Marty, 'Toward a Theological Interpretation and Reading of Film', J. May, *New Image of Religious Film* (Kansas City, MO: Sheed & Ward, 1997), p. 135.

[The teddy bear] has a richly ambiguous psychological location, shimmering with emotion. A good story serves the same purpose for adults, giving us something outside ourselves ... upon which we can project our feelings.[26]

Cinema ... enlivens human dimensions that are somewhat underdeveloped in our scientific, technological and to the bitter end, rationalised cultures: the symbolic and the poetic, sensibility and emotion. It strengthens weakened possibilities that have to do in part with the religious. It brings back to life the sense of mystery by making us love what is not immediately perceivable, what is beyond appearance and evidence.[27]

The liminoid condition is not unfamiliar to religious believers. It psychologically resembles believers' experiences in worship, prayer, meditation and, less commonly, in visions. The state is frequently referenced in spiritual songs and hymns:

Turn your eyes upon Jesus,
Look full on His wonderful face,
And the things of the earth will grow strangely dim,
In the light of His glory and grace.[28]

Purest and highest, wisest and most just,
There is no truth, save only in Thy trust:
Thou dost the mind from earthly dreams recall,
And bring through Christ to Him for whom is all.[29]

St Paul in the epistles, and St. John in Revelation describe being 'caught up' out of earthly reality: St. Paul writes, 'I know a man ... who was caught up to the third heaven. Whether it was in the body or out of the body I do not know ...'[30] The apostle John describes his experience: 'On the Lord's day I was in the Spirit and I heard behind me a loud voice ... and when I turned, I saw seven golden lampstands ... '[31]

William Biernatzki[32] proposes two positive outcomes of the liminoid state. The first is that in the liminoid state negative stereotypes can be bypassed. It is a common phenomenon in life that when individuals become colleagues or friends of 'the stranger', former preconceived notions shift. Biernatzki points out that when positive images of minorities, subcultures or religious groups are presented on television or film, empathy can be created. This is no small achievement and is of value to religious

---

[26] J. Murray, *Hamlet on the Holodeck* (New York: The Free Press, 1997), p. 100.

[27] Murray, *Hamlet*, p. 135.

[28] H. Lemmel, *Hymns for the Living Church*, no. 252. (Carol Stream, IL: Hope, 1922).

[29] R. Graves, 'Purest and Highest' *New English Hymnal*, no. 609 (Norwich: The Canterbury Press, 1920), p. 590.

[30] 2 Cor. 12:2.

[31] Rev. 1:10, 12.

[32] Biernatzki, *Roots of Acceptance*.

communicators who are often working against mass audiences' negative stereotypes of religion and religious believers. The highly popular TV situation comedy series, *The Cosby Show*,[33] depicted life in a middle-class black family with two parents who were professionals (medical doctor and lawyer) who capably managed careers and the parenting of their five children. The series served to dislodge white middle-class stereotypes of African American families as fatherless, dysfunctional and living in poverty.

A second dynamic of the liminoid state is its ability to draw a viewer into unaccustomed worldviews, questions and conflicts. Most people are cloistered within personal social worlds of their daily lives.

Story invites individuals to consider issues and experiences that may be quite different from the familiar. A gripping story which raises metaphysical questions may overcome a viewer's disinterest or antipathy to religious questions or ideas. Emily Dickinson catches this dynamic when she writes, 'Tell all the Truth, but tell it slant, success in circuit lies.'[34]

Meaning in root paradigms

Stories can also be interpreted at an almost unconscious level. Biernatzki points out that films and television can powerfully evoke latent meanings that override cultural and social biases and ideology. They do so because of the presence, imbedded in the media works, of root paradigms which he defines as 'any assumptions about the nature of the world of human beings or any expected patterns for human action which are culturally determined and communicated and accepted from generation to generation'.[35] Regardless of the manifest content of a media product, when it ties into timeless struggles of the human dilemma, audiences will recognise and respond to its latent meaning.

The American television series *Dallas* has provided a fertile case study for media researchers and writers.[36] *Dallas* was broadcast in more than ninety countries, becoming the most popular program in the world.[37] In examining why so many widely differing global audiences were fascinated by the series, Biernatzki examines the 'root paradigms' of *Dallas*. He argues that the cultural symbols in *Dallas* familiar to American viewers, luxurious cars, clothes, homes, appeared so exaggerated and exotic to those in non-Western

---

[33] M. Carsey, T. Wemer and B. Kukoff (Executive Producers), *The Cosby Show*, New York: NBC, (1984–92).

[34] E. Dickinson, 'Tell All the Truth But Tell It Slant', M. Grant, *Poems for a Good and Happy Life* (New York: Grammercy, 1997), p. 21.

[35] Biernatzki, *Roots of Acceptance*, p. 132.

[36] E. Katz and T. Liebes, 'Once Upon a Time in Dallas', *Intermedia* 12 (3) (1984), pp. 28–32; L. Ang, *Watching Dallas* (London: Methuen, 1987); L. Van Wormer, *Dallas: the Complete Ewing Family Saga* (London: Comet/W. H. Allen-Co., 1985); R. Masello, *The Dallas Family Album: Unforgettable Moments from the #1 TV Series* (New York: Bantam Books, 1980); E. Hirschfeld, *Dallas* (Paris: R. Laffont, 1981); A. Silj, *East of Dallas: the European Challenge to American Television* (London: BFI Pub., 1988).

[37] E. Katz and T. Liebes, 'Once Upon a Time in Dallas', *InterMedia* 12 (3) (1984), p. 5.

cultures that they were incidental to the deeper structures within *Dallas*, which viewers recognised: the centrality of family, family permanence and land.[38]

Liebes and Katz, in their study *The Export of Meaning: Cross Cultural Readings of Dallas*, argue that *Dallas* is 'a primordial tale, echoing the most fundamental mythologies'.[39] 'Primordiality evokes in the viewer an echo of the human experience and makes him an instant connoisseur of the *Dallas* variants.'[40] The authors draw from Genesis to illustrate the primeval nature of the program themes. They point out that dynasty is the major preoccupation of the first book of the Bible, and that J. R. and Bobby are simple variations of Cain and Abel. The childbearing problems of the women characters in *Dallas* mirror the fertility crises of key women in Genesis.[41]

A cinematic example of the power of a root paradigm is the *Star Wars* trilogy,[42] which has overtaken *Dallas* in enduring appeal. The films also employ exotic, and in this case, imaginary, fantastical symbols. The events take place cosmically removed from the viewer, 'in a galaxy far away', (as *Dallas* may have been for some global audiences). *Star Wars*'s personification of good and evil dynasties, of struggle culminating in an apocalyptic battle in which good ultimately triumphs, presents themes of mythic scope and appeal, stories 'not so much to entertain ... but rather to reveal something about ourselves and to discover what gives identity, purpose and meaning of our existence'.[43]

Meaning in metaphor, symbol and story

John Shae privileges metaphor and symbol as *the* means of human connection to God.[44] Television, the most powerful dispenser of popular culture in America, is engaged in a ceaseless creation of story, providing a continual supply of symbols and metaphors that are readily understood by mass audiences. Such audiences, however, may make only the weakest connection to biblical narrative images and persons such as shepherds, fig trees, sowers, King David, the apostle Paul. They easily see Mother Teresa as an icon for self-giving love, Nelson Mandela as a symbol of reconciliation, the Red Cross or the Red Crescent as help. The armor of God is an obscure concept to Americans, but home security systems and bulletproof vests are not. The Roman games provided the apostle Paul with a metaphor that does not resonate with audiences today, but the Superbowl does. Angela Tilby observes,

---

[38] Biernatzki, *Roots of Acceptance*, p. 131.

[39] T. Liebes and E. Katz, *The Export of Meaning: Cross Cultural Readings of Dallas* (Cambridge, England: Polity Press, 1993), p. 141.

[40] Liebes and Katz, *The Export of Meaning*, p.144.

[41] Liebes and Katz, *The Export of Meaning*, p. 142.

[42] G. Lucas (Executive Producer), *Star Wars* (1977), *The Empire Strikes Back* (1980), *Return of the Jedi* (1983), Los Angeles: LucasFilm, G. Lucas.

[43] A. MacIntyre, *After Virtue* (Notre Dame, IN: University of Notre Dame Press, 1984), p. 71.

[44] J. Shea, *Stories of Faith* (Allen, TX: Resources for Christian Living, 1996), p. 153.

'[T]elevision is becoming a vital cradle of meaning for most of Western society.'[45]

Biblical metaphors can also contribute to the sense that Christianity is obscure, irrelevant, and alien to the modern age. These negative views of Christianity are easily 'collapsed', in Baudrillard's words, into what for the secular person *is* the reality. Gregor Goethals writes, 'What appears especially difficult, and indeed only rarely achieved, is the use of the most pervasive of cultural languages, television and film, to communicate the Christian faith ... [the challenge is] how to become iconographers in a technological society.'[46] A BBC religious broadcaster writes:

> I have found the search for contemporary images for religious ideas and ideals by far the most satisfying aspect of the work of a television producer. To find a contemporary image for a religious truth is to continue the work of painters, poets, musicians and dramatists ... All we [producers] felt we could do was provide a sufficient richness of imagery for viewers to be at least offered a ride beneath the surface of things; what connections they made were up to them. Little is explained in the programme ... the revelatory power of a combination of images to shock, touch, or alter the sensibilities of viewers is taken away if, as in so much television, they are first told what responses to have.[47]

As is often pointed out, the New Testament is replete with Jesus' use of illustration, metaphor and parable. His audiences were frequently culturally diverse, made up of Jewish leaders steeped in the Old Testament scriptures, common Jewish people who knew the great stories of Jewish history and law, sceptical Romans, rationalistic Greeks, and probably curious travelers from various cities in the ancient world. Jesus knew the language of the synagogue and Old Testament scriptures. The Gospel of Luke makes it plain that from childhood Jesus impressed rabbinical teachers of the law with his learning.[48] Yet in his public ministry, he taught using illustrations, metaphors and parables that were frequently ambiguous stories without explanation or suggestions. He appears to have encouraged his diverse audiences to puzzle over the equivocal meaning of his words and often went away leaving his audience to work out for themselves the meaning of his sayings and stories.

Muggeridge humorously compared the presentation of the gospel on television to 'playing *Abide With Me* in a whore house'. He rightly saw that a religious text or presentation does not necessarily constitute a religious communication and preceded McLuhan in his sense that the medium is the message. He feared that television audiences would take broadcasts of

[45] A. Tilby, 'Like the appearance of lamps', *The Way* 31 (2) (1991), p. 97.

[46] Goethals, *Church and the Mass Media*, p. 77.

[47] P. Armstrong, 'Television as a medium for theology', P. Eaton, *The Trial of Faith* (Worthing, UK: Churchman, 1988), p. 189.

[48] Luke 2:46–7.

religious truth as just another fantastical program offered up for their entertainment. He did, however, have a high view of story as a vehicle for truth. When he wanted to expose the sham of Soviet ideology in his early years, he wrote a novel.[49] When he wanted to decry euthanasia late in life, he wrote a play.[50]

In spite of his glee[51] at the prospect of shocking his audience in his upcoming three London Lectures in Contemporary Christianity,[52] his own writings and numerous religious television programs demonstrate that he actually did believe that the authenticity of the gospel could be communicated through the medium of television.

John Stott, in his remarks following Muggeridge's final London Lecture, graciously countered Muggeridge's disavowal of religious television. Stott observed that Muggeridge was, among other characterisations, a prophet:

> And sometimes, prophets exaggerate. Strict, mathematical accuracy is not their strong point. Now, as I've listened to Malcolm Muggeridge's three lectures, I've found myself casting him in the joint role of Elijah and John the Baptist . . . But you know, the interesting thing is that the Lord God had to make, or help Elijah make, drastic adjustment of his figures . . . I sum it up like this: I believe in the reckoning of God, prophetic faithfulness is more important than strict statistical accuracy.[53]

---

[49] M. Muggeridge, *Winter in Moscow* (Eyre and Spottiswoode: London, 1934).
[50] M. Muggeridge and A. Thornhill, *Sentenced to Life* (Nashville: Thomas Nelson, 1983).
[51] Personal communication, Robertsbridge, Surrey (25 July 1975).
[52] London Lectures on Contemporary Christianity, All Souls, Langham Place, London, November 1976.
[53] J. Stott, 'Chairman's Speech', M. Muggeridge, *Christ in the Media*, p. 122.

PART 4

Media Literacy and Religion

12

Practising Attention in Media Culture

Mary E. Hess

Brian Eno once wrote that 'familiarity breeds content. When you use familiar tools, you draw upon a long cultural conversation – a whole shared history of usage – as your backdrop, as the canvas to juxtapose your work. The deeper and more widely shared the conversation, the more subtle its inflections can be.'[1] In my teaching, which takes place both in seminary and graduate theological contexts, as well as in parish and congregational settings, I am very interested in just what the cultural conversation is that we are engaging. I seek to create as widely and deeply shared a conversation about Christian faith, and as subtle, complex and embodied a conversation as possible.

If Eno is right, that 'familiarity breeds content', then it seems inescapable to me that we need to take seriously the ways in which people live within popular culture – particularly mass-mediated popular culture – as part of the canvas upon which we work as educators. There are some obvious ways in which this canvas is already painted: explicitly religious symbols taken into pop culture (*Dogma, The West Wing, The Simpsons*, and so on), for instance, but there are also ways in which any discussion of faith is painted on a canvas that includes 'secular' images from the news, advertising, the Web, pop music, and elsewhere.[2]

This process of 'familiarity breeding content' is part of the depth and substance behind the notion of 'practices' being constitutive of identity. I am interested in how we think about 'practice' in a mass-mediated age, and in particular, how we think about Christian practice in the context of mass-mediated popular culture. If our familiarity with the basic postures and languages of faith builds, indeed breathes, content through our lives, how is that content shaped through its encounter with mass media? Kathryn Tanner, a Christian theologian who has spent significant time thinking about the various ways in which we currently conceive of 'culture' and then

---

[1] B. Eno, 'The Revenge of the Intuitive', *Wired Magazine* 7.01 (January 1999).

[2] The film *Dogma* was released in the US in 1999 and poked gentle and bathroom humor fun at Catholic notions of papal indulgence, marauding angels, and so on. The television show *The West Wing* is a primetime melodrama that began to air in the US in 2000 and centers on the activities of White House staff. So much has been written about the animated sitcom *The Simpsons* that I would simply suggest a literature search for more information on that particular show. Pinsky, *The Gospel According to the Simpsons* is a good starting point.

in turn how these conceptions interact with theology, has suggested that: 'Christian practices are ones in which people participate together in an argument over how to elaborate the claims, feelings, and forms of action around which Christian life revolves.'[3] This is an interesting definition because it both suggests that there *is* something around which Christian life revolves, and yet it leaves that 'something' to be specified by the arguments in which Christians engage as they enact their ways of being in the world.

Another group of scholars, those working in conjunction with the Valparaiso University *Project on the Education and Formation of People in Faith*, have similarly argued that Christian practices 'are things Christian people do together over time in response to and in the light of God's active presence for the life of the world'.[4] The practices they name in the book that lays out their argument, *Practicing our Faith: A Way of Life for a Searching People*, include: 'honoring the body', 'hospitality', 'household economics', 'saying yes and saying no', 'keeping sabbath', 'testimony', 'discernment', 'shaping communities', 'forgiveness', 'healing', 'dying well' and 'singing our lives'. Each of these practices points to a particular way of being in the world, a specific set of concerns and communicative responses to those concerns, that shapes what it means to be Christian. Yet each of them is also constructed through various mass-mediated representations.

What counts as 'saying yes and no', for instance, within the world of the television drama? How is that process permeated by the agenda-setting effect of the mass media? What might we learn in discerning when it is appropriate to 'say yes and say no' to specific media representations? In what ways might our practices of attention support or interfere with seeking silence? Media literacy educators are fond of saying that our most precious natural resource, that which is scarcest in the US context, is attention. Most of our industries spend an inordinate amount of time attempting to 'capture' our attention, to create 'sticky eyeballs' as they say in the parlance of the WWW. Indeed 'attention', the process of engaging attention, shaping attention, paying attention, and so on, is the practice most at stake and most embodied in our rituals of media.

In our contemporary context many Christians have thought about practising 'attention' in media culture in relation to content. On one end of the Christian spectrum you will find a vast amount of conversation and

[3] K. Tanner, *Theories of Culture: A New Agenda for Theology* (Minneapolis: Fortress, 1997) p. 125.

[4] D. Bass (ed.), *Practicing Our Faith: A Way of Life for a Searching People* (San Francisco: Jossey-Bass, 1998). More information available at: www.practicingourfaith.org In some ways, both Tanner's and the Valparaiso project's definitions draw on the arguments of philosopher Alasdair MacIntyre, who argues that a practice is: 'any coherent and complex form of socially established cooperative human activity through which goods internal to that form of activity are realized in the course of trying to achieve those standards of excellence which are appropriate to, and partially definitive of, that form of activity, with the result that human powers to achieve excellence, and human conceptions of the ends and goods involved, are systematically extended'. A. MacIntyre, *After Virtue* (South Bend, IN: University of Notre Dame Press, 1997) p. 187.

literature devoted to pointing out what is 'dangerous' content for Christians, and a vast number of resources devoted to labeling 'safe' content. There are institutions that put content-rating labels on record albums, and others that rate movies in relation to 'family values'. There are huge industries devoted to creating, marketing and distributing Christian content. I am not arguing that content is unimportant, but content is not so easily quantified or labeled, precisely because of the practices of meaning-making engaged in constructing it.

On the other end of the Christian spectrum, you will find people who are extraordinarily conscious of the ways in which economic factors shape media content. Living in a consumer society, they argue, all media is owned by industries that require the production of more consumers, and hence all media ultimately subordinates meaning-making to practices of commodification. We can not and do not engage in resisting, negotiating, contesting or in other ways frustrating that commodification; we simply fall prey to it. These Christians tend to look with scorn upon the Christian publishing and broadcasting empires as simply further evidence of 'empire building', of the creation of commodification with a Christian label.

I should apologise for the caricatures I am developing here, because either end of this spectrum is more complex than my description. But my point is that neither of these perspectives on the process of attending to mass media sufficiently respects the ways in which people bring mass-mediated materials into their meaning-making processes, into the ways in which we shape and employ our attention.

One of the most interesting aspects of contemporary communications research is the shift scholars are making in the underlying paradigm they use to describe communication, a shift that moves away from an instrumentalist focus to a more expressive one. Rather than using the metaphor of a message 'pipeline' or envisioning information as something the mass media deliver in much the same way that trucks deliver cargo, recent scholarship has begun to talk about communications media as crucial elements of our cultural surround, with the information they 'contain' or 'convey' seen as raw materials from which we then make meaning in complex rituals of representation and interpretation.[5]

From this perspective, religious communities have access to mass-mediated communication at almost any point of the process, rather than simply at the point of production. Perhaps a concrete example will help to make my point more clearly. In my own immediate faith context, that of the Catholic community, a video entitled 'Hollywood vs. Catholicism' was distributed in 1996 that purported to be a documentary showing many ways in which Hollywood has deliberately attempted to create entertainment that is

---

[5] I develop this argument at more length in 'From Trucks Carrying Messages to Ritualized Identities: Implications of the Postmodern Paradigm Shift in Media Studies for Religious Educators', *Religious Education* 94 (3) (Summer 1999).

derogatory of Catholic meaning-making.[6] There are clearly instances within US history where we can point to people and institutions who tried to advance an anti-Catholic agenda, but this documentary did not make an argument from social history. Instead the producers took clips of several films and asserted that the content of these films clearly displayed an anti-Catholic bias. The documentary further argued that the best way to engage such films was by not giving them any attention at all, that is, by boycotting them in movie theaters and not renting them on video. In this case there was concern with 'what' the content was as well as with the economic structures that distributed that content.

Is such a strategy an effective way to structure Christian identity? Perhaps. But my own reaction to the documentary, and that of many other Catholics to whom I have since shown it, is that it actually served to introduce me to films I would like to see. Creative art is not a simple or straightforward process of content manufacture. No producer can be assured that specific content will be 'read' the same way by everyone who engages it. For many of us who are passionately immersed in Catholic community, but all too aware of its flaws and human failings, the films excerpted in this documentary (films such as *Priest, The Last Temptation of Christ, Monty Python's Life of Brian*) highlighted dilemmas that exist within the Christian community, providing opportunities to confront difficult issues, oftentimes with humor or irony that helped ease the pain of doing so.

Paying attention to content is one way to think about the shape of attention in a mass-mediated context. But engaging in arguments over what constitutes appropriate Christian content is an ultimately doomed enterprise, since content is so dependent on context and on the practices used to engage meaning. In my previous example, for instance, the documentary sought to show 'bad' content and suggested that the right response was to boycott (both visually and financially) that content. That tactic backfired, however, because even simply showing the content to point out how bad it was highlighted the inadequacy of the criteria being used to judge it. Asking people to boycott provocative media is counter-intuitive. Indeed, in some ways this documentary 'produced' the opposite of what it was trying to create, because it allowed numbers of progressive Catholics to find films they otherwise might not have been aware of to further solidify their critical stance.

Paying attention solely in terms of critiquing content, or solely as a mode for somehow shortcircuiting consumer commodification, is not sufficient. Are there other ways of engaging our attention, perhaps some that are more productive of Christian identity and community? One in particular is what a group of scholars call a 'responsible imagination'.

---

[6] The videotape 'Hollywood vs. Catholicism' was distributed free of charge to a number of graduate programs in pastoral studies at Catholic universities by the Chatham Hill Foundation in 1996. I have never been able to find more of a citation for it than the Foundation's address, which is: P.O. Box 7723, Dallas, TX 75209.

Daloz et al. spent a number of years interviewing people who have maintained a long-term commitment to the common good (a difficult task in the US context in which commitment to selfish aims often seems more supported than commitment to common aims), and their study pointed to a number of common threads that were found in these people's lives. One that I think is especially pertinent to this discussion is something they termed a 'responsible imagination':

> Their practice of imagination is responsible in two particular ways. First, they try to respect the *process* of imagination in themselves and others. They pay attention to dissonance and contradiction, particularly those that reveal injustice and unrealized potential ...
>
> Second, they seek out sources of worthy images. Most have discovered that finding and being found by fitting images is not only a matter of having access to them but requires discretion and responsible hospitality – not only to what is attractive but also to what may be unfamiliar and initially unsettling ...
>
> Living with these images, the people in our study appear to know that two truths must be held together – that we have the power to destroy the Earth and the power to see it whole. But unlike many who seek escape from the potent tension this act of holding requires, these people live in a manner that conveys a third and essential power: the courage to turn and make promises, the power of a responsible imagination.[7]

For these researchers, the process of imagination is not a trivial one. It is 'imagination' in the richest sense of that word. It is a form of imagination that lives within a community that helps to foster it, that helps to work over the insights that emerge from the process and connect them up with others. It is a seeking out of images: not simply those close to hand, or those that are easy and reassuring, but also those which require 'being sought out' in their dissonance.

This definition of a responsible imagination is full of paradox and ambiguity, not the certainty and clarity that the documentary I mentioned earlier sought to promote. Yet it was this kind of open and fluid perspective that these researchers found necessary for continuing commitment to the common good in the people they studied. It is also this kind of practice of attention that is most open to engaging cultural ritual. Finally, it is a way of thinking about attention that is open to the notion of process and argument that is so much a part of both Tanner's and the Valparaiso project's definitions of Christian practice. Such an understanding suggests that rather than focusing on the 'delivery' of a message (that is, defeating the content we believe is to be delivered, or defeating the distribution itself), we ought to be focusing on engaging culture, on stepping into

---

[7] L. Daloz, C. Keen, J. Keen, and S. Parks, *Common Fire: Lives of Commitment in a Complex World* (Boston: Beacon, 1996) pp. 151–2.

active engagement with the rituals of meaning-making that pervade our culture.

We are already familiar with this shift in more traditional content areas within religious education. We have learned that it is not enough to present doctrine, for instance, simply as an intellectual activity. We have to find ways to make the beliefs and identity of our community of faith come alive to people emotionally. We have to show how they are embodied in concrete practices, and explore them critically. Paulo Freire pointed to this shift in his distinction between 'banking' practices of education and 'praxis'-oriented approaches.[8] Within communications studies, you could call previous understandings of how mass media work a 'banking' approach to communication, and you could suggest that the newer, emerging definitions are praxis-oriented.

What does a praxis-oriented approach, in relation to our emerging understandings of mass-mediated communication, suggest about shaping attention to mass media within religious education? My research suggests that there are three ways in particular that religious educators might work on shaping a responsible imagination using mass-mediated materials, or what some people call 'pop culture objects' in communities of faith. The first of these is as entry points to experiences of transcendence and connection. The second is as clues to social currency. The third is as sources of social conscientisation.

In our media culture, people's desires and yearnings are often given voice at least partially and initially in relation to pop culture objects. In some ways the experience of feeling connected to people beyond one's immediate context, and to experiences beyond one's imagining, occurs more often through mass media technologies than it does in any other way. If we take theologians seriously in their claim that experiences of finitude, of connection beyond self, are essential experiences of religious community, then we must acknowledge that these experiences are occurring in mass-mediated contexts using mass-mediated objects. Indeed, those Christians who have been most intent on critiquing the content of mass media would probably agree that in part they do so because they are so conscious of a particular medium's ability to evoke religious experiences, and they want to ensure that the experiences evoked are authentic and appropriately channeled. Unfortunately, the production of meaning is neither initiated nor controlled so easily.

Along with an acknowledgement of how much religious experience can be evoked by mass-mediated representations, comes the concomitant caution from religious educators and other practitioners who work with people of faith that we must recognise the vulnerability and fragility of feeling that often accompanies such experiences, and almost always accompanies their articulation in speech. Far too often religious leaders make blanket claims negating or trivialising the kinds of experiential encounters made possible

---

[8] P. Freire, *Pedagogy of the Oppressed* (New York: Continuum, 1985).

by mass-mediated representations, thereby turning people away at the precise moment that they are ripe for what is traditionally called 'evangelisation'.

Mass-mediated popular culture is replete these days with so-called secular artists engaging religious themes, often in very specific Christian language. The award-winning album '*All that we can't leave behind*' by the group U2 includes a specific meditation on grace. Moby, whose CD '*Play*' was at the top of the charts for quite a while, encloses an eloquent essay on his Christian beliefs within that album. All of these musicians have been greeted with great skepticism by many institutional church leaders, while the congregants of those same leaders try to express often unarticulated, but no less real, religious feelings through engagement with these albums. The collision between religious meaning-making that occurs in mass-mediated formats and religious meaning-making controlled by church institutions is often so abrupt and painful as to drive younger people far from churches.[9]

The process of translating religious experience into language and beyond that into commitment to a community of faith is always fraught with difficulty, and the opportunity for misunderstanding and confusion is great. Such difficulties and confusion are somewhat eased when bridges are built that allow meaning to be created and sustained in multiple ways and in multiple contexts, when a responsible imagination is at work helping to create a focus for attention that can find God's presence.

A second way in which religious educators can engage media culture is as a source of social insight. Given that religious education is so often confined to 'Sunday School' contexts or other limited venues while mass media surround and immerse us, we need to recognise the ways in which popular culture can provide specific clues to issues of 'social currency'. We can survey the breadth of popular culture and ask ourselves: what themes are emerging as common concerns? In doing so, we need to think about this not only in overt terms: that is, what are the most popular films concerned with right now, but also what desires are television commercials seeking to evoke and respond to? What kinds of stories are news magazines covering? As we live into the months and years following the events of September 11 2001, it is not surprising that films that focus on archetypal clashes between good and evil such as *Harry Potter* and *The Lord of the Rings* should enjoy such phenomenal success.

In my own research projects, participants have genuinely enjoyed permission to engage media culture in these ways. The practitioners who participate in our research workshops have come primarily from Catholic Christian communities, so their experiences flow from those locations, but perhaps their ideas can be evocative for those coming from other faith traditions. These religious educators suggest that the themes of relationality,

---

[9] See for instance M. Miles, *Seeing and Believing: Religion and Values in the Movies* (Boston: Beacon, 1996).

identity, confrontations with illness and death, and a desire for connection beyond oneself, are all themes that consistently emerge within popular culture, and they are also all themes that are easily and naturally explored through engagement with sacred text (understood broadly to include liturgy and tradition as well as scripture).

Their suggestions of how to engage pop culture objects, however, are even more interesting. Rather than simply pointing out themes, or asserting that a religious community must agree to a specific interpretation of a representation embodied in a media object, these religious educators suggest that people need to be supported in environments that allow them to draw the connections themselves and then find ways to embody them in their own practices. They focus on supporting a responsible imagination.

Here are just a few of our participants' suggestions, more of which can be found on our project's web site:

> Gather a group of people to follow a soap opera together and explore the scenes which made people cry by suggesting that tears are one way of sensing God's presence.

> Choose a controversial show, such as *South Park*, and watch it together. Identify what made you laugh and what made you uncomfortable. Why? What do those emotions tell you about norms for our community?

> Tape a television commercial and have a group watch it several times over. To what desires is the commercial responding? How do we fulfill those desires in our community of faith?

> Tape two different national newscasts for the same evening, and then compare their similarities and differences. Think about how people of faith are represented, and then talk about how descriptive – or not – that representation is of your own faith community.

There are many more suggestions, but the similarities among them are important as we think about how to shape practices of attention. In the first place, media culture is engaged by a dialogical group, not in isolation. Second, emotional responses are important raw data from which to work. Third, there is a relationship between the mediated representation and the community of faith, but that relationship is not defined in advance but rather allowed to emerge from the dialogue. And finally, there is someone present who must be fluent in the practices and norms of the faith community to serve as a resource and a facilitator.[10] In these examples the role of the religious educator is to create a space within which dialogue can flourish, in which there can be movement back and forth between the pop culture object and the community of faith, and in which that movement

[10] More information on the research projects referred to here, as well as constructive exercises and other tools for engaging media culture in the context of religious education can be found at my web site: www.luthersem.edu/mhess

builds on existing resonances and relevance. This is precisely the kind of space Daloz et al. are writing about when they suggest that a responsible imagination is fed by trustworthy communities.

A third way in which popular culture objects are useful is as a catalyst for conscientisation. This is a familiar practice for many communities of faith. Media literacy education in the US began, and in some cases still continues, as a project of religious communities. Strategies for deconstructing support for consumer commodification and other destructive processes are well articulated in curricula produced by the Center for Media Literacy and other such organisations. Indeed, this pragmatic effort represents well the end of the Christian spectrum that was most interested in how we 'pay' for our attention.

Clearly the commercial basis upon which most of the mass-mediated popular culture of the United States is created has an impact on imagination, on the ability to focus our attention. In large measure the impact is one of narrowing attention to those images and ways of being represented through and in mass-mediated objects. Another way to think of this effect is as one of channeling attention towards an ever smaller set of ideas and ways of seeing oneself and one's relationship with others and with God.

Critiquing this overt narrowing of focus, however, is only one way in which such media objects can serve the goal of conscientisation. Because an ironic stance towards meaning is now embedded even in texts one suspects the producers intend to be taken in without critique, critiquing *overt* content is only one aspect of the process. Asking what is *not* named or present, what is not represented, what is left out, is an even more important question. Ensuring this kind of discussion requires bringing different viewpoints to the task. The most effective way this happened within my research projects was by ensuring that the people present in the discussion were themselves coming from a diversity of location and perspective.[11]

Questioning the 'taken for granted', the 'common sense', implied within mass-mediated frameworks is a very difficult task, but it is greatly supported by a responsible imagination: both in the sense of an imagination that can focus attention on perceived dissonance and contradiction, and also in the sense of an imagination that is rooted in a community that has a richness of alternative story to share. Here again I hope that you can hear the resonance with Daloz et al., when they talk about engaging in a process of responsible imagination and paying attention to that process, particularly in its ability to identify sources of dissonance and contradiction and the ways in which that dissonance might lead to a recognition of unrealised justice.

Appropriate Christian identity cannot be supported by staying locked away in 'safe' or 'pure' contexts, barricaded against content that is feared

---

[11] See, in particular, chapter 5 of my dissertation, 'Media Literacy in Religious Education: Engaging Popular Culture to Enhance Religious Experience'. Completed in the Program in Religion and Education at Boston College, 1998. It is available both through UMI and via my website: www.luthersem.edu/mhess/diss.html

but never engaged. The biblical injunction to love our enemies requires an identity that can reach out to those from whom we are estranged, whether by structures of dominating power (as in situations of race, class and gender oppression), or by our own fears and ignorance. Such a compassion and engagement is required of Christians; the biblical witness makes it centrally constitutive of our identity.

In each of these cases – experiential transcendence, social currency, conscientisation – a responsible imagination applied to the practice of attending to mass media can shape the process of religious education and build a different focus for attention. Practising this kind of attention is at times great fun, particularly in contexts where pop culture previously was primarily ignored; and at times it is very difficult, particularly where pop culture texts cause us to question ways of seeing the world which we have taken for granted. But whether cause for laughter or for tears, it will always provide the opportunity to engage Christian identity. As I mentioned at the start of this chapter, each of the Christian practices the Valparaiso project identified is embedded in media culture and permeated by meaning-making practices shaped by that culture. How we take up those practices, or to use Tanner's language, the arguments we engage in in our attempts 'to elaborate the claims, feelings, and forms of action around which Christian life revolves', must of necessity engage media culture. Indeed, the central faith claims of Christian life are 'on the table' at this point in time in a way in which they have not been previously.

We now have, courtesy of media technologies, compelling representations of life lived out in multiple faiths, many of which are far distant from Christianity. We now have, courtesy of media technologies, multiple ways in which to capture our imagination and cede its territories to all kinds of dreams. Our struggle is to search out those dreams most worthy of our attention, and those communities most trustworthy and supportive of these dreams. Our struggle is to shape our attention and nurture it in as generous a way as possible; to shape it in, as Daloz et al. remind us, a way that 'resists prejudice and its distancing tendencies on one hand, and avoids messianic aspirations and their engulfing tendencies on the other hand'.[12]

It is my devout hope that in doing so, in practising the shaping of our attention, in bringing popular culture objects into religious education and bringing religious sensibilities to mass-mediated popular culture, we can truly create the familiarity that 'breeds the content' that will continue to nurture and support our communities of faith for some long time to come. In all these ways we stretch and nurture, challenge and sustain, our manner of paying attention in the world. And in all these ways we build familiarity with religious practice by building on and with the familiar images and sounds of media culture. Doing so we will surely deepen, nuance and make more complex the cultural conversation in which we are engaged, renewing and reinvigorating Christian practices along the way.

[12] Daloz et al. p. 151.

13

Mormons and Media Literacy: Exploring the Dynamics of Religious Media Education

Daniel A. Stout and David W. Scott

The impact of mass media is a dominant concern to leaders of the Mormon Church. Numerous articles on the subject appear in church publications, and Sunday class instruction includes a lesson on 'the power of the media'.[1] Soap opera viewing is discouraged in an article in the official church magazine[2] and in one of the Church's world conferences, an entire sermon was devoted to the potentially harmful effects of television.[3] In addition to these warnings, however, there are also invitations to enjoy mass media which inspire and educate. President Gordon B. Hinckley points out a number of benefits of magazines, movies and television programs:

> Let there be good magazines about the house, those which are produced by the Church and by others, which will stimulate their thoughts to ennobling concepts. Let them read a good family newspaper that they may know what is going on in the world ... When there is a good show in town, go to the theatre as a family. Your patronage will give encouragement to those who wish to produce this type of entertainment. And use that most remarkable of all tools of communication, television, to enrich their lives.[4]

This simultaneous praise and criticism of mass media underscores the importance of media literacy in Mormon culture. Media literacy has to do with critical skills used to evaluate films, television and other forms of mediated communication. Are Mormons informed consumers of information? What criteria do they use in evaluating the artistic merits of media texts? How do church members define and resolve conflicts associated with media use? In what ways do they enjoy and learn from media? According to the National Telemedia Council, media literacy is the ability to 'respond

---

[1] 'The Powerful Influence of the Media', *Come Unto Me: Relief Society Personal Study Guide 3.* (Salt Lake City, UT: The Church of Jesus Christ of Latter-day Saints, 1991).
[2] K. Strong-Thacker, 'TV Free: Giving up the Daytime TV habit', *The Ensign* (July 1991), pp. 29–31.
[3] M. R. Ballard, 'The Effects of Television', *The Ensign* (May 1989), pp. 78–81.
[4] G. B. Hinckley, 'Opposing Evil', *The Ensign*, (November 1975) p. 39.

thoughtfully to the media we consume'.[5] To Kubey, it means having sufficient skills to 'appreciate, interpret, and analyse the mass media'.[6] In this
chapter, Mormons identify issues most important to them as they strive
to be media literate; they describe their media use within the context of
religious and family experience.

Popular books such as Medved's *Hollywood vs. America* and Dobson and
Bauer's *Children at Risk* argue that the entertainment industry has almost
limitless power in corrupting youth. However, they rarely give examples of
how this occurs. Their claims are based on content analysis; media depictions are assumed to have particular effects on the audience. However,
content analysis is founded on inference and does not describe what audience members actually do. The role mass media play in the lives of
Mormons, therefore, is not sufficiently understood through content
research alone. Lacking are data describing personal experiences of
audience members.

Studies of the Mormon audience reveal strikingly different opinions
about media effects. For example, Mormon women disagree about the
value of television for children, as well as about its importance as an entertainment medium.[7] There also appears to be considerable variation in time
devoted to television viewing.[8] Given shared religious beliefs and commitments, what accounts for these contrasting views and behaviors? According
to Hall such questions are best addressed by studying the social contexts of
family life:

> Television viewing, the choices which shape it and the many social
> uses to which we put it, now turn out to be irrevocably active and
> social processes. People don't passively absorb subliminal 'inputs'
> from the screen. They discursively make sense or produce 'readings'
> of what they see. Moreover, the 'sense' they make is related to a pat-
> tern of choices ... which is constructed within a set of relationships
> constituted by the domestic and familial settings in which it is taking
> place.[9]

In this article, we ask: 'How do Mormons themselves define what it means
to be media literate?' This way, religious media education can be studied as
a social process with emphasis on media use within social contexts. To this

[5] *Media Literacy Resource Guide.* (Toronto: The Ontario Department of Education,
1992).

[6] R. Kubey, 'The Case for Media Education', *Education Week* X(24) (6 March 1991), p.
1.

[7] D. A. Stout, 'Resolving Conflicts of Worldviews: LDS Women and Television', *AMCAP
Journal* 20 (1) (1994), pp. 61–79.

[8] J. Valenti and D. A. Stout, 'Diversity from Within: an Analysis of the Impact of
Religious Culture on Media Use and Effective Communication to Women', D. A. Stout and J.
M. Buddenbaum (eds.), *Religion and Mass Media: Audiences and Adaptations* (Thousand Oaks,
CA: Sage, 1996), pp. 183–96.

[9] S. Hall, 'Introduction', D. Morley, *Family television: Cultural power and domestic leisure*
(London: Comedia, 1986) pp. 8–9.

point, writers on the topic have focused on *direct effects;* little has been said about how audience members ponder mediated texts, actively resist certain appeals, and appraise artistic and educational merit. Little is known about the issues important to Mormons as they interact with family members and make decisions about media use.

The paradigm shift in Mormon media studies: 'direct effects' to interpretative community

The family is the *sine qua non* of Mormon theology. In Mormon doctrine, the family is eternal, and through obedience to God's laws, family members can live together in the hereafter. The temple ordinance of eternal marriage reflects this idea. Such beliefs form a foundation for media education stressing protection from messages appearing to threaten the family unit. These are the foundational ideas of two popular Mormon writers, Victor B. Cline, Professor Emeritus of Psychology at the University of Utah, and Randal A. Wright, Director of a Mormon Institute of Religion. Both are influential in the Mormon community through books, magazine articles and public lectures. Although they write independently, their basic conclusions are similar: mass media can be highly destructive instruments of manipulation and should be viewed with caution and careful selectivity. Cline makes this point when discussing television:

> A steady diet of television has a powerful influence. Television may subtly brainwash us by shaping the way we and our children understand the world and how people live and act.[10]

In his books, *Protecting your Family in an X-rated World* and *Why Do Good People See Bad Movies?*, Wright[11] makes a similar argument. He concludes that 'youth with televisions in their bedrooms [are] more sexually permissive than those who do not have them' and 'the more movies youth watch, the more they are influenced by media celebrities'.

Efforts by Wright and Cline to isolate media as the primary cause of many social problems is consistent with the 'hypodermic needle' model of mass media fostered by experimental psychology in the 1960s. Based primarily on theories of social learning and attitude change, this perspective assumes a direct causal link between media and behavior. 'The media do have incredible power to influence us and shape the nature of our civilisation ... Our hearts and our minds – and those of our children – are vulnerable.'[12]

---

[10] G. C. Griffin and V. B. Cline, 'Screening out the garbage: How to teach "correct principles" about television in the home', *The Ensign* (August 1976), p. 20.

[11] R. Wright *Protecting your Family in an X-rated World,* (Salt Lake City, UT: Deseret 1988); and R. Wright, *Why Do Good People See Bad Movies? The impact of R-rated movies* (National Family Institute, 1993).

[12] V. B. Cline, 'Obscenity: How it affects us, how we can deal with it', *The Ensign* (April 1984), pp. 32–7.

While Cline and Wright raise valid questions and encourage media selectivity, they overlook a number of dimensions in a church member's experience with media. According to Potter, media literacy has cognitive, emotional, aesthetic and moral dimensions.[13] Audience research is needed to better understand which of these are valued most by Mormons and to identify specific types of educational resources desired. Powerful-effects research reinforces values fundamental to Mormon beliefs; it is not sufficient, however, for the development of skills necessary for optimal use of mass media. For this to occur, a deeper, more thorough analysis of the audience is required.

Recently, a number of professors and graduate students at Brigham Young University (a Mormon university) began exploring an audience-oriented perspective called 'interpretative community'.[14] An interpretative community is a sub-level collectivity of family members, friends, neighbors, co-workers, etc., that identify their own set of problems and opportunities regarding media use in a social and cultural context. Briefly stated, an interpretative community is a group that shares certain strategies of interpretation.[15] By examining some of these interpretative communities, the authors describe different approaches to media literacy by Mormons.

Research questions

In this article, Mormons discuss TV, film and other entertainment media in their own words. Their comments are presented in the context of three research questions:

(1) Is it possible to identify a typology of approaches to media literacy among Mormons?
(2) Which dimensions of media literacy (i.e., cognitive, affective, aesthetic and moral) do these approaches emphasise?
(3) How is a knowledge of these approaches to media literacy valuable in the future planning and design of media education materials?

Method

This article summarises qualitative data obtained in three separate studies. The first is a 1994 intercept study of 238 Mormon students at Brigham

---

[13] W. J. Potter, *Media Literacy* (Thousand Oaks, CA: Sage, 1998).
[14] T. R. Lindlof, 'The passionate audience: community inscriptions of "The Last Temptation of Christ"', D. A. Stout and J. M Buddenbaum (eds.), *Religion and Mass Media: Audiences and Adaptations* (Thousand Oaks, CA: Sage, 1996), pp. 148–68; and T. R. Lindlof, K. Coyle and G. Grodin, 'Is There a Text in this Audience?' in C. Harris and A. Alexander (eds.) *Theorizing Fandom* (Creskill, NJ: Hempton, 1998), pp. 219–47.
[15] S. Fish, *Is There a Text in this Class?* (Cambridge: Harvard University Press, 1980).

Young University in a video rental store in close proximity to the BYU campus. The second is a 1992 analysis of open-ended statements from 428 Mormon women responding to an open-ended question in a mail survey. The third is a focus group study of BYU students from Las Vegas, Nevada, an environment where entertainment media often conflict with Mormon religious values. This study was conducted in 2000.

The three data sets provide cross validation of findings about how Mormons, both younger and older, talk about entertainment media. In all three studies, statements were assigned to categories using a sorting technique developed by Browning.[16] The categories represent dominant themes or frequently mentioned topics regarding media use. In Studies One and Two, the category names were shown to an independent panel of three members who made suggestions and comments. After the panel review, the authors made adjustments and finalised the categories. In Study Three, two researchers commented on the categories and finalised them.

The three data sets were analysed separately, and parts of them are summarised elsewhere in addressing other topics.[17] Although statements from all three studies are used to illustrate various types of media literacy, it is not intended that they be read as a single data set. In the results section, it is made clear which studies the data are from and a code designation (S1=Study One; S2=Study Two; S3=Study Three) is used to identify respondent quotes.

Data collection: Study One

Customers were intercepted at a video rental store near the BYU campus and asked to fill out a survey questionnaire. A total of 326 individuals completed surveys, and non-BYU students were eliminated from the sample. This left 238 surveys which were subjected to analysis. Respondents were given a '$1.00 – Off' coupon for participating. Those completing questionnaires were assured of complete anonymity.

In response to open-ended questions, students wrote about their motivations in selecting various films; they also discussed how values play a role in making acceptable movie choices. Then, respondents were asked to share impressions of the movie *Schindler's List,* Steven Spielberg's Oscar -winning film based on the book by Thomas Keneally, which tells the compelling story of efforts to save European Jews from the Holocaust.

---

[16] L. D. Browning, 'A grounded organizational communication theory derived from qualitative data', *Communication Monographs* 45 (1978), pp. 93–107.

[17] Stout, 'Resolving conflicts of worldviews', Valenti and Stout, 'Diversity from within'; D. A. Stout, D. W. Scott and D. M. Martin, 'Mormons, Media, and the Interpretative Audience' in D. A. Stout and J. M. Buddenbaum (eds.), *Religion and Mass Media: Audiences and Adaptations* (Thousand Oaks, CA: Sage, 1996), pp. 243-58; D. A. Stout and M. McMurray, 'Mormons in Las Vegas: A Study of Entertainment Media and Secularization Defense Strategies', paper presented at the Annual Conference of the Association for Education in Journalism and Mass Communication (AEJMC), (Washington, DC, 2000).

Because 'R-rated' movies are strongly discouraged by church leaders, the critically acclaimed film sparked a controversy in the Mormon community.[18] In this study, *Schindler's List* provides a specific means of gauging which dimensions of media literacy Mormons emphasise when analysing a text of artistic and historical merit.

The study was conducted on a Friday starting late in the afternoon until the store closed. Women comprise 52 per cent of the participants, and men 48 per cent.

Data collection: Study Two

The second study randomly selected names of Mormon women from five congregational lists or 'wards' in each of the three metro areas (i.e., Los Angeles, Houston and Salt Lake City) in the US. They were sent a questionnaire asking respondents to share experiences about 'television viewing and religious life'. The 428 respondents are more representative of highly educated, affluent, and married Mormon women than Mormon women in general. They are comparable, however, to the larger Mormon population in terms of family size and number employed outside the home. Higher levels of education and income are likely attributed to respondents from Los Angeles, where household earnings tend to be greater.

Data collection: Study Three

In the third study, qualitative data were analysed from two focus groups of Brigham Young University students from Las Vegas, Nevada. It is a tourist city centered on gambling and entertainment. The Mormon Church has taken aggressive stands against gambling, pornography and prostitution, three significant industries in Las Vegas. These phenomena are reflected in a wide range of media, from outdoor signs containing nudity to elaborate burlesque dance revues.

A list of 159 students was extracted from the total BYU population using the 1999-2000 Student Directory. Mormon students from the Las Vegas list were telephoned and asked screening questions to qualify them for the focus groups. Questions had to do with length of residence in Las Vegas, religious affiliation, basic familiarity with Las Vegas entertainment/casino industry, and willingness to participate. A total of fourteen were invited to each focus group, with ten women and seven men actually participating. The first focus group consisted of six participants (three women and three

---

[18] R. Broadbent, 'Varsity theatre to resume showing edited R-rated movies', *The Daily Universe* (18 July 1995), p. 1; R. Robinson, '*Schindler's List* pulled from Varsity Theatre schedule, editing difficulties blamed', *The Daily Universe* (28 September 1994), p. 1; and J. Waite, 'R-ratings steal the show', *The Daily Universe* (7 October 1994).

men). Eleven comprised the second group, which included seven women and four men. Each session lasted about ninety minutes.

Results and analysis

Data in all three studies were analysed according to the 'grounded theory' approach of Glaser and Strauss,[19] which allows findings to emerge from the data, rather than framing the results in terms of pre-conceived hypotheses. Specifically, three distinct approaches to media literacy emerged. They include: *belief-based media literacy*, where audience members emphasise religious teachings and predetermined sets of guidelines in their media selections; *personal media literacy*, which is the evaluation of media according to the fulfilment of individual needs and objectives; and *interactional media literacy*, where media use revolves around relationships and church members often defer to other family members in making media selections.

These categories are not mutually exclusive and are not intended as static or fixed definitions of media literacy. Indeed, not all Mormons will fit these descriptions completely; they are starting-points for future exploration of media diversity within conservative religious groups. This article, then, is a useful point of departure for discussions about what is most important to Mormons as they use media within the context of their religious experience; it uncovers additional ideas for enhancing educational materials for media literacy programs and campaigns.

The remainder of the article describes the three types of media selection strategies using actual statements by Mormon viewers. At the end of every section is a brief discussion of how each approach is applied in evaluating the movie *Schindler's List*.

Belief-based media literacy

In belief-based media literacy, critical skills are tied to religious doctrine. That is, the cognitive or knowledge element is stressed in deciding how to use media in the home. Some Mormon viewers, for example, prefer rules and guidelines in selecting television shows or movies. These guidelines are usually set in advance and determine which shows and movies are consistent with religious values. Examples include the US movie rating system (G, PG, PG-13, R, NC-17), or when parents themselves specify the amount of time children can watch television. Enforcement of rules ranges from monitoring viewing to actually placing locks on television sets. An example of rules-based selection comes from a respondent who said that she had instructed her eight-year-old to 'leave the movie theatre if you hear more than five swear words'. (S2)

[19] B. Glaser and A. Strauss, *The Discovery of Grounded Theory* (Chicago: Aldine, 1967).

In belief-based media literacy, the most salient types of media content are violence and explicit sexuality, which are reasons for rejecting entire programs or movies regardless of the context of such depictions. In most cases, media are assumed to have deleterious effects on one's spirituality. For example, a Mormon woman stated:

> I am an advocate of the warnings given ... throughout the years about secret combinations working to destroy and take away the freedom of all lands ... I do not clutter my mind with the pornography of movies or TV so I can have divine inspiration to what is truly happening. (S2)

Why do many Mormon viewers set rules for appropriate television and movie viewing? Analysis of written statements reveals a belief in a strong link between media content and undesirable behaviors. Family arguments, disrespectful children and poor grades in school are all attributed to 'the media' by a number of respondents in Study Two. Often complex personal, family and societal problems are traced directly to television and movie viewing. One mother related how she had fallen away from the Church and was convinced that watching 'tremendous' amounts of television led her to 'live unrighteously'. Another attributed, in part, an incident of sexual abuse to 'TV shows' watched at a young age. Still another respondent said that television was 'the biggest cause of contention' in her home.

Belief-based media literacy seems to encourage scepticism about the value of television in general. Almost anything, some argue, is a better use of time. Of those advocating belief-based media literacy in Study Two, only 8 per cent said television was a valid source of entertainment, and only 15 per cent said television was a legitimate form of escape from everyday cares. One audience member said 'the only reasons to keep the TV' are to watch 'family videos, ... decent movies, ... General Conference, ... and church films ...'

Another interesting manifestation of the belief-based approach was expressed by Mormon students from Las Vegas (Study Three) who spoke of the need to stay away from physical locations where unsavory night clubs, movies and casino shows are offered. Admonitions to reject undesirable media are heeded by physically avoiding main areas of the city. They spoke of going to great lengths to avoid the 'downtown' and 'strip' areas of Las Vegas, which they claimed could be avoided almost entirely:

> [T]here's no point to go down there [to the strip]. (S3)

> [M]ost of the LDS families I know aren't involved in it [Las Vegas entertainment]. (S3)

> I don't go downtown unless I have to. (S3)

> I don't ever go down there. It's an entirely different atmosphere when you're not on the strip. (S3)

> [M]ost locals don't want to go down to the strip all that often. (S3)

Such statements demonstrate the extent that church members go to in applying belief-based media literacy. How entertainment media help define appropriate physical spaces for church members as well as the neighborhoods they live in is an important subject for future research. The point is, belief-based approaches to media can be very strong and have implications beyond media selection alone; they can ultimately affect how religious groups integrate in cities and form out-group ties.

In applying a belief-based approach to the movie *Schindler's List*, several BYU students in Study One emphasised the 'R' rating in making their decision whether to view the film. Typical comments were, 'I would love to see it, but it's rated 'R',' or, 'I don't like to see 'R' movies.' One student said of the film, '(I'm) not going to see it – it's rated 'R' – that's all I need to know.'

In pursuing belief-based media literacy, respondents do not usually speak of artistic, technical or historical dimensions of a media text unless the TV show, film, etc., is acceptable according to written guidelines. Although many are aware of high public praise for *Schindler's List* as a moral commentary, the underlying messages of the film rarely outweigh its 'R' rating which church leaders discourage. A student in Study One asserts, 'I would love to see *Schindler's List,* but it is rated 'R' and I don't see rated 'R' movies.' Another student recognised the film's artistic merit, but said he would only see an edited version: 'I hope that *Schindler's List* comes to ... TV. I won't see it in the movies.'

Belief-based media literacy implies dualistic analysis. Those applying this approach see the 'R' rating as an absolute directive not to be compromised in any situation. Several students in Study One categorise 'R' rated films with labels like, 'wrong and of the devil' and 'degrading and damaging to the spirit'. Data show evidence of a spillover effect, where films are rejected not only for the rating, but the artistic merit of 'R' rated films is discounted. One explained that 'true art' does not contain overt or graphic scenes of sex and violence:

> *Schindler's List* is trying to create an event realistically instead of artistically. I won't see it because of the rating this realism brings. (S1)

These comments uncover important issues for those designing media education materials. That is, it appears that some Mormon viewers tie artistic components of a film directly to the rating or guideline. More research is needed to learn what such behaviors imply in terms of attitudes about art in general.

Personal media literacy

Not all devout Mormons restrict their media use in the ways just described. While belief-based selection stresses uniform guidelines in most situations, *personal media literacy* is an approach that says, 'I am in control, and I decide what is best for me.' Viewers create personal standards for media use and rarely dismiss entire genres. In personal media literacy, function wins out over rules. One respondent illustrates this point:

> My husband thinks we should do away with the TV altogether because the children have disagreements over programs occasionally or don't hear what we say because they are involved in a show. However, it is my only 'link to the outside world' at this time. He feels better when I explain that it gives me entertainment while I do exercises, read and play with the kids, and do housework. (S2)

The skills of personal media literacy revolve more around the accomplishment of religious goals and less around the application of guidelines. TV programs that are highly criticised by some Mormons are praised by others. If they stimulate substantive family discussions, for example, they might be seen as a teaching tool. One illustration is the US animated TV situation comedy *The Simpsons,* whose main character, Bart Simpson, engages in a variety of undesirable behaviors (i.e., cheating in school, being disrespectful to parents, getting into mischief, etc.). Those displaying personal media literacy reveal significant enjoyment of the show, with one mother in Study Two insisting it provides an outlet for 'discussing the [show's] social messages'. Another example relates to daytime talk shows, when a viewer said that although she was aware of criticisms by church leaders, the programs often lead to 'meaningful conversations on political issues' with her daughter.

Like belief-based media literacy, the personal orientation is also grounded in religious teachings. Other dimensions besides rules, however, are referenced in media selection. For example, while daytime talk shows were often criticised, a respondent displaying *religious feeling* defended them on spiritual grounds:

> I like talk shows because it gives me an opportunity to see how others live, the choices they've made and how those choices affected their lives. More often than not, I reaffirm my own beliefs and choices in life as being wise. I feel grateful for the influence of the Church when I see others that don't have it and how unfortunate their lives have turned out. (S2)

The ability to access religiosity in diverse ways also emerged in the study of Mormon students from Las Vegas. Rather than undermining faith, Las Vegas media, they argue, can actually strengthen convictions. Controversial media and entertainment are seen as opportunities to make a stand and overcome temptation. In this sense, Mormons evoke that aspect of religiosity emphasising earthly tests that all must confront in growing to become like God. Examples of this way of thinking are:

> It's kind of nice [being exposed to a negative element in Las Vegas] because it teaches you to stay focused and disciplined. (S3)

I think that because the members live there it does make them stronger… (S3)

Yeah, it's really hard to sit on the fence there [in Las Vegas]. (S3)

I'm partial to Las Vegas, obviously. But, they have a really nice balance, you know living in the world but not of the world. (S3)

The media of Las Vegas were often contrasted with those of Utah, which were deemed insufficient to produce the faith necessary to develop spiritually. For example, a participant said that living in Utah was not as good because in Las Vegas 'you have this opposition and you want to be an example to other people and stuff like that'. Such comments suggest that religiosity is a multidimensional phenomenon that can be divergently accessed to produce oppositional reads by different church members.

Within the perimeters of personal media literacy, evaluation of the movie *Schindler's List* is not restricted to ratings. Perceived artistic merit, an underlying moral and personal interests are all reasons for selecting movies on religious grounds. One respondent in Study One comments: 'if I've heard it's good … I don't care what it is rated. I want to see *Schindler's List* because it is the best picture …'

Why some Mormons choose to overlook the rating system and others do not, remains an interesting question. However, those choosing to see this film mention art and historical realism frequently. Nudity and violence are not litmus tests for rejecting films when the overall premise is intended to inspire or uplift, according to a number of respondents. As one student put it, 'Excessive and distasteful nudity, violence, and sex are turn-offs. I had to see *Schindler's List* because it exposed me to a very disappointing time in the world's history' (S1). Although some respondents ignored the rating system, they indicated that they had researched the film before seeing it. For example, one said that it was important to know something about the 'values' of the film before viewing:

I don't really look at the ratings, but I research the content and the subject matter of the movie before seeing it. The values portrayed in the movie are very important to me … *Schindler's List* is absolutely one of the greatest works of art I have ever seen. Although I've heard complaints of nudity and violence, there was nothing in the film that was added to attract a crowd to those things. It is not pornographic and I believe all the scenes were created to get a message across. (S1)

The assumption that only those using the rating system emphasise moral values is not supported in this analysis. The respondent quoted above, for example, bases his decision on 'values' and does 'research' to assure that the movie is consistent with personal religious standards.

Interactional media literacy

Interactional media literacy is the analysis of media use based on relation-ship dynamics; it is the idea that media are used optimally when they strengthen interpersonal relationships. The assumption is that all family members should have input when it comes to decisions about media use. Imbalances of power in relationships, however, can also retard the devel-opment of media literacy. Respondents in all three studies recognise the influence of others in media selection, and a dominant theme emerges in this regard. A group of Mormon women in Study Two, for example, voice frustration about the inability to influence media decisions in the home. They prefer other activities, but acquiesce to the will of others in order to protect family time or preserve the peace. One Mormon wife and mother expressed it this way:

> I sometimes watch TV with my husband because of his work and church callings. TV takes no effort so it relaxes him. I'd rather be doing something better or different but I feel 'holding hands' helps our relationship at times. (S2)

Other Mormon women say their spouses and children dominate television program and movie choice. Media use, they argue, is something that just happens, whether they prefer it to or not. Consequently, frustrations are reflected in statements such as: 'I'd rather be doing something else ...' or 'it is best not to watch, but ...' or television viewing is 'not necessarily my choice'. These comments indicate a behavior-attitude incongruity which often results in guilty feelings about media use.

Male dominance is the main deterrent to interactive media literacy. In fact, only 12 per cent of Mormon women sampled said they got to use the remote control device during a typical evening of television viewing.[20] Television, according to several women in Study Two, was a favorite activity of their husbands, and in order to be together, they would view also. One viewer states: 'I mostly wind up watching 'Current Affairs' or 'Inside Edition' because my husband puts it on – not my choice.'

Similar views were also expressed about *Schindler's List*. For example, a female viewer deferred to her husband's feelings when asked about her own opinions: 'I want to see *Schindler's List* ... but my husband says it looks too depressing.' These statements reveal that a number of Mormon women have personal views and preferences regarding media use but may find it difficult to express them.

The quest for media literacy often occurs within an environment of inequity, and these data raise important questions about how frequently media selection is based on balanced, fair and substantive family discussion. Given that church leaders admonish parents to instruct their children

---

[20] D. A. Stout *Resolving conflicts of worldviews: LDS women and television* (Unpublished doc-toral dissertation, Rutgers University, 1993).

about appropriate uses of mass media, it appears that relational dynamics could frustrate attempts to teach relevant skills.

Summary and conclusion

Devout, committed Mormons don't always agree about what it means to be media literate and are diverse in the ways they talk about entertainment media. Some advocate a fixed set of rules that can be applied to all media texts, while others argue that media use is a highly individualised process tied to personal goals. Still others define media literacy as a struggle of relationships, where imbalances of power often impede progress. These findings suggest that the richest source of insight about media literacy is not the content of messages, but the expressed needs of the audience member. In summary, there are many approaches to media literacy within the Mormon community, and effective media education materials must address a wide range of issues and problems in order to accommodate the interests of this audience.

Helping church members as they strive for media literacy should be a top priority. Based on the preceding analysis, here are some suggestions to planners of media education programs.

(1) Recognise the wide range of goals family members have for media

Media literacy materials should encourage more than one approach to media use and enjoyment. Several respondents, for example, expressed frustration that other family members were not aware of the things they gleaned from media (e.g., entertainment, information about world affairs, something to talk about with friends, etc.). In fact, a number of Mormon women described television viewing in terms of building family relationships; issues of media selection and use were secondary. Authors of media educational aids might encourage parents to better understand the contexts of media use within the family.

Media literacy resources should reflect an understanding of the multidimensional nature of religiosity and how religious belief, feelings, behavior and interaction facilitate diverse media selections and interpretations. Belief-based media literacy operates within a set of defined guidelines, while personal media literacy implies a wider range of ways in which religiosity defines media use. Interactional media literacy stresses relationships. Rather than a predictor of uniform perceptions, religiosity turns out to be a complex phenomenon through which 'divergently correct'[21] media selections

---

[21] T. R. Lindlof, Coyle, and Grodin, 'Is There a Text in this Audience?'.

and interpretations are possible. If media education programs are to be effective, they must reflect a deeper understanding of religiosity itself.

(2) Balance guidelines with discussion of art and aesthetics

Media rules and guidelines are vital and reinforce high standards of moral conduct; they reject unsavory depictions of sex and violence that are inconsistent with Mormon teachings. As for children, rules are absolutely necessary until more mature critical skills can be acquired. Yet the problem with the application of rules to all situations is the lack of attention to artistic analysis which is also an important dimension of Mormon culture. A 1948 issue of the *Improvement Era* admonishes Mormons to become 'more intelligent critics' of movies and other media. Criticism, according to the article, is the 'art of judging ... works of art and literature'.[22] Yet it is difficult to become intelligent critics if guidelines are interpreted in such a way as to restrict potentially edifying media experiences. If, for example, parents allow only one hour of television a night, and provide no way to adjust, say, when a critically acclaimed program is aired, an opportunity may be missed. The question, then, is not whether or not rules should guide media use, but in which situations they should do so. Media literacy materials should raise these issues.

On the other hand, is it possible to be intelligent consumers of information without any rules or standards? While personal media literacy emphasises independence and individual choice, the absence of any guidelines also restricts the scope and depth of one's media literacy in a religious context. The absence of rules often promotes a sense that one is impervious to influence; that there are no real 'effects' of mass media. This idea is expressed by a mother who said she 'would go crazy' without a TV because her kids would be after her 'constantly to do things with them'. While a personal need is being fulfilled by TV, the comment suggests little concern about what children might be deriving from the viewing experience apart from meeting their mother's need for free time. Rules can ensure that television, for example, does not crowd out valuable time for conversations, chores, personal study and family activities and traditions.

Media literacy programs can encourage a synthesis of critical perspectives that utilise both guidelines and artistic criteria. As psychologist Mary Pipher explains, there are times to shield each other from mass media and there are times to use them to enrich our lives: 'Conservatives emphasise protection; liberals emphasise connection. Both things are important.'[23] Educational materials must reach for a higher standard that transcends both simple rules and goals; they should challenge families to achieve

---

[22] M. C. Josephson, 'And so the movies!' *Improvement Era* (January 1948), pp. 25, 31.
[23] M. Pipher, *The shelter of each other: Rebuilding our families* (New York: Grosset/Putnam, 1996), p. 5.

maximum artistic fulfilment and family enjoyment. A necessary condition for this is a multidimensional approach which emphasises different critical skills in various situations.

Without attention to the balance between art and rules, the aesthetic dimension of media literacy is underdeveloped. This is illustrated by the respondent arguing that *Schindler's List* could not be art because it is rated 'R'. The application of rules in absolutely all cases leaves nowhere to go but to question the artistic merit of all that falls outside the guidelines. It is worth pondering the consequences of such an approach when outlining future media education programs.

(3) Take into account power dynamics in media selection

A common theme expressed by many women sampled was the lack of influence in media selections. Media use, they argue, is controlled by husbands and other family members. This might help explain why some Mormon women have strong feelings of guilt about television viewing.[24] Those preparing educational resources will want to increase awareness of this and promote egalitarian decision-making. Family members should be taught to recognise situations where one might be going along with the choices of others simply to avoid confrontations. Gender-related conflicts suggest that media literacy is as much about interpersonal communication as it is about mass communication. In order to achieve optimal use of mass media, audience members could be taught how to recognise an imbalance of power in the family unit.

(4) Encourage media-related discussions in the home

Critical media skills are often learned in informal conversations. A parent comments on the plot development of a particular movie at dinner, or a teenager asks questions about the appropriateness of a television show popular with peers. Families should set aside time to share ideas about how to enjoy mass media as well as how to resolve the dilemmas they create. In many ways, media literacy is an ongoing discourse that challenges and strengthens one's ability to analyse media texts.

Media discussions allow children to benefit from the experience and insights of their parents. One Mormon teenager said she liked it when her father 'talked back to the TV' in the evenings. Something as simple as explaining why TV stations air commercials or what a movie director does gives young people a foundation upon which their media literacy can mature. Children are often critical, playful and even sarcastic at times; with the right information they can become fairly adept media critics.

---

[24] D. A. Stout, 'Resolving conflicts of worldviews'.

14

The Communication Formation of Church Leaders as a Holistic Concern

Franz-Josef Eilers

In 1995, the General Congregations of the Society of Jesus drafted and approved their first document on social communication. In it they observed that, 'Communication in the Society has usually been considered as a *sector* of apostolic activity, a field for some specialists who often felt isolated or on the margin of the apostolic body. The Society needs to acknowledge that communication is not a domain restricted to a few Jesuit professionals, but a *major apostolic dimension* for all our apostolates ...' Such a statement is significant not only for Jesuit communicators, but also for other religious groups. Unfortunately, training in communication is too often considered a specialised field focused on technical training. A broader vision of communication that sees it as both a dimension of and an attitude in religious life is frequently missing. This chapter puts forward a case for an approach that goes beyond mere technical communication training to a more broadly based formation of religious leaders.

Theological basis

From a Christian perspective, there is also a theological reason for such an approach. Over the years church people and academics have called for a 'Theology of Communication' but it has never really happened. Instead of developing another 'genitive theology', however, one should see communication rather as a theological principle. This means that the whole of Christian theology is seen in the context of communication. Communication is not then just an activity which is 'baptized' by theology. Avery Dulles, in agreement with Karl Rahner, Bernard Lonergan, Carlo Martini, Peter Henrici and others, says that 'theology is at every point concerned with the realities of communication'.[1] Dulles calls the Trinity the 'deepest mystery of communication' where:

---

[1] Avery Dulles, *The Craft of Theology, From Symbol to System* (Dublin: Gill and Macmillan, 1992), p. 22.

159

Our human eyes are blinded by its surpassing brilliance. The created analogies, while falling immeasurably short, point through their convergence to the communicative character of this exalted mystery. The Trinity is communication in absolute, universal perfection, a totally free and complete sharing among equals. In generating the Son as Word, the Father totally expresses himself ... the Holy Spirit completes the intradivine process of communication.'[2]

Concluding, Dulles quotes Bernhard Häring in saying that 'communication is constitutive in the mystery of God. Each of the three divine Persons possesses all that is good, all that is true, all that is beautiful, but in the modality of communion and communication.'[3] Human beings reflect this inner Trinitarian communication, because they are created 'in His image and likeness' and in this way are able to communicate. Häring formulates it thus, 'Creation, redemption and communication arise from this mystery and have as their final purpose to draw us, by this very communication, into communion with God,' and Dulles concludes: 'Because Christianity is first and foremost the religion of the triune God, it is pre-eminently a religion of communication, for God in his inmost essence is a mystery of self-communication.'[4]

God's Trinitarian self-communication manifests itself in revelation and reaches its high point in the incarnation of Jesus Christ. The Church is the continuation of this self-communication into the here and now of every time and place. As Avery Dulles argues:

> The entire work of creation, redemption, and sanctification is a prolongation of the inner processions within the Trinity. Creation is ascribed to the Father, who thereby fashions finite images and vestiges of his Son. Redemption is attributed to his Son, who communicates himself to human nature in the Incarnation. Sanctification is appropriated to the Holy Spirit who communicates himself to the Church, the communion of saints. The mystery of divine communication, therefore, permeates any area of theology ... Because Christianity is the religion of the triune God, it is pre-eminently a religion of communication.'[5]

Communication is thus at the heart of the work of the Trinitarian God and therefore should be at the heart of theology. This communication within the Godhead occurs at several different levels: communication between the persons of the Trinity, communication with humanity through creation and grace (revelation) and the communication with humanity through the incarnation of Christ. The Church was founded to continue this communication in the world, especially as community (*communio, koinonia*), in proclaiming (*kerygma*) and in serving (*diakonia*).

[2] Dulles, *The Craft of Theology*, pp. 37–8.
[3] Dulles, *The Craft of Theology*, p. 39.
[4] Dulles, *The Craft of Theology*, pp. 38–9.
[5] Dulles, *The Craft of Theology*, pp. 38–9.

Such a theology has concrete consequences for the work of the Church and therefore the formation of church members (especially leaders) should be centred on the ideas and concepts of communication. Formation has often included traditional forms of communication such as homiletics and apologetics. In contemporary society it is time that church educators saw media skills as an integral part of formation not only as practical skills for the contemporary Church, but also as part of the theological understanding of the Church.

The duty and role of communication

If the Church is the continuation of God's communication through revelation and incarnation, the ways and means of this communication must also be reflected in her. Christian communicators are called to develop attitudes which go beyond merely technical skills to more sensitive forms of listening and communication. This begins with a self-critical understanding of the different levels of communication in which a Christian leader will be involved. The personal communication of a church leader must be first and foremost grounded in her/his communication with God in prayer and meditation which is finally reflected in her/his communication with others. This has the potential to transform the practice of interpersonal communication, which starts with the 'witness of life' of the individual and the community. The early Church and modern theology see '*koinonia*', '*communio*' as the basis for Christian life. Today in many countries it is especially the local Christian communities which bring life and are the centre of the Church, thus reflecting in a very concrete way this '*communio*'. Here also the Eucharist is seen and experienced as the centre of Christian communication. The Pastoral Instruction *Communio et Progressio* asserts: 'In the institution of the Eucharist, Christ gave us the most perfect, most intimate form of communion between God and humans possible in this life, and, out of this the deepest possible unity between people' (No.11). All principles of group communication apply here. 'Homiletics' as the study and teaching of preaching but also religious instruction ('catechesis') are areas to be considered. Simple means of communication like newsletters and information services can be an expression of committed interpersonal communication and a service to professional communicators.

The modern mass media bring news and information, but normally in a fashion designed to entertain and to hold an audience. Religion and religious practices can be part of stories told, but also part of news, documentaries or the general background of any presentation. They present a new and often daunting arena with which church leaders can engage. Multimedia communication provides a different, more personal experience through computers, the Internet and other means. They offer a new level of communication with increasing challenges to the availability and flexibility of a church leader.

Communication is thus at the heart of theology, but too often different communication activities, especially those of the mass media, are separated and isolated from other church activities. The approaches most churches take towards communication can be generalised and codified into four basic paradigms.

Isolationist approach

The different sections of the communication office work independently of each other. They are also unrelated to other pastoral ministries. The ministries are like 'little kingdoms', each operating on its own. The consequences can be a lack of common vision and collaboration between different media sections and ministires. Sometimes this leads to overlapping and duplication.

Unified approach

The communication office and activities are under one umbrella; in other words there is one director for all the different media. The different media sections are interrelated. The consequences can be a common vision where all communication activities are supportive of each other and related to the overall mission. The use of limited resources can ensure a more effective interaction with other aspects of the Church's life.

Collaborative approach

The communication office, its activities and its ministries are not only interrelated but also interdisciplinary. The consequences can be that communication is brought into all other ministries. This quality infrastructure can lead to a convergence of communication technologies and convergence of ministries.

Integrated approach

Here, communication is seen as an essential dimension of the Church at all levels. The consequences can be that communication as a theological principle underlies all church activities. This approach can ensure that there is less concern about instrumentality of communication. Here, communication is the 'giving of self in love'[4] on all levels and in all church activities.

Of these approaches, it is the 'integrated approach' which places com-

---

[4] *Communio et Progressio*, no. 11 in *Church and Social Communication – Basic Documents*, Franz-Joseph Eilers (ed.), (Manila: Divine Word/Logos, 1997) Second edition.

munication where theology locates it. The development of such an approach depends very much on an overall holistic formation of church leaders who are open to each other and are able to dialogue for the good of the community. This integrated approach brings together personal communication, interpersonal communication, community orientation and eucharistic experience to serve the Church holistically. It requires the Church to take modern mass media seriously and to engage with the opportunities of multimedia.

Such different levels and possibilities of communication demand from church leaders not only a certain professional knowledge but also attitudes and abilities which must be developed and established during their formative years. We need not only an introduction to the basics of professional mass media but also an holistic approach to communication where attitudes and abilities, human as well as Christian, are developed in such a way that they can respond to the changing needs and demands of our times. These attitudes are rooted in the centrality of community to all theology and the theological implications of community in the Church. It is not sufficient simply to concentrate on the technical skills of modern community techniques. These basic attitudes need to be manifest at a personal as well as professional level.

Personal attitudes

The first basic attitude on the personal level is an *openness* to God and others. A church leader must in the final analysis reflect God himself who became flesh through his son Jesus Christ. This is only possible if s/he is grounded in prayer and has developed a personal relationship to the God s/he represents. Such an openness with God leads also to a greater openness towards others, their concerns, needs and expectations. This openness to God leads to a *willingness to listen and learn.* Only a person who is willing to listen and learn can really communicate with others and share their needs and expectations. Only the willingness to listen and learn equips the church leader for *dialogue* and sharing.

Professional attitudes

Attitudes and abilities needed on the professional level flow from the basic personal attitudes of openness and willingness to listen and learn. Beside the technical knowledge appropriate to the means to be used it is essential that a church leader is aware of (a) the situation and needs of the people he has to address, (b) the communicative possibilities of the medium he wants to use, and (c) the message he wants to convey.

Any target audience is determined by the expectations and receptivity of the culture, society and general environment. Audiences are shaped by their cultures, societal relations and perception abilities. Only a church leader who knows the emotional, cultural and professional background of his people can adequately communicate. For the electronic media, this also involves knowing the programme preferences of a given audience for radio, TV and film. It is also useful for a church leader to know which means of communication are appropriate for a given community or situation and how to use them accordingly. This does not only refer to mass media but also to patterns of behaviour which are always influenced by culture and relationships. Finally the church leader needs to know how to formulate and articulate his message. This is a challenge to his theological knowledge and experience. An ability to communicate fully therefore requires the church leader to be fully immersed in the culture and society. S/he must be able to stand alongside those with whom s/he seeks to communicate.

New directions for communication formation

Communication is essential for *every* church member and especially every church leader. It is not just one aspect of the Church's activities but it is 'a major apostolic dimension of all our apostolates'.[5] This therefore places communication at the heart of church leadership training to ensure that the Church realises the centrality of communication in its activities.

This formation will require the development of a healthy personal attitude towards and ability in communication. It means that the *basics of human communication* have to be instilled theoretically and practically in all future ministers of the Church. In a world where communication is increasingly 'unifying humanity and turning it into what is known as a 'global village',[6] it is important that church leaders receive sufficient media education to be able to critically assess, evaluate and also use the modern means of communication, especially the mass media. Besides basic personal communication skills, those leaders with special talents and/or interests should be encouraged and promoted for further professional studies and skills training.

Too often different communication activities, especially those of the mass media, are separate and isolated from other church activities. The holistic attitude outlined above towards communication formation for individual leaders and church members will enable the integration of social communication into the overall structures and activities of the Church.

Communication formation experiences

So far we have discussed the theory and theology of the place of communication within the Church. The centrality of communication at the heart of the gospel requires an integrated approach to be taken towards communication

[5] See *Jesuits' General Congregation*, 1995.
[6] See *Redemptoris Missio*, 37c

within the Church. At a theoretical level we have concluded that the formation of church members and leaders must therefore reflect this theory, but such formation requires a complex interplay of personal attitudes and professional skills which equip the person with the necessary communication skills.

For several years, the theology which places communication at the heart of the Church has inspired the curriculum at the Divine Word School of Theology in Tagaytay City in the Philippines. Although there is neither the time nor space to discuss fully the way this is implemented, I will end with a short overview of this task. Clearly the actual implementation of this theology will be determined by the specific situations in which church leaders are being trained, but this is offered as one way that it can be integrated.

Every student beginning theological studies has in the first semester an obligatory course, 'Introduction to Social Communication'. This course stresses the dimension and basic rules of human communication, considers the theological dimensions and leads from there to the basics of mass media, group communication and multimedia. Students with special interests are offered additional classes with more practical applications. In the course of further studies, beside regular classes in Homiletics, other courses are offered such as Pastoral Communication, Intercultural Communication, Communication Theology, and Religious Broadcasting. Beyond such courses, deeper personal relationships are being developed in regular individual spiritual direction, as well as in group sharing and processing.

The more holistic communication formation is personalised, the more effective it will be, and the more the individual concerned will experience the values of openness and willingness to learn, listen and share. The Divine Word School has seen that through the integration of communication at the heart of church leader formation, the Church can realign itself with communication at its heart. Through the course, holistic communication formation is personalised to the skills and future experience of the individual and necessarily teaches the individual to experience the values and willingness to learn, listen and share. As we saw earlier, these personal attributes are at the heart of an integrated approach to communication and will prevent the relegation of communication to the margins of church activity and structure. Only through such techniques will the Church be able and competent to communicate with the rapidly changing world and be able to assess critically and to influence the mass media market. Only through such an holistic attitude to Church formation which places communication at its centre will the Church be able to reflect the centrality of communication in its theology, reflecting the communication at the heart of the Trinitarian Godhead.

PART 5

Film and Religion

15

Towards a New Religious Film Criticism: Using Film to Understand Religious Identity Rather than Locate Cinematic Analogue

Steve Nolan

The earliest attempts to relate theology and film coincide with an important shift in film theory.[1] The late 1960s/early 1970s mark the beginnings of film theory's encounter with 'Marxism and psychoanalysis on the terrain of semiotics'.[2] This encounter may not have yielded the scientific base film theorists desired, but it was productive of a more philosophically sophisticated and self-consciously analytical approach to film and its operation as a vehicle for ideology and system of meaning. It also came to dominate film theory through the 1970s and continues to give shape to analysis through its categories and vocabulary.

Regrettably, 'religious film criticism' has been little touched by film theory. This is in large part because the ideological-semiotic-psychoanalytic trajectory of contemporary film theory developed in Europe.[3] On the other hand, the early religious film critics were North American, where *auteur* theory had become pervasive as a theoretical tool in film studies. With notable exceptions,[4] US religious film critics have been preoccupied with the 'vision of the director', and have largely drawn on categories familiar to theology, biblical studies and literature.

In this chapter I will suggest that religious film criticism has been seduced into a futile pursuit of cinematic analogue from which it needs to escape. I will begin by reviewing and evaluating the main contributions to religious film criticism to date. I will suggest that despite claims to treat film *qua* film,

---

[1] John May suggests that theological interest developed in the US with the introduction of European directors to American film-goers. For alternative overviews of this literature see John R. May, 'Contemporary theories regarding the interpretation of religious film,' John R. May (ed.), *New Image of Religious Film* (Kansas City, MO: Sheed & Ward, 1997), pp. 17–37; Robert K. Johnston, *Reel Spirituality: Theology and Film in Dialogue* (Grand Rapids, Baker Academic, 2000), pp. 41–62.

[2] Stephen Heath, '*Jaws*, ideology, and film theory', Bill Nichols (ed.), *Movies and Methods: an Anthology*, Vol. 2 (Berkeley: University of California Press, 1985), p. 511.

[3] The British film journal *Screen* played a prominent role through the 1970s in pursuing the semiotic-psychoanalytic trajectory.

[4] See Thomas M. Martin, *Images and the Imageless: a Study in Religious Consciousness and Film* (Lewisburg, PA: Bucknell University Press, 1981).

religious film criticism has largely regarded film in terms of literary theory, and that this has led to a certain predictability in its findings. As a way forward, I will argue that religious film criticism should engage with the categories of film theory rather than those of literary theory.

Wall, May and Hurley: director's 'vision' and 'cinematic theology'

Early religious film critics were influenced by the 'Death of God' debates and the development of 'secular theology'. Writers like Wall and Hurley took seriously the contemporary cultural challenges to Christian faith and the associated haemorrhage of disenfranchised young people from the church. With apologetic and missiological purpose, they regarded cinema as expressing cultural values and began to address what they understood to be the key concerns of a generation, articulated through cinema. Their methodological concern was to secure a place for film as a legitimate partner with which to dialogue.

James Wall

As editor of *Christian Century*, Wall has made a sustained contribution to religious film criticism through editorials, articles and reviews. Foundational to his approach is his view that, while 'secular man' is no longer interested in biblical spectaculars like *The Greatest Story Ever Told* (George Stevens, 1965), he is nonetheless able to find considerable meaning in 'religious' films.

Implicitly, Wall raises the question: What is a religious film? His answer is to conceive the experience of viewing film as a point on a 'continuum of perception'. One end of the continuum picks up what the film is about, and the other what the film is. These ends correspond with the ways in which films can be made: either as *discursive* films, which function like audio-visual aids to transmit information; or as *presentational* films, which transcend information and present their theme implicitly and so share the filmmaker's vision.

Wall's purpose is to distinguish 'overall vision' from plot structure through which vision is projected, on the basis that, as art, film should not 'mean' but 'be'. In other words, film is artistic product which communicates artistic vision and makes us feel. For Wall, biblical spectaculars fail as religious films precisely because they are discursive, whereas, for example, *The Pawnbroker* (Sidney Lumet, 1965) or *Nothing But a Man* (Michael Roemer, 1964), are presentational films with genuine religious merit.

From this Wall attempts a definition of the religious film as 'that motion picture which manages, through artistic utilisation of its medium, to celebrate what it means to be human'.[5] In short, a religious film communicates the artist's vision through which we come to feel what it is to be human. For Wall the specifically Christian vision in a film is the specifically Christian vision of the human. But he also acknowledges the part played by context in that, while each of us approaches the cinematic experience from a particular background and history, for a Christian, particular experience is encountered from a context of a history shared with other Christians.

John R. May

Like Wall, May holds to the centrality of the director's vision and argues that by attending to this vision it is possible to find the religious significance in the film. May's methodology is informed by an occupational interest in literature, which leads him to interpret films as visual stories and discuss film in terms of the 'language of film'.

May employs an interdisciplinary model drawn from theology and literature to discern three theoretical approaches to theology and film: *heteronomy, theonomy* and *autonomy*. Heteronomy names the position apparent in T. S. Eliot's conviction that literature should be judged by Christian faith, since the greatness of literature can only be measured by a standard outside itself. Theonomy describes Paul Tillich's belief that literature and religion are unable to judge each other, because neither is an absolute. Against these, autonomy locates the norms for judging the achievement of a given discipline within that discipline. In these terms, '[a]ny discussion of the religious or sectarian dimension of cinema ought to be confined, as far as possible, to the language of film itself. *The critic's task is to discover the cinematic analogue of the religious or sectarian question.*'[6]

The difficulty with May's literary approach is as fundamental as it is obvious: film is not literature. Literary theory does not deal with the operations of the medium on the subject nor is it as sympathetic to film as he assumes. Consequently, his conception of film as 'visual story' entirely misses the specific operations of film as experience.

May's later approach displays a shift from his emphasis on autonomy to heteronomy, and in *Images and Likeness* he appears to share Eliot's conviction that literature and film can be judged by Christian faith. Attending to cinematic analogue of religious concerns, May and his collaborators search for Judaeo-Christian 'visions' in American film classics. However, the editorial definition of 'religious' is very broad, allowing directors to be

---

[5] James Wall, 'Biblical spectaculars and secular man', John C. Cooper and Carl Skrade (eds.), *Celluloid and Symbols* (Philadelphia: Fortress, 1970) p. 55.
[6] John R. May, 'Visual story and the religious interpretation of film', John R. May and Michael Bird (eds.), *Religion in Film* (Knoxville: University of Tennessee, 1982), p. 26, emphasis added.

selected because of their concern with those questions which are 'most fundamental'.

Neil Hurley

Hurley is motivated by a conviction that theology is the playground of an élite, but movies are for the masses. He attempts to connect theology and movies on the basis that they both deal with transcendence. Hurley understands transcendence to be rooted, not in the metaphysics of divine otherness, but in encounter. For him the critic who exercises insight and criticism exercises transcendence, and the moviewatcher's 'transcendental faculties [are] remarkably close to what religion has traditionally termed faith, prophecy, and reverence'.[7] However, this theological sleight of hand transforms unsuspecting moviewatchers into 'anonymous believers', trivialising the concerns of those young people he wants to engage, and reducing genuine differences to a matter of emphasis or perspective.

Hurley's 'cinematic theology' is a type of systematic theology in which he reviews contemporary cinematic statements on universal themes: freedom, conscience, sex, evil, death, grace and the future. In each case he moves swiftly from film to theology, interpreting film through a hermeneutic of transcendence, to develop a 'cinematic theology' specific to each given theme. For example, considering how the subject exercises transcendence in social situations, he finds insights for developing a 'behavioural theology' in Lindsay Anderson's *If* (1968).

Hurley's strategy is problematic. Redefining a particular theological category, and then using this as a hermeneutical analytic tool, masks the already committed nature of his method. He tellingly betrays this 'committedness' in discussing the work of Jacques Tati: 'Tati's films offer cogent theological insights *for those capable of deciphering them.*'[8] Hurley begs the question about the source of such theological insight: do theological insights already exist in the text, or are they supplied by the reader? Is it in Tati or in Hurley? Hurley further betrays himself in his search for a cinematic 'sexual theology' in the exercise of transcendence in sexual encounters on film. Given that he considers Anderson, Fellini, Bergman and Antonioni, the principles he elicits for a cinematic sexual theology are remarkable for the way they accord with traditional Roman Catholic values.

Kreitzer and Jewett: film and biblical studies

Recent theological interest in film has extended to biblical studies, with attention focusing in two directions. Some have written historiographically

---

[7] Neil Hurley, *Theology Through Film* (New York: Harper and Row, 1970), p. x.
[8] Hurley, *Theology Through Film*, p. 35, emphasis added.

about the cinematic treatment of Jesus and/or biblical stories, while others, like Kreitzer and Jewett, have worked imaginatively at a dialogue between biblical studies and film. This does not mark an immediate return to a concern for those outside the church, but it may indicate that postmodern deconstruction of the high/low culture opposition is opening a way for theologians and biblical students to engage meaningfully with contemporary culture.

Larry J. Kreitzer

Kreitzer is not primarily interested in film, but in the processes of interpretation and the insights to be gained by interpreting biblical texts in the light of contemporary literature and film. For this reason, he starts from the premise that there can be a '[reversing] of the flow of influence within the hermeneutical process', in such a way as to allow us to re-examine 'NT passages or themes in the light of some of the enduring expressions of our own culture, namely great literary works and their film adaptation'.[9]

There are two elements to Kreitzer's method. First, he makes the general observation that the Bible and biblical themes have informed our culture and its art forms. These art forms have in turn reflected back interpretations of the biblical themes on which they have drawn, to such a degree that understanding of those themes has been reinforced. This new understanding has once more informed culture, new art has been created, and so the cycle continues. (Kreitzer's specific example is Holman Hunt's *The Light of the World.*) In terms of his own strategy, Kreitzer locates his chosen literary and cinematic art Janus-like between New Testament texts and our contemporary setting. In this way they lubricate the hermeneutical flow. Kreitzer's second element is to see cinematic interpretation as a kind of performance of the interpretative process, which he describes but does not go on to theorise.

Kreitzer's strength is in detailing the way fiction and film can inform the process of interpretation. He demonstrates, for example, how William Wyler's film *Ben Hur* (1959) interprets Lew Wallace's novel and may 'provide a helpful doorway through which to enter the hermeneutical arena of NT studies'.[10] To the extent that he is discussing the intertextuality that may provide flashes of interpretative insight between texts, biblical, literary and filmic, John Barton can reasonably term Kreitzer's approach mishradic.[11]

Ultimately, however, Kreitzer's methodology disappoints. Typical of his results is his consideration of Romans 7: 'Dr Jekyll and Mr Hyde: Re-reading the Pauline model of the duality of human nature'. After

---

[9] Larry Kreitzer, *The New Testament in Fiction and Film: On Reversing the Hermeneutical Flow* (Sheffield: Sheffield Academic Press, 1993), p. 19.

[10] Kreitzer, *Fiction and Film*, p. 18.

[11] John Barton, Preface to Kreitzer, *Fiction and Film* (1993), p. 8.

impressively detailed consideration of the dark side of human nature personified in Mr Hyde, read by some as sexual immorality, Kreitzer concludes: 'Is it too much to suggest that the words in Romans 7, although they almost certainly will not bear the interpretative weight of sexuality sometimes thrown upon them, nonetheless do so speak to us of moral struggles that characterised not only the apostle's life, but ours as well?'[12]

The weakness is Kreitzer's analytical method. He appears to suggest a reader-response approach to the texts that moves from 'facets of our cultural heritage, and then to apply it to our understanding of the NT materials'.[13] Instead, his meticulous investigation of sources and nuances of adaptation reveals the redaction critical preoccupation with authorial intention of New Testament scholarship. Kreitzer seems uncritically innocent of the theory around either authorial intent or the concept of the *auteur*.[14]

Robert Jewett

Jewett's aim is to develop a 'dialogue in a prophetic mode'. Adopting a starting point in St Paul's missionary strategy, Jewett argues that contemporary Americans are shaped more by popular culture than by formal education or religious training. Given that Paul's method of gospel communication was to put himself where people are, Jewett's contention is that for us this should involve engaging with cinema, and that, had they been available in his time, Paul would certainly have been a discerning critic of secular movies. Jewett's method is to regard films as capable of disclosing truth in their own right, and on this basis he proposes to 'deal with a film in tandem with a specific biblical passage, treating both with equal respect, and bringing their themes and metaphors into relationship so that a contemporary interpretation for the American cultural situation may emerge'.[15] To this end Jewett is 'not as much interested in evaluating films on the basis of aesthetic criteria as in discerning the message these interacting "stories" disclose for our society'.[16]

---

[12] Kreitzer, *Fiction and Film* (1993), p. 126.

[13] Kreitzer, *Fiction and Film* p. 19.

[14] In defence Kreitzer asserts: 'I take it for granted that a well-grounded understanding of the author's intent in producing a piece of literature, however difficult that is to determine, can contribute significantly to our appreciation of his or her writing.' Larry J. Kreitzer, *Pauline Images in Fiction and Film: On Reversing the Hermeneutical Flow* (Sheffield: Sheffield Academic Press, 1999), p. 28. However, the experiments of Russian Formalist Lev Kuleshov persuasively demonstrate that cinematic meaning emerges for the spectator in the juxtaposition of shots in a way that is beyond the intention of the director/editor. Realist film theorist André Bazin concedes that 'The meaning is not in the image, it is in the shadow of the image projected by montage onto the field of consciousness of the spectator.' André Bazin, 'The evolution of the language of cinema', André Bazin, *What is Cinema?*, Vol. 1, trans. Hugh Gray (Berkeley and London: University of California Press, 1967), pp. 25, 26.

[15] Robert Jewett, *St Paul at the Movies: the Apostle's Dialogue with American Culture* (Louisville, KY: Westminster John Knox, 1993), p. 7.

[16] Jewett, *St Paul at the Movies*, p. 8.

Jewett represents an extension of May's project into the arena of biblical studies. His concern to treat film and biblical texts with equal respect maps with May's approach of autonomy; and Jewett's stress on treating 'stories' and seeking analogies clearly continues May's own approach.[17] An example of such analogy is found in the juxtaposition of 2 Timothy (1:3–7) with *Dead Poets Society* (Peter Weir, 1989), both of which Jewett argues deal with 'the force of ancestral tradition and the reigniting of the charismata received from God'.[18]

Martin and Ostwalt: film and religious studies

If Wall, May and Hurley represent a theological strand of religious film analysis, and Jewett and Kreitzer a biblical strand, Martin and Ostwalt offer a more generally religious studies direction. Their multidisciplinary approach examines film in a manner which connects well with trends in cultural studies (and has the potential to interact with contemporary psychoanalytic and poststructural film theory). To this extent they mark a return to the early concerns of Wall, May and Hurley, and to questions of methodology.

Martin proposes a threefold critique to match the three branches in the study of religion: *theological*, equating religion with specific religious traditions; *mythological*, defining religion in the broad terms of universal mythic archetypes; and *ideological*, focusing on the political and social effects of religion.

Theological Criticism issues from a committed position within a particular theological tradition, making explicit the premise of May's *Images and Likeness*: 'Theological criticism hinges upon the notion that the critic, director, screenplay writer, or some other creative force behind the film develops a certain theological agenda or concept, and the distinctive goal of the theological critic is to uncover that concept.'[19] As such, theological criticism draws on traditional theological concepts like good and evil, redemption, grace, etc., and relies on allegorical interpretation to find traces of familiar religious stories. Authentic theological reading will demonstrate how the film communicates religious meanings even to viewers unfamiliar with religious texts and traditions. *Mythological Criticism* explores religious myth in popular film and assumes that film meaningfully communicates archetypes (universal symbols) to contemporary audiences. Mythic criticism probes for such archetypes, explicating the myths which narrate encounters with the mysteriously unknowable. *Ideological Criticism* draws on Althusserian theory

[17] 'I therefore understand a Pauline text in the light of its bearing on a specific cultural and historical context, and I look for modern analogies not just to the words Paul wrote but also to the situations he addressed,' Jewett, *St Paul at the Movies*, p. 9.

[18] Jewett, *St Paul at the Movies*, p. 148.

[19] Joel W. Martin and Conrad E. Ostwalt, *Screening the Sacred: Religion, Myth, and Ideology in Popular American Film* (Boulder, CO: Westview, 1995), p. 14.

of ideology to argue that, because 'religious symbols and values are diffused throughout popular culture and continue to shape contemporary subjects',[20] religion needs to be taken seriously in ideological analysis. To this end Martin's essay, 'Redeeming America: *Rocky* as ritual racial drama', argues that much of the film's ideological power depends upon the scapegoating ritual.

For Martin and Ostwalt none of these critical postures is sufficient on its own. Each being commendable in part though inevitably weak, they hint at a necessary (if as yet unknown) fourth type of criticism which will synthesise these three criticisms: 'Such a synthesis will be a criticism deeply grounded in generations of thought about the sacred, broadly open to the diverse ways in which the sacred manifests itself, and acutely sensitive to the political and social effects of religious and mythological texts.'[21]

Ostwalt's argument is that religion and film are independent modes implicated in the search for meaning; they represent 'forms of life that define society and thereby constitute valid sources of investigation for the search for meaning in culture'.[22] Ostwalt predicates his position on 'a theory of culture that is holistic and interrelated', and quotes anthropologist Clifford Geertz: '[M]an is an animal suspended in webs of significance he has spun, I take culture to be those webs, and the analysis of it to be therefore not an experimental science in search of law but an interpretative one in search of meaning.'[23] Ostwalt is also clear that the critical postures presented are functional and descriptive, not methodological or programmatic, with each of the tripartite divisions attending to how it interacts with film.

The new criticism at which Martin and Ostwalt hint will have methodological procedures based on an agenda broad enough to 'deal with the interconnectedness of a complex cultural matrix – one that draws on strengths from film criticism, religious studies, and cultural studies in general'.[24] Interestingly, Ostwalt's argument makes use of psychoanalytic language (referring to 'otherness', dreams as the 'cultural unconscious' and film as 'mirror'), and he suggests a way forward that is concerned with film as performance, 'what happens or might happen when one watches a film and what consequences these happenings might hold for society'[25] (an approach anticipated by Robert Wagner some twenty-five years earlier).[26]

---

[20] Martin and Ostwalt, *Screening the Sacred*, p. 121.

[21] Martin and Ostwalt, *Screening the Sacred*, p. 12.

[22] Martin and Ostwalt, *Screening the Sacred*, p. 153.

[23] Clifford Geertz, 'Thick description: toward an interpretive theory of culture', *The Interpretation of Cultures* (New York: Basic, 1973: p. 5), cited in Martin and Ostwalt, *Screening the Sacred*, p. 152.

[24] Martin and Ostwalt, *Screening the Sacred*, p. 154.

[25] Martin and Ostwalt, *Screening the Sacred*, p. 156.

[26] Robert W. Wagner, 'Film, reality and religion', Skrade and Cooper (eds.), *Celluloid and Symbols*, p. 137.

Film as film: the consumption of representation

From this brief review it is clear that several interests preoccupy religious film critics: the director's artistic vision as defining the meaning of a film; the search for cinematic analogue to religious questions or doctrines; the possibility of using theological categories as hermeneutical tools. I suggest that these interests are inappropriate to any engagement with film precisely because they regard film from within essentially literary categories. In fact religious film criticism must treat film *qua* film and engage with the large and highly theorised body of film studies literature.

Much film theory has been concerned with understanding how spectators consume cinematic representation. Analysing films in terms of the spectator's construction of meaning has highlighted the fact that cinematic meaning is located, not in its production, but in its consumption. And psychoanalytic film theory has stressed that cinematic representation is consumed at the level of the unconscious where film contributes to the construction of subjectivity (self-identity). I suggest that this offers religious studies with an alternative methodology that will enable it to escape the fruitless pursuit of cinematic analogue to religious questions.

My own approach has been to work with Lacanian film theory.[27] This highly theoretical approach is not without its detractors,[28] but it has the strength of regarding film as *experience* rather than *text*, and critically appropriated it can illuminate the unconscious operation of cinematic representation. Using Lacanian film theory, I want to suggest an alternative methodology based on the premise that film and liturgical theorists share certain questions in common. These include a shared concern with the perception of, and identification with, aesthetically represented reality. Various of Lacan's theories may illuminate how aesthetically represented reality is perceived and identified with: his notion of anticipated certainty, his category of the Real, and his concept of paranoiac knowledge (the well known 'Mirror Stage' in which individuals' [pseudo]identity is constructed in relation to a [mis]representation of themselves in an other).

For example, in terms of identification, cinema spectators relate to film stars as to signifying images. Just as dream images condense and displace narcissistic identifications, star images condense and displace spectators' identifications with the stars' ideological effect. Thus, when the fans of Sylvester Stallone identify with their star image (icon) he condenses and displaces for them a series of identifications within an ideological economy of alterities. Stallone's characters attain self-identity (subjectivity) by being

---

[27] This film theory was developed in the British film journal *Screen* and came to dominate British theoretical discourse during the 1970s.

[28] Notably, Noel Carroll, *Mystifying Movies: Fads and Fallacies in Contemporary Film Theory* (New York: Columbia University Press, 1988); and David Bordwell, *Making Meaning: Inference and Rhetoric in the Interpretation of Cinema* (Cambridge and London: Harvard University Press, 1989).

othered and objectified, in turn othering and objectifying, struggling with and ultimately overcoming, all within an ideological economy.

The church worshipper similarly relates to signifying images, in this case religious heroes. Thus, Roman Catholic theology of priestly representation positions the priest in his 'heroic' role representing Christ to the people (*in persona Christi*) and the people to Christ (*in nomine totius populi*). As such, worshippers identify with the priest and through this identification participate in sacramental reality. Again, in Protestant Unionism the Rev. Ian Paisley is cast as 'heroic' Calvinist pastor/politician. Visitors to Martyrs Memorial Church encounter him leading them in worship in hymns and prayers that articulate their religious representation. The primary representation may be Christ, but given the power and presence of 'the Big Man', the secondary identification is with Paisley himself. As with Stallone, identification with Paisley is to a signifying image that condenses and displaces narcissistic identifications with the 'hero's' ideological effect. Liturgically, Paisley represents the Protestant cause with which worshippers identify in a liturgical ideology constructed by the religio-political mix.

I lack here the space to develop this method further.[29] But I suggest that this common concern with the experience of aesthetically represented reality, rather than the preoccupation with supposed directorial 'vision', or the search for cinematic analogue, offers an alternative and potentially more productive basis on which religious studies can engage with film. Examining film and liturgy through the theoretical categories of Lacanian film theory could deepen religious studies' understanding of the construction of liturgical subjectivity. In addition, the insights gained by 'doing theology from experience' could facilitate more significant engagement between theology and contemporary culture than has so far been the case.

---

[29] For examples of this approach see Steve Nolan, 'Worshipping (wo)men, liturgical representation and feminist film theory: an *Alien/s* identification?', *Bulletin of the John Rylands University Library of Manchester* 80 (3) (Autumn 1998), pp. 195–213; '*Carpe phallum*: (male) salvation meta-narrative and the Renewal', Michael A. Hayes, Wendy Porter and David Tombs, (eds.), *Religion and Sexuality* (Sheffield: Sheffield Academic Press, 1998), pp. 285–311. For a discussion of eucharistic theology and film theory that theorises the worshipper's relation to liturgical 'reality', see Steve Nolan, 'Representing realities: theorising reality in liturgy and film', *Worship* (forthcoming).

16

The Catholic Church and its Attitude to Film as an Arbiter of Cultural Meaning

Gaye Ortiz

Introduction

This chapter contributes to the thesis that, alongside the more commonly perceived tendency toward censorship, the Catholic Church has held a little-known but nevertheless positive attitude toward film as a means of cultural expression which 'enriches both [the Church] and the cultures them-selves'.[1] Since the invention of motion pictures over one hundred years ago, the Church has recognised film as an instrument of catechesis, but she has also respected cinema's power to enthral and inspire audiences. The Church realised almost from the start that she must not ignore the film industry; indeed, she could not, because of the Church's tradition of involvement with the great art emerging from the two thousand years of her history. Underlying this involvement is nothing less than a commitment to imagination through metaphor and analogy, but this commitment does not mean uncritical acceptance of all flights of imagination. As Andrew Greeley puts it:

> If a religious tradition commits itself to metaphor (for which another word is analogy) then it has to be open to all possible metaphors and to be willing to judge each one as it comes along, aware that some unsuitable metaphors cannot be resisted, and that the suitability of others will be certain only after the passage of time, and that finally the rejection of other metaphors may be a catastrophic mistake.
>
> Catholicism is a religious tradition that is enthralled by metaphors and at the same time constantly uneasy about the metaphors that it finds itself using.[2]

Thus, the Church could be seen to be full of praise for film, and she embarked very early on upon a strengthening of relationship between herself and the film industry; at the same time, the censorious attitude the

---

[1] Austin Flannery (ed.), *Vatican Council II* (Northport, NY: Costello, 1984), p. 963.
[2] Andrew Greeley, *The Catholic Myth* (New York: Collier, 1990), p. 276.

Church has shown toward film is not confined to the era of the American Legion of Decency. It has been in evidence through much of the Church's work on national film classification codes and, as I will discuss, through the hierarchy's adverse reaction to certain films and filmmakers. A positive attitude toward film, although congruent with the Church's appreciation of art and her pronouncements on the merits of contemporary culture, is often challenged by a confrontational and reactionary response from those in the Church who object to films that address a range of contemporary cultural, social and ethical issues in ways which challenge Church teaching or practice.

Catholicism and art

I believe that the 'Catholic (artistic) heritage of the past two thousand years has attempted to articulate its people's quest for the sacred'.[3] Art can express our search for meaning and identity, as well as attempt to communicate our most profound ecstatic spiritual experiences. The tremendous legacy of artistic genius, dedicated to the glory of God, has of course had slightly more prosaic, and even profane, functions: from catechetical education (as in stained glass communicating the Christian story for an illiterate congregation) to status symbols of papal power and grandeur. That art can be a means of expression and an appropriate instrument of searching for answers to the questions of life is perhaps due to its place within a Catholic theological framework. There are three theological concepts which can be seen to link art with Catholicism: analogy, sacramentalism and incarnation.

Firstly, the idea of a particular 'Catholic imagination', which relies upon the use of analogy to create and sustain a worldview in which God is present in the world, 'disclosing himself [sic] in and through creation',[4] may be seen in the works of classic writers such as Aquinas (who put the analogous relationship between God and creation into perspective by saying that the differences between God and the world were as great as the similarities). This analogical worldview gives value to the activities and creativity of humans; the 'similarity-in-difference' points to the assertion in Genesis 1 that humanity was made in the image of God. Therefore, humans can be said to be like God in their attempts to express themselves in the act of creating beauty.

David Tracy's seminal work, *The Analogical Imagination* (1981), explores the Catholic tendency to aestheticism and symbolism in the Church's religious make-up. In doing so he brings into play a second theological concept, that of sacramentalism. Greeley defines this instinct as a belief that 'the whole of creation and all its processes, especially its life-giving and

---

[3] Gaye Ortiz, *The Catholic Imagination in Film* (M.Th. thesis, unpublished, 1993), p. 1.
[4] Greeley, *The Catholic Myth*, p. 45.

life-nurturing processes, reveal the lurking and passionate love of God'.[5] Because Jesus Christ is believed to be 'fully God and fully man' (from the doctrinal statement at Chalcedon) this leads to an understanding of all creation as potentially a symbol of divine in-dwelling: 'each thing is itself but as itself, it is also something else.'[6] The use of natural elements, such as water, wine and bread, in Catholic sacraments, shows how fundamental and pervasive this tendency is in the theology of the Church. The reaction against this tendency is iconoclastic, characterising the Reformation and defined by Tillich as the 'Protestant principle': the concern to keep the finite in its place 'lest it believe' itself to be infinite.

Connected with the sacramentality of natural elements is the concept of the incarnation: that God would think the human state worthy of his Son implies that the created order is of value. Again, the Protestant sensibility veers away from this idea, promoting instead the radical difference of humanity from God. The disclosure of the divine within the ordinary is an assumption of the Catholic imagination, which, Greeley says, is catholic (with a small 'c') in the sense of being radically open to the world and therefore accepting that existence can be both beautiful and degraded.

The creativity of the human spirit is therefore appreciated in greater depth by the Catholic tradition, because, according to Greeley, 'religion operates in the same area of personality where artistic expression and scientific insight flourish; image, experience and story inform the Catholic heritage.'[7] The Catholic tradition, which has not only provided a place for inspired works of art, but which has also appropriated art from other traditions, is committed to a religious imagination in which film too can find a home.[8]

Catholicism and film

However wonderful it is to theologise about art and the Catholic tradition, we are jolted back to reality when we consider the occasions throughout history when artists clashed with the authorities of the Church:

> Throughout the history of the Church there have been movements against new artistic media, from the theatre to verse, the novel and new forms of music, and now to film. At the same time that the Church ... cautions filmmakers about the potential dangers of film as a corrosive influence on society, films emerge ... which will be recognised as masterpieces of Christian art for at least the next 100 years.[9]

[5] Greeley, *The Catholic Myth*, p. 253.
[6] Sallie McFague, *Metaphorical Theology* (Philadelphia: Fortress, 1997), p. 11.
[7] Greeley, *The Catholic Myth*, p. 36.
[8] see Greeley on pagan art, pp. 284ff.
[9] Peter Fraser, *Images of the Passion* (Trowbridge, UK: Flicks, 1998), p. 12.

The Church was quick to recognise the power of cinema, and in several European countries, during the first thirty years of the new medium, the Church became heavily involved in exhibition and production of films. In 1928 a Catholic International Congress on Cinema took place in the Hague, and this congress saw the establishment of the Office Catholique International du Cinéma (OCIC, but later Office was changed to Organisation). Eighteen countries voted to establish this Office, which formally combined activities already existing in several countries in Europe as well as in the Americas.[10]

The establishment of a Catholic organisation to deal with cinema was encouraged by Pope Pius XI, in a letter to Canon Brohee of the Belgian Catholique Centrale. In it the activities of OCIC were applauded as a form of Catholic Action. This positive view of OCIC's work was boosted by a papal encyclical in 1936, *Vigilanti Cura*, 'the first official papal document relating to the cinema and ... social communications'.[11] The encyclical was addressed especially to the United States hierarchy and contained papal approval of the Legion of Decency's 'holy crusade against the abuses of motion pictures'; but the pope went on immediately to praise the artistic values of film, which he saw as a powerful modern medium of the diffusion of ideas.[12]

He declared that 'the motion picture should not be simply a means of diversion, a light relaxation to occupy an idle hour. With its magnificent power, it can and must be a bearer of light and a positive guide to what is good.'[13] Yet another phrase, 'Scientific progress is also a gift from God to be used for his glory and the spread of his kingdom,'[14] is indicative of the tone of the document, which ended by urging bishops to set up a national film-reviewing office in each country, comprised of 'persons who are familiar with the technique of the motion picture and who are, at the same time, well grounded in the principles of catholic morality and doctrine'.[15] This was a call for expert (not ecclesiastical) judgement on films: 'It seems clear that not every priest is qualified to pass expert judgement on a film ... and that special knowledge is absolutely essential for the difficult task of reviewing and classifying films.'[16]

OCIC's permanent secretariat was also established in Brussels in 1936, and *Vigilanti Cura* was instrumental in giving it the authority for its work in 'promoting moral films' and supporting the work of Christians in the film

---

[10] *Fifty Years of OCIC 1928–1978* (unpublished report, 1978), p. 1.

[11] *Fifty Years of OCIC*, p. 2.

[12] Pius XI, *Vigilanti Cura* (1936), No. 1.

[13] Pius XI, *Vigilanti Cura*.

[14] *Fifty Years of OCIC*, p. 2.

[15] Pius XI, *Vigilanti Cura*, No. 52.

[16] J. C. Reid, *Catholics and Their Films* (Auckland, NZ: Whitcomb and Tombs, 1949), p. 16. (However, at every stage of Church involvement with film, there has been a strong clerical personality liaising between the hierarchy and the film industry.)

industry.[17] Later Vatican writings, such as *Miranda Prorsus* (1956), continued to confirm a positive view of cinema's role in society.

The Second World War curtailed many of OCIC's activities, but its postwar objectives included two projects: the creation of an international OCIC prize[18] and the publication of an international cinematographic journal.[19] The impetus was provided by the OCIC General Secretary André Ruszkowski, whose philosophy was evident in this statement from the inaugural issue of *International Film Review.*

> We are eager and anxious to be of service, not only to Catholics who are engaged in work for the cinema but to the industry as a whole. To all those philosophical, aesthetic, cultural, social and economic problems which the industry is called upon to solve, we should like to bring the impact of Christian thought and study, thus demonstrating clearly that no basic difference exists between their moral and material prosperity and the keen interest which the Church and its followers display towards the cinema.[20]

Film festivals have been seen as an important focus of OCIC activity, beginning with a plan to create such an OCIC prize to be awarded in recognition of a work of cinema which is 'la plus capable de contribuer a l'élévation spirituelle et morale de l'humanité' ('the most capable of contributing to the moral and spiritual elevation of humanity').[21] In addition, from the very beginning OCIC wanted to signal by the award that the organisation is not a censoring body: 'Il est certain que l'attribution de ce Prix démentira de façon éclatante le reproche, souvent adressé aux organismes catholiques, de ne jouer qu'un rôle negatif de censeur' ('It is certain that the award of the prize will demolish in brilliant fashion the reproach often addressed to Catholic bodies, of playing only (after 'reproach') the negative role of the censor' [author's translation]).[22] The OCIC award has been given by Catholic juries at prestigious film festivals around the world to many directors, including Catholics like John Ford and Francis Coppola, for their filmmaking and professional dedication to the craft.

In 1932 the Biennale Internationale d'Arte in Venice included film for the first time in its festival programme; in 1948 OCIC gave its first prize at the Mostra festival to *The Fugitive* by John Ford. Occasionally there have been political and ideological disagreements about the Church's participation in the festival (for example, in 1951 the Communists 'keenly criticised the Mostra as being clerical' and felt it selected too many films with a

---

[17] François Quenin, 'Le film religieux' in *CinemAction* No. 49 (Paris: Corlet, 1985), p. 52.

[18] Léo Bonneville, *Soixante-dix ans au service du cinema et de l'audiovisuel* (Quebec: Fides, 1998), pp. 108ff.

[19] *OCIC Bulletin V* 8 and 9 (1946), p. 9; Bonneville, *Soixante-dix ans,* pp. 57–63.

[20] André Ruszkowski, *International Film Review* No.1 (Brussels: OCIC, 1949), p. 1.

[21] Bonneville, *Soixante-dix ans,* p. 51.

[22] *OCIC Bulletin V* 8 and 9 (1946).

'religious coloration'). But OCIC's objective was to work with Venice to create a forum for films 'which, by their themes and artistic qualities, contribute to promoting true human values and enable man [sic] and his world to be better understood'.[23]

The number of festivals at which OCIC is annually represented, whether through a dedicated OCIC jury or within the framework of an ecumenical jury, has risen to more than eighteen. The most established juries serve at the festivals of Cannes (since 1952), Berlin (1954) and Venice. Over the years some decisions of the OCIC juries in awarding Catholic prizes have been controversial: the OCIC jury at Venice in 1964 had to consider (in the words of Leo Bonneville) whether a Marxist could make an honest film about the Gospel of St Matthew. The jury, he says, had to consider the film, not the filmmaker, and so Pier Paolo Pasolini's *The Gospel According to Saint Matthew* was given the OCIC festival prize. The following year Catholic national film offices voted to give it the annual OCIC Grand Prize. Plans to screen *The Gospel According to Saint Matthew* for the hierarchy amassed for the Second Vatican Council in Rome that year were almost scuppered by alarmed officials in the Vatican Curia, but it was eventually shown to eight hundred bishops at a remarkable screening in Rome.[24]

In 1968 the OCIC jury at Venice gave the prize to Pasolini's *Theorem*. A majority decision, the award was justified in the accompanying text as being given to the film that, more than any other film in the festival, provided an experience which could be described as 'religious'. The jury intended 'to recognise the authentic spiritual search evident' in the work of Pasolini, especially in *Theorem*, and also commended the cinematographic language and its 'profound human dimension'.[25] A letter from the Cardinal of Venice to the director of the Venice International Film Festival on the occasion of its 50th anniversary contains a potted history of its OCIC prizes, and enigmatically states that 'in 1968 unfortunate incidents followed the presentation of the OCIC prize to Pasolini's film *Theorem*, a decision which surprised Catholics as much as non-Catholics'.[26] What actually happened over the course of that year and the next was an unprecedented exchange of letters between OCIC and the Pontifical Council for Social Communications, which reacted adversely to the award because it had grave reservations about *Theorem*'s moral content (the film was actually banned in Italy for some time). The Venice OCIC jury president, Marc Gervais, a Jesuit priest, wrote to Mgr. Jean Bernard, the OCIC secretary general, to explain the decision and to disassociate the jury from the pursuant widespread media reviews of the film using the OCIC award as evidence for commending or condemning the film. In defence of the jury, the OCIC secretary general reassured the Vatican that OCIC would continue to play a vital role in

---

[23] Franz Ulrich, 'La Mostra de Venezia and OCIC', *NewsOCIC* No. 4 (Brussels: OCIC, 1982), p. 5.

[24] Bonneville, *Soixante-dix ans*, pp. 112–14.

[25] Bonneville, *Soixante-dix ans*, p. 115.

[26] Ulrich, 'La Mostra de Venezia', p. 5.

contact and dialogue with the film industry; if OCIC is to do its work, he said, then it must be left to get on with its remit of reading 'the signs of the times' in film. OCIC seemed to ride out the storm until July 1969, when the OCIC jury at the Berlin Film Festival gave its prize to John Schlesinger's *Midnight Cowboy*. The jury (which included two priests) stated that the film presented 'a treatment of a contemporary social problem in a form at once artistic yet accessible to a vast public'.[27]

With Catholic prizes going to *Theorem* and *Midnight Cowboy* in consecutive years, it is interesting to note that a statement from Paul VI followed in September 1969 during a papal audience, denouncing 'inadmissible' films. A series of long discussions continued into 1970, with Mgr. Bernard effectively troubleshooting for OCIC and guaranteeing the future of OCIC festival awards. In the coming years the original criteria received a much-needed broadening, perhaps in anticipation of the rise of the ecumenical jury containing both Protestants and Catholics. There are now four points for all Catholic juries to consider. Awards are:

(1) to encourage films which contribute to human progress and the recognition of spiritual, social and human values;
(2) to draw attention to the cinematographic works which express new personal and social dimensions of the evangelical message;
(3) to take into account the artistic talent and technical skill manifested by the director and his team in the production;
(4) to favour quality films whose commercial future seems uncertain; also those about less favoured peoples or regions.[28]

These broadened criteria allow for an openness to film in a way that keeps open the lines of communication between Church and cinema and that encourages cultural interests. The autonomy of the OCIC prizes is notable by the absence of any restrictions on the types of films that can be given awards.

What is most interesting when considering the three films and the controversies which grew up around the OCIC awards is the timeframe: the Second Vatican Council in the early 1960s had introduced into the Catholic world a totally fresh re-evaluation of the Church and its interaction with culture. In the final section of this paper I would like to consider some of the main themes of the document *Gaudium et Spes* (Pastoral Constitution on the Church in the Modern World, 1965), and the implications for the Church in its future appreciation of and dialogue with contemporary culture.

It is no secret in the history of the Second Vatican Council that the Church Fathers who wrote *Gaudium et Spes* threw out the preliminary framework presented to them and devised their own draft. The second chapter of Part II comprises a tenth of the text and focuses on the sole topic of culture: 'culture intimately linked with the dignity of the human person and with the call of

---

[27] Bonneville, *Soixante-dix ans*, p. 125.
[28] OCIC 'Regulations for Juries' leaflet, undated.

freedom to become more fully human'.[29] The Fathers recognise difficulties and challenges in contemporary culture, such as balancing dynamic cultural change with tradition, and the hostility to religion that secularism may bring. However, it affirms an approach to culture that is less elitist and offers a recognition of the diversity in social structures and cultures.[30] An optimistic and perhaps quite naive attitude to culture is revealed by the Fathers' assertion that 'cultural activities are central to the Christian calling',[31] but later writings by Popes Paul VI and John Paul II confirm the basic worth of human culture. They see it as a place for artistic and intellectual contact and dialogue, especially with nonbelievers. And their stress on the importance of culture shows the *Gaudium et Spes* text to be a prophetic one.

In his 1999 Easter letter addressed to artists, Pope John Paul II reiterated the importance of the renewal of the relationship between the Church and culture effected by the *Gaudium et Spes* document. When considering the separation in today's world between art and faith, John Paul II praised the ability of artists to 'seek the beautiful', but went on to say that 'even when they explore the darkest depths of the soul or the most unsettling aspects of evil, artists give voice in a way to the universal desire for redemption'.[32] His remark could apply to the genre that we often see in contemporary film which Peter Malone calls 'de profundis', a cry from the depths. This genre, as seen in *Theorem* and *Midnight Cowboy*, is controversially recognised by Catholic juries, who perhaps have been decades in advance of the Church in their understanding of film as an arbiter of cultural meaning.[33]

Reflecting upon Andrew Greeley's remark that a religious tradition which commits itself to analogy has to be open to all possible metaphors, there are bound to be confrontations between two sections of the Church: the traditional hierarchy which seeks to uphold 'Catholic values' and to prevent contamination from worldly ones, and the Church which, because of her identity within an incarnational and sacramental theology, sees her place in the midst of contemporary culture, seeking to read 'the signs of the times'. Film indeed is an arbiter of cultural meaning that the Church must heed, but even as recently as 1995 it was clear that some sections of the Church still resist the cultural dialogue of which Pope John Paul speaks so glowingly: the release of the film *Priest* (directed by Antonia Bird) provoked a range of reactions within the Church. Cardinal John O'Connor of the United States condemned *Priest* without having seen it, by saying it was 'as viciously anti-Catholic as anything that has ever rotted on the silver screen'.[34] His comments were given prominence in a reaction throughout

---

[29] Michael Paul Gallagher, *Clashing Symbols* (London: Darton, Longman & Todd, 1997), p. 37.

[30] Gallagher, *Clashing Symbols*, p. 39.

[31] Gallagher, *Clashing Symbols*, p. 39.

[32] John Paul II, 'Letter of his Holiness Pope John Paul II to Artists', No. 10 (1999).

[33] Peter Malone and Robert Molhant, *Cinema, Religion and Values* (Brussels: OCIC, 1999), p. 15.

[34] J. C. O'Connor, '*Priest* and Real Priests', *Cine et Media* (Brussels: OCIC, 1995), p. 8.

America against the film that saw a boycott of the distributor Disney and even fire bombings.

In contrast, *Priest* was shown that year at the Berlin Film Festival, and although it was not in a category eligible for consideration for an Ecumenical jury award, the OCIC members of that jury issued a press release about the importance of the film for the Church:

> *Priest* is a picture of priestly life and ministry in a Liverpool parish. Jimmy McGovern's screenplay shows an authentic and detailed experience of British Catholic life. It is undeniable that clerical celibacy and homosexual relationships of priests are a real problem of the Catholic Church in different countries and continents. All media in these countries deal openly and at length with these questions. *Priest*, from filmmaker Antonia Bird, also raises these issues and thematises them in the form of a dramatic story. A number of aspects of sexuality and sexual relationships are shown and discussed. The treatment is frank, sometimes explicit, but not sensational.
>
> The issues, as well as the film, are provocative and controversial. The Church shouldn't avoid or deny these issues, but confront, reflect on and clarify them. Many positive Christian themes and values are strongly present in this film: the search for God, the involvement of the faith community, prayer, the Eucharist, solidarity, forgiveness, reconciliation.
>
> The lively response of the large audience at the festival at the screening of the film and during the press conference afterwards indicated that there are a clear interest in and need for dramatising these religious values. The Church still seems to have great opportunities, when it is aware and involves itself in this complex and controversial area.[35]

The statement was endorsed by the Bishop of Berlin. The film was then scheduled for screenings to Catholic communities throughout Germany, followed by seminars and discussions arranged by the media office of the National Conference of Bishops.

The reaction of the Church to this film vividly shows the two sides of the Church in its dealings with film. One side clearly voices disapproval at the content or ideology of the filmmakers. But as this history of the last hundred years shows, the Church appreciates film's creativity, progress and cultural importance. There is no doubt that the Church recognises cinema as an arbiter of cultural meaning, and that this alternately poses a threat and an opportunity to the Church as she begins her third millennium in dialogue with 'the things of the world'.

---

[35] Statement on behalf of the OCIC members of the ecumenical jury at the Berlin Film Festival, Berlin, 17 January 1995.

Further Reading

G. Black, *Hollywood Censored: Morality Codes, Catholics and the Movies* (Cambridge: Cambridge University Press, 1994).

—————— *The Catholic Crusade Against the Movies, 1940–1975* (Cambridge: Cambridge University Press, 1997).

A. Flannery, (ed.), *Vatican Council II* (Northport, NY: Costello, 1984).

P. Fraser, *Images of the Passion* (Trowbridge, UK: Flicks Books, 1998).

M. P. Gallagher, *Clashing Symbols* (London: Darton, Longman & Todd, 1997).

P. Giles, *American Catholic Arts and Fiction* (Cambridge: Cambridge University Press, 1992).

A. Greeley, *The Catholic Myth* (New York: Collier, 1990).

L. and B. Keyser, *Hollywood and the Catholic Church* (Chicago: Loyola University Press, 1984).

S. McFague, *Metaphorical Theology* (Philadelphia, Fortress, 1997).

D. Tracy, *The Analogical Imagination* (New York: Crossroad, 1981).

17

From Popular to Arthouse: An Analysis of Love and Nature as Religious Motifs in Recent Cinema[1]

Jörg Herrmann

The success of popular films in the nineties was marked by the worldwide box-office hit list, where one finds seven titles from the nineties were in the all time top ten.[2] Near the top of the list is James Cameron's *Titanic*, which remains one of the world's most successful films. With a budget of two hundred million dollars, it took receipts of nearly two billion dollars.[3] In Germany alone the number of cinema goers for this film since its release on 8 January 1998 amounts to over 18 million.[4]

But *Titanic* was not only economically successful. In Hollywood this film equalled with its eleven Oscars the previous hit *Ben Hur*.[5] The public made a cult out of Cameron's film spectacle. Teenagers went to see it four or five times.[6] The portrait of the leading actor Leonardo DiCaprio became temporarily the icon of a whole generation of teenagers (the cinema's core audience is sixteen to twenty-one year olds).

Cameron's film represents a new dimension of popular cinema. Its cultic reception indicates that this phenomenon has religious aspects. The film's advertising slogans reinforce this religious impression: the PR strategists invite the audience to 'collide with destiny!' and offer at the same time consolation for the forthcoming catastrophe by hinting at the absolute love of

---

[1] This article presents some observations and considerations from my dissertation 'Sinnmaschine Kino. *Sinndeutung und Religion im populären Film* (Gütersloh: Gütersloher Verlagshaus, 2001), which in February 2000 was accepted by the theological department of the Ruhr-Universität Bochum. It is meant to contribute to the theological hermeneutics of popular culture with the example of the popular film. With this the dissertation takes up a cultural-theological deficit – at least in the German-speaking context.

[2] The Internet Movie Database, *The Top Grossing Movies of All Time at the Worldwide Box Office* (www.imdb.com).

[3] Internet Movie Database, *Top Grossing Movies*.

[4] Spitzenorganisation der Filmwirtschaft e.V. *Die 50 erfolgreichsten Kinofilme in Deutschland seit 1985, Wiesbaden* (7 December 1998, gefaxte Liste).

[5] cf. Georg Seeßlen, 'Der Höhenflug des sinkenden Schiffs: Das Medienereignis "Titanic"', *epd Film* (May 1998), pp. 8–9.

[6] Erik Fosnes Hansen, 'Der magische Schiffbruch. Die "Titanic" – Legende verzaubert Schriftsteller und Filmemacher – durch ihren Schatz von mächtigen Archetypen: Meer, Tod und Liebe', *Der Spiegel*, No. 13 (23 March 1998), pp. 234–9, 235.

the heroic couple: 'Nothing on earth could come between them.'[7] Thus it is about the intrusion of a disturbing event and love's response, both of which are classic themes of religion.

In this *Titanic* is not an exception. It is rather typical of popular cinema, which does not restrict itself to provoking strong emotions. At the same time it touches on fundamental questions. This makes popular films simultaneously entertainment products as well as media for interpreting the world and for conveying meaning. They fulfil a purpose which is comparable to religion.

In this respect, popular cinema belongs within the wide spectrum of cultural resources for exploring meaning, which covers everything from therapy through esotericism to art. 'The foundation of the attributions of meaning which are meant to make contingency bearable have taken plural forms in modern western societies,' suggests the theologian Wilhelm Gräb.[8] Against this background he can interpret the attributions of meaning in contemporary culture as 'lived religion'.

To interpret the cinema in particular as a form of 'lived religion' is not a new thesis. Recently the prominent American writer John Updike confessed in an interview: 'In any case the cinema has done more for my spiritual life than the church. My ideas of fame, success and beauty all originate from the big screen. Whereas Christian religion is retreating everywhere and losing more and more influence; film has filled this vacuum and supports us with myths and action-controlling images. During a certain phase in my life film was a substitute for religion.'[9]

In the German-speaking context it was naturally those in the church involved in film production that were interested in the connection between religion and film, and between the church and the cinema. At the centre of their interest stood the European arthouse film.[10] Only lately has attention been moved towards the popular film. Its present boom is also one of the reasons for it becoming a theological issue. Only through a careful analysis can one demonstrate, within the tradition of natural theology, the plausibility of theological contents.

---

[7] The Internet Movie Database, http://us.imdb.com/Taglines?Titanic+ (1997)

[8] Wilhelm Gräb, *Lebensgeschichten – Lebensentwürfe – Sinndeutungen. Eine praktische Theologie gelebter Religion* (Gütersloh: Gütersloher Verlagshaus, 1998), pp. 88–9.

[9] John Updike, '"Amerika hat sein Versprechen gehalten". Star-Autor John Updike über Kirche, Kino und das Land der unbegrenzten Möglichkeiten', *Focus* 31 (1998), pp. 88–9..

[10] From this perspective the author of this article has been organising, on behalf of the Evangelical media work, together with the Hamburg 'Abaton Cinema' and the Evangelical and Catholic Academies, the dialogue projects in Hamburg since 1990. cf. Jörg Herrmann, 'Götter auf der Durchreise'. Hamburger Dialoge zwischen Kirche und Kino, *epd Film* (May 1998), pp. 6–7; Dietrich Kuhlbrodt, 'Kino auf dem Evangelischen Kirchentag', *epd Film* (August 1995), pp. 2–3. The analysis on hand, which is presented here in the form of selected excerpts, originated from the desire on the one hand to reflect the practical work from a cultural-hermeneutic point of view, and on the other hand to supply and complete it with a hitherto neglected debate on popular film.

Implicit and explicit religion in film

Part of my research intends to discover the religious connections in some of the successful popular films of the nineties. In the context of this undertaking I have distinguished between explicit and implicit religion. One question was whether religious traditions were explicitly drawn on and how they were used. The main focus of the investigation, however, was to bring out the implicit religion, that is, those structures of meaning which can be interpreted as religious only from the perspective of a specific concept of religion. To this end I have based my study on a functional concept of religion which defines it as the 'culture of symbolising final horizons of meaning'.[11] On the basis of such a broad concept, I have first of all identified factual connections between film culture and religious culture. Next I have tried to develop approaches to a dialogue in which the patterns of meaning in the cinema and in Protestant religious culture derive from, criticise and challenge each other. The films were selected on the basis of attendance figures for the fifty most successful feature films in Germany since 1985. I have selected six of those films that had the largest audiences between 1990 and 1998. In order of ranking, these films are: *Titanic, The Lion King, Pretty Woman, Jurassic Park, Independence Day* and *Forrest Gump.* One exception is the film *Pulp Fiction* (1994), by Quentin Tarantino. It ranks among the also-rans, but is interesting for aesthetic reasons, because it is right on the borderline between popular and advanced film aesthetics. This film therefore represents another example of arthouse cinema's trend to mirror the aesthetics and content of postmodernism. Against this background the specific characteristics of popular cinema can be brought out more clearly.

In almost all these films one can find explicit traces of the Jewish-Christian tradition. In *Jurassic Park* the symbol of creation is alluded to, in *Titanic* the book of Revelation is quoted, in *Forrest Gump* they pray and talk about Jesus, in *The Lion King* a ritual occurs which is strongly reminiscent of baptism, in *Pulp Fiction* one finds the book of Ezekiel together with a miracle and a conversion. These are mere traces and, apart from *Pulp Fiction,* they do not touch the heart of the film's story. One can conclude that the Jewish-Christian tradition does still belong to the nineties repertoire of film symbols and is referred to in a sporadic and eclectic manner. Nevertheless its significance is of a rather marginal nature. The religious significance of specific films cannot be deduced from its use of Jewish-Christian symbolism.

One example of a relatively explicit reference to Christianity is the film *Pulp Fiction.* In it the black killer Jules pretends to quote from the book of Ezekiel before his weapon is heard. This supposed quote from the Bible was imported (according to one news magazine[12]) from a kung fu film. The reference to religious tradition has thus already been mediated by popular

---

[11] Gräb, Lebensgeschichten, p. 51.
[12] cf. Susanne Weingarten, 'Der Killer als Plünderer', Der Spiegel (3 October 1994), pp. 237–42.

culture. The formal inner logic of the religious system is obviously not of interest here, since the dialogue only partly matches the quoted section of the Bible. Either Tarantino did not check whether the kung fu film quoted the Bible correctly, or he misquoted it on purpose to establish a difference by which the reference to the biblical tradition was broken. The deliberate differentiation is probable, for it would be characteristic of *Pulp Fiction* to refer to and break with traditions of popular culture.

Tarantino samples set pieces from popular culture like a DJ, manipulating them in order to create ironic and unexpected contrasts. On the dramatic level this approach corresponds with the principle of surprise: it always turns out differently from what the audience and the protagonists expect. The killers are spared by a miracle, Marvin is accidentally shot in the car, Mia mixes up heroin and cocaine, Fabienne crucially forgets Butch's watch, and so on. Tarantino's ensemble reflects a statement by the philosopher Odo Marquard: 'We human beings are always rather our coincidences than our choices.'[13] Tarantino continually confronts us in his story with a network of unexpected incidents and mostly unpleasant coincidences which destroy the continuity of meaning and expectation. For this *Pulp Fiction* uses biblical references to depict its negative gospel of absolute contingency with even greater contrast. This lust for coincidences which frustrate any sort of meaning corresponds with current social developments: it can be interpreted as a reflection of the increasing experience of chance in a world which gets more and more complex.

The implicit catechism of popular cinema

The cinema of powerful emotions is also the cinema of powerful issues. It revolves around the issues of love, death and meaning. Popular cinema covers these themes by narrating exciting stories in a simple but impressive manner. 'Simple' means, amongst other things, that it refers to familiar things, to famous actors, established views and conventional narrative strategies. 'Impressive' means that it aims at visual sensations and intense experiences. Due to its interest in success, the popular film has to deal with common wishes and anxieties. Therefore popular films can be labelled, according to Siegfried Kracauer, as 'the daydreams of society'.[14] They might also be regarded as society's religion, for they give symbolical answers to existential questions. Two themes were singled out in my analysis: the framework of natural order and the meaning of love. These two issues seem to be especially central to the catechism of the popular cinema of the nineties.

[13] Odo Marquardt, 'Apologie des Zufälligen. Philosophische Überlegungen zum Menschen', Odo Marquardt, *Apologie des Zufälligen* (Stuttgart: Reclam, 1986), pp. 117–139, p. 131.
[14] Siegfried Kracauer, 'Die kleinen Ladenmädchen gehen ins Kino', Siegfried Kracauer, *Das Ornament der Masse* (Frankfurt am Main: Suhrkamp, 1977), pp. 279–94, p. 280.

Nature

In *Jurassic Park* nature is explicitly the central issue.[15] The dinosaur preserve can be interpreted as a symbol for our utilitarian approach to the natural world, in which an interest in profits, scientific ambition, a desire for sensation and an instinct for play dictate our relationship to nature. Man as *alter deus* proves himself in creating his own apocalypse. The film shows how nature violated by genetic engineering strikes back and how self-interested intervention causes destruction. But the film also shows scenes with examples of an alternative relationship to nature, which is characterised by the phrase 'humility towards nature', chiefly by Malcolm, Grant and the children. Altogether *Jurassic Park* reflects in its depiction of humankind's relationship to nature the insights of certain members of the ecological movement. The film symbolises the criticism of instrumentalising the relationship to nature for economic profit.

In *The Lion King* nature is not so obviously the central theme. Nevertheless on closer examination nature's quasi-religious significance as a prized and meaningful frame of reference is expressed more strongly in *The Lion King* than in *Jurassic Park*. Nature as equilibrium, law and 'eternal circle of life' is the force behind the origin and order of things in this film. Rites, kingdoms and battles have their permanent place in the eternal cycle of nature. Social, political and religious life form a fundamental network and are mirrored in this mythical frame of reference. This concept of nature also corresponds with the development in society of an ecological and religious interest in nature. From this perspective *The Lion King* might be seen as the fundamentalist answer of popular cinema to the issue which *Pulp Fiction* raises: the increase of random experiences.

A similar transposing of the social, political and religious into a nature-religious frame of reference as in *The Lion King* can also be detected in *Forrest Gump*. Nature also appears here as a final point of reference, as solid ground and the protecting cover of 'Sweet Home Alabama'. In *Titanic*, however, nature principally shows its other, threatening face. The ship, embodiment of humankind's creative power and technical progress, collides with an iceberg and thus with the superior strength of nature. As in *Jurassic Park*, nature shows the limits of human hubris and is thus defined as a significant higher order.

The recapitulation of the views of nature in these four films agrees with current ecological-spiritual trends. Looking at the whole spectrum of the present nature-renaissance, Norbert Bolz concludes: 'The worries about health these days are articulated as worries about the ecological equilibrium. And the meaning is clear: for the Green Party nature itself is super-nature. The demoted God is called environment, at whom the worries and hopes for salvation are directed. This system of belief is of course much

---

[15] Here and elsewhere I have omitted parts of the film plot – hoping that the films mentioned are known to most of the readers.

more stable than communism, which it supersedes.'[16] Later Bolz reflects on the causes of the present focus on nature which are worth considering:

> I assume that the fascination with the concept of Nature lies in its suggestion of a norm for a correct order, similar to the former concept of cosmos. One only has to utter the word 'nature' to bring order into the chaos of our social systems, through the effective suggestion of something fundamental and essential, which is that nature does not need us but we need it. This cannot even be invalidated by science. 'Nature' therefore functions as some sort of stop sign for the eternal struggle of observing and calculating. If one utters the word 'Nature', one drops anchor in the sea of complexity.[17]

Bolz's evaluation fits with the concept of nature in *The Lion King* and *Forrest Gump*. Both films emphasise the orderly and saving character of nature. In criticising the trend towards fundamentalist credence in such concepts of nature in popular culture, one should nevertheless not ignore the legitimate demand of the nature-renaissance for a response to the symptoms of an ecological crisis. The other side of eco-religion however is the long history of the exploitation and devaluation of nature. Against this background, nature's canonisation is a rash but understandable attempt to re-instate it which, despite reservations, one must acknowledge is a cultural matter of critical concern.

In theology this insight has been reflected in the form of approaches to an 'ecological theology'.[18] These approaches are meant to concede Christianity's share in the genesis of the modern violent relationship to nature and to develop nature-theological perspectives. The nature-religious tendencies of the analysed films can be taken as further evidence of the necessity for these debates.

Conversely the way Christian belief differentiates between the Creator and the Creation can alert us to how nature is portrayed as the ultimate source of meaning in a film like *The Lion King*. This elevation of nature to an absolute frame of reference in the course of its neo-pagan canonisation avoids on the one hand the fact that it is culturally mediated, and on the other hand its fundamental ambivalence. Nature is in no way identical with a good ethic but is to a very high degree ambivalent.

In the ambivalence of nature lies the ambivalence of beauty and a menacing strength. The feeling for the sublime is connected with the experience of nature's power. Contemporary popular cinema can be interpreted on several levels within the aesthetic category of the sublime.[19] The dominant theme, however, is love.

---

[16] Norbert Bolz, *Die Sinngesellschaft* (Düsseldorf: Econ, 1997), pp. 15–16.

[17] Bolz, *Die Sinngesellschaft*, p. 16.

[18] cf., e.g., Günter Altner (Hg.), *Ökologische Theologie. Perspektiven zur Orientierung* (Stuttgart: Kreuz, 1989).

[19] S. Jörg Herrmann, *Sinnmaschine Kino*, pp. 221–9.

Love

Love is the first commandment of the popular film of the nineties. In *Pretty Woman* it saves a fallen girl from the gutter and a lonely manager from dying of exposure to a world ruled by money. It changes the protagonists, surmounts social barriers and fills life with meaning. This gospel of love can be found in a similar form in *Titanic*. Here, too, love surmounts class barriers, rescues the unhappy upper-class girl Rose from the dead world of capitalism and changes her despair into pure happiness. The transcendent character of this love proves its romantic origin. Ulrich Beck explains: 'Love is, due to its romantic origin, a community of conspirators against society. Love knows no barriers. Neither those of status and class nor those of law and morality.'[20] The religiosity of the *Titanic* love shows in the face of the ship's sinking. Rose risks her life when she frees Jack, who is kept in chains under the deck. His love, as often in the popular cinema a love at first sight, goes as far as leaving the only safe spot on the drifting door to his lover. Even in the face of death he affirms his sacrifice and thus the utter disgust of his love with a voice shivering from the cold: winning the ticket for the Titanic was the best thing that ever happened to him, for this ticket brought him to Rose.

Titanic preaches the gospel of a love which is stronger than death. It is the consequence of this conception that, after the ship's sinking and thus Jack's death, Rose dreams of his resurrection. One of the two advertising slogans of the film gets to the point: 'Nothing on earth could come between them.' Not even the unscrupulous Cal Hockley, who still tries, even during the sinking, to insinuate that Jack is a thief so that he can leave him under the deck to his certain death, nor the sinking of the Titanic, nor Jack's death. The love of the two protagonists is the supreme virtue in the world of the Titanic. Just as the biblical tradition offers comfort with the conviction that nothing can separate us from the love of God which is to be found in Jesus Christ (Rom. 8:39), so Cameron's film gives comfort in the name of the religion of love: Nothing on earth could come between them. The telling parallels make it obvious that the lovers of popular cinema have to achieve for one another what in Christianity comes from God, unconditional love.

In this context it is remarkable how precisely the two central advertising slogans of the film parallel the two religious motifs and thus point to the structural affinity to religion. Clifford Geertz has emphasised that on the one hand religious symbols specifically acknowledge contingency and suffering and on the other hand they challenge it in the name of a more extensive reality.[21] Both aspects can be found in *Titanic* and are expressed

---

[20] Ulrich Beck, 'Die irdische Religion der Liebe', Ulrich Beck/Elisabeth Beck-Gernsheim, *Das ganz normale Chaos der Liebe* (Frankfurt am Main: Suhrkamp, 1990), pp. 222–66, p. 248.

[21] cf. Clifford Geertz, 'Religion als kulturelles System', Clifford Geertz, *Dichte Beschreibung. Beiträge zum Verstehen kultureller Systeme* (Frankfurt am Main: Suhrkamp, 1995), pp. 44–95, p.72.

concisely in the slogans 'Collide with destiny!' in terms of the contingency and in 'Nothing on earth could come between them' in terms of love. Here the counter-force is not God but love. *Titanic* preaches the gospel of a love which is stronger than death, but it evokes a particular pathos against the background of a testing catastrophe. If we turn to other films, it becomes evident that we are dealing with a widespread leitmotif in popular cinema if not its most central message.[22]

But the love motif is also dominant in arthouse cinema. The film *Dancer in the Dark*, by Lars von Trier (2000), offers an impressive example of contemporary workings of this theme. After his *Breaking the Waves* (1995), this latest film of the converted Catholic Dane again polarises the audiences. The retrospective, in which fourteen critics rank the films of the year 2000, awards it two completely opposite ratings, 'gold' and 'trash'.[23] For some this film 'makes the invisible visible' (Kerstin Decker); others just find it ridiculous (Frank Noack). Is someone recycling here a trite myth, or has the embodiment of maternal self-sacrifice been dramatised in a way that even hardened hearts may be touched? A film so perfect it hurts to watch, commented a moviegoer in the American 'Internet Movie Database'.[24] Again, like *Titanic*, it is about a sacrifice. And again the story takes place in the past, the sixties in the US where Selma, a Czech immigrant, lives with her 12-year-old son in a trailer. The life of the single mother is a race against time: a hereditary disease, which also threatens her son Gene, turns her blind. So the fragile Selma, impressively played by the Icelandic singer Bjoerk, works like one possessed. She insists on getting together the money for the operation that can save her son from this disease. This depressing situation is lightened up by Selma's passion for musicals (she knows that nothing bad ever happens in those), whereas at the same time everything is ultimately doomed by a complex plot in which Selma commits a murder in self-defence, and ends up getting sentenced to death and finally hanged. She rejects the possibility of re-opening the case since it would cost exactly the amount of money which she had scrimped and saved for the operation.

Von Trier pulls out all the stops of his art to make this mixture of melodrama and musical a postmodern passion play which gets under one's skin. Through a complex intertwining of filmic strategies which either create intimacy or distance from a figure stylised as the maternal sacrifice, he also makes her an icon, 'a Jeanne d'Arc of Pop-modernism' (Georg Seesslen). One could also say that 'the hanged' becomes the synonym for 'the crucified'. A touch of feminist re-interpretation of the theology of the cross is mixed with early Protestant family theology. For it was Martin Luther who declared a woman's self-sacrificing devotion to the family as her central act

---

[22] The analysis of the narrative of popular films has shown that a heterosexual love story belongs to the standards of mainstream conventions. cf. Jens Eder, *Dramaturgie des populären Films. Konventionen des Handlungsaufbaus in Drehbuchpraxis und Filmtheorie* (Münster/Hamburg/London: Lit, 1999).

[23] *Der Tagesspiegel* is a Berlin daily newspaper.

[24] www.imdb.com

of worship: 'Children are the churches, the altar, the testament, the vigil and the masses of the soul, which you leave behind, which will also lighten your path to death and to wherever you will end up.'[25] A woman's devotion has to be expressed in her self-sacrificing care for the child and the family, for house and home. Against this background Barbara Vinken remarks: 'As the world-saving agent the mother figure in predominantly Protestant countries becomes the final secularisation, the secularised reason of a formerly religious purpose.' In her religious promises of salvation she embraces motherhood.[26] In this she follows the call of nature. Thus the mother is the figure in whom biology becomes ethical and ethics become biological.

It is this mixture of ontologism, religion-based patriarchy and fundamentalism in von Trier's film which, despite all artificial advances, creates an uneasy shiver down one's spine. The suspicion remains that the artist is trying to impose on us medieval certainties in postmodern packaging. At times like this, when even journalists of the left-wing liberal weekly 'Die Zeit' write hymnic biographies of the pope and give several pages to Ratzinger's lectures, this fundamentalist tendency towards the archetypal, this escapism from the never-ending discourses of postmodernism fits perfectly.

Titanic and *Dancer in the Dark* are two examples of the heroic act of sacrifice for love. This is for 'the good', according to von Trier, for *Dancer in the Dark* is also the final part of his trilogy on 'the good'. Could one, in the light of these examples, speak of hints within the discourse on love of an ethical renaissance at the end of the millennium, of a new longing for the seriousness of religion and sacrifice? Could this be interpreted as a reaction to the hyper-aestheticism of postmodernism, to the emptiness of a society dedicated to pure fun, to the coldness of the New Economy?

In any case the central position of love as equivalent to a religious authority in conveying meaning is evident in the popular films of the nineties. It corresponds with the observations of the literature on the development of the love theme within a chronological framework. Ulrich Beck's analysis places the filmic findings in a broader context and therefore gives it a plausible explanation. Beck interpreted love as 'earthly religion' which makes post-Christian and inner-modern sense,[27] and is in keeping with our own analyses, which aim to discover patterns of meaning that are analogous to religion. Beck identifies a number of factors in this promotion of love into a religion in today's culture.[28] The decline of economic constraints, the loss of traditional meaning, the increasing individualisation and the shattering of functionally differentiated working worlds create freedoms and at the same time give rise to a longing for meaning, common ground and authentic experience. In this situation the concept of a religion of love, which was formerly explored by the Romantics, develops into a mass phenomenon. As

---

[25] Quoted by Barbara Vinken, 'Mütter, Kinder und Karriere', *Lettre International* Heft 51, Volume 4 (2000), pp. 78–81, p.80.

[26] Vinken, p. 81.

[27] Beck, *Die irdische Religion der Liebe*, pp. 223–32.

[28] cf. Beck, *Die irdische Religion der Liebe*, pp. 258–61., 243–7.

far as Beck is concerned, the quasi-religious valency of love shows itself, amongst other things, in increasingly asserting that it has a higher value in conflict within the family. 'To leave one's own children does not mean to break with love but to fulfil it. Love demands a break with its false form. This accurately illustrates the force with which by now the earthly religion of love reigns in the hearts and actions of the people.'[29]

Various theological criticisms of the religion of love are possible. One could say a lot more, but I only want to mention a more fundamental criticism of the popular film from the perspective of a Christian religious culture. Popular film constructs its stories without exception as *heilsgeschichten* (salvation history) with a happy ending, which is a concession to the needs and desires of the consumer. In contrast Christian religious culture perceives social realities in which the contradictions and discontinuity are apparent. It represents a culture of narration and perception which is determined by *memoria passionis*. Johann Baptist Metz has repeatedly drawn attention to this.[30] According to Metz, 'Christian belief articulates itself as *memoria passionis, mortis et resurrectionis Jesu Christi* [memorial of the passion, death and resurrection of Jesus Christ]. In the centre of this belief stands the memory of the crucified Lord, a certain *memoria passionis*, on which the promise of future freedom for all is founded.'[31] This *memoria passionis* constitutes a perspective of pity. This cannot only be deduced from the *memoria* of the *heilsgeschichte* but also from the behaviour of Jesus: 'Originally Christianity was a community of memory and narration in the succession of Jesus, whose first glance was aimed at someone else's misery.'[32]

With regard to film one could, against this background of perception, raise the question of how its depiction relates to concrete experiences in everyday life, especially the experience of misery. In this context the increasing mediation of everyday life has to be taken into consideration and with it the interaction between actual and vicarious experience.

Conclusion

Popular cinema is booming, whereas the churches in many part of Europe become increasingly empty. Is popular cinema about to replace the church as cultural agent of meaning? One can observe that the cinema has a great impact on conversations in everyday life. Film provides viewers with resources to make sense of their own autobiographies and other

---

[29] Beck, *Die irdische Religion der Liebe*, p. 229.

[30] First in his essay 'Kleine Aplogie des Erzählens' (concilium September 1973, pp. 329–33), then again in *Glaube in Geschichte und Gesellschaft, Studien zu einer praktischen Fundamentaltheologie* (Mainz: Grünewald, 1984), pp. 87–92 and pp. 181–8.

[31] Metz, *Glaube in Geschichte*, p. 97.

[32] Johann Baptist Metz, 'Kirche in der Gotteskrise. Oder: Entlaubte Bäume in der postmodernen Landschaft. Eine Einladung zu elementaren Vergewisserungen', *Frankfurter Rundschau* (27 June 1994), p. 12.

biographies. Nevertheless religious culture is still responsible for the area which religious sociologist Thomas Luckmann describes as 'great transcendences'. Births, deaths and weddings cannot be celebrated well in the cinema, nor can existential crises be coped with in mainstream movies.

Against this background one can conclude that the function of interpreting everyday experiences, which was previously fulfilled by religion, has in many contexts been replaced by aspects of popular culture. Nevertheless interpretation of the great transcendences at the turning points of life are often still the domain of the church. But for how much longer?

If one concedes that the religious tradition is responsible for existential matters, the question arises about the future role of the church as an interpretative and communicative agent. For the Jewish-Christian tradition can be understood by a wider public only if the interplay of references between present-day culture and religious culture can be mutually recognised and if it can be shown to be plausible that the experiences of contemporaries have something to do with traditional religious culture and vice versa. Through a brief analysis of the themes of 'nature' and 'love' in both recent popular and arthouse films I have attempted to demonstrate that this is not only possible, but also a fruitful exercise.

Further Reading

R. Barthes, *Mythen des Alltags* (Frankfurt am Main: Suhrkamp, 1981).

J. Eder, *Dramaturgie des populären Films. Konventionen des Handlungsaufbaus in Drehbuchpraxis und Filmtheorie* (Münster/Hamburg/London: Lit, 1999).

W. Gräb, *Lebensgeschichten – Lebensentwürfe – Sinndeutungen. Eine praktische Theologie gelebter Religion* (Gütersloh: Gütersloher Verlagshaus, 1998).

J. Herrmann, *Sinnmaschine Kino. Sinndeutung und Religion im populären Film* (Gütersloh: Gütersloher Verlagshaus, 2001).

J. Staiger, *Interpreting Films. Studies in the Historical Reception of American Cinema* (Princeton: Princeton University Press, 1992).

18

Paradise Lost or Paradise Learned?: Sin and Salvation in *Pleasantville*

Christopher Deacy

In the weeks leading up to its release in British cinemas on 12 March 1999, critics were swift to draw parallels between *Pleasantville*, the directorial debut of Gary Ross, screenwriter of the Capraesque comedies *Big*[1] and *Dave*,[2] and Peter Weir's *The Truman Show*.[3] Both are media satires which feature protagonists trapped within a perennial 'sit-com' universe, who, in albeit different ways, struggle to discover and create some semblance of authenticity and humanity in what amounts to an artificial, reactionary and, above all, oppressive milieu. While *The Truman Show* was nominated for three Academy Awards and for seven BAFTAs and opened to uniformly positive reviews worldwide, *Pleasantville*, despite its sophistication and innovation on both a theoretical and visual level, was largely overlooked by the critics and gained just three Academy Award nominations in the technical categories (for its art direction, costume design and original score). In America, *Truman* grossed nearly $130 million at the box office and a respectable £10 million in the UK, compared to *Pleasantville*'s $40 million in the US and a paltry £800,000 in British cinemas (where it ran in most theatres for no more than a week). In this paper, I will attempt to redress the balance, by concentrating on some of *Pleasantville*'s most distinctive, albeit neglected, motifs and themes in the light of what Ross, who directed, produced and wrote the film, and a range of critics and Internet movie reviewers, have discussed. While, as I will evince, not all viewers may have gone to see the film for its (at times) overt religious connotations (indeed, this may actually have deterred many people from seeing it), it is the film's manifold religious possibilities and considerations that have attracted many of *Pleasantville*'s most vociferous and passionate responses.

---

[1] *Big*, dir. Penny Marshall, 1988.
[2] *Dave*, dir. Ivan Reitman, 1993.
[3] *The Truman Show*, dir. Peter Weir, 1998.

The religious subtext of Pleasantville

In the first scene, the viewer is presented with a montage of different tele-vision channels, which, as Ross explains in his DVD commentary on the film, amounts to an opportunity to 'surf' and wander through the wasteland and dissonance of contemporary society before settling upon the 'homely', com-forting, easychair world of ersatz 1950s situation comedy, *Pleasantville*. This sets the standard for the first half of the film, in which a contrast is set up between the fractured and frenetic 1990s, where job insecurity, sexually transmitted diseases and global warming are all introduced into the narra-tive, and the hermetically sealed world of 1950s television fantasy, where there is no sex, no crime, no chaos, and every family is nuclear. Indeed, this is a world in which the sun always shines, the rain never falls, the tempera-ture is always 72 degrees, the high school basketball team never loses a game, teenagers enthusiastically do their homework, and, regular as clock-work, the father, and breadwinner, returns home from the office at a quar-ter to six, yells 'Honey, I'm home', before promptly being served up another wholesome meal, which his wife has spent the afternoon zealously prepar-ing in the kitchen. The stability and order of this world may, as Ross notes, initially prove irresistible, not least when we witness the juxtaposition in one early scene of two women, one the mother of the male protagonist, David (Tobey Maguire), who is involved in an angry and tearful telephone con-versation with her ex-husband; the other, the sitcom mother, Betty Parker (Joan Allen), a woman of animation and gaiety, whose only affliction is having to remind her son that there is no such word as 'swellest'. Pleasantville is, at least upon a superficial rendering, a utopian and paradisal realm, epitomised by David when he explains its allure to a friend at school, 'Nobody's homeless in Pleasantville, because that's just not what it's like.'

As the film develops, however, *Pleasantville* takes issue with the values and precepts of this ostensibly idealistic universe. Upon being magically trans-ported into the *Pleasantville* show, arguably the only point in the film in which the viewer is required to suspend disbelief, David and his chain-smoking, promiscuous sister, Jennifer (Reese Witherspoon), slowly but inexorably bring chance, risk and imperfection to this hitherto unspoiled Eden, as is visualised by the gradual transformation of this black-and-white universe into resplendent colour. No sooner has Jennifer introduced sex into the community than roses turn red, a rainbow appears over the town for the first time, and pink cherry blossoms fall on the (for the moment) black-and-white road to Lovers Lane. For once, the inhabitants of the small town begin to question and challenge the limitations of their worldview. Consequently, rather than a utopian world, Ross points out that Pleasantville is, at heart, a sterile environment, where it is the fear of embracing the unknown and the uncertainty bound up with yielding to that which is unstable that is responsible for the clear-cut, black-and-white morality that at first sight may have seemed so alluring and seductive. It is a milieu where sex is prohibited, whereas, in fact, sexual awakening is one of the most primal and basic human instincts, and, as the film suggests, has the capacity to give rise to a flourishing and creative world of nuance and beauty that is non-sexual, in the form of other kinds of knowledge. Indeed, the film depicts many of the town's teenagers turning into colour when they embark upon reading works of literature for the first time. Previously, all the pages of books in the library were blank, while Bill Johnson (Jeff Daniels), proprietor of the local soda store, discovers he has a penchant for art, and paints a mural on his shop window which reflects the new cultural awakening, containing as it does images ranging from Adam and Eve to *Moby Dick*, *Catcher in the Rye*, *Huckleberry Finn* and D. H. Lawrence.

Ultimately, as David proclaims to some of the other teenagers in Pleasantville, 'There are places where the road doesn't go in a circle. There are some places where the road keeps going.' For the first time, the characters realise they have a chance to create their own futures, rather than live a static, preordained existence where everything functions like clockwork. It may entail the dissolution of established practices and conventions, but Ross uses the film to argue this can only be a positive advance. After all, as he puts it, the 'glue' that holds the nuclear family together in this context is merely a 'mythological glue', since it is not based on understanding or reciprocation. Hence, Betty's position is untenable when she finds herself unable to find fulfilment with her husband, George (William H. Macy), for whom, in his defiantly black-and-white universe – he is one of the last inhabitants to turn to colour – she can only ever be a stereotype, whose *raison d'être* is to fulfil her duties submissively as a wife and mother, rather than a potentially fully-fledged and expressive human being. When, in relation to her beauty, George tells her to pretend nothing has changed, 'It'll just go away,' Betty stands up to and confronts her husband for the first time, and avows, 'I don't want it to go away.' It is, then, the challenge of engagement, and their preparedness, despite the inevitable risks, to open themselves up to the random nature of things, that enables these characters to be transformed into colour.

It is for this reason that *Pleasantville* may be read as a cinematic analogy of the Fall. Indeed, according to Thomas Hegel, although in the Genesis story, humankind lost its state of innocence and bliss by eating the fruit of the tree of the knowledge of good and evil, the Fall narrative nevertheless has a message and a prediction of reconciliation and redemption. It is of a kind, moreover, that the characters in *Pleasantville* may be seen to emulate. Hegel considered paradise to be no more than a 'dreaming innocence', which is lacking in the knowledge of good and evil, lacking in self-consciousness and lacking in an ability to choose. In his words, 'Innocence implies the absence of will, the absence of evil, and consequently the absence of goodness.'[4] The movement from innocence to knowledge has positive as well as negative connotations, in so far as it may not simply lead

---

[4] Quoted in James C. Livingston, *Modern Christian Thought: From the Enlightenment to Vatican II* (London: Collier MacMillan, 1971), p. 151.

to spiritual hardening and death but is the catalyst and the prerequisite for awakening a person from innocence and towards self-consciousness and the attendant possibilities for redemption and renewal.

The Fall is, in short, a necessary experience for human development. As Roger Ebert has remarked in his review of *Pleasantville* in the *Chicago Sun-Times*, 'The film observes that sometimes pleasant people are pleasant simply because they have never, ever been challenged,' and that, for such people, it is 'scary and dangerous to learn new ways'.[5] Ebert acknowledges that we may have more problems in the present day than we did in the so-called 'good old days'. Ross labours this point in the film when he raises questions pertaining to ecological, sexual and sociological anxieties, but as Ebert argues, crucially, we also have 'more solutions, more opportunities and more freedom'.[6] He continues:

> I grew up in the '50s. It was a lot more like the world of *Pleasantville* than you might imagine. Yes, my house had a picket fence, and dinner was always on the table at a quarter to six, but things went wrong that I didn't even know the words for. There is a scene in this movie where it rains for the first time. Of course it never rained in 1950s sitcoms. *Pleasantville*'s people in color go outside and just stand in it.[7]

Life is not, nor should be, entirely 'tidy' or 'neat'[8] and, albeit paradoxically, it is this very erratic aspect of our existence which makes human life and endeavour so potentially beautiful, exciting, and, to borrow the film's metaphor, 'colourful'. It is for this reason that the film does not succumb to a contrived 'happy ending', in which all the tensions and vicissitudes that have been generated during the course of the narrative are magically resolved, in the manner of a film such as *The Wizard Of Oz*,[9] whose 'it was all a dream' ending fails, in its affirmation of certainty and the status quo, to embrace the more realistic uncertainty and diversity of human existence. Indeed, whereas *Oz* concludes with the sentiment that 'There's No Place Like Home', *Pleasantville* ends with a failure to concede that we can ever know what the future holds. Sitting on a park bench, in glorious 'technicolored' surroundings, George asks Betty, 'So, what's going to happen now?', and she significantly responds, 'I don't know. Do you?' George then retorts, 'No, I don't,' while the camera moves back over to Betty, before then returning to where George sat, only this time Bill Johnson is at her side, and he attests, in the last words of the film, 'I guess I don't either.'

---

[5] Roger Ebert's review of *Pleasantville* in the *Chicago Sun-Times*, at www.suntimes.com/ebert/ebert_reviews/1998/10/102302.html

[6] Ebert's review of *Pleasantville*.

[7] Ebert's review of *Pleasantville*.

[8] Gary Ross, Director's Commentary of *Pleasantville*, DVD (New Line Cinema, released 1999).

[9] *The Wizard Of Oz*, dir. Victor Fleming, 1939.

This ending concurs in many respects with the spirit of the Old Testament book of Ecclesiastes, which posits the unconventional and un-Hebraic notion that there is no more to human existence than the seeming meaninglessness and irrationality we observe all around us. As a result, it is not possible for human beings to fathom and make sense of the temperament of the universe, wherein 'what is crooked cannot be made straight, and what is lacking cannot be numbered.' (Eccles. 1:15). However, despite this somewhat entrenched, cynical perspective, the author, *Qoheleth*, affirms that, despite the limits of our knowledge, ability and circumstances, and our transitory life span, humans can strive to learn to live authentically within the prescribed limitations and boundaries of our existence. While accepting that we are 'no more the master'[10] of our lives than we are of the day of our death, we can nonetheless come to appreciate and value, even enjoy, our 'good fortune if and when it comes',[11] and 'relish the satisfactions and joys of life',[12] even though we know we cannot depend on them. Returned in the penultimate scene to the 1990s and the plight and unhappiness of his (single) mother, David comforts her in her grief at never having found a durable and fulfilling relationship, or of not possessing or being able to possess the 'right house' and the 'right car'. In David's words, 'There is no right house. There is no right car ... It's not supposed to be anything.' In this light, Matt Wolf makes an astute point in his article on *Pleasantville* in *The Times* newspaper[13] when he refers to 'the emotional daring of a film whose message is that the pain and disorder of life are ultimately preferable to an ordered, black-and-white existence'.

The diversity of audience responses to the film

Invariably, however, though recognising and apprehending *Pleasantville*'s religious subject matter, this is not the verdict or the conclusion that all viewers have reached. Having searched the Internet, and in particular the (to date) 400 reviews of *Pleasantville* that appear on the Internet Movie Database (IMDb),[14] not only are audiences sharply divided as to whether or not they enjoyed the film, but it is the way the film handles its religious motifs that in many cases has informed the various discussions. On the positive side, a reviewer in Houston, Texas, discerns that: 'For years we have blamed Eve for the Apple, but are we really so sure we want to *live* in an

---

[10] R. B. Y. Scott, *The Way of Wisdom in the Old Testament* (New York: Macmillan, 1971), p. 187.

[11] Scott, *The Way of Wisdom*.

[12] Scott, *The Way of Wisdom*.

[13] Matt Wolf, 'Playing the world and his wife: interview with Joan Allen', *The Times*, (11 March 1999), p. 36.

[14] The *Internet Movie Database*, www.imdb.com. Reviews are mostly from members of the public, yet there are a number of reviews from professional critics and journalists whose columns have been passed on to the site.

untainted Eden?' Another, anonymous reviewer raises the discerning point that the catalyst behind the characters' transformation into colour is 'one's acceptance of change', in the respect that colour encroaches into the *Pleasantville* universe when they realise that they want, and need, things to change. This is actually a crucial point, and one that not all commentators have acknowledged. In the British film magazine *Empire*, for instance, the reviewer, Kim Newman, presumes that the profusion of colour emanates from *passion*, such as when one of the characters, the town's reactionary mayor, is 'driven to a fury'.[15] If this was the case, however, then all of those characters who initially resist change, and do so vociferously, in the form of book-burning, street riots, and the drafting of legislation restricting the spread of colour would have 'changed' at the outset. It is, rather, only when the possibility of change is accepted and authentically embraced that the transformation into colour, and the seeds of redemption and renewal, is able to ensue.

On the other hand, *Pleasantville* has been interpreted by some reviewers as a film *devoid* of redemption. One contributor argues, for instance, that the picture never convinces as anything other than a gimmick and a one-joke premise and, perhaps surprisingly, 'a tired and obvious retread of ideas thoroughly past their sell-by date'. While, according to another on the same Internet site, Gary Ross has produced 'a smug, sappy movie with ideas as shallow and black-and-white as the 50s milieu he was trying to satirize'. This reviewer continues:

> The 'feel good ending' is beyond redemption, in its way even sappier than the mythical sit-com it tries to improve upon. Yes, it is kind of neat to see things turn from black and white to color accompanied by stirring orchestral strings ... But where are the shades of gray?[16]

Many of the other negative reviews follow this line, seeing the film's conclusion not as one that is willing to embrace the random nature of existence, but as one which, in the words of a New York reviewer, 'solves its problems so easily and unambiguously you'd think the author forgot [what] he was writing about a moment before'. Likewise, according to David Walsh's review on the 'World Socialist Web Site', reproduced on the IMDb, *Pleasantville* 'is too nebulous' and 'too tame' for rounding off 'life's rough edges'. He objects that 'A work that argues for spontaneity and change' is, in the event, 'fatally ordered and tidy', and he is especially severe regarding the conclusion, which he designates as 'inexcusable, sentimental' and 'banal', such that *Pleasantville* amounts to a 'film about nonconformism with a thoroughly conformist conclusion!'

Individuals who identify themselves as Christians have raised some of the most extreme responses to the film. On the Internet site 'Christian Spotlight on the Movies', which is part of Arizona-based Eden

---

[15] Kim Newman, review of *Pleasantville*, *Empire* No. 124 (October 1999), p. 142.
[16] From the *Internet Movie Database*, www.imdb.com

Communications, 'an interdenominational, non-profit, evangelical ministry active for over 40 years ... specializing in evangelism and discipleship through mass media',[17] the respondents are almost exclusively disparaging in their response to *Pleasantville*. One categorises it as 'a twisted allegory of Genesis' where the characters are saved by sin, and concludes that 'any Christian paying to see this movie should regret that his money will go into the pockets of people who scream hate speech [sic] against the Bible'. In the words of another, the film is no more than 'filth and embarrassment', whereas it should, she says, have been 'wholesome' and 'fun'. In like manner, one Christian reviewer on this site claims that 'this movie was an unpleasant, brutal assault on traditional biblical morality and our Christian values', and warns her fellow Christians that in going to see *Pleasantville* they are contributing money to push immorality, unfaithfulness and profanity. In like manner, another Christian critic encourages her fellow Christians not to 'see this movie for it must grieve God's heart and soul, ours too'. And, finally, another draws attention to the absence of references in the film to God or the church, and castigates the film for its depiction of morality and family values 'as simple, unenlightened and ... stupid', and adds that this 'literally makes me sick to my stomach'.

In contrast, however, there are other Christian groups and individuals who, in reviewing the film, do not denounce Ross for failing to restore at least the image of an innocent, prelapsarian America. On the 'Hollywood Jesus' web site,[18] which aims to look 'for the deeper' and 'more profound meaning behind blockbuster hits', and to explore 'pop culture from a spiritual point of view', the reviewer, David Bruce, refers to a plethora of constructive biblical parallels and themes located in the film. The fact that Betty Parker has never heard of sex makes her, Bruce suggests, an Eve-figure, while one scene reveals David picking an apple from a tree and then eating it, in a clear (literal) analogy of Genesis 3. An image in the film of a burning bush invokes, further, the story of God's appearance to Moses in Exodus 3, while the rainbow that follows the first rainfall in the town of Pleasantville, with its attendant motif of promise and hope, may be said to resemble Genesis 9, where, following the Flood, God establishes the rainbow as 'a sign of the covenant between me and the earth' (Gen. 9:12). One of the respondents to this site even identifies David as a Christ-figure and Jennifer as a serpent-figure. She introduces seduction (in the form of sexual activity) into this universe, while he wants to preserve it in its 'holiness', for fear that 'if we don't play along we may alter their universe, and may never get out of here', though he cannot prevent her from exercising her free will. Furthermore, whereas Jennifer acts out of self-interest, David, like Christ, finds purpose in teaching others to use their free will for good and beneficent purposes. He even acts as an exemplar when he protects his

---

[17] *Christian Spotlight on the Movies*, www.christiananswers.net/spotlight/movies/pre2000/i-pleasantville.html

[18] *Hollywood Jesus*, www.hollywoodjesus.com/pleasantville.htm

'screen' mother from being persecuted because she is a 'coloured' person in what is still (at this stage) a militantly black-and-white universe. According to the reviewer, his punching of her oppressor 'is symbolic of the decisive blow against evil dealt with on the cross'.

While issue could be taken with this interpretation, in that Christ *suffered* violence on the cross, rather than *inflicted* it, and, as the Sermon on the Mount testifies, Christ vehemently rejected violence, there is a modicum of support for this point of view. According to S. G. F. Brandon[19] there was a close association between Christ and the Zealot movement of the first century C.E. If this is so, then Jesus may be said to have *literally* and *physically* engaged with and confronted this 'sinful' world in his capacity as a political and revolutionary Messiah. The 'Hollywood Jesus' reviewer then seals the analogy between David and Christ by pointing out that, in his courtroom speech towards the end, when he defends the rights of the 'coloured' population, David 'becomes an Advocate (like Christ) before the Judge, loving all men', which is 'the greatest Commandment Christ gave us'. It is only apt that, having accomplished and fulfilled his new-found mission as the catalyst which enables the entire town to blossom into colour, David should then 'ascend', in the manner of the Logos, back to the 'real' world (of the 1990s) from which he came (cf. Luke 24:51).

Conclusion

At the end of the day, of course, no two individuals, or even two Christians, will interpret the film in the same way. One contributor to the Internet Movie Database can say that *Pleasantville* 'displays complex social issues, and lets you decide what you think rather than spoon-feeding you the correct way to think'. Another can criticise it precisely for telling the audience 'how to think' and 'how to feel', to the effect that 'a movie that purports to be about freewill and expression sure doesn't show much faith in its audience to figure it out on their own'. This diversity of opinion only serves to demonstrate that there can be no easy understanding of where and to what extent, in our increasingly media-saturated landscape, Christian truths and values may be seen to reside. Nonetheless, outside of traditional ecclesiastical agencies and institutions, it is apparent that a film such as *Pleasantville* has, at the very least, the capacity to convey and impart fundamental truths and insights pertaining to the human condition. Indeed, it is notable in this regard that, on the 'Hollywood Jesus' site, one of the respondents sees in Ross' film a reminder that 'the Fall didn't unleash just the knowledge of Evil, but the knowledge of *Good* and Evil' (my italics). Consequently, in line with the Hegelian understanding of human nature, he attests that 'God Himself seemed to have something much, much more glorious in mind by

---

[19] S. G. F. Brandon, *Jesus and the Zealots: A Study of the Political Factor in Primitive Christianity* (Manchester: Manchester University Press, 1967).

giving us free will than for us to stay in unaware innocence forever'. This reviewer continues that, in line with St. Paul's affirmation in Romans 5:20 that 'where sin abounded, grace abounded all the more', so 'this wonderful Grace brought to us by our Saviour gives *Pleasantville* its triumph'. Irrespective of whether or not one is prepared to go this far, it is easy to see why some commentators have identified in the film a distinctive theological dimension.

I would, however, take issue with the film's slightly facile premise that, once the characters have chosen to engage with the unknown and uncertain possibilities of existence, they could or would simply transform from black-and-white into various resplendent shades of 'technicolor'. In the Christian tradition, even where signs and glimmers of redemption are apparent, the process is not necessarily simply understood 'to happen suddenly, but gradually and by steps, as ... the process of improvement and correction advances by different degrees in different individuals'.[20] Redemption is not a once-for-all activity, but a process which, as Origen suggests, is 'gradually effected by stages during the passing of countless ages'.[21] It would, perhaps, make more sense, therefore, if the characters in *Pleasantville* were not simply to undergo a process of transformation from black-and-white into colour, but had the capacity to alternate between black-and-white and colour to mark the different stages, progressive and regressive, of their condition and predicament. In a way this is already addressed within the narrative, in that, for some of the characters, only parts of their anatomy, or parts of their clothing, tend to turn into colour, with a fully-fledged transformation only taking place at a later stage. Nevertheless, there is a certain veracity in the observation of one Internet Movie Database reviewer from Los Angeles that, at the film's denouement, 'every citizen is just as happy and docile on the surface as they appeared in their black-and-white beginning'. So, although 'everybody changed', Ross has contrived that 'everybody changed in the exact same way'.

To its credit, however, *Pleasantville* constitutes a departure from the mainstream Hollywood fantasy-oriented picture, which, in the form of, for example, *Forrest Gump*,[22] dissolves recent American history into 'a bleak yet saccharine tale of simple-minded goodness triumphing over the social ills associated with the Vietnam era'.[23] Indeed, it was Zemeckis' Oscar-winning film that prompted *Empire*'s Philip Thomas to witness and perceive in Hollywood an increasingly 'inward-looking, blinkered spirit', and a re-presentation of 'America's idea of itself as opposed to how it really is'.[24] *Pleasantville* may not have been as much of a critical or commercial success

---

[20] Origen, *On First Principles*, 3.6.9, Brian E. Daley, *The Hope of the Early Church: A Handbook of Patristic Eschatology* (Cambridge: Cambridge University Press, 1991), p. 49.

[21] Origen, *On First Principles*, 3.3.6, Henry Bettenson, *The Early Church Fathers* (Oxford: Oxford University Press, 1991), p. 257.

[22] *Forrest Gump*, dir. Robert Zemeckis, 1994.

[23] J. Hoberman, 'Under the rainbow', *Sight and Sound* (Volume 9, January 1999), p. 16.

[24] Philip Thomas, review of *Forrest Gump*, *Empire* No. 72 (June 1995), p. 104.

as *The Truman Show*, which was on release in the same period, but maybe its more modest achievements are only to be expected from a film which dares to challenge an audience and to introduce motifs and to explore intellectual terrain not normally expected from a film of this kind. Just as John May laments the fact that *Forrest Gump*'s international success 'seems, to me at least, to be a true barometer of cinema's current illness'[25], so *Pleasantville* may be said to hold out real promise. It represents a tangible hope for the future of commercial (and specifically Hollywood) film-making, with its all-too-rare combination of impressive computer-generated digital effects and a well-crafted, intelligent, though shamefully under-estimated, screenplay. It may even be possible to go so far as to claim that *Pleasantville* has successfully bridged the gap between entertainment and art and between escapism and authentic, redemptive possibility.

[25] John May, 'Cinema at 100 is alive and well,' *Media Development* XLII, Autumn 1995), p. 5.

PART 6

New Media and Religion

19

Approaches to Religious Research in Computer-Mediated Communication

Heidi Campbell

Approaching religion online

Within the past decade many have sounded a call for the church to become active in utilising the Internet in its mission. Anthropologist and journalist from the Religious Studies Institute of Rio de Janeiro, Andre Mello claimed:

> Religious groups that remain outside [the Internet communication revolution] will become ghettos, like some Puritan communities in the eighteenth and nineteenth centuries, who tried to halt the message of time to preserve tradition ... Changes arising from computer technology are irreversible.[1]

Many Christian groups have readily appropriated Internet technology into their ministries. George Barna in 1998 claimed the challenge facing Christian leaders was not how to stop new forms of church, but how to meet the challenge of ensuring 'those forms are tied in to the founda-tional theology and principles that reflect the basis of the existing church'.[2] Findings in a 2001 Barna Research Group survey on net-based faith experiences in the USA showed 8 per cent of the surveyed adult population and 12 per cent of teenagers now use the Internet for religious purposes. Barna predicted the American church would drastically change in the next decade as their research found 'Christian Internet users already spend more time surfing the Net than they do communicating with God through prayer'.[3]

---

[1] 'Join the Internet or become a ghetto, pastor tells Christians', Ecumenical News International News Service (26 May 1998).

[2] Barna Research Group, 'The Cyberchurch is Coming. National Survey of Teenagers shows Expectation of Substituting Internet for Corner Church' (5 May 1998) www.barna.org/PressCyberChurch.htm

[3] Barna Research Group, 'More Americans Are Seeking Net-Based Faith Experiences' (21 May 2001) www.barna.org/cig-bin/PageP...asp?PressReleaseID=90&Reference=A

While online religion is predicted to have a significant effect on religious culture in the coming decades, religious research on the Internet and its effects is still in its infancy. The purpose of this chapter is to summarise the responses made by the Christian community to the emergence of the Internet and describe the state of religious research in computer-mediated communications. First, responses to Internet technology by Christian writers and researchers are discussed. Secondly, a summary of four trends within current religious Internet research is given. Thirdly, a research project in the social ethnography of Christian online communities is highlighted to demonstrate the significance of research in this area for the church and religion.

Response to the Internet

When a new technology is created a spectrum of responses emerge: advocates who promote its use, critics who are sceptical of its effects and those who stand between these viewpoints. This range of responses has been mirrored in the Christian community's reaction to the Internet.[4]

Advocates

Advocates promote the Internet's ability to make the world a better place, often describing it as a communicative nirvana, a place where access to information equals freedom. Christian advocates, such as British researcher Patrick Dixon, characterise the Internet as a place of opportunity and challenge for the church. He outlines possible applications of Internet technology within the church and gives a general critique of its influence on church and societal relationships. Dixon sees the Internet as a 'God-given means of proclamation and explanation' and states: 'The Internet world needs cyberchurch, not as a substitute for local church life, but as a vibrant electronic expression of the life found in the body of Christ worldwide.'[5]

This is echoed in *The Internet Church*, by Walter Wilson, who stresses that the church should utilise the Internet for the task of world evangelism. He describes the Internet as empowered by God for his purposes. 'He is here with us in this moment of history, this information age, equipping us and empowering us for the creation of the Internet church.'[6] Advocates' enthusiasm is tempered with only a hint of caution. Dixon states that a 'clear call

---

[4] The categories have been adopted from other sources. Similar categorisations can be found in Gregor Goethals, 'Media Mythologies', Chris Arthur (ed.), *Religion in the Media* (Cardiff: University of Wales, 1993). Also consult Jolyon Mitchell, *Deconstructing Religious Stereotypes in Popular Television* (University Publication Pontifica of Salamanca, 2000).

[5] Patrick Dixon, *Cyberchurch, Christianity and the Internet* (Eastborne: Kingsway, 1997), p. 162.

[6] Walter Wilson, *The Internet Church* (Nashville: Word, 2000), p. 120.

from God'[7] should be sought before incorporating the Internet into church life, and stresses that the cyberchurch is no substitute for real-life membership and involvement.[8] Christian advocacy of the Internet involves more than promoting its technological use; it proposes using it as a tool of God for his manifest purposes.

Critics

Critics denounce the Internet, often portraying it as a de-humanising medium, a threat to 'real' community and communication. They point to the weakness of technology which they see most people overlooking or brushing aside. Tal Brooke, director of the Spiritual Counterfeits Project (SCP) in California, offers such a response in *Virtual Gods*. He argues that virtual reality and the Internet will lead 'towards the spiritual landscape' of Genesis before the great flood where 'man creates his own universe with no god in it but himself'.[9] Describing global computer networking as the Tower of Babel, Brooke sees cyberspace as a breeding ground for delusion, 'the worst kind of alienation – from reality and from God', as people are encouraged to hide from reality and play God.[10]

Similarly SCP founder Brooks Alexander identifies what he calls 'instrumental Gnosticism' in the techno-culture where illusory forms of knowledge exist and are encouraged, as reality is mediated through new media technology. Both Brooke and Alexander argue that cyberspace introduces problematic practices and conceptions of reality for those seeking to live by 'biblical truths'. They suggest Christians approach technology from a perspective of 'sanctified cynicism', meaning they hold a 'realistic, clear-eyed view of the fallen world without succumbing to the bleak despair that normally accompanies such knowledge'.[11] Others have offered critiques with less fervour, such as in *Hidden Dangers of the Internet*, which investigates Internet pornography.[12] Christian critics evaluate the Internet not simply as a tool, but also as a conveyer of spiritual doctrines and ideas. Their critique rests heavily on the danger of technology for believers, relationships with God and the church.

---

[7] Dixon, *Cyberchurch*, p. 162.

[8] Dixon, *Cyberchurch*, p. 94.

[9] Tal Brooke, 'Virtual Gods, Designer Universes', Tal Brooke (ed.), *Virtual Gods* (Eugene, OR: Harvest House, 1997), p. 126.

[10] Tal Brooke, 'Lost in the Garden of Digital Delights', *Virtual Gods*, p. 176.

[11] Tal Brooke, 'The Other Half', *Virtual Gods*, p. 188.

[12] Gregory L. Jantz, *Hidden Dangers of the Internet: Using It Without Abusing It* (Wheaton, IL: Harold Shaw, 1998).

Critical friends

While technophiles rave and technophobes rant, others offer 'reflection' as an approach.[13] Critical friends attempt to reflect on both the advantages and disadvantages introduced by Internet technology. Nardi and O'Day use the label 'critical friends' to describe the school of thinking attempting to address 'different ways of doing and being that emerge with technological change'.[14] Critical friends suggest individuals embrace technology with caution. Denver Seminary theologian Douglas Groothuis endeavours to offer a balanced critique. In *The Soul in Cyberspace* he calls his efforts an attempt at 'reflection'.[15] He states that 'given the present tendency to worship technology, some negativity is necessary in order to bring some balance.'[16] Groothuis evaluates the Internet on a spiritual level, calling for the Christian community to ask if the Internet is an appropriate medium for the Christian message, especially manifestations of cyberchurch and e-vangelism. He argues that all technologies extensively alter human forms of life, sees cyberspace technology as affecting 'our souls and our society' and challenges Christians to consider how it may affect our relationship with God as well as earthly lifestyle.[17]

Graham Houston also takes this approach, focusing on ethical issues surrounding virtual reality (VR). He argues that in an age where reality is broken down into images, Christians who interact with VR are caught in a tension between affirming the *imago Dei* or creating a new 'sense of centred selfhood'.[18] He endeavours to develop an ethical framework of 'Christian realism' which presupposes that the moral order is based on the created order and technological determinism is not necessary.[19] Houston encourages Christians to engage with discernment, so they can inform the technology rather than letting it inform their worldview. Being a Christian critical advocate means identifying how technology influences society and individual beliefs and values as well as behaviour and lifestyle. This means being 'friendly' and familiar with technology, while being critical of the path down which it may lead.

The Christian response to technology not only considers just how the Internet affects social and communicative relationships, it also reflects on how its use shapes the soul and cultural values. The most desirable position is that of a critical friend, as it highlights both advantages and disadvantages and responds to both extremes by trying to bring balance to the debate. It

---

[13] The term 'reflecter' is taken from Douglas Groothuis, *The Soul in Cyberspace* (Grand Rapids: Baker, 1997), p. 155.

[14] Bonnie Nardi and Vicki O'Day, *Information Ecologies – Using Technology with Heart* (Cambridge: MIT Press, 1999), p. 27.

[15] Groothuis, *Soul in Cyberspace*, p. 155.

[16] Groothuis, *Soul in Cyberspace*.

[17] Groothuis, *Soul in Cyberspace*, p. 15.

[18] Graham Houston, *Virtual Morality* (Leicester: Apollos, 1998), p. 185.

[19] Houston, *Virtual Morality*, p. 183.

is from this perspective that most religious online research has been approached.

Approaches to religious research online

The Internet has created a fascinating new area for study: computer-mediated communication (CMC). CMC is defined by John December as 'a process of human communication via computers, involving people, situated in particular contexts, engaging in processes to shape media for a variety of purposes'.[20] This field investigates the process of capturing, storing, reproducing and delivering computer-mediated coded messages; it also considers the effects this process has on senders, receivers and social structures. CMC is an interdisciplinary field of study encompassing diverse areas such as psychology, informatics and philosophy. While it often focuses on similar issues of identity and social structure, it typically integrates different methodologies and approaches.

In the 1990s interest and scholarly study in CMC began to surface within theological and religious studies disciplines. Issues such as the authenticity of online relationships, effects of disembodied communication and the potential of online interactions to replace face-to-face communication have become areas of concern for many Christian researchers and theologians such as Houston, Brooke and Gene Veith.[21] The way traditional and non-traditional religions utilise Internet technology in their spiritual pursuits has also been of interest, exemplified by Gary Bunt's work on Islam in cyberspace[22] and Joshua Hammerman's writing on Judaism online.[23] CMC researchers have taken a number of different approaches which can be broadly described as observational analysis, philosophical/theological examinations, theoretical development and social ethnography. A brief summary of each of these approaches provides a summary of topics and a focus of current religious online research.

Observational analysis

Observational analysis focuses on the general phenomenon of cyber-religion, evaluating the extent of its influence and effects by taking a survey

[20] John December, 'Notes on Defining of Computer-Mediated Communication' *Computer-Mediated Communication Magazine* Vol. 4, No. 1 (January 1997) www.december. com/cmc/mag/1997/jan/december.html
    [21] See Gene Edward Veith and Christopher L Stamper, *Christians in a .com World: Getting Connected without Being Consumed* (Wheaton, IL: Crossway, 2000).
    [22] Gary Bunt, *Virtually Islamic: Computer-Mediated Communication and Cyber Islamic Environments* (Lampeter: University of Wales Press, 2000).
    [23] See Joshua Hammerman, *thelordismyshepherd.com: Seeking God in Cyberspace* (Deerfield Beach, FL: Simcha, 2000).

analysis approach. This combines web site analysis with online observation of and interviews with webmasters and users. These projects offer either reflection on how specific religions are being transformed online, such as Jeff Zaleski's survey of major religions online, or broad reflection on the overall phenomenon of cyber-religion. A key question asked is how the Internet is shaping individual religious beliefs and practices.

An example of observational analysis is Brenda Brasher's work, *Give Me That Online Religion*, which explores the meaning of electronic faith and spirituality in the age of the Internet. She contends that online religion is 'a crucial contemporary cultural outlet for our meaning heritage from the past' and can 'make a unique contribution to global fellowship' and inter-religious understanding.[24] Her central thesis is that religious expression online should be protected and supported because religious people and their traditions 'make a valuable, necessary contribution to civil society' and online religion is crucial for the positive future of religion.[25] She argues that cyber-religion is invigorating concepts of sacred time, presence and spiritual experience by offering snapshots of web sites dealing with Y2K prophecies, descriptions of virtual shrines, along with essays of individuals' cyber-pilgrimages. In essence her research is a virtual tour of cyber-religion and spiritual expression online, providing justification for her argument that cyberspace is a public domain fit for religious expression. Observational analysis provides broad surveys of examples from the Internet to illustrate or answer general questions about online religion.

Philosophical/theological examination

Philosophical/theological examination investigates basic philosophical issues raised by the Internet and how this technology can be used to reconnect people to religious ideas or beliefs. These studies draw heavily on literature reviews and historical surveys of underlying theories and spiritual concepts emanating from computer technology. They often focus on a single issue or concept, such as grace or conceptions of space, and examine how the digital world re-informs it or calls for its re-examination.

Two clear examples of this approach are the works of Margaret Wertheim and Jennifer Cobb. In *The Pearly Gates of Cyberspace*[26] Wertheim, a science historian, explores the historic development of conceptions of space. She argues that cyberspace revives a medieval understanding of physical and spiritual space, in which the immaterial soul was central. Using Dante's *Divine Comedy*, the artwork of Giotto and the writing of Nicholas of Cusa, she

---

[24] Brenda Brasher, *Give Me That Online Religion* (San Francisco: Jossey-Bass, 2001), p. 6.

[25] Brasher, *Give Me That Online Religion*, p. 11.

[26] Margaret Wertheim, *The Pearly Gates of Cyberspace* (London: Virago, 1999).

outlines how philosophical ideas of space and time have been shaped and can be used to frame contemporary understanding of cyberspace. Jennifer Cobb's project is to demonstrate 'the sacred is present in computers' and to attempt to create a 'theology of Cyberspace' by exploring the Internet as a spiritual network. In *Cybergrace: The Search for God in a Digital World*, she encourages people to find a way to bring computers into their 'sacred lives'. Her arguments bring together Teilhard de Chardin's idea of the noosphere, the process theology of Alfred North Whitehead and chaos theory. Cobb portrays cyberspace as a place for society to find healing by reconnecting the spheres of science and religion. These examples show that philosophical/theological examination draws on extensive historical and literature reviews to build its arguments; online examples are given as illustrations of the specific concept being argued.

Theoretical development

Theoretical development recognises the need for tested conceptual frameworks to be developed in order to interpret the empirical data emerging in CMC studies. These draw on literature analysis of recognised communication theories such as semiology (F. de Sausseure) or social interactionism (G. H. Mead) and original empirical online studies. Empirical observation is used to test and refine the theoretical perspective being developed. These studies emphasise the importance of developing a research framework within which other data can be tested and interpreted.

Alf Linderman and Mia Lövheim of Uppsala University (Sweden) exemplify this in their work on religious identity and community formation online. One of their projects involves the application and adaptation of social semiology, which, they argue, is an appropriate and useful method for studying meaning-making in the online context. Semiotics focuses on how individuals construct meaning though symbols and sign systems. Employing aspects of Mead's work on interactions within social semiology, they have developed a model that can be applied to CMC studies investigating issues of meaning and identity construction. In their paper 'Internet and Religion. The Making of Meaning, Identity and Community through Computer Mediated Communication', they describe how such a model was used to study people who have established traditional and non-traditional religious web sites. The application of a social semiotic framework led to the conclusion that 'the degree of social trust experienced in computer-based social networks seems to be significant for the construction of identity and meaning in CMC'.[27] Their continued work seeks to outline how religion

---

[27] Alf Linderman and Mia Lövheim, 'Internet and Religion. The Making of Meaning, Identity and Community through Computer Mediated Communication', Paper presented to the *Media, Religion and Culture Conference*, Edinburgh, Scotland, 1998. This research article is adapted in their chapter 'Internet, Religion and the Attribution of Social Trust' chapter 20.

and CMC affects existing theories about late modernity and media reception studies. Theoretical development is vital, as little work has been done to establish credible and tested frameworks for studies of method and ethical questions in cyberculture.

Social ethnography

In the late 1990s social interaction became a key research focus in mainstream CMC. This hinged on the observation that 'distinct cultures that emerge in CMC are grounded in communicative practice'.[28] From this, the study of online communities has emerged where questions of social information, group meanings and identities, forms of relationship and social negotiation are explored. This research is microanalytic and ethnographic, often involving the in-depth analysis of a single online community, as illustrated by Jennifer Mnookin's study of the emergence of law in LamdaMOO.[29] Social ethnography involves a variety of research techniques such as online observation/participation and comparison of findings of other cyberculture studies. Though some research has taken this approach in exploring online religious practice and groups, such as Schroeder, Heather and Lee's study of religion in multi-user virtual reality,[30] few in-depth examples are currently available within strictly Christian CMC studies.

This is the approach that I have taken in my PhD research entitled *An Investigation of the Nature of the Church Through an Analysis of Selected Email-Based Christian Online Communities*, an ethnographic investigation of online community relationships utilising a three-phase case study research strategy of online participant-observation, online questionnaires and face-to-face interviews with selected community members.[31] This methodology proved effective in identifying individual and communal online communication patterns and determining how online relationships influence involvement within offline communities and the church. The research project and its findings are the focus of the remainder of this chapter demonstrating what insights this approach can offer into the state of religious online research.

[28] Nancy Baym, 'The Emergence of Community in Computer-mediated Communication', Steven Jones (ed.), *CyberSociety* (Thousand Oaks, CA: Sage, 1995), p. 139.

[29] Jennifer Mnookin, 'Virtual(ly) Law: The Emergence of Law in LamdaMOO', *Journal of Computer Mediated Communication* Vol. 2, No. 1, www.ascusc.org/jcmc/vol2/issue1/lamda.html

[30] Ralph Schroeder, Noel Heather and Raymond M. Lee, 'The Sacred and the Virtual: Religion in Multi-User Virtual Reality', *Journal of Computer Mediated Communication* 4 (December 1998), www.ascusc.org/jcmc/vol4/issue2/schroeder.html#LANGUAGE

[31] Heidi Campbell, *An Investigation of the Nature of the Church Through an Analysis of Selected Email-Based Christian Online Communities*, unpublished PhD thesis, University of Edinburgh, 2001.

We are one in the network: a social ethnography of online Christian community

My research was an interdisciplinary study bringing together the fields of computer-mediated communication, practical theology and sociology. Online communities challenge the traditional view of what constitutes a community, raising questions as to how this technology may contribute to the redefinition of personal and community relationships in both religious and public spheres. Internet technology is influencing people's conceptions of community. This thesis investigated Christian online communities, with special emphasis on studying the nature of community and cyberspace. The purpose was to identify the characteristics of community which individuals are seeking to cultivate in the online setting, showing possible implications for individuals in the 'real world' church and offline communities.

One approach to online community research is to identify and describe specific group narratives through researcher immersion in the online environment. Ethnographic study seeks to present a picture of a specific people group or organisation. Online social ethnography typically involves immersion in a given online community in order to understand and explain its social structure and issues of identity. Findings are presented through describing a community's overall narratives or highlighting a specific topic in the community such as gender or power relations. This study focused on identifying online groups' understanding of community and how that was lived out online. The key research questions being asked were: 'What does online communication offer individual Christians and groups of Christians? How is the Internet changing Christians' interaction with the real world Christian church?'

In order to address these questions a literature review on the topics of community, cyberculture and online religion was conducted to answer the basic questions: 'What is community?'; 'What is the Internet/cyberspace?'; and 'What happens when the two come together?' Theological definitions of community were brought together with a social network analysis of community; this is a sociological method with the underlying assumption that communities are social, not spatial structures. The result was that community was defined as a network of relationships between individuals connecting to a common purpose, whose bonds are created and sustained through shared traits and/or beliefs. The Internet, the 'network of all connected networks', was described as more than a communication tool used to connect to computer networks, it was also shown to transport ideas and values about the online and offline world. Cyberspace is a metaphorical space behind the computer screen, laden with distinct interpretations of what is real and what is virtual in a technological world. Together they can be seen as a reality laboratory, as the Internet becomes a place used to explore new ways of communicating and being. The online community combines traditional traits of community with a new technological setting. An online community is defined as individuals who assemble through

Internet technology and form a network of interdependent relationships based on a common vision, care and communication. This serves as background for specifically studying online Christian communities. These are interactive online groups who share a common Christian commitment and unite through a specific faith-based discussion topic.

Next, case study methodology was used to explore three Christian email communities. Communities were selected on the basis of common online practices, yet they represented diverse theological groups. The Community of Prophecy represented a Charismatic-Renewal group focused around the gift of prophecy. The Online Church was an evangelical group of visually impaired individuals. The Anglican Communion Online represented a group, as the name suggests, with links to the Anglican Church. A three-phase research strategy was employed in each case study. Phase one involved participant-observation in selected online communities. Phase two involved distribution and analysis of online questionnaires to online communities' members. Phase three involved face-to-face interviews with selected members in order to verify online observations and observe how individuals link their online and 'real world' communities. The goal was to define the characteristics of Christian online communities and discover how members' online involvement influences their interactions with the real world church.

Each case study was analysed with data presented under four themes. First, *The Online Community and the Online Context* examines how each community has used Internet technology and adapted to the online environment. Members described feeling freed in their communication online, having more time to reflect, not being judged by their physical appearance and gaining access to greater numbers of social contacts. However, anti-social online behaviour, such as spamming and flamming, was exhibited in some communities due to the lack of boundaries provided by the technology. Overall, community members also indicated a desire for more intimate/personal communication than this non-verbal medium allows; this was achieved through the use of emoticons, typed symbols relaying emotions, and cyber-hugs.

Secondly, *The Online Community and the Real World* investigates how each community links online experiences with real world activities. Members in all communities expressed the desire to reach beyond the screen for more intimate contact with their online friends; the result was that many sent personal emails, established contact via the phone and even arranged frequent face-to-face meetings with members. Sharing personal details about individuals' offline lives was encouraged; sharing real world needs through prayer requests also fostered members' concern and knowledge of each other's lives. Identification as a 'Christian' community boosted trust levels of members in the information and perceptions they received from other members.

Thirdly, *The Online Community as a Community* considers how each online group developed unique patterns of behaviour and a common identity. The overarching narrative for all three communities was identified as 'The Internet as Social Network', highlighting the Internet as a communal network encouraging members to invest emotionally in online community relationships. Each online community could also be summarised by a unique descriptive narrative highlighting the focus of each community: The Community of Prophecy as a spiritual network, The Online Church as a support network and the Anglican Communion Online as an Anglican network.

Fourthly, *The Online Community Reflects on the Church* demonstrates how members critique the real world church community through the positive characteristics of the online community they highlighted. Overall, members described online community as valuable in their spiritual lives and growth. Many emphasised experiencing more care, fellowship and encouragement online than they received in their real world church. Members also valued online prayer support and having access to teaching/discussion on topics not available in their local church. Yet most stressed that online fellowship was 'incomplete' because it lacked non-verbal feedback and touch. Another key finding was that while online Christian community structures are quite different from local church manifestations with similar theological backgrounds, it can be argued that the focus and message of their ministry are often quite similar. In this study online community could be linked to specific theological church models as outlined by Avery Dulles:[32] The Community of Prophecy with the Church as Mystical Communion, The Online Church with Church as Servant/ Herald, and the Anglican Communion Online with Church as Sacrament.

Three key conclusions about the nature of online Christian community and the church were drawn through the findings summarised above; a synthesis of these is presented in the next section.

Key findings

(1) *Online involvement is not causing people to leave their local church or shy away from real world participation.*

The majority of community members in this study described their online involvement as a 'supplement' to, rather than a substitute for, local church involvement. Most indicated that they were active in a local congregation, many stating they held leadership positions such as Sunday School teachers, lay readers, prayer team members and a few even served as ministers/ priests. Others indicated they frequently shared teaching and prayer requests they received online with their church. Identifying online participation as supplemental was often qualified in respondents' explanations, since members saw local church participation as important.

[32] Avery Dulles, *Models of the Church* (New York: Doubleday, 1974).

One Anglican Communion Online (AC) member used the phrase 'companion parish' to describe how it enabled them to connect with the real world church online and the wider body of Christ. Another AC member said online community had been valuable for her self-esteem, since she was judged by 'the ideas I put in print' and not her clothes or mannerisms. Yet she said the AC was lacking because, 'I can't share Communion with the List, and I can only very rarely hug them.' Labelling online community as a supplement to real world church highlighted members' desire for face-to-face contact.

Embodied interaction was referred to as the 'Chocolate Chip Cookie Factor' by a Community of Prophecy (CP) member in response to the survey question 'Do you believe you can care for members of the community as you do in a "real world" (face-to-face) community?' He stated:

> I believe a person can care and minister as much [but] not in a complete way. It would be difficult to email you a plate of chocolate chip cookies, or help you move to a new apartment. But listening, praying and communicating can be carried out online.[33]

The 'Chocolate Chip Cookie Factor' highlights the strengths and limitations of online relationships. Email offers fast and instantaneous communication; thus many CP members indicated how the frequency of contact they have with Christians online is more significant than in their local church. Yet, while anonymity enables people to be more open one-to-one, not being able to look someone in the eyes can effect the process of building trust in relationships for some. 'Trustworthiness must be demonstrated ... because of the lack of physical connection online, trust is more difficult, but not impossible to build.' For many the 'Chocolate Chip Cookie Factor' is the main reason online community supplements, but does not become a full substitute for, local church participation.

(2) *People join online communities primarily for relationships, not information; relationships are often noted as lacking in the offline church.*

While members stress that online community is supplemental, what they highlighted as being supplemented was personal interaction and relationships, and not just information exchange. When describing an email list as a community, members often said how online groups facilitate higher levels of intimacy, care and commonality than is often found in their real world faith communities. The value placed on online relationships and socialising was dependent on members' past or current church experiences and job circumstances.

Online Church (OLC) members noted relational support as the primary area that online community supplemented; the OLC provided a 'listening ear', people who understood their physical limitations, Christian counsel, and a place to receive support and encouragement. Online relationships

---

[33] CP Email Questionnaire Response, Mon, 30 March 1998.

were often described as more dynamic, especially for those with sensory impairments. One member who was active in a local church commented, 'OLC members know how I feel, because they feel much the same. I do not have a chance to share at this level in my local church.' The local church was described as a place to receive teaching, and the OLC was where members found Christian friendships and spiritual or emotional input.

In the AC the ability to interact at a deeper level online was also noted. Several members made comments such as, 'I know more about many of the people on AC than I do members of my parish.' This was explained because online community is focused on dialogue at a level many find hard to facilitate in offline parishes. One member commented, 'It takes a very, very long time in a parish face-to-face to talk with people about the kinds of things we talk with each other instantly about online.' The local parish, she said, often facilitates few opportunities to discuss personal issues of faith and theology in-depth unless you are involved in church ministry. Many individuals are drawn to online Christian community because of their experience of being cared for and the opportunity to communicate and form relationships with like-minded people.

(3) *Descriptions given by members of online communities, stating their reasons for online involvement and benefits they receive, provide critiques of the real world church. The characteristics of online communities highlighted offer a picture of what individuals envision and hope a church or Christian community would be like.*

Online community can provide a model for what individuals desire in an offline church. Online Christian communities are often consciously trying to create an open or family atmosphere of care and acceptance. AC members frequently refer to each other as 'listsibs', for 'list siblings in Christ'. An OLC member describes their community as the kind of group I would call a loving Christian family.' Engagement with Christian brothers and sisters who would normally be separated by geography or physical limitation is helping members understand church relationships in new and exciting ways.

Involvement in an online community helps widen many Christians' vision of what it means to be part of the 'body of Christ'. One CP member from the Philippines said, 'Like in the "real world" community, I meet various kinds of people in the online community, some that I can relate better to than others. For me the exciting feature of the "online community" is that it is international in scope so it brings greater immediacy to the "abstract" doctrine of the universal Body of Christ.' An AC online discussion also highlighted this fact, as one member wrote, 'This Anglican Church of ours is getting more and more like one big family. You don't suppose this list could have anything to do with it, do you?'[34] Access to other Christians was not the only attribute of online community highlighted as desirable.

---

[34] Email sent to AC, Sun, 13 June 1999.

Members indicated that they felt cared for, valued and accepted by their online communities. Email enables individuals to receive frequent and instantaneous responses to their prayer requests or confession of personal struggles. Postings offering encouragement made to an entire email list, but directed towards specific members, portray the community as a supportive place where people are loved and understood. OLC members indicated that offline church is not an easy place for those with disabilities to find acceptance. Online community provides a social outlet where they are judged on the basis of their written words and not on physical appearance or the ability to express themselves verbally. Others in the AC and CP also expressed disappointment with the real world church, which encouraged them to go online in search of Christians they could trust. One AC member stated, 'I have to say that I do not find a lot of honesty and trust in my present in-the-flesh congregation. I guess some of my online searching for community goes towards compensating for this lack.' Online community was described as a place people can find empathetic Christian support that many have identified as lacking in their offline experience.

Online community focuses on building and supporting relationships; this was frequently highlighted as the key attribute of community. Many of the definitions of community given by online community members were people-focused and relationship-centred. Common phrases used were 'bound together by beliefs and interests', 'a group of people who get together for a fellowship', 'come together for a common purpose' and 'having a common sense of care for one another'. Community is held together through the connection people make with others. Christian community was expressed as 'a group of people who recognise that connection, of being in the body, and see themselves as brothers and sisters in Christ, supporting one another in their worship and devotion'. Members desired investment and involvement in their lives by others as well as the ability to share in others' lives.

This study demonstrates that while online community is incomplete in certain respects, when real world options do not provide the spiritual connection many individuals long for, it can be a 'Godsend'[35] to know there is another realm where these desires can be realised. For this reason many individuals will continue to invest in online community, thus posing a challenge to the church and the culture of religion.

Conclusion

This chapter has provided a survey of current religious research trends and reactions by the Christian community to the Internet. Spotlighting a specific example of social ethnography demonstrates that the religious community can benefit not only from utilising the online environment in

---

[35] Response given by an OLC member in an online questionnaire.

its worship and ministry, but also from asking how this engagement may shape people's views and involvement with the religious community. Here it is shown how research into online Christian community can illustrate how individuals conceive of offline community and evaluate contemporary church culture. More study needs to be carried out by researchers interested in religious issues to uncover these beliefs and the potential effects online religion may have on society.

Further reading

N. Baym, 'The Emergence of Community in Computer-mediated Communication', Steven Jones (ed.), *CyberSociety* (Thousand Oaks, CA: Sage, 1995).

Barna Research Group,'The Cyberchurch is Coming. National Survey of Teenagers shows Expectation of Substituting Internet for Corner Church' (5 May 1998) www.barna.org/PressCyberChurch.htm

Barna Research Group, 'More Americans Are Seeking Net-Based Faith Experiences' (21 May 2001) www.barna.org/cig-bin/PageP...asp? PressReleaseID=90&Reference=A

B. Brasher, *Give Me That Online Religion* (San Francisco: Jossey-Bass, 2001).

T. Brooke (ed.), *Virtual Gods* (Eugene, OR: Harvest House, 1997).

G. Bunt, *Virtually Islamic: Computer-Mediated Communication and Cyber Islamic Environments* (Lampeter: University of Wales Press, 2000).

J. Cobb, *Cybergrace. The Search for God in the Digital World* (New York: Crown, 1998).

J. December, 'Notes on Defining of Computer-Mediated Communication', *Computer-Mediated Communication Magazine* Vol. 4, No. 1 (January 1997) www.december.com/cmc/mag/1997/jan/december.html

P. Dixon, *Cyberchurch, Christianity and the Internet* (Eastborne: Kingsway, 1997).

G. Goethals, 'Media Mythologies', Chris Arthur (ed.), *Religion in the Media* (Cardiff: University of Wales, 1993).

D. Groothuis, *The Soul in Cyberspace* (Grand Rapids: Baker, 1997).

J. Hammerman, *thelordismyshepherd.com: Seeking God in Cyberspace* (Deerfield Beach, FL: Simcha, 2000).

G. Houston, *Virtual Morality* (Leicester: Apollos, 1998).

G. L. Jantz, *Hidden Dangers of the Internet: Using It Without Abusing It* (Wheaton, IL: Harold Shaw, 1998).

J. Mitchell, *Deconstructing Religious Stereotypes in Popular Television* (University Publication Pontifica of Salamanca, 2000).

J. Mnookin, 'Virtual(ly) Law: The Emergence of Law in LamdaMOO', *Journal of Computer Mediated Communication* Vol. 2, No. 1, www.ascusc.org/jcmc/vol2/issue1/lamda.html

B. Nardi and V. O'Day, *Information Ecologies – Using Technology with Heart* (Cambridge: MIT Press, 1999).

R. Schroeder, N. Heather, and R. M. Lee, 'The Sacred and the Virtual: Religion in Multi-User Virtual Reality', *Journal of Computer Mediated Communication* 4 (December 1998) www.ascusc.org/jcmc/vol4/issue2/schroeder.html#LANGUAGE

G. E. Veith and C. L. Stamper, *Christians in a .com World: Getting Connected without Being Consumed* (Wheaton, IL: Crossway, 2000).

M. Wertheim, *The Pearly Gates of Cyberspace* (London: Virago, 1999).

W. Wilson, *The Internet Church* (Nashville: Word, 2000).

J. Zaleski, *The Soul of Cyberspace: How Technology is Changing our Spiritual Lives* (San Francisco: HarperSanFrancisco, 1997).

'Join the Internet or become a ghetto, pastor tells Christians', Ecumenical News International News Service (26 May 1998).

20

Internet, Religion and the Attribution of Social Trust

Alf Linderman and Mia Lövheim

In recent years, the Internet has become a site where churches and other established religious groups, together with those representing alternative religion and spirituality, have explored new approaches to religious proclamation, communication and interaction. As religious groups of various kinds turn to the Internet, several questions of interest to sociologists of religion arise. Consequently, the study of Internet and religion has emerged as a new field of research into the social and cultural aspects of computer-mediated communication (CMC). This field has developed alongside the growing public interest in the possibilities of the use of information technology in order to connect people. As described in the previous chapter, one-sided utopian and dystopian images have often dominated the public discussion on these issues, but research within the field has increasingly come to emphasise the need for more empirical work and less speculation in order to understand the complexity of social and cultural aspects of CMC.[1]

Based on the general assumption that more empirical work is needed, a research project was initiated in 1998 to address issues concerning CMC, community and identity in Sweden, and this chapter draws on work within this project. The project's objective is to develop our general understanding of how people 'make sense' of CMC and what their uses of these new modes of communication are in terms of community and identity construction. Religion is chosen as the area of study, and there are several reasons for this. Religion is a fundamental dimension of culture and is, as such, interesting when exploring cultural change and development. Religion is also a social phenomenon, and it is relatively straightforward to find groups to compare. Furthermore, new technologies have historically time after time been referred to as 'sacred' in their own right, and it appears appropriate to explore this dimension further in the area of CMC.

---

[1] cf. M. A. Smith and P. Kollock (eds.), *Communities in Cyberspace* (London and New York: Routledge, 1999), p. 4.

The impact of new technology and new modes of communication must be related to processes of social and cultural change taking place in late modern society, changes which imply new and often ambiguous conditions for the formation of community and individual identity.[2] This chapter will therefore start with a discussion of changing conditions for community formation in late modernity. The second section deals with the theoretical perspective that is applied in the study. Then we will turn to some empirical observations and finally conclude with some inferences based on the work within the project.

Changing conditions for community and identity construction

Our preconceived understanding of the concept of community is of course based on previous research where community is related to boundaries in time and space. But, as scholars like Anthony Giddens and Manuel Castells have pointed out, things are not what they used to be. The local setting can no longer be seen as the only context for social interaction. For a growing number of people, work, relationships and social activities are organised through networks emancipated from time and space. Furthermore, the mediation of symbols, values and norms concerning identity and meaning increasingly takes place through global commercial companies and media networks. Religious groups as we traditionally know them have fulfilled functions of expressing, controlling and transmitting symbols, values and norms for the construction of collective and individual identity in a society.[3] Thus, religious groups have constituted community in its quintessential form. The study of religion in late modern society indicates that the transformations briefly delineated here challenge the dominant position and the legitimacy of such traditional authorities. How, then, will we in the midst of this development deal with the concept of community?

On the one hand, our understanding of community is primarily based on experiences in and studies of the local social world. We are trying to understand the implications of ongoing social, economic and cultural changes, and therefore our previous knowledge has to remain an important part of our frame of reference. On the other hand, we are studying CMC with an interest in exploring whether this kind of communication can generate new ways of interaction through which people can establish a sense of community that is similar to, but not necessarily the same as, the sense of community established through traditional social interaction. If so, it is not unlikely that the quality of communities developed through CMC might have both similarities to and differences from that which the concept of community is thought to imply when applied to interaction experienced in a traditional social setting. Thus, we are entering the study of CMC with a

---

[2] cf. J. Slevin, *The Internet and Society* (Cambridge: Polity Press UK, 2000).
[3] cf. E. Durkheim, *The Elementary Forms of Religious Life* (New York: Free Press, 1965).

conception of community that might be, and most likely is, in need of refinement or redefinition. Developing a more elaborate understanding of how community could be defined when applied to CMC is part of the project.

In terms of its definition, the concept of religion parallels the problem related to the concept of community. We need to start with what we know about religion, but we are just as interested in what we do not know as to where and how religion can emerge. We will focus below on one aspect of that which binds religious communities together, the attribution of social trust, and consider if and how social trust is attributed in the context of religion mediated through CMC.

Previous studies in the field of media, religion and culture have begun to explore the significance of electronic media in particular as an increasingly important site for the mediating of religious symbols and values and the construction of meaning and identity.[4] However, previous research exploring the implications of CMC for religion is still limited, even though there is a growing interest in the field.[5] The issues addressed in these studies can roughly be grouped into three related areas: how religious institutions that also exist in the offline world use CMC, the possibilities and the problems of computer-based networks fulfilling functions similar to traditional religious communities, and the possible emergence of alternative forms of religious practices and beliefs through CMC.[6]

One of the advantages of CMC for religious organisations is its ability to transcend time and place, thereby connecting people in different places who share the same interests. Previous studies show that new or alternative religious movements[7] as well as more established religious organisations[8] have taken advantage of these possibilities. In most cases, CMC has been used in order to spread information in more effective ways, but there are also examples of networks being set up for contact and support, more so among alternative religious movements which often lack the resources for such interactions offline.

As argued by, for example, Wellman and Gulia[9] new forms of socially meaningful relationships can and do emerge in such sites as email discussion lists, conferencing systems, text chat, web sites and graphical worlds,

---

[4] cf. S. M. Hoover and K. Lundby (eds.), *Rethinking Religion, Media and Culture* (Thousand Oaks, CA: Sage, 1997).

[5] e.g. J. K. Hadden and D. E. Cowan (eds.), *Religion on the Internet. Research Prospects and Promises* (Amsterdam, London and New York: JAI Press, 2000).

[6] cf. L. L. Dawson, 'Researching Religion in Cyberspace. Issues and Strategies', J. K. Hadden and D. E. Cowan (eds.), *Religion on the Internet*, pp. 25–51.

[7] L. L. Dawson and J. Hennebry, 'New Religions and the Internet. Recruiting in a New Public Space', *Journal of Contemporary Religion* 1 (1999), pp. 17–39.

[8] E. Larsen (principal author). 'Wired Churches, Wired Temples: Taking Congregations and Missions into Cyberspace', Report from the *Pew Internet & American Life Project*, Washington, DC, (2000) www.pewinternet.org/

[9] B. Wellman and M. Gulia, 'Virtual Communities as Communities. Netsurfers Don't Ride Alone', M. A. Smith and P. Kollock (eds.), *Communities in Cyberspace*, pp. 67–162.

even though these relationships might be more sparsely knit and based on less frequent and direct forms of social interaction than those that make up traditional communities. Studies of neo-pagan computer-mediated news groups[10] and charismatic Christian groups using email discussion lists[11] or multi-user virtual worlds[12] indicate that this kind of interaction might provide a sense of shared identity organised around something that is set apart as 'sacred'. However, these studies also point to the problem of constructing a sense of community through a medium in which relationships are constructed not as in the local context, but according to the choices made by individual members in terms of invested time, interaction and commitment.

The masking of markers such as race, gender, status and age in a way other than interaction face-to-face shapes interaction in CMC. Early texts on this issue anticipated that the flexible and pluralistic character of relationships in such contexts might foster more innovative and experimental expressions of identity and community.[13] In more recent studies, however, such anticipation has been disputed and modified. There seems to be far more continuity between online identities and relationship and offline contexts than was expected.[14] In the case of religious computer-based networks, the studies referred to above indicate that practices and symbols seem to be transferred from the local religious context to the online context, possibly fulfilling similar functions. However, there are also indications of how religious symbols and practices have been used in ways that differ from their traditional use. These indications point to the possibility of more reflective, eclectic and experimental expressions of religiosity emerging in CMC.[15]

So far previous studies have just scratched the surface of the areas listed above and indicated the need for more thorough research on questions such

[10] cf. J. Fernback, 'Internet Ritual: A Case Study of the Construction of Computer-Mediated Neo-Pagan Religious Meaning', in M. Hoover and L. Schofield Clark (eds.), *Practicing Religion in the Age of Media* (New York: Columbia University Press, 2002), pp. 254–275; and S. D. O'Leary, 'Cyberspace as Sacred Space. Communicating Religion on Computer Networks', *Journal of the American Academy of Religion* 64 (1996), pp. 781–808.

[11] H. Campbell, 'Congregation of the Disembodied: A Look at a Religious Community on the Internet', Paper presented to the *Sociology of Religion Study Group at the British Sociological Association* 1998 Conference, and see also chapter 19 of this volume.

[12] R. Schroeder, N. Heather, and R. M. Lee, 'The Sacred and The Virtual: Religion in Multi-User Virtual Reality', *Journal of Computer Mediated Communication* 4 (1998) www.ascusc.org/jcmc/vol4/issue2/schroeder.html

[13] cf. S. Turkle, *Life on the Screen. Identity in the Age of the Internet* (New York: Simon & Schuster, 1995); and S. D. O'Leary and B. Brasher, 'The Unknown God of the Internet: Religious Communication from the Ancient Agora to the Virtual Forum', C. Ess (ed.), *Philosophical Perspectives on Computer-Mediated Communication* (Albany: SUNY Press, 1996), pp. 238–63.

[14] cf. S. C. Herring, 'The Rhetorical Dynamics of Gender Harassment Online', *The Information Society* 3 (1999), pp. 151–68; and B. Burkhalter, 'Reading Race Online: Discovering Racial Identity in Usenet Discussions.' M. A. Smith and P. Kollock (eds.), *Communities in Cyberspace*, pp. 60–75.

[15] cf. O'Leary, 'Cyberspace as Sacred Space'; and Dawson and Hennebry, 'New Religions and the Internet'.

as: How is the interaction between the individual believer and the community structured in CMC? What is the significance of practices and symbols used in offline religious contexts online? What happens to questions of authority and control on the part of the community versus individual believers? What happens to the individual's need of support and legitimacy from the community? Do different forms of religious tradition differ in this respect?

The attribution of social trust – in theory

When individuals engage in social interaction and, through that interaction, establish rules and conventions for the use of language and signs in general, these individuals take part in the creation and maintenance of social meaning systems. Thus, shared social meaning systems are manifestations of communities. It seems obvious that various kinds of communities have different qualities, and the manifestations of these differences are reflected on the individual level in terms of how the individual relates to the interaction and the social meaning systems. One concept through which such differences could be discussed is social trust.

The theoretical foundation for this study draws on a previously developed theoretical perspective for television reception: social semeiology.[16] According to this perspective, the first key-notion is the idea of conventional sign systems as the factor facilitating human communication. Each act of communication is related to one (or several) socially established meaning system(s). Any 'text' resulting from an act of communication will signal its belonging to a meaning system in that its elements will be organised according to rules and conventions within this particular system. This relation to a meaning system constitutes constraints on the individual construction of meaning. However, this does not mean that the process of meaning construction is completely determined by this circumstance. 'Divergent readings' are possible since each reader has a variety of ways to relate the text to different meaning systems, and to combine elements from different meaning systems. The emphasis on the individual (mental) process of meaning-construction and reconstruction constitutes the second key-notion for social semeiology. Through this continuous use of signs in social interaction, socially established meaning systems can undergo continuous change and development, and central to this process is the concept of social trust.

With reference to psychologists like Winnicott, Erikson and Sullivan, Giddens[17] points out that a sense of security and trust in the social

---

[16] cf. A. G. Linderman, 'The Reception of Religious Television: Social Semeiology applied to an Empirical Case Study', *Acta Universitatis Upsaliensis, Psychologia et Sociologia Religionum* 12 (Stockholm: Almqvist & Wiksell, 1996); and A. G. Linderman, 'Making Sense of Religion in Television', S. M. Hoover and K. Lundby (eds.), *Rethinking Religion, Media and Culture* (Thousand Oaks, CA: Sage, 1997), pp. 263–83.

[17] A. Giddens, *Modernity and Self-identity. Self and Society in the Late Modern Age* (Cambridge: Polity, UK, 1991).

environment of the child is the very foundation for the development of a sense of the self. This basic social trust is founded upon the relation between the child and its caretakers. If it were not for the development of this basic trust, the child would not develop a sense of self that is defined through a process of interaction between the child and its significant others. The very existence of significant others presupposes a certain level of trust.

In accordance with the role trust plays in the initial phase of construction of meaning and identity, trust continues to be vital for the construction of meaning and identity in the adult life, but in a context that becomes more and more differentiated and diversified. Trust directed toward others, i.e., social trust, is that which sets the scene for or determines the preconditions of the process of constructing meaning and the continuous reflexive process of identity formation. One could conceptually describe social trust as a filter through which communication and interaction take place. When there is a high degree of social trust between an individual and those with whom the individual communicates, this communication will be more significant in the mind of this individual. This, in turn, leads to the development of kinship. The individual becomes part of the group in a sense that also implies commitment and moral obligations toward the group. Social trust can, of course, be established through many different kinds of interaction, but it is likely that the mode of communication through which social trust is established has significance for the level and quality of community that is established. Our exploratory study of interaction in religious sites on the Internet is thus in fact a study of if, how, and to what degree community can be developed through the individual attribution of social trust (with regard to the interaction) through CMC.

The attribution of social trust – in practice

How are we then to study the development of social trust and related implications for the process of constructing religious identity and community in CMC? The first issue discussed here is how individuals experience the kind of CMC in which they take part, and if, in what way, and to what degree they find it meaningful. With this focus, we want to explore the foundation for the individual's attribution of social trust to this particular interaction. The second issue discussed in this study is whether a common understanding of religious symbols and practices is expressed in these computer-mediated interactions. To what degree can we find indications of the development of social meaning systems that could be interpreted as manifestations of individuals' attribution of social trust in this context of interaction?

The theoretical discussion points out that the individual's previous experience of social interaction plays an important role in the process of attributing social trust to other kinds of interaction. We know from previous research that gender and different organisational patterns has had an impact on how individuals relate to religious communities. Previous research in the area of CMC also suggests that gender, the type of organisation and also the type of CMC used[18] may have implications for social interaction online. However, we need to know more about how factors such as these might frame the process of constructing religious identity and meaning in CMC. Therefore, we have in this study chosen to focus on young men and women who relate to either an established or an alternative religious context in their lives offline. Also, we have chosen to focus on two different forms of religious CMC: an email discussion list devoted to issues about Wicca, alternative spiritualities, magical practices, etc., and a news group devoted to discussions about Christian (Lutheran) faith and theology.

The study started with an ethnographic methodological approach, in which data from several techniques were interrelated. First, an online questionnaire was sent to a number of sites supplying information and opportunities for discussing religious issues. The questionnaire was followed by in-depth interviews offline and online with a smaller group of the individuals answering the questionnaire. Most of the answers to the questionnaire were derived from two sites; one supplied access to the email discussion list and the other to the news group mentioned above. The interaction in these two sites was observed for a period of four months. Our aim has thus been to focus on processes of meaning-making on an individual as well as on a social level.

When asked about the significance of the computer-mediated interaction in which they participated, the majority of those answering the questionnaire mentioned that they had encountered new types of information, explored new issues and thereby expanded their knowledge in matters of religion and spirituality. Some of the informants emphasised the extended ability to get into contact with people with similar interests and experiences in the area of religion. Several informants also found the religious dialogue interesting since the computer-mediated interaction allowed for a wider array of possible input compared to interaction taking place within traditional religious contexts.

These answers given in the questionnaire were confirmed as well as complemented by the interviews. Computer-mediated interaction can thus be considered meaningful in that it widens the possibilities for encountering people who relate to religious symbols, practices and traditions in a way that is beyond what these young men and women encounter in their local context. Thereby interaction in these sites might offer extended possibilities to reflect on one's own and other people's faiths.[19] Furthermore, computer-mediated interaction can be considered meaningful in that it provides relationships in which one's own religious identity can be confirmed and

[18] cf. N. Baym, 'The Emergence of Online Community', S. Jones (ed.), *Cybersociety 2.0: Revisiting Computer-Mediated Communication and Community* (Thousand Oaks, CA: Sage, 1998), pp. 35–68.

[19] This corresponds to studies of the implications of religious television, cf. S. M. Hoover, *Mass Media Religion* (London: Sage, 1988).

strengthened. This happens through finding and establishing contact with others who share the same thoughts and experiences, which might provide some sort of legitimacy and also a common identity to which one can relate; or through the opportunity to discuss and reflect further upon a religious tradition to which one is already affiliated (in the interaction) with people of other convictions who bring new ideas and perspectives.

These findings suggest that the individuals involved consider interaction through CMC meaningful in several ways. Thus, there seems to be a foundation which allows for the attribution of social trust in the interaction through CMC. We can now turn to the second issue dealing with actual indications of social meaning being established through the computer-mediated interaction. In accordance with the present theoretical perspective, such indications are interpreted as manifestations of social trust being attributed by the individuals involved.

The Christian news group was dominated by young men who felt restricted or not satisfied by the kind of tradition present in the local setting where they lived. Therefore, they oriented themselves toward an alternative, more conservative Christian tradition. The purpose and norms of the group, as a forum for theological discussions in which intellectual acumen and academic learning were highly valued, were seldom discussed or questioned. Although the meaning of certain parts of the Bible and the role of the church were often discussed, postings that radically questioned the fundamental authority of these were very rare. The discussions many times tended to end up in a consensus regarding a certain interpretation of these issues, often with a critical stance towards more 'liberal' or divergent perspectives.

The email discussion list aimed at issues about Wicca, alternative spiritualities and magical practices was dominated by women who were self-taught and without affiliation to any particular group or tradition. Here many different ways of relating to and interpreting the meaning of religious symbols and practices were represented. In the period during which the observation was carried out, a fierce debate over two conflicting authoritative claims concerning a certain tradition took place. Also, the purpose, values and norms of the list were continuously being questioned and discussed. Still, certain values and norms could be discerned in the discussions, such as the value of religious tolerance and the depreciation of any restrictions on individual freedom of choice in relation to religious beliefs and practices.

Processes of developing common meanings, values and norms that take place through the interaction on the list as well as in the news group indicate that some kind of social trust can be established through different kinds of CMC. However, the function of these common meanings, values and norms and the quality of the community established seems to be different depending on the character of the social trust attributed to the interaction by the participants. How do we explain those differences? Differences in the way participants approach a news group and an email discussion list might of course be useful to consider. In an email discussion list, every new posting gets distributed to all participants. In the case of a news group, participants have to log on to the group in order to read new postings. This might imply that an email discussion list has a greater potential for a larger and perhaps more diverse number of participants taking part in the discussions.

The data, however, also indicate that religious context and gender might have some implications for the character of the social trust attributed to the interaction in these computer-based sites. In the questionnaire, trust in the ability of CMC to generate some kind of community was most strongly expressed by the users whose religious identification was in line with alternative spirituality or neo-paganism. Only a few of these had a relationship to some kind of religious community in their local context. Few of the users who identified themselves as Christians mentioned this possibility. Rather, they emphasised CMC as a complement to, but not a replacement for, religious community offline. The users with a Christian background emphasised more than those with an alternative religious background the possibility of spreading the Christian faith and answering questions about their faith from people they would not have encountered without CMC. These indications also correspond with initial interviews made within the present project regarding the expectations of the people who set up sites for interaction related to religious issues.

More men than women answered the questionnaire. In the Christian group the number of women who answered was less than 25 per cent. Among the users relating to alternative religious traditions the numbers were almost equally balanced between men and women. The male users tended to emphasise the possibility of discussing with people of other, opposing beliefs as meaningful. The female users tended to emphasise more the possibility of giving and receiving support and confirmation from others. These differences emerged as more salient in the interviews, where the women also expressed dislike of discussion turning into a display of intellectual acumen and a lack of tolerance towards 'stupid' questions.

In the case of the news group, the transference of symbols as well as norms and values familiar to all the participants seemed to be an important part of what made them attribute social trust to the interaction. Even though the participants themselves were critical towards certain parts of their respective local religious settings, the social trust attributed to the interaction is perhaps related more to the possibility of strengthening and developing a religious identity which is already established than to the potential of CMC to open up a space for alternative perspectives, beliefs and practices. The news group can thus be seen as a community in which a collective identity and a common system of beliefs and practices, in this case a conservative Christian tradition, can be maintained and strengthened. The lack of alternative voices in this group might, however, also affect the social trust attributed to the interaction by participants who feel excluded by such a tradition. This was indicated by some of the young women in the group who seldom took part in the discussions since they felt intimidated by a lack of knowledge or support.

In the case of the email discussion list, the plurality of perspectives made possible by CMC seemed to be the main reason for the participants to attribute a sense of social trust to the list. The seemingly heterogeneous, disputed and fugitive character of meanings, values and norms might be seen as fulfilling a function of maintaining fundamental values of tolerance and plurality. Thereby the list can become a community that provides an opportunity to express and further explore alternative religious identities, beliefs and practices, in a way that gives legitimacy to the common quest of the participants but also acknowledges the right of every member to do this in his/her own way. Thus, the sense of community established on the list seemed to refer more to a sense of being in opposition to, or questioned by, the established religious institutions than with sharing a certain system of religious beliefs and practices. Constructing a more consistent meaning system might in this case imply the risk of excluding someone from the community. However, this also implies the possibility of the list becoming more of a place to try out different beliefs and practices than a place to which the individual attributes the social trust traditionally associated with religious communities.

Conclusion

The above account of some initial findings of the present project indicates that the significance and potential of CMC differs according to a variety of factors and variables. Therefore, a more fruitful approach than trying to determine whether CMC fosters a certain or different kind of religion is to look into the question of whether CMC facilitates or renders more difficult certain forms of social relations and identities than others. In late modern society the individual is faced with a multitude of symbols, values and norms, of which some might be confronting traditional religious beliefs and practices. As proposed by James Slevin and Lorne Dawson, CMC might empower people in the process of constructing religious identity and meaning under such conditions in ways that might connect to the processes of religious change already under way in late modern society. As we continue to explore religion and computer-mediated communication and interaction, we will learn more about the complex ways these new modes of interaction play into ongoing processes of religious community and identity formation. At this stage, the conceptualisation of this research as an exploration of how social trust is attributed to different forms of CMC and how community is formed in the process seems to be a fruitful approach. Such exploration will shed light not only on the implications of computer-mediated communication and interaction for religious identity and community formation, but on the overall potential and implications of these new modes of communication for the general culture.

Further reading

N. Baym, 'The Emergence of Online Community', S. Jones (ed.), *Cybersociety 2.0: Revisiting Computer-Mediated Communication and Community* (Thousand Oaks, CA: Sage, 1998), pp. 35–68.

B. Burkhalter, 'Reading Race Online: Discovering Racial Identity in Usenet Discussions', M. A. Smith and P. Kollock (eds.), *Communities in Cyberspace* (London and New York: Routledge, 1999), pp. 60–75.

H. Campbell, 'Congregation of the Disembodied: A Look at a Religious Community on the Internet', Paper presented to the *Sociology of Religion Study Group at the British Sociological Association* 1998 Conference.

M. Castells, *The Rise of the Network Society* (Oxford: Blackwell, 1996).

M. Castells, *The Power of Identity* (Oxford: Blackwell, 1997).

L. L. Dawson, 'Researching Religion in Cyberspace. Issues and Strategies', J. K. Hadden and D. E. Cowan (eds.), *Religion on the Internet. Research Prospects and Promises* (Amsterdam, London and New York: JAI Press, 2000), pp. 25–51.

L. L. Dawson, 'Doing Religion in Cyberspace: The Promise and the Perils', *The Council of Societies for the Study of Religion Bulletin* Vol. 30, No. 1 (February 2001), pp. 3–9.

L. L. Dawson and J. Hennebry, 'New Religions and the Internet. Recruiting in a New Public Space', *Journal of Contemporary Religion*, 1 (1999), pp. 17–39.

E. Durkheim, *The Elementary Forms of Religious Life* (New York: Free Press, 1965).

J. Fernback, 'Internet Ritual. A Case Study of the Construction of Computer-Mediated Neo-Pagan Religious Meaning', Unpublished paper (1995).

A. Giddens, *Modernity and Self-identity. Self and Society in the Late Modern Age* (Cambridge: Polity Press UK, 1991).

J. K. Hadden and D. E. Cowan (eds.), *Religion on the Internet. Research Prospects and Promises* (Amsterdam, London and New York: JAI Press, 2000).

S. C. Herring, 'The Rhetorical Dynamics of Gender Harassment Online', *The Information Society* 3 (1999), pp. 151–68.

S. M. Hoover, *Mass Media Religion* (London: Sage, 1988).

S. M. Hoover and K. Lundby (eds.), *Rethinking Religion, Media and Culture* (Thousand Oaks, CA: Sage, 1997).

E. Larsen (principal author). 'Wired Churches, Wired Temples: Taking Congregations and Missions into Cyberspace', Report from the *Pew Internet & American Life Project*, Washington, DC, (2000) www.pew internet.org/

A. G. Linderman, 'The Reception of Religious Television: Social Semeiology applied to an Empirical Case Study', *Acta Universitatis*

Upsaliensis, Psychologia et Sociologia Religionum 12 (Stockholm: Almqvist & Wiksell, 1996).

A. Linderman, 'Making Sense of Religion in Television', S. M. Hoover and K. Lundby (eds.), *Rethinking Religion, Media and Culture* (Thousand Oaks, CA: Sage, 1997), pp. 263–83.

S. D. O'Leary, 'Cyberspace as Sacred Space. Communicating Religion on Computer Networks', *Journal of the American Academy of Religion* 64 (1996), pp. 781–808.

S. D. O'Leary and B. Brasher, 'The Unknown God of the Internet: Religious Communication from the Ancient Agora to the Virtual Forum', C. Ess (ed.) *Philosophical Perspectives on Computer-Mediated Communication* (Albany, NY: SUNY Press, 1996) pp. 238–63.

R. Schroeder, N. Heather and R. M. Lee, 'The Sacred and The Virtual: Religion in Multi-User Virtual Reality', *Journal of Computer Mediated Communication* 4 (1998) www.ascusc.org/jcmc/vol4/issue2/schroeder.html

J. Slevin, *The Internet and Society* (Cambridge: Polity Press UK, 2000).

M. A. Smith and P. Kollock (eds.), *Communities in Cyberspace* (London and New York: Routledge, 1999).

S. Turkle, *Life on the Screen. Identity in the Age of the Internet* (New York: Simon & Schuster, 1995).

B. Wellman and M. Gulia, 'Virtual Communities as Communities. Netsurfers Don't Ride Alone', M. A. Smith and P. Kollock (eds.), *Communities in Cyberspace* (London and New York: Routledge 1999), pp. 67–162.

21

The Decent Society and Cyberspace

Cees Hamelink

Choices

Whatever breathtaking advances technological innovations offer, they are never without trouble. Technology inevitably brings both great benefits and awesome risks. This essential ambivalence raises a challenging question about human governance of technological development. Can a balance be struck between progress and plague? How should social choices be made to shape technology towards humanitarian aspirations? Choices have to be made about the design, development and innovation of technology. Choices have to be made among a range of possible applications. Choices have to be made about the usage of such applications. These choices can have far-reaching and long-lasting effects upon individual lives, societies, and even the sustainability of all life on earth. Social choices are particularly urgent in the light of the very real social risks the pervasive application of cyberspace technology implies.

Cyberspace

Science-fiction author William Gibson invented the term cyberspace in 1981 to describe a new, virtual world. It is 'a consensual hallucination experienced daily by billions of legitimate operators, in every nation, by children being taught mathematical concepts ... a graphic representation of data abstracted from the banks of every computer in the human system ...'[1] John Perry Barlow, one of the founders of the Electronic Frontier Foundation, and lyrics writer for the pop group Grateful Dead, referred to cyberspace as 'that place you are in when you are talking on the telephone'.[2]

Cyberspace is a geographically unlimited, non-physical space independent of time, distance and location in which transactions take place between

---

[1] D. B. Whittle, *Cyberspace. The Human Dimension* (New York: W. B. Freeman, 1997), p. 4.

[2] Whittle, *Cyberspace*, p. 6.

people, between computers and between people and computers. Characteristic of cyberspace is the impossibility of pointing to the precise place and time where an activity occurs or where information traffic happens to be.

We participate in cyberspace whenever we surf on the Web, but also when our personal data get stored in a databank, when we pay with a credit card, reserve a seat on a flight, or when neurologists make a three-dimensional computer scan of our brains. It is important to note that there is no single cyberspace. There are 'cyberspaces'. People live, love, play and work in multiple virtual spaces that are sometimes complementary and sometimes conflicting.

Cyberspace encompasses all forms of computer-mediated communications and thus consists of six components:

- digital computers (from laptops to expert systems)
- networks that connect telephones and fax machines through digital electronics
- digitally operated transportation systems (such as cars, trains, airplanes, elevators)
- digitally operated control systems, such as are applied in chemical processes, health care or energy provision
- digitally operated appliances such as watches, microwave ovens and video recorders
- digitally operated robots that independently run automated systems

Cyberspace creates the fictional world in which most of today's financing takes place. Through cyberspace flow 2 trillion dollars daily in a complex money game.

Since more and more objects are provided with digital facilities, they acquire forms of intelligence, can communicate with each other (the toaster with the microwave oven, for example), and thus create a permanent virtual space in which time and space lose their absolute significance. Business is done outside hours and off the physical premises, prisoners can be surveyed from outside the prison without their knowledge.

Unequal access to cyberspace technology

Cyberspace is rapidly expanding across the globe, but in highly unequal ways. There are today stark inequalities in both access and use. 'The network society is creating parallel communication systems: one for those with income, education and (literally) connections, giving plentiful information at low cost and high speed; the other for those without connections, blocked by high barriers of time, cost and uncertainty and dependent on outdated information.'[3]

[3] UNDP (United Nations Development Programme), *Human Development Report 1999* (New York: Oxford University Press, 1999), p. 63.

Unequal access holds for all new networks and services. In rich countries one finds 84 per cent of the population are users of cellular phones, 91 per cent of fax machines, and 97 per cent of all Internet host computers.[4] In 1999 there were an estimated 170 million people with access to the Internet. This represents some 4 per cent of the world population. Over 80 per cent are in North America and Europe. Access to the global network society is available mainly to those with good education and those living in the OECD countries with sufficient disposable income. In most countries men dominate access to the Internet and young people are more likely to have access than the elderly. Ethnicity is an important factor, and in many countries the differences in use by ethnic groups has widened. 'English is used in almost 80 per cent of web sites and in the common user interfaces – the graphics and instructions. Yet fewer than one in ten people worldwide speaks the language.'[5]

A particularly skewed distribution of ICT (information and communication technologies) resources and uses concerns the position of women across the world. An immediate problem is the fact that ICT skills are largely based on literacy. Actually, 'it seems likely that the vast majority of the illiterate population will be excluded from the emerging knowledge societies'.[6] This affects women especially, since around the world illiteracy rates for women are higher than for men. According to the latest data from UNICEF, there are, among one billion illiterates in the world, some 130 million children. Among these kids for whom there are no schools, two out of every three in the developing world are girls.[7]

The digital vulnerability

Where cyberspace is more readily available, its many different applications ranging from electronic mail to e-commerce pervade a wide range of social domains and have serious impact on national economies and private lives. As more and more social domains (like banking, telecommunications, air traffic or energy supply) become dependent upon cyberspace technology, society's vulnerability to malfunctioning of the technological infrastructure raises the possibility of serious destabilisation. Among the possible causes are software failures and deliberate destruction of computer systems.

We find today that digital systems are applied in a wide variety of applications, from microwave ovens to cockpits of airplanes. Such systems are guided by software. This implies that the instructions for the actions that systems must perform are written in thousands of rules in a computer

[4] OECD (1998), *Cross-ownership and Convergence: Policy Issues*, DSTI/ICCP/TISP (98)3/Final, Paris, OECD.

[5] UNDP, p. 62.

[6] R. Mansell and U. Wehn, *Knowledge Societies. Information Technology for Sustainable Development* (Oxford: Oxford University Press, 1998), p. 35.

[7] UNICEF, State of the World's Children, (New York: United Nations, 1999).

programme. The obvious intention is that the systems do precisely what they are instructed to do. Often this works well. But all computer users are familiar with the nuisance of computer programmes that malfunction or with programmes that upon their installation delete existing software. Since even the simple PC is never fully reliable, users are constantly advised to make so-called 'backups'.

In general, it has to be said that digital systems are unreliable. In many big projects, the software demonstrates serious flaws. In 1992 the manager of British Nuclear Fuels announced that in an essential part of the system's software several thousands of errors had been detected, hundreds of which pose a serious threat to the secure operation of the company.[8] Such problems have been known since the 1960s but have still not been satisfactorily resolved.

Much work is at present being done to improve the reliability of essential software. All kinds of control mechanisms are being explored that would detect failures much earlier. The production of software has certainly improved in recent years and will be further refined by the application of more strict methodologies in software design. One important problem in this context is that measures to make software more secure always cost time and money. There is always the need to balance these costs against the consequences of possible failure. However it is not possible to completely avoid errors. Error-free software remains, possibly forever, a dream.

Virus and warfare

Some risks to security are caused by deliberate efforts to wreak damage in computer systems. Acts of digital vandalism may include denial of service attacks whereby outsiders instruct computer systems to crash. Special programmes (among them WinNuke) have been designed to send so much information to other computers that they stop functioning. The popular Microsoft operating system Windows is particularly vulnerable to such attacks as it makes it fairly easy for outsiders to infiltrate hard disks as soon as users log on to the Internet. Computer security is the essential topic in current debates on new forms of warfare. The development of digitally run weapons systems makes 'cyberwar' an attractive and 'clean' alternative to conventional armed conflicts. A deceptive aspect, though, is that in a digital war there may be fewer victims in the short term than with old-fashioned bombing, but the numbers of victims will rapidly increase as the effects of cyberwar set in. A successful digital attack would, among other things, lead to disruption of the provision of electricity and water. A cyberattack could close all international communications of a country, render all air traffic impossible, sabotage the provision of electricity and water, paralyse the country's financial system. A scary prospect is the possibility that organised

[8] J. Leslie, *The End of the World* (London: Routledge, 1996), p. 95.

crime or terrorist groups equip themselves with cyberspace weapons. Societies that apply many digital systems are extremely vulnerable to 'cyberterror'. With relatively simple tools the key functions of such societies can be disrupted.

Surveillance in cyberspace

In many countries electronic surveillance is mushrooming. As Gumpert and Drucker formulate, 'the sanctity of privacy has been eroded by the increasing intrusion of the technology of surveillance.'[9] This happens through video cameras in public spaces, bugging of telephone calls, credit card firms, scanners in supermarkets, 'cookies' on the World Wide Web and international spy satellites. As the scope of 'surveillance' in a society grows, the confidentiality of communications diminishes. Digitisation renders surveillance easy and attractive. It facilitates what governments have always wanted to do: to collect as much information as possible about those they govern. Because of technological limitations this was always a difficult job. However, recent technological innovations have made grand scale spying rather simple. One consequence is that the trading of surveillance technology from rich to poor countries has become an attractive sideline for the world's arms traders. Digitisation facilitates the monitoring of all communications through fax machines, telephones (particularly mobile phones) and computers. It has become technically relatively easy to register all traffic that uses Global System for Mobile Communication (GSM) cellular telephones. Swiss telecom operator Swisscom admitted at the end of 1997 that it had registered the communications traffic of more than one million users of cellular phones in the GSM network. In other European countries also, police forces use the technical possibility to establish the presence of mobile telephones. The computer systems of telecom service providers can register where mobile phones are, even when they are not used for calls but switched on to receive voice mail.

According to the report 'An Appraisal of the Technologies of Political Control',[10] the US National Security Agency (NSA) surveillance through the use of intelligence searches the communications traffic of European politicians and citizens. The British research bureau Omega Foundation (in Manchester) prepared this report for the European Commission. The report found that the US espionage computer network 'ECHELON' detects keywords in military and political information as well as in economic information used by commercial firms, and stores relevant data for later analysis. For a long time there had been indications of eavesdropping on world

---

[9] G. Gumpert and S. Drucker, 'The Demise of Privacy in a Private World: From Front Porches to Chat Rooms', *Communication Theory* 8 (4) (1998), p. 409.

[10] 'An Appraisal of the Technologies of Political Control', The US National Security Agency (February 1998).

communication networks by the NSA, and the Omega report provided the evidence. The British-American surveillance programme targets all the Internet satellites that carry the major portion of worldwide telephone calls, fax communications and Internet traffic. The main justification is the struggle against terrorism and crime. There is, however, little hard evidence that there are indeed positive law enforcement effects. In the meantime European Parliament members were informed that the NSA routinely intercepts valuable private commercial data about investments, tenders and mergers. Besides ECHELON there is also an EU–FBI surveillance system (for police, security and immigration services) that facilitates interception of worldwide communications by the US National Security Agency. In September 1998 the European Parliament discussed the NSA surveillance and adopted a consensus resolution asking for more openness and accountability for electronic spying activities.

Interestingly enough, in early 1999 a working group of the European Parliament proposed the establishment of an extensive tapping network for police and intelligence organisations to intercept all telecommunication traffic among citizens and companies. According to the working group, the permanent surveillance of all data traffic in real time is a 'must' for law enforcement purposes. In May 1999 the European Parliament resolved to approve the establishment of a comprehensive surveillance system for all European telecommunications traffic on mobile phones, faxes, pagers and the Internet. The electronic system that is being designed for this massive interception programme will track data on phone numbers, email addresses, credit card details, PIN codes and passwords. Also in 1999 the European Parliament was informed[11] about the planning by the NSA, the FBI and the European Union through the International Law Enforcement Telecommunication Seminar of a vast surveillance network that would combine national security and law enforcement activities.

In many of the digitally advanced countries the state has a strong desire to monitor civil electronic communications. The crucial argument is that although this violates people's privacy it is inevitable to guarantee security. As state institutions can compose rather precise profiles of the communications traffic of their citizens, the inequality in power relations between states and citizens increases. The civil claim to the confidentiality of personal communications is violated and the principle of information security is seriously eroded. The permanent surveillance of people hampers their free participation in communication and information traffic. When personal data about individuals are collected, processed, stored and retrieved without their consent, their information security is under threat.

Information security also means that people are free to determine what information about themselves they want to share with others. The standard implies that others cannot gather information about people without their consent. In a decent society, citizens know who collects what information,

---

[11] Report to European Parliament, 'Interception Capabilities' (2000).

where, how and to what purpose about them. In this context, the notion of privacy-protection refers to the space that societies accord to individual autonomy. Even though there are important cultural variations in the appreciation of privacy, we can observe that in almost all societies people show the desire to have a small space where they can withdraw from the gaze of others. Also, most people will keep at least some of their personal secrets to themselves. It is also a sensible strategy that we keep some thoughts about others to ourselves and do not share all our thinking with them. If we did not do this, there would be even more civil wars in the world. This protection of the intimate sphere of human life has to be balanced with participation in social networks.

The individual preference to be left alone conflicts with the wish of societal institutions to gather information about the individual. The development of digital technologies has increased the tension of this conflict and made it more urgent. The protection of personal data has always been a difficult challenge, but with recent developments such as the Internet the effort has become very discouraging. Information about how people use the Net is collected though a variety of means (such as the so-called 'cookies'), and each act in cyberspace contains the real danger of privacy intrusion. Using electronic mail, for example, inevitably implies a considerable loss of control over one's privacy unless users are trained in the use of encryption techniques and as long as law does not prohibit these. Engaging in cyberspace transactions implies we leave a digital trace through credit cards, bonus cards and client cards. And as online transactions grow, the collecting of personal data will increase. Not only is it attractive for entrepreneurs to know the preferences of their clients, it is also lucrative to sell such data to third parties. Acquiring data about people's biogenetical profiles as well as consumer data can be of great value to, among others, insurance companies. The combined information about high blood pressure and the purchase of alcoholic beverages helps the insurer to define the level of risks and therefore the amounts the client will pay for the insurance policy.

Today we face a rapid proliferation and globalisation of uncontrollable forms of electronic control by law enforcement agencies and commercial companies. The current practices of both governments (the increasing use of surveillance technologies for law enforcement and national security purposes) and commercial companies (the use of surveillance technologies for management purposes and the use of data mining technologies for marketing purposes) erode the principle of information security. In connection with the protection of privacy, there are only very general legal principles as codified in human rights agreements and regional agreements (under such institutions as the OECD or the Council of Europe). There are no effective global rules and institutions and no globally co-ordinated efforts to protect information security.

The issue of sustainability

An important concern that has arisen in connection with the possible proliferation of digital technologies across the world, is the question of whether
cyberspace technology can be applied in environmentally sustainable ways.
If, as a result of the deployment of digital technologies, economic productivity increases, does this imply that levels of consumption also increase?
And, is this an acceptable course from the perspective of sustainable
development? It would seem naïve to assume that the mere deployment of
cyberspace technology implies the sustainable development of societies.
There are both environmentally positive and negative scenarios.

When information replaces tangible goods, production processes
could emerge with lower levels of environmental pollution. However, the
rise in economic productivity (even assuming this could be done with
lower pollution levels per unit produced), implies the strong likelihood
that more industrial output leads to higher levels of consumption and
therefore, in the end, to more pollution.[12] If, for example, one assumes
that digital technologies would improve the productivity of the automo-
bile industry, then even if cars were manufactured with lower levels of
pollution, the overall increase in car purchase and use would probably
lead to overall higher pollution levels. The core problem with a more
equitable global access to cyberspace technology is that this would
increase the level of energy use (per capita) in the developing countries
to the average levels in the rich countries. As Makridakis[13] suggests, 'it is
doubtful that the climatic equilibrium of the earth can be sustained' if
this were to happen. The global use of digital technology would also
drastically increase the emission of carbon dioxide (by printers, copiers
and computers) to environmentally untenable levels. Providing more
access to more cyberspace technology implies producing more computers. The production of a single PC requires approximately as much
energy as the average electricity consumption of a mid-European
household per year.[14]

IBM presented a technology in 1998 that makes it possible to diminish
the energy use of chips. The production of low-energy chips is primarily
intended for the cellular phone market. For some time to come most computers (with Pentium processors and Microsoft operating systems) will function without such chips. With the ever higher speeds at which they operate,
their energy use will increase. PCs are obsolete after three to four years, and
the question is what to do with a rapidly growing mountain of electronic
garbage that contains all kinds of poisonous materials like PVC, bromide,

[12] P. Jokinen, 'The Promise of the Information Society for Sustainable Development',
Paper for the Conference on Challenges of Sustainable Development', University of
Amsterdam (22–25 August 1996).
[13] S. Makridakis, 'The forthcoming information revolution: its impact on society and
firms', *Futures* (27 August, 1995), p. 800.
[14] P. Jokinen, 'The Promise of the Information Society'.

antimony, lead and cadmium.[15] All this has to be seen in the light of an expanding world population which could by the mid-twenty-first century amount to some 8 to 10 billion people. For policy makers this may be one of the toughest questions: can a global digital grid, accessible for all, be combined with environmentally sustainable development?

Fun shopping in the electronic shopping mall

The Internet has begun to attract the attention of the major forces in the global market place, as it has been discovered as a major vehicle for commercial advertising. Money-making on the Net will require turning it into an advertising medium. In order for companies to re-coup their enormous investments, advertising and sales will be essential. The competition to attract advertising dollars is already on its way. The World Wide Web has begun to target children who go online as potential consumers and asks them to fill in questionnaires that provide good marketing profiles.

With the largest players preparing themselves for the interactive possibilities of digital networks and the Hollywood majors and companies like Time Warner and News Corporation getting ready for grand investments to ride the information superhighway, a communicative structure that so far has been public, non-commercial, un-regulated, un-censored, anarchistic and very pluralistic may soon turn into a global electronic shopping mall and become the world's largest advertising medium. Global advertising proclaims a single cultural standard for the world: consumption fulfils people's basic aspirations and fun shopping is an essential cultural activity. It subjects all the world's cultural differences to the dominance of a consumption-oriented lifestyle. People's fundamental cultural identity is that of consumer. Global advertising teaches people around the world the values of materialism and the practices of consumerism. As markets open worldwide and more advertising for consumer products arrives, there develops an explosive disparity between visibility and availability around the world. In the global shopping mall the world spent some 24 trillion dollars in 1998 on consumer expenditures. Over 80 per cent of this was spent by 20 per cent of the world's population. The result is that the global shopping mall has many clients who merely gawk and only a few that can buy. This is likely to create an enormously dangerous social fragmentation.

The cyborg species

Let us assume that new types of human intelligence could be developed that would be superior to the capacities of the human species. The

---

[15] J. Malley, *Introductory Paper*, Telecommunications and Sustainability Workshop at the Conference on Challenges of Sustainable Development, Amsterdam (22–25 August, 1996).

confrontation between the human being and the humanoid digital system (the 'cyborg') creates a fundamentally new situation for moral philosophy. The cyborg presupposes a development by which digital electronics is deployed within the human body and human brainpower is linked to cybernetic systems. This would seem to belong to the realm of science fiction, and there is indeed no possibility of predicting with any certainty which forms of digital life this might lead us to. Since there are no indications that human beings will be held back by moral considerations in the search for 'virtual people', one cannot discard the possibility of the evolution of a new humanoid species more intelligent than human beings. This would raise the prospect of a future in which the human species is no longer needed.

The decent society

Like any other technology, cyberspace has both positive and negative potential. The negative dimensions have so far been highlighted because in many treatises on the subject, the attention gravitates towards the socially beneficial applications. Indeed, there are in many different fields, from commerce, to health care and education, many benefits to be expected as the result of a technology that significantly lowers the costs and increases speed and ease of global communications.

If, however, the risks are not taken seriously, indulging in prophecies about future benefits may be wasting our time. A society that would deal responsibly with future technological developments and applications should realise that the core of the matter is indeed not the technology itself but the quality of its governance. A characteristic of the decent society is that its governance of technology will be guided by Article 28 of the Universal Declaration of Human Rights. This declares that 'everyone is entitled to a social and international order in which the rights and freedoms set forth in this Declaration can be fully realised'. This claim is equally valid for the organisation of physical as well as of virtual societies. The relevant question is thus which standards should guide the social and international order that guarantees the protection of human rights and freedoms in cyberspace?

In recent years the notion of 'good governance' has become very fashionable in international development co-operation. In this context it has often amounted to a rather paternalistic assessment of the performance of governments in poor countries by standards such as respect for human rights, rule of law, multi-party democracy and accountable administration. To judge one's partners by standards of social morality seems in itself a useful idea lest one ends up with parties that demonstrate more talent for corruption and gross human rights violations than for sustainable social development. However, within the framework of international human rights law such standards would apply equally to all the parties involved. They would thus be the moral measure for governments in both poor and rich countries, for intergovernmental development agencies, but also for non-state actors such as transnational corporations and the development assistance non-governmental organisations (NGOs). This is not the case today. International institutions such as the IMF and the World Bank have in the past years not contributed to the development of democratic institutions in poor countries. Most of their programmes have rather undermined such institutions.[16] They have also themselves not been paragons of democratic governance.[17] One also finds in the world of the NGOs a lack of public accountability and democratic structure that rivals authoritarian government institutions.[18] Equally, most global business corporations do not live up to the standards of good governance. Moreover, development assistance agencies tend to be most cavalier in applying good governance standards in countries where they hurt good business prospects.

Key requirements for good governance of cyberspace

The international human rights bodies point to a democratic organisation of societies as a prerequisite for the realisation of human rights. Human rights cannot be realised without involving citizens in the decision-making processes about the spheres in which freedom and equality are to be achieved. This moves the democratic process beyond the political sphere and extends the requirement of participatory institutional arrangements to other social domains. It claims that culture and technology should be also subject to democratic control. This is particularly important in the light of the fact that current democratisation processes (the 'new world order' processes) tend to delegate important areas of social life to private rather than to public control and accountability. Increasingly large volumes of social activity are withdrawn from public accountability, from democratic control, and from the participation of citizens in decision-making.

The requirement of broad participation in social decision-making processes needs to be complemented with the requirement of public accountability. The Universal Declaration of Human Rights (1948) states in Article 1: 'All human beings are born free and equal in dignity and rights. They are endowed with reason and conscience and should act towards one another in a spirit of brotherhood.' This conception of the human being as gifted with reason and conscience leads to the obligation of accountability. The gift of reason and conscience means that people can know what they are doing, can reflect on their actions in terms of normative categories, and can

---

[16] D. C. Korten, *When Corporations Rule the World* (West Hartford, CT: Kumarian, 1995), p. 171.

[17] Korten, *When Corporations Rule*, p. 165.

[18] See J. Mertus, *Human Rights and the Promise of Transnational Civil Society*, B. H. Westen and S. P. Marks (eds.), *The Future of International Human Rights* (New York, Transnational, 1999), pp. 452–4. Also A. Colas, *International Civil Society* (Oxford: Polity, 2002), p. 155 and passim.

thus be held responsible for what they are doing! They should act in a certain way ('in a spirit of brotherhood' which could be translated as 'with compassion') and can be held accountable for their conduct. If one accepts the position that government institutions and business corporations are 'moral agents', then they can and should be held accountable by those who are affected by their moral choices.

In line with the proposal to base social morality upon the normative standards of internationally adopted human rights and freedoms, the social and international order within which this can be realised should be guided by global governance 'with a human face'. At a minimum this implies that global governance of cyberspace should have democratic and inclusive structures and should recognise the public responsibility of all participators.

This conflicts with the observation that there is presently a widening gap between the domains of technological development and political decision-making.[19] As Ulrich Beck notes, 'Faith in progress replaces voting.'[20] The development of biotechnology provides a good illustration. Scientists and investors cooperate to produce artificial tissue, blood vessels and organs such as hearts and livers. Charles Vacanti, a top scientist in the field of 'regenerative' medicine thinks enough experimentation has been carried out with animals. It is time to begin the renovation of human beings. *Business Week* expects that the bio-industry will soon bring a veritable 'body shop' with human spare parts on the market.[21] Irrespective of possible advantages versus disadvantages, the whole process evolves outside any form of social control. The German sociologist Beck points out that social concerns and anxieties about developments in genetic technology have no impact on the real decisions in this domain. These decisions have already been taken because the question of whether certain developments were socially desirable was never posed. 'One can say "no" to progress, but that does not change its course at all.'[22] This course is determined outside the political domain. Policies on technology are not made by the political system. 'No votes are taken in parliament on the employment and development of microelectronics, genetic technology or the like; at most it might vote on supporting them in order to protect the country's economic future (and jobs). It is precisely the intimate connection between decisions on technological development and those on investment, which forces the industries to forge their plans in secret for reasons of competition. Consequently, decisions only reach the desks of politicians and the public sphere after being taken.'[23]

There is today a worldwide trend for governments to delegate the responsibility for basic social choices to the marketplace. The democratic

---

[19] L. Winner, 'Citizen Virtues in a Technological Order', E. R. Winkler and J. R. Coombs (eds.), *Applied Ethics* (Oxford: Blackwell, 1993), p. 61.

[20] U. Beck, *Risk Society. Towards a New Modernity* (London: Sage, 1992), p. 214.

[21] *Business Week*, Editorial: 'Bio-tech Bodies', 27 July 1998, pp. 42–49.

[22] Beck, *Risk Society*, p. 203.

[23] Beck, *Risk Society*, p. 213.

control of important social domains is thus increasingly eroded without any major societal debate. Following their desire to deregulate, liberalise and privatise, many governments are leaving the governance of the new information and communication technologies in the hands of private entrepreneurs. The European Commission's Action Plan, 'Europe's Way to the Information Society',[24] for example, states that European regulation must promote the mechanisms of the marketplace. The Commission proposes that through liberalisation a competitive climate can be created within which the forces of the market can freely operate. 'The creation of the information society will be entrusted to the private sector . . .'[25]

One implication is that the realisation of the social potential of cyberspace technology comes to depend more on investment decisions than on considerations of common welfare. For anyone who cherishes the democratic ideal, this is a regrettably short-sighted position that demonstrates a basic lack of democratic sensitivity. If democracy represents the notion that all people should participate in those decisions that shape their future welfare, such social forces as the new technologies cannot just be left to the interests and stakes of commercial parties on the market. If we are serious about the democratic nature of our societies, there should be public responsibility in such a crucial domain as the design, development and deployment of cyberspace technology.

Since the choices that are made in this domain have a far-reaching impact on societies, the political process requires the broadest possible participation of all those concerned. In other words, there is an urgent need for an extensive public dialogue about 'our common digital future'. The success of this dialogue will depend largely upon the degree to which societies are successful in teaching their members the 'culture of dialogue' which is the essence of a (communicative) democracy in which citizens deliberate and decide about the social choices they prefer. In order to effectively conduct this dialogue it is vital that participants learn to distance themselves from their common prejudices and certainties. They will also have to acquire the capability to judge social choices from a variety of perspectives. In a fundamental sense this dialogue is different from the conventional adversarial political debate where winning is essential and where all kinds of deceptive debating methods and tricks are used.

For the dialogue to be different from the debate, the participants should observe such rules as:

- Let others finish what they want to say.
- Ask questions instead of merely offering opinions.
- Do not think against but with each other.
- First analyse, then offer solutions.
- State what you really think.

[24] European Commission's Action Plan, 'Europe's Way to the Information Society' (Brussels, 17 July 1994).
[25] As above, p. 10.

Even such seemingly simplistic rules are not normally applied in daily practice. They require that people learn the skills of the culture of dialogue. In
this learning process the Socratic method is a crucial tool. The essence of
Socratic thought is found in a statement Socrates makes during his defence
before the Athenian judges. He proposes that the unexamined life is not
worth living.

This is the mindset of preparation for the 'culture of dialogue' that the
democratic process requires. It means that the deliberating citizens should
be able to distance themselves from their own assumptions. They need the
capacity to reason through their own positions and justify their preferences.
This requires 'Socratic qualities' of all participants in the dialogue. The
American philosopher Martha Nussbaum argues this in her book
Cultivating Humanity. She writes, 'In order to foster a democracy that is
reflective and deliberative, rather than simply a marketplace of competing
interest groups, a democracy that genuinely takes thought for the common
good, we must produce citizens who have the Socratic capacity to reason
about their beliefs.'[26] For Socrates the critical investigation of our own
assumptions is the essence of all serious reflection. Socrates establishes that
our positions are often more determined by beliefs than by knowledge and
we often fail to explain these beliefs. The Socratic approach does not ignore
the significance of factual knowledge, but wants to explore its meaning.
Socrates is in search of wisdom, and therefore he asks whether we know
what our knowledge represents. His investigations ruthlessly reveal that we
often talk about matters we have little understanding of and that frequently
we do not even understand our own thinking.

Conclusion

Whether societies will deal responsibly with the future potential of cyberspace technology will be determined by the mental maps that guide their
moral choices. These could be defined by the market-centred culture of
money or by the people-centred culture of human rights. At the core of the
prevailing neo-liberal world order stands the belief in the constructive role
market forces play in the realisation of a decent society. The common reasoning goes as follows. The society that respects the defence of human
rights is a democratic society. Democracy is a political arrangement in
which people's needs and aspirations are freely expressed. The market is an
economic arrangement by which people's needs and aspirations are satisfied. A marriage made in heaven! But is the market the perfect tool for a
democratic social order? The trouble is that the market caters to the needs
and aspirations only of those people who can pay for their satisfaction. The
market is selective and exclusive in its treatment of people, whereas a

---

[26] M. C. Nussbaum, *Cultivating Humanity. A Classical Defense of Reform in Liberal
Education*, (Cambridge: Harvard University Press, 1997), p. 19.

human rights-inspired democratic order should be inclusive and egalitarian. Moreover, the market does not meet all needs and aspirations equally well. It prioritises some needs and aspirations over others. Priorities are not determined by substantial moral standards such as human security but by monetary value. Those needs and aspirations that can be defined in hard monetary terms are the definite winners. Characteristic of 'free market' societies is the 'money culture' that judges all human activity in terms of its monetary value.

Everything is provided with a price tag: even basic resources, such as water, air, maternal care, security, time. Everything can be acquired through money and can be traded in against more money. In this culture people engage in contractual and calculating relations with each other. Its greatest problem is the totalitarian nature of the money culture. It is worldwide the most prominent model for the organisation of societies. As a result the relations that people have in the market place spill over into domains such as education, health care, care for the elderly, science and culture. By applying market principles in more and more social domains people are not merely calculating consumers, but become calculating citizens. This poses a serious obstacle to the implementation of a human rights-based type of governance. On the market people entertain contractual relations because they expect to gain from these exchanges. Within this mental map human rights fit only in so far as respect for them yields a profit. It holds little promise for a decent governance of cyberspace!

It is essential to a humanitarian future of cyberspace that societies adopt the moral guidance of a human rights culture. Given the currently prevailing neo-liberal political agenda, this would seem a tall order indeed. However, there is a great deal of serious concern in the world about the possible consequences of this agenda. Social activists from around the globe have recently expressed this in Seattle, Washington, Nice, Prague and Davos. It would not seem unrealistic to hope that this civil promotion of a global humanitarian agenda may also affect the development of cyberspace technology!

Further reading

Barnet and Cavanagh, *Global Dreams: Imperial Corporations and the New World Order* (New York: Simon & Schuster, 1994).

U. Beck, *Risk Society. Towards a New Modernity* (London: Sage, 1992).

G. Gumpert and S. Drucker, 'The Demise of Privacy in a Private World: From Front Porches to Chat Rooms,' *Communication Theory* 8 (4) (1998), pp. 408–25.

C. Hamelink, *The Ethics of Cyberspace* (London: Sage, 2000).

D. C. Korten, *When Corporations Rule the World* (West Hartford, CT: Kumarian, 1995).

J. Leslie, *The End of the World* (London: Routledge, 1996).

S. Makridakis, 'The forthcoming information revolution: its impact on society and firms', *Futures* (27 August 1995), pp. 799–821.

J. Malley, *Introductory Paper*, Telecommunications and Sustainability Workshop at the Conference on Challenges of Sustainable Development, Amsterdam (22–25 August, 1996).

R. Mansell and U. Wehn, *Knowledge Societies. Information Technology for Sustainable Development* (Oxford: Oxford University Press, 1998).

M. C. Nussbaum, *Cultivating Humanity. A Classical Defense of Reform in Liberal Education*, (Cambridge: Harvard University Press, 1997).

OECD, *Cross-ownership and Convergence: Policy Issues*, DSTI/ICCP/TISP (98)3/Final, (Paris: OECD, 1998).

UNDP (United Nations Development Programme) *Human Development Report 1999* (New York: Oxford University Press, 1999).

UNICEF, *State of the World's Children*, (New York: United Nations, 1999).

D. B. Whittle, *Cyberspace. The Human Dimension* (New York: W. B. Freeman, 1997).

L. Winner, 'Citizen Virtues in a Technological Order', E. R. Winkler and J. R. Coombs (eds.), *Applied Ethics* (Oxford: Blackwell, 1993) pp. 46–68.

22

Myth and Ritual in Cyberspace

Gregor Goethals

Human history is uniquely marked by traces of myth and ritual. Sacred stories of the beginning and the beyond are found in all cultures, and ritual spaces range in complexity from simple ground paintings to magnificent architectural monuments. With the explosion of electronic visual communication came a transformation of the enactment of myth and ritual through the medium of television. Live TV images allowed people to 'transcend' time and space and 'gather' collectively and individually before the screen for common 'participation' in sports, entertainment events and religious services. Does cyberspace now offer a more authentic, intensive ritualistic participation? Has the Web become a major source for meaningful stories around which communities are formed?

Discerning myth and ritual in cyberspace will depend very much upon how these forms of religious communication are defined and upon the expectations with which one enters the electronic universe. To aid our search, we will use some of the elements of religious ritual as they have been defined and mapped by scholars in anthropology and religious studies over the last two decades. These fundamental elements include: first, entry into specially designated zones of time and space; second, the attentive, dynamic engagement of persons in a participatory event; third, the formation of community which emerges from shared attentiveness and participation in symbolic temporal and spatial zones; fourth, a renewal of spirit experienced by individuals taking part in ritual.

In addition, some liturgical theologians would assert that ritual is the embodied enactment of myth, the form through which it is most meaningfully experienced. Moreover, for some theorists, though certainly not all, there is no 'ritual' as such apart from an engagement with a divine, transcendent order of being.

I suspect that these last two elements will be the most problematic in our search for electronic ritual in mass media and in cyberspace. As we explore and critique sites in cyberspace, we will refer back to these structural elements to inform and organise our inquiry.

Electronic transformations of traditional ritual space and time

Before the development of the Web, earlier media technologies, first radio and later television, demonstrated that the enclosed time and space of traditional religious or political rituals could be transformed and enlarged to include hundreds of thousands of people. Although situated in many different time zones and distant places, people could 'enter' the extraordinary time and space of ritual. Through their television monitors they were able to experience a sense of 'being there'.

Video cameras, for example, became portals through which ordinary individuals could, to some degree, move into and be 'present' at the coronation of Queen Elizabeth or at the funeral of John F. Kennedy. For many Americans the shocking loss of a president was made more bearable by the communion of shared grief through uninterrupted televised images of the stately ceremonies.[1] In addition, television quickly began to reshape certain secular events and transform them into ritual-like occasions. Popular sports in particular lent themselves to such ritualisation. Each year the Super Bowl, for example, becomes a secular hallowed space, not simply for Americans but for people worldwide. Similarly, televised matches of World Cup competitions enable fans around the globe to enter its 'sacred' zones of time and space. Animated TV viewers 'take their place' alongside the cheering crowds in the stadium and collectively experience a feeling of community. Like ancient rites, the telecast games galvanise the attention of disparate individuals, evoking feelings of belonging and egalitarianism. One commentator referred to the televised soccer matches as the great 'equaliser,' drawing millions of diverse ethnic, national, religious and social groups into a collective whole.

Are some web sites doing the same thing? Do they offer more or less? One fundamental difference, of course, is that millions of individuals turn on their computers and log on to particular sites, setting up their own customised spatial and temporal zones. The sites are constantly out there in cyberspace, but people choose diverse, separate moments of entry. We may contrast this solitary approach with the gathering of friends around the TV monitor in a local pub, awaiting the opening of a soccer match.

We will now examine a few web sites. Although different in style and focus, they share a concern for the life of the spirit and take myth seriously. Some are created by specific religious institutions. Others have no religious affiliation; yet they feature mythologies and often give vision and voice to a spiritual dimension of life. All offer an opportunity for engagement and response. Ultimately, however, an evaluation of these sites as ritual spaces will depend upon the structural and theological elements one considers absolutely essential.

---

[1] G. Goethals, *The TV Ritual: Worship at the Video Altar* (Boston: Beacon, 1981).

A functionalist perspective: social cohesion and identification

A functionalist concept of religion is perhaps the most inclusive. It allows the broadest spectrum for defining and identifying mythic and ritualistic components in a secular society.[2] Some theorists thus use ritual as an analogical lens through which we observe and analyse events and gatherings of various sorts. From this perspective, we may refer to participation on web sites as 'ritual-like', even if there is nothing inherently sacred in the time, space or participatory events. Emphasising a functionalist perspective enables us to recognise the importance of shared symbols for the formation and maintenance of community. Bracketing the transcendent element of ritual, we underscore the power of particular web sites to identify and reinforce shared beliefs and commitments.

In focusing on the functional elements of ritual, we shift the emphasis from theological mystery in ritual to its power to promote and maintain certain values and thus to foster a community of shared interests. In this respect, we can identify a number of sites which feature various cyberspace myths and offer opportunities for ritualistic experiences. Viewers are encouraged to return repeatedly to the site for changing information, entertainment or shopping.

Following this overview we then turn to an evaluation of cyber myth and ritual from two theological perspectives.

(i) The Millennium Matters: www.mm2000.nu/intro.html

On its home page (see Fig. 5) this site is described as a 'repository of source material and information about the new millennium'. Icons at the bottom identify specific topics and enable the viewer to navigate throughout the site. Clicking on the icon 'Spirit', for example, takes us to 'Matters of Spirit', which 'explores the many manifestations of spirit'. In this section, we discover 'voices old and new' which share experiences of spirituality. 'Envision yourself as a seeker on a journey. You meet other colourful and learned wayfarers along the paths. Gather with them in a sacred circle as they share their stories with you. Approach the fire and listen with respect to guidance from the Elders.' This page lists other areas to explore, such as 'The Himalayan Gardens', 'where we may share the insights of the editors and spiritual family regarding the matters of Spirit'.

The 'Vision' icon takes us to 'The Vision of Temenos', which seeks to establish a philosophical foundation for living in harmony with the world ecosystems. On this page we may select 'Gaia', for example, which features 'scientific bases for learning about our changing earth and skies'. Another major section, 'Earth Prophecy', juxtaposes prophecy and prediction with

---

[2] B. Wilson, *Religion in Sociological Perspective* (New York: Oxford, 1982). See chapter 2, 'The Functions of Religion in Contemporary Society'.

Figure 5   The Millennium Matters home page

facts about today's changing earth. Finally, The Millennium Matters has its own shopping center. We reach it by clicking on an icon, 'MISC'. The 'MM Bazarre' is described as 'a cyber vision of the old-fashioned bazarre [sic], the global village's neighbourhood fair'. There we find 'good stuff from good people at good prices'.

(ii) Star Wars: www.starwars.com

Accessible in several languages, the web site is intended for people all over the world who remain captivated by the Lucas films. 'Starwars.com' is a gathering place in cyberspace for fans. It reinforces the continuing interest and involvement of viewers through an online comic, chat room, 'Star Wars News', and a storehouse of information about all the films. There is a feature in which George Lucas, in making his next film, 'shares some personally selected moments of the process' with those who log on. There is also a cyber shop where one finds toys, gifts, books and magazines.

In 1997, KQED Television in San Francisco aired an interview of George Lucas by Bill Moyers. At one point Moyers questioned Lucas: 'Is *Star Wars* the expression of a kind of religion?' Lucas dismissed the notion of *Star Wars* as a religion. At the same time, the filmmaker said that he saw the films as an opportunity to take the 'mysteries', the ancient myths and hero stories, and to communicate them in modern language. Inspired by his mentor, Joseph Campbell, Lucas described his work as a recasting, a re-creation of ancient myths to deal with the issues that exist today. Later in the interview, he reflected on the great theme of his movies, noting that *Star Wars* is about transformation. In the Lucas films evil is always redeemed.

These two sites, The Millennium Matters and Starwars, exemplify one dimension of a functionalist concept of religion: communicating and reinforcing mythological material with which viewers can identify. These cyber communities are easily accessible 'places' where viewers share stories and interests, and 'meet' like-minded individuals. While the chat-room conversations are largely anonymous, they nevertheless provide attentive viewers with an opportunity to express their commitments.

Are there, however, web sites oriented toward traditional religious beliefs and values? If so, what kinds of images, myths and rituals are associated with these? Do they mirror or transform historical forms of worship? How has cyber technology affected the accepted symbolic forms of religious communication?

The New Media Bible: www:newmediabible.org

In 1989 the American Bible Society established the Newmedia Project in its Translations Department to explore multimedia translations of biblical texts. The early experiments resulted in three CD-ROMs, and one of their translations, 'The Neighbor' (based on the parable of the Good Samaritan), was turned into a web site. On this site one can find a film translation of the parable, as well as historical background of the text, study guides and articles by biblical scholars.

One member of the creative team responsible for the music direction of the new translations, J. Ritter Werner, speculated that for Logos- or Word-centered worship, the Web may become an authentic ritual space, particularly for the 'ritual reading of biblical texts in the Judeo-Christian tradition'. For him, the Web is potentially a ritualistic event whenever a sacred text is central to worship. Werner notes that the key to the translation process lies in finding the auditory and visual analogies for aesthetic and other elements of Word-centered worship. Prescribed movements, liturgical prayers, music and environmental images can be analysed and transformed into new media translations. Collectively these linguistic and para-linguistic expressions may establish 'a ritual matrix in cyberspace that mirrors traditional Logos-worship'.[3]

Does the Web, however, provide religious communication for traditions which emphasise the centrality of Eucharistic liturgy? Can religious communities which are sacramental, rather than Word-centered, find Web communication useful? Various groups and individuals have created sites that highlight and reinforce forms of worship in which liturgy is paramount. We will look at two of these.

(i) Christworld: www.christworld.com

Even a brief glance at this site reveals a deep concern for the integration of the visual arts and meditation. For many years Fr. John Render and researchers at the Passionist Research Center in Chicago have built up a collection of religious images from Western and non-Western, folk and popular culture. The site now uses these images to establish a context for prayer and meditation based upon the drama and rhythm of the Christian liturgical year.

The site offerings displayed on the home page (see Fig. 6) include, for example, 'Stations of the Cross', 'Sunday Scripture and Meditations', along with weekly devotional images organised around the themes of 'Passion', 'Jesus', 'Mary', and 'Icons'. Each page provides viewers with text and images for reflection. While there are other features on this site, carefully selected religious symbols from all artistic traditions are its major feature. They are ordered to guide viewers through the Christian liturgical year and to focus and enrich their spiritual reflections.

---

[3] J. Ritter Werner, 'Sacred Scripture, Ritual, and Cyberspace', Unpublished paper (1998), pp. 8–9.

Weekly Images for 9/30/01

Passion | Jesus | Mary | Icon

CybeRetreat

Passionists Around the World

Spiritual Links

Awards

Passionist Research Center

Updated September 25, 2001

Figure 6   Christworld home page

(ii) The Monastery of Christ in the Desert: www.christdesert.org/pax.html

This web site is distinguished by its breadth, complexity and integration of the visual and music arts. While informative, it also attempts to sustain and to encourage participation in a Catholic liturgical tradition in which the Sacrament is primary.

The home page of this Benedictine monastery (see Fig. 7) allows viewers to follow the changing emphases of each day of the liturgical calendar. Also on the home page are icons indicating the major areas: 'Seeking God', 'The Porter', and 'Monastic Studies'. From this page one can also access 'Monastic News' and 'The Gift Shop'.

The icon 'Seeking God' offers several options: Chant, Vocation, Prayers, Desert Fathers, Homily and Dominican Retreat House. On accompanying pages are prayers, chants, stories of the lives of saints, guides to reflection, and opportunities to follow the Liturgy of the Hours. Viewers may also learn more about the Rule of St. Benedict and the particular kinds of prayers and liturgies of the monastic community.

Through this site the Benedictine monks reach out to a broader public. Pages are designed to inform the laity and to introduce them into the life and worship of the monastery. The church year unfolds in a daily rhythm of devotional materials through which viewers may share the richness of Benedictine liturgical life. Using the Web, the monks have updated the ancient medieval *scriptorium*, even providing something like an electronic 'Book of Hours' for those who want to follow the ebb and flow of daily liturgies.

Certain questions remain, however, for this as well as the previously mentioned web sites. Is it possible, even with the most sophisticated virtual reality, to replace the phenomenal reality of embodied religious ritual?

Turning now to a critical look at the mythic and ritualistic dimensions of web sites, we will question the degree to which they expand or fall short of their traditional functions. The first critique assumes the position of an evangelical, conversionist religious tradition; the second views cyberspace myths and ritual from a sacramental religious perspective.

Worship and Word: the Centrality of Conversion

At the outset I suggested that a functionalist definition of religion would offer the most inclusive perspective. Emphasis upon shared myths as an organising principle of a social group allows us to include web sites, such as The Millennium Matters and Starwars, which are not necessarily identified with what we think of as 'religious' communities. These sites simply draw like-minded viewers together as a cyber-community of shared loyalties and values. This concept of religion emphasises the creation of a social 'whole' that emerges from common concerns and convictions. Such a social entity

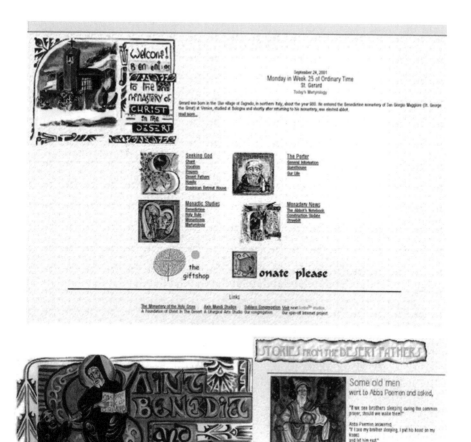

Figure 7   The Monastery of Christ in the Desert home page.

is revealed and expressed in its meaningful stories, heroes and role models. Following this concept of community formation, we may identify a web site as a 'place' where like-minded individuals may 'gather'. For regular viewers the site affords a sense of identity and belonging.

There are many theologians, however, who would object to a functionalist definition of religion, especially when it is the sole criterion applied to the concept of myth and ritual on web sites. They might argue, for example, that while interest groups may be developed by attentive Web watchers, it would take more than that to make it a 'religious' community. This critique is frequently voiced by evangelical groups which emphasise the intimate connection between scripture, evangelisation and community formation.

A large number of sites on the Web can be identified with religious traditions which have little or no interest in myths, rituals or visual imagery. The major emphasis for many Protestant churches in America is scripture-centered worship. For these groups, the question of a Eucharistic ritual is moot. What is important is the transmission of biblical messages aimed at conversion. Individual spiritual guidance, study guides and devotional materials serve a major goal of evangelisation. Numerous Christian groups, therefore, see the Web as an extension of spreading the Word. Like the printing press in the post-Reformation era, the Web, radio and television introduce wider audiences to scripture and sow the seeds of conversion and spiritual renewal. Regardless of the medium or technology, the focus remains the same: proclamation, witnessing and persuasion.

Both ritual and myth may thus be largely irrelevant to religious traditions which concentrate primarily on conversion or renewal and which emphasise charismatic preaching and scripture. The Web is, indeed, overflowing with sites featuring sermons and testimonials of faith. Upon reflection, however, current Web technology may actually be less effective than radio and television in communicating the persuasive rhetoric of a Spirit-filled preacher. The sounds of radio enable individual listeners to follow the emotional tones of sermons and readings from scripture. Television evangelists extend and enhance such a personalised, direct appeal through intense visual engagement. TV cameras move in close to provide eyeball-to-eyeball images, fiery expressions and gestures and tear-filled countenances. To the degree that evangelisation and spiritual renewal are dependent upon powerful sermons and dramatic readings from scripture, there will have to be a significant technological leap if the Web is to compete with the more sophisticated television imaging.

The Sacramental Liturgical Tradition

For some liturgical scholars, genuine religious ritual presupposes the existence of a divine, transcendent being, whose presence is the defining element of the rite. For example, through the gift of the Eucharist participants take part in the mystery of the Incarnation, Passion and Resurrection, that is, they participate in divine life. Central to the divine/human encounter, the Sacrament is an affirmation of the indissoluble unity of flesh and spirit.

From this perspective, contemporary theologians such as Catherine Pickstock, Phillip Blond, Graham Ward, John Milbank and others have become identified by their 'Radical Orthodoxy' project. These scholars emphasise in various ways the mystery of creation and the Incarnation, and the centrality of the Eucharist to the divine/human encounter. They are each concerned with a wholeness of human experience in which the physical and spiritual coalesce; they also emphasise the ways in which human beings participate in the mystery of creation.

At the same time, individual theologians within this group approach these issues in different ways. In this paper, I am drawing principally upon an essay by Phillip Blond on perception.[4] Among the issues in this essay, and the most relevant to our discussion of ritual on the Web, Blond poses a re-evaluation of the world because it is created by God and seen as a gift of God, and insists upon the inseparability of the visible and invisible, and upon the possibility of discerning objective, transcendent form in material reality.

The focus of Blond's essay is twentieth-century art, which he criticises for its solipsistic subjectivity and its separation of form from the materiality of the world. If we transpose some of Blond's ideas, applying them to the Web, we may question the validity of cyberspace ritual in two respects. First, an intensive preoccupation with spirituality on the Web further encourages a de-materialisation of reality and continues to underscore a disconnected, abstract engagement with the phenomenal world. For example, even as we 'chat' with others on the Web, the cyberspace world and the communities within it are essentially cerebral and frequently anonymous. While the Web may be a unique, and now an invaluable, source of obtaining information, it falls short of ritual activity because it is essentially disembodying. Human beings moving, touching, praying, singing, lamenting, praising and gesturing in concrete liturgical settings, in real space and time: this is genuine ritual experience.

Second, for these theologians, the animating element of Christian ritual is human engagement with transcendent being. Through ritual, God speaks in the language and material substance of the world, communicating and mediating the ultimate mystery of the Incarnation. Catherine Pickstock, for example, views Christian ritual as a gift of participation in the life of the divine.[5] While sites such as Christworld and Christdesert provide information, devotional materials, visual and musical sources for meditation and ritual, and even an email community of like-minded

---

[4] P. Blond, 'Perception: From modern painting to the vision in Christ', J. Milbank, C. Pickstock and G. Ward (eds.), *Radical Orthodoxy* (London: Routledge, 1999).

[5] C. Pickstock, *After Writing: On the Liturgical Consummation of Philosophy* (Oxford: Blackwell, 1998), pp. 203–13 and pp. 242–7.

individuals, some liturgical theologians would assert that authentic ritual is essentially antithetical to the abstractions of cyberspace. Ultimately, of course, an evaluation of Web interactivity and resources as mythic or 'ritual-like' depends on the liturgical theology and forms of religious communication associated with particular faith communities.

Are there not, however, certain analytical advantages in adopting a broad functionalist definition of religion in order to understand the symbolic forms present not only on the Web but also in other popular electronic media? Acknowledging the concerns of both 'Radical Orthodoxy' and evangelical theology, we may employ it to detect powerful and widely accepted 'secular' myths and rituals flourishing in cyberspace. Used as a critical tool, a functionalist approach will enable us to identify the latent role of religion in cultural symbols.

The mega myths and rituals of consumer culture

Perhaps the most pervasive, and unquestioned, public mythologies and rituals are those which we never stop to think about. So ingrained are they in our uncritical behavior and consciousness that we have ceased to recognise them as fundamental mythologies of a belief system. Unnoticed and serving as an overarching canopy over both religious and secular sites is an uncritical public commitment to a religion of consumerism. Following the patterns of print and all electronic media, the Web reinforces the central dynamic of our society: consuming. Endlessly repeated themes of advertising and entertainment center on success, beauty, health, wealth and commodities that will insure happiness and a sense of belonging. These mythic stories structure our personal lives and society. In the United States we identify these mythic themes with the American Way of Life; and the rituals of buying confirm our participation in that social whole. As the Web is increasingly associated with commerce, our 'click and buy' quickly becomes the basic sacramental act of cyberspace. Through Web shopping we make the tangible connection to an intangible cyberspace realm and thus become members incorporate of the mystical body of faithful consumers.

Perhaps the irony of this argument may prompt theologians to say that this is precisely the blindness of our materialist culture: we do not understand, or even recognise, the gift that cannot be bought, one that is freely given – the awesome, sacramental gift of creation. Similarly, Word-centered theologians, amid the growing commercialisation of all electronic communication, may be moved to intensify their prophetic efforts to witness to and proclaim alternative values and visions.

While Word-centered and Sacramental traditions emphasise different forms of religious communication, they share the same basic need, the need of complex body-spirit, earthbound creatures to find a meaningful place in the cosmos. This quintessential human search for attunement with the transcendent, marked by wonderment and awe, has left tangible traces throughout known time, from prehistoric carvings of simple linear contours, circles and spirals to monumental architectural forms. It may, in fact, make us uneasy to contemplate that we share with the least technological people something that W. E. H. Stanner has described as a fundamentally human metaphysical gift: the drive to make sense of reality.[6]

Today, robots, artificial intelligence and space exploration may tempt us to think that this expressly human search is being carried out and fulfilled through science and technology. Clearly scientific revolutions in all areas appear to offer almost limitless information about ourselves and our world. But can they address the timeless, non-technological question posed by Leibniz: Why is there something and not nothing?

Regardless of technological sophistication, the confrontation with mystery and with the uncertainty of life gives birth to a quest for meaning that arises from the depths of human consciousness. Capturing a sense of the precarious and the ultimately unknown questions, Blaise Pascal described human existence as lying between the Infinite and the Nothing.[7] It is in this fragile creaturely realm that we may expect to find myth and ritual. Yet, with our insatiable appetite for technological progress and for commodities, it is far more entertaining, and less risky, to explore the astrophysical universe and cyberspace than to explore the capricious human space between Infinity and Nothing where genuine myth and ritual reside.

[6] W. E. H. Stanner, 'The Dreaming', W. A. Lessa and E. Z. Vogt (eds.), *Reader in Comparative Religion, An Anthropological Approach* (Evanston, IL: Row, Peterson, 1958), p. 518.
[7] B. Pascal, *Pensées/The Provincial Letters* (New York: Random House: Modern Library, 1941), p. 23.

23

Electronic Media and the Past-Future of Christianity

Peter Horsfield

The late twentieth century saw a significant decline in the membership and social position of mainline Christian churches in many Western societies. A significant aspect of this decline was its generational character. In Australia, for example, the past two decades have seen the virtual disappearance of people under the age of forty from mainline churches, as illustrated below.[1]

This disappearance of younger people from churches has both practical and symbolic effects. Practically it means a major drop in finances, in the number of people providing voluntary labour for church activities, and future renewal of current membership. Symbolically, young people and children represent new life, vitality and the hope of the future. The disappearance of young people from many traditional churches therefore has created a crisis of faith, hope and morale among those adults who remain.

Are we entering post-Christianity?

There are those who suggest that this crisis is a sign of the end of institutionalised faith. Sociologist Steve Bruce, for example, sees the decline in churches as a consequence of the steady progress of secularisation, characteristic of society in the modern industrialised world.[2] Bruce argues that the

TABLE 2: **Ages of Australian church attendees**

	Uniting Church	**Anglican**	**Pentecostal**
50 years +	66%	61%	25%
30–49 years	24%	27%	48%
15–29 years	10%	13%	28%

[1] Australian National Church Life Survey, 1997.
[2] Steve Bruce, *Religion in the Modern World: From Cathedrals to Cults* (Oxford: Oxford University Press, 1996). Bruce writes, 'The basic elements of what we conveniently refer to as 'modernisation' fundamentally altered the place and nature of religious beliefs, practices, and organisations so as to reduce their relevance to the lives of nation-states, social groups, and individuals, in roughly that order.' p. 1.

Reformation introduced the voluntary principle into Christianity, opening the way for the element of choice in religious belonging. This led to the phenomenon of selective church membership and even optional belief, relocating faith authority away from society to the individual.[3]

While individualism has always had a place in modern religious practice, it has previously meant the freedom to dissent. Now individualism means the right of the individual to determine. According to Bruce, this favours the cult type of religious expression more than that of church, denomination or sect.[4]

In the light of these changes and the decline in Christianity's social and institutional forms, a number of thinkers argue for the abandonment of the past forms altogether and the creation of something totally new. Don Cupitt makes this point:

> Until very recently it was a matter of great grief to me that the Church seemed unwilling and even unable to reform itself: but now it seems that people in general have decided that there is not enough left to salvage. Reform isn't worth trying for: let the dead bury their dead. It wasn't I who decided that it is now too late, but the general public. In which case it is time to describe something new.[5]

I agree with those who see many of the current institutional forms of the Christian church as well past their use-by date. I see great value in the post-modern exposé and dismantling of some of the Christian patriarchal super-structures that over the centuries have been the agency of colonial exploitation, destruction of indigenous cultures, suppression of dissent, the abuse and murder of women and the suppression of human sexuality. Strategically also, there is great value in Cupitt's suggestion that concerned people of faith should cease bothering about trying to change the old and concentrate on facilitating the emergence of the new.

But I also have some questions about the concept of the de-institutionalisation of religious faith, not because it undermines the power of the current institutions, but because I suspect that it is not a de-institutionalising at all, but a *re-institutionalising* of religious faith *within the institutions of commercial mass media*. Social health, I believe, lies in the maintenance of diversity,

---

[3] The fragmentation of religious culture that took place in the Reformation and post-Reformation period, according to Bruce, 'was, in time, to see the widespread, taken-for-granted, and unexamined Christianity of the pre-Reformation period replaced by an equally widespread, taken-for-granted, and unexamined indifference to religion'. Bruce, *Religion in the Modern World*, p. 4.

[4] 'Modernisation makes the church form of religion impossible. The church requires either cultural homogeneity or an elite sufficiently powerful to enforce conformity ... Modernisation also undermines the hierarchical and rigid social structures which permit the maintenance of mono-cultures.' Steve Bruce, 'Cathedrals to Cults: The Evolving Forms of the Religious Life', Paul Heelas (ed.), *Religion, Modernity and Postmodernity* (Oxford: Blackwell, 1998), pp. 23–4.

[5] Don Cupitt, 'Post-Christianity', Heelas (ed.), *Religion, Modernity and Postmodernity*, pp. 218–19.

and that involves maintaining robust social institutions that contend with the institutional forms constructed and preferred by commercial media.

I believe there is great potential in the current ferment. In faith terms, it can be seen as a creative God pruning the old in order for new life and new forms to come forth. Continuing the gardening metaphor, this process of composting what has died to feed the living has been part of the Christian heritage since its beginnings.

Church analyses of the crisis

A range of Christian missiologists, strategists and theological writers have been addressing themselves to this changing social position of churches. Part of this response has involved strategies for helping churches redefine and reposition themselves. Many of these strategies are retrograde – their operating assumption seems to be a Christendom model of social dominance, political coercion, patriarchal imposition and moral imperialism. It seems as if a major commercial industry has now arisen around selling solutions to churches in crisis.

For many thinkers, Thomas Kuhn's[6] concept of paradigm shift has become a common device for explaining the changed social relationships most Western churches now find themselves in. In missiology, for example, Loren Mead of the Alban Institute identifies three paradigms: the Apostolic, the Christendom, and the Emerging paradigms.[7] In theology and church history, Hans Küng's recent major survey of Christian history uses a paradigmatic approach, describing six major paradigms in Christian history.[8]

While this paradigmatic approach falls into all the traps and restrictions of grand narrative constructions, it can provide a useful bridge and construct of coherence for many from which to conceptualise the specifics of the present situation.

The missing factor: the place of media

What is missing from most church analyses of the present situation, however, is any sort of consideration of the part played by changes in the social

---

[6] Thomas Kuhn, *The Structure of Scientific Revolutions* (Chicago: Chicago University Press, 1970).

[7] Loren Mead, *The Once and Future Church: Reinventing the Congregation for a New Mission Frontier* (New York: The Alban Institute, 1991).

[8] Hans Küng, *Christianity: The Religious Situation of Our Time* (London: SCM, 1994). Küng's paradigms are: The Jewish Apocalyptic Paradigm of Earliest Christianity; The Ecumenical Hellenistic Paradigm of Christian Antiquity; The Roman Catholic Paradigm of the Middle Ages; The Protestant Evangelical Paradigm of the Reformation; The Paradigm of Modernity, Orientated on Reason and Progress; and The Present Paradigm.

structures of mediated communication. Five years ago I surveyed ten recent theological texts addressing issues of theology and culture. Of the ten, only one made any mention of media as a significant factor in their cultural analysis. I think this represents more than an oversight. From my work and conversations with church leaders, I have identified a number of methodological or structural factors that blind many church leaders to the importance of media within culture and cultural change. There is a tendency to view media within an instrumental rather than a cultural framework and to disdain electronic media as a lower form of culture that is unworthy of theological consideration. Their view of faith is framed by Enlightenment ideas and institutional forms, so that other important expressions of faith such as everyday practices, visual and material culture are neglected. Just as the age and education of most church leaders place them in different media-cultural subgroups from those of later generations and affect their personal media preferences, so too their professional practices lock them into a particular media culture. Many church leaders tell me – sometimes proudly, sometimes dismissively – that they are too busy to watch television or go to the movies. Their major media activities are reading books and journals, activities that put them out of touch with the most common media practices of the people to whom they are supposed to be communicating.

Reframing perspectives

Part of my professional role for a number of years was to try to reframe these dominant perceptions so that churches could begin to engage electronic media culture in a more positive and less oppositional way.

One of the practical difficulties in doing this is that there is no single, nor simple coherent theory of media and cultural change that one can draw on in order to break open the firm instrumental ideological mindset of most church leaders and theologians. One needs to be true to the complexity of media-culture theory, but if one is too complex or goes into too much detail, one reinforces the instrumental view because it is at least simple and usable.

Elizabeth Eisenstein notes the difficulties of finding a good balance in her analysis of the social impact of printing on fifteenth- and sixteenth-century Europe. She writes:

> When dealing with these transformations it is important to strike the right balance between the uninformed enthusiasts who assume printing changed almost *everything* and the scholarly skeptics who hold it changed *nothing*. The enthusiasts overestimate the initial changes wrought by print and forget that pre-literate folk were not much affected... The skeptics... do not appreciate the danger that comes from *under*estimating its true dimensions.[9]

[9] Elizabeth L. Eisenstein, 'The Emergence of Print Culture in the West', *Journal of Communication* (Winter 1980), pp. 99–106.

The approach I have used in consultations and workshops with church leaders has the following theoretical framework. First, I use a concept gained from Stewart Hoover,[10] challenging the metaphor of the media as instruments and proposing the metaphor of media as the web of culture, the framework upon which all other cultural activities and institutions are located and constructed. Second, drawing on the work of theorists such as Walter Ong, I explore ways in which the characteristics of different media shape or influence the cultural characteristics of those activities constructed through their mediation, and ways in which changes in cultural forms can be correlated with changes in structures of mediation.[11] Third, I explore ways in which electronic-based technologies of communication are contributing to changes in the fabric and shape of the cultural web. Fourth, I propose that these changing patterns of mediated culture are producing major consequences for faith ideologies, practices and institutional forms that were developed to be relevant to the web of previous media cultural contexts. The structural blindness of religious thinkers and leaders to the social constructive role of media means that religious institutions, which are significantly affected by these changes, lack an adequate analysis on which to respond to them.

Media contests in the development of Christianity

The lack of appreciation for the culturally constructive role of media means that the significant role that media have played in the cultural and institutional development of Christianity over the centuries has been relatively unexplored. As a result, valuable lessons that could be drawn from Christian history to provide useful perspectives on current developments and possible future responses are simply undeveloped. Two specific instances from Christian history may serve to illustrate that the current turmoil being experienced within churches today, prompted by the electrifying of the global media web, has precedents in Christian history.

---

[10] Stewart Hoover, 'What Do We Do about the Media?' *Conrad Griebel Review* (Spring 1993), pp. 97–107.

[11] See for example, Walter Ong, *Orality and Literacy: The Technologising of the Word* (London: Routledge, 1982). There is a range of criticisms of Ong's approach, such as Ruth Finnegan in *Literacy and Orality: Studies in the Technology of Communication* (London: Blackwell, 1988). Where appropriate it is important to address those criticisms. But for those who have never given consideration to any other view than that media are simply instruments for getting across one's message, Ong's work is useful for exploring the correlations between the characteristics of the form by which reality is mediated and the shape and character of cultural forms, practices and ethos that form around, through and within those mediations.

Opposition to writing in the early church

A persistent issue I have found in working with church leaders around the subject of electronic media is their fear that engaging with electronic media seriously will compromise Christian faith. Most Christian leaders I work with are strongly influenced in their cultural thinking by the framework articulated by Richard Niebuhr in his book *Christ and Culture*. There, Niebuhr defines faith (or Christ) and culture as separate entities – overlapping and intertwined certainly, but still capable of separate identification. For most church leaders, Christianity is a distinct body of ideas and practices, defined and defended most effectively in theological books and journals. In this common view, electronic media are seen as more than just another form of mediation: their very structure as well as common content are seen as a significant threat to Christianity as a thoughtful, ordered and authoritative faith structure.

One of the useful perspectives of postmodern criticism has been to challenge this view. Far from being a single, unitary, discreetly bounded entity that has moved systematically and paradigmatically through history, writers such as Kathryn Tanner[12] argue, Christianity has always been a diverse, messy and often contradictory movement of individuals, institutions, sentiments and practices that are continually in the process of being constructed, de-constructed and re-constructed in the concrete lives of its adherents and institutions. Christian identity is a continual task, not an accomplishment.

Within this complex dynamic, differences generated by variations in how faith was mediated, and the various power contests associated with those forms of mediation, have been significant factors in how Christianity has developed.

Given the current hegemonic identification of Christianity with written and printed text, it is instructive to note that the adoption of text in the transmission of Christian teaching was controversial in the first several centuries of Christianity. The opposition to writing was such that one of the early fathers, Clement of Alexandria, in the early third century, felt it necessary to name these objections and respond to them explicitly when writing the first chapter of his book, *Stromateis*.

The objections being voiced, as identified by Clement were these:

> The living voice was the best medium for the communication of Christian truth. Writings were public and it was wrong to cast pearls before swine. To write implied that one was inspired by the Holy Spirit and this was a presumptuous claim. If one must write, it were better

[12] Kathryn Tanner, *Theories of Culture: A New Agenda for Theology* (Minneapolis: Fortress, 1997).

that one should write badly. The heretics had shown that a clever style could mislead and corrupt.[13]

These objections indicate an implicit recognition by those with roots in oral forms of discourse that adopting a different mediation of faith would involve significant changes to how faith is understood, embodied, communalised and passed on.

Clement in his work provided counter arguments for each of these objections. Writing had distinct advantages, and not to write simply abandoned the field to those who would use it anyway for adverse purposes. It is obvious that Clement's view won out. Christian men in this period, particularly highly literate men such as Clement and Origen from the literate cultural centre of Alexandria, played a major role in intentionally moving Christianity from the cultural fringes of the Greco-Roman world into the very centre of its cultural life and philosophy.

Writing was not the only influence in this, but it was a very significant one. Writing provided liberties of action that were fundamental to the formulation and ascendancy of Christian ideas and organisational structures within the Roman Empire. Origen, for example, is said to have assembled a team of trained word processors who churned out by hand a massive 6,000 works, only a few of which have survived.

'Stenographers copied his sermons and lectures in shorthand, secretaries transcribed the notes, and calligraphers produced elegant copies.' The stature of biblical studies was increased by Origen's *Hexapla*, 'a kind of study of the Old Testament. It had six parallel columns, one of the Scripture in Hebrew, and the other five of various Greek translations.'[14]

In this deliberate strategy of cultural re-mediation of faith, the formal defining features of Christianity were changed profoundly and the die was cast for its future development into a universal religion within the universal culture of Hellenism. Hans Küng notes the changes brought by these influential Christian men of letters:

> The centre of Christian theology is now no longer, as in Paul, Mark and the New Testament generally, the cross and resurrection of Jesus. Now largely speculative questions stand in the centre: how the three hypostases in the one Godhead are related; how the incarnation of the divine Logos and the bridging of the Platonic gulf between the true, ideal, heavenly world and the untrue, material, earthly world is to be envisaged; how Jesus can be described as the God-man ... There is no mistaking the fact that already among the early Greek fathers the main theological interest shifted from the concrete salvation history of the people of Israel and the Rabbi from Nazareth to the great soteriological system.[15]

---

[13] Eric Osborn, 'Teaching and Writing in the First Chapter of the *Stromateis* of Clement of Alexandria', *Journal of Theological Studies* 10 (1959), pp. 335–43.

[14] Stephen Miller, 'Mavericks and Misfits', *Christian History* 43 (1994), pp. 18–21.

[15] Küng, *Christianity*, pp. 167–8.

This universalising of Christian thought laid the basis for Christianity to become the religion of the Empire, and the imposition of an institutional order and credal ideology that has been normative to this day. There were many alternative understandings and interpretations of what being Christian meant, but they were never able to exert the same influence in a centralised manner because their mediation of faith was decentralised, contextual and fluid.

One of those streams of alternative understanding and organisation was in the oral-charismatic Christian communities, whose leadership included a high proportion of women. In the dynamic messiness of contestation, the power brought by writing was an important factor in determining who had access to the processes within which significant decisions were made. This included, for example, specific actions to ban Christian women from writing and to suppress and declare as heretical women-led oral-prophetic communities, such as the Montanists. The contest around oral and written mediation of Christian faith in early Christian communities is a rich area waiting further research.

What reality do words of faith refer to?

Several years ago I viewed a quite gruesome but powerful commercial film called *Butterfly Kiss*. It tells the story of a sexually-abused and self-abusive young woman called Eunice who is travelling through northern England in search of a mother-like figure called Judith. On her travels, she is propositioned sexually by a number of men, to whom she responds by killing them. A waitress called Miriam, a symbol of the good, befriends her and travels with her to help her find Judith and prevent her from killing people. In the middle of the movie, there is a scene in which Eunice discloses to Miriam her deep anguish:

> I've been forgotten. I kill people, and nothing happens ... You'd think that God would smite me, or take me into bondage. But nowt! He doesn't see me. He doesn't see me. It's like I've disappeared and become invisible.

The scene struck me particularly powerfully at the time because of work with people who were survivors of sexual abuse within church communities, for whom these are common existential and theological questions. Eunice's experience also struck me as emblematic of a recurring question I hear, particularly from young people, of faith validation. What 'reality' do words of faith refer to or invoke?

In her study, *Seeing the Lord: Resurrection and Early Christian Practice*, Marianne Sawicki provides an analysis of the construction of faith meaning in the New Testament period and the influences of different mediations of faith in that construction.

Sawicki notes that the earliest sayings and stories of Jesus travelled across Palestine and across social frontiers for the most part as oral recitations, not as written texts. These oral recitations shared characteristics common to many forms of oral history and storytelling, in which the past was recounted, adapted and continually made real in the present in the person and actions of the storyteller or the oral prophet.

Jesus himself stood in this tradition. He was itinerant, validating his words by deeds: exorcising demons, healing and performing wonders. His teachings were improvised and adapted for the situation. The earliest Christian prophets and storytellers followed this teaching and working style of Jesus: they travelled, exorcised demons, healed, preached in the name of Jesus, and uttered new sayings as if they came from the mouth of Jesus himself. Resurrection was proclaimed as a real-time experience: Jesus was not remembered as someone from out of the past whose life had closed. 'The prophetic way was to proclaim that one now lives and works among the people, who is Jesus, who died.'[16] The Jesus who died was identical with this person speaking and making things happen in the midst of the people.

There were a range of advantages in this mode of communicating faith. It located faith within people through the richness of presence, voice and personal actions that produced physical effects. It also allowed for the past to be continually adapted relevantly to the present through the process of creative re-membering and re-telling.

But there were also a number of disadvantages. If the power of one's words was dependent on making things happen, things had to keep happening in order for the communication to be validated. If Jesus was continually saying new things through the prophets, there was an emerging problem of maintaining continuity between the new things Jesus was saying and the words of the original Jesus. Prophets were also notoriously undependable. Fired by the spontaneity of the Spirit, they could often disappear just when you needed them.

These disadvantages created the practical need to locate the faith within something more stable. Writing had liberties of action that appeared to provide that stability. The original sayings and stories of Jesus began to be written down in order to preserve them. The past was stabilised and fixed in the written text. In many ways the process of writing down the stories and sayings of Jesus was continuous with and complementary to oral tradition.[17]

But writing also created discontinuities with oral practices of faith. Writing down stories and sayings was an innovation and a significant

---

[16] Marianne Sawicki, *Seeing the Lord: Resurrection and Early Christian Practice* (Minneapolis: Fortress, 1994), pp. 85–6.

[17] 'These [Gospel] texts should be read as traces of oral practices occurring before the writing, continuing alongside the writing, and often persisting independently after the writing. Each saying had plenty of variants, and they could bundle with other sayings or stand alone, depending on the needs of the occasion. A Gospel writer had quite a few to choose from; or to put it another way, the writer had ample precedent to mix and match and improvise in accordance with traditional oral practices.' Sawicki, *Seeing the Lord*, p. 29.

departure from the style and method of Jesus.[18] While fixing the past in written text solved the problem of stabilising the past against continual modifications and the unpredictability of the Spirit, it created a problem of its own: that is, once Jesus was fixed in the past, how was one to have real-time contact with Jesus in the present? How can Jesus be risen Lord, how can Jesus perform present wonders, if Jesus is buried once again in the text?

The solution for the writers of the Gospel of Matthew and of Luke-Acts was through obedience. Jesus comes to life out of the text by readers and listeners following Jesus' teachings and by ritualising his presence. How do you know what Jesus' teachings are in a textual community? You need somebody who can interpret the text – a teacher.

The process of writing down the sayings and stories of Jesus therefore involved a gradual displacement of the mediation role of oral prophets with the mediation role of teachers and leaders of the ritual. It involved also a realignment of the relationship between words and actions: away from the miracle-working presence of the oral prophets towards a focus on ethical behaviour and ritualised presence within the community.

As noted earlier, this shift did not happen without contestation, and this contestation can be seen in various places. The writer of Matthew's Gospel warns in a number of places against the danger of false prophets and prophetic signs. Gradually the kinds of works that were to be done in Jesus' name were no longer wonder works but deeds of justice and compassion.

Within a textual community, teaching takes on a new significance. Sawicki notes how, in Matthew's Gospel, Jesus' actions as a prophet were downplayed in the text as Jesus was constructed more as a teacher, consistent with the known Greek social practice of *paidea*. So Jesus was made 'real' by reconstructing Jesus in the text in a way that resonated with known cultural practices and roles. In the process, the role of the teacher became a significant one, for 'in the days before widespread literacy and inexpensive printed bibles, access to the text is through teachers alone.'[19]

Within this framework, the early Gospels can be seen as more than just a written record of events. They represent a constructive media exercise, an effort to found the Christian movement on a particular media-based methodology of making faith real, i.e., grounded in the written text as a basis for teaching and ritualised presence. In this context Matthew's attacks on the prophets, like the later attacks on the oral-prophetic Christian

---

[18] 'There was a time when a textual, written Gospel was an oddity, a curious innovation amid the Jesus movements. Sayings of and about Jesus ordinarily were recited to the accompaniment of certain distinctive practices, which could not be replicated in texts. The textual practice of writing itself does not come from Jesus; writing Gospels was an innovation introduced in several early churches. This new way of remembering Jesus severed the traditional interaction among spoken words and their context. The "old" way, the way that arguably came from Jesus, was to vary the sayings about God's kingdom and to improvise.' Sawicki, *Seeing the Lord*, p. 29.

[19] Sawicki, *Seeing the Lord*, p. 87.

communities by those who were trying to establish Christianity through cen-tralised, hierarchical structures, reflect more than just a difference of ideas. They reflect a polemic by particular groups who were grounded in a par-ticular mediation of faith against differently mediated faith cultures that were seen as potentially subversive or damaging.

Continuation of contested mediation

The method of making faith real by grounding it in a text, interpreted by accredited teachers into ethical actions and re-membering rituals has remained a very effective method for making faith real within Christianity to this point. To a significant extent, the 'reality' of the words of textual faith have been validated by the development of powerful religious institutions aligned with significant political, military and economic forces. Reality was constructed in the words through the churches' political and social power to discipline, socially ostracise or even execute those who ignored them.

Today there is a convergence of factors that are undermining these text-based strategies of making faith real. One of these is the decline in the social and political power of churches to coerce acceptance of preferred meanings in Christian words and symbols. The second is a radical shift in the mediation and construction of social reality, away from the social and cognitive characteristics of text-based mediation within which 'official' Christianity has largely been based, to the more dynamic, transient and sensory fluidity of electronically mediated reality.

The consequence is that the social and cosmological view that gave mean-ing to Christian words and ritual practices is no longer there. The crisis in much of traditional Christianity is not just a crisis of institutions: it is a crisis of meaning. Faith words continue to have their own consistent internal logic for those who know the grammar, but increasingly they are losing their power to evoke material meaning for those whose feet are in differently mediated cultures.

The changes taking place in a major faith tradition like Christianity today cannot be fully understood without an analysis of the crucial role of differ-ent forms of mediation in the construction of culture and cultural meaning and the shifts that occur when that structure of mediation changes.

Further reading

P. Babin, *The New Era in Religious Communication* (Minneapolis: Fortress, 1991).

S. Bruce, *Religion in the Modern World: From Cathedrals to Cults* (Oxford: Oxford University Press, 1996).

M. Edwards Jr., *Printing, Propaganda and Martin Luther* (Berkeley: University of California Press, 1994).

P. Heelas (ed.), *Religion, Modernity and Postmodernity* (Oxford: Blackwell, 1998).

S. Hoover and K. Lundby (eds.), *Rethinking Media, Religion, and Culture* (Thousand Oaks, CA: Sage, 1997).

C. McDannell, *Material Christianity: Religion and Popular Culture in America* (New Haven: Yale University Press, 1997).

David Morgan, *Visual Piety: A History and Theory of Popular Religious Images* (Berkeley: University of California Press, 1998).

W. Ong, *Orality and Literacy: The Technologising of the Word* (London: Routledge, 1982).

M. Sawicki, *Seeing the Lord: Resurrection and Early Christian Practice* (Minneapolis: Fortress, 1994).

K. Tanner, *Theories of Culture: A New Agenda for Theology* (Minneapolis: Fortress, 1997).

PART 7

Media Ethics and Religion

24

The Emerging 'Communitarian' Ethics of Public Communication

Robert A. White

The thesis which I would like to explore in this chapter is that we are experiencing a fundamental paradigm shift in the ethical foundations of public communication, the formation of the 'communitarian' ethic of public communication. The social responsibility and public service paradigms, which came into existence gradually from about 1870 to 1970, are no longer considered an adequate normative foundation for consensus on norms of public communication. More fundamentally, the communitarian ethic is challenging the libertarian tradition which has been the foundation of democratic communication since the inauguration of the printing press and our present era of popular mass media.

Most of the partners in the current debate are aware of the arguments of communitarian normative theory of public communication, and many would tend to think that the thesis enunciated above is, at best, exaggerated. Some would argue that we live in an era of deregulation, neo-liberalism and growing domination of media by an increasingly small number of media barons. More than ever the Murdochs, Ted Turners, and the faceless managers behind agencies such as Reuters control not only the national but the international flow of information. There is much evidence, however, that deregulation is not just a reversion to the libertarian ethic but is a symptom of the breakdown of old certainties about how the free flow of public opinion should be maintained.

Let me begin with a brief definition of a paradigm of ethics of public communication as a formula which guarantees to all major actors in the public communication arena the recognition of the moral claims of each.[1] Examples of major actors are the communicating public, the media professionals, media proprietors, etc. The moral claims of members of the public are not just to be informed but to be able to dialogue with other members of the public. The moral claim of professionals is to be able to serve their clients and the public according to their conscience and

---

[1] For a more in-depth discussion of the concept of normative paradigm, cf. Robert White, 'New Approaches to Media Ethics: Moral Dialogue, Creating Normative Paradigms and Public Cultural Truth', Bart Pattyn (ed.), *Media Ethics* (Leuven, Belgium: Peeters, 2000), pp. 47–67.

according to the best tenets of their science. A brief review of current discussions of media ethics reveals a widespread feeling among major actors that their moral claims are not being satisfied. Few are happy with the public communication order which we now have.

Increasingly, members of the public feel more competent and responsible for direct communication in the public sphere. There is increasing hesitancy about blind delegation of public communication to professionals and to media proprietors. Members of the public want more direct discussion and dialogue among major actors of a given cultural community. This is generating an increasing amount of horizontal communication in communities but is also generating a new normative foundation for public communication which is widely defined as 'communitarian'.

The sources of the communitarian normative theory of communication

The end of political colonialism and the growth of a multicultural worldview

The political independence of the new nations after World War II meant that the non-European cultures no longer had a vertical, dependent relationship, but were all officially considered equally valid. The principles involved in the formation of the United Nations meant that nations and cultures had to enter into a communication relationship of dialogue in order to form a community of cultures. The unilinear evolution model of development may have persisted for some decades in the modernisation paradigm of development, but the logic of this collapsed, especially in the 1970s.

The new logic began to recognise that the agreement of the European Enlightenment to keep cultural values, especially religious beliefs, in the private sphere was no longer valid. Values had to be brought out in the open, and they had to be recognised and respected by others, not swept under the rug as if they did not exist. The hope that the world would be brought together in one instrumental form of rationality was finished. The social contract model of intercommunication which assumes that values and culture are a private matter and that we could never agree on them publicly is increasingly questioned. It is not enough to have a pragmatic arrangement of 'you help me attain my values and I will help you attain your values'. We must have an open discussion about values which enables every cultural group to preserve its own values, but then to discover higher levels of common symbols in which we can all truly agree. This new logic began to sweep through the world so that minority religious groups, subcultural regions and minority movements at the grass-roots level also affirmed a dialogical model of public communication.

Philosophical movements that question the liberal premises of modernity

The libertarian conception of the public sphere began to be questioned on all sides from the beginning of the nineteenth century. The socialist ideal was one of the strongest generators of alternative models until about the 1930s. Although the communist political model maintained its place until 1989 and supported many movements against liberal capitalism around the world, the contradictions of communism were already widely evident in the 1930s. The model of liberal democracy with its principle of public service and universal professionalisation (implying the conscience-binding pledge to use scientific knowledge to serve society) emerged after 1850 and became dominant in the world by the 1930s. This brought with it the social responsibility and public service normative paradigms of mass communication.

By the 1960s, however, social philosophers such as Habermas began to show that a professionalisation based on bureaucratic rationalism was 'colonising our life space' and destroying a sense of community. This was not simply a nostalgia for past days. From this observation that communication in the public sphere was happening less and less, there began to emerge communitarian approaches cutting across all disciplines. Some of the most inspiring sources of a new public philosophy, especially in the area of communication, have come from Martin Buber, John MacMurray, Paolo Freire and Charles Taylor, but there are a host of others who have various degrees of importance.

The new community media experiences

Community media have been with us for centuries; the community newspapers of the US are but one example. In the late 1950s and the 1960s, however, there began a new worldwide movement of community radio, television (usually via cable) and other media. These are owned and administered by a cooperative community association or by a public service, non-profit organisation. They are staffed largely by volunteers, and their chief objective is to create *dialogue* in the community. They have a strong commitment to become a 'voice for the voiceless' and make a special effort to develop the communication competencies of less-educated minorities or people who have not learned to articulate their issues.

Community media have a strong commitment to help less powerful groups develop organisational capacity so that they will be able to participate from a base of greater power in the cultural, socioeconomic and political decision-making process. In order to develop capacity for organisation they frequently engage in formal and non-formal educational programmes. Community media also become the major intercommunication facility for people's grass-roots organisations.

Radio has been one of the prime community media because it requires less investment and a lower level of personal training to reach a fairly high level of aesthetical expression in the radio media language. Radio most easily adapts to the conditions of community media. Radio also has the advantage of being a 'personally expressive' medium because it is oral. As Walter Ong has explained, oral expression is more deeply involving and touches the deeper sources of personal identity.[2] Oral communication is also much more oriented toward interpersonal and community communication.

The Internet is another example of a more direct-access, community medium. Although there are problems of access for poorer people and a lack of 'orality' in the use of the medium, it is a process of creating virtual communities. The Internet is shown to be a medium in which social status is less important and all participants are considered equal, something which is important in building community.

Group communication, group media and 'consciousness raising' approaches

Closely associated with community media is group communication (often with the use of group media and the Freirian 'conscientisation' value-clarification and educational approaches).[3] Group communication began with the poor who are dependent on the decision-making structure of the more powerful and who have not developed the capacity for articulating their own values. The method has gradually extended to all 'system-dependent' people whose lives and immediate living spaces are 'colonised', to use Habermas' term – most recently including executives in Silicon Valley. The primary objectives are to create a space of freedom at the interpersonal level where people can voice their deeper alienations and create a group-level consciousness of the structural factors that are causing this alienation from their own identities and values. The intention is to help people in the group value their own personal and cultural identities and to value the identities of others. The ability to habitually become aware of personal identity and perceptions of the world and express this in the group context is of central importance. Thus, the leadership is that of the non-directive *animator* whose main task is to help people learn to express themselves and formulate a position understandable to others in the group.

A further objective is therefore to learn to *dialogue* and to learn to value dialogue as the heart of human existence. Freire would say that once one has experienced deeply the value of dialogue, it is not possible to instrumentalise others again. The heart of the consciousness-raising method is to

---

[2] Walter J. Ong, *Orality and Literacy: The Technologising of the Word* (London: Methuen, 1982).

[3] Paolo Freire, *Pedagogy of the Oppressed* (New York: Continuum, 1970, 1993).

encourage participants to define their personal and group problems from the perspective of their own valued identities and then to gradually construct the line of structural causes which have caused a deep alienation from their identities. By sharing information that members of the group already have (you do not have to become information-dependent) or by carrying out strategic participatory research, participants can discover the falseness of many of the ideologically-oriented explanations of their problems. From this comes the conviction of the necessity of social change and the commitment to work toward change.

Group communication uses media, but not to 'transport' information. Rather participants are encouraged to produce their own media – often audiovisual – which embody their logic and understanding of values (generative terms in the language of Freire). The media production essentially presents the problem they are facing and the line of causes of the problem. The participants can then look at their own constructed world in order to deconstruct it and then reconstruct with another media production how they should face the problem from the perspective of dignity and dialogue.

Obviously, group communication has great importance as a means of socialisation in communitarian communication. Many educational systems working with the poor and marginalised will use a combination of community media, group communication and interpersonal consultation in order to create an interaction of all the communitarian media.

Communitarian approaches in the theory and methodology of academic communication studies

In the mid-1970s there began to be a major paradigm shift in the field of communication challenging the linear, author-centred and media/message-centred conception of communication. Particularly important are the following shifts:

(1) The convergence model of communication, which owes much to social interaction approaches to social science.
(2) The ritual, communion model of mass communication proposed by James Carey[4] and the forum model put forward by Horace Newcomb.[5]
(3) The continued development of the critical-democratic approaches in communication theory with the emphasis on reception theory, audience reception networks, the new semiotic approaches to the complexity of the text, the importance of alternative construction of

[4] James W. Carey, 'Mass Communication and Cultural Studies', James Curran, Michael Gurevitch and Janet Woollacott (eds.) *Mass Communication and Society* (London: Edward Arnold, 1977), pp. 409–26.
[5] Horace Newcomb and Robert Alley, *The Producer's Medium: Conversations with Producers of American TV* (New York: Oxford University Press, 1983). cf. chapter 1.

meaning of fan networks and other perspectives that have an origin in French and British Marxist cultural studies.

The critical tradition has also provided a foundation for developing qualitative methods of research which emphasise subjective meaning.

The development of the alternative communication movement

At times, in contexts of enormous concentration of power, it has not been possible to develop community, people-controlled media. Examples of this are the totalitarian communist regimes, apartheid regimes such as that of South Africa, or the modernising state-centred governments in many countries of Africa and Asia. In these contexts systems of grass-roots, alternative communications have arisen in an underground, illegal form. These alternative networks are often able to become the major communication network and to be considered the only legitimate communication system of their countries. Often the governments which control the mass media so lack legitimacy that media simply disappear.

Alternative media have also developed a specific communitarian mode: they are small, inexpensive and mobile; they are controlled democratically within a particular movement; and they use a discourse which systematically analyses the dominant ideology and presents a valued appreciation of the identities of oppressed people.

The growing importance of normative theory in both academic and professional circles

The field of sociology opted in the 1920s to take a value-free, positivist stance that tended to separate theory and research from the professions and policy. These human sciences located value issues in the area of the 'applied' sciences. Sociology has attempted to achieve scientific status by adopting an essentially value-free, functionalist logic that enables the social sciences to ignore the human and social consequences. Communication sciences, however, developed normative theory as an integral part of the theoretical research approach. This has kept communication close to the issues of professional evaluation, public policy and the needs of the public. Communication theory has become inherently committed to the development of democracy, human rights and communitarian values, so that theory and method which is not oriented to these commitments is considered inadequate theory.

This has enabled communication studies to be heavily involved with issues of democratisation, the communication rights of nations of the South, the communication rights of the poor and minorities. This has also permitted communication studies to engage in a debate about the quality or performance of public media – one of which is the public journalism movement.

The public journalism movement

The current debate about public journalism is interesting because it involves both academics and editors in the publishing industry.[6] The central notion of public journalism is that local media should promote in local communities dialogue about the issues and problems in those communities and develop a political life which serves community discussion and decision-making. The movement deliberately distances itself from a journalism which simply enables politicians to get into power and remain there, regardless of whether this serves community interests.

Public journalism began with the observation of the decline in participation in public decision-making (political, social, cultural and economic) and the decline in the circulation and use of newspapers. Editors argue that newspaper circulation will not grow again until it is possible to engage the public in democracy again.

The public, it is argued, is not interested because the politicians and public relations firms are manufacturing pseudo-events which are not of interest to the people, and the newspaper industry has allowed this to happen. Public journalism is introducing a new approach, namely, finding out what issues are of interest to the people and making this the agenda of the newspapers. The newspapers then force public figures to respond to these issues.

A major objection to current practice is that the news media are tending, for economic reasons, to simply present news items straight off the wires, but defend themselves in terms of objectivity and value-free stances. This also enables newspapers to take a neutral uncontroversial position, more convenient for advertising. There is no attempt to present a 'connected' view of events. That is, journalists have an obligation to present a view of the causes and consequences of events so that people can make a more intelligent judgement about these events. In general, journalists are criticised for self-interested agenda-setting in the news rather than serving the interests of the public.

A major problem: the colonialisation of our human life space

Most human interaction in groups such as the family, friends, religious groups, etc., is under tremendous pressure today from the demands of the productive system. The media are part of the invasion of the life space,

---

[6] Theodore L. Glasser (ed.) *The Idea of Public Journalism* (New York: Guilford, 1999).

especially in the area of advertising, and the decisions about media content. If it does not produce profit or if it does not support the dominant capitalist ideology, it has no place. What is happening is that the quality of our human relations is being destroyed. Those who suffer the most are those with less valuable cultural capital, women, minority racial and ethnic groups, etc. Everything is subjected to the rules of commodities for consumption. Even our privacy has become a commodity to be sold to the highest bidder.

So far community communication approaches have not responded to this. There is some interest on the part of those promoting media education, but this has generally not had much success. This remains one of the weakest points in the communitarian ethic.

Conclusion

The movement toward communitarian communication is part of a much broader trend toward a new foundation of civil society. In the face of receding nationalism and the receding power of overarching ideologies, there is much greater emphasis on the active subject of human relations. On the one hand, the large institutional organisations with voluntary memberships, such as the labour union, the political party, the professional association or the institutional churches, seem to be a less attractive and probably less functional form of social identity today. The flexible contracting of services makes people extremely mobile not only geographically but in terms of careers or belief systems. People identify most easily with a fairly open, flexible, geographically based or virtual community which they can enter to co-operate in improving the conditions of their life space, but also leave fairly easily if life calls them elsewhere. These human relations are quite intense and affective, but also fairly loose and mobile.

Further reading

C. G. Christians, J. P. Ferre and P. M. Fackler, *Good News: Social Ethics and the Press* (New York: Oxford University Press, 1993).

T. Glasser and S. Craft, 'Public Journalism and the search for democratic ideals', Tamar Liebes and James Curran (eds.), *Media, Ritual and Identity* (London: Routledge, 1998), pp. 203–18.

M. Kieran (ed.), *Media Ethics* (London: Routledge, 1998).

E. B. Lambeth, P. E. Meyer and E. Thorson (eds.), *Assessing Public Journalism* (Columbia: University of Missouri Press, 1998).

S. Mulhall and A. Swift, *Liberals and Communitarians* (Oxford: Blackwell, 1992).

R. A. White, 'A Communitarian Ethic of Communication in a Postmodern Age', *Ethical Perspectives. Journal of the European Ethics Network* Vol 3, No. 4, (1996), pp. 207–18.

25

Cross-Cultural Ethics and Truth

Clifford G. Christians

The primary challenge at present is to replace the Eurocentric axis of communication ethics with a comparative model instead. International approaches are increasing, but a transformation to multicultural ethics has not been completed.[1] And in the process of developing a global non-Western media ethics, several contentious issues are dominating the theoretical agenda.

The first area of debate involves a shift from individualistic rationalism to social ethics. Mainstream communication ethics has presumed that autonomous agents are obliged to apply formal rules self-consciously to moral decisions. Social and feminist ethics are making a radical break with the individual autonomy and mental abstractions of canonical morality, toward a deeply holistic, gender inclusive and culturally constituted ethics instead.[2]

A second issue, less well developed, is the status and character of narrative ethics. Situating moral agents discursively is an attractive alternative to the ethics of rationalism. Switching from principle to story often invigorates our analysis, especially in communication ethics. Social constructions and contextual values do not seek ultimate standards, but investigate the conditions under which we consider our value judgments

---

[1] Examples of internationalising communication ethics are Fred Casmir (ed.), *Ethics in Intercultural and International Communication* (Mahwah, NJ: Lawrence Erlbaum, 1997); Clifford Christians and Michael Traber (eds.), *Communication Ethics and Universal Values* (Thousand Oaks, CA: Sage, 1997); Thomas Cooper, *Communication Ethics and Global Change* (New York: Longman, 1989); Thomas Cooper, *A Time Before Deception: Truth in Communication, Culture and Ethics* (Santa Fe, NM: Clear Light, 1998); Bart Pattyn (ed.), *Media Ethics: Opening Social Dialogue* (Leuven, Belgium: Peeters, 2000); Cees J. Hamelink, *World Communication: Disempowerment and Self-Empowerment* (New York: St. Martin's 1996); Kaarle Nordensteng and Hifzi Topuz (eds.), *Journalist: Status, Rights and Responsibilities* (Prague: International Order of Journalists, 1989); and Claude-Jean Bertrand, *L'arsenal de la Démocratie: Médias, déontologie et MARS* (Paris: Economica, 1999).

[2] Daryl Koehn, *Rethinking Feminist Ethics* (New York: Routledge, 1998); Charlene Siegfried, *Pragmatism and Feminism: Reweaving the Social Fabric* (Chicago: University of Chicago Press, 1996); Virginia Held, *Feminist Morality: Transforming Culture, Society, and Politics* (Chicago: University of Chicago Press, 1993); Carol Gilligan, *In a Different Voice: Psychological Theory and Women's Development* (Cambridge, MA: Harvard University Press, 1982); and Nel Noddings, *Caring: A Feminine Approach to Ethics and Moral Education* (Berkeley: University of California Press, 1984).

warranted.[3] However, narrative ethics entails the conundrum that whatever is identified experimentally cannot itself yield normative guidelines. To assert prescriptive claims from an experimental base is contradictory. Therefore, despite the intellectual power of narrative ethics, an ethics of being is emerging as a new path away from both.

A third issue is the possibility and credibility of universals in cross-cultural ethics. Universal imperatives that claim to be rooted in the shared features of human beings as a whole have been largely discredited. Abstract notions of the good are now recognised as the 'morality of a dominant gender and class'.[4] Must we therefore presume that moral principles have no validity outside the societies within which they are constituted? Does cultural diversity entail philosophical relativism? In confronting these questions, entirely new kinds of universalism are being developed; they are not rooted in human reason nor do they presuppose essentialist human nature.[5]

Fourth, in the face of today's massive multimedia conglomerates, can we articulate a legitimate version of distributive justice? A new world information order is coming into its own, and only a sophisticated and complex notion of social justice can respond to it adequately. The dominant conception under private ownership is allocating to each according to ability to pay. The open marketplace of supply and demand determines who obtains the service, and justice means equitable access to products at a fair price. In contrast, an ethics of social justice based on need allocates to everyone according to essential needs, regardless of income or geographical location. Therefore as a necessity of life in an increasingly global society, information systems ought to be distributed impartially, regardless of income, race, religion or merit. This view of social justice must be established up front at the head of the information revolution.

A fifth difficult issue on the media ethics agenda is identified by Charles Taylor as the politics of recognition.[6] Democratic societies are committed by definition to equal representation for all. Each individual counts, and in principle everyone is given equal access to the procedures of democratic institutions. Thus the crucial question is whether democracies are culpable if their institutions do not take account of specific cultural and social

[3] W. Ellos, *Narrative Ethics* (Oxford: Blackwell, 1994); John Dewey, *Human Nature and Conduct* (New York: Henry Holt, 1948, 1992); and Richard Rorty, *Contingency, Irony and Solidarity* (Cambridge, UK: Cambridge University Press, 1989).

[4] Gene Outka and J. P. Reeder, Jr. (eds.), *Prospects for a Common Morality* (Princeton: Princeton University Press, 1993), p. 4.

[5] Benhabib's interactive universalism, Nussbaum's capabilities approach, Wiredu's common biological identity, and sacredness of life as a protonoun in Christians and Traber are illustrations: Seyla Benhabib, *Situating the Self: Gender, Community and Postmodernism in Contemporary Ethics* (Cambridge, UK: Polity Press, 1992); Martha Nussbaum, *Women and Human Development: The Capabilities Approach* (Cambridge, UK: Cambridge University Press, 2000); Kwasi Wiredu, *Cultural Universals and Particulars: An African Perspective* (Bloomington, IN: Indiana University Press, 1996); Christians and Traber, *Communication Ethics and Universal Values*.

[6] Charles Taylor, et al., *Multiculturalism: Examining the Politics of Recognition* (Princeton: Princeton University Press, 1994).

identities. In what sense do our race, gender and religion require explicit recognition? With the rise of democratisation and the collapse of social hierarchies, the challenge of multiculturalism becomes inescapable. Democratic citizens in principle share an equal right to education, police protection, political liberties, religious freedom, due process and health care. But beyond equal rights, the foundational question about the character of cultural identity must be resolved for democracy to remain vital over the long term.

These complicated issues in communication ethics need further development. As voices are heard and perspectives articulated from around the world, additional issues will enter the discourse. In the midst of these clarifications and expansions of the agenda in communication ethics, a believable concept of truth is the primary need. The central question as we develop a cross-cultural ethics is whether scholars of communication and culture can recover the idea of truth. As the norm of healing is to medicine, justice to politics, and critical thinking to education, so truthtelling is the occupational norm of the media professions. Without articulating a sophisticated notion of truth, any new model of comparative ethics will have an empty center.

As a way of stimulating further research and scholarship on this foundational issue, I develop an argument for truth as disclosure. In constructing this alternative to the mainstream view, I consider a theological framework to be inescapable. In that sense, this essay on the state of communication ethics at present challenges philosophical and sociological perspectives to match theological ones on the question of truth.[7] Clearly the theistic worldview represented here must meet the standard of religious diversity to be credible, as communication ethics becomes international in scope. In order to sharpen dialogue, truth will be approached from a Christian perspective, but out of a commitment to pluralism. Therefore, rather than merely identifying the issue of truth as important for multicultural ethics, the concept of truth and its nuances will be elaborated below. For the sake of specificity the focus will be on news, though the argument by extension applies to communication institutions, technologies and practices as a whole.

Definitions

Historically the mainstream media have defined themselves in terms of an objectivist worldview. Centered on human rationality and armed with the scientific method, the facts in the news have been said to mirror reality. The aim has been true and incontrovertible accounts of a domain separate from human consciousness. In Bertrand Russell's formula, 'truth consists in

---

[7] For an elaboration of the concept of truth from a non-theological perspective, see Clifford Christians, 'Social Dialogue and Media Ethics', *Ethical Perspectives* 7:2–3 (September 2000), pp. 182–93.

some form of correspondence between belief and fact'.[8] In the received view, truth is defined in elementary epistemological terms as accurate representation and precision with data, that is, verisimilitude. News corresponds to neutral algorithms, and professionalism is equated with impartiality.

In the objective Greek view of truth, Plato saw it as reality and for Aristotle truth was correct or accurate statement. Truth was mathematical and non-contingent for Descartes, an ontological category. This prevailing view of human knowledge in the West has been attacked steadily since the Counter-Enlightenment of the eighteenth century, until the antifoundationalism of our own day indicates a crisis in correspondence perspectives on truth. The demise of correspondence views has created a predicament for the notion of truth altogether. However, instead of appealing to coherence versions or abandoning the concept, truth needs to be relocated in the moral sphere. Truth is a problem of axiology rather than epistemology. With the dominant scheme no longer tenable, truth should become the province of communication ethicists who can reconstruct it as the news media's contribution to public discourse.

When truth is articulated in terms of a moral framework, it is most richly textured in the Hebrew *emeth* (trustworthy, genuine, dependable, authentic) and the Greek *aletheia* (openness, disclosure). But there are reflections of this moral accent across the human family. In Serbo-Croation the true is justified as with a plumbline in carpentry. In the powerful wheel imagery of the Buddhist tradition, truth is the immovable axle. The Truth and Reconciliation Commission in South Africa presumes that sufferings from apartheid can be healed through truthful testimony. In Gandhi's *satyagrapha*, the power of truth through the human spirit eventually wins over force.[9] Dietrich Bonhoeffer's *Ethics* contends correctly that a truthful account lays hold of the context, motives and presuppositions involved. For him, telling the truth depends on the quality of discernment so that penultimates do not gain ultimacy.[10] Truth means, in other words, to strike gold, to get at 'the core, the essence, the nub, the heart of the matter'.[11] For Kierkegaard, truth is subjective, and Brunner speaks of truth as encounter. Buber finds truth in the I-Thou relationship. For the former Secretary General of the United Nations, Dag Hammarskjold, 'the most dangerous of all moral dilemmas is when we are obliged to conceal truth in order to help the truth be victorious'.[12] In the Talmud, the liars' punishment is that no one believes them.

---

[8] Bertrand Russell, *Problems of Philosophy* (New York: Henry Holt, 1912), p. 121. Cf. Richard L. Kirkham, *Theories of Truth* (Cambridge, MA: MIT Press, 1992), ch. 4.

[9] Vernon Jensen, 'Bridging the Millennia: Truth and Trust in Human Communication', Sixth National Communication Ethics Conference, Gull Lake, Michigan, USA. (May 2000), p. 6.

[10] Dietrich Bonhoeffer, *Ethics*, trans. N. H. Smith (New York: Macmillan, 1955), ch. 5.

[11] Wesley Pippert, *An Ethics of News: A Reporter's Search for Truth* (Washington, DC: Georgetown University Press, 1989), p. 11.

[12] Jensen, 'Bridging the Millennia,' p. 7.

Augustine (AD 354–430), professor of rhetoric at Milan and later Bishop of Hippo, illustrates a non-correspondence view of truth. His rhetorical theory is a major contribution to the philosophy of communication, contradicting the highly secular and linear view of the ancient Greeks. As with Aristotle, rhetoric entails reasoned judgment for Augustine; however, he 'break[s] away from Graeco-Roman rhetoric, moving instead toward ... rhetoric as *aletheiac* act'.[13] Rhetoric for him is not knowledge-producing or opinion producing but truth producing (*aletheia*). Truth is not fundamentally a value-neutral prescriptive statement. *Aletheia* in Augustine 'tends to be more relational than propositional, a dialogically interpersonal, sacramental act rather than a statement ... taking into account and being motivated by [the cardinal virtues] faith, hope, and charity'.[14] The truth for him does not merely make things clear, but motivates us to belief and action. In truthful communication, for Augustine, '[I]t is not enough to move our minds, merely for the sake of power; instead this power must be used to lead us to truth.'[15] He conceived of truth as reason irradiated by love, the rhetorical process informed and directed by *caritas*. The Augustinian legacy subverts contemporary discourse which defines truth as facticity. His truth as *aletheia* has a constructive ambience while linking truth with moral discernment.

Created order

As biblical theism enters the world of truth through the New Testament's *aletheia*, special revelation is engaged as an integrated whole: creation, redemption, the eschaton. Jesus' resurrection, as St. Paul presents it, is God's decisive word on his creature Adam.[16] Adam's choice of sin and death is reversed. The work of the creator who brought into being an order of things in which humanity has a place is affirmed once for all. Through the empty tomb God stands by the world he made and will not allow it to be brought to nothing. In the second Adam the world of the first Adam is restored. 'As in Adam all die, so in Christ shall all be made alive' (I Cor. 15:22). The resurrection is the assurance that the world God has made is stable and permanent.

Thus a worldview of the Kingdom has the created order as its foundation. The very act of God which ushers in his Kingdom is the resurrection of Christ, which itself reaffirms creation. With faith one knows the created

---

[13] Glenn Settle, 'Faith, Hope and Charity: Rhetoric as Aletheiac Act in *On Christian Doctrine*', *Journal of Communication and Religion* 17:2 (September 1994), p. 49.

[14] Settle, 'Faith, Hope and Charity', pp. 49, 57.

[15] James J. Murphy, *Rhetoric in the Middle Ages: A History of Rhetorical Theory from St. Augustine to the Renaissance* (Berkeley: University of California Press, 1974), p. 62.

[16] The integrated connection of resurrection and creation is developed here following Oliver O'Donovan, *Resurrection and Moral Order*, 2nd ed. (Leicester: Apollos, 1994), chs. 1–3, esp. pp. 13–17, 31–5.

order in its wholeness; but all God's creatures find it structuring their existence. The resurrection of believing individuals apart from creation would
be a purely gnostic and world-denying gospel. So the resurrection of Christ
directs our attention back to the creation which it vindicates, and it would
be meaningless if creation were no more than undifferentiated energy. It is
not created energy as such that is renewed in the resurrection of Christ, but
the order in which created energy was disposed by the hand of the creator.
Creation is not merely raw material, but is ordered by its creator's design.
There is a world that exists as his creation and in no other way.

Moreover, just because it is ordered vertically, it must have an internal
horizontal ordering among its parts. The creation forms, over against the
creator, an ordered whole in which created parts are determined in their
existence by their maker. Through the six days of creation a complex and
intelligible network of relations binds the universe into a cosmic oneness.
Vegetables and people are both created, but vegetables are ordered to
people as food. Rocks and trees are both created entities, but rocks are
ordered to trees as the foundation for the soil in which they grow.

Some kinds are hierarchical, subspecies within species, and species within
genus. But relations among humans are horizontal: no slave race is created
to serve a master race. Work is creation's gift. Speech is ordered to truth
and marriage to fidelity. And in its orderedness, creation is the complete,
given totality which forms the presupposition of historical existence. The
created order is not negotiable when the course of history unfolds. Chance
will not destroy the creation, and the human species will not transmogrify
into something else. The created order is history's source, its beginning, an
intelligible order that makes history intelligible.

The eternal creator of all things is the source and norm of all truth about
everything. The creator of all knows all truth and he knows it as a coherent
whole. While God alone is omniscient and human knowledge partial, the
created order affirms that truth is knowable and life ultimately makes sense.
Humans 'created as intelligent beings in God's image can hope to understand in measure a world intelligently made'[17] by the supremely intelligent
being. It means that although we know in part and see it all dimly, yet what
we see and know will ideally fit together into the intelligible whole God himself knows it to be.

The doctrine of creation affirms that truth is as wide as reality itself.
Historic Christianity affirms the 'truthfulness of Scripture, not as ... an
exhaustive revelation of everything we can know, but as a sufficient rule of
faith and conduct'.[18] The truth of Civil War history in the United States and
the electromagnetic spectrum, for example, are known apart from scripture. Revelation occurs on two planes, special and general. From Clement
of Alexandria to Jonathan Edwards, from John Calvin to Arthur Holmes, all
truth is God's truth wherever it may be found.

---

[17] Arthur Holmes, *All Truth is God's Truth* (Grand Rapids: Eerdmans, 1977).
[18] Holmes, *All Truth*, p. 8.

The biblical writers themselves have an intimate knowledge of nature, society and human culture. Moses was well trained in the learning of Egyptians, Daniel in Babylonian scholarship and Paul in the Rabbinical schools. Within 'the admixture of wheat and tares in human thought' after the Fall, 'all creaturely activities and all human learning bear witness' to the God of Truth.[19]

Truth rooted in creation means that 'truth is inherently personal, not autonomous like the ideal forms of Plato's *Republic*, nor an abstract ideal approached with detachment' as in the Enlightenment. Biblical *emeth* and *aletheia* are primarily ethical rather than epistemological terms.[20] Theism emphasises less the static quality of objects than the human act of knowing. Knowledge is life-related. We know and have moral convictions in the process. Being personal and not detached means we measure up to what we know and act accordingly. Thus for *aletheia* Jesus used a strange language. He spoke of 'doing the truth', 'living the truth', 'abiding in' and thus 'being in the truth', and of knowing the truth will set us free. *Aletheia* is not the correspondence of intellectual knowledge and facts. It must be done. It is *in actu*.[21] Truth as disclosure and authenticity is rooted in our creatureliness. The biblical view of truth is not personal 'in the sense of being individually relative but rather in the sense of being a deeply meaningful and even a religious concern'.[22]

In Descartes' mathematical reasoning, it is the mind alone which knows. In the fuller understanding of biblical *emeth* and *aletheia*, there is no propositional truth independent of human beings as a whole. Truthtelling is not considered a problem of cognition *per se*, but is integrated into human consciousness and social formation.

Human existence is impossible without an overriding commitment to truth. As a primary agent of the lingual world in which we live, the news media have no choice but to honor this norm as obligatory for their mission and rationale.

Interpretive sufficiency

Truth as *emeth* and *aletheia* is known to us in special revelation, but grounded in creational truth that by God's common grace has intrinsic value universally. This releases the news media from objectivism and correspondence. What exactly does the redeemed mind propose as guidelines instead? Forsaking the quest for precision journalism does not mean imprecision, but precision in *aletheia*, in disclosure and authenticity, in getting to the heart of the matter. To replace news gathering rooted in empiricism,

[19] Holmes, *All Truth*, pp. 21, 23.
[20] Holmes, *All Truth*, p. 34.
[21] Philip C. Holtrop, 'A Strange Language: Toward a Biblical Conception of Truth', *The Reformed Journal* (February 1977), p. 9.
[22] Holmes, *All Truth*, pp. 35–6.

fiction and fabrication are not acceptable substitutes. In terms of authenticity and disclosure, reporters will seek what might be called 'interpretive sufficiency'. They will polish their investigative and writing skills in terms of interpretive strategies. They will ensure the news story's deeper reading.

In *aletheia*, human knowing is grounded historically and biographically, so that complex cultures are represented adequately. The reporters' frame of reference is not derived from a free-floating mathematics, but resonates with the attitudes, definitions and language of the people and events they are actually reporting. In a fundamental sense, interpretive sufficiency is a temperament of mind. C. Wright Mills called it 'the sociological imagination', rather than merely a series of techniques for handling the telephone, minicam or interview pad.

Interpretive sufficiency seeks to open up public life in all its dynamic dimensions. Ethnographic accounts have the 'depth, detail, emotionality, nuance, and coherence' that permit 'a critical consciousness to be formed' by readers and viewers. Rather than reducing social issues to the financial and administrative problems defined by politicians, the news media disclose and lay open to enable people to judge authenticity themselves.[23]

Sensitised concepts are a crucial dimension of truth as disclosure. These categories are formulated from the research area itself, yet are sufficiently powerful to explain large domains of social experience. They generate an insightful picture and distinctively convey the meaning of a series of events. They get at the essence, the heart of the matter. Quantitative research traditionally produces law-like abstractions through fixed procedures designed to isolate concepts from the experience, attitudes and language of the people being studied. IQ, for example, becomes the operational definition of intelligence.

Sensitised concepts are a different device for ordering empirical instances. They display an integrating scheme from within the data themselves. The truth of authenticity unveils their inner character. Examples of those well known in the literature are Charles Cooley's 'primary group', 'James Carey's 'ritual vs. transmission' view of communication, Alexis de Tocqueville's 'equalitarianism', Antonio Gramsci's 'hegemony', Jean Jacques Rousseau's 'noble savage', Thomas Kuhn's 'paradigm', Thorsten Veblen's 'conspicuous consumption', Jean Baudrillard's 'simulacra', Harold Innis' 'monopoly of knowledge', and Irving Janis' 'group think'.

With sensitised concepts, the theory–practice relationship is not linear but dialectical. This is grounded theory, integrating the existential and conceptual, emphasising the interpretive character of theorising in natural settings. Experience alone is not the same as understanding it. It aims for compelling generalisations that are grounded in the language, definitions

[23] Norman Denzin, *Interpretive Ethnography: Ethnographic Practices for the 21st Century* (Thousand Oaks, CA: Sage, 1997), p. 283. Clifford Christians, John Ferré and Mark Fackler, *Good News: Social Ethics and the Press* (New York: Oxford University Press, 1993), pp. 120–2.

and attitudes of those who are studied. It requires a reflexive form of writing that turns ethnographic and theoretical texts back onto each other.[24] In the process of weaving a tapestry of truth, reporters will attempt to reduce as much as possible the distance between the concepts of social science and those of the particular news context itself. The deeper disclosures will ring true on both levels; that is, they will be theoretically credible and realistic to the natives. Sensitised concepts are the most lasting contribution the news media can make.

Ellul's la technique

Jacques Ellul provides an example of *aletheia* – in this case, the truth as disclosure of social structures. His work illustrates interpretive sufficiency as he cuts through today's technology to the fundamental issues underneath.

In our commonplaces, technology is neutral. Technology is seen in mechanistic terms as an instrument that can be used for good or ill, artifacts apart from values. If whales become extinct because of modern hunting weapons and if television is excessively violent, we are not to blame those who designed and manufactured the tools. Politicians and consumers use bad judgment. Technology *per se* is not at fault, but the uses to which we put it. A knife in the surgeon's hands saves life; among criminal gangs it kills. The same video player shows pornography and educational specials in science.

Technics are not thought to have any meaning in themselves; they are a means to something else. Technology is extrinsic to a person's being and society's character. Its purpose derives from non-technological goals. What it produces is not necessary or innate. Musical instruments are for enjoyment, television promotes the visual arts, and the telescope in astronomy expands human knowledge. But in all cases technical products receive their justification from the uses to which they are put. Technology itself is subordinate, a lower human activity, pedestrian.

Aletheia – disclosure – interpretive sufficiency probes beneath this neutrality model to the heart of the issue. The whole technological phenomenon must be called into question, not just some of its positive or negative consequences. Jacques Ellul understands the technological order in terms of the instrumentalist worldview it represents. Technological societies are fundamentally amoral. Their social infrastructure conforms to *la technique*, to the spirit of machineness.[25] The issue is not technological products, but the mystique of efficiency that underlies them. As 'in ancient days they put out the eyes of nightingales in order to make them sing better', we skewer

---

[24] Norman Denzin, *Interpretive Ethnography*, p. xii.
[25] Jacques Ellul, *The Technological Society*, trans. J. Wilkinson (New York: Vintage, 1964).
[26] Jacques Ellul, *Presence of the Kingdom*, trans. O. Wyon (New York: Seabury, 1967), p. 75.

commitments, freedom and ethics for the machine-like imperative of efficiency.[26] The information system, itself co-opted by *la technique,* subtly manipulates the citizens to accept it, even welcome it eagerly.

Abundant data, far from permitting people to make judgments and form opinions, actually keeps them busy within an instrumentalism alien to moral obligation. Global realities demand global communications. Information is a social necessity for a modern planet, but as the system is expanded, its content thickened, and transmission speeded up, its normative base is being undermined though needed now more than ever. Efficiency and morality are a contradiction in terms.

Rather than being neutral, technology is value-laden throughout. Value judgments penetrate all technological activity, from our selecting the needs to address and which materials to use, through the processes of design and fabrication, to the resulting tools and products. Technology proceeds from our whole human experience and is directed by our ultimate commitments. Technological objects are unique, not universal. The problems of x and not y are addressed. Certain resources are used and not others.

The values underlying the technological enterprise are the question for *aletheia.* We value progress, technical expertise and natural reality as a resource. And only when these values, these dimensions of the instrumental worldview, are revolutionised, will radical changes occur in our technological society. The mainstream neutrality definition is driven by a logical fallacy. It confuses the part with the whole. The product, tool or artifact is substituted for the technological enterprise, as though the tip of the iceberg is the iceberg itself. Truth as disclosure focuses for us on the values that drive the technological society, calling for a transformation in our commitments to progress, expertise, unlimited natural resources and efficiency.

Conclusion

I am contending that truth in creational terms be the media's defining feature. To the extent we achieve it, we have available the public resources for solidarity, enriched dialogue and peace. And among these social goods truth is foundational; truth pulls them together. As prophetic wisdom puts it, 'Justice stands far off; for truth has fallen in the public square, and righteousness cannot enter' (Isa. 59:14–15). Truth is a basic principle integrating other norms.

We face what Jürgen Habermas calls a crisis of legitimation. With correspondence theories of truth in disrepute, what counts as valid? It is far from settled whether a credible version of normative values in general, and of truthtelling in particular, can be established for cross-cultural ethics. But this is a worthwhile goal, even an essential one, given the centrality of truth to communications as a scholarly field and professional practice.

This chapter represents a theological attempt to wrest the concept of truth away from its Enlightenment moorings and to understand it in creational, cross-cultural terms. It is premised on confessional pluralism, that is, with intellectual integrity it articulates a Christian worldview within a plethora of worldviews and ideologies. While the other issues continue to be researched and resolved, this chapter is one way to reinvigorate truth as the axis of a new model of comparative communication ethics.

Further reading

Z. Bauman, *Postmodern Ethics* (Oxford: Blackwell, 1993).

S. Benhabib, *Situating the Self: Gender, Community and Postmodernism in Contemporary Ethics* (New York: Routledge, 1992).

N. Fraser, *Justus Interruptus* (New York: Routledge, 1997).

J. Habermas, *Justification and Application: Remarks on Discourse Ethics,* trans. C. Cronin (Cambridge: MIT Press, 1993).

C. J. Hamelink, *The Ethics of Cyberspace* (Thousand Oaks, CA: Sage, 2000).

A. Heller, *Beyond Justice* (Oxford: Blackwell, 1988).

A. Holderegger (ed.), *Ethik der Medienkommunitkation: Grundlagen* (Freiburg-Wien: Universitätsverlag Freiburg Schweiz, 1992).

D. Koehn, *Rethinking Feminist Ethics: Care, Trust and Empathy* (London: Routledge, 1998).

E. F. Paul, F. D. Miller and J. Paul (eds.), *Cultural Pluralism and Moral Knowledge* (Cambridge: Cambridge University Press, 1994).

C. Taylor, *Sources of the Self: The Making of the Modern Identity* (Cambridge: Harvard University Press, 1989).

26

Foundation of Communication in Islamic Societies

Hamid Mowlana

Introduction

The phenomenon of communication and culture has been the subject of many heated discussions and debates during the last several decades. Although numerous studies have been carried out in this somewhat general and prolific area, the comparative aspect of this concern has remained fairly underdeveloped, particularly by the students of communication theories. There are a number of distinct reasons for this neglect, among them, conceptual unclarity, epistemological rigidity, insufficient skill in language and area studies, a high level of ethnocentrism and parochialism, and a good deal of ideological bias. Consequently, our knowledge of communication, culture and social systems is provincial rather than universal. There is not time and space in this chapter to dwell on this issue, which requires a separate thesis of its own. Suffice it to say that if human communication as a discipline remains the focus of our attention, we must strive to understand and study cultural and social systems in a comparative and universal context, and pay particular attention to those cultural and geo-social areas with which we are less familiar. In my own work as an international relations researcher and teacher, working at the level of the general theory of international communication, I have found this comparative perspective completely indispensable.

This chapter is a study of a social system and a value system within an Islamic context. A social system is a process of interaction of individuals within a larger unit called society, which exhibits the property that Ibn Khaldun, an Islamic thinker, called solidarity ('*assabieh*'), a term also employed later by Durkheim in his works. As Kroeber and Parsons have noted, a social system is not the value itself, but a system of values and actions of individuals which are associated in terms of symbolic meaning. On the other hand, values maintain the cultural integrity and cohesion of society, serving to legitimise the modes of more concrete actions. Here, we are concerned with the question of cultural systems and how they interact

305

with problems of conceptualisation, theorisation and practices of infor-mation and communication. What impact do cultural settings have on the studies of communication? What communication theories and practices do they foster?

The Islamic world

The Islamic world consists of a vast and diverse geo-political area stretching from Indonesia and the Pacific Ocean in the east to Morocco and the Atlantic coast in the west, from Central Asia and the Himalayas in the north to the southern African nations and the Indian Ocean. As one of the major religions of the world, Islam encompasses one quarter of the world's popu-lation, over a billion and a half people. From the death of the prophet Mohammad (AD 572–632) and the period of the first four Caliphs (AD 632–61), to the end of World War I and the demise of the Ottoman Empire, the Islamic community has been a major world power. In the context of decolonisation and increasing numbers of sovereign nation-states, the Islamic world politically, economically and often culturally began to inte-grate into the existing sphere of the Western-dominated modern world system. The contacts between the Islamic world and the West in the nine-teenth and twentieth centuries increased the absorption of many Islamic countries into quasi-secular political entities ranging from hereditary monarchies to modern Western and/or military-style republics. This also resulted in pronounced conflicts between modern secularism and the Islamic tradition of *al shari'a*, the canonical law of Islam.

In order to understand the current social communication processes in the Islamic world and to assess their future directions, it is necessary to examine a number of the fundamental principles upon which the Islamic *tabligh* (propagation) framework has been built, and how the Islamic soci-eties have come under constraint as a result of global political, economic and cultural developments over the last century. In this chapter the study of Islamic communication and ethics in general and the Islamic *tabligh* or propagation in particular, is not directed towards a single country or a geo-graphical area, although a number of Islamic countries are mentioned. Rather, the central foci of analysis will be on the fundamental principles of Islamic ethical methods in communication and on the objectives and aims of *tabligh*. This understanding should help clarify the function of some of the modern institutions of communication in contemporary Islamic societies.

Definition of terms

A distinction should be made between the Islamic term '*tabligh*' (propagation) and the general concepts of communication, propaganda and agitation commonly used in contemporary literature. The word 'communication' comes from the Latin *communico* – meaning 'to share', and it is essentially a social process referring to the act of imparting, conveying or exchanging ideas, knowledge or information. It is a process of access or means of access between two or more persons or places. Also implicit and explicit in this definition is a notion of some degree of trust without which communication cannot take place. In its reductive approach (mathematical, technical and some scientific analysis) communication is associated with the concept of information linking the process with chance events and various possible outcomes. This 'atomic' view gives emphasis to quantitative and linear aspects of the process and not to its cultural and cognitive meanings.[1]

The term 'propaganda' is a Western concept and was used for the first time by a committee of cardinals (founded in 1622 by Pope Gregory) of the Roman Catholic Church having the care and oversight of foreign missions. Propaganda comes from the Latin word *propagare* and originally meant propagating the gospel and establishing the Church in non-Christian countries. The contemporary usage of the term in its political, sociological and commercial contexts, however, dates back to the beginning of the twentieth century. Since World War I, its definition has evolved to connote an instrument of persuasion and manipulation of individuals and collective behaviour in national and international scenes.[2]

Thus, according to French sociologist Jacques Ellul, 'propaganda is a set of methods employed by an organised group that wants to bring about the active or passive participation in its action of a mass of individuals psychologically unified through psychological manipulations and incorporated in an organization'.[3] In a somewhat similar fashion, Harold D. Lasswell, an American political scientist, has defined propaganda as 'the manipulation of symbols as a means of influencing attitudes on controversial matters'.[4] This follows the common definition of propaganda as spreading ideology,

---

[1] A. L. Kroeber and Talcott Parsons, 'The Concepts of Culture and of Social System', *American Sociological Review* 23 (October 1958), pp. 582–3.

[2] See Norbert Wiener, *Cybernetics, or Control and Communication in Animal and Machine* (Cambridge: MIT Press, 1961) and his *The Human Use of Human Beings: Cybernetics and Society* (New York: Avon, 1967). Also Colin Cherry, *On Human Communication* (Cambridge: MIT Press, 1961); Claude E. Shannon and Warren Weaver, *The Mathematical Theory of Communication* (Urbana: University of Illinois Press, 1961); and Peter Payl Kirschemann, *Information and Reflection: On Some Problems of Cybernetics and How Contemporary Dialectical Materialism Copes with Them* (Dordrencht, The Netherlands: D. Reidel, 1970).

[3] Jacques Ellul, *Propaganda: The Formation of Men's Attitudes* (New York: Vintage Books, 1965), p. 61.

[4] Harold D. Lasswell, Daniel Lerner and Hans Speier (eds.), *Propaganda and Communication in World History*, Three volumes (Honolulu: University of Hawaii Press, 1980). (The first volume deals with 'The Symbolic Instrument of Early Times', while the second volume concerns the 'Emergence of Public Opinion in the West'. The third volume deals with the contemporary world situation.) Also Harold D. Lasswell, 'Communication Research and Politics,' Douglas Waples (ed.), *Print, Radio, and Film in a Democracy* (Chicago: University of Chicago Press, 1942), p. 106.

doctrine or ideas and of agitation as an instrument for arousing people to spontaneous action. The communist position on propaganda and agitation differs methodologically from that of Lasswell. As defined by Vladimir I. Lenin, 'a propagandist presents many ideas to one or a few persons; an agitator presents only one or a few ideas, but he presents them to a mass of people'.[5]

Note that contemporary propagandists, therefore, do not need to be believers in an ideology or a doctrine. Here propagandists are people in the service of the state, the party, the political or commercial campaign, or any other organisation that is ready to use their expertise. Propagandists are technicians, bureaucrats and specialists who may eventually come to despise the ideology itself. The aim is the objective of propaganda and the method is utilitarian.

Tabligh or propagation, on the other hand, is dissemination and diffusion of some principle, belief or practice. It is the increase or spread of a belief by natural reproduction; it is an extension in space and time. It is the action of branching out. *Tabligh* in an Islamic context has an ethical boundary and a set of guiding principles. In a broader sense, *tabligh* is a theory of communication and ethics. This theory of communication and global community integration is well stated by Ibn Khaldun (1332–1406, a great Islamic thinker and social philosopher) in *The Muqaddimah* (*An Introduction to History*). Here he cites 'truthful propagation' (*tabligh*) and group cohesion (*assabieh*) as two fundamental factors in the rise of world powers as states and large communities.[6]

Communication and ethics: their boundaries and frontiers

A study of *tabligh* in Islamic society in the early days and certainly before the rise of the modern nation-state system has a unique element to it.[7] This is because it was rooted in oral and social traditions and the notion of '*ummah*' or greater Islamic community. Also the geographical entities now called Islamic countries were not heavily influenced by Western methods, conducts and regimes in conflict with the major tenets of Islam. With the exception of the Islamic Republic of Iran, which is founded on the Islamic notion of the state, the remaining Islamic countries have state systems which are a mixture of the modern and traditional monarchical

---

[5] Vladimir I. Lenin, *Selected Works II*, J. Fineberg (ed.), (New York: Macmillan, 1935–9), p. 85.

[6] Ibn Khaldun, *The Introduction to History: The Muqaddimah*, trans. Franz Rosenthal, abridged and edited N. J. Dowood (London: Routledge & Kegan, Paul, 1967), pp. 123–7. Also, Abdulrahman Ibn Khaldun, *Muqaddimah* (translated into Persian by Muhammad Parvin Gonabadi), Vol. I (Tehran: Bongah-e-Tarjumeh va Nashreh Ketab, [1336] 1957) pp. 301–16.

[7] Murtaza Mutahhari, *Majmo-e-Ghoftaha* (*Collection of Speeches*) (Tehran: Sadra [1361] 1982); and *Nahjul Balagha: Sermons, Letters and Sayings of Hazrat Ali*, trans. Syed Mohammed Ashari Jafery, (Elmhurst, New York: Tahrik-e-Tarsile Quran, 1977).

or republican systems. Thus their legal and ethical codes are heavily influenced by non-Islamic frames of reference. In many current analyses, great confusion arises from the failure to make a distinction between a nation-state and an Islamic state. It should be emphasised that while the nation-state is a *political* state, the Islamic state is a *muttagi* or religio-political and 'God-fearing' state. The ecological terrain of *tabligh* in an Islamic state emphasises intrapersonal/interpersonal communication over impersonal types, social communication over atomistic communication and intercultural communication over nationalism.

Moving from the process of *tabligh* to the definition of ethics, it must be emphasised that the boundaries of the study called 'ethics' vary from culture to culture. For the purpose of the present study, a method of ethics is defined as any rational procedure by which we determine what an individual human being as a person and as a member of a community ought to do as a 'right' action by voluntary means. By using the word 'individual' as a member of community, this definition does not make a distinction between ethics and politics. From an Islamic perspective, the study and conduct of politics cannot be separated from the methods of ethics; the need is to determine what ought to be and not to analyse what merely is. Consequently, the concept of ethics here essentially deals with the Islamic perceptions of conduct as an inquiry into the nature of '*tawhid*' – the unity of God, humankind and nature and the method of attaining it.[8]

Since the Enlightenment, the West has gradually divorced religion from secular life. Ethical conduct in everyday life was left to an individual's conscience as long as such actions did not conflict with perceived public morality. In Islam, this separation of the religious from the secular sphere did not materialise, and if attempts were made by the late modernisers to do this, the process was never completed. Thus, throughout Islamic societies not only did religion encompass a person wholly, but also the conduct of individuals in general was shaped by Islamic socio-religious ethics. In short, whereas modern ethics in the West became predominantly social in nature, in Islamic societies that power remained religious as well as social. As the Qur'an says: 'The noblest of you in the sight of Allah is the best of you in conduct' (49:13). In the Islamic tradition the word '*adab*' means discipline of the mind or every praiseworthy conduct by which a person excels.

Until the nineteenth century Islamic canonical law, *al shari'a*, provided the main if not the complete legal underpinning of social and economic conduct in Muslim societies. The intimate contact between Islam and modern Western industrial countries, coupled with the process of colonisation of substantial parts of Asia and Africa, introduced a number of Western standards and values to these societies. Thus at the beginning of the twentieth century and with the introduction of modern means of communication, transportation and technologies, the fields of civil and commercial

---

[8] Murtaza Mutahhari, *Fundamentals of Islamic Thought: God, Man and the Universe*, trans. R. Campbell (Berkeley, CA: Mizan, 1985).

transactions proved particularly ripe for change and new methods of con-duct. The first foothold of European law, criminal and commercial, in the Islamic countries (particularly in the Ottoman Empire) was advanced as a result of the system of Capitulations, which ensured that the European citizens residing in the Middle East and a large part of Africa would not be governed by the Islamic laws and conduct of ethics but by their own laws and traditions. Furthermore, the reform movements such as the Tanzimat in the Ottoman (1839–76) and the Constitutional reform in Iran (1906–11) were indeed direct translations of French and other European codes which tended to establish secularism and injected the kinds of rules of conduct that were particularly European. In Egypt that process, from 1875 onward, went even further in the adaptation of European laws in such fields as commerce and navigation and included the enactment of civil codes which were basically modelled on French laws and contained only a few provisions drawn from *shari'a.*

Communication and ethical thinking in Islamic societies

The current ethical thinking and practices in Islamic societies, especially as they might relate to *tabligh,* communication and social interactions, are usually based on two different but important dimensions: (1) normative religious ethics as explained in the primary source of Islam, the Qur'an and the traditions (*al-sunna*) of the Prophet and the Imams; and (2) normative secular ethics ranging from the Greek tradition of popular Platonism, to the Persian tradition of giving advice to sultans and *wazirs* about government and politics, to the more contemporary ethical frameworks introduced by the West through 'modernisation', 'development', 'industrialisation' and 'secular humanism'.

In the first category, the study of ethical principles in the religious tradition dates back to the eighth and ninth centuries, during which two lines of argument were developed: the rationalist, which subscribed to rational opinion (*ra'y*), argued that where there is no clear guidance from the Qur'an or tradition, the Islamic judges and lawyers might make their own rational judgements on moral and ethical questions. The traditionalist insisted that ethical and moral judgements can be based only on the Qur'an and tradition. This led to major debates among and between the various groups which are well known in the study of the Mu'tazilites, the Asharis, the Shafi'is and the Hanbalis, who took different positions on the questions of ethics in classical Islam. In addition to these varied schools of thought, there is also a strong tradition in the mainstream of Islamic philosophy, mainly the contribution on *akhlag* (character) in the works of Islamic philosophers such as Farabi (870–950), Ibn Sina or Avicenna (980–1037) and Ibn Rushd or Averroes (1126–98), who have contributed significantly to our knowledge about the sources of mystical as well as Sufi and Hellenic traditions in the classical Islamic system of ethics.

Indeed, ethics occupied an important field in the system of knowledge among the early philosophers of Islam. For example, the Ikhwan al-Safa group, which was composed of an association of scientists and philosophers at Basra (Iraq) around 983, had three main areas in their teaching: theory of knowledge, cosmology and ethics. In fact, the whole system of this group, the so-called Brethren, was based around their methods of ethics and was spiritual and ascetic in nature. This group had leanings towards the rational philosophy of Mu'tazilism and Shi'ism and towards a very extensive eclecticism. Abubakr Mohammad Ibn Zakariya Razi (864–924), an Iranian Muslim philosopher and scientist, was against all forms of asceticism, but he believed that philosophy was not a mere learning but a way of life, a way of knowing and acting together. On the other hand Abubakr Ibn Bajjah, a prominent Spanish Muslim philosopher known as Avenepace or Avenpace both in Latin and in English (1106–38), believed that moral action is the action which belongs to the nature of man, and his study of ethics was concerned mainly with the problem of the relation of humankind to society. He believed in the capacity of people to associate among themselves with mutual advantage. Like Hegel he believed that thought is a human being's highest conceptual experience; experiences of this world are deceptive. It was Ibn Khaldun, the father of sociology, however, who theorised about *tabligh* as a social institution which grew according to the need of the community. *Tabligh* provided for a vast number of people from diverse races, languages and histories a common forum for participation in a shared culture which was Islam. According to Ibn Khaldun, the states, governments and political systems of wide power and authority have their origin in religious principles based either on prophethood and propagation or on a 'truthful *tabligh*' carried out by '*khatibs*' (orators/communicators).[9] Ibn Khaldun was one of the first thinkers to point out that communication based on ethics is the web of human society and that the flow of such communication determines the direction and the pace of dynamic social development. To him combinations of the '*assabieh*' (group feelings and cohesion) and '*tabligh*' (propagation) approach provided a more dynamic view of organisational behaviour than can be readily derived from the more conventional concepts of states, of hierarchical position and of role which had usually been used in the discussion of politics, government and large social organisation. He thus concluded that propagation cannot materialise without group feeling. The relationship of *tabligh* and Islam, therefore, emerges from the very nature of these two institutions. One is the source of society's values; the other propagates, disseminates and maintains the value system of society, the '*ummah*' or community.

In the Islamic tradition of epistemology, the sustained discussion on ethics in Islam has been discussed in the '*kalam*' literature, the theologians' discussion and debate on the sources of right. The review of this development and other factors' contribution to the literature are outside the scope

---

[9] Ibn Khaldun, *The Introduction to History.*

of this chapter; however, an attempt will be made here to outline a number of fundamental Islamic concepts that have been the basis of Islamic *tabligh* and ethics and are the sources of much of the contemporary social, political and economic debates in the Muslim world, especially in regard to normative secular ethics and in relation to the influences and values coming from the West and the non-Islamic traditions.

Rights of communication in Islam

Communication has been an instrumental and integral part of Islam since its inception as a religio-political movement. Islamic civilisation, indeed, is associated with a high level of oral communication, an unprecedented number of reproduced books and manuscripts and the first attempt in history to bring oral and written cultures into a unified framework, laying the groundwork for the scientific revolution that followed in Europe.

The art of oral communication in Islam derives its origins from the Qur'an (The Holy Book), Sunnah (tradition), and Hadith (sayings of the Prophet and his companions, the *ahl-al-bayt*). According to these three sources the basic rights of communication in Islam include the following: (1) the right to know, (2) the right to read (*iqra*), (3) the right to write (*ghalam*), (4) the right to speak (*khutbah*), (5) the right to knowledge (*ilm*), (6) the right to consult (*showra*), (7) the right to disseminate (*tabligh*) and (8) the right to travel (*hijrah*). During the last fourteen centuries the Islamic culture thus was characterised by the Qur'anic and Arabic language as the basis for international language, Muslim aesthetic culture and arts as a framework for a global culture, Muslim literature, poetry and scholasticism as the foundation of major literature, Sufis and Sufism as a branch of mysticism, and an incredibly vast area of science, technology and philosophy rooted in Islamic epistemology and scientific thought.

The first and most fundamental outlook regarding man and universe in Islam is the theory of '*tawhid*', which implies the unity, coherence and harmony among all parts of the universe. Thus one of the most basic ethical pillars of the Islamic world is born: the existence of purpose in the creation, liberation and freedom of humankind from bondage and servitude to multiple varieties of non-Gods. It stands for the necessity of exclusive servitude to God and it negates any communication and messages, intellectual, cultural, economic or political, that subjugate humankind to creatures. Under the principle of *tawhid* another fundamental ethical consideration in communication becomes clear: the destruction of thought structures based on dualism, racism, tribalism and familial superiority. The function of communication order in Islamic society, according to the principle, is to break idols, to break dependence on outsiders and to set the *ummah* or community in motion towards the future.

A second principle guiding the ethical boundaries of communication in Islam is the doctrine of '*amr bi al-ma'ruf wa nahy'an al munkar*' or 'commanding to the right and prohibiting from the wrong'. Implicit and explicit in this principle is the notion of individual and group responsibility for preparing the succeeding generation to accept the Islamic precepts and make use of them. Muslims have the responsibility of guiding one another, and each generation has the responsibility of guiding the next. The Qur'anic verse explains this: 'Call people to the path of your Lord with wisdom and mild exhortation. Reason with them in the most courteous manner. Your Lord best knows those who stray from His path and best knows those who are rightly guided' (16:125). This points out the responsibilities of Muslims in guiding each other, especially those individuals and institutions who are charged with the responsibilities of leadership and propagation of Islamic ideals. This includes all the institutions of social communication such as the press, radio, television and cinema as well as the individual citizens of each community. Thus, a special concept of social responsibility theory is designed around the ethical doctrine of 'commanding to the right and prohibiting from the wrong'.

A third fundamental concept in determining the nature and boundaries of communication and of social ethics, particularly as it might relate to the political life of the individual and Islamic society, is '*ummah*' or community. The concept of *ummah* transcends national borders and political boundaries. Islamic community transcends the notion of the modern nation-state system: an Islamic community is a religio-economic concept and is only present when it is nourished and governed by Islam. The notion of community in Islam makes no sharp distinction between public and private; therefore, what is required of the community at large is likewise required of every individual member. Under the concept of *ummah*, race is not accepted as a foundation of the state. Values follow piety, and the social system of Islam is based on equity, justice and ownership of the people. There is no individual or class of individuals to dominate, exploit or corrupt the state. Intercultural and international communication (the emphasis here is on nationality and not the nation-state) is the necessary ingredient of Islamic *ummah*. The Qur'an says: 'We created you from a single (pair) of a male and a female and made you into nations and tribes, that you may know each other (not that you may despise each other). Verily the most honoured of you in the sight of God is (he who is) the most righteous of you' (49:13). In the Islamic *ummah* the sovereignty of the 'state' belongs to God and not to the ruler or even to the people themselves. The ruler or leaders are only acting executives chosen by the people to serve them according to the Law of Islam and the concept of *tawhid*. Every citizen in the Islamic 'state' is required to offer his best advice on common matters and must be entitled to do so.

A fourth and a final principle outlined in this paper to explain the ethical framework of communication in Islamic societies is the concept of '*taqwa*' or, roughly translated, piety. In Islamic societies *taqwa* is commonly used in reference to individual 'fear of God' and the ability to guard oneself against the unethical forces which might surrender the environment;

however, the concept of *taqwa* goes beyond this common notion of piety. It is the individual, spiritual, moral, ethical and psychological capacity to raise oneself to that higher level which makes a person almost immune from the excessive material desires of the world, elevating the individual to a higher level of prophetic self-consciousness. The assumption is that human beings possess in their nature a set of divine elements which are other than the material constituents that exist in animals, plants and inanimate objects. Human beings are endowed with innate greatness and dignity. Recognising that freedom of choice is a condition for the fulfilment of obligation, the person is held responsible for performing his or her obligations within the Islamic framework of ethics. In short, it is recognised that human beings perform some of their actions only under the influence of a series of ethical emotions rather than with the intention of gaining a benefit or of repelling a harm. Thus, as a virtue and as an important element in the ethical framework of Islamic *tabligh*, on both the individual and community levels, *taqwa* should be the underpinning ingredient in almost every action of a Muslim.

Communication media in Islam

Communication media in Islam during the first six centuries (630–1200) were characterised by the growing number of *warragin* (intellectual scribes), the development of the paper industry, the expansion of book-making, the creation of great public libraries, the establishment of major medieval universities, the expansion of public schools, postal communications, navigation and transportation and above all, development of the first truly worldwide system of commerce. In the early sixteenth century modern printing presses were introduced into a number of Islamic countries, and during the eighteenth century the first newspapers were published in India, Egypt and Turkey. The first cinema and screenings were introduced into the Ottoman Empire (Turkey) in the late nineteenth century and other Islamic countries during the first decade of the twentieth century (Iran, Tunisia, Egypt, Algeria and Nigeria.)

Colonialism and subjugation of Islamic lands and their people by the European powers had a profound impact on the nature of the modern media in the Islamic world. For example, the first newspaper in Egypt, *Courier de L'Egypte*, was established by Napoleon in 1789 after he invaded the country. The development of Islamic magazines began in 1884 when Jamal al-din al-Afghani and Muhammad Abduh, living in exile in Paris, published the monthly *Al-urwat al-withga* (*The Firm*). The history of Islamic journalism in the Indian subcontinent goes back to 1866, when Sir Sayyid Ahmad Khan founded the oldest Indian review, *Aligrah Institute Gazette*. However, newspapers were published in India a century earlier, during the late 1700s.

Over the last century, however, a dualism and contradiction has been created within the Islamic countries as a result of the introduction of a secular nationalist framework and the accompanying new concepts and methods of communication and ethics from the West. A crisis of legitimacy has been created as a result of a conflict between the 'official culture' of the ruling elites, which in many cases now represents and promotes Western influence, and the 'Islamic culture' of the masses rooted in centuries of religio-political and socio-ethical experience. The current social and political movements in the Islamic world, beginning with the Islamic revolution in Iran, are simply a continuation of the pre-modernist movements which tried to resolve contradictions created by exogenous and non-Islamic forces.

Conclusion

This historical and theoretical exposition may at first sight appear to be distant from some of the earlier more empirical studies in this book. Rubina Ramji's thought-provoking discussions of the stereotyping of Islam in various Hollywood films and news reports (chapter 6), Mark Silk's careful analysis of the coverage of Islam post September 11 in the American Press (chapter 7) and Rosalind Hackett's insightful consideration of the role of different media in religious conflict in Nigeria (chapter 5) are indirectly complementary to my project here. These earlier chapters demonstrate the importance of sustained study of the representations of Islam, and other religions, in both local and international media. The way in which the tragic cycle of violence in the Middle East, West Africa and North America is portrayed demands careful investigation.

Nonetheless, the ideals and foundations that underlie Islamic theories of communication require careful attention if such media stories, practices and events are to be fully understood. This chapter has demonstrated that certain Islamic foundational theories are much more sophisticated than many journalistic accounts allow for. An interpretative framework from a distinctively Islamic perspective is a rich resource not to be ignored. Only if this framework is properly appreciated will scholars, broadcasters and journalists develop a more comprehensive interpretation of Islamic approaches to communication and the development of peaceful media.

27

Communitarian Media Theory with an African Flexion

Mark Fackler

Four theories of press and society have dominated American media scholarship since the publication in 1956 of Wilbur Schramm's famous afterthought, pulled together with funding left over from research for the National Council of Churches.[1] Indeed, that slim volume, with its overbroad generalisations and glaring innocence, defined the field until liberalism was deconstructed and no longer able to carry the freight of explaining the most influential and least understood institution in modern history, the free press.

Social Responsibility theory was the first stage in the critique of liberalism. The Hutchins Commission Report[2] provided initial scholarly impetus to begin the search for an alternative theory. Yet it lacked popular appeal, folded into classical liberalism, lost its reforming fire and smoldered into arcane disuse, rarely cited as a variable in academic research.[3]

The second stage in liberalism's demise was the dual influence of postmodernism and pragmatism. As American intellectuals emerged from the re-evaluation of the 1960s and the malaise of the 1980s, they abandoned liberalism's confidence in human reason and progressive goodness as quaint and unfruitful. Now liberalism can no longer propose that more information available to more people invariably produces better democracy, or that negative freedom is the test of healthy public discourse.[4]

The third and definitive stage, argued here, is the recovery (not the invention) of communitarian theory, which we summarise as the ontological priority of relationship, that is, relationship precedes personhood.[5]

---

[1] Fred S. Siebert, Theodore Peterson, and Wilbur Schramm, *Four Theories of the Press* (Urbana: University of Illinois Press, 1956).

[2] Robert D. Leigh (ed.), *A Free and Responsible Press: A General Report on Mass Communication by the Commission on Freedom of the Press* (Chicago: University of Chicago Press, 1947).

[3] John C. Nerone (ed.), *Last Rights: Revisiting Four Theories of the Press* (Urbana: University of Illinois Press, 1995), p. 31.

[4] Nerone, *Last Rights*, p. 75.

[5] Clifford Christians, John Ferré and Mark Fackler, *Good News: Social Ethics and the Press* (New York: Oxford University Press, 1993).

This chapter focuses on three themes, with a concluding note on the storm center of modern information technology. The argument here is that Western communitarian theory is a recovery, not an invention; that much of the current malaise in sub-Sahara Africa is explained by the difficulty of projecting communitarianism from village and tribe to nation-state; and that Africa needs a nuanced theory of the press to provide grounding for civic discourse and public justice.

Communitarian theory and African media

Humankind traces its earliest movement to the spread of peoples across the continent of Africa. These 'frontiersmen have colonized an especially hostile region of the world on behalf of the entire human race'.[6] The prehistory of these early human societies includes the emergence of food-producing and food-gathering communities which tilled poor soils through unpredictable rainfall, insects and disease. Indeed, the central themes of African history are the 'achievement of human coexistence with nature' and the 'building up of enduring societies'. From this perspective, the history of humankind itself is a 'single story' begun there.[7]

Agriculture and food-sharing cooperatives, examples of communitarian social behaviors, first appear in sub-Sahara Africa. Long before the atomistic individual of the Western Enlightenment was invented, people of conscience and self-reflection learned that survival required strategies of interdependence and mutual aid. While communitarian practice in the US has been primarily the marginalised enclave or utopian sect, and communitarian theorising has generated a literature only recently, communitarian practice has been evident in Africa from the beginning. Neither empire nor individualism, writ large across Western history, has distracted Africans from the sense of mutuality and social interdependence that have been integral to the earliest expressions of cultural development there.

Independence changed the way mass media were deployed there. Kenya in 1963, for example, followed the British model of parliamentary democracy. With its borders already established by European powers in 1884, Kenyan leaders faced the daunting task of uniting tribal and language groups, some of which crossed the arbitrary national boundaries into neighboring states. A large pastoral and agricultural population and the difficulty of transporting print media to remote locations gave preference to radio for national development. The expense of television reception and the poor quality of most national programming further tended to favor radio as the primary medium for connecting Kenya's peoples.[8]

---

[6] John Iliffe, *Africans: The History of a Continent* (Cambridge: Cambridge University Press, 1995), p. 1.

[7] Iliffe, *Africans*.

[8] Levi Obonyo, 'Living Dangerously: An Assessment of Journalism in Kenya', Conference paper, unpublished (1999) p. 23.

Elsewhere in Africa mass media played a vital role in developing national identity and centering power in single-party governments. The controversial Kwame Nkrumah, Ghana's founding president, started the first national news agency in black Africa, developed radio broadcasting and began a television service before he was ousted in 1966.[9]

In other locations, political power rallied vertically but failed to spread horizontally. Where political debate flourished initially, as in Nigeria from 1960 to 1966, the contentiousness of media voices failed to move that country's three regions toward agreements and contributed to its first military coup.[10] In Tanzania, the socialist visionary Julius Nyerere eventually exerted control over media, and in Zambia, the independence government simply appropriated media, renamed it and turned it into a party propaganda tool. The dissident Kenyan journalist Hilary Ng'weno observed: 'In respect to the all-pervading power of government, nothing has really changed from the bad old days of colonialism. Only the actors have changed: the play remains the same ... [Media] opposed to being incorporated into the government propaganda machinery were closed down.'[11]

In forty years of African independence, this pattern of state control and periodic calls for reform continues. Francis Kasoma, former head of the department of mass communication at the University of Zambia, still urges his government ministries to privatise state-owned media: 'When government funds media, all hell breaks loose.'[12]

Regrettably, even as the millennial calendar turned across the world's longitudes, Africa remained economically and dialogically underdeveloped. Sierra Leone, a killing field for journalists, is 'an extreme, but untypical example of a state with all the epiphenomena and none of the institutions of government. It has poverty and disease in abundance, and riches, too'.[13] Political change occurs commonly through military coup, and the 'Big Man' theory of political leadership forecloses any chance for broad-based leadership to emerge. Liberia is, in fact, Charles Taylor Inc.[14] Today, private independent media in Africa are co-opted by consumerism directed to a narrow range of elites, or regarded as voices of political instability. State control in most countries guarantees a homogenous presentation of information and opinion to peoples whose constitutive sense of community still needs considerable nurture to broaden from local and tribal to national and global.

---

[9] William Hachten, *The Growth of Media in the Third World: African Failures, Asian Successes* (Ames: Iowa State University Press, 1993), p. 23.

[10] Hachten, *Growth of Media*, p. 25.

[11] Hilary Ng'weno, 'The Third World Dilemma: Can a State Press be Free?' *The Weekly Review* (Nairobi) (22 June 1979).

[12] Anthony Kundal, 'Where to, Zambian media?' *Africa Law Review* No. 76 (January 1999), p. 25.

[13] *The Economist*, 'Hopeless Africa' and 'Africa: The Heart of the Matter' (13 May 2000), p. 17.

[14] *The Economist*, 'Hopeless Africa' and 'Africa', p. 22.

Recovering African communitarianism

In the West, the right to express the beliefs of conscience emanates from a doctrine of the individual as locus of being, rooted in natural law but explained in the Christian doctrine of the grant of God's image (*imago Dei*) to each beloved person in the creation.[15] The 'image' has generally been interpreted as the moral conscience, self-awareness, reflectivity, and its grant underscores the inherent value of each person, other qualifications aside.

African theological reflection fixes human worth at a different point and interprets the 'image' as a grant of essential human relatedness. In his dramatic re-reading of the early North African theologian Tertullian, the Nigerian Ogbonnaya argues that divine essence is communal, and thus the grant to humankind is community akin to that of the Godhead – fundamentally related and ontologically equal while distinct in person and function.[16] Ogbonnaya grounds human intersubjectivity on the theological assertion that prior to creation, the Godhead was dialectical yet undivided. 'In that oneness was a plurality of personal entities seeking actualization and self-realization through various historical functions.'[17] That same process explains human culture and provides the moral ground for communitarian care-giving and accountability.

The Ghanaian philosopher Kwasi Wiredu insists that African communitarianism requires no theological grounding. The intellectual orientation of the Akan people of Ghana, he contends, is fundamentally empirical.[18] For Africans, the divine does not exist outside the known universe. To link ethical universals to a supernatural 'other' is to think gibberish and to speak nonsense.[19] For the Akan, morality is what promotes social well-being by harmonising interests. Had the ancient Akan written a classic ethic, mutual aid would have been the keynote, not rationalist appeals to duty or injunction revealed by special circumstances.[20]

If communitarianism in the West is a reaction to Enlightenment individualism, in sub-Sahara Africa it is the way the world is constituted, whether cast in terms of theological interrelatedness, as Ogbonnaya argues, or in humanist common-faith terms, as Wiredu prefers. From all sides, the African would appear to regard community as nothing less than 'the way things are', a presupposition, a *prima facie* truth. To speak meaningfully is to address social reality in communitarian terms.

---

[15] John Calvin, *Institutes of the Christian Religion* (1545), vol 1, trans. Henry Beveridge (Grand Rapids: Eerdmans, 1972), p. 164.

[16] A. Okechukwu Ogbonnaya, *On Communitarian Divinity* (New York: Paragon, 1994), p. 23.

[17] Ogbonnaya, *On Communitarian Divinity*, p. 69.

[18] Kwasi Wiredu, *Cultural Universals and Particulars: An African Perspective* (Bloomington: Indiana University Press, 1996), p. 99.

[19] Wiredu, *Cultural Universals.*

[20] Wiredu, *Cultural Universals*, p. 72.

Several questions now apply. Could a social theory based on communitarian assumptions provide media professionals with principles to build a dynamic, transformative system which serves universal human interests? Can participatory democracy emerge in Africa with even greater clarity than in the West, given that region's long embrace of communitarian praxis? Is mediated communication tenable in a communitarian context? Across the African continent, as elsewhere, media corporations seek maximised profits and global audiences, while state-run systems languish and political propaganda becomes mere entertainment.

First, communitarian theory supports accessible media channels. Philip Ochieng, one of Kenya's most forceful press critics, allows no quarter to an élite news media. 'There can be no freedom of the press where only a handful of people exist who can efficiently and quickly collect, process, and sell ideas. No country can enjoy freedom of expression in a situation of underdevelopment.'[21] Wiredu observes that power and accountability are distributed through a complex social network of speakers and elders. As villages grow into metropolis, the technology of speaking and writing must be available to representative political communities. Media systems homogenised by political gatekeepers cannot reach to the threshold of dialogue, and without dialogue the community withers.

Urbanisation has reshaped the village, scattered youth, marginalised elders and fragmented the clan. Young workers flood major cities seeking employment, all the while keeping official residence (and often family) in a rural home area. They are displaced residents of a city to which they feel no loyalty whatsoever; rather, the city is their obstacle, opponent and only opportunity for salaried work. Its institutions provide them no protection from crime and too little care during sickness. Living is hazardous, and job-seekers far outnumber jobs.

In settings like this, arguing accessible media channels may seem superfluous. Clean water and sewage treatment become arguable priorities. But communitarian theory insists that urbanisation (and health care, education, police power, taxation and small business entrepreneurship) are issues about which all interested parties must be speaking and working. Media literacy and 'many voices' are not elixirs, but they are surely a component of public well-being.[22] Accessible media is the modern invitation to join the village palaver.[23]

Second, communitarian theory respects the integrity of conscience. Because conscience cannot be purged, the human condition must reflect the social role of conscience and open discourse to the reflections of conscience. In African communalism, no human life is a prop to another's

---

[21] Philip Ochieng, *I Accuse the Press* (Nairobi: ACTS, 1992), p. 155.
[22] Christians, Ferré and Fackler, *Good News.*
[23] Benezet Bujo, *The Ethical Dimensions of Community* (Nairobi: Paulines, 1997), p. 41.

happiness; life is sacred.[24] Every democratically inspired statement of human rights supports free expression and the duty of each person to speak truthfully in context. African communitarianism needs a recovery of confidence in the rightness of peaceful political change, in the necessity of dialogue including oppositional voices, and in the core concept of human sympathy around which all morality revolves.[25] The half-dozen African wars in the last decade, with their seven million refugees and brutal treatment of non-combatants, scoff at notions of communitarian revival. But what are the alternatives?

Third, community-based media development projects have been effective in Africa when initiated and designed for maximum grass-roots participation and ownership.

Louise Bourgault describes several projects in the concluding chapter of her survey of sub-Saharan media. In Ghana, a UNESCO project in partnership with Legon University has created self-help organisations which have built daycare centers, clinics and latrines – infrastructure essential to other parts of a productive economy.[26] AIDS is a killer throughout the region. Sexual activity is largely unprotected. Information concerning sexually transmitted disease has been pathetically unavailable, a taboo subject. Thus the Karate Kids project, using video drama and discussion to reach children and adolescents, is life-saving media offered to Africa's most vulnerable viewers. Bourgault applauds the low-tech, low-cost effectiveness of this program, available in major languages of East and West Africa.[27] She concludes her review by reiterating the conceptual advantages of traditional African interdependence:

> Although the present decade is fraught with perils for Africa, the prospects for the next century appear brighter. Africa's pre-colonial, community-based values of harmony, plurality, and balance are well suited to a steady state communitarian world order toward which the planet must inevitably move or face perdition. This notion alone is the basis for hope for the continent and the empowerment of its people.[28]

In Kenya, politically oppositional reading is available in the capital and other major cities. *People* newspaper is produced by a lean staff of editors and reporters who daily challenge the policies and news bias of KANU, the ruling party, under the banner 'Fair, Frank, and Fearless'. Bylines are used, but mastheads often do not appear. *African Law Review*, calling itself 'a magazine of legal education and citizen rights awareness', hammers on matters

---

[24] Andrew Azukaego Momeka, 'Community and Self-Respect as African Values', Clifford Christians and Michael Traber (eds.), *Communication Ethics and Universal Values*, (Thousand Oaks, CA: Sage, 1997), p. 176.

[25] James Q. Wilson, *The Moral Sense* (New York: Free Press, 1993), p. 29.

[26] Louise M. Bourgault, *Mass Media in Sub-Saharan Africa* (Bloomington: Indiana University Press, 1995), p. 250.

[27] Bourgault, *Mass Media*, p. 248.

[28] Bourgault, *Mass Media*, p. 256.

of judicial integrity and constitutional reform. These examples (not to mention politically courageous reporting from the church-based press) suggest that dialogue is alive, often vibrant, sometimes rancorous, dangerous and confrontational.

While Nigeria splits more deeply along religious traditions, Zimbabwe struggles with land issues and Rwanda nurses the wounds of genocide. Communitarianism may be Africa's most naturalised ideology[29] and its peoples' most effective public appeal. Cultural transformation is essential in every institution, and the growing power of its press will play a central role in shaping the participatory dialogue that may yield solutions to seemingly intractable problems.[30]

The Internet age arriving

Sub-Sahara Africa is opening to the information age with ready access to multi-channel discourse without significant interference from vested political authority. Will traditional African communitarianism shape this new era, or be colonised and commercialised by it?

Within North American communication studies, few lights represent the scholarly interests of religion, media and culture so dramatically as the ever-creative technophile Marshall McLuhan. To him we owe most of the concepts that have popularised the study of new information technology. Largely forgotten is the context in which he developed those ideas, a context that wrapped Catholic commitments and scholarship into a mastery of Western literature and a prescience concerning information technology as formative and mysterious.[31]

In his first book, *The Mechanical Bride*, McLuhan adopted a metaphor from Edgar Allen Poe's short story 'Descent into the Maelstrom'. In it, three Norwegian fishermen are caught in the vortex of the century's most vicious hurricane. One perishes immediately; another lashes himself to the boat, hoping to save himself and the enterprise, but he dies on the rocks of the exposed sea floor. The other fisherman, despite the terrifying descent, is fascinated by the power of the storm yet still applies analytical skill which enables his near escape. He alone survives to tell the world of this monster whirlwind, knowing all the while that none will believe. As in several Poe tales, once natural tragedy is overcome the protagonist faces intransigent social tragedy: people resist acknowledging powerful forces just beyond the reach of ordinary experience. McLuhan observes that 'Poe's sailor saved himself by studying the action of the whirlpool and by cooperating with it'.[32]

[29] Bujo, *Ethical Dimensions*, pp. 53–7.

[30] Nadim Rouhana and Daniel Bar-Tal, 'Psychological Dynamics of Intractable Ethnonational Conflicts', *American Psychologist* (July 1998), pp. 761–70.

[31] W. Terence Gordon, *Marshall McLuhan: Escape into Understanding* (New York: Basic, 1997).

[32] Gordon, *Marshall McLuhan*, p. 14.

McLuhan himself lived within a maelstrom of intellectual currents that generated a legacy of ideas still important to communications studies. His confidence in human renewal through information technology foreshadowed the Internet and the new region of reality we call cyberspace. We may fault McLuhan today for his glib invocations and mosaic prose. His best work has been reduced to cliché, and his inventiveness, for all its cross-disciplinary genius, never surrendered to the discipline of replicable and verifiable hypothesis-testing. He was a prophet-scholar, pointing forward always, calling a culture to see the world as it would be. And his vision throughout embraced the intersubjectivity of a technological future he spent a career describing. In that important sense, he presents Africa with a challenge and a warning.

In the centre of Addis Ababa, ancient capital of the only African country never colonised, sits a technological edifice fit for a future which has never appeared. Built by the United Nations, the Economic Commission of Africa's state-of-the-art communications center is unstaffed, unused, its potential unexplored. It is, as it were, a whirlpool waiting to begin its irresistible spin. What happens in Africa when information technology sweeps past ancient tribal boundaries? Will community thrive in an information future bound to break upon the continent with whirlwind fury? Several elements of African communitarianism seem well suited to surviving the storm.

First, African communitarianism is characterised as open.[33] Dialogue within communities is open to innovation, creativity and new meanings. Communal societies may be transformed by 'historical experiments undertaken by persons'. Authentic community recognises that existence is a process 'of being in the world', not merely of occupying space and utilitarian function. Cultural shift in every place is a slow and often costly process, no mere 'turn of a kaleidoscope'.[34] But change happens irrevocably, as human societies sift and sort their values, through dialogue and violence, seeking incremental adjustments that address new sensitivities toward the right and the good, or at least toward the pragmatic and efficient. Even the 'tenacious though irrational beliefs' associated with ethnic and religious hatred are amenable to change through civic dialogue, though history's record of peaceful change at this level is fearfully short.[35] Nonetheless, Africans writing about their own communitarian climate suggest that it is less bound than the West by commercial, privacy or class constraints which stifle public dialogue. In this regard, McLuhan's new information era translates optimistically for Africa's future. We simply need a solid case study to verify theoretical projections.

Even in the aftermath of Rwandan bloodlust and the imploding of Zaire, the open-to-change atmosphere of African communitarianism permits

---

[33] A. Okechukwu Ogbonnaya, *On Communitarian Divinity*, p. 9.

[34] Richard A. Posner, *Overcoming Law* (Cambridge: Harvard University Press, 1995), p. 578.

[35] Posner, *Overcoming Law*.

moments of hopefulness. In South Africa, apartheid is overcome. In Uganda, former lunacy in Kampala has been replaced by steady, diplomatic, though still arbitrary, national leadership. In Africa, communitarian dialogue may seem lost in the percussion of upheaval and cruelty, but its fragile presence is replacing the sound of guns here and there.

Second, the international dialogue concerning human rights is heard more frequently than ever before. The vigor of rights-talk is strong, and international calls to free speech and civil rights, the rule of law, the special needs of children, universal suffrage, the integrity of tribal and cultural traditions, literacy and education are frequently heard.[36]

Translating the United Nations Charter into public policy will be realised neither quickly nor easily, but skilled dialogue and a growing recognition of mutuality – the heart of communitarianism – are evident in Africa and need only anchoring in normative universals.

Third, religious experience grounds African communitarianism as nowhere else in the world. The Malawian bishop Patrick Kalilombe situates African religious life in community solidarity, egalitarianism and hospitality:

> Where Descartes said, 'I think, therefore I am,' the African would rather say, 'I am related, therefore, we are.' In African spirituality, the value of interdependence through relationships comes high above that of individualism and personal independence ... the practice of cooperation is more relied upon than competition.[37]

From a feminist perspective, the Ghanaian theologian Mercy Amba Oduyoye locates Africa's struggle around patriarchalism and authentic faith:

> The most fundamental issues of feminism ... relate to autonomy – naming ourselves – and integrity, and both have roots in religion. Feminism itself is not a priority among the competing ideologies in Africa, but religion is ... Religion remains integral to the various political ideologies that seek to inform our budding nationalism.[38]

The Nigerian church leader Tokunboh Adeyemo sums up the core belief of nearly all African groups: 'God is, hence man is.'[39] In traditional manifestations, this core declaration works itself out in elaborate interconnections of spirit and nature, animistic and fetishistic, but Christianity recalibrates those relationships around a beneficent creator-redeemer. In many parts of black Africa, Islam is a growing presence also.

---

[36] Charles A. Khamalla, 'Half a Century of Human Rights', *Africa Law Review* No. 76 (January 1999), p. 8.

[37] Patrick A. Kalilombe, 'Spirituality in the African Perspective', Rosino Gibellini (ed.), *Paths of African Theology* (Maryknoll, NY: Orbis, 1994), p. 122.

[38] Mercy Amba Oduyoye, 'Feminist Theology in an African Perspective,' *Paths of African Theology*. p. 175.

[39] Tokunboh Adeyemo, 'Unapproachable God: The High God of African Traditional Religion,' *The Global God* (Grand Rapids: Baker, 1998), p. 138.

In the West and Middle East, religious conflict has confounded communitarianism. But as a primary motivation, religion in Africa has served to build the village and preserve life.[40] The indelible care-providing meta-ethic arising from Africa's sense of connectedness to the divine will provide African communitarianism with a more substantial sense of human responsibility than modern empiricist ideologies can provide the West.

In the West, the epitome of humanness is symbolised in Michelangelo's *David*, a biblical figure of immense and 'perfect' proportion. In the Makerere University library, Kampala, East Africa's oldest university, stands a human form that tells a different story. It is one-legged, both arms missing, bullet holes puncture the headless torso. Yet the figure stands and seems to move forward, dedicated to the resilience of the human spirit. It is community-violated, but community-preserving. Nothing here speaks of Renaissance perfectionism; it is enough to live and stand scarred, mutilated, upright, as if to say, there will be another day.

As infrastructure develops and the Internet connects African villages to the wider world of Asian, Latin and Western cultures, the response and result could be a heightened awareness of public accountability and participation, an expanding sense of human care, and a more fulsome mutuality for all. Whether capitalist consumerism will eventually whirl even Africa into its vortex is the unanswered issue.

Further reading

T. Adeyemo, 'Unapproachable God: The High God of African Traditional Religion,' *The Global God* (Grand Rapids: Baker, 1998).

G. B. N. Ayittey, *Africa in Chaos* (New York: St. Martin's, 1998).

L. M. Bourgault, *Mass Media in Sub-Saharan Africa* (Bloomington: Indiana University Press, 1995).

B. Bujo, *The Ethical Dimensions of Community* (Nairobi: Paulines, 1997).

B. V. Brady, *The Moral Bond of Community: Justice and Discourse in Christian Morality* (Washington, DC: Georgetown University Press, 1998).

J. Calvin, *Institutes of the Christian Religion* (1545), vol. 1, trans. Henry Beveridge (Grand Rapids: Eerdmans, 1972).

C. Christians, J. Ferré and M. Fackler. *Good News: Social Ethics and the Press* (New York: Oxford University Press, 1993).

The Economist, 'Hopeless Africa' and 'Africa: The Heart of the Matter' (13 May 2000), pp. 17–24.

Jacques Ellul, *Propaganda*, trans. Konrad Keller and Jean Lerner (New York: Vintage, 1965).

P. Freire, *Pedagogy of the Oppressed*, trans. Myra Bergman Ramos (New York: Seabury, 1970).

---

[40] Adeyemo, 'Unapproachable God', p. 128.

W. Terence Gordon, *Marshall McLuhan: Escape into Understanding* (New York: Basic, 1997).

J. Iliffe, *Africans: The History of a Continent* (Cambridge: Cambridge University Press, 1995).

P. A. Kalilombe, 'Spirituality in the African Perspective', Rosino Gibellini (ed.), *Paths of African Theology*, (Maryknoll, NY: Orbis, 1994).

C. A. Khamalla, 'Half a Century of Human Rights', *Africa Law Review* No. 76 (January 1999).

F. G. Kirkpatrick, *Community: A Trinity of Models* (Washington, DC: Georgetown University Press, 1986).

A. Kundal, 'Where to, Zambian media?' *Africa Law Review* No. 76 (January 1999).

R. D. Leigh (ed.), *A Free and Responsible Press: A General Report on Mass Communication by the Commission on Freedom of the Press* (Chicago: University of Chicago Press, 1947).

A. Azukaego Momeka, 'Community and Self-Respect as African Values', Clifford Christians and Michael Traber (eds.), *Communication Ethics and Universal Values*, (Thousand Oaks, CA: Sage, 1997), pp. 170–93.

J. C. Nerone (ed.), *Last Rights: Revisiting Four Theories of the Press* (Urbana: University of Illinois Press, 1995).

H. Ng'weno, 'The Third World Dilemma: Can a State Press be Free?' *The Weekly Review* (Nairobi) (22 June 1979).

J. Nyirenda, 'The Relevance of Paulo Freire's Contributions to Education and Development in Present Day Africa', *African Media Review.* Vol 10, No. 1 (1996), pp. 1–20.

L. Obonyo, 'Living Dangerously: An Assessment of Journalism in Kenya', Conference paper, unpublished (1999).

Philip Ochieng, *I Accuse the Press* (Nairobi: ACTS, 1992).

M. Amba Oduyoye, 'Feminist Theology in an African Perspective', Rosino Gibellini (ed.), *Paths of African Theology.* (Maryknoll, NY: Orbis, 1994).

A. Okechukwu Ogbonnaya, *On Communitarian Divinity* (New York: Paragon, 1994).

N. Onishi, 'Democracy Sprouts in Ghana', *New York Times* (7 July 1999).

P. J. Paris, *The Spirituality of African Peoples* (Minneapolis: Fortress, 1995).

Richard A. Posner, *Overcoming Law* (Cambridge: Harvard University Press, 1995).

N. Rouhana and D. Bar-Tal, 'Psychological Dynamics of Intractable Ethnonational Conflicts', *American Psychologist* (July 1998), pp. 761–70.

F. S. Siebert, Theodore Peterson and Wilbur Schramm, *Four Theories of the Press* (Urbana: University of Illinois Press, 1956).

J. Q. Wilson, *The Moral Sense* (New York: Free Press, 1993).

K. Wiredu, *Cultural Universals and Particulars: An African Perspective* (Bloomington: Indiana University Press, 1996).

28

A Brief Look at the Ethics of Broadcasting

Richard Holloway

Ted Hughes' book *Tales from Ovid,* contains many good things, but one of the poems has a particular resonance for anyone interested in the role of broadcasting in our culture. It is the poem *Erisychthon,* and it is about the curse of gluttony. According to the poem, Erisychthon '*Gave to the gods nothing but mockery*'. In particular, he cuts down every tree in the sacred grove of Ceres. In revenge, Ceres sends Hunger:

> to the house of Erisychthon
> And bends above the pillow where his face
>
> Snores with open mouth.
> Her skeletal embrace goes around him.
> Her shrunk mouth clamps over his mouth
> And she breathes
>
> Into every channel of his body
> A hurricane of starvation.

Erisychthon wakes to a devastating and insatiable hunger that engulfs his entire wealth. At the end he is left with nothing except a daughter, his last chattel, so he cashes her in for food. She is saved by the pity of Neptune, who enables her to change her shape, so she constantly escapes the various types of bondage into which her father sells her. Hughes tell us that Erisychthon:

> Elated, saw business. After that
> On every market he sold her in some new shape.
> A trader bought a horse,
> Paid for it and found the halter empty.

Using this means of supply, however demeaning and unnerving to his daughter, Erisychthon continues to feed his hunger. Hughes finishes the poem:

> But none of it was enough. Whatever he ate
> Maddened and tormented that hunger
> To angrier, uglier life. The life
>
> Of a monster no longer a man. And so
> At last, the inevitable.

He began to savage his own limbs.
And there, at a final feast, devoured himself.[1]

I would like to suggest that poem as a parable of the devouring, unsatisfi-
able power of the communications media in our day. I am thinking, in particular, about broadcasting in this chapter, but the modalities of
broadcasting, and the opportunities and excesses that accompany it, provide us with a particular example of a generalised trend in prosperous cultures. Broadcasting inevitably mirrors society and its values; but, since it is a
two-way mirror, broadcasting creates as well as reflects values. The difficulty
always lies in separating the two elements, the causal from the reflective, in
calculating responsibility for cultural change. A good example of this ambiguity was the night Kenneth Tynan used, for the first time on BBC, a four-
letter word that has now become a necessary punctuation mark for
comedians. Did he coarsen the tone of public discourse that night, as some
would suggest, or was he honestly reflecting a change that had already
occurred in society? It is clearly impossible to answer that question without
thinking about the nature of society and the way it influences and is influenced by broadcasting. That is why I want to spend some time thinking
about the nature of our society today, and the new global culture, a culture
that has been largely created by the revolution in telecommunications and
information technology.

I would like to suggest that there is present in liberal capitalist societies
today a constant pressure towards addictive behaviour, towards radical dis-
content and a consequent hunger for constant stimulus, of which the
appetite for news and entertainment is merely a symptom. Addiction is one
of the characteristics of our era, and it probably has a lot to do with the
apparently limitless productiveness of global capitalism, which has to generate new needs all the time, because the one thing it cannot do is stand
still. I am not suggesting that human nature has, in our time, become more
prone in itself to these distressing dependencies; I am suggesting that the
human disposition to pathologise otherwise neutral activities is exacerbated
in our time by our almost manic productiveness as a species. I have no
doubt that, at this very moment, somewhere in California a group of
Internet abusers is convening for therapy. G.K. Galbraith has described the
prosperous sections of Western society as inhabiting a culture of contentment that insulates them from the misery of the poor; and that is undoubtedly a valid reading of our society. But it is not the only way to describe what
is going on. The flip side is a radical hunger among the prosperous for
more and more of what they like. Most of us are now prone to the weaknesses that once only characterised the idle rich: boredom, the constant
search for stimulus and entertainment, a weary superficiality and inattentiveness that craves the repeated provocation of the new and different. Our
discontents lead us into fresh experiences that begin by exhilarating us,

---

[1] Ted Hughes, *Tales from Ovid* (London: Faber & Faber, 1997), p. 85.

gradually turn into habits that bore us, and can end by trapping us in processes that imprison us. And there is nothing on earth that cannot be the vehicle of this addicting dynamic: natural substances, sex, emotional entanglements, food, greed for status and the toys it buys, work, spirituality, religion, and the shallow celebrity that the communications media can endow on its unwilling, as well as on its willing, victims.[2] As far as the broadcasting and general media side of the new culture goes, there is a sort of double whammy effect at work: the communications industry creates new hungers in us, but the machine itself, like Erisychthon, is insatiable and promises, in the end, to devour itself. One of the earliest commentators on this phenomenon was the historian Daniel Boorstin. In the 1970s I read a little book of his called *The Image*,[3] which captured the nature of what was beginning to happen to the consumerist societies of the West.

He offered three examples of the way our society was in danger of compulsively trivialising important aspects of the human experience, along with a look at the way almost everything gets commodified in capitalist cultures. The first distinction he applied is the difference between travelling and tourism. The traveller goes to the strange country in order to encounter otherness, and usually comes back changed and enriched by it. The tourist, on the other hand, never really encounters the other place at all. She occupies a bubble that may move over the surface of the strange country, but never really encounters it, preferring instead to take advantage of the photo opportunities that are conveniently provided by the tour guide, so that she can create an image of the other country to inflict on her friends back home, rather than really try to have a genuine encounter with it. The other example he offered was the difference between fame and celebrity. The famous used to be famous for something: battles fought, books written, symphonies composed. Nowadays, he pointed out, the communications machine has created the phenomenon of people who are famous for being famous, what he called *celebrity*, a celebrity being someone who is known for being known, such as a news reader or weather person or quiz show presenter.

But his most trenchant criticism was levelled at the media machine itself. Its main characteristic is its insatiability, and the appetite has grown exponentially since Boorstin's book came out. This colossal and incessant need for news and entertainment, not to say news as entertainment, leads to a systemic freneticism in the media, an intrinsic haste, that can lead to lazy and unethical journalism. Nothing human has ever been pure, of course, but the original theory behind news reporting, for example, must have been based on an ethic of objectivity. Events were out there happening and they needed to be interpreted, but basically a reporter was just that, a person who brought back an objective report of something that was going on. We know, of course, that pure objectivity was never possible, and that even

[2] Richard Holloway, *Godless Morality* (Edinburgh: Canongate, 1999), pp. 157ff.
[3] Daniel Boorstin, *The Image: A Guide to Pseudo-Events in America* (New York: Vintage, 1992).

scientific experiments are affected by the observer, but there was a sense in which the reporter prided him or herself on the honesty or objectivity of the reports that were written. In more leisurely days this was probably fairly true, so that there would be a distinct difference between the reporting side and the opinion or editorialising side of a programme. But when the appetite for news increased in the way it has in our era, there was an inevitable trend towards creating events in order to report them. The traditional reporter, with his raincoat and shorthand notebook, went out looking for news that was happening in order to report it; the modern media machine is sometimes tempted to set about creating news in order to be able to report it.

There is a genuine dilemma here that is created by the intrinsically theatrical nature of television journalism. If you are making a documentary about the drug trade, for example, and you know that human donkeys are recruited to smuggle drugs, it must be tempting to stretch the truth by staging something you know goes on anyway, so you get those fraudulent documentaries from time to time. More subtle, and less easy to police, are the human reaction shots that can be faked, most famously by William Hurt in the film *Broadcasting News*, where he fakes tears while interviewing a rape victim. Anyone who has been involved in television programme making knows how important the editorial input is. To distil several hours of conversation into twenty minutes of really watchable material is the programme maker's art, but it is a creative art, and by what ethic do we apply it, so that what we say genuinely expresses the truth of the recorded encounter, even if it is heavily edited? We all know how important context is to the evaluation of any act, but the demands of the media can totally decontextualise anything in order to get a story out of it.

For instance, you may write a book or deliver a lecture from which the reporter has derived an excerpt. Already an inevitable distortion has occurred, because a point of view can only really honestly be interpreted within its complete context, and, ultimately, all the facts in the universe provide the context. But we do not have to be as ambitious as that. We can stick to the context of a five thousand word lecture which has, embedded within pages of argument, a conclusion or an opinion. That becomes the kernel of the phone ploy. The reporter gets hold of it. To be fair, he or she will usually check the source. They will phone up and ask: 'Did you say this?' 'Well, yes, I did, but it came at the end of a piece of argumentation, from which it logically proceeded, and taken out of context it makes a completely different impression from when it's heard in its complete context.' 'Yes, but you did say it?' 'Yes.' 'Thank you,' and that call is concluded, but the calling goes on. Next morning it is announced that a damaging row has broken out in this or that institution, because the enterprising reporter, by phoning up a list of the usual suspects, has got a number of people to say what they think of the original decontextualised utterance.

The other thing that is worth noting about all of this is that the communications industry creates a permanent sense of crisis, a mood of perpetual uproar. There *are* rows, of course, and they can be extremely enjoyable to take part in or just to witness; but they are not really as common as the media machine makes us believe. Politicians and theologians, to name but two subsections of the chattering classes, are used to and even believe in the processes of conflict and disagreement. There is no way of arriving at even relative or approximate truth without the necessary clash of idea with idea. It is the clash of ideas that is the process whereby intellectual evolution takes place. To be fair, broadcasting networks can be very good at assisting this process. Most of them have skilled science or medical correspondents, for instance, who can help their viewers or listeners engage in the debate on new developments in science or medical technology. Often, however, the crisis-driven approach to complex subjects creates a mood of hysteria that makes it difficult for real debate to take place. The main advantage of the broadcasting media in this process is that they can give the protagonists time on air with their opponents, sometimes on phone-in shows, that let people hear the offending opinion delivered directly. I was involved in a few programmes of this sort, particularly after the publication of my book *Godless Morality* in 1999. Many of my listeners were offended by my views, but I found it re-assuring to know that it was the real views that had put them off, and not some version delivered by a newspaper reporter. I know that phone-ins can be the hunting ground for wandering obsessives, but they do offer access broadcasting to people in a way that creates real dialogue and the learning that flows from it.

Let me conclude by looking at three areas that present real ethical challenges to us. The first is the ability of the broadcasting media to usurp life itself. Given the staggering growth of networks in our time, this is set to increase and present us with new human pathologies. In his parable of the cave, Plato talked about a people who mistook shadows for reality. Modern broadcasting universalises that insight. Theoretically, it would be possible to spend most of your free time not in living, but in watching others live. It is all innocent enough, but it is intriguing the way the fate of characters in a popular soap can achieve reality in the minds of a nation. Some people may remember from the 1970s the furore that surrounded the death of JR in *Dallas*. We all need a bit of escape from time to time. The trouble with the omnivorous nature of broadcasting is that it may offer too many people a permanent escape from reality. Related to that is the fiction that television celebrities are people we actually know, so that there is a blurring of the distinction between the public and the personal into Auden's public faces in private places. It is well known that actors who play tough guys or unattractive people on film or TV are sometimes assaulted by people for whom the acted fiction has replaced reality. Of course, people can lose themselves in anything. There was an amusing article in the *New York Times* some years ago about a man who, rather than living his own life, decided to read Proust instead.

More important is the ethical problem of the power of the broadcasting media. Broadcasters and the owners of broadcasting empires all have

Conclusion

29

Emerging Conversations in the Study of Media, Religion and Culture

Jolyon Mitchell

Humans have already changed the world several times by changing the way they have had conversations. There have been conversational revolutions which have been as important as wars and riots and famine. When problems have appeared insoluble, when life has seemed meaningless, when governments have been powerless, people have sometimes found a way out by changing the subjects of their conversation, or the way they talked, or the persons they talked to. In the past that gave us the Renaissance, the Enlightenment, modernity and postmodernity. Now it's time for the New Conversation.[1]

Theodore Zeldin's call for the New Conversation that transforms the way we work and relate to people with different perspectives is an intriguing vision. Whilst not fully embodying Zeldin's New Conversation, many of the chapters in this volume celebrate the art of the written conversation through a range of lively and developing discussions. They raise numerous significant questions: Is there a specifiable set of common conversations in the study of Media, Religion and Culture? What are the major threads in this rapidly evolving field of research and debate? And, closely related to these two questions: what are promising future topics for research and discussion? Out of the wide range of current conversations and possible areas for further study, I shall describe seven.

The participative turn

One significant theme that emerged is the turn towards the audience, described here as *the participative turn*. This move goes beyond a simple critique of the 'passive audience' paradigm, in which the audience supposedly absorbs material like a sponge, to a more sophisticated analysis of how active audiences participate in the making of meaning. The qualitative research by Stewart Hoover on patterns of audience interaction with the media is a crucial resource for understanding how individuals create their

---

[1] Theodore Zeldin, *Conversation* (Harvill Press, London, 1998), p. 7.

own identities with the help of mediated narratives (chapter 2). Lynn Clark's research on adolescents demonstrates what a rich quarry this is to mine (chapter 3). Both Hoover and Clark provide original data and interpretations on what audiences do with the media that they consume. The different modes of engagement with the media, set out by Hoover in chapter 2, are well worth further consideration: experiences *in* the media, interactions *about* the media and accounts *of* the media. Through investigations on how audiences participate in media use, Hoover tests the robustness and precision of these categories.

How can the work of Hoover, Clark and company be translated into new cultural contexts? In other words, how can such extensive research rooted in North America be developed in different situations? There is a range of research developing, as yet largely unpublished, in a variety of new locations. Other scholars currently working in related areas include Sham Thomas and Ailsa Hollinshead. Thomas investigates how television is used in everyday life amongst Mar-Thoma Christians in Kerala, South India, showing how the recent advent of television in many rural contexts is transforming traditional attitudes towards practices of religion, such as family prayer or corporate worship. His research includes interviews with several Hindu and Moslem families and shows that there are surprising similarities across distinct faith traditions. The work in progress of Hollinshead on perceptions of religious figures in popular British television points towards another future direction of research[2]. Both Hollinshead and Thomas offer valuable counterpoints to the work of Hoover and Clark and others involved in the Lifecourse project.[3]

The participative turn can also be discerned in some emerging work on religion and film. In this book, Steve Nolan outlines a new religious film criticism that makes a persuasive case for 'understanding how spectators consume cinematic representation' (chapter 15). He claims that 'analysing films in terms of the spectators' construction of meaning has highlighted the fact that cinematic meaning is located not in its production but in its consumption'. As he himself admits this assertion merits further research.[4] Extended analysis of how audiences use, or do not use, particular media for their own spiritual development in different cultural contexts would enrich our understanding of religious practice in a media age.

The narration of identity

A second area, closely connected to research on reception and the participative turn, concerns *the narration of identity*. For work on narrating religious

---

[2] Ailsa Hollinshead, *The Production and Reception of Discourses Concerning Religion in Fictional Broadcasting*, University of Glasgow, unpublished PhD (2003).

[3] For more information see www.colorado.edu/Journalism/MEDIALYF.

[4] For an example of research that demonstrates how the emerging Media, Religion and Culture discussions could interact with film and religion studies see: Krzystof Jozajtis, *Religion and Film in American Culture: The Birth of a Nation*, University of Stirling, unpublished PhD (2001), especially chapters 1 and 2.

identity, Clark's examination of the role of the media in religious identity construction amongst US teens offers a valuable model. On the basis of her careful analysis of teenagers' narratives, her five categories of traditionalist teens, intrigued teens, mystical teens, experimenters and resisters offer rich insights into how media engagement is a highly diverse and complex phenomenon.[5] As Clark emphasises, these categories are fluid, and many teenagers may fit into more than one grouping. This suggestion raises questions about which factors might move a teenager from being a traditionalist, who uses their religious beliefs to critique the media, to a resister, who finds resources in the media to challenge traditional religious values. A similar issue about what causes transformation in media-use habits can be asked of Stout and Scott's research on Mormons and their different forms of media literacy (chapter 13). Their narratives of transformation help us to see more clearly which factors move a Mormon from belief-based media criticism via individualised media consumption to communal and interactive media literacy.

The narration of identity is by no means a new topic of conversation. Both the philosopher Charles Taylor and the sociologist Anthony Giddens provide valuable resources for understanding the narratives that form our self-identities.[6] For Taylor 'the issue of our condition can never be exhausted for us by what we are, because we are always changing and becoming'.[7] In his eyes the formation of moral identity presupposes a 'narrative understanding' of our lives.[8] For Giddens 'the self forms a trajectory of development from the past to the anticipated future'.[9] From his perspective the creation of self-identity as a 'coherent phenomenon presumes a narrative'.[10] These two writers provide a significant background conversation for the authors in this book who explore the narration of identity.

A number of writers use individual personal narratives to illustrate how interactions with religious and mainstream media have been transformed over the last twenty years. This helps us to understand how viewers account for their uses of the media. In my own research I was fascinated to interview Aoife, a twenty-three-year-old Irish woman, who described her relation to the televised *Angelus* on Irish mainstream television. As background it is helpful to know that the *Angelus* is a devotion consisting in the 'repetition three times daily (early morning, noon and evening) of three Ave Marias with versicle and collect as a memorial of the incarnation. A bell is rung three times for each Ave and nine times for the collect.'[11] Originally television audiences saw

---

[5] See the conclusion of Clark's article for three suggested areas for further research.

[6] See Anthony Giddens, *Modernity and Self-Identity: Self and Society in the Late Modern Ages* (Stanford: Stanford University Press, 1991) and Charles Taylor, *Sources of the Self: The Making of the Modern Identity* (Cambridge: Cambridge University Press, 1989).

[7] Charles Taylor, *Sources of the Self*, pp. 46–7.

[8] Taylor, *Sources of the Self*, p. 48.

[9] See Anthony Giddens, *Modernity and Self-Identity*, p. 75.

[10] Giddens, *Modernity and Self-Identity*, p. 77.

[11] E. A. Livingstone (ed.), *The Concise Oxford Dictionary of the Christian Church* (Oxford: Oxford University Press, 1977), p. 21.

only a still image as the bells rang: a single picture of the Madonna and Child. More recently this has been replaced by a series of images, reflecting a somewhat idealised view of Catholic Ireland. These tightly edited broadcasts include shots of churches, Celtic crosses, people looking up from their work or thoughtfully staring into the middle distance as the chimes are heard. Inevitably, this creates a much greater sense of movement than the original single image. The 'real' *Angelus* happens at six o'clock in churches around Ireland, as does the televised version on RTE 1, delaying the six o'clock news by one minute. Aoife remembers that as a child her strict Catholic grandmother encouraged her to watch this after her tea. 'It used to be so strange, because it was such a *still* image, compared to so many other *moving* pictures on television. Interestingly, we wouldn't look at her, the Madonna, we'd just be quiet and listen to the bells.' Nevertheless, some fifteen years later, she feels guilty about changing channels on the television once the broadcast has begun, so she now tries to 'avoid getting stuck with the *Angelus*'. The result is that, along with many of her friends, she misses the opening of the news in order to avoid having to turn off the *Angelus*. This narrative helps Aoife to understand her own religious self-identity, as in the context of telling this story she described herself as a 'distanced rather than a lapsed Catholic'.

There are at least four ways of reading this narrative. The first can be described as a *narrative of textual transformation*, in other words the way in which the televised *Angelus* itself has changed over a period of time. The second, closely related to the first, could be termed as a *narrative of institutional change*. Here the Catholic Church, other Irish churches and the Irish broadcasters responsible for this broadcast have changed their policy and practice over a period of years. The third narrative shifts from describing the story of textual and institutional transformation to a *narrative of audience engagement*, in this case Aoife's description of her engagement with the *Angelus*. The fourth might be described as a *narrative based on expressive reflection*. This is produced through interaction between the interviewee and the interviewer with reference to the media text. In some cases there may be a moment of insight and subsequent reinterpretation that is created through the retelling of the story.

The first three kinds of narratives have been described and discussed in detail in earlier stages of this book. For example, consider Christopher Deacy's analysis of *Pleasantville* (chapter 18) and Jörg Hermann's thematic reflection on popular and arthouse film (chapter 17). Both deal in different ways with cinematic texts and narratives where transformation is inherent. Gaye Ortiz's description of positive Catholic interactions with film (chapter 16), and Peter Horsfield's discussion of the historical views towards Christianity tackle issues related to institutional transformation (chapter 23). Jim McDonnell's essay on English Catholics' interaction with the media (chapter 4) and David Morgan's piece on visual piety could be seen as narratives of audience engagement (chapter 10).

How the narrative of expressive reflection is described, analysed and interpreted is a common area of discussion amongst those attempting to develop a sophisticated anthropology of the audience.[12] This narrative raises questions on a number of levels. First, on the process level, how might the researcher change the nature of the interviewee's responses by altering, through mere presence or through questions, the original interaction with a particular media text? Second, on the analytical level, upon what criteria are these new situations or moments of reflection to be celebrated as opportunities of insight or avoided as constructed descriptive narratives? Third, on the interpretative level, how can researchers go beyond simply redescribing subjects' narratives or practices in relation to religion and media? This is much more than an academic question. If a Jewish viewer in Tel Aviv draws his or her primary understanding of religious elements of the conflict on the West Bank from pro-Israeli news reporting, whilst a viewer in Ramallah hears only pro-Palestinian stories from an Arabic news source, then both may be implicitly accepting a narrative that demands a violent response.[13] This problem may be compounded if, as Johan Galtung asserts, the media not only have a 'perverse fascination with war and violence; [but] they also neglect the peace forces at work'.[14] On these grounds, how far is it legitimate for a researcher exploring questions of identity narration to affirm patterns of resistance to what is sometimes described as war journalism? And to push this question further, can researchers go beyond uncritical descriptions to critical narratives of how violent religious identities are nurtured, shaped and encouraged?

The multi-religious perspective

The example cited above from the West Bank and the subsequent questions point towards a third area of emerging research and conversation. *The multi-religious perspective* is used in this context primarily to refer to emerging work on separate religious traditions and the media. For example, deepening the study of the relationship between Islam and the media has now become an urgent requirement in the shadow of September 11, 2001 and the current crisis in the Middle East, as Mark Silk's essay makes abundantly clear (chapter 7). Rubina Ramji's chapter about representations of Islam in North American mass media (chapter 6) offers a contrasting view of the news media and popular Hollywood films. Hamid Mowlana's more theoretically grounded chapter on an Islamic approach to media ethics (chapter 26) provides a sustained alternative foundation. The problems raised by the stereotyping of religious traditions and figures have long proved a fertile field for

---

[12] See Stewart M. Hoover, 'Media and the Construction of the Religious Public Sphere', Stewart M. Hoover and Knut Lundby, *Rethinking Media, Religion and Culture* (London: Sage, 1997). 'What is needed is a religious anthropology of the audience to stand alongside the more rationalist anthropologies.' p. 287.

[13] See 'Reporting the Israeli/Palestinian Conflict' in *Media Development*, 3/2002.

[14] Johan Galtung, in Colleen Roach (ed.), *Communication and Culture in War and Peace* (London: Sage, 1993), p. xi.

scholars of Islam and media.[15] More recently some scholars have investigated not only Western stereotyping of the Islamic world, but also Muslim stereotyping of the West.[16]

Analysis of the representation, caricaturing and stereotyping of religious traditions and figures is an important component of developing any multi-religious approach to media, religion and culture.[17] It is by no means the only approach to this subject. Recent books have marked out several alternative methods,[18] though none to date have attempted to investigate in detail whether media can become a catalyst for religiously motivated violence or peacemaking. Rosalind Hackett's essay considering whether the media accentuates the religious divide in Nigeria is a rarity (chapter 5). Her first conclusion bears repeating: 'The growth of media coverage and production at the local and national levels [in Nigeria], and in ever more varied forms, has accentuated the (perceived or real) religious fault lines by projecting them to a wider public.' If this judgement is correct, as I believe it is, then more research is needed into why certain media fail to cover peaceful patterns of co-existence between different religious groups.

It is also interesting to note that other rich, historic religious traditions have not to date received such extensive treatment as Islam and the media or Christianity and media. Apart from a few books such as *Media and the Transformation of Religion in South Asia*,[19] which analyses printed images, audio recordings and visual media in India, few texts investigate the uses of media in non-Abrahamic religions. There is a real need for scholars to investigate in greater depth the relationships between diverse traditions found within Indian religions and the media. The reason for this can be seen clearly in the extraordinary popularity of the televised versions of the *Ramayana* and *Mahabharata*. Sunday, especially before midday, became television day for millions of Hindus, who 'felt a need to sacralize their television screens each week in order to make them "a frame for sacred events"'.[20] It is surprising that recent studies such as *Television and Social Change in Rural India*[21] virtually ignore the religious significance of these televised epics and their uses in the western Indian state of Maharashtra. It

[15] See, for example, Edward W. Said, *Covering Islam: How the Media and the Experts Determine How We See the Rest of the World,* second edition (New York: Vintage Books, 1997).

[16] Kai Hafez (ed.), *Islam and the West in the Mass Media: Fragmented Images in a Globalizing World* (Cresskill, NJ: Hampton Press, 2000); Malise Ruthven, *Fury for God: the Islamist Attack on America* (London: Granta, 2002).

[17] See, T. Parfitt (ed.), *Imagining the Other: Representations of Jews, Muslims and Christians in the Media* (London: Curzon, 2002).

[18] See, for example, Dale F. Eickelman and Jon W. Anderson (eds.), *New Media in the Muslim World – Emerging Public Sphere* (Bloomington and Indianapolis: Indiana University Press, 1999) or *Virtually Islam.*

[19] Lawrence A. Babb and Susan S. Wadley (eds.), *Media and the Transformation of Religion in South Asia* (Philadelphia: University of Pennsylvania Press, 1995).

[20] Philip Lutgendorf, 'All in the (Raghu) Family: A Video Epic in Cultural Context', Babb and Wadley, *Media and the Transformation of Religion in South Asia,* pp. 217–53.

[21] Kirk Johnson, *Television and Social Change in Rural India* (New Delhi: Sage, 2000).

is also surprising to see how little attention religion has received in the study of cinema in India and Bollywood.[22] Equally, there is a need for understanding what part television, film and other media play in religious transformation in South Asian contexts. The same is true in other Asian settings. For example, what is television's role in, use by and impact upon Theravada Buddhism in Cambodia, Laos, Myanmar and Thailand, or Mahayana Buddhism in Bhutan, China, Japan, Nepal, Taiwan, Tibet and Vietnam? Are different expressions of Buddhism more suited to particular media, and are modern Mahayana Buddhists more at ease with media than Theravada Buddhists?

Perhaps one of the most significant foundations for developing a multi-religious approach to media, religion and culture is recognition of the distinct nature of separate religious traditions and practices. This can be seen by comparing Peter Horsfield's essay which draws upon Patristic sources to understand Christianity's interaction with media technologies (chapter 23) and Hamid Mowlana's handling of medieval sources for outlining Islamic approaches to communication (chapter 26). Taken together these two articles demonstrate that the cause of dialogue is not served by pretending that the Christian and Islamic traditions and practices are identical, nor that they embrace ancient or modern media in the same fashion.

Nevertheless, a number of recent writers have pointed out that distinct religious traditions do have points of connection or elements of similarity in response to various media. These are manifested in attitudes and practices towards both the visual and verbal media.[23] In this book, Clifford Christians' thought-provoking essay on 'Cross-Cultural Ethics and Truth' and Robert White's chapter on developing a normative approach to media ethics illustrate how the search for common norms across religious and cultural divides remains a live issue (chapters 25 and 24 respectively). This is a hotly debated topic. Some researchers and practitioners believe that the search for such universal norms is doomed to failure while others celebrate it as the way forward in a religiously violent and fragmented world.

The quest for communicative justice

The fourth topic of conversation frequently provokes passionate debate: *the quest for communicative justice*. Economic injustice divides the communication rich and communication poor. Well over half the world's population

---

[22] Rachel Dwyer's developing work on Religion and Indian Cinema is an exception. See 'Representing the Muslim: the "courtesan film" in Indian Popular Cinema', T. Parfitt (ed.), *Imagining the Other*.

[23] For a tracing of Pagan [sic], Jewish, Christian and Muslim attitudes towards iconoclasm see: Alain Beançon, *The Forbidden Image: An Intellectual History of Iconoclasm* (Chicago: University of Chicago Press, [1994] 2000). For an analysis of the oral aspects of scripture in the history of religions see: William A. Graham, *Beyond the Written Word* (Cambridge: Cambridge University Press, 1987).

has never made a phone call. There are one billion telephone lines for some 5.7 billion people.[24] It is not surprising therefore that in 2002 little more than 5 per cent of the world has access to the Internet, 80 per cent of whom live in North America and Europe. Young Western men dominate access to the Internet. These and connected points are well made by Cees Hamelink in his chapter on the ethics of the Internet (chapter 21). As he demonstrates, the issue becomes more complicated when the environmental implications of widened access and increased computer construction are considered. Given that most computers supposedly become 'dinosaurs' after a few years, and that they each leave a long shadow on the environment, will it ever be environmentally sustainable for the entire world's population to possess a computer? How can religion and media research highlight the contradiction between these areas of communicative injustices and the environmental implications of massively increased computer production and ownership? Are there resources within the world's religious traditions that point to alternative ways of sharing and consuming media technologies?

The issue of communicative inequalities can be seen in two other closely related spheres, those of news coverage and news flow. According to Rosalind Hackett's chapter on Nigerian media, both Muslims and Christians in Nigeria perceive that their side of the story is covered unjustly. In many settings this is a matter of life and death. The challenge remains for journalists in such situations to cover the story of the 'other' with as much compassion and sympathy as they tell the news of their own communities. Unjust narratives, as suggested earlier, have the potential to accentuate the perception and reality of divided communities. News coverage that is dominated by Western stories and flows out of Western news agencies can also heighten the sense of injustice felt by many of the world's impoverished groups. The 1970s' debates on NWICO (New World Information Communication Order), and the voices shouting 'media imperialism' and 'cultural imperialism' may appear quieter, but they continue to echo in questions asked about news balance. Why, for example, did the genocide of nearly one million people in Rwanda receive comparatively little coverage compared to more recent terrorist atrocities in North America? This is not to lighten the seriousness of the tragic events of September 11, 2001. Nevertheless, there is clearly a role for scholars of media and religion to analyse the religious significance of why many tragic news stories, such as the death of thousands of Iraqi children, are buried in the Western news trivia of film stars' re-marriages, royal peccadilloes and naughty vicars.

These questions about news coverage and news flow initially return us to familiar questions about news values, but could scholars bring new insights into why certain stories are ignored whilst others are put under the spotlight?

---

[24] See chapter 21 of this book and for a more extended discussion of these issues see Cees J. Hamelink, *The Ethics of Cyberspace* (London: Sage, 2000) p. 81.

The media, religion and culture discussion may be able to contribute to Michael Traber's observation that 'the fundamental problem with these criteria of news-worthiness [e.g., Prominence, Proximity, Timeliness, Conflict, Oddity and Sex] is that they distort reality. They create some kind of surface to social reality, which has very little to do with the world we live in. And above all they exclude the vast majority of people, but especially manual labourers, women and children from the media.'[25] Scholars of media, religion and culture could usefully explore why certain religious leaders receive more coverage than others, and why the piety of millions can often be caricatured or patronised by journalists.[26]

The historical perspective

A fifth significant strand, evident in this book and other recent publications, is the development of *the historical perspective*.[27] One of the keys to understanding situations of conflict is to develop a historical perspective. News that simply tells the immediate story, such as that there has been a suicide bombing in Jerusalem, a wave of killings in Nigeria or an explosion in Bali, without contextualising them in their religious and historical context, fail to provide adequate coverage. Likewise discussion of the religious implications of the uses of specific media without reference to their historical background will only offer thin descriptions. In short, ahistorical approaches to the interactions between media and religion will inevitably lead to shallow insights.

Peter Horsfield's discussion of the opposition towards writing in the early church (chapter 23) supplies a stimulating model of how historical analysis can contribute to current debates about the future of the church in post-Christian environments. Research as to why the churches have historically held an iconoclastic approach to specific media provides valuable insights into current theological debates over both new and old media. In the last century, the initial response by many religious leaders and commentators to the advent and use of radio, cinema and television was one of suspicion, caution or avoidance. Malcolm Muggeridge's argument, discussed by Myrna Grant, that television is inevitably a medium of fantasy and illusion is an example of one such iconoclastic response (chapter 11).

Whilst this negative response has not entirely abated, many religious

[25] Michael Traber, 'Communication Ethics' (Ch. 18), George Gerbner, Hamid Mowlana and Karle Nordenstreng (eds.), *The Global Media Debate: Its rise, fall and renewal* (NJ: Ablex, 1993).

[26] For example, see Matt Frei's report for BBC 2's *Correspondent* (28 January 1995) of the Pope's visit to the Philippines where Frei was clearly shocked by the size of the crowd and claimed that the Pope 'needed the adoring crowds as much as they needed him. An Opium for the masses and for the Pope.' Jolyon Mitchell, *Deconstructing Religious Stereotypes in Popular Television* in *Cultura Y Medios De Comunicación. Actas del III Congreso Internacional*, 2000, p. 784.

[27] See, for example, Stewart Hoover and Lynn Schofield Clark, *Practicing Religion in the Age of the Media* (New York: Columbia University Press, 2002) especially chapters 2, 5, 6, 13 and 15.

leaders have embraced communication technologies over the past eighty years, believing that they can offer effective communication of faith messages. It is useful to analyse the historical roots of these iconoclastic and iconographic responses in order to demonstrate how both of these approaches are problematic, and to offer an alternative audience-centred model for interacting with the media.[28] David Morgan's work both in this book (chapter 10) and elsewhere exemplifies how a historical approach can inform understandings of how audiences interpret and appropriate images.[29] Another way of describing this *oeuvre* is as a 'visual turn' or 'material move', reflecting historians' study of how audiences use what they see.

Two other books recently widened our understanding of issues of media and religion from a historical perspective. *Readings on Religion as News*, edited by Judith Buddenbaum and Debra L. Mason, takes the reader on a journey through three hundred years of American history.[30] This anthology of over a hundred articles illustrates the rich original materials available to those wishing to trace the evolution of religious and religion journalism. *Media and Religion in American Religion*, edited by W. David Sloan, provides a series of articles that challenge the assumption that media and religion have always been natural enemies. On the basis of these books and several of the articles in this volume, I would like to make a plea for more historical research that takes us beyond the borders of the USA. There are, for example, many gaps in the history of global and national religious broadcasting. Likewise to date there is no book that attempts to chart the religious implications of the evolution of communication technologies from oral via printing to electronic communication. Both Eisenstein's work on *The Printing Press as an Agent of Change* and Walter Ong's research on *Literacy and Orality* raise a whole set of significant research questions for those concerned with the interaction between media, religion and culture.[31]

The transformation of religious and theological reflection

Deepening our historical perspective is not the only way of ensuring that there is a *transformation of religious and theological reflection* on the media. This sixth topic of research can be seen clearly through reading Fran Plude's useful annotated bibliography on texts for the study of Communication Theology. John Ferré's chapter on 'The Media of Popular Piety' provides a helpful interpretative framework

[28] For a more detailed discussion of iconography and iconoclasm see: Jolyon Mitchell 'Deconstructing Religious Stereotypes in Popular Television', *Cultura Y Medios De Comunicación. Actas del III Congreso Internacional*, pp. 769–75.

[29] See, for example, David Morgan, *Visual Piety* (Los Angeles: University of California Press, 1998) and *Protestants and Pictures* (Oxford University Press: New York, 1999).

[30] Judith Buddenbaum and Debra L. Mason, *Readings on Religion as News* (Ames: Iowa State University Press, 2000).

[31] Elizabeth L. Eistenstein, *The Printing Press as an Agent of Change: Communications and Cultural Transformations in Early Modern Europe* (Cambridge: Cambridge University Press, 1979); and Walter Ong, *Orality and Literacy: The Technologizing of the Word* (New York: Routledge, 1982). (See also Peter Horsfield's discussion in chapter 23 of this book.)

for understanding those religious communicators who see the media as a neutral conduit, a mode of knowing or a social institution (chapter 8). Many of the early books on religion and media tended to work on instrumental approaches to communication, concentrating upon either the effective potential of particular media to 'reach the world' or the danger of specific media corrupting viewers. The underlying assumption appears to have been the bigger the technology, the better it could be used to communicate the message. Or the more sophisticated the communicative forms employed, the greater the potential for seducing the viewers into patterns of unhealthy or unholy behaviour. In both cases, the underlying assumption was that modern forms of communication were powerful tools or instruments for communication. This led to a concentration upon the content of messages, so that the mythmaking power of media such as television was deconstructed and then severely criticised.[32]

This approach still informs close textual analysis of specific films, and does provide enriching insights into the religious significance of various films. Christopher Deacy's article on *Pleasantville* is an example of one such approach (chapter 18). It also leads scholars to set out advice on how religious leaders should be trained in the art of communication in a media age. Eilers, for example, focuses on assisting broadcasters to develop their skills as communicators in order to improve the quality or clarity of the message itself (chapter 14). Mary Hess recognises the importance of moving away from an instrumentalist understanding of communication and recommends careful attention to the media (chapter 12). This is a significant argument in an increasingly distracted age.

Outside this book and from a more Protestant perspective, writers such as Jacques Ellul have gone further. In *The Humiliation of the Word*, influenced by the Swiss theologian Karl Barth, Ellul sets out an uncompromising case for rejecting television as a medium for Christian communication. As I showed in greater detail in *Visually Speaking*, for Ellul, television may be useful in terms of communicative efficacy, but it undermines what is at the very heart of Christianity: the word.[33] For many critics this is too restrictive an understanding of the foundations of Christianity and results in an overly narrow theological reflection on the media. Nevertheless, as Christians shows in his discussion of Ellul and truth (chapter 25), there is clearly considerably more work to be done in setting out the theological foundations for understanding the nature and practice of communication.

From a more Catholic perspective, writers beyond this volume such as Michael Budde suggest that Christians should spend more time learning the language and habits of the gospel and the church, and less time consuming the 'products of commercial culture industries' and thereby 'distance' themselves

---

[32] William Fore, *Television and Religion: The Shaping of Faith, Values and Culture* (Minneapolis: Augsburg, 1987).

[33] Jolyon Mitchell, *Visually Speaking: Radio and the Renaissance of Preaching* (Edinburgh: T&T Clark, 1999).

[34] Michael Budde, *The (Magic) Kingdom of God: Christianity and Global Culture Industries* (Boulder, CO: Westview, 1997), pp. 150, 151.

from 'the consumerist worldview upon which they depend'.[34] But is shunning the products of culture industries the most effective form of media engagement? Like many other writers in this area, Budde underestimates the creative role of the audience in his forceful analysis of the power of the media industries. There are distinctive resources in specific religious traditions for interacting with both media producers and audiences. Within the Christian tradition, for example, there are insights that can be discerned not only from traditional biblical material, but also from the practice of theological engagement articulated by theologians such as Augustine, Aquinas and Balthasar. More work is required to identify, outline and creatively critique the resources provided by such theologians for further cultural engagement and criticism.

The ethics of the audience

A seventh strand of conversation is only recently beginning to emerge. The chapters by Heidi Campbell (chapter 19), and Alf Linderman and Mia Lövheim (chapter 20), demonstrate the dynamic way in which Internet users create their own virtual communities. These communities often take responsibility for each other's welfare despite not being physically present. Their conclusions point towards the benefit of an extended study on the responsibilities of media users: an *ethics of the audience*. As can be seen by Clifford Christians' annotated bibliography, the existing literature in media ethics is overwhelmingly producer-oriented. Stories or images of suffering are often used to explore the rights and wrongs of specific courses of action taken by journalists and editors. By approaching the subject this way they tend to highlight the act of their decision-making, what Cartier-Bresson described in 1952 as the 'the decisive moment'. This action-centred approach continues in contemporary writing. Others concentrate more on the agency of journalists themselves. These agent-centred approaches, influenced perhaps by MacIntyre's now classic *After Virtue,* tend to go beyond questions of journalistic codes of conduct, to recognisably Aristotelian questions such as 'What sort of journalist should I be?' Agent-centred media ethicists identify a wide range of virtues from being competent and committed to becoming truthful, humane and just. These two methods, the action-centred and agent-centred approach, which are sometimes brought together, are currently the dominant paradigms in media ethics. But we need a new paradigm: an *ethics of the audience.* This will avoid the pitfall of turning ethical decision-making into highly individualised and privatised acts, where the final arbiter is often 'gut feeling'. Mark Fackler's chapter on the value of African communitarianism for transforming elements of media theory is a valuable reminder of the significance of the community in assisting audiences to participate more fully in media use (chapter 27).

No single text adequately outlines an audience-centred approach to media ethics, nor is there a book that has sufficiently explored whether media literacy can equip audiences to transform the apparently secularised media into sites and sources of theological or religious insight. There is need for further research that will complement and draw critically upon a range of sociological, religious and theological studies, including some of the themes set out in this chapter: the increased sophistication in interpreting audiences through reception work and identity questions; the developing research on separate religious traditions; the increasing interest in religion and media history; the growing concerns about communicative justice and the multifaceted attempts to extend religious and theological questions about the media. My hope is that other scholars involved in discussions around media, religion and culture will find the essays in this book suggestive for their own research projects. For example, it would be fascinating to explore in greater depth how audiences evolve from passive voyeurs to compassionate participants, ready to challenge and resist the hegemony of certain media institutions.

A few weeks prior to the publication of *Mediating Religion* a second Gulf War exploded onto television screens around the world. Unlike the 1991 war in Kuwait where most journalists were confined to tightly confined reporting 'pools', the 2003 war has seen the embedding of journalists with frontline American and British forces. The result: unprecedented public access to the sights and sounds of fighting. The original intention may have been to show rapid 'liberation' of the Iraqi people and their euphoric welcome to coalition forces. With unexpectedly strong resistance these often 'live' pictures are far more ambiguous, revealing not only the fog of battle, but also that war is never simple or clean as a smart-bomb video pretends it to be. This impression of the real cost of war is reinforced by stations such as *al-Jazeera*, providing graphic representations of the results of the bombing on Baghdad's civilian population. Apart from the pressing ethical questions about how suffering and the effects of violence are framed in news, it is also useful to analyse how audiences can reframe the images with which they are presented. An audience-centred approach will take into account how the world's religious traditions are used by viewers for making sense of the violence that they consume.

Conclusion

This chapter is not intended to be a comprehensive survey of all the possible new directions in the study of media, religion and culture. It has rather aimed to sketch some of the emerging areas that are currently being explored and which merit further exploration. It is clear from the range of conversations clustered around the seven themes of the participative turn, the narration of identity, the multi-religious perspective, the quest for communicative justice, the historical perspective, the transformation of religious and theological reflection, and the ethics of the audience, that developing a single coherent methodology is premature if not impossible. This book has instead offered a wide range of essays and methodologies on

Annotated Bibliographies

Media Ethics

Clifford G. Christians

Further Reading

J. B. Atkins (ed.), *The Mission: Journalism, Ethics and the World* (Ames: Iowa State University Press, 2002).

> Essays by international journalists and scholars on the ethical dilemmas they face, including societies which have experienced profound change.

L. W. Baker, *The Credibility Factor: Putting Ethics to Work in Public Relations* (Homewood, IL: Business One Irwin, 1993).

> The major theme is that ethics – ethics codes, individual conscience, company guidelines, careful decision-making – are the foundation for achieving credibility. Provides examples of companies that prospered by taking ethics seriously.

A. Belsey and R. Chadwick (eds.), *Ethical Issues in Journalism and the Media* (New York: Routledge, 1992).

> Ethics for journalism and the media is built on such fundamental values as democracy, freedom, truth, honesty, objectivity and privacy. This textbook emphasises the idea that the press's role is to provide information, and therefore, its ethical purpose is maintaining the quality of its content.

C-J. Bertrand (ed.), *L'arsenal de la démocratie: Médias, déontologie et M*A*R*S* (Paris: Economica, 1999).

> Essays by a range of scholars and professionals on the various forms of accountability for the media – such as codes of ethics, press councils, media critics, review magazines and ombudsmen.

C-J. Bertrand, *Media Ethics & Accountability Systems* (New Brunswick, NJ: Transaction, 2000).

> A textbook outlining the self-regulation and media-criticism systems in different parts of the world for making the press accountable and responsible.

F. L. Casmir (ed.), *Ethics in Intercultural and International Communication* (Mahwah, NJ: Lawrence Erlbaum, 1997).

> Seven essays, plus a case study on the Hanshin earthquake in Japan. The editor introduces and concludes the book, and contributes a chapter on 'the third culture building model'.

C. G. Christians, M. Fackler, K. B. Rotzoll and K. B. Mckee, *Media Ethics: Cases and Moral Reasoning,* 6th ed. (New York: Longman, 2001).

Seventy-eight case studies and commentaries on the major ethical issues in news, advertising, public relations and entertainment. Ethical theories are used to reach ethically justified conclusions.

C. G. Christians, J. P. Ferre and P. J. Fackler, *Good News: Social Ethics and the Press* (New York: Oxford University Press, 1993).

This book develops a communitarian model for the press's context and structure. It is designed as a theoretical alternative to the individualistic approaches to media ethics that have dominated under the Enlightenment's influence.

C. G. Christians and M. Traber (eds.), *Communication Ethics and Universal Values* (Thousand Oaks, CA: Sage, 1997).

Based on essays from thirteen countries, bedrock principles across cultures are identified: human dignity, truthtelling and non-violence.

E. D. Cohen and D. Elliott (eds.), *Journalism Ethics: A Reference Handbook* (Santa Barbara, CA: ABC-Clio, 1997).

Reviews the major issues in journalism morality today, including intrusion into privacy, graphic media, computer technology and misleading reporting. Reference chapters on important court cases, codes of ethics and media organisations.

T. W. Cooper, *Communication Ethics and Global Change* (New York: Longman, 1989).

Essays from sixteen countries on important issues in media ethics. Overview chapters on the crucial international issues are included in sections I and III. Codes of ethics included in appendix.

P. J. Creedon, *Women in Mass Communication: Challenging Gender Values* (Beverly Hills, CA: Sage, 1989).

A book accounting for the increased number of women in mass media occupations, with several chapters contributed by public relations scholars.

L. A. Day, *Ethics in Media Communication: Cases and Controversies,* 2nd ed. (Belmont, CA: Wadsworth, 1997).

Three opening chapters introduce students to ethical theory and to a model of moral reasoning. Seventy hypothetical cases are included, each with a brief commentary. They are selected from across the media professions, including news, advertising, public relations and film entertainment.

J. P. Ferré and C. W. Shirley, *Public Relations and Ethics: A Reference Guide* (Boston: G. K. Hall, 1991).

A comprehensive annotated bibliography of 295 English-language sources on public relations and ethics.

D. T. Elliott (ed.), *Responsible Journalism* (Beverly Hills, CA: Sage, 1986).
Nine essays by academics, examining issues in press theory and social responsibility.

J. Ellul, *Propaganda* (New York: Vintage, 1973).
Always innovative, Ellul explores public attitude formation as part of the larger social issue surrounding *la technique.*

C. Ess (ed.), *Philosophical Perspectives on Computer-Mediated Communications* (Albany: State University of New York Press, 1996).
Examines the assumptions and core issues in the current rush to the information age. Various chapters deal with the ethical consequences for gender, pornography, privacy, religious life and democracy.

J. A. Ettema and T. L. Glasser, *Custodians of Conscience: Investigative Journalism and Public Virtue* (New York: Columbia University Press, 1998).
This book is based on extensive interviews with award-winning newspaper and television reporters. The authors conclude that investigative journalists are custodians of the public conscience.

C. Frost, *Media Ethics and Self-Regulation* (London: Longman, 2000).
Concentrates on everyday problems of working journalists in Britain. He advocates self-regulation rather than media legislation, and in reviewing ethical theory promotes the approach of the British twentieth century moral philosopher W. D. Ross and rejects utilitarianism.

P. G. Gomes, *Direto de Ser: A Ética da communicao na América Latina (The Right to Be: An Ethics of Communication in Latin America)* (São Paulo: Ediciones Paulinas, 1990).
Gomes applies the principles of liberation theology to journalism in the Latin American context. Advocating justice for the poor is the central concept for media professionals, and only if they help sustain hope can the dignity of the oppressed be maintained.

A. D. Gordon, J. M. Kittross and C. Reuss, *Controversies in Media Ethics*, 2nd ed. (White Plains, NY: Longman, 1998).
An overview of media ethics in general, but focuses on real life issues and the specific responsibilities of those who work in the various forms of mass media. The authors debate two sides of the issue, and John Merrill offers commentary.

G. Gjelsten, *Mote eller manipulasjon? Om etikk I massemedia* (Forlaget, Norway: NKS, 1988).
The opposite of manipulation is a normative model for mass communication built on the principles of promoting mental health and social adjustment. The author develops his perspective historically and theoretically and uses illustrations from various media.

L. Gross, J. S. Katz and J. Ruby, *Image Ethics: The Moral Rights of Subjects in Photographs, Film, and Television* (New York: Oxford University Press, 1991).
Original essays on the ethics of representation reviewing moral questions in terms of the subject rather than the rights of producers and filmmakers.

C. J. Hamelink, *The Ethics of Cyberspace* (Thousands Oaks, CA: Sage, 2000). (Originally published as *Digitaal Fatseon*, The Netherlands, Uitgeverij Boom).
Puts computer networks and digital information into a broad socio-political context, and argues for international human rights standards for governing cyberspace.

A. Holderegger (ed.), *Ethik der Medienkommunikation: Grundlagen* (Freiburg-wein: Universitätsverlag Freiburg Schweiz, 1992).
Eight theological ethicists examine the underlying assumptions of the mass media system from a critical cultural perspective.

J. Hurst and S. A. White, *Ethics and the Australian News Media* (South Melbourne: Macmillan Education Australia, 1994).
Discusses the ethics and morality of the Australian press in terms of the roles that the media and journalists play in Western society generally. Covers all aspects of reporting and journalism, including topics such as privacy, business, pressures, the press's role in guarding and informing society, the confidentiality of sources and reporting on gender and race.

J. Iggers, *Good News, Bad News: Journalism Ethics and the Public Interest* (Boulder, CO: Westview, 1998).
This volume argues that the traditional standards of journalism and morality (avoiding conflicts of interest, accuracy, objectivity, fairness, etc.) are outdated. Develops a pragmatist ethical theory worked out in the context of public journalism.

M. F. Jacobson and L. A. Mazur, *Marketing Madness* (Boulder, CO: Westview, 1995).
A highly critical analysis of such advertising-related topics as targeting children, sexism and sexuality, cigarettes and alcohol, etc.

J. A. Jaksa and M. S. Pritchard, *Communication Ethics: Methods of Analysis*, 2nd ed. (Belmont, CA: Wadsworth, 1994).
A variety of case studies are included in each chapter, ranging from interpersonal to organisational communication. The central issue is the current crisis of confidence in spoken and written words as it affects the professions, public figures and institutions.

S. Jhally and J. Lewis, *Enlightened Racism: The Cosby Show, Audiences, and the Myth of the American Dream* (Boulder, CO: Westview, 1992).
How prime-time television presents race and class images. This case

study examines the popular show that starred Bill Cosby and Felicia Rashad.

R. L. Johannesen, *Ethics in Human Communication*, 5th ed. (Prospect Heights, IL: Waveland, 2002).
Places ethical responsibility into the context of political philosophy and communication theory. Includes cases and analysis of ethics codes.

P. Juusela, *Journalistic Codes of Ethics in the CSCE Countries* (Finland: University of Tampere, 1991).
Juusela discusses the codes and morality of journalism in contemporary Europe. He focuses on the thirty-five states that signed the Helsinki Act in 1975 (Conference on Security and Cooperation in Europe). Twenty-four nations' ethical codes or systems are included.

F. P. Kasoma (ed.), *Journalism Ethics in Africa* (Nairobi: African Council for Communication Education, 1994).
Five chapters on theoretical issues from African perspectives, and four chapters of application to photojournalism and news reporting.

M. Kieran (ed.), *Media Ethics* (New York: Routledge, 1998).
Academics and professionals from Britain and the US examine the difficult issues in journalism, such as truth, privacy, human rights, war reporting, violence, pornography, photojournalism and the tabloid press.

M. Kieran, *Media Ethics: A Philosophical Approach* (Westport, CT: Praeger, 1997).
The philosophical literature and a dialectical method are used to analyse the main ethical issues in all types of media.

S. Klaidman and T. L. Beauchamp, *The Virtuous Journalist* (New York: Oxford University Press, 1987).
Built around real-life cases, this volume describes the character traits and professional virtues needed for fair, truthful and competent journalism.

S. R. Knowlton, *Moral Reasoning for Journalists: Cases and Commentary* (Westport, CT: Praeger, 1997).
Part One gives the bases for moral reasoning, and Part Two examines real-life cases to apply the author's call for balancing competing interests.

S. R. Knowlton and P. R. Parsons (eds.), *The Journalist's Moral Compass: Basic Principles* (Westport, CT: Greenwood, 1995).
An anthology of twenty-four readings, from John Milton to John Merrill. Together they seek to describe the basic principles that govern contemporary American journalism. These common

principles (many of them embodied in the SPJ Code of Ethics) are set against the major issues that challenge them.

E. B. Lambeth, *Committed Journalism: An Ethic for the Profession*, 2nd ed. (Bloomington: Indiana University Press, 1992).
Outlines a framework for ethical journalism from the codes, ideas and best practice in the field.

L. Z. Leslie, *Mass Communication Ethics: Decision Making in Postmodern Culture* (Boston: Houghton Mifflin, 2000).
A major section on philosophical foundations from classical Greece to the present. Case studies are used from the press, broadcasting, cinema, advertising and public relations, and the Internet to apply ethical theory.

P. Lester (ed.), *Images That Injure: Pictorial Stereotypes in the Media* (Westport, CT: Praeger, 1996).
This collection of essays explores the impact of age, gender, and racial, ethnic and social stereotypes perpetuated in advertising, television, film and journalistic photography with illustrations from an ethical and social perspective. The conclusion offers examples of 'images that heal' as well.

V. E. Limburg, *Electronic Media Ethics* (Boston: Focal, 1994).
Critical issues in broadcast ethics are examined – in radio, television, entertainment, broadcast news, advertising and telecommunications. Uses historical and theoretical approaches, as well as professional codes, for ethical guidelines.

B. MacDonald and M. Petheram, *Key Guide to Information Sources in Media Ethics* (London: Cassell, 1998).
A reference handbook on media ethics around the world. Part I gives an overview, Part II is an annotated bibliography of books and other printed materials. Part III is a directory of organisations and institutions.

M. P. McElreath, *Managing Systematic and Ethical Public Relations Campaigns*, 2nd ed. (Madison, WI: Brown & Benchmark, 1997).
Text offers practical discussion of tools and techniques in campaigns through the lens of ethical analysis. Numerous hypothetical and industry case studies are included.

J. M. Makau and R. C. Arnett (eds.), *Communication Ethics in an Age of Diversity* (Urbana: University of Illinois Press, 1997).
Essays dealing with cultural diversity from the perspective of moral principles, new technologies, and demographic change.

M. Medved, *Saving Childhood* (New York: Harper Collins, 1998).
Plenty of evidence in this well written book that children are not well served by television and film.

J. C. Merrill, *Journalism Ethics: Philosophical Foundations for New Media* (New York: St. Martin's, 1997).

> Explores such concepts as individualism, communitarianism, propaganda and responsibility in order to understand the foundations of everyday journalism practice.

R. L. Moore, *Mass Communication Law and Ethics* (Hillsdale, NJ: Lawrence Erlbaum, 1994).

> Media law and ethics are combined explicitly. Chapters include prior restraint; government policy; broadcasting; libel; right of privacy; public access to records, judicial process, and meetings; intellectual property; and indecency and obscenity.

H. Newcomb and R. Alley, *The Producer's Medium: Conversations with Creators of American TV* (New York: Oxford University Press, 1993).

> Interviews with notable producers (e.g., Norman Lear, Richard Levinson, William Link and Garry Marshall) about the values they express as artists.

J. H. Newton, *The Burden of Visual Truth: The Role of Photojournalism in Mediating Reality* (Mahwah, NJ: Lawrence Erlbaum, 2001).

> Examines the notion of visual truth particularly in the news media by combining research on photojournalism and imagery with visual communication theory.

K. Nordenstreng (ed.), *Reports on Media Ethics in Europe* (Finland: University of Tampere, 1995).

> A collection of empirical studies on the way self-regulation is done in the European region. It includes surveys of European media councils, examination of media codes of ethics in general and regarding racism and xenophobia in Europe, and a study of the Finnish journalists' adoption of their own code of ethics.

P. Patterson and L. Wilkins, *Media Ethics: Issues and Cases*, 3rd ed. (Boston: McGraw-Hill, 1998).

> Thoughtful case studies and analyses from several media ethicists. Includes simulated cases, three levels of questions, and contemporary responses to long-standing issues.

B. Pattyn (ed.), *Media Ethics: Opening Social Dialogue* (Leuven, Belgium: Peeters, 2000).

> Essays by an international array of scholars on the history and theory of media ethics, professional journalism, popular culture, teaching, codes of ethics and audiences.

M. Phillips, *Ethics and Manipulation in Advertising* (Westport, CT: Quarum, 1997).

> A thoughtful analysis of the ethical positions of critics and defenders of advertising.

I. Preston, *The Great American Blow-up,* rev. ed. (Madison: University of Wisconsin Press, 1996); I. Preston, *The Targeted Web They Weave: Truth, Falsity, and Advertisers* (Madison: University of Wisconsin Press, 1996).

Provocative and analytical examination of the role of 'puffery' (exaggeration) and deception in advertising.

D. C. Robinson, E. B. Buck, M. Cuthbert and the International Communication and Youth Consortium, *Music at the Margins: Popular Music and Global Cultural Diversity* (Newbery Park, CA: Sage, 1991).

Forty scholars from twenty countries analyse popular music and the industrial structure that produces and distributes the product.

W. D. Romanowski, *Pop Culture Wars: Religion and the Role of Entertainment in American Life* (Downers Grove, IL: InterVarsity Press, 1996).

At issue is Medved's thesis of warfare between Hollywood and traditional values, seen through the lens of an informed (culturally and theologically) Reformed worldview.

P. Rossi and P. Soukup, *Mass Media and the Moral Imagination* (Kansas City, MO: Sheed & Ward, 1994).

A collection of scholarly essays that probes spirituality and religious conviction en route to insights on media and morality.

N. Russell, *Morals and the Media: Ethics and Canadian Journalism* (Vancouver: University of British Columbia Press, 1994).

Public concern over the media and journalism's proper roles is discussed in this handbook. Russell addresses various issues – such as sensationalism, misquoting sources, violence, commercialism and reporting only bad news – while staying focused on ethical codes and standards.

P. Sieb and K. Fitzpatrick, *Journalism Ethics* (New York: Harcourt Brace, 1997).

Through various case studies and applications the duties of journalists are explored, including such issues as tabloids, conflicts of interest, deception and diversity.

P. Sieb and K. Fitzpatrick, *Public Relations Ethics* (Fort Worth, TX: Harcourt Brace, 1995).

Examines public relations ethics from the perspective of professionals, with attention given to moral theories and professional codes of ethics.

U. Sinclair, *The Brass Check* (Pasadena, CA: Classic, 1920).

No advocate of the profession of public relations, Sinclair was one of the first to tell us why we should be watchful.

C. Taylor, *The Ethics of Authenticity* (Cambridge: Harvard University Press, 1991).

Taylor recognises the danger in contemporary appeals to authenticity, to self-fulfillment, to rights. But he argues for their possibilities and promise also, using thinkers from Nietzsche to Foucault.

N. Thomassen, *Communicative Ethics in Theory and Practice*, trans. J. Irons (London: Macmillan, 1985). (Originally published as *Samvoer og Solidaritet*, Copenhagen, 1985).

Presents a theoretical model of communicative solidarity dealing with the good of all, shaped by hermeneutics and Habermas' discourse ethics.

A. Valerie, B. Brennan and B. Hoffmaster (eds.), *Deadlines and Diversity: Journalism Ethics in a Changing World* (Halifax, Nova Scotia: Fernwood, 1996).

Contributors from both practitioners and academics in Canada deal with broad issues such as objectivity, ethnic diversity and codes, and with particular problems such as radio talk shows, sports journalism, art criticism and editorial cartoons.

J. Willis and A. A. Okunade, *Reporting on Risks: The Practice and Ethics of Health and Safety Communication* (Westport, CT: Praeger, 1997).

Discusses issues in journalism that surround health, risk, disasters and safety. The book explores problems with accuracy in reporting as well as other ethical dilemmas that surround health care policy, matters of life and death, sexual abuse, AIDS and the environment.

W. Wunden (ed.), *Medien Zwischen Markt und Moral: Beitrage zur Medienethik* (Stuttgart: J. F. Steinkopf Verlag, 1989).

Chapters from twenty academics and practitioners on the ethics of media institutions and professionals. News reporting, children's pro-gramming, entertainment film, new technologies, teaching of ethics, and biblical perspectives are included.

New Media and Religion

Heidi Campbell

Further Reading

Barna Research Group, 'The Cyberchurch is Coming. National Survey of Teenagers shows Expectation of Substituting Internet for Corner Church' (5 May 1998). www.barna.org/PressCyberChurch.htm

An American survey targeting teenagers found one out of six teens said they expected to use the Internet as a substitute for current church-based religious experience within the next five years. Common uses included interactions with others in chat rooms or email exchanges about religious beliefs.

Barna Research Group, 'More Americans Are Seeking Net-Based Faith Experiences' (21 May 2001). www.barna.org/cig-bin/PageP...asp? PressReleaseID=90&Reference=A

A survey of net-based faith experiences, found 8 per cent of the surveyed adult population and 12 per cent of teens used the Internet for religious purposes. Barna predicts the American church will drastically change in the next decade as their research found 'Christian Internet users already spend more time surfing the Net than they do communicating with God through prayer'.

M. Bauwens, 'Spirituality and Technology: Exploring the Relationship', *First Monday* (4 November 1996). www.firstmonday.dk/issues/issue5/ bauwens/index.html

Bauwens presents three characterisations of how Internet technology is conceived of in spiritual pursuits online: Technology as Gaia, Technology as God Project and Technology as Sacramental Cyberspace.

D. Bell, *An Introduction to Cybercultures* (London: Routledge, 2001).

Bell offers a comprehensive synopsis of the key debates and research issues emerging in the field of cyberculture studies including examining identity, the body, community and computer subcultures.

M. Benedikt (ed.), *Cyberspace: First Steps* (Cambridge: MIT Press, 1992).

This foundational book offers prophetic pictures on how cyberspace technologies might emerge and where these developments might lead, popularised in the 1990s. It has a diverse interdisciplinary range of authors coming from philosophical and computer programming backgrounds.

B. Brasher, *Give Me That Online Religion* (San Francisco: Jossey-Bass, 2001).
Brasher provides a survey of the ways the Internet is used in religious contexts, as well as exploring issues of online pilgrimage and religious millennial fears. This is a good general introduction to the topic of online religion.

T. Brooke (ed.), *Virtual Gods* (Eugene, OR: Harvest House, 1997).
Brooke, director of the Spiritual Counterfeits Project in California, offers a critical Christian response to the Internet, arguing virtual reality and the Internet will lead 'towards the spiritual landscape' similar to that before the great flood in Genesis where 'man creates his own universe with no god in it but himself' (p. 126).

G. Bunt, *Virtually Islamic: Computer-Mediated Communication and Cyber Islamic Environments* (Lampeter: University of Wales Press, 2000).
Bunt presents an overall survey of how the Islamic community has utilised the Internet as well as non-Muslims' perceptions of Islam as demonstrated online. He offers examples of various cyber Islamic environments and their influence on sacred texts, religious identity and religious perceptions.

A. Carega, *E-vangelism: Sharing the Gospel in Cyberspace* (Lafayette, LA: Vital Issues, 1999) and e *Ministry: Connecting with the Net Generation* (Grand Rapids, MI: Kregel Publications, 2001).
Carega explores the Internet as a new mission field for Christians by addressing issues raised by doing 'friendship evangelism' in online conferences or 'surf evangelism' on web sites. He advocates online missionaries be fluent in the language of technology as well as being informed about the culture of the Internet before venturing into cyberspace.

J. C. Chama, 'Finding God on the Web', *TIME* (6 Dec 1996).
One of the first significant articles to appear in mainstream press about online religion.

J. Cobb, *Cybergrace. The Search for God in the Digital World* (New York: Crown Publishers, 1998).
Cobb argues that cyberspace as a spiritual network can aid humanity's spiritual progression. She describes the Internet as a medium in which we can experience grace in humanity's journey towards a greater spiritual evolution (p. 97). Her theology of cyberspace employs diverse, interreligious sources and interviews offering an interesting overview of spirituality online.

E. Davis, *Techgnosis* (New York: Random House, 1998).
Davis is noted for his writing on Technopaganism ('Technopagan', *WIRED*, June 1997 www.wired.com/wired/archive/3.07/technopa

gans.html) and looking at the similarities between online usage and magic. In *Techgnosis* he demonstrates that computers become for many pagans the holding ground for myths of the 'ancient ways', and 'spiritual powers' can be sought out online.

P. Dixon, *Cyberchurch, Christianity and the Internet* (Eastbourne: Kingsway, 1997).

Dixon advocates Christian involvement in the Internet, stating the Internet needs a 'cyberchurch'. He speculates on the positive outcomes Christian involvement online might lead to and offers examples of ways the church could utilise the Internet in its ministry.

D. Groothuis, *The Soul in Cyberspace* (Grand Rapids: Baker, 1997).

Groothuis, who is a seminary professor, reflects on how involvement in cyberspace may influence our perceptions of human identity, community and religious/theological reflection. He tries to offer a middle of the road approach to other critics' and advocates' claims, while admitting a tendency to rant rather than rave about the Internet.

J. K. Hadden and D. E. Cowan (eds.) *Religion on the Internet. Research Prospects and Promises* (Amsterdam, London and New York: JAI Press, 2000).

A noteworthy collection of research studies on how organisations and individuals are presenting religion online, including reflection on both traditional and new religious movements.

C. Hamelink, *The Ethics of Cyberspace* (London: Sage, 2000).

An overall analysis of ethical issues related to Internet technology such as the Digital Divide, issues of copyright and information access. Consult Hamelink's chapter, 'The Decent Society and Cyberspace', for fuller details. [Also included in Media Ethics bibliography.]

J. Hammerman, *thelordismyshepherd.com: Seeking God in Cyberspace* (Deerfield Beach: Simcha, 2000).

Hammerman offers a Jewish perspective on using the Internet for spiritual reflection and development, using analytical and experiential approaches. He stresses that computer use is changing the ways we think about God and personal faith.

G. Houston, *Virtual Morality* (Leicester: Apollos, 1998).

Houston takes a critical friend approach, focusing on ethical issues surrounding virtual reality. *Virtual Morality* is based on his PhD thesis, where he seeks to define a Christian ethical interface between technology and postmodernity.

G. L. Jantz, *Hidden Dangers of the Internet: Using It Without Abusing It* (Wheaton, IL: Harold Shaw, 1998).

Investigates the dangers of Internet pornography from a Christian perspective.

S. Jones (ed.), *Cybersociety*. (Thousand Oaks, CA: Sage, 1995).
    Cybersociety was one of the first collections of essays of this work in the area of social formation online. Chapters such as Baym's 'The Emergence of Community in Computer-mediated Communication' offer helpful descriptions of issues related to social interaction and community formation emerging within CMC studies in the 1990s.

S. Jones (ed.), *Virtual Culture* (Thousand Oaks, CA: Sage, 1997).
    The Internet as a social sphere is a significant trend in CMC research and is exemplified in Jones' research, see his chapter 'The Internet and its Social Landscape'. Here he describes the Internet as a 'human constructed' sphere. 'Cyberspace is promoted as social space because it is made by people and thus as the "new public space" it cojoins traditional mythic narratives of progress with the strong modern impulses towards self-fulfilment and personal development' (p. 22).

D. Lochhead, *Shifting Realities: Information Technology and the Church* (Geneva: WCC, 1997).
    Presents how computer enthusiasts in the church began in the 1980s to explore using computers as tools for ministry. Lochhead offers specific examples of different Bulletin Board Services and discussion groups formed around topics of religion, providing a short history of the development of Christian online communities.

A. Markham, *Life Online* (Walnut Creek, CA: AltaMira, 1998).
    Provides a good overview of issues arising from the study of life online. Markham also offers a helpful categorisation of the Internet as a tool, place, and state of mind.

J. Mnookin, 'Virtual(ly) Law: The Emergence of Law in LamdaMOO' *Journal of Computer Mediated Communication* Vol. 2, No. 1. www.ascusc. org/jcmc/vol2/issue1/lamda.html
    A key case study in the 1990s focusing on issues of community formation online and describing patterns of life found on MUD and MOOs.

B. Nardi and V. O'Day, *Information Ecologies, Using Technology with Heart* (Cambridge: MIT Press, 1999).
    Provides a reflective look at how information technologies should be approached. The authors use the label of 'critical friend' as an alternative response emerging between dystopian and technophile perspectives.

D. Pullinger, *Information Technology and Cyberspace. Extra Connected Living* (London: Darton, Longman & Todd, 2001).
    While questioning the kind of relationship that can be cultivated when limited to words, Pullinger sees the potential of the Internet creating new communities of faith. He argues for the development of 'networks of concern', groups that develop an understanding of the ben-

efits and challenges posed by using their specific type of technology 'from the perspective of lived experience' (p. 133).

H. Rheingold, *The Virtual Community* (New York: HarperPerennial, 1993).
This landmark book earned Rheingold the title of the first 'philosopher of the virtual community'. A personal reflection of his experiences with the online community known as the WELL (the Whole Earth 'Lectronic Link), based in California.

R. Rosenzweig, 'Wizards, Bureaucrats, Warriors and Hackers: Writing the History of the Internet', *American Historical Review* 103.5 (December 1998).
This article provides a survey of written accounts of the emergence of the Internet detailing the bias and perspectives from which they were written.

R. Schroeder, N. Heather and R. M. Lee, 'The Sacred and the Virtual: Religion in Multi-User Virtual Reality', *Journal of Computer Mediated Communication* 4 (December 1998). www.ascusc.org/jcmc/vol4/issue2/schroeder.html#LANGUAGE
Schroeder, Heather and Lee present a case study of a prayer group in a multi-user virtual reality environment offering insight into the challenges posed by study in the online context.

'Technorealism: get real! A manifesto from a new generation of cultural critics', in *The Nation* (6 April 1998).
Technorealism is a school of cyber-thought, representing a middle ground between neo-luddism and techno-utopianism, defined by a group of Generation X cultural critics. The *Technorealism Manifesto* went public in 1998 when it was launched on the web. www.technorealism.org

S. Turkle, *Life on the Screen: Identity in the Age of the Internet* (London: Phoenix Paperbacks, 1995).
Turkle was one of the first researchers on computer cultures, focusing on a psychological analysis of how computer usage influences issues of identity. Well known for her work studying hacker culture at MIT.

G. E. Veith and C. L. Stamper, *Christians in a .com World: Getting Connected without Being Consumed* (Wheaton, IL: Crossway, 2000).
A general survey of how the Internet is influencing mainstream culture as well as Christianity.

B. Wellman, 'An Electronic Group is Virtually a Social Network', Sara Kielser (ed.), *Culture of the Internet* (Mahwah, NJ: Lawrence Erlbaum, 1997).
Wellman has pioneered the application of Social Network Analysis (addressing communities as loosely knit, frequently changing networks) as a way to describe and study online communities and culture. He demonstrates how a computer network can be viewed as a social network.

M. Wertheim, *The Pearly Gates of Cyberspace* (London: Virago, 1999).

>Wertheim argues the Internet can be used to reconnect with the spiritual side of life by demonstrating that the Internet is providing a bridge between the worlds of science and religion. As a science historian she argues that cyberspace contains a conception of space 'outside the physical space that science has articulated' (p. 9). She claims cyberspace brings us back to a powerful understanding of 'Christian soul space' and the immaterial world lost in modern science.

W. Wilson, *The Internet Church* (Nashville: Word, 2000).

>Wilson stresses that the Internet's pervasive nature, ability to cross social and cultural borders and non-threatening environment make it an ideal medium for individuals to engage in spiritual searching. Through the Internet 'we have the opportunity to reach every man, woman and child on the face of the earth in the next decade' (p. 154).

J. Zaleski, *The Soul of Cyberspace: How Technology is Changing our Spiritual Lives* (San Francisco: HarperSanFrancisco, 1997).

>Best survey to date of how major world religions view Internet technology and use the Internet in their worship or religious practices. Book currently out of print.

A. Zukowski and P. Babin, *The Gospel in Cyberspace: Nurturing Faith in the Internet Age* (Chicago, IL: Loyola Press, 2002).

>This is the first book to combine rigorous reflection on the outcomes of mixing the gospel and new technologies with an investigation of contemporary media culture, drawing on relevant communication models and theory. The dialogue is grounded in a tradition of Catholic communication study, offering thoughtful discussion on how evangelism is being reshaped in the Internet age.

Film and Religion

Steve Nolan

Further Reading

J. W. Arnold, *Seen Any Good Dirty Movies Lately? a Christian Critic Looks at Contemporary Films* (Cincinnati: St Anthony Messenger Press, 1972).

B. Babington and P.W. Evans, *Biblical Epics: Sacred Narrative in the Hollywood Cinema* (Manchester: Manchester University Press, 1993).
> Survey of biblical epics of Hebrew and Christian testaments, and the Roman period. Offers analysis of the relation of religion and Hollywood film, with reference to gender issues, representation of Christ, and star meanings.

L. Baugh, *Imaging the Divine: Jesus and Christ-Figures in Film* (Kansas City, MO: Sheed & Ward, 1997).
> A more academic treatment than that of Malone. Includes extensive bibliography listing articles from European writers.

K. L. Billingsley, *The Seductive Image: a Christian Critique of the World of Film* (Westchester, IL: Crossway, 1989).

G. Black, *Hollywood Censored: Morality Codes, Catholics, and the Movies* (New York: Cambridge University Press, 1994).

R. A. Blake, *Screening America: Reflections on Five Classic Films* (New York: Paulist, 1991).
> 'Blake emphasises the autonomy of movies "that must not and cannot be baptised and then coerced into ecclesial servitude" [and attempts] to use the history of film to provide access to American culture' (Jewett [1993], p. 8).

A. Butler, *Religion in the Cinema* (New York: A.C. Barnes, 1969).
> An historical survey of the cinematic treatment of biblical and religious themes from the earliest days of cinema. Includes 'Christ in the cinema': from early passion play recordings, through the development of 'Lives' to Pasolini; and 'Satirical comment': the anti-religious films of, among others, Buñuel and Fellini.

J. Butler, *TV, Movies, and Morality: a Guide for Catholics* (Huntington, IN: Our Sunday Visitor, 1984).

R. H. Campbell and M. R. Pitts, *The Bible on Film: a Checklist 1897–1980* (Metuchen, NJ, and London: The Scarecrow Press, 1981).
　　A resource list of films which deal with biblical themes.

J. C. Cooper and C. Skrade (eds.), *Celluloid and Symbols* (Philadelphia: Fortress, 1970).
　　Written from the perspective of 'secular theology' and predicated on an existential analytic perspective. Skrade's methodological essay considers the basis of dialogue between film and theology, and Wall raises the question: What is a religious film?

R. Cosandey, A. Gaudreault and T. Gunning (eds.), *An Invention of the Devil? Religion and the Early Cinema. Une Invention du Diable? Cinéma des Premiers Temps et Religion* (Sainte Foy, Canada: Les Presses de l'Université Laval, 1992).

C. Deacy, *Screen Christologies: Redemption and the Medium of Film* (Cardiff: University of Wales Press, 2001)
　　Premised on the idea that film offers one more secular site of religious activity, Deacy's thesis is that *film noir* protagonists can be considered as redeemer-figures, a 'functional equivalent of Christ'. An up-dating of May, Deacy is interested in the cinematic analogue of redemption.

D. J. Drew, *Images of Man: a Critique of the Contemporary Cinema* (Downers Grove, IL: InterVarsity, 1974).

E. Ferlita and J. May, *Film Odyssey: the Art of Film as Search for Meaning* (New York: Paulist Press, 1976).
　　The result of an undergraduate course, Ferlita and May approach film through the Judaeo-Christian value of fundamental hope. This hope, itself expounded by existential psychotherapy, is hope in suffering and is explored on the assumption that cinema represents a potent source of contemporary insight into life's meaning.

P. Fraser, *Images of the Passion: the Sacramental Mode in Film* (Trowbridge: Flicks, 1998).
　　Fraser regards the essential mode of 'religious films' to be the introduction of the 'incarnational gesture' to disrupt and make 'holy' the primary narrative. This disruption 'typically transforms the narrative of the film into the most recognisable of all Christian narrative patterns: the Passion'.

F. Getlein and H. C. Gardiner, *Movies, Morals and Art* (New York: Sheed & Ward, 1961).
　　May regards this moral evaluation of films as a classic text, 'at least in the sense that it antedates by a decade the flood of books that responded to the new freedom in American film' (May, 1997, p. 20).

A. Gibson, *The Silence of God: Creative Response to the Films of Ingmar Bergman* (New York: Harper & Row, 1969).

Gibson argues that Bergman articulates the modern human experience of the silence of God, which, he argues, atheists claim as the basis for their disbelief. Gibson offers a 'theoaesthetic' response to Bergman intended as a dialogue with modern atheists.

A. Greeley, *God in Popular Culture* (Chicago: Thomas More, 1988).

R. Holloway, *Beyond the Image: Approaches to the Religious Dimension in the Cinema* (New York: WCC, 1977).
Film historian Holloway offers ten approaches to the religious dimension in the cinema, each an attempt at finding 'the deeper meaning in film esthetics and a better appreciation of the contemporary human condition'.

N. P. Hurley, *Theology Through Film* (New York: Harper & Row, 1970). Reprinted as *Toward a Film Humanism* (New York: Dell, 1975).
Starting from his conviction that movies are for the masses what theology is for an elite, Hurley uses the theological category of transcendence to review contemporary cinematic statements on universal themes. His 'cinematic theology' includes 'A cinematic theology of freedom', 'Toward a cinematic theology of sex' and 'Grace on the screen'.

N. P. Hurley, *Soul in Suspense: Hitchcock's Fright and Delight* (Metuchen, NJ, and London: The Scarecrow Press, 1993).
Highly idiosyncratic interpretation of the 'master of suspense' through the paradigm of Jesuit theology. Hurley finds that 'Hitch' plants 'hidden sacreds' as clues to the religious interpretation of his films!

R. Jewett, *St Paul at the Movies: the Apostle's Dialogue with American Culture* (Louisville, KY: Westminster John Knox Press, 1993).
Jewett aims at developing a 'dialogue in a prophetic mode' by 'seeking analogies between ancient and modern texts and situations'. To this end he attends to the cultural and historical context of a given biblical passage, setting this alongside a contemporary popular film with 'thematic and narrative similarities'.

R. Jewett, *Saint Paul Returns to the Movies: Triumph over Shame* (Grand Rapids: Eerdmans, 1999).
Jewett's tracing of biblical themes is more populist than Kreitzer's with films like *Forrest Gump* (1994), *Groundhog Day* (1993) and *The Firm* (1993).

R. K. Johnston, *Reel Spirituality: Theology and Film in Dialogue* (Grand Rapids: Baker Academic, 2000).
Johnston has helpful introductory chapters on the history of the church and Hollywood, and a review of theological approaches to film criticism. He offers some account of general film criticism. Finally, he sets out a method for responding theologically to movies.

G. W. Jones, *Sunday Night at the Movies* (Richmond: John Knox, 1967).

R. Kahle and R. E. A. Lee, *Popcorn and Parables: a New Look at the Movies* (Minneapolis: Augsburg, 1971).

R. Kinnard and T. Davis, *Divine Images: a History of Jesus on the Screen* (New York: Citadel, 1992).
>   A survey of the whole range of cinematic portrayals of Christ from Oberammergau recordings to *Jesus of Montreal* (1989), including renderings of Christ-types and many of the little referenced Christ films. Most treatments give credits, commentary, reviews and stills.

R. G. Konzelman, *Marquee Ministry: the Movie Theatre as Church and Community Forum* (New York: Harper & Row, 1972).

L. J. Kreitzer, *Pauline Images in Fiction and Film: on Reversing the Hermeneutical Flow* (Sheffield: Sheffield Academic Press, 1999).
>   Kreitzer reverses the hermeneutical flow with Pauline texts in relation to *Dracula* and *The Picture of Dorian Gray*.

L. J. Kreitzer, *The New Testament in Fiction and Film: on Reversing the Hermeneutical Flow* (Sheffield: Sheffield Academic Press, 1993).
>   Kreitzer's intertextual approach attempts a '[reversal] of the flow of influence within the hermeneutical process' in order to allow a re-examination of biblical passages or themes in the light of our culture, its literature and film. Directed by the concerns of redaction criticism, Kreitzer subtly differs from Jewett in attending to authorial intent over cultural context.

L. J. Kreitzer, *The Old Testament in Fiction and Film: on Reversing the Hermeneutical Flow* (Sheffield: Sheffield Academic Press, 1994).
>   Kreitzer extends his methodology to Old Testament themes and among others considers creation in relation to *Mary Shelley's Frankenstein* (1994).

C. McClain, *Morals and the Movies* (Kansas City, MO: Beacon Hill, 1970).

A. MacDonald, *Films in Close-Up* (Leicester: Frameworks, 1991).
>   First British commercially published treatment of theological themes in popular film. Considers films as powerful and potentially 'negative' persuaders, and attends to what the 'message' of the film is saying.

I. Maher, *Reel Issues: Engaging Film and Faith* (Swindon: British and Foreign Bible Society, 1998).
>   Using themes from the Bible Society's Open Book Project, Maher suggests ten worked examples with practical suggestions for using film in group discussion/study.

P. Malone, *Movie Christs and Antichrists* (New York: Crossroad, 1990).
>   Malone distinguishes the *Jesus-figure* (a portrayal of Jesus) from the *Christ-figure* (a character made to resemble Jesus) as a basic method of religious film analysis.

C. Marsh and G. Ortiz (eds.), *Explorations in Theology and Film: Movies and Meaning* (Oxford: Blackwell, 1997).

The first major offering from British writers (but including US and Australian contributions), the book is concerned to theologically read 'popular' films such as *Shirley Valentine, Dead Poets Society* and *Babette's Feast.* The approach is sympathetic to that of May, but includes a critique of this approach from Jaspers and an editor's response to Jaspers. Useful bibliography.

J. W. Martin and C. E. Ostwalt Jr (eds.), *Screening the Sacred: Religion, Myth and Ideology in Popular American Film* (Boulder, CO: Westview, 1995).

Martin and Ostwalt propose a threefold critical approach to religious film criticism: theological, mythological and ideological. Their significance is in their departure from seeking cinematic analogues or biblical connection, and their acceptance of religion and film as independent modes implicated in a search for meaning.

T. M. Martin, *Images and the Imageless: a Study in Religious Consciousness and Film* (Lewisburg, PA: Bucknell University Press, 1981).

The first study to treat film and theology from within a framework of philosophy of religion. Martin argues that humans need stories to make sense of life, and considers the role of filmic stories in the development of religious consciousness.

J. R. May (ed.), *Images and Likeness: Religious Visions in American Film Classics* (New York/Mahwah, NJ: Paulist Press, 1991).

A collection of religious film reviews, built around the idea that each of the films considered offers an image of the transcendent in the director's vision. Attention is given to finding the cinematic analogue to religious concerns.

J. R. May and M. Bird (eds.), *Religion in Film* (Knoxville: University of Tennessee, 1982).

Introductory essays include contributions to methodology from Bird and May; Ferlita develops his thinking in *Film Odyssey.* Further attention is given to considering film by genre and by director.

J. R. May (ed.), *New Image of Religious Film* (Kansas City, MO: Sheed & Ward, 1997).

The proceedings of an international symposium, the papers concentrate on developments over the last fifteen to twenty years. Includes methodological discussion and insights from the Third World, and a useful bibliography listing articles from European writers.

H. Miles, *Movies and Morals* (Grand Rapids: Zondervan, 1947).

M. R. Miles, *Seeing and Believing: Religion and Values in the Movies* (Boston: Beacon, 1996).

From the premise that religion is about relationships, Miles concerns herself with the values by which people conduct their relationships. She argues that films address the question of how human beings should live, that they foster debate in which film-going friends can negotiate the film's multiple meanings. Her significance is in attempting to develop a methodology within a cultural theory perspective in which films are scrutinised as 'products of the culture's social, sexual, religious, political, and institutional configurations'.

A. Pavelin, *Fifty Religious Films* (Chislehurst, Kent: A. P. Pavelin, 1990).
Reviews of 'high-brow' films whose 'religious' content includes that which reaches 'to the very fundamentals of the human condition'.

A. Schillaci, *Movies and Morals* (Fides, Notre Dame, 1968).

P. Schrader, *Transcendental Style in Film: Ozu, Bresson, Dreyer* (Berkeley: University of California, 1972).
Director (*American Gigolo*, 1980) and scriptwriter (Scorsese's *The Last Temptation of Christ*, 1988), Schrader argues for the possibility of encountering the transcendent through the film style of three (non-Hollywood) directors.

J. Skinner, *The Cross and the Cinema: the Legion of Decency and the National Office for Motion Picture, 1933–1970* (Westport, CT: Greenwood, 1993).

J. M. Wall, *Church and Cinema: a Way of Viewing Film* (Grand Rapids: Eerdmans, 1971).
Wall develops and applies his critical methodology for approaching film. Based around a distinction between plot-driven 'discursive' and artistic 'presentational' films, he seeks the director's vision of reality as a mode of revelation.

F. Walsh, *Sin and Censorship: the Catholic Church and the Motion Picture Industry* (New Haven and London: Yale University Press, 1996).
Historical survey of the attitudes, actions and influence of the Roman Catholic Church on the film business.

D. Wilkinson, *The Power of the Force: the Spirituality of the* Star Wars *Films* (Oxford: Lion, 2000).
Wilkinson attempts to find relationships between Christian faith and contemporary culture. The first half is a well researched Lucas-legend goldmine of facts and anecdotes culled from reviews and interviews. The second half explores the connections between the films and the faith.

Communication Theology[1]

Frances Forde Plude

Further Reading

E. Arens, *Christopraxis: A Theology of Action* (Minneapolis: Fortress, 1995).
    A work that builds upon the social-scientifically and philosophically
    oriented theory of action developed by Jürgen Habermas. Arens dis-
    cusses a communicative theory of action and biblical foundations of a
    theological theory of action.

Asian Research Center for Religion and Social Communication, *Media,
Religion and Culture* newsletter (St. John's University, Bangkok,
www.stjohn.ac.th/arc)
    This is a valuable link to web sites and research underway throughout
    Asia.

T. Beaudoin, *Virtual Faith: The Irreverent Spiritual Quest of Generation X* (San
Francisco: Jossey-Bass Publishers, 1998).
    Beaudoin, himself a member of Generation X, explores fashion, music
    videos and cyberspace and concludes that his generation has fash-
    ioned a theology radically different from but no less potent or valid
    than that of their elders.

R. Bellah, R. Madsen, W. Sullivan, A. Swidler and S. Tipton, *Habits of the
Heart: Individualism and Commitment in American Life* (New York: Harper &
Row, 1985).
    This work analyzes aspects of American culture, along with utilitarian
    individualism (the isolated self) and urges a return to 'the common
    good'.

---

[1] Increasingly, the study of theology, popular culture, audience-reception analysis and
communication systems is provoking new conversations. Some writers believe that these discussions are generating original perspectives on Communication and Theology. As this new
area of interdisciplinary thought develops it will help with the challenge of interpreting a
wired world of local theologies, cultural pluralism and religious conflict. Some of the authors
included in this bibliography are part of emerging conversations around Media, Religion and
Culture. Others are more directly a part of what has been described as a Communication
Theology movement.

A. Besançon, *The Forbidden Image: An Intellectual History of Iconoclasm* (Chicago: University of Chicago Press, 2000).

> The book's thesis is that iconoclasm comes in many kinds (Pagan, Jewish, Christian, Muslim and Secular), but is always religious in one manner or another. It also includes a wide-ranging study of iconophilia and iconoclasm in the West.

J. Bowker, *The Religious Imagination and the Sense of God* (Oxford: Clarendon, 1978).

> Explores the distinctive sense of God in Judaism, Christianity, Islam and Buddhism. It notes the importance of information process and systems behavior for the analysis of religious belief, applying information systems analysis to religion studies.

M. Budde, *The (Magic) Kingdom of God: Christianity and Global Culture Industries* (Boulder, CO: Westview, 1997).

H. Campbell and J. Mitchell (eds.), *Interactions: Theology Meets Film, TV and the Internet* (Edinburgh: Centre for Theology and Public Issues, 1999).

> This journal explores a spiritual renaissance in popular culture, film, TV and the Internet. It also includes information about the Media and Theology Project at New College, University of Edinburgh.

J. Carey, *Communication as Culture: Essays on Media and Society* (Winchester: Unwin Hyman, 1989).

> This work helped to establish the ground for cultural approaches to the study of communication and modern society.

C. Christians and J. Van Hook (eds.), *Jacques Ellul: Interpretive Essays* (Urbana: University of Illinois Press, 1981).

> A series of essays on the work of the Protestant lay theologian, Jacques Ellul. The volume includes an extensive bibliography of Ellul's works and an Epilogue by Ellul.

H. De Vries and Samuel Weber (eds.), *Religion and Media* (Stanford, CA: Stanford University Press, 2001).

> Twenty-five contributors to this volume, who include Jacques Derrida, Jean-Luc Nancy, Talad Asad, and James Siegel, confront the conceptual, analytical and empirical difficulties involved in addressing the complex relationship between religion and media.

A. Dulles, *The Craft of Theology: From Symbol to System* (New York: Crossroad, 1992).

> The author explores theology as symbolic communication and seeks a dynamic equilibrium between continuity and innovation. He explores the cultural-linguistic aspects of theology and notes that religions are predominantly characterised by their symbols.

A. Dulles, *The Reshaping of Catholicism: Current Challenges in the Theology of Church* (San Francisco: Harper & Row, 1998).

In the chapter 'The Church and Communications: Vatican II and Beyond' Dulles notes that a theology of communication is closely connected with ecclesiology. His five models include: hierarchical, herald, sacramental, *communio,* and that of church studying the signs of the times.

F. J. Eilers, (ed.), *Church and Social Communication: Basic Documents* 2nd ed. (Manila: Logos, 1997).

This volume contains all basic documents of the Catholic Church on Social Communication, including messages from the Pope on World Communication Days from 1967–1996. Eilers provides a helpful introduction for each document and a document text-numbering system making discussion easy.

F. J. Eilers, *Communicating in the Community: An Introduction to Social Communication* (Manila: Logos, 2002).

A text for the introduction of social communication for ministry leaders based on a training program developed by the author. Helpful suggested readings and appendices. Included is a chapter on video planning for churches.

F. J. Eilers, *Communication Between Cultures* (Manila: Divine Word, 1992).

Helpful information about sharing knowledge, sentiments and experience by people of different cultures, moving from ethnocentrism to mutual respect. The author notes his interactive perspective 'is developed from Carey's cultural view while the theological basis is derived from Kierkegaard's concept of indirect communication'.

D. Emmanuel, *Challenges of Christian Communication and Broadcasting: Monologue or Dialogue?* (London: Macmillan Press, 1999).

This volume examines the nature of true dialogue through an analysis of the historical development of attitudes towards communicative practices of Christian churches, particularly the Catholic Church.

T. Farrell and P. Soukup (eds.), *Communication and Lonergan: Common Ground for Forging the New Age* (Kansas City, MO: Sheed & Ward, 1993).

An interdisciplinary attempt to explore how Lonergan's thought might apply to communication. Approaches include: rhetoric, 'intercultural communication, interpretation, interpersonal communication, postmodernist questions, and the ways in which communication interacts with culture'. A helpful glossary of Lonerganian terminology is included.

D. Felton, *The Unavoidable Dialogue: Five Interfaces Between Theology and Communication* (*Media Development,* October 1984).

This document outlines interfaces and gives sources, determinants or horizons, concepts and categories, and frameworks for future study for each interface. The five are: theology and communication, communicative theology, systematic theology of communication, pastoral theology of communication, and Christian moral vision of communication.

B. Forbes and J. Mahan, *Religion and Popular Culture in America* (Berkeley: University of California Press, 2000).

> Ranging from the religious themes in cowboy fiction to Madonna's 'Like a Prayer', from televangelism to the world of sports, contributors offer insights into what popular culture reveals about the nature of American religion today.

D. F. Ford, *Self and Salvation: Being Transformed* (Cambridge: Cambridge University Press, 1999)

> Rich multi-disciplinary text with several pertinent sections on communication.

W. Fore, *Mythmakers: Gospel, Culture and the Media* (New York: Friendship, 1990).

> Includes reflections on Christian culture, US mass media and the religious aspects of communication and media.

R. Gaillardetz, 'The Reception of Doctrine and New Perspectives,' in B. Hoose (ed.) *Authority in the Roman Catholic Church* (London: Ashgate, 2002).

> This essay explores the ways modern hermeneutics, literary theory, communication theory and the study of popular religion can enrich the theology of reception and the teaching of authority.

G. Goethals, *The TV Ritual: Worship at the Video Altar* (Boston: Beacon, 1981).

> This volume explores the symbolic environment in the US created by the TV culture and how media challenge the communication of religious values.

G. Goethals, *The Electronic Golden Calf* (Cambridge, MA: Cowley, 1990).

> This book is 'an attempt to understand the transformation and dispersal of the sacramental functions of images in a secular and pluralistic society'. Goethals moves from high art to the advertisements on television in her exploration of the making of meaning and myths through visual media.

R. Goizueta, *Caminemos con Jesús: Toward a Hispanic Latino Theology of Accompaniment* (Maryknoll NY: Orbis Books, 1995).

> An appreciation of cultural differences in Hispanic Latino Theology.

P. Granfield (ed.), *The Church and Communication* (Kansas City: Sheed & Ward, 1994).

> Viewing the centrality of communication in the Catholic Church, this volume covers various themes: dialogue and participation, the communicative dimension of ecumenism, evangelisation, the status of church communicators, and how interactive technologies are a metaphor for a more dialogic church.

A. Greeley, *God in Popular Culture* (Chicago: Thomas More, 1988).

> The author develops a theology of popular culture and speaks of a theology of religious imagination. Many examples are media-based.

J. Habermas, *The Structural Transformation of the Public Sphere* (Cambridge: Polity, 1989).

B. Häring, 'Ethics in Communication', *Free and Faithful in Christ,* Vol. 2 (New York: Crossroad, 1982).

In Chapter 3 Häring outlines a communication theology, along with a discussion of the mass media and the new situation presented by media.

J. Healey and D. Sybertz (eds.), *Towards an African Narrative Theology* (Maryknoll: Orbis, 1996).

This work deals with the challenge of inculturation in Africa today and describes the characteristics of a local African narrative theology of inculturation. Jesus is placed within the African context of healer, brother-intercessor and victor over death.

M. Hess, *Media Literacy in Religious Education: Engaging Popular Culture to Enhance Religious Experience,* (Doctoral Dissertation, Boston College 1998).

The author uses Robert Kegan's theorising and participatory action research as a structure. She analyses mass-mediated popular culture as a transformative resource for religious education in an age of pluralism.

S. Hoover, *Mass Media Religion: The Social Sources of the Electronic Church* (Newbury Park: Sage, 1988).

An analysis of religious television in the light of the new religious consciousness in America, with special emphasis on Pat Robertson. A concluding chapter concerns the impact of the electronic church on American culture.

S. Hoover and K. Lundby (eds.), *Rethinking Media, Religion and Culture* (Thousand Oaks, CA: Sage, 1997).

These significant essays show 'there is a substantive, ontological, and authentic dimension to meaning making that accompanies media behavior'. The authors do not argue that media *constitute* religion, but that media play a quasi-religious role in everyday life. There is a valuable bibliographical review chapter and a concluding analysis of areas needing more study in the field.

S. Hoover and L. Clark (eds.), *Practicing Religion in the Age of Media: Explorations in Media, Religion, and Culture* (New York: Columbia University Press, 2002).

Topics range from Islam on the Internet to the quasi-religious practices of Elvis fans, from the uses of popular culture by the Salvation Army in its early years to the uses of interactive media technologies at the Simon Wiesenthal Center's Beit Hashoah Museum of Tolerance. The issues these essays address include the public / private divide and the distinctions between the sacred and the profane.

P. Horsfield, *Religious Television: The American Experience* (New York: Longman, 1984).

> The author writes of the development of religious television and covers research up to that time on effects of paid-time religious programs, the size of the audience, audience characteristics, and the impact on the local church and on American culture.

International Study Commission on Media, Religion and Culture, www.jmcommunications.com (Commission link).

> This commission is a group of scholars and practitioners who have gathered to consider the shape and direction of both productive and reflective work on these three intersecting fields.

I. Lawrence, *Linguistics and Theology: The Significance of Noam Chomsky to Theological Construction* (Metuchen, NJ: The American Theological Library Association, 1980).

> A review of Chomsky's work as a model for theological problems with emphasis upon pluralism and God language.

B. Lonergan, *Method in Theology* (London: Darton, Longman & Todd, 1972).

L. Luzbetak, *The Church and Culture: New Perspectives in Missiological Anthropology* (Maryknoll NY: Orbis Books, 1988).

> A study of contextualization – the process by which a local church integrates its understanding of the Gospel ('text') with local culture ('context').

D. Lyon, *Jesus in Disneyland: Religion in Postmodern Times* (Cambridge, UK; Malden, MA: Polity Press in association with Blackwell Publishers, 2000).

> A thoughtful analysis of the changing fortunes of religion in postmodern times.

J. McDonnell and F. Trampiets (eds.), *Communicating Faith in a Technological Age* (Slough: St Paul, 1989).

J. Martin-Barbero, *Communication, Culture and Hegemony: From the Media to Mediations*, trans. E. Fox and R. White (Newbury Park: Sage, 1993).

> This work emphasizes the *mediation* process (defined as 'the articulation between communication practice and social movements'), rather than media content or ownership. This theory of sociocultural mediations opens up a new approach to audience reception theory. The author notes: 'the receiver in the communication process is not simply a decoder of what the sender has put into the message but is also a producer of meaning.'

C. Martini, *Communicating Christ to the World* (Kansas City, MO: Sheed & Ward, 1994).

> A series of pastoral letters by the Archbishop of Milan.

J. Mitchell, *Visually Speaking: Radio and the Renaissance of Preaching* (Edinburgh: T&T Clark, 1999).

> This volume explores, homiletics, radio history, music videos, British and American religious radio broadcasting, and communication theology. Mitchell investigates what preachers can learn from radio broadcasters in a media age. He stresses the importance of listening and translating public speech into 'accessible, conversational, and visual' language.

D. Morgan, *Protestants and Pictures: Religion, Visual Culture, and the Age of American Mass Production* (Oxford: Oxford University Press, 1999).

> This finely illustrated book examines the important role that American Protestants played in the formation of visual mass culture between 1820 and 1920.

D. Morgan, *Visual Piety: A History and Theory of Popular Religious Images* (Berkeley: University of California, 1998).

> One of the first, if not the first, book to examine the important role popular images have played in the formation and maintenance of American religious life.

H. R. Niebuhr, *Christ and Culture* (New York: Harper & Row, 1951).

> Recent communication/cultural studies research adds significant insights that go beyond this classic study. His model proposes: Christ Against Culture; The Christ of Culture; Christ Above Culture; Christ and Culture in Paradox (Dualists); and Christ and the Transformation of Culture. The author concludes: the world of culture exists within the world of grace.

W. Ong, *Orality and Literacy: Technologizing the World* (London; New York: Methuen, 1982).

> A study of language and culture, oral tradition, writing, and oral-formulaic analysis.

J. Peters, *Speaking into the Air: A History of the Idea of Communication* (Chicago: University of Chicago Press, 1999).

> Peters analyses the teachings of Socrates and Jesus, the theology of Saint Augustine, philosophy in the wake of Hegel, and the American tradition from Emerson to William James in relation to understanding communication today.

M. Pinsky, *The Gospel According to the Simpsons* (Louisville, KY: Westminister John Knox, 2001).

> Pinsky considers several of the show's central characters, interviews a number of the show's writers and producers, and concludes with an examination of whether the show is subversive or supportive of faith.

F. Plude, *Communication Theology* (Vol. 12 (4) of *Catholic International*, Baltimore, November 2001).

J. Raja, *Facing the Reality of Communication: Culture, Church and Communication* (Delhi: ISPCK, 2001).

> Drawing both on recent New Testament scholarship on parables and cultural studies findings on reception, Joshva Raja makes a case for re-imaging the nature of Christian communication. He offers a number of signposts for understanding the audience for today's church.

P. Rossi and P. Soukup (eds.), *Mass Media and the Moral Imagination* (Kansas City, MO: Sheed & Ward, 1994).

> This collection of essays examines four topics: the context of mass media and moral reflection, moral dimensions of public life, using the media for moral development, and the importance of moral imagining (philosophically and theologically). Gender issues are considered – the shifting roles of women and the media, along with media economics.

R. Schreiter, *The New Catholicity: Theology Between the Global and the Local* (Maryknoll, NY: Orbis, 1997).

> This volume examines the impact of globalisation on the contexts of theology, including the impact of new communication technologies. The work includes many communication-related issues such as codes, cross-cultural issues, hierarchical control, intercultural issues, and communication flows. Schreiter is a leader among theologians, incorporating communication and cultural studies concepts into his thinking and writing.

Q. Schultze, *Communicating for Life: Christian Stewardship in Community and Media* (Grand Rapids: Baker Academic, 2000).

> This book sets out to offer a 'perspective on communication that is anchored in a Christian world view'. Schultze believes that 'God created us to be stewards of symbolic reality'. His use of the steward-ship theme is one of the most original elements of his argument.

P. Soukup, *Communication and Theology: Introduction and Review of the Literature* (London: World Association for Christian Communication, 1983).

> This is a key review of the literature of theology and communication (as of 1983), and it includes a thoughtful analysis of the growing dialogue between the two fields. Soukup establishes a framework for analysis including the following analogues: linguistic, aesthetic, cultural, dialogic, broadcast/mechanical, and theological. The author summarises the main questions raised by the literature at this stage. An extensive bibliography is arranged in helpful categories.

P. Soukup (ed.), *Media, Culture and Catholicism* (Kansas City, MO: Sheed & Ward, 1996).

> These essays highlight 'a significant shift for theology as it engages culture'. The volume includes Ong's important document on 'Communications Media and the State of Theology', Greeley's analysis

of Catholic Imagination concepts, along with other practical applications in liturgy, preaching, pastoral education, and dialogical forums.

D. Stout and J. Buddenbaum (eds.), *Religion and Mass Media: Audiences and Adaptations* (Thousand Oaks, CA: Sage, 1996).
   A collection of essays on how religious audiences react to and use the mass media.

D. Stout and J. Buddenbaum (eds.), *Religion and Popular Culture: Studies on the Interaction of Worldviews* (Ames: Iowa State Press, 2001).
   Divided into three parts, this book first offers theoretical discussion of the interplay between religion and the media of popular culture. The second part describes several world religions' (Christianity, Judaism, Islam and Eastern philosophies) teachings about media use. The third part presents case studies analysing media uses, including the Southern Baptists' boycott of Disney products, as well as a study of the uses of contemporary Christian music.

Symbolism, Media and the Lifecourse Project (University of Colorado, Boulder).
   This is one of the largest ongoing research projects in the US on the meaning-making function of individuals and families as they view media. Papers and meeting summaries are available at www.colorado.edu/Journalism/MEDIALYF

K. Tanner, *Theories of Culture: A New Agenda for Theology* (Minneapolis: Fortress, 1997).
   An exploration of the historical notion of culture and its modern meaning. She explores theology as a part of culture, interactions between Christian culture and society, commonalities in Christian practice, and issues of diversity and its implications for theological creativity. The author contends that the anthropological notion of culture 'can be profitably employed in theology, setting new questions and new directions for theological research'.

T. Tilley, *Story Theology* (Collegeville: Liturgical Press, 1991).
   This work attempts to show 'that Christian stories provide the central and distinctive strength and content of Christian faith'. It constructs a narrative theology for Christians.

A. Van der Meiden, 'Appeal for a More Communicative Theology', *Media Development* 28 (4) (1981) pp. 43–5.
   The author calls for a communication-centered theology where communication is included *in* theology – rather than speaking of a 'theology *of* communication'.

R. Wuthnow, *Cultural Analysis in the Work of Peter Berger, Mary Douglas, Michel Foucault and Jürgen Habermas,* (London: Routledge and Kegan Paul, 1984).
   Cultural and social change through the perspective of four analysts.

Name Index

Subject Index